A to Zoo

A to Zoo

Subject Access to Children's Picture Books

Supplement to the 7th Edition

Carolyn W. Lima and Rebecca L. Thomas

Children's and Young Adult Literature Reference

LIBRARIES
UNLIMITED
A Member of the Greenwood Publishing Group

Westport, Connecticut • London

Library of Congress Cataloging-in-Publication Data
Lima, Carolyn W.
  A to zoo. Supplement to the 7th edition / Carolyn W. Lima and Rebecca L. Thomas.
      p. cm. – (Children's and young adult literature reference)
  "Subject access to children's picture books."
  Includes bibliographical references and indexes.
  ISBN 978-1-59158-672-2 (alk. paper)
  1. Picture books for children–Indexes. 2. Children's literature, English–Indexes. I. Thomas,
Rebecca L. II. Title.
  Z1037.L715 2006 Suppl.
  011.62–dc22   2008006033

British Library Cataloguing in Publication Data is available.

Library of Congress Catalog Card Number: 2008006033
ISBN: 978-1-59158-672-2

First published in 2008

Libraries Unlimited, 88 Post Road West, Westport, CT 06881
A Member of the Greenwood Publishing Group, Inc.
www.lu.com

Printed in the United States of America

The paper used in this book complies with the
Permanent Paper Standard issued by the National
Information Standards Organization (Z39.48–1984).

10 9 8 7 6 5 4 3 2 1

In Memoriam
John Lima (1935–2007)

Contents

Preface

A new edition of *A to Zoo: Subject Access to Picture Books for Children* has typically appeared every four years, and many users have expressed the desire to see a more frequent publication schedule. This supplement to the 7th edition of *A to Zoo* (Libraries Unlimited, 2006) is a response to these requests and provides users with subject access to picture books published in 2005, 2006, and 2007.

This supplement includes 2,451 titles cataloged under 769 subjects, and will be useful for public and school librarians developing collections, preparing bibliographies and classroom units, and for reader's advisory. Its arrangement is the same as that of the main edition, and the familiar subject headings are used.

Rebecca Thomas, a school librarian and university teacher and author in the field of children's literature, has joined Carolyn Lima as coauthor in the preparation of this supplement.

HOW TO USE THIS BOOK

A to Zoo can be used to obtain information about children's picture books in two ways: to learn the titles, authors, and illustrators of books on a particular subject, such as "dragons" or "weddings"; or to ascertain the subject (or subjects) when only the title, author and title, or illustrator and title are known. For example, if the title *Knuffle Bunny Too* is known, this volume will enable the user to discover that *Knuffle Bunny Too* is written and illustrated by Mo Willems, and published by Hyperion in 2007, and that its subject areas are Animals — rabbits; Caldecott award honor books; School — nursery; and Toys.

For ease and convenience of reference use, *A to Zoo* is divided into five sections:

Subject Headings
Subject Guide
Bibliographic Guide
Title Index
Illustrator Index

SUBJECT HEADINGS: This section contains an alphabetical list of the subjects cataloged in this book. The subject headings reflect the established terms used commonly in public libraries, originally based on questions asked by parents and teachers and then modified and adapted by librarians. To facilitate reference use, and because subjects are requested in a variety of terms, the list of subject headings contains numerous cross-references. Subheadings are arranged alphabetically under each general topic, for example:

Animals (general topic)
Animals — apes *see* Animals — baboons; Animals — chimpanzees; Animals — gorillas; Animals — monkeys (cross-reference)
Animals — babies (subheading)
Animals — baboons (subheading)

SUBJECT GUIDE: This guide to 2,451 picture books is cataloged under 769 subjects. The guide reflects the arrangement in the Subject Headings, alphabetically arranged by subject heading and subheading. Many books, of course, relate to more than one subject, and this comprehensive list provides a means of identifying all those books that may contain any information or material on a particular subject.

If, for example, the user wants books on flies (insects), the Subject Headings section will show that Insects is a subject classification with many subheadings. A look in the Subject Guide reveals that under Insects there are 3 titles listed alphabetically by author, plus a number of additional titles under related subheadings.

BIBLIOGRAPHIC GUIDE: Each book is listed with full bibliographic information. This section is arranged alphabetically by author, or by title when the author is unknown, or by uniform (classic) title.

Each entry contains bibliographic information in order: author, title, illustrator, publisher and date of publication, miscellaneous notes when given, International Standard Book Number (ISBN), and subjects, listed according to the alphabetical classification in the Subject Headings section.

The user can consult the Bibliographic Guide to find complete data on each of the titles listed in the Subject Guide under the subheading of Insects — flies, as for example:

> **Cronin, Doreen.** *Diary of a fly* ill. by Harry Bliss. HarperCollins, 2007. ISBN 978-0-06-000156-8 Subj: Activities — writing. Insects — flies.

In the case of joint authors, the second author is listed in alphabetical order, followed by the book title and the name of the primary author or main entry. The user can then locate the first-named author for complete bibliographic information. For example:

> **Page, Robin.** *Move!* (Jenkins, Steve)

Bibliographic information for this title will be found in the Bibliographic Guide section under "Jenkins, Steve."

Titles for an author who is both a single author and a joint author are interfiled alphabetically. Where the author is not known, the entry is listed alphabetically by title with complete bibliographic information following the same format as given above.

TITLE INDEX: This section contains an alphabetical list of all titles in the book with authors in parentheses, followed by the page number of the full listing in the Bibliographic Guide, such as:

> *I lost my tooth in Africa* (Diakité, Penda), 103

If a title has no known author, the name of the illustrator is given if available. When multiple versions of the same title are listed, the illustrator's name is given with the author's name (when known) in parentheses:

> *The night before Christmas*, ill. by Lisbeth Zwerger (Moore, Clement Clarke), 129
> *The night before Christmas*, ill. by Richard Jesse Watson (Moore, Clement Clarke), 129

ILLUSTRATOR INDEX: This section contains an alphabetical list of illustrators with titles and authors, followed by the page number of the full listing in the Bibliographic Guide. For example:

> **Dewey, Ariane.** *The last laugh* (Aruego, Jose), 91

Titles listed under an illustrator's name appear in alphabetical sequence. When the author is the same as the illustrator, the author's name is not repeated.

ACKNOWLEDGMENTS

The authors wish to express their thanks for the assistance provided by many people in bringing this book together. Special thanks to Barbara Ittner of Libraries Unlimited, to series editor Catherine Barr, and to Julia C. Miller and Christine McNaull, who worked on the database, sorting, editing, and typesetting.

Subject Headings

Main headings, subheadings, and cross-references are arranged alphabetically and provide a quick reference to the subjects used in the Subject Guide section, where author and title names appear under appropriate headings.

ABC books
Abused children *see* Child abuse
Accidents
Accordions *see* Musical instruments — accordions
Activities
Activities — babysitting
Activities — baking, cooking
Activities — ballooning
Activities — bargaining *see* Activities — trading
Activities — bartering *see* Activities — trading
Activities — bathing
Activities — cooking *see* Activities — baking, cooking
Activities — dancing
Activities — drawing
Activities — driving
Activities — eating *see* Food
Activities — flying
Activities — gardening *see* Gardens, gardening
Activities — jumping
Activities — kissing *see* Kissing
Activities — knitting
Activities — making things
Activities — painting *see also* Careers — artists
Activities — photographing
Activities — picnicking
Activities — playing
Activities — reading *see* Books, reading
Activities — sewing
Activities — shopping *see* Shopping
Activities — singing
Activities — storytelling
Activities — swapping *see* Activities — trading
Activities — swimming *see* Sports — swimming
Activities — talking
Activities — trading
Activities — traveling
Activities — vacationing
Activities — walking
Activities — weaving
Activities — wood carving
Activities — working
Activities — writing
Actors *see* Careers — actors
Adoption
Afghanistan *see* Foreign lands — Afghanistan
Africa *see* Foreign lands — Africa
African Americans *see* Ethnic groups in the U.S. — African Americans
Aged *see* Old age
AIDS *see* Illness — AIDS

Airplane pilots *see* Careers — airplane pilots
Airplanes, airports
Airports *see* Airplanes, airports
Alaska
Aliens
All Souls' Day *see* Holidays — Day of the Dead
Allergies *see* Illness — allergies
Alligators *see* Reptiles — alligators, crocodiles
Alphabet books *see* ABC books
Alzheimer's *see* Illness — Alzheimer's
Ambition *see* Character traits — ambition
American Indians *see* Indians of North America
Amphibians *see* Frogs & toads; Reptiles
Amusement parks *see* Parks — amusement
Anatomy
Anatomy — faces
Anatomy — feet
Anatomy — skeletons
Anatomy — skin
Anatomy — tails
Anatomy — teeth *see* Teeth
Anatomy — toes
Anatomy — wings
Angels
Anger *see* Emotions — anger
Animals *see also* Birds; Frogs & toads; Reptiles
Animals — apes *see* Animals — baboons; Animals — chimpanzees; Animals — gorillas; Animals — monkeys
Animals — babies
Animals — baboons
Animals — badgers
Animals — bandicoots
Animals — bats
Animals — bears
Animals — beavers
Animals — bison *see* Animals — buffaloes
Animals — bonobos
Animals — buffaloes
Animals — bulls, cows
Animals — camels
Animals — cats
Animals — chimpanzees
Animals — cougars
Animals — cows *see* Animals — bulls, cows
Animals — coyotes
Animals — deer
Animals — dislike of *see* Behavior — animals, dislike of
Animals — dogs
Animals — donkeys
Animals — elephants

Animals — endangered animals
Animals — ferrets
Animals — foxes
Animals — giraffes
Animals — goats
Animals — gorillas
Animals — groundhogs
Animals — guinea pigs
Animals — hamsters
Animals — hedgehogs
Animals — hippopotamuses
Animals — horses, ponies
Animals — kangaroos
Animals — kindness to animals *see* Character traits — kindness to animals
Animals — koalas
Animals — leopards
Animals — lions
Animals — llamas
Animals — marsupials
Animals — meerkats
Animals — mice
Animals — migration *see* Migration
Animals — moles
Animals — monkeys
Animals — moose
Animals — mountain lions *see* Animals — cougars
Animals — muskrats
Animals — octopuses *see* Octopuses
Animals — opossums *see* Animals — possums
Animals — orangutans
Animals — otters
Animals — pack rats
Animals — pandas
Animals — panthers *see* Animals — leopards
Animals — pigs
Animals — platypuses
Animals — polar bears
Animals — porcupines
Animals — possums
Animals — prairie dogs
Animals — prairie wolves *see* Animals — coyotes
Animals — pumas *see* Animals — cougars
Animals — rabbits
Animals — raccoons
Animals — rats
Animals — rhinoceros
Animals — seals
Animals — service animals
Animals — sheep
Animals — skunks
Animals — slugs
Animals — snails
Animals — snow leopards *see* Animals — leopards

Animals — squid *See* Squid
Animals — squirrels
Animals — swine *see* Animals — pigs
Animals — tigers
Animals — wallabies
Animals — weasels
Animals — whales
Animals — wolves
Animals — wombats
Animals — woodchucks *see* Animals — groundhogs
Animals — wooly mammoths
Animals — worms
Animals — yaks
Antarctica *see* Foreign lands — Antarctica
Ants *see* Insects — ants
Apartments *see* Homes, houses
Apes *see* Animals — baboons; Animals — chimpanzees; Animals — gorillas; Animals — monkeys
Appearance *see* Character traits — appearance
Arab Americans *see* Ethnic groups in the U.S. — Arab Americans
Arabia *see* Foreign lands — Arabia
Arachnids *see* Spiders
Architects *see* Careers — architects
Arctic *see* Foreign lands — Arctic
Arguing *see* Behavior — fighting, arguing
Arithmetic *see* Counting, numbers
Art
Artists *see* Careers — artists
Asian Americans *see* Ethnic groups in the U.S. — Asian Americans
Assertiveness *see* Character traits — assertiveness
Astrology *see* Zodiac
Astronauts *see* Careers — astronauts; Space & space ships
Astronomy
Aunts *see* Family life — aunts, uncles
Australia *see* Foreign lands — Australia
Authors *see* Careers — authors
Automobiles
Autumn *see* Seasons — fall
Award-winning books *see* Caldecott award books; Caldecott award honor books

Babies *see also* Animals — babies
Babies, new *see* Family life — new sibling
Baboons *see* Animals — baboons
Babysitting *see* Activities — babysitting
Bad day *see* Behavior — bad day
Badgers *see* Animals — badgers
Bakers *see* Careers — bakers
Baking *see* Activities — baking, cooking
Ballet
Ballooning *see* Activities — ballooning
Balloons *see* Toys — balloons
Balls *see* Toys — balls
Bandicoots *see* Animals — bandicoots
Banjos *see* Musical instruments — banjos
Barns
Bartering *see* Activities — trading
Baseball *see* Sports — baseball
Bashfulness *see* Character traits — shyness
Basketball *see* Sports — basketball
Bathing *see* Activities — bathing
Bats *see* Animals — bats
Beaches *see* Sea & seashore — beaches
Bears *see* Animals — bears
Beasts *see* Monsters
Beauty shops
Beavers *see* Animals — beavers

Beds *see* Furniture — beds
Bedtime
Bedwetting *see* Behavior — bedwetting
Beekeepers *see* Careers — beekeepers
Bees *see* Insects — bees
Beetles *see* Insects — beetles
Behavior
Behavior — animals, dislike of
Behavior — bad day
Behavior — bedwetting
Behavior — boasting
Behavior — boredom
Behavior — bossy
Behavior — bullying
Behavior — cheating
Behavior — collecting things
Behavior — dissatisfaction
Behavior — fighting, arguing
Behavior — forgetfulness
Behavior — forgiving
Behavior — gossip
Behavior — greed
Behavior — growing up
Behavior — hiding
Behavior — imitation
Behavior — indifference
Behavior — lost
Behavior — lost & found possessions
Behavior — lying
Behavior — messy
Behavior — misbehavior
Behavior — mistakes
Behavior — misunderstanding
Behavior — name calling
Behavior — naughty *see* Behavior — misbehavior
Behavior — potty training *see* Toilet training
Behavior — resourcefulness
Behavior — running away
Behavior — secrets
Behavior — sharing
Behavior — solitude
Behavior — stealing
Behavior — talking to strangers
Behavior — toilet training *see* Toilet training
Behavior — trickery
Behavior — wishing
Behavior — worrying
Being different *see* Character traits — being different
Belarus *see* Foreign lands — Belarus
Bereavement *see* Death; Emotions — grief
Bible *see* Religion
Bicycling *see* Sports — bicycling
Bigotry *see* Prejudice
Birds
Birds — chickens
Birds — cranes
Birds — crows
Birds — doves
Birds — ducks
Birds — falcons
Birds — finches
Birds — flamingos
Birds — geese
Birds — hawks
Birds — herons
Birds — owls
Birds — parrots
Birds — pelicans
Birds — penguins
Birds — pigeons
Birds — puffins
Birds — robins

Birds — sandpipers
Birds — seagulls
Birds — storks
Birds — swallows
Birds — swans
Birds — turkeys
Birds — vultures
Birth
Birthdays
Bison *see* Animals — buffaloes
Blindness *see* Handicaps — blindness; Senses — sight
Blizzards *see* Weather — blizzards
Board books *see* Format, unusual — board books
Boasting *see* Behavior — boasting
Boats, ships
Bonobos *see* Animals — bonobos
Books *see* Books, reading; Libraries
Books, reading
Boredom *see* Behavior — boredom
Bossy *see* Behavior — bossy
Boxing *see* Sports — boxing
Bravery *see* Character traits — bravery
Brazil *see* Foreign lands — Brazil
Bridges
British Columbia *see* Foreign lands — British Columbia
Brothers *see* Family life — brothers & sisters; Sibling rivalry
Buffaloes *see* Animals — buffaloes
Bugs *see* Insects
Buildings
Bulldozers *see* Machines
Bulls *see* Animals — bulls, cows
Bullying *see* Behavior — bullying
Bumble bees *see* Insects — bees
Burglars *see* Crime
Burros *see* Animals — donkeys
Bus drivers *see* Careers — bus drivers
Buses
Butterflies *see* Insects — butterflies, caterpillars

Cafés *see* Restaurants
Caldecott award books
Caldecott award honor books
Calendars
Camels *see* Animals — camels
Camouflages *see* Disguises
Camps, camping
Canada *see* Foreign lands — Canada
Cancer *see* Illness — cancer
Cards *see* Letters, cards
Careers
Careers — actors
Careers — airplane pilots
Careers — architects
Careers — artists *see also* Activities — painting
Careers — astronauts
Careers — authors
Careers — bakers
Careers — beekeepers
Careers — bus drivers
Careers — chefs, cooks
Careers — construction workers
Careers — cooks *see* Careers — chefs, cooks
Careers — custodians, janitors
Careers — dentists
Careers — detectives
Careers — doctors
Careers — explorers
Careers — farmers

Careers — firefighters
Careers — fishermen
Careers — fur traders
Careers — garbage collectors *see* Careers
— sanitation workers
Careers — illustrators
Careers — inventors
Careers — janitors *see* Careers —
custodians, janitors
Careers — jockeys
Careers — librarians
Careers — magicians
Careers — mail carriers *see* Careers —
postal workers
Careers — meteorologists
Careers — migrant workers
Careers — military
Careers — miners
Careers — musicians
Careers — painters *see also* Activities —
painting; Careers — artists
Careers — physicians *see* Careers —
doctors
Careers — police officers
Careers — postal workers
Careers — principals *see* Careers —
school principals
Careers — ranchers
Careers — salesmen
Careers — sanitation workers
Careers — school principals
Careers — scientists
Careers — sculptors
Careers — shepherds
Careers — sheriffs
Careers — shoemakers
Careers — singers
Careers — soldiers *see* Careers — military
Careers — tailors
Careers — teachers
Careers — truck drivers
Careers — veterinarians
Careers — waiters, waitresses
Careers — weather reporters *see* Careers
— meteorologists
Caribbean Islands *see* Foreign lands —
Caribbean Islands
Carnivals *see* Fairs, festivals
Carousels *see* Merry-go-rounds
Cars *see* Automobiles
Caterpillars *see* Insects — butterflies,
caterpillars
Cats *see* Animals — cats
Cerebral palsy *see* Handicaps — cerebral
palsy
Chairs *see* Furniture — chairs
Chameleons *see* Reptiles — chameleons
Change *see* Concepts — change
Character traits
Character traits — ambition
Character traits — appearance
Character traits — assertiveness
Character traits — being different
Character traits — bravery
Character traits — cleanliness
Character traits — cleverness
Character traits — clumsiness
Character traits — confidence
Character traits — cooperation
Character traits — courage *see* Character
traits — bravery
Character traits — cruelty to animals *see*
Character traits — kindness to animals
Character traits — curiosity
Character traits — foolishness
Character traits — fortune *see* Character
traits — luck

Character traits — freedom
Character traits — generosity
Character traits — helpfulness
Character traits — honesty
Character traits — incentive *see*
Character traits — ambition
Character traits — individuality
Character traits — kindness
Character traits — kindness to animals
Character traits — laziness
Character traits — luck
Character traits — meanness
Character traits — orderliness
Character traits — ostracism *see*
Character traits — being different
Character traits — patience
Character traits — perfectionism
Character traits — perseverance
Character traits — persistence
Character traits — pride
Character traits — questioning
Character traits — resourcefulness
Character traits — responsibility
Character traits — selfishness
Character traits — shyness
Character traits — smallness
Character traits — stubbornness
Character traits — willfulness
Cheating *see* Behavior — cheating
Chefs *see* Careers — chefs, cooks
Cherokee Indians *see* Indians of North
America — Cherokee
Cherubs *see* Angels
Chickens *see* Birds — chickens
Child abuse
Chile *see* Foreign lands — Chile
Chimpanzees *see* Animals —
chimpanzees
China *see* Foreign lands — China
Chinese Americans *see* Ethnic groups in
the U.S. — Chinese Americans
Chinese New Year *see* Holidays —
Chinese New Year
Choctaw Indians *see* Indians of North
America — Choctaw
Christmas *see* Holidays — Christmas
Cinco de Mayo *see* Holidays — Cinco de
Mayo
Circular tales
Circus
Cities, towns
Cleanliness *see* Character traits —
cleanliness
Cleverness *see* Character traits —
cleverness
Clocks, watches
Clothing
Clothing — coats
Clothing — costumes
Clothing — dresses
Clothing — gloves, mittens
Clothing — hats
Clothing — neckties
Clothing — pajamas
Clothing — scarves
Clothing — shoes
Clothing — socks
Clothing — sweaters
Clouds *see* Weather — clouds
Clowns, jesters
Clubs, gangs
Clumsiness *see* Character traits —
clumsiness
Coats *see* Clothing — coats
Cockroaches *see* Insects — cockroaches
Cold *see* Concepts — cold & heat;
Weather — cold

Cold (disease) *see* Illness — cold
(disease)
Collecting things *see* Behavior —
collecting things
Color *see* Concepts — color
Communication
Communities, neighborhoods
Competition *see* Sibling rivalry; Sports;
Sportsmanship
Computers
Concepts
Concepts — change
Concepts — cold & heat
Concepts — color
Concepts — counting *see* Counting,
numbers
Concepts — measurement
Concepts — motion
Concepts — opposites
Concepts — patterns
Concepts — perspective
Concepts — self *see* Self-concept
Concepts — shape
Concepts — size
Concepts — up & down
Confidence *see* Character traits —
confidence
Conservation *see* Ecology
Construction workers *see* Careers —
construction workers
Contests
Cooking *see* Activities — baking, cooking
Cooks *see* Careers — bakers; Careers —
chefs, cooks
Cooperation *see* Character traits —
cooperation
Costumes *see* Clothing — costumes
Couches, sofas *see* Furniture — couches,
sofas
Cougars *see* Animals — cougars
Counting, numbers
Countries, foreign *see* Foreign lands
Country
Courage *see* Character traits — bravery
Cousins *see* Family life — cousins
Cowboys, cowgirls
Cows *see* Animals — bulls, cows
Coyotes *see* Animals — coyotes
Crabs *see* Crustaceans — crabs
Crafts *see* Activities — making things
Cranes (birds) *see* Birds — cranes
Creation
Creatures *see* Monsters; Mythical
creatures
Cree Indians *see* Indians of North
America — Cree
Crickets *see* Insects — crickets
Crime
Criminals *see* Crime
Crippled *see* Handicaps — physical
handicaps
Crocodiles *see* Reptiles — alligators,
crocodiles
Crows *see* Birds — crows
Cruelty to animals *see* Character traits —
kindness to animals
Crustaceans — crabs
Crustaceans — lobsters
Crustaceans
Crying *see* Emotions
Cuba *see* Foreign lands — Cuba
Cumulative tales
Curiosity *see* Character traits — curiosity
Currency *see* Money
Custodians *see* Careers — custodians,
janitors

Cycles *see* Motorcycles; Sports — bicycling

Dancing *see* Activities — dancing; Ballet
Daniel *see* Religion — Daniel
Dark *see* Night
Darkness — fear *see* Emotions — fear
Daughters *see* Family life — daughters
Day
Day care *see* School — nursery
Days of the week, months of the year
Deafness *see* Handicaps — deafness
Death
Deer *see* Animals — deer
Demons *see* Devil; Monsters
Dentists *see* Careers — dentists
Department stores *see* Shopping; Stores
Desert
Detective stories *see* Mystery stories; Problem solving
Detectives *see* Careers — detectives
Devil
Diggers *see* Careers — construction workers; Machines
Diners *see* Restaurants
Dinosaurs
Disabilities *see* Handicaps
Diseases *see* Illness
Disguises
Dissatisfaction *see* Behavior — dissatisfaction
Divorce
Doctors *see* Careers — doctors
Dogs *see* Animals — dogs
Dolls *see* Toys — dolls
Donkeys *see* Animals — donkeys
Doves *see* Birds — doves
Down & up *see* Concepts — up & down
Dragonflies *see* Insects — dragonflies
Dragons
Drawing *see* Activities — drawing
Dreams *see also* Nightmares
Dresses *see* Clothing — dresses
Driving *see* Activities — driving
Droughts *see* Weather — droughts
Drums *see* Musical instruments — drums
Ducks *see* Birds — ducks
Dwarfs, midgets
Dwellings *see* Buildings; Homes, houses
Dying *see* Death
Dyslexia *see* Handicaps — dyslexia

Ears *see* Handicaps — deafness
Earth
East Africa *see* Foreign lands — East Africa
East Indian Americans *see* Ethnic groups in the U.S. — East Indian Americans
Easter *see* Holidays — Easter
Eating *see* Food
Ecology
Education *see* School
Eggs
Egypt *see* Foreign lands — Egypt
Elderly *see* Old age
Elections
Elephant seals *see* Animals — seals
Elephants *see* Animals — elephants
Elves *see* Mythical creatures — elves
Embarrassment *see* Emotions — embarrassment
Emotions
Emotions — anger
Emotions — embarrassment

Emotions — envy, jealousy
Emotions — fear
Emotions — grief
Emotions — happiness
Emotions — jealousy *see* Emotions — envy, jealousy
Emotions — loneliness
Emotions — love
Emotions — sadness
Emotions — unhappiness *see* Emotions — happiness; Emotions — sadness
Emperors *see* Royalty — emperors
Endangered animals *see* Animals — endangered animals
Engineered books *see* Format, unusual — toy & movable books
England *see* Foreign lands — England
Environment *see* Ecology
Envy *see* Emotions — envy, jealousy
Eskimos *see also* Indians of North America — Inuit
Ethiopia *see* Foreign lands — Ethiopia
Ethnic groups in the U.S. — African Americans
Ethnic groups in the U.S. — Arab Americans
Ethnic groups in the U.S. — Asian Americans
Ethnic groups in the U.S. — Chinese Americans
Ethnic groups in the U.S. — East Indian Americans
Ethnic groups in the U.S. — Hispanic Americans
Ethnic groups in the U.S. — Jamaican Americans
Ethnic groups in the U.S. — Japanese Americans
Ethnic groups in the U.S. — Jewish Americans
Ethnic groups in the U.S. — Korean Americans
Ethnic groups in the U.S. — Mexican Americans
Ethnic groups in the U.S. — Puerto Rican Americans
Ethnic groups in the U.S. — Racially mixed
Etiquette
Exercise *see* Health & fitness — exercise
Explorers *see* Careers — explorers
Extraterrestrial beings *see* Aliens
Eye glasses *see* Glasses
Eyes *see* Handicaps — blindness; Senses — sight

Fables *see* Folk & fairy tales
Faces *see* Anatomy — faces
Fairies
Fairs, festivals
Fairy tales *see* Folk & fairy tales
Falcons *see* Birds — falcons
Fall *see* Seasons — fall
Family life
Family life — aunts, uncles
Family life — brothers *see* Family life; Family life — brothers & sisters; Sibling rivalry
Family life — brothers & sisters
Family life — cousins
Family life — daughters
Family life — fathers
Family life — grandfathers
Family life — grandmothers
Family life — grandparents

Family life — mothers
Family life — new sibling
Family life — only child
Family life — parents
Family life — single-parent families
Family life — sisters *see* Family life; Family life — brothers & sisters; Sibling rivalry
Family life — step families
Family life — stepchildren *see* Divorce; Family life — step families
Family life — stepparents *see* Divorce; Family life — step families
Farmers *see* Careers — farmers
Farms
Father's Day *see* Holidays — Father's Day
Fathers *see* Family life — fathers; Family life — parents; Family life — single-parent families; Family life — step families
Fear *see* Emotions — fear
Feelings *see* Emotions
Feet *see* Anatomy — feet
Ferrets *see* Animals — ferrets
Fighting *see* Behavior — fighting, arguing
Finches *see* Birds — Finches
Fire
Fire engines *see* Careers — firefighters; Trucks
Firefighters *see* Careers — firefighters
Fireflies *see* Insects — fireflies
Fish
Fish — seahorses
Fish — sharks
Fishermen *see* Careers — fishermen
Fishing *see* Sports — fishing
Fitness *see* Health & fitness
Flags
Flamingos *see* Birds — flamingos
Flies *see* Insects — flies
Floods *see* Weather — floods
Flowers
Flowers — roses
Flying *see* Activities — flying
Fog *see* Weather — fog
Fold-out books *see* Format, unusual — toy & movable books
Folk & fairy tales
Food
Foolishness *see* Character traits — foolishness
Football *see* Sports — football
Foreign lands
Foreign lands — Afghanistan
Foreign lands — Africa
Foreign lands — Antarctica
Foreign lands — Arabia
Foreign lands — Arctic
Foreign lands — Australia
Foreign lands — Belarus
Foreign lands — Brazil
Foreign lands — British Columbia
Foreign lands — Canada
Foreign lands — Caribbean Islands
Foreign lands — Chile
Foreign lands — China
Foreign lands — Cuba
Foreign lands — Czechoslovakia
Foreign lands — East Africa
Foreign lands — Egypt
Foreign lands — England
Foreign lands — Ethiopia
Foreign lands — France
Foreign lands — Galapagos Islands
Foreign lands — Germany
Foreign lands — Ghana
Foreign lands — Haiti
Foreign lands — Hungary

Foreign lands — Iceland
Foreign lands — India
Foreign lands — Indonesia
Foreign lands — Iran
Foreign lands — Iraq
Foreign lands — Ireland
Foreign lands — Israel
Foreign lands — Italy
Foreign lands — Japan
Foreign lands — Kenya
Foreign lands — Korea
Foreign lands — Latin America
Foreign lands — Mali
Foreign lands — Mexico
Foreign lands — Middle East
Foreign lands — Mongolia
Foreign lands — Morocco
Foreign lands — Nepal
Foreign lands — Palestine
Foreign lands — Panama
Foreign lands — Persia
Foreign lands — Poland
Foreign lands — Puerto Rico
Foreign lands — Russia
Foreign lands — Siam *see* Foreign lands
    — Thailand
Foreign lands — Somalia
Foreign lands — South Africa
Foreign lands — Spain
Foreign lands — Switzerland
Foreign lands — Tanzania
Foreign lands — Thailand
Foreign lands — Trinidad
Foreign lands — Venezuela
Foreign lands — Vietnam
Foreign lands — Yukon Territory
Foreign languages
Forest, woods
Forgetfulness *see* Behavior —
    forgetfulness
Forgiving *see* Behavior — forgiving
Format, unusual
Format, unusual — board books
Format, unusual — toy & movable books
Fortune *see* Character traits — luck
Fossils
Fourth of July *see* Holidays — Fourth of
    July
Foxes *see* Animals — foxes
France *see* Foreign lands — France
Freedom *see* Character traits — freedom
Friendship
Frogs & toads
Frontier life *see* U.S. history — frontier &
    pioneer life
Fur traders *see* Careers — fur traders
Furniture — beds
Furniture — chairs
Furniture — couches, sofas

Galapagos Islands *see* Foreign lands —
    Galapagos Islands
Games
Gangs *see* Clubs, gangs
Garbage collectors *see* Careers —
    sanitation workers
Gardens, gardening
Geese *see* Birds — geese
Gender roles
Generosity *see* Character traits —
    generosity
Genies *see* Mythical creatures — genies
Geography
Germany *see* Foreign lands — Germany
Ghana *see* Foreign lands — Ghana

Ghosts
Giants
Gifts
Giraffes *see* Animals — giraffes
Glasses
Gloves *see* Clothing — gloves, mittens
Goats *see* Animals — goats
Gorillas *see* Animals — gorillas
Gossip *see* Behavior — gossip
Grammar *see* Language
Grandfathers *see* Family life —
    grandfathers; Family life —
    grandparents
Grandmothers *see* Family life —
    grandmothers; Family life —
    grandparents
Grandparents *see* Family life —
    grandfathers; Family life —
    grandmothers; Family life —
    grandparents
Grasshoppers *see* Insects — grasshoppers
Greed *see* Behavior — greed
Grief *see* Emotions — grief
Grocery stores *see* Shopping; Stores
Groundhog Day *see* Holidays —
    Groundhog Day
Groundhogs *see* Animals — groundhogs
Growing up *see* Behavior — growing up
Guinea pigs *see* Animals — guinea pigs
Gymnastics *see* Sports — gymnastics

Hair
Haiti *see* Foreign lands — Haiti
Halloween *see* Holidays — Halloween
Hamsters *see* Animals — hamsters
Handicaps
Handicaps — blindness
Handicaps — cerebral palsy
Handicaps — deafness
Handicaps — dyslexia
Handicaps — physical handicaps
Hanukkah *see* Holidays — Hanukkah
Happiness *see* Emotions — happiness
Hares *see* Animals — rabbits
Hats *see* Clothing — hats
Hawaii
Hawks *see* Birds — hawks
Health & fitness
Health & fitness — exercise
Hearing *see* Handicaps — deafness
Heat *see* Concepts — cold & heat
Heavy equipment *see* Machines
Hedgehogs *see* Animals — hedgehogs
Helpfulness *see* Character traits —
    helpfulness
Hens *see* Birds — chickens
Herons *see* Birds — herons
Hibernation
Hiccups
Hiding *see* Behavior — hiding
Hiking *see* Sports — hiking
Hippopotamuses *see* Animals —
    hippopotamuses
Hispanic Americans *see* Ethnic groups in
    the U.S. — Hispanic Americans
Hockey *see* Sports — hockey
Hogs *see* Animals — pigs
Holidays
Holidays — Chanukah *see* Holidays —
    Hanukkah
Holidays — Chinese New Year
Holidays — Christmas
Holidays — Cinco de Mayo
Holidays — Day of the Dead
Holidays — Easter

Holidays — Father's Day
Holidays — Fourth of July
Holidays — Groundhog Day
Holidays — Halloween
Holidays — Hanukkah
Holidays — Independence Day *see*
    Holidays — Fourth of July
Holidays — New Year's
Holidays — Passover
Holidays — Ramadan
Holidays — Rosh Hashanah
Holidays — Rosh Kodesh
Holidays — Seder
Holidays — Thanksgiving
Holidays — Valentine's Day
Homeless
Homes, houses
Homework
Homosexuality
Honesty *see* Character traits — honesty
Honey bees *see* Insects — bees
Hope
Horses *see* Animals — horses, ponies
Hospitals
Hotels
Houses *see* Homes, houses
Hugging
Humorous stories
Hungary *see* Foreign lands — Hungary
Hurricanes *see* Weather — hurricanes
Hygiene *see* Character traits —
    cleanliness; Health & fitness

Ice skating *see* Sports — ice skating
Iceland *see* Foreign lands — Iceland
Identity *see* Self-concept
Iguanas *see* Reptiles — iguanas
Illness
Illness — AIDS
Illness — allergies
Illness — Alzheimer's
Illness — cancer
Illness — cold (disease)
Illness — poliomyelitis
Illustrators *see* Careers — illustrators
Imaginary friends *see* Imagination —
    imaginary friends
Imagination
Imagination — imaginary friends
Imitation *see* Behavior — imitation
Immigrants
Incentive *see* Character traits — ambition
Independence Day *see* Holidays —
    Fourth of July
India *see* Foreign lands — India
Indians, American *see* Indians of North
    America
Indians of North America
Indians of North America — Cherokee
Indians of North America — Choctaw
Indians of North America — Cree
Indians of North America — Inuit
Indians of North America — Lenape
Indians of North America — Metis
Indians of North America —
    Passamaquoddy
Indians of North America — Pima
Indians of North America — Powhatan
Indians of North America — Tiwa
Indians of North America — Tlingit
Indifference *see* Behavior — indifference
Individuality *see* Character traits —
    individuality
Indonesia *see* Foreign lands — Indonesia
Insects

Insects — ants
Insects — bees
Insects — beetles
Insects — butterflies, caterpillars
Insects — cockroaches
Insects — crickets
Insects — dragonflies
Insects — fireflies
Insects — flies
Insects — grasshoppers
Insects — lightning bugs *see* Insects — fireflies
Insects — moths
Inuit Indians *see* Indians of North America — Inuit
Inventions
Inventors *see* Careers — inventors
Iran *see* Foreign lands — Iran
Iraq *see* Foreign lands — Iraq
Ireland *see* Foreign lands — Ireland
Irish Americans *see* Ethnic groups in the U.S. — Irish Americans
Islam *see* Religion — Islam
Islands
Israel *see* Foreign lands — Israel
Italy *see* Foreign lands — Italy

Jamaican Americans *see* Ethnic groups in the U.S. — Jamaican Americans
Janitors *see* Careers — custodians, janitors
Japan *see* Foreign lands — Japan
Japanese Americans *see* Ethnic groups in the U.S. — Japanese Americans
Jealousy *see* Emotions — envy, jealousy
Jesters *see* Clowns, jesters
Jewish Americans *see* Ethnic groups in the U.S. — Jewish Americans
Jewish culture
Jobs *see* Careers
Jockeys *see* Careers — Jockeys
Jokes *see* Riddles & jokes
Jumping *see* Activities — jumping
Jungles

Kangaroos *see* Animals — kangaroos
Karate *see* Sports — karate
Kenya *see* Foreign lands — Kenya
Kindness *see* Character traits — kindness
Kindness to animals *see* Character traits — kindness to animals
Kings *see* Royalty — kings
Kissing
Kites
Knights
Knitting *see* Activities — knitting
Koalas *see* Animals — koalas
Korea *see* Foreign lands — Korea
Korean Americans *see* Ethnic groups in the U.S. — Korean Americans

Lakes, ponds
Lambs *see* Animals — babies; Animals — sheep
Language
Language — sign language *see* Sign language
Languages, foreign *see* Foreign languages
Latin America *see* Foreign lands — Latin America
Laundry
Law *see* Careers — police officers; Crime

Laziness *see* Character traits — laziness
Legends *see* Folk & fairy tales
Lenape Indians *see* Indians of North America — Lenape
Leopards *see* Animals — leopards
Leprechauns *see* Mythical creatures — leprechauns
Letters, cards
Librarians *see* Careers — librarians
Libraries
Light, lights
Lightning *see* Weather — lightning, thunder
Lightning bugs *see* Insects — fireflies
Lions *see* Animals — lions
Littleness *see* Character traits — smallness
Lizards *see* Reptiles — lizards
Llamas *see* Animals — llamas
Lobsters *see* Crustaceans — lobsters
Loneliness *see* Emotions — loneliness
Losing things *see* Behavior — lost & found possessions
Lost *see* Behavior — lost
Love *see* Emotions — love
Luck *see* Character traits — luck
Lullabies
Lying *see* Behavior — lying

Machines
Magic
Magicians *see* Careers — magicians
Mail *see* Letters, cards
Mail carriers *see* Careers — postal workers; Letters, cards
Making things *see* Activities — making things
Mali *see* Foreign lands — Mali
Manners *see* Etiquette
Marionettes *see* Puppets
Markets *see* Stores
Marriages *see* Weddings
Mars *see* Planets
Marsupials *see* Animals — marsupials
Masks
Math *see* Counting, numbers
Mazes
Meanness *see* Character traits — meanness
Measurement *see* Concepts — measurement
Meerkats *see* Animals — meerkats
Memories, memory
Mermaids *see* Mythical creatures — mermaids, mermen
Merry-go-rounds
Messy *see* Behavior — messy
Metamorphosis
Meteorologists *see* Careers — meteorologists
Metis Indians *see* Indians of North America — Metis
Mexican Americans *see* Ethnic groups in the U.S. — Mexican Americans
Mexico *see* Foreign lands — Mexico
Mice *see* Animals — mice
Middle Ages
Middle East *see* Foreign lands — Middle East
Migrant workers *see* Careers — migrant workers
Migration
Military *see* Careers — military
Miners *see* Careers — miners
Minorities *see* Ethnic groups in the U.S.
Misbehavior *see* Behavior — misbehavior

Missions
Mist *see* Weather — fog
Mistakes *see* Behavior — mistakes
Misunderstanding *see* Behavior — misunderstanding
Mittens *see* Clothing — gloves, mittens
Moles *see* Animals — moles
Money
Mongolia *see* Foreign lands — Mongolia
Monkeys *see* Animals — monkeys
Monsters
Months of the year *see* Days of the week, months of the year
Moon
Moose *see* Animals — moose
Morning
Morocco *see* Foreign lands — Morocco
Moses *see* Religion — Moses
Mothers *see* Family life — mothers; Family life — parents; Family life — single-parent families; Family life — step families
Moths *see* Insects — moths
Motion *see* Concepts — motion
Motorcycles
Mountain climbing *see* Sports — mountain climbing
Mountain lions *see* Animals — cougars
Mountains
Moving
Multiple births — triplets
Multiple births — twins
Mummies
Museums
Music
Musical instruments
Musical instruments — accordions
Musical instruments — banjos
Musical instruments — drums
Musical instruments — fiddles *see* Musical instruments — violins
Musical instruments — orchestras
Musical instruments — saxophones
Musical instruments — tubas
Musical instruments — violins
Musicians *see* Careers — musicians
Muskrats *see* Animals — muskrats
Mystery stories
Mythical creatures
Mythical creatures — elves
Mythical creatures — genies
Mythical creatures — leprechauns
Mythical creatures — mermaids, mermen
Mythical creatures — ogres
Mythical creatures — trolls
Mythical creatures — unicorns

Name calling *see* Behavior — name calling
Names
Napping *see* Sleep
Native Americans *see* Indians of North America
Nativity *see* Religion — Nativity
Nature
Naughty *see* Behavior — misbehavior
Neckties *see* Clothing — neckties
Negotiation *see* Activities — trading
Neighborhoods *see* Communities, neighborhoods
Nepal *see* Foreign lands — Nepal
New Year's *see* Holidays — New Year's
Night
Nightmares

No text *see* Wordless
Noah *see* Religion — Noah
Noise, sounds
North Pole *see* Foreign lands — Arctic
Noses *see* Senses — smell
Numbers *see* Counting, numbers
Nursery rhymes
Nursery school *see* School — nursery

Occupations *see* Careers
Oceans *see* Sea & seashore
Octopuses
Odors *see* Senses — smell
Ogres *see* Mythical creatures — ogres
Old age
Olympics *see* Sports — Olympics
Only child *see* Family life — only child
Opossums *see* Animals — possums
Opposites *see* Concepts — opposites
Orangutans *see* Animals — orangutans
Orchestras *see* Musical instruments — orchestras
Orderliness *see* Character traits — orderliness
Orphans
Otters *see* Animals — otters
Outer space *see* Space & space ships
Owls *see* Birds — owls

Pack rats *see* Animals — pack rats
Painters *see* Activities — painting; ; Careers — painters
Painting *see* Activities — painting
Pajamas *see* Clothing — pajamas
Palestine *see* Foreign lands — Palestine
Panama *see* Foreign lands — Panama
Pandas *see* Animals — pandas
Panthers *see* Animals — leopards
Parades
Parks
Parks — amusement
Parrots *see* Birds — parrots
Parties
Passamaquoddy Indians *see* Indians of North America — Passamaquoddy
Passover *see* Holidays — Passover
Patience *see* Character traits — patience
Patterns *see* Concepts — patterns
Pelicans *see* Birds — pelicans
Pen pals
Penguins *see* Birds — penguins
Perfectionism *see* Character traits — perfectionism
Perseverance *see* Character traits — perseverance
Persia *see* Foreign lands — Persia
Persistence *see* Character traits — persistence
Perspective *see* Concepts — perspective
Pets
Photography *see* Activities — photographing
Physical handicaps *see* Handicaps — physical handicaps
Physicians *see* Careers — doctors
Picnics *see* Activities — picnicking
Picture puzzles
Pigeons *see* Birds — pigeons
Pigs *see* Animals — pigs
Pilots *see* Careers — airplane pilots
Pima Indians *see* Indians of North America — Pima
Pioneer life *see* U.S. history — frontier & pioneer life

Pirates
Planes *see* Airplanes, airports
Planets
Plants
Platypuses *see* Animals — platypuses
Playing *see* Activities — playing
Plays *see* Theater
Poetry
Poland *see* Foreign lands — Poland
Polar bears *see* Animals — polar bears
Police officers *see* Careers — police officers
Polio *see* Illness — poliomyelitis
Ponds *see* Lakes, ponds
Ponies *see* Animals — horses, ponies
Poor *see* Homeless; Poverty
Pop-up books *see* Format, unusual — toy & movable books
Porcupines *see* Animals — porcupines
Possums *see* Animals — possums
Postal workers *see* Careers — postal workers
Potty training *see* Toilet training
Poverty
Powhatan Indians *see* Indians of North America — Powhatan
Prairie dogs *see* Animals — prairie dogs
Prehistory
Prejudice
Preschool *see* School — nursery
Pride *see* Character traits — pride
Princes *see* Royalty — princes
Princesses *see* Royalty — princesses
Problem solving
Puerto Ricans *see* Ethnic groups in the U.S. — Puerto Rican Americans
Puerto Rico *see* Foreign lands — Puerto Rico
Puffins *see* Birds — puffins
Pumas *see* Animals — cougars
Puppets
Puzzles *see also* Picture puzzles; Rebuses; Riddles & jokes

Queens *see* Royalty — queens
Questioning *see* Character traits — questioning
Quilts

Rabbits *see* Animals — rabbits
Raccoons *see* Animals — raccoons
Race relations *see* Prejudice
Racially mixed *see* Ethnic groups in the U.S. — Racially mixed
Racing *see* Sports — racing
Railroads *see* Trains
Rain *see* Weather — rain
Ramadan *see* Holidays — Ramadan
Ranchers *see* Careers — ranchers
Rats *see* Animals — rats
Reading *see* Books, reading
Rebuses
Religion
Religion — Daniel
Religion — Islam
Religion — Moses
Religion — Nativity
Religion — Noah
Remembering *see* Memories, memory
Repetitive stories *see* Cumulative tales
Reptiles — alligators, crocodiles
Reptiles — chameleons
Reptiles — crocodiles *see* Reptiles — alligators, crocodiles

Reptiles — iguanas
Reptiles — lizards
Reptiles — snakes
Reptiles — turtles, tortoises
Resourcefulness *see* Behavior — resourcefulness; Character traits — resourcefulness
Responsibility *see* Character traits — responsibility
Restaurants
Rhinoceros *see* Animals — rhinoceros
Rhyming text
Riddles & jokes
Roads
Robbers *see* Crime
Robins *see* Birds — robins
Robots
Rockets *see* Space & space ships
Rocking chairs *see* Furniture — chairs
Rocks
Rodeos
Roosters *see* Birds — chickens
Rosh Hashanah *see* Holidays — Rosh Hashanah
Rosh Kodesh *see* Holidays — Rosh Kodesh
Royalty
Royalty — kings
Royalty — princes
Royalty — princesses
Royalty — queens
Royalty — sultans
Running *see* Sports — racing
Running away *see* Behavior — running away
Russia *see* Foreign lands — Russia

Sadness *see* Emotions — sadness
Safety
Sailing *see* Sports — sailing
Salesmen *see* Careers — salesmen
Sandpipers *see* Birds — sandpipers
Sanitation workers *see* Careers — sanitation workers
Santa Claus
Saxophones *see* Musical instruments — saxophones
School
School — field trips
School — first day
School — nursery
School principals *see* Careers — school principals
School teachers *see* Careers — teachers
Science
Scientists *see* Careers — scientists
Sculptors *see* Careers — sculptors
Sea & seashore
Sea & seashore — beaches
Seagulls *see* Birds — seagulls
Seahorses *see* Fish — seahorses
Seals *see* Animals — seals
Seashore *see* Sea & seashore — beaches
Seasons
Seasons — fall
Seasons — spring
Seasons — summer
Seasons — winter
Secrets *see* Behavior — secrets
Seder *see* Holidays — Seder
Seeds
Seeing *see* Glasses; Handicaps — blindness; Senses — sight
Seeing eye dogs *see* Animals — service animals

Self-concept
Self-esteem *see* Self-concept
Self-image *see* Self-concept
Self-reliance *see* Character traits — confidence
Selfishness *see* Character traits — selfishness
Senses
Senses — sight
Senses — smell
Service animals *see* Animals — service animals
Sewing *see* Activities — sewing
Sex instruction
Sex roles *see* Gender roles
Shadows
Shape *see* Concepts — shape
Sharing *see* Behavior — sharing
Sharks *see* Fish — sharks
Sheep *see* Animals — sheep
Shepherds *see* Careers — shepherds
Sheriffs *see* Careers — sheriffs
Ships *see* Boats, ships
Shoemakers *see* Careers — shoemakers
Shoes *see* Clothing — shoes
Shopping
Shops *see* Stores
Shows *see* Theater
Shyness *see* Character traits — shyness
Siam *see* Foreign lands — Thailand
Sibling rivalry
Siblings *see* Family life — brothers & sisters; Family life — step families
Sickness *see* Health & fitness; Illness
Sight *see* Glasses; Handicaps — blindness; Senses — sight
Sign language
Singers *see* Careers — singers
Singing *see* Activities — singing
Single-parent families *see* Family life — single-parent families
Sisters *see* Family life; Family life — brothers & sisters; Sibling rivalry
Size *see* Concepts — size
Skating *see* Sports — ice skating
Skeletons *see* Anatomy — skeletons
Skiing *see* Sports — skiing
Skin *see* Anatomy — skin
Skunks *see* Animals — skunks
Sky
Slavery
Sledding *see* Sports — sledding
Sleep
Sleep — snoring
Sleepovers
Sleight-of-hand *see* Magic
Slugs *see* Animals — slugs
Smallness *see* Character traits — smallness
Smell *see* Senses — smell
Smiles, smiling *see* Anatomy — faces
Snails *see* Animals — snails
Snakes *see* Reptiles — snakes
Snoring *see* Sleep — snoring
Snow *see* Weather — blizzards; Weather — snow
Snowmen
Soccer *see* Sports — soccer
Socks *see* Clothing — socks
Sofas *see* Furniture — couches, sofas
Soldiers *see* Careers — military
Solitude *see* Behavior — solitude
Somalia *see* Foreign lands — Somalia
Songs
Sorcerers *see* Wizards
Sounds *see* Noise, sounds

South Africa *see* Foreign lands — South Africa
South Pole *see* Foreign lands — Antarctica
Space & space ships
Spain *see* Foreign lands — Spain
Spectacles *see* Glasses
Spiders
Sports
Sports — baseball
Sports — basketball
Sports — bicycling
Sports — boxing
Sports — fishing
Sports — football
Sports — gymnastics
Sports — hiking
Sports — hockey
Sports — ice skating
Sports — karate
Sports — mountain climbing
Sports — Olympics
Sports — racing
Sports — sailing
Sports — skiing
Sports — sledding
Sports — soccer
Sports — swimming
Sports — T-ball
Sports — tennis
Sportsmanship
Spring *see* Seasons — spring
Squid
Squirrels *see* Animals — squirrels
Stage *see* Theater
Stars
Stealing *see* Behavior — stealing; Crime
Step families *see* Divorce; Family life — step families
Stepchildren *see* Divorce; Family life — step families
Stepparents *see* Divorce; Family life — step families
Stones *see* Rocks
Stores
Stories in rhyme *see* Rhyming text
Storks *see* Birds — storks
Storms *see* Weather — storms
Storytelling *see* Activities — storytelling
Strangers *see* Behavior — talking to strangers
Streets *see* Roads
Stubbornness *see* Character traits — stubbornness
Sultans *see* Royalty — sultans
Summer *see* Seasons — summer
Sun
Superstition
Surfing *see* Sports — surfing
Swallows *see* Birds — swallows
Swamps
Swans *see* Birds — swans
Swapping *see* Activities — trading
Sweaters *see* Clothing — sweaters
Swimming *see* Sports — swimming
Switzerland *see* Foreign lands — Switzerland

T-ball *see* Sports — T-ball
Tailors *see* Careers — tailors
Tails *see* Anatomy — tails
Talking *see* Activities — talking
Talking to strangers *see* Behavior — talking to strangers
Tall tales

Tanzania *see* Foreign lands — Tanzania
Teachers *see* Careers — teachers
Teasing *see* Behavior — bullying
Teddy bears *see* Toys — bears
Teeth
Television
Telling stories *see* Activities — storytelling
Telling time *see* Clocks, watches; Time
Temper tantrums *see* Emotions — anger
Tennis *see* Sports — tennis
Texas
Thailand *see* Foreign lands — Thailand
Thanksgiving *see* Holidays — Thanksgiving
Theater
Thunder *see* Weather — lightning, thunder; Weather — storms
Tigers *see* Animals — tigers
Time
Tiwa Indians *see* Indians of North America — Tiwa
Tlingit Indians *see* Indians of North America — Tlingit
Toads *see* Frogs & toads
Toes *see* Anatomy — toes
Toilet training
Toilets
Tools
Tornadoes *see* Weather — tornadoes
Tortoises *see* Reptiles — turtles, tortoises
Towns *see* Cities, towns
Toy & movable books *see* Format, unusual — toy & movable books
Toys
Toys — balloons
Toys — balls
Toys — bears
Toys — dolls
Toys — pandas *see* Toys — bears
Toys — teddy bears *see* Toys — bears
Tractors
Trading *see* Activities — trading
Trains
Transportation
Traveling *see* Activities — traveling
Trees
Trickery *see* Behavior — trickery
Tricks *see* Magic
Trinidad *see* Foreign lands — Trinidad
Trolls *see* Mythical creatures — trolls
Truck drivers *see* Careers — truck drivers
Trucks
Tsunamis
Tubas *see* Musical instruments — tubas
Turkeys *see* Birds — turkeys
Turtles *see* Reptiles — turtles, tortoises
TV *see* Television
Twins *see* Multiple births — twins

U.S. history
U.S. history — frontier & pioneer life
Umbrellas
Uncles *see* Family life — aunts, uncles
Unhappiness *see* Emotions — happiness; Emotions — sadness
Unicorns *see* Mythical creatures — unicorns
Unusual format *see* Format, unusual
Up & down *see* Concepts — up & down

Vacationing *see* Activities — vacationing
Valentine's Day *see* Holidays — Valentine's Day
Venezuela *see* Foreign lands — Venezuela

Veterinarians *see* Careers — veterinarians
Vietnam *see* Foreign lands — Vietnam
Violins *see* Musical instruments — violins
Volcanoes
Vultures *see* Birds — vultures

Waiters *see* Careers — waiters, waitresses
Waitresses *see* Careers — waiters,
    waitresses
Walking *see* Activities — walking
Wallabies *see* Animals — wallabies
War
Watches *see* Clocks, watches
Water
Weasels *see* Animals — weasels
Weather
Weather — blizzards
Weather — clouds
Weather — cold
Weather — droughts
Weather — floods
Weather — fog
Weather — hurricanes
Weather — lightning, thunder

Weather — mist *see* Weather — fog
Weather — rain
Weather — snow
Weather — storms
Weather — thunder *see* Weather —
    lightning, thunder
Weather — tornadoes
Weather — wind
Weather reporters *see* Careers —
    meteorologists
Weaving *see* Activities — weaving
Weddings
Weekdays *see* Days of the week, months of
    the year
West *see* U.S. history — frontier &
    pioneer life
Whales *see* Animals — whales
Wheels
Willfulness *see* Character traits —
    willfulness
Wind *see* Weather — wind
Wings *see* Anatomy — wings
Winter *see* Seasons — winter
Wishing *see* Behavior — wishing
Witches
Wizards

Wolves *see* Animals — wolves
Wombats *see* Animals — wombats
Woodcarving *see* Activities — wood
    carving
Woodchucks *see* Animals — groundhogs
Woods *see* Forest, woods
Wooly mammoths *see* Animals — wooly
    mammoths
Word games *see* Language
Wordless
Working *see* Activities — working; Careers
World
Worms *see* Animals — worms
Worrying *see* Behavior — worrying
Writing *see* Activities — writing
Writing letters *see* Letters, cards

Yaks *see* Animals — yaks
Yukon Territory *see* Foreign lands —
    Yukon Territory

Zodiac
Zoos

Subject Guide

This is a subject-arranged guide to picture books. Under appropriate subject headings and subheadings, titles appear alphabetically by author name, or by title when author is unknown. Complete bibliographic information for each title cited will be found in the Bibliographic Guide.

ABC books

Alberti, Theresa Jarosz. *Vietnam ABCs*
Aylesworth, Jim. *Little Bitty Mousie*
Belle, Jennifer. *Animal stackers*
Blackstone, Stella. *Alligator alphabet*
Bruel, Nick. *Bad Kitty*
   Poor puppy
Butler, Dori Hillestad. *F is for firefighting*
C is for caboose
Cleary, Brian P. *Peanut butter and jellyfishes*
Compestine, Ying Chang. *D is for dragon dance*
Crane, Carol. *D is for dancing dragon*
Cronin, Doreen. *Click clack, quackity-quack*
Delessert, Etienne. *A was an apple pie*
Demarest, Chris L. *Alpha Bravo Charlie*
DiTerlizzi, Tony. *G is for one gzonk!*
Domeniconi, David. *M is for masterpiece*
Downie, Mary Alice. *A pioneer ABC*
Doyle, Charlotte Lackner. *The bouncing, dancing, galloping ABC*
Dugan, Joanne. *ABC NYC*
Elya, Susan Middleton. *F is for fiesta*
   N is for Navidad
Engelbreit, Mary. *Mary Engelbreit's A merry little Christmas*
Freymann, Saxton. *Food for thought*
Herzog, Brad. *R is for race*
Janovitz, Marilyn. *A, B, see!*
Jocelyn, Marthe. *ABC x 3*
Kontis, Alethea. *Alpha oops!*
Layne, Steven L. *T is for teachers*
Lobel, Anita. *Animal antics*
London, Jonathan. *Do your ABC's, Little Brown Bear*
MacDonald, Suse. *Edward Lear's A was once an apple pie*
McLeod, Bob. *Super hero ABC*
McLimans, David. *Gone wild*
Marino, Gianna. *Zoopa*
Melmed, Laura Krauss. *New York, New York!*
Michaels, Pat. *W is for wind*
Minor, Wendell. *Yankee Doodle America*
Mora, Pat. *Marimba!*
Murphy, Liz. *ABC doctor*
Nickle, John. *Alphabet explosion!*
O'Keefe, Susan Heyboer. *Hungry monster ABC*
Pallotta, Jerry. *The construction alphabet book*
Raczka, Bob. *3-D ABC*
Rogalski, Mark. *Tickets to ride*
Sanders, Nancy. *D is for drinking gourd*
Seeger, Laura Vaccaro. *Walter was worried*
Shindler, Ramon. *Found alphabet*

Shoulders, Michael. *D is for drum*
Shulman, Mark. *A is for zebra*
   Aa is for Aardvark
Slate, Joseph. *Miss Bindergarten celebrates the last day of kindergarten*
   Miss Bindergarten has a wild day in kindergarten
Smith, Marie. *N is for our nation's capital*
   Z is for zookeeper
Sobel, June. *Shiver me letters*
Spirin, Gennady. *A apple pie*
Stewig, John Warren. *The animals watched*
Sweet, Melissa. *Carmine*
Wallace, Nancy Elizabeth. *Alphabet house*
Wells, Rosemary. *Max's ABC*
Wood, Audrey. *Alphabet rescue*

Abused children *see* Child abuse

Accidents

Lujan, Jorge. *Sky blue accident / Accidente celeste*
Pulver, Robin. *Axle Annie and the speed grump*

Accordions *see* Musical instruments — accordions

Activities

Day, Alexandra. *Carl's sleepy afternoon*
Franco, Betsy. *Summer beat*
O'Connor, Jane. *Ready, set, skip!*

Activities — babysitting

Kromhout, Rindert. *Little Donkey and the baby-sitter*
Ward, Nick. *Don't eat the babysitter!*

Activities — baking, cooking

Cazet, Denys. *The perfect pumpkin pie*
Cooper, Helen (Helen F.). *Delicious!*
   A pipkin of pepper
Denise, Anika. *Pigs love potatoes*
Evans, Lezlie. *The bunnies' picnic*
Grey, Mini. *Ginger bear*
Howe, James. *Houndsley and Catina*
The little red hen. *The little red hen*
   The little red hen: an old fable
McAlister, Caroline. *Holy Molé!*
Manushkin, Fran. *How Mama brought the spring*
Martin, David. *All for pie, pie for all*
Mother Goose. *Pat-a-cake*
Mozelle, Shirley. *The bear upstairs*
Park, Linda Sue. *Bee-bim bop!*
Reynolds, Aaron. *Buffalo wings*
   Chicks and salsa
Roberts, Bethany. *Cookie angel*
Rosenthal, Amy Krouse. *Cookies*
Shulman, Lisa. *The moon might be milk*
Simmonds, Posy. *Baker cat*
Smalls, Irene. *My Pop Pop and me*

Stadler, Alexander. *Beverly Billingsly takes the cake*
Stowell, Penelope. *The greatest potatoes*
Teevin, Toni. *What to do? What to do?*
Wellington, Monica. *Mr. Cookie Baker*
    Pizza at Sally's
Wilson, Karma. *Whopper cake*
Wolff, Nancy. *Tallulah in the kitchen*
Yamada, Utako. *The story of Cherry the pig*

Activities — ballooning

Priceman, Marjorie. *Hot air*
Rawlinson, Julia. *A surprise for Rosie*
Sakai, Komako. *Emily's balloon*

Activities — bargaining *see* Activities — trading

Activities — bartering *see* Activities — trading

Activities — bathing

Ehrlich, Fred. *Does an elephant take a bath?*
Esbaum, Jill. *Estelle takes a bath*
Ficocelli, Elizabeth. *Kid tea*
Harper, Jamie. *Splish splash, baby bundt*
Jones, Sylvie. *Who's in the tub?*
Landstrom, Lena. *A hippo's tale*
Neubecker, Robert. *Beasty bath*
Pelletier, Andrew T. *The amazing adventures of Bathman!*
Teckentrup, Britta. *Big smelly bear*
Weninger, Brigitte. *"No bath! No way!"*

Activities — cooking *see* Activities — baking, cooking

Activities — dancing

Baryshnikov, Mikhail. *Because . . .*
Bell, Cece. *Sock Monkey boogie-woogie*
Bradley, Kimberly Brubaker. *Ballerino Nate*
Capucilli, Alyssa Satin. *Katy Duck*
    Katy Duck, big sister
Chaconas, Dori. *Dancing with Katya*
DePalma, Mary Newell. *The Nutcracker doll*
Durango, Julia. *Cha-cha chimps*
Elliott, David. *One little chicken*
French, Jackie. *Josephine wants to dance*
Grimm, Jacob. *The twelve dancing princesses*
Gruska, Denise. *The only boy in ballet class*
Hager, Sarah. *Dancing Matilda*
Headley, Justina Chen. *The patch*
Holabird, Katharine. *Christmas in Mouseland*
Hutchins, Pat. *Barn dance!*
Knister. *Sophie's dance*
Pinkwater, Daniel Manus. *Dancing Larry*
Quattlebaum, Mary. *Sparks fly high*
Ryder, Joanne. *Dance by the light of the moon*
Schaefer, Carole Lexa. *Dragon dancing*
Thomas, Joyce Carol. *Shouting*
Thompson, Lauren. *Ballerina dreams*
Wheeler, Lisa. *Hokey pokey*
Young, Amy. *Belinda and the glass slipper*
    Belinda begins ballet
    Belinda in Paris

Activities — drawing

Edwards, Pamela Duncan. *The neat line*
Ericsson, Jennifer A. *A piece of chalk*
Freedman, Deborah. *Scribble*
Gretz, Susanna. *Riley and Rose in the picture*
Johnson, D. B. (Donald B.). *Eddie's kingdom*
McDonnell, Patrick. *Art*
Mills, Claudia. *Ziggy's blue-ribbon day*
Watt, Melanie. *Chester*
Wing, Natasha. *Go to bed, monster!*

Activities — driving

Pulver, Robin. *Axle Annie and the speed grump*
Timmers, Leo. *Who is driving?*
Wilson, Karma. *Sakes alive!*

Activities — eating *see* Food

Activities — flying

Berkeley, Jon. *Chopsticks*
Hodgkins, Fran. *How people learned to fly*
Johnson, Angela. *Wind flyers*
Kinerk, Robert. *Clorinda takes flight*
McCarty, Peter. *Moon plane*
Morison, Toby. *Little Louie takes off*
Rau, Dana Meachen. *Flying*
Stanley, Mandy. *Lettice the flying rabbit*
Willard, Nancy. *The flying bed*
Willems, Mo. *Today I will fly!*

Activities — gardening *see* Gardens, gardening

Activities — jumping

Cronin, Doreen. *Bounce*

Activities — kissing *see* Kissing

Activities — knitting

Bunge, Daniela. *The scarves*
Waterton, Betty. *A bumblebee sweater*

Activities — making things

Kleven, Elisa. *The apple doll*
Lin, Grace. *Lissy's friends*
Michelin, Linda (Donald B.). *Zuzu's wishing cake*
Rylant, Cynthia. *If you'll be my Valentine*
Sturges, Philemon. *I love tools!*
Ziefert, Harriet. *Grandma, it's for you!*
    Knick-knack paddywhack

Activities — painting *see also* Careers — artists

Arnold, Katya. *Elephants can paint, too!*
Beaumont, Karen. *I ain't gonna paint no more!*
Demi. *The boy who painted dragons*
Hong, Chen Jiang. *The magic horse of Han Gan*
Johnson, Angela. *Lily Brown's paintings*
Sweet, Melissa. *Carmine*

Activities — photographing

Perkins, Lynne Rae. *Pictures from our vacation*
Scotton, Rob. *Russell and the lost treasure*

Activities — picnicking

Cronin, Doreen. *Click clack, quackity-quack*
Elya, Susan Middleton. *Oh no, gotta go #2*
Evans, Lezlie. *The bunnies' picnic*
Goode, Diane. *The most perfect spot*
Graham, Bob. *Oscar's half birthday*
Lies, Brian. *Bats at the beach*
Livingston, Irene. *Finklehopper Frog cheers*
Murphy, Mary. *Panda Foo and the new friend*
Webster, Christine. *Otter everywhere*

Activities — playing

Anderson, Peggy Perry. *Joe on the go*
Ayres, Katherine. *Matthew's truck*
Baguley, Elizabeth. *Meggie moon*
Beaty, Andrea. *When giants come to play*
Brown, Jo. *Hoppity skip Little Chick*
Brown, Susan Taylor. *Oliver's must-do list*

Butler, John. *Ten in the meadow*
Capucilli, Alyssa Satin. *Little spotted cat*
Crews, Nina. *Below*
Cuyler, Margery. *Please play safe!*
Doyle, Charlotte Lackner. *The bouncing, dancing, galloping ABC*
Eaton, Maxwell. *Superheroes*
Ellery, Amanda. *If I had a dragon*
Greenfield, Eloise. *The friendly four*
Gutierrez, Akemi. *The mummy and other adventures of Sam and Alice*
Heide, Iris van der. *The red chalk*
Konnecke, Ole. *Anthony and the girls*
Lakin, Patricia. *Rainy day*
Lawler, Janet. *A father's song*
MacLennan, Cathy. *Chicky Chicky Chook Chook*
McPhail, David. *Emma in charge*
Merz, Jennifer J. *Playground day*
Milgrim, David. *Time to get up, time to go*
O'Connor, George. *Ker-splash!*
Ohi, Ruth. *And you can come too*
O'Keefe, Susan Heyboer. *Baby day*
Portis, Antoinette. *Not a box*
Ritchie, Alison. *What Bear likes best!*
Rodman, Mary Ann. *My best friend*
Schertle, Alice. *The adventures of old Bo Bear*
Schwartz, Corey Rosen. *Hop! Plop!*
Smalls, Irene. *My Nana and me*
Smith, Lois T. *Carrie and Carl play*
Stein, David Ezra. *Monster hug!*
Thompson, Lauren. *Little Quack's new friend*
Weeks, Sarah. *Overboard!*
Wolff, Nancy. *It's time for school with Tallulah*
Wood, Douglas. *Nothing to do*
Yolen, Jane. *Dimity Duck*
      Soft house

Activities — reading *see* Books, reading

Activities — sewing

Cotten, Cynthia. *Abbie in stitches*

Activities — shopping *see* Shopping

Activities — singing

Bolliger, Max. *The happy troll*
Daly, Niki. *Ruby sings the blues*
Elya, Susan Middleton. *Sophie's trophy*
Martin, Jacqueline Briggs. *Chicken joy on Redbean Road*
Watts, Leslie Elizabeth. *The Baabaasheep Quartet*

Activities — storytelling

Aska, Warabe. *Tapicero tap tap*
Banks, Kate (Katherine A.). *Max's words*
Downey, Lynn. *Matilda's humdinger*
Kurtz, Jane. *In the small, small night*
Muth, Jon J. *Zen shorts*
Robberecht, Thierry. *Sam tells stories*
Say, Allen. *Kamishibai man*
Taback, Simms. *Kibitzers and fools*

Activities — swapping *see* Activities — trading

Activities — swimming *see* Sports — swimming

Activities — talking

Hindley, Judy. *Baby talk*

Activities — trading

Heide, Iris van der. *The red chalk*

Activities — traveling

Alsenas, Linas. *Mrs. Claus takes a vacation*

Brunhoff, Laurent de. *Babar's world tour*
Dunbar, Joyce. *Shoe baby*
Egan, Tim. *Dodsworth in New York*
Eschbacher, Roger. *Road trip*
Faller, Regis. *The adventures of Polo*
      Polo
Hobbie, Holly. *Toot and Puddle*
Krebs, Laurie. *Off we go to Mexico*
      We're riding on a caravan
      We're sailing down the Nile
      We're sailing to Galapagos
Louis, Catherine. *Liu and the bird*
Neubecker, Robert. *Courage of the blue boy*
Ohi, Ruth. *A trip with Grandma*
Orona-Ramirez, Kristy. *Kiki's journey*
Pattison, Darcy. *Searching for Oliver K. Woodman*
Rosen, Michael J. (1954[EN]). *A drive in the country*
Skinner, Daphne. *All aboard!*
Smath, Jerry. *Sammy Salami*
Wood, Audrey. *Silly Sally*
Ziefert, Harriet. *From Kalamazoo to Timbuktu!*

Activities — vacationing

Alsenas, Linas. *Mrs. Claus takes a vacation*
Becker, Suzy. *Manny's cows*
Chapra, Mimi. *Sparky's bark / El ladrido de Sparky*
Davies, Jacqueline. *The house takes a vacation*
Koch, Ed. *Eddie's little sister makes a splash*
Perkins, Lynne Rae. *Pictures from our vacation*
Puttock, Simon. *Goat and Donkey in the great outdoors*
Smath, Jerry. *Sammy Salami*
Stock, Catherine. *A porc in New York*

Activities — walking

Briggs, Raymond. *The puddleman*
Cooper, Elisha. *A good night walk*
Frazee, Marla. *Walk on!*

Activities — weaving

Shah, Idries. *Fatima the spinner and the tent*

Activities — wood carving

Martín, Hugo C. *Pablo's Christmas*

Activities — working

Ancona, George. *Mis quehaceres / My chores*
Asim, Jabari. *Daddy goes to work*
Cordsen, Carol Foskett. *The milkman*
Ericsson, Jennifer A. *Home to me, home to you*
Gershator, Phillis. *Sky sweeper*
Hartland, Jessie. *Night shift*
Purmwell, Ann. *Christmas tree farm*
Taber, Tory. *Rufus at work*

Activities — writing

Christelow, Eileen. *Letters from a desperate dog*
Cronin, Doreen. *Click clack, quackity-quack*
      Diary of a fly
      Diary of a spider
Danneberg, Julie. *Cowboy Slim*
Dubosarsky, Ursula. *Rex*
Howe, James. *Houndsley and Catina*
Kempter, Christa. *Dear Little Lamb*
Kirk, David. *Library mouse*
Louis, Catherine. *Liu and the bird*
Morgan, Michaela. *Dear bunny*
Muntean, Michaela. *Do not open this book!*
O'Malley, Kevin. *Once upon a cool motorcycle dude*
Pearson, Susan. *Slugs in love*
Wallner, Alexandra. *Lucy Maud Montgomery*
Watt, Melanie. *Chester*

Activities – playing

Cronin, Doreen. *Bounce*

Actors *see* Careers — actors

Adoption

Carlson, Nancy L. *My family is forever*
Coste, Marion. *Finding Joy*
Friedrich, Molly. *You're not my real mother!*
Garden, Nancy. *Molly's family*
Joosse, Barbara M. *Nikolai, the only bear*
Krishnaswami, Uma. *Bringing Asha home*
Lears, Laurie. *Megan's birthday tree*
Lewis, Rose A. *Every year on your birthday*
Lin, Grace. *The red thread*
McMahon, Patricia. *Just add one Chinese sister*
Parr, Todd. *We belong together*
Stoeke, Janet Morgan. *Waiting for May*
Sugarman, Brynn Olenberg. *Rebecca's journey home*
Thomas, Eliza. *The red blanket*
Wynne-Jones, Tim. *The boat in the tree*
Xinran, Xue. *Motherbridge of love*
Young, Ed. *My Mei Mei*

Afghanistan *see* Foreign lands — Afghanistan

Africa *see* Foreign lands — Africa

African Americans *see* Ethnic groups in the U.S. — African Americans

Aged *see* Old age

AIDS *see* Illness — AIDS

Airplane pilots *see* Careers — airplane pilots

Airplanes, airports

Hodgkins, Fran. *How people learned to fly*
McCarty, Peter. *Moon plane*
Stanley, Mandy. *Lettice the flying rabbit*

Airports *see* Airplanes, airports

Alaska

Aillaud, Cindy Lou. *Recess at 20 below*
Gill, Shelley. *Up on Denali*
Joosse, Barbara M. *Wind-wild dog*
London, Jonathan. *Sled dogs run*

Aliens

Breathed, Berkeley. *Mars needs moms!*
O'Malley, Kevin. *Captain Raptor and the moon mystery*
Schories, Pat. *Jack and the night visitors*

All Souls' Day *see* Holidays — Day of the Dead

Allergies *see* Illness — allergies

Alligators *see* Reptiles — alligators, crocodiles

Alphabet books *see* ABC books

Alzheimer's *see* Illness — Alzheimer's

Ambition *see* Character traits — ambition

American Indians *see* Indians of North America

Amphibians *see* Frogs & toads; Reptiles

Amusement parks *see* Parks — amusement

Anatomy

Henderson, Kathy. *Look at you!*
Jenkins, Steve. *Prehistoric actual size*
Moore, Julianne. *Freckleface Strawberry*
Saltz, Gail. *Amazing you*
Schwartz, Amy. *A beautiful girl*

Anatomy — faces

Ehrlich, Fred. *Does a seal smile?*
Rayner, Catherine. *Augustus and his smile*

Anatomy — feet

Crocker, Nancy. *Betty Lou Blue*
Ellis, Sarah. *The queen's feet*
Pearson, Susan. *Hooray for feet!*
Vail, Rachel. *Righty and Lefty*
Young, Amy. *Belinda and the glass slipper*
    Belinda begins ballet
    Belinda in Paris

Anatomy — skeletons

Pickering, Jimmy. *Skelly the skeleton girl*

Anatomy — skin

Tyler, Michael. *The skin you live in*

Anatomy — tails

Duvall, Deborah L. *The opossum's tale*
Feiffer, Kate. *Henry, the dog with no tail*

Anatomy — teeth *see* Teeth

Anatomy — toes

Madison, Alan. *The littlest grape stomper*

Anatomy — wings

Tanaka, Shinsuke. *Wings*

Angels

Arrigan, Mary. *Mario's angels*
dePaola, Tomie. *Angels, Angels everywhere*
Durango, Julia. *Angels watching over me*
Morpurgo, Michael. *On angel wings*
Roberts, Bethany. *Cookie angel*
Spinelli, Eileen. *City angel*

Anger *see* Emotions — anger

Animals *see also* Birds; Frogs & toads; Reptiles

Alborough, Jez. *Tall*
Allen, Jonathan. *"I'm not cute!"*
Anderson, Peggy Perry. *Chuck's truck*
Arnosky, Jim. *Babies in the bayou*
Ashman, Linda. *Babies on the go*
Baddiel, Ivor. *Cock-a-doodle quack! Quack!*
Bailey, Linda. *The farm team*
Barretta, Gene. *Dear deer*
Bauer, Marion Dane. *If frogs made the weather*
Beaver steals fire
Behrens, Janice. *Let's find rain forest animals*
Belle, Jennifer. *Animal stackers*
Berkes, Marianne Collins. *Over in the jungle*
Blackstone, Stella. *Alligator alphabet*
Bonnett-Rampersaud, Louise. *How do you sleep?*

Brooks, Erik. *Slow days, fast friends*
Brown, Lisa. *How to be*
Bunting, Eve (Anne Evelyn). *Hurry! Hurry!*
Butler, John. *Can you growl like a bear?*
  Ten in the den
  Ten in the meadow
Butler, M. Christina. *One winter's day*
Cabrera, Jane. *If you're happy and you know it*
Calmenson, Stephanie. *Birthday at the Panda Palace*
Carlson, Nancy L. *Get up and go!*
Carris, Joan. *Welcome to the bed and biscuit*
Carter, David A. *Whoo? Whoo?*
Cartwright, Reg. *What we do*
Casey, Dawn. *The great race*
Chernaik, Judith. *Carnival of the animals*
Chicken Little. *Henny Penny*
Conway, David. *The most important gift of all*
Cooper, Helen (Helen F.). *Delicious!*
  A pipkin of pepper
Côté, Geneviève. *With you always, Little Monday*
Cousins, Lucy. *Maisy, Charley, and the wobbly tooth*
Cowley, Joy. *Mrs. Wishy-Washy's Christmas*
Crawford, Laura. *In arctic waters*
Cronin, Doreen. *Click clack, quackity-quack*
  Click, clack, splish, splash
  Dooby dooby moo
Crum, Shutta. *A family for Old Mill Farm*
Dale, Penny. *The boy on the bus*
Daly, Niki. *Welcome to Zanzibar Road*
Demers, Dominique. *Every single night*
Denslow, Sharon Phillips. *In the snow*
Derrick, Patricia. *Riley the rhinoceros*
Díaz, Katacha. *Badger at Sandy Ridge Road*
Downey, Lynn. *Matilda's humdinger*
Downing, Johnette. *Down in Louisiana*
Dutton, Sandra. *Dear Miss Perfect*
Edwards, Pamela Duncan. *Ms. Bitsy Bat's kindergarten*
Egan, Tim. *Dodsworth in New York*
  The pink refrigerator
Ehrlich, Fred. *Does a baboon sleep in a bed?*
  Does a camel cook?
  Does a chimp wear clothes?
  Does a duck have a daddy?
  Does a giraffe drive?
  Does a mouse have a mommy?
  Does a seal smile?
  Does an elephant take a bath?
Eriksson, Eva. *A crash course for Molly*
Farber, Norma. *How the hibernators came to Bethlehem*
Fisher, Aileen Lucia. *Do rabbits have Christmas?*
  Know what I saw?
Fitzgerald, Joanne. *Yum! Yum!*
Fleming, Denise. *The cow who clucked*
Florian, Douglas. *Zoo's who*
Foley, Greg. *Thank you, Bear*
Freedman, Claire. *One magical day*
  One magical morning
  Snuggle up, sleepy ones
A frog he would a-wooing go (folk-song). *Froggy went a-courtin'*
George, Lindsay Barrett. *In the garden*
  The secret
Gerstein, Mordicai. *Leaving the nest*
Gillham, Bill. *How many sharks in the bath?*
Giogas, Valarie. *In my backyard*
Gorbachev, Valeri. *Red red red*
Greene, Rhonda Gowler. *Noah and the mighty ark*
Griessman, Annette. *Like a hundred drums*
Grimm, Jacob. *The Bremen town musicians*
  Musicians of Bremen
  Musicians of Bremen / Los musicos de Bremner
  Snow White
Hague, Michael. *Animal friends*
Hamilton, Martha. *The hidden feast*
Harper, Jamie. *Miss Mingo and the first day of school*
Harper, Jessica. *A place called Kindergarten*
Harper, Jo. *I could eat you up!*
Harris, Robie H. *Maybe a bear ate it!*

Hayward, Linda. *The King's chorus*
Henkes, Kevin. *A good day*
Himmelman, John. *Mouse in a meadow*
Hindley, Judy. *Sleepy places*
Hogg, Gary. *Beautiful Buehla and the zany zoo makeover*
Horacek, Petr. *Silly Suzy Goose*
Horowitz, Dave. *Soon, Baboon, soon*
Horton, Joan. *Hippopotamus stew*
Hutchins, Pat. *Barn dance!*
Isaacs, Anne. *Pancakes for supper!*
Janovitz, Marilyn. *A, B, see!*
Jenkins, Steve. *Living color*
  Move!
  Prehistoric actual size
Jocelyn, Marthe. *Eats*
Johnson, D. B. (Donald B.). *Four legs bad, two legs good!*
Johnson, Paul Brett. *On top of spaghetti*
Jones, Sylvie. *Who's in the tub?*
Kangas, Juli. *The surprise visitor*
Keller, Holly. *Help!*
Keller, Laurie. *Do unto otters*
Kelly, Mij. *Where's my darling daughter?*
Khing, T. T. *Where is the cake?*
Kinerk, Robert. *Clorinda takes flight*
Klise, Kate. *Why do you cry?*
Krebs, Laurie. *We're sailing to Galapagos*
Kroll, Steven. *Jungle bullies*
Krosoczka, Jarrett J. *Punk Farm*
  Punk Farm on tour
Kudlinski, Kathleen V. *The sunset switch*
Kumin, Maxine W. *Mites to astodons*
Kurtz, Jane. *Do kangaroos wear seat belts?*
Larios, Julie Hofstrand. *Yellow elephant*
Lewis, J. Patrick. *Tulip at the bat*
The little red hen. *The little red hen*
  The little red hen: an old fable
Lloyd-Jones, Sally. *Time to say goodnight*
Lobel, Anita. *Animal antics*
Lobel, Gillian. *Little Honey Bear and the smiley moon*
Louise, Tina. *When I grow up*
MacDonald, Alan. *Wilfred to the rescue*
MacDonald, Margaret Read. *A hen, a chick, and a string guitar*
  The squeaky door
McDonald, Megan. *When the library lights go out*
MacLennan, Cathy. *Chicky Chicky Chook Chook*
Marino, Gianna. *Zoopa*
Martin, Bill, Jr. (William Ivan). *Baby bear, baby bear, what do you see?*
Mayo, Margaret. *Roar!*
Merz, Jennifer J. *Playground day*
Meyers, Susan. *This is the way a baby rides*
Milgrim, David. *Young MacDonald*
Miller, Pat. *Substitute groundhog*
Miranda, Anne. *To market, to market*
Mitchell, Susan K. *The rainforest grew all around*
Mitton, Tony. *All afloat on Noah's boat!*
Mora, Pat. *Marimba!*
  The song of Francis and the animals
Newman, Leslea. *Skunk's spring surprise*
Numeroff, Laura Joffe. *When sheep sleep*
Olson, David J. *The thunderstruck stork*
Olson, Nathan. *Animal patterns*
Onishi, Satoru. *Who's hiding*
Owens, Mary Beth. *Panda whispers*
Pallotta, Jerry. *Ocean counting*
Parker, Kim. *Counting in the garden*
Parker, Marjorie. *Your kind of mommy*
Paul, Ann Whitford. *Fiesta fiasco*
Peck, Jan. *Way up high in a tall green tree*
Pfister, Marcus. *Charlie at the zoo*
Pipe, Jim. *Farm animals*
Polacco, Patricia. *Mommies say shhh!*
Prap, Lila. *Animal lullabies*
  Animals speak
  Daddies
Prelutsky, Jack. *Behold the bold umbrellaphant and other poems*
Raye, Rebekah. *The very best bed*
Rempt, Fiona. *Snail's birthday wish*

Rex, Michael. *Dunk skunk*
Reynolds, Aaron. *Buffalo wings*
Ross, Michael Elsohn. *Mama's milk*
Rueda, Claudia. *Let's play in the forest while the wolf is not around*
Ruurs, Margriet. *In my backyard*
Ryder, Joanne. *Dance by the light of the moon*
St. Pierre, Stephanie. *What the sea saw*
Salley, Coleen. *Epossumondas saves the day*
Schaefer, Carole Lexa. *Cool time song*
Schwartz, Amy. *A beautiful girl*
  Starring Miss Darlene
Schwartz, David M. *Where in the wild*
Schwartz, Roslyn. *Tales from Parc la Fontaine*
Serfozo, Mary. *Whooo's there?*
Shahan, Sherry. *Cool cats counting*
Shannon, George. *Rabbit's gift*
Shulman, Lisa. *The moon might be milk*
Slate, Joseph. *Miss Bindergarten celebrates the last day of kindergarten*
  Miss Bindergarten has a wild day in kindergarten
Sockabasin, Allen. *Thanks to the animals*
Soule, Jean Conder. *Never tease a weasel*
Spinelli, Eileen. *The best time of day*
  Polar bear, arctic hare
Stewig, John Warren. *The animals watched*
Stock, Catherine. *A porc in New York*
Straaten, Harmen van. *Duck's tale*
  For me?
Tang, Greg. *Math fables too*
Tankard, Jeremy. *Grumpy Bird*
Tarlow, Ellen. *Pinwheel days*
Taylor, Eleanor. *Beep, beep, let's go!*
Tildes, Phyllis Limbacher. *Eye guess*
Timmers, Leo. *Who is driving?*
Toft, Kim Michelle. *The world that we want*
Vestergaard, Hope. *Hillside lullaby*
Votaw, Carol. *Good morning, little polar bear*
  Waking up down under
Walsh, Melanie. *Do lions live on lily pads?*
Ward, Jennifer. *Forest bright, forest night*
  Way up in the Arctic
Warhola, James. *If you're happy and you know it*
Weninger, Brigitte. *Bye-bye, Binky*
Williams, Brenda. *Home for a tiger, home for a bear*
Wilson, Karma. *Animal strike at the zoo, it's true!*
  Bear feels sick
  Mama always comes home
  Moose tracks!
Wise, William. *Zany zoo*
Wolff, Ferida. *It is the wind*
Wood, Audrey. *Silly Sally*
Yee, Wong Herbert. *Detective Small in the amazing banana caper*
Yolen, Jane. *Sleep, black bear, sleep*
Zane, Alexander. *The wheels on the race car*
Ziefert, Harriet. *Be fair, share!*
  Beach party!

Animals — apes *see* Animals — baboons; Animals — chimpanzees; Animals — gorillas; Animals — monkeys

Animals — babies

Baddiel, Ivor. *Cock-a-doodle quack! Quack!*
Baillie, Marilyn. *Small wonders*
Bogue, Gary. *There's an opossum in my backyard*
Bunting, Eve (Anne Evelyn). *The baby shower*
Cabrera, Jane. *Mommy, carry me please!*
Chaconas, Dori. *Christmas mouseling*
Fisher, Doris. *Happy birthday to whooo?*
Freymann, Saxton. *Baby food*
Krauss, Ruth. *The growing story*
Morton-Shaw, Christine. *Wake up, sleepy bear!*
Olson, David J. *The thunderstruck stork*
Pipe, Jim. *Baby animals*
Rose, Deborah Lee. *Ocean babies*
Sturges, Philemon. *How do you make a baby smile?*
Tafuri, Nancy. *Five little chicks*

Tatham, Betty. *Baby Sea Otter*

Animals — baboons

Horowitz, Dave. *Soon, Baboon, soon*

Animals — badgers

Brett, Jan. *Honey, honey — lion!*
Díaz, Katacha. *Badger at Sandy Ridge Road*
Kasza, Keiko. *Badger's fancy meal*
Odone, Jamison. *Honey badgers*

Animals — bandicoots

Fox, Mem. *Hunwick's egg*

Animals — bats

Edwards, Pamela Duncan. *Ms. Bitsy Bat's kindergarten*
Lies, Brian. *Bats at the beach*
Lunde, Darrin. *Hello, bumblebee bat*
Markle, Sandra. *Little lost bat*

Animals — bears

Bedford, David. *I've seen Santa!*
Berenstain, Jan. *The Berenstain bears trim the tree*
Bryan, Sean. *A bear and his boy*
Butler, M. Christina. *Snow friends*
Chen, Chih-Yuan. *The best Christmas ever*
Cooper, Elisha. *Bear dreams*
Duval, Kathy. *The Three Bears' Christmas*
  The Three Bears' Halloween
Dyer, Jane. *Little Brown Bear and the bundle of joy*
Foley, Greg. *Thank you, Bear*
Freedman, Claire. *One magical morning*
Gravett, Emily. *Orange Pear Apple Bear*
Greene, Rhonda Gowler. *Firebears*
Hayes, Karel. *The winter visitors*
Horvath, David. *Bossy bear*
Joosse, Barbara M. *Nikolai, the only bear*
Krauss, Ruth. *Bears*
Kroll, Virginia L. *On the way to kindergarten*
Lamb, Albert. *Sam's winter hat*
Landa, Norbert. *Little Bear and the wishing tree*
Lobel, Gillian. *Little Honey Bear and the smiley moon*
London, Jonathan. *Do your ABC's, Little Brown Bear*
McPhail, David. *Big Brown Bear goes to town*
  Big Brown Bear's birthday surprise
  Emma in charge
Mahoney, Daniel J. *A really good snowman*
Martin, Bill, Jr. (William Ivan). *Baby bear, baby bear, what do you see?*
Marzollo, Jean. *Little Bear, you're a star!*
Miles, Victoria. *Old mother bear*
Moss, Miriam. *Bare bear*
Mozelle, Shirley. *The bear upstairs*
Nolan, Janet. *A Father's Day thank you*
O'Keefe, Susan Heyboer. *Baby day*
Peters, Lisa Westberg. *Sleepyhead bear*
Ritchie, Alison. *Me and my dad!*
  What Bear likes best!
Rockwell, Anne F. *Backyard bear*
Rogers, Gregory. *The boy, the bear, the baron, the bard*
  Midsummer knight
Rosen, Michael. *Bear's day out*
Ryder, Joanne. *Bear of my heart*
Schertle, Alice. *Very hairy bear*
Stein, David Ezra. *Leaves*
Teckentrup, Britta. *Big smelly bear*
The three bears. *Goldilocks and the three bears*
Waddell, Martin. *Sleep tight, Little Bear*
Wallace, Nancy Elizabeth. *Shells! Shells! Shells!*
Wilson, Karma. *Bear feels sick*
Wright, Cliff. *Bear and ball*
  Bear and kite
Yolen, Jane. *Baby Bear's big dreams*

Baby Bear's books
Baby Bear's chairs

Animals — beavers

Harper, Charise Mericle. *When Randolph turned rotten*

Animals — bison *see* Animals — buffaloes

Animals — bonobos

Napoli, Donna Jo. *Bobby the bold*

Animals — buffaloes

Arnosky, Jim. *Grandfather Buffalo*

Animals — bulls, cows

Becker, Suzy. *Manny's cows*
Borgo, Lacy. *Big Mama's baby*
Bunting, Eve (Anne Evelyn). *The baby shower*
Chaconas, Dori. *When cows come home for Christmas*
Ditchfield, Christin. *Cowlick!*
Fleming, Denise. *The cow who clucked*
Fox, Mem. *A particular cow*
Hamilton, Arlene. *Only a cow*
Hill, Ros. *Shamoo*
Hoberman, Mary Ann. *Mrs. O'Leary's cow*
Hume, Lachie. *Clancy the courageous cow*
Kinerk, Robert. *Clorinda takes flight*
Korchek, Lori. *Adventures of Cow, too*
Neubecker, Robert. *Courage of the blue boy*
Newman, Marlene. *Myron's magic cow*
Shannon, George. *The Secret Chicken Club*
Steffensmeier, Alexander. *Millie waits for the mail*
Weis, Carol. *When the cows got loose*
Willis, Jeanne. *Misery Moo*
Wilson, Karma. *Sakes alive!*

Animals — camels

Alsenas, Linas. *Peanut*

Animals — cats

Almond, David. *Kate, the cat and the moon*
Asch, Frank. *Mrs. Marlowe's mice*
Berry, Lynne. *The curious demise of a contrary cat*
Bruel, Nick. *Bad Kitty*
    Poor puppy
Cabrera, Jane. *Kitty's cuddles*
Capucilli, Alyssa Satin. *Little spotted cat*
Carmody, Isobelle. *Magic night*
Catalanotto, Peter. *Kitten red, yellow, blue*
Cecka, Melanie. *Violet comes to stay*
    Violet goes to the country
Chichester Clark, Emma. *Will and Squill*
Christian, Mary Blount. *If not for the calico cat*
Cooper, Helen (Helen F.). *Delicious!*
    A pipkin of pepper
Crawley, Dave. *Cat poems*
Dick Whittington and his cat. *Dick Whittington and his cat*
Downey, Lynn. *Matilda's humdinger*
Egan, Tim. *Roasted peanuts*
Elschner, Geraldine. *Mark's messy room*
Ford, Bernette G. *Ballet Kitty*
Friend, Catherine. *The perfect nest*
Gay, Marie-Louise. *Caramba*
Grant, Joan. *Cat and Fish*
Gretz, Susanna. *Riley and Rose in the picture*
Grimes, Nikki. *When Gorilla goes walking*
Hamilton, Martha. *Priceless gifts*
Harper, Anita. *It's not fair!*
Hicks, Barbara Jean. *The secret life of Walter Kitty*
Hodgkins, Fran. *The cat of Strawberry Hill*
Hogg, Gary. *Look what the cat dragged in!*

Hooper, Meredith. *Celebrity cat*
Howe, James. *Houndsley and Catina*
    Houndsley and Catina and the birthday surprise
Janovitz, Marilyn. *We love school!*
Jenkins, Emily. *Love you when you whine*
Jenkins, Steve. *Dogs and cats*
Kleven, Elisa. *The wishing ball*
Kuskin, Karla. *So, what's it like to be a cat?*
    Toots the cat
Kwon, Yoon-duck. *My cat copies me*
Lear, Edward. *The owl and the pussycat*
Lloyd, Sam. *Mr. Pusskins*
Lobel, Anita. *Nini here and there*
McCarty, Peter. *Fabian escapes*
McDonnell, Patrick. *The gift of nothing*
    Just like Heaven
McKinlay, Penny. *Flabby Tabby*
Manzano, Sonia. *A box full of kittens*
Martin, David. *All for pie, pie for all*
Meyers, Susan. *Kittens! Kittens! Kittens!*
Mockford, Caroline. *Cleo's color book*
Montes, Marissa. *Los gatos black on Halloween*
Penner, Fred. *The cat came back*
Root, Phyllis. *Lucia and the light*
Rymond, Lynda Gene. *Oscar and the mooncats*
Saltzberg, Barney. *I love cats*
Samuels, Barbara. *Dolores meets her match*
    Happy Valentine's Day, Dolores
Santoro, Scott. *Farm-fresh cats*
Schachner, Judith Byron. *Skippyjon Jones and the big bones*
    Skippyjon Jones in mummy trouble
Seki, Sunny. *The tale of the lucky cat*
Sidman, Joyce. *Meow ruff*
Simmonds, Posy. *Baker cat*
Smath, Jerry. *Sammy Salami*
Smiley, Norene. *That stripy cat*
Soto, Gary. *Chato goes cruisin'*
Spinelli, Eileen. *Callie Cat, ice skater*
    Hero cat
Stainton, Sue. *The chocolate cat*
    I love cats
Sturges, Philemon. *Waggers*
Taber, Tory. *Rufus at work*
Thomas, Shelley Moore. *Take care, Good Knight*
Thomas, Valerie. *Winnie the witch*
Umansky, Kaye. *I don't like Gloria!*
Varon, Sara. *Chicken and Cat*
Walton, Rick. *The remarkable friendship of Mr. Cat and Mr. Rat*
Watt, Melanie. *Chester*
Weaver, Tess. *Cat jumped in!*
Wells, Rosemary. *McDuff's wild romp*
Weninger, Brigitte. *Good night, Nori*
Wheeler, Lisa. *Castaway cats*
Wilson, Karma. *Hello, Calico!*
    Sleepyhead
Wolff, Nancy. *It's time for school with Tallulah*
    Tallulah in the kitchen
Yolen, Jane. *Soft house*

Animals — chimpanzees

Alborough, Jez. *Yes*
Anholt, Catherine. *Happy birthday, Chimp and Zee*
Durango, Julia. *Cha-cha chimps*
Napoli, Donna Jo. *Bobby the bold*

Animals — cougars

Mora, Pat. *Doña Flor*

Animals — cows *see* Animals — bulls, cows

Animals — coyotes

Arnosky, Jim. *Coyote raid in Cactus Canyon*
Beaver steals fire

The gingerbread boy. *The Gingerbread Cowboy*
Lowell, Susan. *Josefina javelina*

Animals — deer

Scott, Nathan Kumar. *Mangoes and bananas*

Animals — dislike of *see* Behavior — animals, dislike of

Animals — dogs

Bailey, Linda. *Stanley's wild ride*
Bartoletti, Susan Campbell. *Nobody's diggier than a dog*
Beaumont, Karen. *Move over, Rover*
Bedford, David. *The way I love you*
Bluemle, Elizabeth. *My father the dog*
Boelts, Maribeth. *Before you were mine*
Bradley, Kimberly Brubaker. *Ballerino Nate*
Broach, Elise. *Wet dog!*
Brown, Peter. *Chowder*
Bruel, Nick. *Poor puppy*
Bunge, Daniela. *Cherry time*
Calmenson, Stephanie. *May I pet your dog?*
Casanova, Mary. *Some dog!*
Catalanotto, Peter. *Ivan the terrier*
Chapra, Mimi. *Sparky's bark / El ladrido de Sparky*
Chess, Victoria. *The costume party*
Chichester Clark, Emma. *Melrose and Croc*
    Piper
Christelow, Eileen. *Letters from a desperate dog*
Church, Caroline Jayne. *Digby takes charge*
Clements, Andrew. *Dogku*
    Naptime for Slippers
    Slippers at School
    Slippers loves to run
Cochran, Bill. *The forever dog*
Coffelt, Nancy. *Fred stays with me!*
    Pug in a truck
Cole, Barbara Hancock. *Anna and Natalie*
Conahan, Carolyn. *The twelve days of Christmas dogs*
Consentino, Ralph. *The story of Honk-Honk-Ashoo and Swella-Bow-Wow*
Crisp, Marty. *The most precious gift*
Cronin, Doreen. *Bounce*
Crummel, Susan Stevens. *Ten-gallon Bart*
Cullen, Lynn. *Moi and Marie Antoinette*
Daly, Niki. *Pretty Salma*
Day, Alexandra. *Carl's sleepy afternoon*
Dewdney, Anna. *Grumpy Gloria*
Ehlert, Lois. *Wag a tail*
Estefan, Gloria. *Noelle's treasure tale*
Faller, Regis. *The adventures of Polo*
    Polo
Fearnley, Jan. *The search for the perfect child*
Feiffer, Kate. *Henry, the dog with no tail*
Foreman, Michael. *Mia's story*
French, Jackie. *Pete the sheep-sheep*
Freymann, Saxton. *Dog food*
Gay, Marie-Louise. *What are you doing, Sam?*
Goldfinger, Jennifer P. *My dog Lyle*
Goode, Diane. *The most perfect spot*
Graham, Bob. *"The trouble with dogs," said Dad*
Gretz, Susanna. *Riley and Rose in the picture*
Grogan, John. *Bad dog, Marley!*
Guy, Ginger Foglesong. *Perros! Perros! Dogs! Dogs!*
Heiligman, Deborah. *Fun dog, sun dog*
Herman, R. A. (Ronnie Ann). *Gomer and Little Gomer*
Hewitt, Kathryn. *No dogs here!*
Hodge, Marie. *Are you sleepy yet, Petey?*
Holt, Kimberly Willis. *Skinny brown dog*
Hornsey, Chris. *Why do I have to eat off the floor?*
Howe, James. *Houndsley and Catina*
    Houndsley and Catina and the birthday surprise
Huneck, Stephen. *Sally's snow adventure*
Imai, Ayano. *Chester*
Jahn-Clough, Lisa. *Little dog*
Jenkins, Emily. *That new animal*

Jenkins, Steve. *Dogs and cats*
Joosse, Barbara M. *Wind-wild dog*
Kasza, Keiko. *The dog who cried wolf*
Keller, Holly. *Sophie's window*
Kinerk, Robert. *Timothy Cox will not change his socks*
King, Stephen Michael. *Mutt dog!*
Kirwan, Wednesday. *Nobody notices Minerva*
Kovacs, Deborah. *Katie Copley*
Kroll, Steven. *Pooch on the loose*
Kroll, Virginia L. *Selvakumar knew better*
Lacombe, Benjamin. *Cherry and Olive*
Lee, Spike. *Please, puppy, please*
Leedy, Loreen. *It's probably penny*
Lewis, Kim. *A puppy for Annie*
London, Jonathan. *Sled dogs run*
Loupy, Christophe. *Wiggles*
McCarty, Peter. *Fabian escapes*
MacDonald, Margaret Read. *The great smelly, slobbery small-toothed dog*
McDonnell, Patrick. *The gift of nothing*
    Just like Heaven
McGuirk, Leslie. *Tucker's spooky Halloween*
McHenry, E. B. *Has anyone seen Winnie and Jean?*
Magoon, Scott. *Hugo and Miles in I've painted everything!*
Manuel, Lynn. *The trouble with Tilly Trumble*
Masurel, Claire. *Domino*
Meserve, Adria. *No room for Napoleon*
Meyers, Susan. *Puppies! Puppies! Puppies!*
Newgarden, Mark. *Bow-Wow bugs a bug*
    Bow-Wow orders lunch
Nez, John. *One smart Cookie*
O'Connor, Jane. *Fancy Nancy and the posh puppy*
Paraskevas, Betty. *Chocolate at the Four Seasons*
Parr, Todd. *Otto goes to school*
Pickering, Jimmy. *Skelly the skeleton girl*
Pipe, Jim. *Dogs*
Pitzer, Susanna. *Not afraid of dogs*
Postgate, Daniel. *Smelly Bill*
Rankin, Laura. *Fluffy and Baron*
Reiser, Lynn. *Hardworking puppies*
    Two dogs swimming
Ries, Lori. *Aggie and Ben*
Rowe, John A. *Moondog*
Saltzberg, Barney. *I love dogs*
Sayre, April Pulley. *Hush, little puppy*
Schachner, Judith Byron. *Skippyjon Jones and the big bones*
    Skippyjon Jones in mummy trouble
Schmidt, Karen Lee. *Carl's nose*
Schneider, Christine M. *I'm bored!*
Schories, Pat. *Jack and the night visitors*
Seeger, Laura Vaccaro. *Dog and Bear*
Shannon, David. *Good boy, Fergus!*
Sidman, Joyce. *Meow ruff*
Simmons, Jane. *Together*
Simon, Charnan. *Big bad Buzz*
Soto, Gary. *Chato goes cruisin'*
Stohner, Anu. *Brave Charlotte*
Sturges, Philemon. *Waggers*
Swaim, Jessica. *The hound from the pound*
Sweet, Melissa. *Carmine*
Tanaka, Shinsuke. *Wings*
Taylor, Eleanor. *Beep, beep, let's go!*
Tellis, Annabel. *If my dad were a dog*
Umansky, Kaye. *I don't like Gloria!*
Ward, Helen. *Little Moon Dog*
Watt, Melanie. *Scaredy Squirrel makes a friend*
Wells, Rosemary. *McDuff's wild romp*
Wishinsky, Frieda. *Please, Louise!*
Wood, Audrey. *A dog needs a bone*
Ziefert, Harriet. *Knick-knack paddywhack*
    Mommy, I want to sleep in your bed!
    Murphy jumps a hurdle

Animals — donkeys

Kromhout, Rindert. *Little Donkey and the baby-sitter*
    Little Donkey and the birthday present

Puttock, Simon. *Goat and Donkey in strawberry sunglasses*
  Goat and Donkey in the great outdoors
Tarlow, Ellen. *Pinwheel days*
Ziefert, Harriet. *Buzzy had a little lamb*

Animals — elephants

Alsenas, Linas. *Peanut*
Arnold, Katya. *Elephants can paint, too!*
Bachelet, Gilles. *My cat, the silliest cat in the world*
  When the silliest cat was small
Beake, Lesley. *Home now*
Brunhoff, Laurent de. *Babar's world tour*
Côté, Geneviève. *What elephant?*
Daly, Niki. *Welcome to Zanzibar Road*
D'Amico, Carmela. *Ella sets the stage*
  Ella takes the cake
Ginkel, Anne. *I've got an elephant*
Hillenbrand, Will. *My book box*
Kilaka, John. *True friends*
Kitamura, Satoshi. *Pablo the artist*
Lewis, Kim. *Hooray for Harry*
McGrory, Anik. *Kidogo*
Magoon, Scott. *Hugo and Miles in I've painted everything!*
Murphy, Jill. *Mr. Large in charge*
Ormerod, Jan. *When an elephant comes to school*
Polacco, Patricia. *Emma Kate*
Prince, April Jones. *Twenty-one elephants and still standing*
Schubert, Leda. *Ballet of the elephants*
Schwartz, Amy. *A beautiful girl*
Schwartz, Corey Rosen. *Hop! Plop!*
Vere, Ed. *The getaway*
Willems, Mo. *I am invited to a party!*
  My friend is sad
  There is a bird on your head!
  Today I will fly!

Animals — endangered animals

Jenkins, Steve. *Almost gone*
Lunde, Darrin. *Hello, bumblebee bat*
McLimans, David. *Gone wild*

Animals — ferrets

Jenkins, Emily. *Num, num, num!*
  Plonk, plonk, plonk!
  Up, up, up!

Animals — foxes

Banks, Kate (Katherine A.). *Fox*
Church, Caroline Jayne. *One smart goose*
Heinz, Brian J. *Red Fox at McCloskey's farm*
Keller, Holly. *Nosy Rosie*
Lobel, Gillian. *Too small for honey cake*
Palatini, Margie. *Three French hens*
Puttock, Simon. *Miss Fox*
Rankin, Laura. *Ruthie and the (not so) teeny tiny lie*
Rawlinson, Julia. *Fletcher and the falling leaves*
Weston, Carrie. *If a chicken stayed for supper*

Animals — giraffes

Ommen, Sylvia van. *The surprise*
Tourville, Amanda Doering. *A giraffe grows up*
  A jaguar grows up

Animals — goats

Church, Caroline Jayne. *Little Apple Goat*
Crummel, Susan Stevens. *Ten-gallon Bart*
Elschner, Geraldine. *Pashmina the little Christmas goat*
Garland, Michael. *King Puck*
Gorbachev, Valeri. *That's what friends are for*
Kimmel, Eric A. *The three cabritos*
Palatini, Margie. *The three silly billies*
Puttock, Simon. *Goat and Donkey in strawberry sunglasses*

  Goat and Donkey in the great outdoors
Shepard, Aaron. *One-eye! Two-eyes! Three-eyes!*

Animals — gorillas

Anderson, Derek. *Gladys goes out to lunch*
Harvey, Damian. *Just the thing!*
Willis, Jeanne. *Gorilla! Gorilla!*

Animals — groundhogs

Cuyler, Margery. *Groundhog stays up late*
Hill, Susanna Leonard. *Punxsutawney Phyllis*
Miller, Pat. *Substitute groundhog*
Swallow, Pamela Curtis. *Groundhog gets a say*

Animals — guinea pigs

Berenzy, Alix. *Sammy*
Katz, Susan. *Oh, Theodore!*
Meade, Holly. *John Willy and Freddy McGee*
Ohi, Ruth. *Clara and the Bossy*
  The couch was a castle
  A trip with Grandma
Roth, Susan L. *Great big guinea pigs*
Weigelt, Udo. *Super Guinea Pig to the rescue*

Animals — hamsters

Bateman, Teresa. *Hamster Camp*
Kimmel, Eric A. *The great Texas hamster drive*
Rubel, Nicole. *Ham and Pickles*

Animals — hedgehogs

Anderson, Lena. *The hedgehog, the pig, and their little friend*
Brett, Jan. *Hedgie blasts off!*
Butler, M. Christina. *One winter's day*
Petz, Moritz. *Wish you were here*
Wheeler, Lisa. *Hokey pokey*

Animals — hippopotamuses

Bauer, Marion Dane. *A mama for Owen*
Jenkins, Emily. *Num, num, num!*
  Plonk, plonk, plonk!
  Up, up, up!
Landstrom, Lena. *A hippo's tale*
Loomis, Christine. *Hattie hippo*
Meng, Cece. *The wonderful thing about hiccups*
Rox, John. *I want a hippopotamus for Christmas*
Schwartz, Amy. *Starring Miss Darlene*
Winter, Jeanette. *Mama*

Animals — horses, ponies

Armstrong, Jennifer. *Magnus at the fire*
Bradley, Kimberly Brubaker. *The perfect pony*
Clayton, Elaine. *A blue ribbon for Sugar*
Egan, Tim. *Roasted peanuts*
Gray, Rita. *The wild little horse*
Hamilton, Arlene. *Only a cow*
Hammerle, Susa. *Let's try horseback riding*
Hong, Chen Jiang. *The magic horse of Han Gan*
Murphy, Stuart J. *Same old horse*
Otsuka, Yuzo. *Suho's white horse*
Pipe, Jim. *Horses*
Stein, David Ezra. *Cowboy Ned and Andy*
  Ned's new friend
Trollinger, Patsi B. *Perfect timing*

Animals — kangaroos

French, Jackie. *Josephine wants to dance*
McAllister, Angela. *Mama and Little Joe*
McBratney, Sam. *Yes we can!*

Animals — kindness to animals *see* Character traits — kindness to animals

Animals — koalas

Sutton, Jane. *The trouble with cauliflower*

Animals — leopards

Poppenhäger, Nicole. *Snow leopards*

Animals — lions

Hartman, Bob. *Dinner in the lions' den*
Horacek, Petr. *Silly Suzy Goose*
Kanevsky, Polly. *Sleepy boy*
Knudsen, Michelle. *Library lion*
Markham, Beryl. *The good lion*

Animals — llamas

Dewdney, Anna. *Llama Llama mad at mama*
   Llama, Llama red pajama

Animals — marsupials

Sill, Cathryn P. *About marsupials*

Animals — meerkats

Lunde, Darrin. *Meet the meerkat*

Animals — mice

Asch, Frank. *Mrs. Marlowe's mice*
Aylesworth, Jim. *Little Bitty Mousie*
Baker, Keith. *Hickory dickory dock*
Baum, Louis. *The mouse who braved bedtime*
Berkeley, Jon. *Chopsticks*
Bonnett-Rampersaud, Louise. *Bubble and Squeak*
Bynum, Janie. *Nutmeg and Barley*
Cain, Sheridan. *By the light of the moon*
Calmenson, Stephanie. *Birthday at the Panda Palace*
Carlson, Nancy L. *First grade, here I come!*
   Henry's 100 days of kindergarten
   I don't like to read!
Chaconas, Dori. *Christmas mouseling*
Cousins, Lucy. *Ha ha, Maisy!*
   Happy Easter, Maisy!
   Maisy big, Maisy small
   Maisy, Charley, and the wobbly tooth
   Maisy goes to the hospital
   Maisy goes to the library
   Maisy's amazing big book of words
   Maisy's wonderful weather book
   More fun with Maisy!
   Stop and go, Maisy
   Sweet dreams, Maisy
   With love from Maisy
Deedy, Carmen Agra. *Martina the beautiful cockroach*
Demas, Corinne. *Two Christmas mice*
Donofrio, Beverly. *Mary and the mouse, the mouse and Mary*
Duke, Kate. *The tale of Pip and Squeak*
Emmett, Jonathan. *I love you always and forever*
Engelbreit, Mary. *Mary Engelbreit's A merry little Christmas*
Esbaum, Jill. *Estelle takes a bath*
Foley, Greg. *Thank you, Bear*
Fraser, Mary Ann. *I.Q. gets fit*
   I.Q., it's time
Garland, Michael. *Hooray José!*
   How many mice?
Gerritsen, Paula. *Nuts*
Henkes, Kevin. *Lilly's big day*
Holabird, Katharine. *Angelina at the palace*
   Christmas in Mouseland
Kangas, Juli. *The surprise visitor*
Keller, Holly. *Help!*

Kirk, David. *Library mouse*
Krupinski, Loretta. *Pirate treasure*
Lithgow, John. *Mahalia Mouse goes to college*
McCully, Emily Arnold. *School*
MacDonald, Alan. *Wilfred to the rescue*
McFarland, Lyn Rossiter. *Mouse went out to get a snack*
Martin, David. *All for pie, pie for all*
Mayer, Mercer. *The little drummer mouse*
Modesitt, Jeanne. *Little Mouse's happy birthday*
Morgan, Michaela. *Bunny wishes*
   Dear bunny
Nikola-Lisa, W. *Magic in the margins*
Numeroff, Laura Joffe. *Merry Christmas, Mouse!*
Pennypacker, Sara. *Pierre in love*
Petz, Moritz. *Wish you were here*
Schoenherr, Ian. *Pip and Squeak*
Schwartz, Corey Rosen. *Hop! Plop!*
Simmonds, Posy. *Baker cat*
Tashiro, Chisato. *Five nice mice*
Thompson, Lauren. *Mouse's first fall*
   Mouse's first snow
   Mouse's first spring
Vere, Ed. *The getaway*
Wallace, Nancy Elizabeth. *Look! Look! Look!*
Walsh, Ellen Stoll. *Mouse shapes*
Weninger, Brigitte. *Double birthday*
   Miko goes on vacation
   Miko wants a dog
   "Mom, wake up and play!"
   "No bath! No way!"
Willems, Mo. *Time to say "please"!*
Willis, Jeanne. *Gorilla! Gorilla!*
Wilson, Karma. *Mortimer's Christmas manger*
Ziefert, Harriet. *Messy Bessie*

Animals — migration *see* Migration

Animals — moles

Delessert, Etienne. *Alert!*
Emmett, Jonathan. *Diamond in the snow*
Hillenbrand, Jane. *What a treasure!*
McAllister, Angela. *Take a kiss to school*

Animals — monkeys

Alborough, Jez. *Tall*
Bell, Cece. *Sock Monkey boogie-woogie*
   Sock Monkey rides again
Christelow, Eileen. *Five little monkeys go shopping*
DiCamillo, Kate. *Great joy*
Duquette, Keith. *Little Monkey lost*
Durant, Alan. *I love you, little monkey*
Elliott, George. *The boy who loved bananas*
Hapka, Cathy. *Margret and H. A. Rey's Merry Christmas, Curious George*
Heck, Ed. *Monkey lost*
Landstrom, Lena. *A hippo's tale*
LaReau, Kara. *Rocko and Spanky have company*
Schwartz, Amy. *Oscar*
Scott, Nathan Kumar. *Mangoes and bananas*
Williams, Suzanne. *Ten naughty little monkeys*

Animals — moose

Gannij, Joan. *Elusive moose*
Haseley, Dennis. *The invisible moose*
Love, Pamela. *A moose's morning*
Root, Phyllis. *Looking for a moose*
Segal, John. *The lonely moose*
Wilson, Karma. *Moose tracks!*

Animals — mountain lions *see* Animals — cougars

Animals — muskrats

Chaconas, Dori. *Cork and Fuzz*

Cork and Fuzz: good sports
Cork and Fuzz: short and tall

Animals — octopuses *see* Octopuses

Animals — opossums *see* Animals — possums

Animals — orangutans

Daddo, Andrew. *Goodnight, me*

Animals — otters

Bedford, David. *Little Otter's big journey*
Tatham, Betty. *Baby Sea Otter*
Webster, Christine. *Otter everywhere*

Animals — pack rats

Ruzzier, Sergio. *The room of wonders*

Animals — pandas

Briant, Ed. *A day at the beach*
Calmenson, Stephanie. *Birthday at the Panda Palace*
Dowson, Nick. *Tracks of a panda*
Morrow, Tara Jaye. *Panda goes to school*
Murphy, Mary. *Panda Foo and the new friend*
Muth, Jon J. *Zen shorts*

Animals — panthers *see* Animals — leopards

Animals — pigs

Addy, Sharon Hart. *Lucky Jake*
Anderson, Lena. *The hedgehog, the pig, and their little friend*
Bailey, Linda. *Goodnight, sweet pig*
Carlson, Nancy L. *Get up and go!*
Cazet, Denys. *Will you read to me?*
Denise, Anika. *Pigs love potatoes*
Downey, Lynn. *The tattletale*
Eaton, Maxwell. *Best buds*
    Superheroes
Ernst, Lisa Campbell. *Sylvia Jean, drama queen*
Falconer, Ian. *Olivia forms a band*
Geisert, Arthur. *Lights out*
    Oops
Gorbachev, Valeri. *That's what friends are for*
Harris, Trudy. *Twenty hungry piggies*
Harrison, David Lee. *Piggy Wiglet*
Hobbie, Holly. *Toot and Puddle: let it snow*
    Toot and Puddle: wish you were here
Lowell, Susan. *Josefina javelina*
Muntean, Michaela. *Do not open this book!*
Norac, Carl. *Monster, don't eat me!*
Numeroff, Laura Joffe. *If you give a pig a party*
Odanaka, Barbara. *Smash! Mash! Crash! There goes the trash!*
Oxenbury, Helen. *Pig tale*
Palatini, Margie. *Oink?*
Polacco, Patricia. *Ginger and Petunia*
Ransom, Jeanie Franz. *Don't squeal unless it's a big deal*
Rockwell, Anne F. *Brendan and Belinda and the slam dunk!*
Saltzberg, Barney. *Cornelius P. Mud, are you ready for bed?*
    Cornelius P. Mud, are you ready for school?
Santore, Charles. *Three hungry pigs and the wolf who came to dinner*
Sillifant, Alec. *Farmer Ham*
Simon, Charnan. *A greedy little pig*
Stein, Mathilde. *Monstersong*
Sturges, Philemon. *This little pirate*
Thaler, Mike. *Pig Little*
The three little pigs. *The three little pigs / Los tres cerditos*
Vischer, Phil. *Sidney and Norman*
Weeks, Sarah. *Ella, of course!*
    I'm a pig
Wild, Margaret. *Piglet and Mama*
    Piglet and Papa
Willems, Mo. *I am invited to a party!*

My friend is sad
There is a bird on your head!
Today I will fly!
Yamada, Utako. *The story of Cherry the pig*

Animals — platypuses

Collard, Sneed B. *A platypus, probably*
Fuge, Charles. *Swim, Little Wombat, swim!*

Animals — polar bears

Anderson, Derek. *Romeo and Lou blast off*
Bloom, Suzanne. *A splendid friend, indeed*
Brett, Jan. *The three snow bears*
Davies, Nicola. *Ice bear*
Floyd, Madeleine. *Cold paws, warm heart*
Pinkwater, Daniel Manus. *Bad bear detectives*
    Bad bears go visiting
    Dancing Larry
    Sleepover Larry
Ryder, Joanne. *A pair of polar bears*

Animals — porcupines

Rowe, John A. *I want a hug*
Wheeler, Lisa. *Hokey pokey*
Wilson, Karma. *Sweet Briar goes to camp*

Animals — possums

Bogue, Gary. *There's an opossum in my backyard*
Chaconas, Dori. *Cork and Fuzz*
    Cork and Fuzz: good sports
    Cork and Fuzz: short and tall
deGroat, Diane. *Brand-new pencils, brand-new books*
    Last one in is a rotten egg!
Duvall, Deborah L. *The opossum's tale*
Salley, Coleen. *Epossumondas saves the day*

Animals — prairie dogs

Stevens, Janet. *The great fuzz frenzy*

Animals — prairie wolves *see* Animals — coyotes

Animals — pumas *see* Animals — cougars

Animals — rabbits

Aesop. *The hare and the tortoise / La liebre y la tortuga*
Anderson, Derek. *How the Easter Bunny saved Christmas*
Asher, Sandy. *Too many frogs!*
Berger, Barbara. *Thunder Bunny*
Bottner, Barbara. *Raymond and Nelda*
Brown, Margaret Wise. *Goodnight moon 123*
Burg, Sarah Emmanuelle. *One more egg*
Carlson, Nancy L. *Loudmouth George earns his allowance*
Cate, Annette LeBlanc. *The magic rabbit*
Côté, Geneviève. *With you always, Little Monday*
Cowell, Cressida. *That rabbit belongs to Emily Brown*
Crimi, Carolyn. *Henry and the Buccaneer Bunnies*
Dijkstra, Lida. *Cute*
Evans, Lezlie. *The bunnies' picnic*
Fleming, Candace. *Tippy-tippy-tippy, hide!*
Ford, Bernette G. *First snow*
    No more bottles for Bunny!
Gore, Leonid. *Danny's first snow*
Grambling, Lois G. *Here comes T. Rex Cottontail*
Gravett, Emily. *Wolves*
Hample, Stoo. *I will kiss you (lots & lots & lots!)*
Henkes, Kevin. *So happy!*
Horse, Harry. *Little Rabbit runaway*
Ives, Penny. *Rabbit pie*
Keller, Holly. *Pearl's new skates*
Klise, Kate. *Imagine Harry*
    Why do you cry?

Kortepeter, Paul. *Oliver's red toboggan*
Krensky, Stephen. *Milo and the really big bunny*
Krishnaswami, Uma. *Remembering Grandpa*
Kroll, Virginia L. *Really rabbits*
Larsen, Andrew. *Bella and the bunny*
Lasky, Kathryn. *Tumble bunnies*
Layne, Steven L. *Love the baby*
Lillegard, Dee. *Balloons, balloons, balloons*
Livingston, Irene. *Finklehopper Frog cheers*
Luthardt, Kevin. *You're weird!*
MacDonald, Margaret Read. *Conejito*
McPhail, David. *Sylvie and True*
Montanari, Eva. *A very full morning*
Morgan, Michaela. *Bunny wishes*
    Dear bunny
Moroney, Trace. *When I'm feeling angry*
    When I'm feeling happy
    When I'm feeling sad
    When I'm feeling scared
Müller, Birte. *I can dress myself!*
Nishimura, Kae. *Bunny Lune*
Novak, Matt. *Too many bunnies*
Park, Linda Sue. *What does Bunny see?*
Pennypacker, Sara. *Pierre in love*
Portis, Antoinette. *Not a box*
Raschka, Chris. *Five for a little one*
Rawlinson, Julia. *A surprise for Rosie*
Russo, Marisabina. *The bunnies are not in their beds*
Saltzberg, Barney. *Hi, Blueberry!*
Schoenherr, Ian. *Pip and Squeak*
Schwartz, Amy. *Oscar*
Segal, John. *Carrot soup*
Shannon, George. *Rabbit's gift*
Stanley, Mandy. *Lettice the flower girl*
    Lettice the flying rabbit
Stewart, Amber. *I'm big enough*
    Rabbit ears
Tingle, Tim. *When turtle grew feathers*
Waechter, Phillip. *Rosie and the nightmares*
Wakeman, Daniel. *Ben's bunny trouble*
Wallace, Nancy Elizabeth. *Alphabet house*
    Snow
Walton, Rick. *Bunny school*
Weeks, Sarah. *Overboard!*
Wells, Rosemary. *Carry me!*
    Max counts his chickens
    Max's ABC
Whybrow, Ian. *Bella gets her skates on*
Willems, Mo. *Knuffle Bunny*
    Knuffle Bunny too
Winget, Susan. *Tucker's four-carrot school day*

Animals — raccoons

Elliott, Laura Malone. *Hunter and Stripe and the soccer showdown*
    Hunter's big sister
Hubery, Julia. *A friend for all seasons*
Mitchard, Jacquelyn. *Ready, set, school!*
Modarressi, Mitra. *Stay awake, Sally*

Animals — rats

Hamilton, Martha. *Priceless gifts*
Kilaka, John. *True friends*
McPhail, David. *Big Brown Bear goes to town*
    Big Brown Bear's birthday surprise
Walton, Rick. *Just me and 6,000 rats*
    The remarkable friendship of Mr. Cat and Mr. Rat

Animals — rhinoceros

Brown, Susan Taylor. *Oliver's must-do list*
Derrick, Patricia. *Riley the rhinoceros*
Mammano, Julie. *Rhinos who rescue*
Newman, Jeff. *Hippo! No, rhino!*

Animals — seals

Mitton, Tony. *Playful little penguins*

Animals — service animals

Kovacs, Deborah. *Katie Copley*

Animals — sheep

Church, Caroline Jayne. *Digby takes charge*
Edwards, David. *The pen that Pa built*
French, Jackie. *Pete the sheep-sheep*
Imai, Ayano. *The 108th sheep*
Kelly, Mij. *One more sheep*
Kempter, Christa. *Dear Little Lamb*
Landstrom, Lena. *Boo and Baa have company*
Lester, Helen. *The sheep in wolf's clothing*
Lunge-Larsen, Lise. *Noah's mittens*
Numeroff, Laura Joffe. *When sheep sleep*
Olsen, Sylvia. *Yetsa's sweater*
Ommen, Sylvia van. *The surprise*
Puttock, Simon. *Miss Fox*
Schroeder, Lisa. *Baby can't sleep*
Scotton, Rob. *Go to sleep, Russell the sheep*
    Russell and the lost treasure
    Russell the sheep
    Russell's Christmas magic
Smallman, Steve. *The lamb who came for dinner*
Stohner, Anu. *Brave Charlotte*
Urbigkit, Cat. *A young shepherd*
Watts, Leslie Elizabeth. *The Baabaasheep Quartet*
Weeks, Sarah. *Counting Ovejas*
Willis, Jeanne. *Misery Moo*

Animals — skunks

Newman, Leslea. *Skunk's spring surprise*
Reed, Lynn Rowe. *Please don't upset P.U. Zorilla!*
Wilson, Karma. *Sweet Briar goes to camp*

Animals — slugs

Krosoczka, Jarrett J. *My buddy, Slug*
Pearson, Susan. *Slugs in love*

Animals — snails

Leedy, Loreen. *The great graph contest*
Loomis, Christine. *The best Father's Day present ever*
Rempt, Fiona. *Snail's birthday wish*
Veit, Barbara. *Who stole my house?*

Animals — snow leopards *see* Animals — leopards

Animals — squid *See* Squid

Animals — squirrels

Bottner, Barbara. *Raymond and Nelda*
Bynum, Janie. *Nutmeg and Barley*
Chichester Clark, Emma. *Will and Squill*
Cooper, Helen (Helen F.). *Delicious!*
    A pipkin of pepper
Freeman, Don. *Earl the squirrel*
Glaser, Linda. *Hello, squirrels!*
Raye, Rebekah. *The very best bed*
Shore, Diane Z. *Look both ways*
Tafuri, Nancy. *The busy little squirrel*
Watt, Melanie. *Scaredy Squirrel*
    Scaredy Squirrel makes a friend

Animals — swine *see* Animals — pigs

Animals — tigers

Bee, William. *Whatever*

Blackford, Harriet. *Tiger's story*
Fore, S. J. *Tiger can't sleep*
Gliori, Debi. *Where did that baby come from?*
Rayner, Catherine. *Augustus and his smile*

Animals — wallabies

Wild, Margaret. *Bobbie Dazzler*

Animals — weasels

George, Jean Craighead. *Frightful's daughter meets the Baron Weasel*

Animals — whales

Hill, Ros. *Shamoo*
Lucas, David. *Whale*
Pinkney, Andrea Davis. *Peggony-Po*

Animals — wolves

Bevis, Mary. *Wolf song*
Egielski, Richard. *St. Francis and the wolf*
Godkin, Celia. *Wolf island*
Gravett, Emily. *Wolves*
Grimm, Jacob. *Little Red Riding Hood*, retold & ill. by Andrea Wisnewski
    Little Red Riding Hood, retold & ill. by Jerry Pinkney
Helakoski, Leslie. *Big chickens*
Hennessy, B. G. (Barbara G.). *The boy who cried wolf*
Kasza, Keiko. *The dog who cried wolf*
Kelly, Mij. *One more sheep*
Kempter, Christa. *Dear Little Lamb*
Krensky, Stephen. *Big bad wolves at school*
Kulka, Joe. *Wolf's coming*
Langton, Jane. *Saint Francis and the wolf*
Lester, Helen. *The sheep in wolf's clothing*
McGee, Marni. *Winston the book wolf*
Mallat, Kathy. *Papa pride*
Melling, David. *The Scallywags*
Murphy, Yannick. *Ahwoooooooo!*
Palatini, Margie. *Bad boys get cookie!*
Perret, Delphine. *The Big Bad Wolf and me*
Rocco, John. *Wolf! Wolf!*
Rueda, Claudia. *Let's play in the forest while the wolf is not around*
Santore, Charles. *Three hungry pigs and the wolf who came to dinner*
Sierra, Judy. *Mind your manners, B. B. Wolf*
Smallman, Steve. *The lamb who came for dinner*
Sweet, Melissa. *Carmine*
The three little pigs. *The three little pigs / Los tres cerditos*
Whybrow, Ian. *Badness for beginners*

Animals — wombats

Fuge, Charles. *Swim, Little Wombat, swim!*
    Where to, Little Wombat?
Lester, Helen. *Batter up Wombat*
McAllister, Angela. *Found you, Little Wombat!*

Animals — woodchucks *see* Animals — groundhogs

Animals — wooly mammoths

Wheeler, Lisa. *Mammoths on the move*

Animals — worms

Bruel, Robert O. *Bob and Otto*

Animals — yaks

Kromhout, Rindert. *Little Donkey and the birthday present*
Stryer, Andrea Stenn. *Kami and the yaks*

Antarctica *see* Foreign lands — Antarctica

Ants *see* Insects — ants

Apartments *see* Homes, houses

Apes *see* Animals — baboons; Animals — chimpanzees; Animals — gorillas; Animals — monkeys

Appearance *see* Character traits — appearance

Arab Americans *see* Ethnic groups in the U.S. — Arab Americans

Arabia *see* Foreign lands — Arabia

Arachnids *see* Spiders

Architects *see* Careers — architects

Arctic *see* Foreign lands — Arctic

Arguing *see* Behavior — fighting, arguing

Arithmetic *see* Counting, numbers

Art

Arrigan, Mary. *Mario's angels*
Dawes, Kwame Senu Neville. *I saw your face*
Domeniconi, David. *M is for masterpiece*
FitzGerald, Dawn. *Vinnie and Abraham*
Hong, Chen Jiang. *The magic horse of Han Gan*
Hooper, Meredith. *Celebrity cat*
Hopkins, Lee Bennett. *Behind the museum door*
Kamm, Katja. *Invisible*
Kitamura, Satoshi. *Pablo the artist*
Lee-Tai, Amy. *A place where sunflowers grow / Sabaku ni saita himawari*
Lin, Grace. *Robert's snowflakes*
McDonnell, Patrick. *Art*
Magoon, Scott. *Hugo and Miles in I've painted everything!*
The Metropolitan Museum of Art, NY. *Museum shapes*
Nikola-Lisa, W. *Magic in the margins*
Nolan, Janet. *A Father's Day thank you*
Reynolds, Peter H. *Ish*
Rodríguez, Rachel Victoria. *Through Georgia's eyes*
Wallace, Nancy Elizabeth. *Look! Look! Look!*

Artists *see* Careers — artists

Asian Americans *see* Ethnic groups in the U.S. — Asian Americans

Assertiveness *see* Character traits — assertiveness

Astrology *see* Zodiac

Astronauts *see* Careers — astronauts; Space & space ships

Astronomy

Gibbons, Gail. *The planets*
Pettenati, Jeanne K. *Galileo's journal, 1609–1610*

Aunts *see* Family life — aunts, uncles

Australia *see* Foreign lands — Australia

Authors *see* Careers — authors

Automobiles

Ernst, Lisa Campbell. *This is the van that Dad cleaned*
Herzog, Brad. *R is for race*
Hubbell, Patricia. *Cars*

Hurd, Thacher. *Sleepy Cadillac*
Mitton, Tony. *Cool cars*
Soto, Gary. *My little car / Mi carrito*
Timmers, Leo. *Who is driving?*
Zane, Alexander. *The wheels on the race car*

Autumn *see* Seasons — fall

Award-winning books *see* Caldecott award books; Caldecott award honor books

Babies *see also* Animals — babies
Archer, Peggy. *From dawn to dreams*
Arnosky, Jim. *Babies in the bayou*
Ashman, Linda. *Babies on the go*
　　Mama's day
Aston, Dianna Hutts. *Mama outside, Mama inside*
Bertrand, Lynne. *Granite baby*
Broach, Elise. *What the no-good baby is good for*
Bunting, Eve (Anne Evelyn). *Baby can*
Chichester Clark, Emma. *Will and Squill*
Creech, Sharon. *Who's that baby?*
Downes, Belinda. *Baby days*
Dunbar, Joyce. *Shoe baby*
Dyer, Jane. *Little Brown Bear and the bundle of joy*
Elya, Susan Middleton. *Bebe goes shopping*
English, Karen. *The baby on the way*
Frazee, Marla. *Hush, little baby*
　　Walk on!
Gershator, Phillis. *This is the day!*
Gliori, Debi. *Where did that baby come from?*
Grimes, Nikki. *Welcome, Precious*
Hawkes, Kevin. *The wicked big toddlah*
Henderson, Kathy. *Look at you!*
Hindley, Judy. *Baby talk*
Holt, Kimberly Willis. *Waiting for Gregory*
Jenkins, Emily. *That new animal*
Katz, Karen. *Ten tiny tickles*
Krishnaswami, Uma. *Bringing Asha home*
Layne, Steven L. *Love the baby*
Lloyd-Jones, Sally. *How to be a baby — by me, the big sister*
Lobel, Gillian. *Too small for honey cake*
MacDonald, Ross. *Bad baby*
McElmurry, Jill. *I'm not a baby!*
McNaughton, Colin. *Captain Abdul's little treasure*
Manzano, Sonia. *A box full of kittens*
Meyers, Susan. *This is the way a baby rides*
Milord, Susan. *Love that baby*
Newman, Marjorie. *Just like me*
O'Hair, Margaret. *Star baby*
O'Keefe, Susan Heyboer. *Baby day*
Patricelli, Leslie. *Binky*
　　Blankie
Patz, Nancy. *Babies can't eat kimchee!*
Peddicord, Jane Ann. *That special little baby*
Pinkney, J. Brian. *Hush, little baby*
Robberecht, Thierry. *Back into Mommy's tummy*
Ross, Michael Elsohn. *Mama's milk*
Savadier, Elivia. *Time to get dressed!*
Schroeder, Lisa. *Baby can't sleep*
Shannon, David. *David smells*
　　Oh, David!
　　Oops!
Shapiro, Jody Fickes. *Family lullaby*
Sheldon, Annette. *Big sister now*
Singer, Marilyn. *City lullaby*
Slater, Dashka. *Baby shoes*

Smith, Maggie (Margaret C.). *One naked baby*
Sockabasin, Allen. *Thanks to the animals*
Sullivan, Sarah. *Dear Baby*
Taylor, Sean. *When a monster is born*
Thong, Roseanne. *Tummy girl*
Van Leeuwen, Jean. *Benny and beautiful baby Delilah*
Weeks, Sarah. *Overboard!*
Wheeler, Lisa. *Jazz baby*
Wigersma, Tanneke. *Baby brother*
Withrow, Sarah. *Be a baby*
Yolen, Jane. *Grandma's hurrying child*

Babies, new *see* Family life — new sibling

Baboons *see* Animals — baboons

Babysitting *see* Activities — babysitting

Bad day *see* Behavior — bad day

Badgers *see* Animals — badgers

Bakers *see* Careers — bakers

Baking *see* Activities — baking, cooking

Ballet

Bradley, Kimberly Brubaker. *Ballerino Nate*
Chaconas, Dori. *Dancing with Katya*
DePalma, Mary Newell. *The Nutcracker doll*
Ford, Bernette G. *Ballet Kitty*
French, Jackie. *Josephine wants to dance*
Gruska, Denise. *The only boy in ballet class*
Headley, Justina Chen. *The patch*
Holabird, Katharine. *Angelina at the palace*
　　Christmas in Mouseland
Lowell, Susan. *Josefina javelina*
Pennypacker, Sara. *Pierre in love*
Pinkwater, Daniel Manus. *Dancing Larry*
Polacco, Patricia. *Rotten Richie and the ultimate dare*
Schubert, Leda. *Ballet of the elephants*
Shulman, Lisa. *Over in the meadow at the big ballet*
Thompson, Lauren. *Ballerina dreams*
Weeks, Sarah. *Ella, of course!*
Young, Amy. *Belinda and the glass slipper*
　　Belinda begins ballet
　　Belinda in Paris

Ballooning *see* Activities — ballooning

Balloons *see* Toys — balloons

Balls *see* Toys — balls

Bandicoots *see* Animals — bandicoots

Banjos *see* Musical instruments — banjos

Barns

Schubert, Leda. *Here comes Darrell*

Bartering *see* Activities — trading

Baseball *see* Sports — baseball

Bashfulness *see* Character traits — shyness

Basketball *see* Sports — basketball

Bathing *see* Activities — bathing

Bats *see* Animals — bats

Beaches *see* Sea & seashore — beaches

Bears *see* Animals — bears

Beasts *see* Monsters

Beauty shops

Caseley, Judith. *In style with Grandma Antoinette*
Schotter, Roni. *Mama, I'll give you the world*

Beavers *see* Animals — beavers

Beds *see* Furniture — beds

Bedtime

Alborough, Jez. *Yes*
Anderson, Christine. *Bedtime!*
Arnold, Marsha Diane. *Roar of a snore*
Ashman, Linda. *Starry safari*
Bailey, Linda. *Goodnight, sweet pig*
Baker, Roberta. *Olive's first sleepover*
Baum, Louis. *The mouse who braved bedtime*
Bean, Jonathan. *At night*
Bergman, Mara. *Oliver who would not sleep!*
Bonnett-Rampersaud, Louise. *Bubble and Squeak*
Brown, Margaret Wise. *Goodnight moon 123*
Brunelle, Nicholas. *Snow Moon*
Butler, John. *Can you growl like a bear?*
Cabrera, Jane. *Ten in the bed*
Cain, Sheridan. *By the light of the moon*
Cousins, Lucy. *Sweet dreams, Maisy*
Daddo, Andrew. *Goodnight, me*
Davies, Jacqueline. *The night is singing*
Demers, Dominique. *Every single night*
Dewdney, Anna. *Llama, Llama red pajama*
Dodds, Dayle Ann. *The prince won't go to bed*
Donaldson, Julia. *One Ted falls out of bed*
Durango, Julia. *Dream hop*
Fancher, Lou. *Star climbing*
Ferreri, Della Ross. *How will I ever sleep in this bed?*
Fore, S. J. *Tiger can't sleep*
Fox, Mem. *Where the giant sleeps*
Freedman, Claire. *Snuggle up, sleepy ones*
Geisert, Arthur. *Lights out*
Glass, Beth Raisner. *Noises at night*
Hächler, Bruno. *What does my teddy bear do all night?*
Harper, Jamie. *Night night, baby bundt*
Harris, Peter. *The night pirates*
Harris, Robie H. *Maybe a bear ate it!*
Hicks, Barbara Jean. *Jitterbug jam*
Hindley, Judy. *Sleepy places*
Hodge, Marie. *Are you sleepy yet, Petey?*
Hurd, Thacher. *Sleepy Cadillac*
Imai, Ayano. *The 108th sheep*
Inches, Alison. *The stuffed animals get ready for bed*
Ives, Penny. *Rabbit pie*
Johnson, Lindan Lee. *The dream jar*
Kanevsky, Polly. *Sleepy boy*
Kloske, Geoffrey. *Once upon a time, the end (asleep in 60 seconds)*
Kono, Erin Eitter. *Hula lullaby*
Kurtz, Jane. *In the small, small night*
Landry, Leo. *Space boy*
LaReau, Kara. *Snowbaby could not sleep*
Lloyd-Jones, Sally. *Time to say goodnight*
MacDonald, Margaret Read. *The squeaky door*
Markes, Julie. *Shhhhh! Everybody's sleeping*
Modarressi, Mitra. *Stay awake, Sally*
Morales, Yuyi. *Little night*
Morrissey, Dean. *The crimson comet*
Newman, Leslea. *Daddy's song*
Numeroff, Laura Joffe. *When sheep sleep*
Owens, Mary Beth. *Panda whispers*

Peck, Jan. *Way up high in a tall green tree*
Prap, Lila. *Daddies*
Raye, Rebekah. *The very best bed*
Rex, Michael. *You can do anything, Daddy!*
Robbins, Maria Polushkin. *Mother, Mother, I want another*
Rockwell, Anne F. *Here comes the night*
Rohmann, Eric. *Clara and Asha*
Russo, Marisabina. *The bunnies are not in their beds*
Saltzberg, Barney. *Cornelius P. Mud, are you ready for bed?*
Sayles, Elizabeth. *The goldfish yawned*
Sayre, April Pulley. *Hush, little puppy*
Schroeder, Lisa. *Baby can't sleep*
Schubert, Ingrid. *There's a crocodile under my bed!*
Scotton, Rob. *Go to sleep, Russell the sheep*
 Russell the sheep
Slater, Dashka. *Firefighters in the dark*
Smee, Nicola. *No bed without Ted*
Sobel, June. *The goodnight train*
Sperring, Mark. *Mermaid dreams*
Stein, Mathilde. *Monstersong*
Tafuri, Nancy. *Goodnight, my duckling*
Vestergaard, Hope. *Hillside lullaby*
Waddell, Martin. *Sleep tight, Little Bear*
Weeks, Sarah. *Counting Ovejas*
Weninger, Brigitte. *Good night, Nori*
 "No bath! No way!"
Willems, Mo. *Don't let the pigeon stay up late!*
Wilson, Karma. *Sleepyhead*
Wing, Natasha. *Go to bed, monster!*
Withrow, Sarah. *Be a baby*
Wolff, Ferida. *It is the wind*
Wright, Michael. *Jake stays awake*
Yolen, Jane. *Baby Bear's chairs*
 Sleep, black bear, sleep
Ziefert, Harriet. *Mommy, I want to sleep in your bed!*

Bedwetting *see* Behavior — bedwetting

Beekeepers *see* Careers — beekeepers

Bees *see* Insects — bees

Beetles *see* Insects — beetles

Behavior

Cooper, Ilene. *The golden rule*
Dutton, Sandra. *Dear Miss Perfect*
Fearnley, Jan. *The search for the perfect child*
Harley, Bill. *Dear Santa*
Keller, Laurie. *Do unto otters*
Kroll, Virginia L. *Cristina keeps a promise*
 Good citizen Sarah
 Good neighbor Nicholas
Rosenthal, Amy Krouse. *Cookies*
Yolen, Jane. *How do dinosaurs play with their friends?*

Behavior — animals, dislike of

Pitzer, Susanna. *Not afraid of dogs*
Simon, Charnan. *Big bad Buzz*

Behavior — bad day

Agee, Jon. *Terrific*
Friday, Mary Ellen. *It's a bad day*
Henkes, Kevin. *A good day*
Lubner, Susan. *Ruthie Bon Bair, do not go to bed with wringing wet hair!*
Rodman, Mary Ann. *First grade stinks!*
Rosen, Michael. *Totally wonderful Miss Plumberry*
Rosenthal, Amy Krouse. *One of those days*
Slate, Joseph. *Miss Bindergarten has a wild day in kindergarten*
Tankard, Jeremy. *Grumpy Bird*

Behavior — bedwetting

Clarke, Jane. *Dippy's sleepover*

Behavior — boasting

Auch, Mary Jane. *Beauty and the beaks*

Behavior — boredom

Elschner, Geraldine. *Max's magic seeds*
Heide, Iris van der. *The red chalk*
Lakin, Patricia. *Rainy day*
Rosenthal, Marc. *Phooey!*

Schneider, Christine M. *I'm bored!*
Yolen, Jane. *Soft house*

Behavior — bossy

Choldenko, Gennifer. *Louder, Lili*
deGroat, Diane. *Last one in is a rotten egg!*
Horvath, David. *Bossy bear*
Ohi, Ruth. *Clara and the Bossy*
Palatini, Margie. *Shelly*
Zemach, Margot. *Eating up Gladys*

Behavior — bullying

Aruego, Jose. *The last laugh*
Buehner, Caralyn. *Would I ever lie to you?*
Church, Caroline Jayne. *One smart goose*
Crocker, Nancy. *Betty Lou Blue*
Dolenz, Micky. *Gakky Two-Feet*
Emberley, Ed (Edward Randolph). *Ed Emberley's bye-bye, big bad bullybug!*
Garden, Nancy. *Molly's family*
Keller, Holly. *Nosy Rosie*
Kroll, Steven. *Jungle bullies*
Kroll, Virginia L. *Ryan respects*
Lacombe, Benjamin. *Cherry and Olive*
LaReau, Kara. *Ugly fish*
Levert, Mireille. *Eddie Longpants*
McBratney, Sam. *Yes we can!*
Nolen, Jerdine. *Plantzilla goes to camp*
O'Connor, George. *Ker-splash!*
Pendziwol, Jean. *The tale of Sir Dragon*
Pinkwater, Daniel Manus. *Yo-yo man*
Polacco, Patricia. *Rotten Richie and the ultimate dare*
Sauer, Tammi. *Cowboy camp*
Smith, Stu. *The bubble gum kid*
Soule, Jean Conder. *Never tease a weasel*
Winstead, Rosie. *Ruby and Bubbles*

Behavior — cheating

Bailey, Linda. *The farm team*

Behavior — collecting things

Banks, Kate (Katherine A.). *Max's words*
Delessert, Etienne. *Alert!*
McGinty, Alice B. *Eliza's kindergarten surprise*
Major, Kevin. *Aunt Olga's Christmas postcards*
Manuel, Lynn. *The trouble with Tilly Trumble*
Ruzzier, Sergio. *The room of wonders*
Slingsby, Janet. *Hetty's 100 hats*

Behavior — dissatisfaction

Agee, Jon. *Terrific*

Behavior — fighting, arguing

Alborough, Jez. *Yes*
Dorros, Alex. *Número uno*
Gretz, Susanna. *Riley and Rose in the picture*
Johnson, D. B. (Donald B.). *Eddie's kingdom*

Kortepeter, Paul. *Oliver's red toboggan*
Lyon, George Ella. *No dessert forever!*
Mayer, Pamela. *The Grandma cure*
Ransom, Jeanie Franz. *Don't squeal unless it's a big deal*

Behavior — forgetfulness

Ashman, Linda. *To the beach!*
Cruise, Robin. *Little Mama forgets*
Lindbergh, Reeve. *My little grandmother often forgets*
Plourde, Lynn. *Pajama day*

Behavior — forgiving

Kroll, Virginia L. *Forgiving a friend*

Behavior — gossip

Bowen, Anne. *The great math tattle battle*
Chicken Little. *Henny Penny*
Downey, Lynn. *The tattletale*
Ransom, Jeanie Franz. *Don't squeal unless it's a big deal*
Waldman, Debby. *A sack full of feathers*

Behavior — greed

Ahmed, Said Salah. *The lion's share / Qayb Libaax*
Bardhan-Quallen, Sudipta. *The Mine-o-saur*
Bolliger, Max. *The happy troll*
Brett, Jan. *Honey, honey — lion!*
Carr, Jan. *Greedy apostrophe*
Gregory, Nan. *Pink*
Lasky, Kathryn. *Pirate Bob*
MacDonald, Margaret Read. *Little Rooster's diamond button*
Metz, Lorijo. *Floridius Bloom and the planet of Gloom*
Norac, Carl. *Monster, don't eat me!*
Oxenbury, Helen. *Pig tale*
Scott, Nathan Kumar. *Mangoes and bananas*
Simon, Charnan. *A greedy little pig*
Smallman, Steve. *The very greedy bee*
Stevens, Janet. *The great fuzz frenzy*
Willard, Nancy. *The flying bed*

Behavior — growing up

Banks, Kate (Katherine A.). *Fox*
Best, Cari. *Sally Jean, the Bicycle Queen*
Blackford, Harriet. *Tiger's story*
Emmett, Jonathan. *I love you always and forever*
Ferri, Giuliano. *Little Tad grows up*
Ford, Bernette G. *No more bottles for Bunny!*
Frazee, Marla. *Walk on!*
Gerstein, Mordicai. *Leaving the nest*
Krauss, Ruth. *The growing story*
Kroll, Virginia L. *On the way to kindergarten*
Louise, Tina. *When I grow up*
McElmurry, Jill. *I'm not a baby!*
McGhee, Alison. *Someday*
Patz, Nancy. *Babies can't eat kimchee!*
Pearson, Debora. *Sophie's wheels*
Schwartz, Amy. *Begin at the beginning*
Shea, Bob. *New socks*
Sloat, Teri. *I'm a duck!*
Stewart, Amber. *I'm big enough*
Taylor, Sean. *When a monster is born*
Thermes, Jennifer. *Sam Bennett's new shoes*
Thong, Roseanne. *Tummy girl*
Weninger, Brigitte. *Bye-bye, Binky*
Yolen, Jane. *Baby Bear's big dreams*

Behavior — hiding

Butler, John. *Ten in the meadow*
Egan, Tim. *Dodsworth in New York*
Fleming, Candace. *Tippy-tippy-tippy, hide!*
Mayr, Diane. *Run, Turkey, run*
Mazer, Norma Fox. *Has anyone seen my Emily Greene?*

Oliver, Narelle. *Twilight hunt*
Wong, Janet S. *Hide and seek*

Behavior — imitation

Brown, Lisa. *How to be*
Harper, Jamie. *Me too!*
Merz, Jennifer J. *Playground day*
Meyers, Susan. *This is the way a baby rides*

Behavior — indifference

Bee, William. *Whatever*
Konnecke, Ole. *Anthony and the girls*

Behavior — lost

Anderson, Lena. *The hedgehog, the pig, and their little friend*
Bauer, Marion Dane. *A mama for Owen*
Bedford, David. *Little Otter's big journey*
Brennan-Nelson, Denise. *Grady the goose*
Buckingham, Matt. *Bright Stanley*
Côté, Geneviève. *With you always, Little Monday*
Duquette, Keith. *Little Monkey lost*
Emmett, Jonathan. *This way, Ruby!*
Grimm, Jacob. *Hansel and Gretel*
    Hansel and Gretel / Hansel y Gretel
Heck, Ed. *Monkey lost*
Hodgkins, Fran. *The cat of Strawberry Hill*
Huneck, Stephen. *Sally's snow adventure*
Jeffers, Oliver. *Lost and found*
Kelly, Mij. *Where's my darling daughter?*
Kimmel, Eric A. *Rip Van Winkle's return*
Kroll, Steven. *Pooch on the loose*
Lobel, Gillian. *Little Honey Bear and the smiley moon*
McAllister, Angela. *Found you, Little Wombat!*
    Mama and Little Joe
MacDonald, Alan. *Wilfred to the rescue*
McDonald, Megan. *When the library lights go out*
McHenry, E. B. *Has anyone seen Winnie and Jean?*
Mitton, Tony. *Playful little penguins*
Skalak, Barbara Anne. *Waddle, waddle, quack, quack, quack*
Sockabasin, Allen. *Thanks to the animals*
Tafuri, Nancy. *Goodnight, my duckling*
Wheeler, Lisa. *Castaway cats*
Whybrow, Ian. *Harry and the dinosaurs at the museum*

Behavior — lost & found possessions

Alborough, Jez. *Duck's key where can it be?*
Blankenship, Lee Ann. *Mr. Tuggle's troubles*
Cate, Annette LeBlanc. *The magic rabbit*
DeSeve, Randall. *Toy boat*
DiFiori, Lawrence. *Jackie and the Shadow Snatcher*
Dunbar, Joyce. *Where's my sock?*
George, Margaret. *Lucille lost*
Kovacs, Deborah. *Katie Copley*
Lamb, Albert. *Sam's winter hat*
Lewis, Kim. *Hooray for Harry*
McClintock, Barbara. *Adele and Simon*
Mahy, Margaret. *Down the back of the chair*
Moss, Miriam. *Bare bear*
Plourde, Lynn. *A mountain of mittens*
Quattlebaum, Mary. *Winter friends*
Simon, Charnan. *Messy Molly*
Smee, Nicola. *No bed without Ted*
Willems, Mo. *Knuffle Bunny*

Behavior — lying

Abercrombie, Barbara. *The show-and-tell lion*
Buehner, Caralyn. *Would I ever lie to you?*
Hennessy, B. G. (Barbara G.). *The boy who cried wolf*
Rankin, Laura. *Ruthie and the (not so) teeny tiny lie*
Robberecht, Thierry. *Sam tells stories*
    Sarah's little ghosts
Rocco, John. *Wolf! Wolf!*

Behavior — messy

Blankenship, Lee Ann. *Mr. Tuggle's troubles*
Elschner, Geraldine. *Mark's messy room*
Gay, Marie-Louise. *What are you doing, Sam?*
Harris, Robie H. *I love messes!*
Lichtenheld, Tom. *What's with this room?*
Simon, Charnan. *Messy Molly*
Ziefert, Harriet. *Messy Bessie*

Behavior — misbehavior

Ashman, Linda. *Desmond and the naughtybugs*
Bruel, Nick. *Bad Kitty*
Burningham, John. *Edwardo*
Carlson, Nancy L. *Loudmouth George earns his allowance*
Catalanotto, Peter. *Ivan the terrier*
Cecka, Melanie. *Violet comes to stay*
Christelow, Eileen. *Letters from a desperate dog*
Church, Caroline Jayne. *Digby takes charge*
Dodds, Dayle Ann. *The prince won't go to bed*
Funke, Cornelia. *Princess Pigsty*
Grogan, John. *Bad dog, Marley!*
Jenkins, Emily. *Love you when you whine*
Joosse, Barbara M. *Please is a good word to say*
Kirwan, Wednesday. *Nobody notices Minerva*
Offill, Jenny. *17 things I'm not allowed to do anymore*
Russo, Marisabina. *The bunnies are not in their beds*
Schneider, Josh. *You'll be sorry*
Schotter, Roni. *When the Wizzy Foot goes walking*
Shannon, David. *Good boy, Fergus!*
    Oh, David!
Weaver, Tess. *Cat jumped in!*
Weis, Carol. *When the cows got loose*
Weston, Carrie. *If a chicken stayed for supper*
Whybrow, Ian. *Badness for beginners*
Ziefert, Harriet. *There was a little girl who had a little curl*

Behavior — mistakes

Schwartz, Amy. *Starring Miss Darlene*

Behavior — misunderstanding

Willis, Jeanne. *Gorilla! Gorilla!*

Behavior — name calling

Luthardt, Kevin. *You're weird!*

Behavior — naughty *see* Behavior — misbehavior

Behavior — potty training *see* Toilet training

Behavior — resourcefulness

Keller, Holly. *Help!*
McMillan, Bruce. *How the ladies stopped the wind*
    The problem with chickens
Stohner, Anu. *Brave Charlotte*

Behavior — running away

Ahlberg, Allan. *The runaway dinner*
Bailey, Linda. *Stanley's wild ride*
Bunting, Eve (Anne Evelyn). *Emma's turtle*
Chichester Clark, Emma. *Piper*
The gingerbread boy. *The Gingerbread Cowboy*
    The gingerbread girl
The gingerbread man. *Can't catch me*
Harrison, David Lee. *Piggy Wiglet*
Horse, Harry. *Little Rabbit runaway*
Ichikawa, Satomi. *I am Pangoo the penguin*
Imai, Ayano. *Chester*
Lloyd, Sam. *Mr. Pusskins*
Long, Kathy. *The runaway shopping cart*
McHenry, E. B. *Has anyone seen Winnie and Jean?*

Ohi, Ruth. *And you can come too*
Shulman, Goldie. *Way too much challah dough*
Waddell, Martin. *Bee frog*

Behavior — secrets

Asch, Frank. *Mrs. Marlowe's mice*
Coombs, Kate. *The secret-keeper*
George, Lindsay Barrett. *The secret*
Gray, Kes. *006 and a half*

Behavior — sharing

Bardhan-Quallen, Sudipta. *The Mine-o-saur*
Beaumont, Karen. *Move over, Rover*
deGroat, Diane. *Last one in is a rotten egg!*
Kortepeter, Paul. *Oliver's red toboggan*
Kroll, Steven. *Jungle bullies*
Landa, Norbert. *Little Bear and the wishing tree*
LaReau, Kara. *Ugly fish*
The little red hen. *The little red hen*
    The little red hen: an old fable
McDaniels, Preston. *A perfect snowman*
McKissack, Patricia C. *The all-I'll-ever-want Christmas doll*
Martin, David. *All for pie, pie for all*
Meserve, Adria. *No room for Napoleon*
Shannon, George. *Rabbit's gift*
Smallman, Steve. *The very greedy bee*
Stein, Mathilde. *Mine!*
Ziefert, Harriet. *Be fair, share!*

Behavior — solitude

Asher, Sandy. *Too many frogs!*
van Lieshout, Elle. *The wish*

Behavior — stealing

Amado, Elisa. *Tricycle*
Beaver steals fire
Khing, T. T. *Where is the cake?*
MacDonald, Margaret Read. *Tunjur! Tunjur! Tunjur!*
Pinkwater, Daniel Manus. *Bad bear detectives*
Vere, Ed. *The getaway*

Behavior — talking to strangers

Grimm, Jacob. *Little Red Riding Hood*, retold & ill. by Andrea Wisnewski
    Little Red Riding Hood, retold & ill. by Jerry Pinkney

Behavior — toilet training *see* Toilet training

Behavior — trickery

Bateman, Teresa. *Keeper of soles*
Beaver steals fire
Chicken Little. *Henny Penny*
Daly, Niki. *Pretty Salma*
Friend, Catherine. *The perfect nest*
Hennessy, B. G. (Barbara G.). *The boy who cried wolf*
Kelly, Mij. *One more sheep*
MacDonald, Margaret Read. *Conejito*
Nadimi, Suzan. *The rich man and the parrot*
Rocco, John. *Wolf! Wolf!*
Scott, Nathan Kumar. *Mangoes and bananas*
Tingle, Tim. *When turtle grew feathers*
Willey, Margaret. *A Clever Beatrice Christmas*

Behavior — wishing

Kleven, Elisa. *The wishing ball*
Klinting, Lars. *What do you want?*
Landa, Norbert. *Little Bear and the wishing tree*
Meddaugh, Susan. *The witch's walking stick*
Michelin, Linda (Donald B.). *Zuzu's wishing cake*
Morgan, Michaela. *Bunny wishes*

Moser, Lisa. *Watermelon wishes*
Napoli, Donna Jo. *The wishing club*
Newman, Marlene. *Myron's magic cow*
Rose, Marion. *The Christmas tree fairy*
Souhami, Jessica. *Sausages*
Stanley, Diane. *The trouble with wishes*
van Lieshout, Elle. *The wish*
Wishinsky, Frieda. *Please, Louise!*

Behavior — worrying

Browne, Anthony. *Silly Billy*
Clarke, Jane. *The best of both nests*
Cocca-Leffler, Maryann. *Jack's talent*
Gavril, David. *Penelope Nuthatch and the big surprise*
Graves, Keith. *The unexpectedly bad hair of Barcelona Smith*
Jacobs, Julie. *My heart is a magic house*
Kelley, Marty. *Winter woes*
Montanari, Eva. *A very full morning*
Ohi, Ruth. *A trip with Grandma*
Poydar, Nancy. *The bad-news report card*
    The biggest test in the universe
Viorst, Judith. *Just in case*
Whybrow, Ian. *Bella gets her skates on*

Being different *see* Character traits — being different

Belarus *see* Foreign lands — Belarus

Bereavement *see* Death; Emotions — grief

Bible *see* Religion

Bicycling *see* Sports — bicycling

Bigotry *see* Prejudice

Birds

Aston, Dianna Hutts. *Mama outside, Mama inside*
Brett, Jan. *Honey, honey — lion!*
Charles, Veronika Martenova. *The birdman*
Franco, Betsy. *Birdsongs*
Friend, Catherine. *The perfect nest*
Gavril, David. *Penelope Nuthatch and the big surprise*
Haas, Irene. *Bess and Bella*
Harper, Charise Mericle. *Amy and Ivan*
Ruddell, Deborah. *Today at the bluebird cafe*
Segal, John. *The lonely moose*
Tafuri, Nancy. *Whose chick are you?*
Tankard, Jeremy. *Grumpy Bird*
Teevin, Toni. *What to do? What to do?*
Valckx, Catharina. *Lizette's green sock*
Winstead, Rosie. *Ruby and Bubbles*

Birds — chickens

Arnold, Tedd. *The twin princes*
Auch, Mary Jane. *Beauty and the beaks*
    Chickerella
Baddiel, Ivor. *Cock-a-doodle quack! Quack!*
Brown, Jo. *Hoppity skip Little Chick*
Bunting, Eve (Anne Evelyn). *Hurry! Hurry!*
Burg, Sarah Emmanuelle. *One more egg*
Chaconas, Dori. *Dori the contrary hen*
Chen, Chih-Yuan. *The featherless chicken*
Chicken Little. *Henny Penny*
Daly, Niki. *Welcome to Zanzibar Road*
Denchfield, Nick. *Charlie Chick*
Diakité, Penda. *I lost my tooth in Africa*
Edwards, Pamela Duncan. *The mixed-up rooster*
Elliott, David. *One little chicken*
Harrington, Janice N. *The chicken-chasing queen of Lamar County*
Hayward, Linda. *The King's chorus*
Helakoski, Leslie. *Big chickens*
Himmelman, John. *Chickens to the rescue*

Hutchins, Pat. *Bumpety bump*
Johnston, Tony. *Chicken in the kitchen*
Kelley, Ellen A. *My life as a chicken*
Kromhout, Rindert. *Little Donkey and the baby-sitter*
Lin, Grace. *Olvina swims*
The little red hen. *The little red hen*
   The little red hen: an old fable
MacDonald, Margaret Read. *Little Rooster's diamond button*
McMillan, Bruce. *The problem with chickens*
Manning, Mick. *Cock-a-doodle hooooooo!*
Martin, Jacqueline Briggs. *Chicken joy on Redbean Road*
Matthews, Tina. *Out of the egg*
O'Malley, Kevin. *Gimme cracked corn and I will share*
Palatini, Margie. *Shelly*
   Three French hens
Reynolds, Aaron. *Buffalo wings*
   Chicks and salsa
Ruurs, Margriet. *Wake up, Henry Rooster!*
Scillian, Devin. *Brewster the rooster*
Shannon, George. *The Secret Chicken Club*
Shea, Bob. *New socks*
Sidjanski, Brigitte. *Little Chicken and Little Duck*
Stoeke, Janet Morgan. *Minerva Louise and the colorful eggs*
   Minerva Louise on Christmas Eve
Tafuri, Nancy. *Five little chicks*
Valentina, Marina. *Lost in the roses*
Varon, Sara. *Chicken and Cat*
Weston, Carrie. *If a chicken stayed for supper*
Why did the chicken cross the road?

Birds — cranes

George, Jean Craighead. *Luck*

Birds — crows

Appelt, Kathi. *Merry Christmas, merry crow*
Kleven, Elisa. *The wishing ball*
Paul, Alison. *The crow (a not so scary story)*
Sillifant, Alec. *Farmer Ham*
Spirin, Gennady. *Martha*

Birds — doves

Yang, Belle. *Always come home to me*

Birds — ducks

Alborough, Jez. *Duck's key where can it be?*
   Hit the ball duck
Andersen, H. C. (Hans Christian). *The ugly duckling*
Aruego, Jose. *The last laugh*
Barry, Frances. *Duckie's ducklings*
Bates, Ivan. *Five little ducks*
Berry, Lynne. *Duck skates*
Capucilli, Alyssa Satin. *Katy Duck*
   Katy Duck, big sister
Chae, In Seon. *How do you count a dozen ducklings?*
Cooper, Helen (Helen F.). *Delicious!*
   A pipkin of pepper
Cronin, Doreen. *Click clack, quackity-quack*
   Duck for President
Egan, Tim. *Dodsworth in New York*
Emmett, Jonathan. *Ruby in her own time*
   This way, Ruby!
Ford, Bernette G. *No more diapers for Ducky!*
Hills, Tad. *Duck and Goose*
   Duck, Duck, Goose
Johansen, Hanna. *The duck and the owl*
Pfister, Marcus. *Charlie at the zoo*
Rankin, Laura. *Fluffy and Baron*
Sidjanski, Brigitte. *Little Chicken and Little Duck*
Skalak, Barbara Anne. *Waddle, waddle, quack, quack, quack*
Sloat, Teri. *I'm a duck!*
Straaten, Harmen van. *Duck's tale*
   For me?
Tafuri, Nancy. *Goodnight, my duckling*

Thompson, Lauren. *Little Quack*
   Little Quack's hide and seek
   Little Quack's new friend
Urbanovic, Jackie. *Duck at the door*
Willems, Mo. *The Pigeon finds a hot dog!*
Yolen, Jane. *Dimity Duck*

Birds — falcons

George, Jean Craighead. *Frightful's daughter meets the Baron Weasel*

Birds — finches

Pericoli, Matteo. *The true story of Stellina*

Birds — flamingos

Guiberson, Brenda Z. *Mud city*
Harper, Jamie. *Miss Mingo and the first day of school*

Birds — geese

Bloom, Suzanne. *A splendid friend, indeed*
Brennan-Nelson, Denise. *Grady the goose*
Church, Caroline Jayne. *One smart goose*
Dunrea, Olivier. *Gossie's busy day*
Harper, Charise Mericle. *When Randolph turned rotten*
Hills, Tad. *Duck and Goose*
   Duck, Duck, Goose
Horacek, Petr. *Silly Suzy Goose*
Kindermans, Martine. *You and me*

Birds — hawks

McCarthy, Meghan. *City hawk*
Winter, Jeanette. *The tale of pale male*

Birds — herons

Gorbachev, Valeri. *Heron and Turtle*
Quigley, Mary. *Granddad's fishing buddy*

Birds — owls

Allen, Jonathan. *"I'm not cute!"*
   "I'm not scared!"
Brunelle, Nicholas. *Snow Moon*
Davies, Nicola. *White owl, barn owl*
Gibbons, Gail. *Owls*
Johansen, Hanna. *The duck and the owl*
Lear, Edward. *The owl and the pussycat*
Lears, Laurie. *Nathan's wish*
Manning, Mick. *Cock-a-doodle hooooooo!*
Oliver, Narelle. *Twilight hunt*
Serfozo, Mary. *Whooo's there?*

Birds — parrots

Agee, Jon. *Terrific*
Bee, William. *And the train goes . . .*
Kennedy, Kim. *Pirate Pete's giant adventure*
Nadimi, Suzan. *The rich man and the parrot*
Rawson, Katherine. *If you were a parrot*

Birds — pelicans

Johnson, Rebecca. *The proud pelican's secret*

Birds — penguins

Anderson, Derek. *Romeo and Lou blast off*
Arnold, Caroline. *A penguin's world*
Barner, Bob. *Penguins, penguins, everywhere!*
Cuyler, Margery. *Please play safe!*
Dunbar, Polly. *Penguin*
Fromental, Jean-Luc. *365 penguins*
Ichikawa, Satomi. *I am Pangoo the penguin*
Jeffers, Oliver. *Lost and found*

Lester, Helen. *Tacky and the Winter Games*
Lin, Grace. *Olvina swims*
Markle, Sandra. *A mother's journey*
Mitton, Tony. *Playful little penguins*
Morison, Toby. *Little Louie takes off*
Richardson, Justin. *And Tango makes three*

Birds — pigeons

Farmer, Nancy. *Clever Ali*
Keller, Holly. *Sophie's window*
San Souci, Daniel. *The Mighty Pigeon Club*
Willems, Mo. *Don't let the pigeon stay up late!*
   The Pigeon finds a hot dog!
   The Pigeon has feelings, too!
   The Pigeon loves things that go!

Birds — puffins

Zecca, Katherine. *A puffin's year*

Birds — robins

Schwartz, Amy. *A beautiful girl*

Birds — sandpipers

Willis, Nancy Carol. *Red knot*

Birds — seagulls

Clark, Katie. *Seagull Sam*

Birds — storks

Clarke, Jane. *The best of both nests*
Olson, David J. *The thunderstruck stork*

Birds — swallows

Ryan, Pam Muñoz. *Nacho and Lolita*

Birds — swans

Andersen, H. C. (Hans Christian). *The ugly duckling*
   The wild swans
Shulman, Lisa. *Over in the meadow at the big ballet*
Tafuri, Nancy. *Whose chick are you?*

Birds — turkeys

Anderson, Derek. *Over the river*
Archer, Peggy. *Turkey surprise*
Auch, Mary Jane. *Beauty and the beaks*
Mayr, Diane. *Run, Turkey, run*
Reed, Lynn Rowe. *Thelonius Turkey lives!*

Birds — vultures

Sayre, April Pulley. *Vulture view*

Birth

Aston, Dianna Hutts. *Mama outside, Mama inside*
Holt, Kimberly Willis. *Waiting for Gregory*
Saltz, Gail. *Amazing you*
Tillman, Nancy. *On the night you were born*
Van Steenwyk, Elizabeth. *Prairie Christmas*
Yolen, Jane. *Grandma's hurrying child*

Birthdays

Anholt, Catherine. *Happy birthday, Chimp and Zee*
Asher, Sandy. *What a party!*
Baker, Roberta. *Olive's pirate party*
Beck, Scott. *Happy birthday, Monster!*
Calmenson, Stephanie. *Birthday at the Panda Palace*
Cheng, Andrea. *The lemon sisters*

Chodos-Irvine, Margaret. *Best best friends*
Daly, Niki. *Happy birthday, Jamela!*
Elya, Susan Middleton. *F is for fiesta*
Evans, Cambria. *Martha moth makes socks*
Foreman, George. *Let George do it!*
Frasier, Debra. *A birthday cake is no ordinary cake*
Graham, Bob. *Oscar's half birthday*
Harper, Charise Mericle. *When Randolph turned rotten*
Howe, James. *Houndsley and Catina and the birthday surprise*
Kroll, Virginia L. *Jason takes responsibility*
Kromhout, Rindert. *Little Donkey and the birthday present*
Kulka, Joe. *Wolf's coming*
Lears, Laurie. *Megan's birthday tree*
Lewis, Rose A. *Every year on your birthday*
McElligott, Matthew. *Backbeard and the birthday suit*
McPhail, David. *Big Brown Bear's birthday surprise*
Martin, Bill, Jr. (William Ivan). *"Fire! Fire!" Said Mrs. McGuire*
Modesitt, Jeanne. *Little Mouse's happy birthday*
Patricelli, Leslie. *The birthday box*
Paul, Ann Whitford. *Fiesta fiasco*
Pilgrim, Elza. *The china doll*
Rempt, Fiona. *Snail's birthday wish*
Saltzberg, Barney. *Hi, Blueberry!*
Schoenherr, Ian. *Pip and Squeak*
Schotter, Roni. *Mama, I'll give you the world*
Slingsby, Janet. *Hetty's 100 hats*
Sperring, Mark. *The fairytale cake*
Stanton, Karen. *Papi's gift*
Thomas, Shelley Moore. *Happy birthday, Good Knight*
Weninger, Brigitte. *Double birthday*
Williams, Barbara. *Albert's gift for grandmother*
Wilson, Karma. *Whopper cake*
Yaccarino, Dan. *The birthday fish*

Bison *see* Animals — buffaloes

Blindness *see* Handicaps — blindness; Senses — sight

Blizzards *see* Weather — blizzards

Board books *see* Format, unusual — board books

Boasting *see* Behavior — boasting

Boats, ships

Arnosky, Jim. *Parrotfish and sunken ships*
Blackstone, Stella. *Ship shapes*
Christian, Mary Blount. *If not for the calico cat*
Clark, Mary Higgins. *Ghost ship*
Floca, Brian. *Lightship*
Greene, Rhonda Gowler. *Noah and the mighty ark*
Mitton, Tony. *All afloat on Noah's boat!*
Soto, Gary. *Chato goes cruisin'*
Stewig, John Warren. *The animals watched*
Wynne-Jones, Tim. *The boat in the tree*

Bonobos *see* Animals — bonobos

Books *see* Books, reading; Libraries

Books, reading

Bertram, Debbie. *The best time to read*
Briant, Ed. *Seven stories*
Carlson, Nancy L. *I don't like to read!*
Cazet, Denys. *Will you read to me?*
Child, Lauren. *But, excuse me, that is my book*
Cousins, Lucy. *Maisy goes to the library*
Crimi, Carolyn. *Henry and the Buccaneer Bunnies*
Donaldson, Julia. *Charlie Cook's favorite book*
Edwards, Pamela Duncan. *The neat line*
Elya, Susan Middleton. *Fairy trails*
Finchler, Judy. *Miss Malarkey leaves no reader behind*
Garland, Michael. *King Puck*
   Miss Smith reads again!

Harris, Robie H. *Maybe a bear ate it!*
Hayward, Linda. *I am a book*
Hillenbrand, Will. *My book box*
Hodge, Deborah. *Lily and the mixed-up letters*
Ivey, Randall. *Jay and the bounty of books*
Jeffers, Oliver. *The incredible book eating boy*
Kanninen, Barbara. *A story with pictures*
Kirk, David. *Library mouse*
Kloske, Geoffrey. *Once upon a time, the end (asleep in 60 seconds)*
Lakin, Patricia. *Rainy day*
McGee, Marni. *Winston the book wolf*
McQuinn, Anna. *Lola at the library*
Montanari, Eva. *My first . . .*
Morris, Carla. *The boy who was raised by librarians*
Muntean, Michaela. *Do not open this book!*
Nez, John. *One smart Cookie*
Nikola-Lisa, W. *Magic in the margins*
Orozco, Jose-Luis. *Rin, rin, rin / do, re, mi*
Palatini, Margie. *The three silly billies*
Parr, Todd. *Reading makes you feel good*
Pinkney, Sandra L. *Read and rise*
Plourde, Lynn. *Book Fair Day*
Sperring, Mark. *The fairytale cake*
Straaten, Harmen van. *Duck's tale*
Thomas, Shelley Moore. *Take care, Good Knight*
Wallner, Alexandra. *Lucy Maud Montgomery*
Yolen, Jane. *Baby Bear's books*

Boredom *see* Behavior — boredom

Bossy *see* Behavior — bossy

Boxing *see* Sports — boxing

Bravery *see* Character traits — bravery

Brazil *see* Foreign lands — Brazil

Bridges

Prince, April Jones. *Twenty-one elephants and still standing*

British Columbia *see* Foreign lands — British Columbia

Brothers *see* Family life — brothers & sisters; Sibling rivalry

Buffaloes *see* Animals — buffaloes

Bugs *see* Insects

Buildings

Beaty, Andrea. *Iggy Peck, architect*
Curlee, Lynn. *Skyscraper*
Hudson, Cheryl Willis. *Construction zone*

Bulldozers *see* Machines

Bulls *see* Animals — bulls, cows

Bullying *see* Behavior — bullying

Bumble bees *see* Insects — bees

Burglars *see* Crime

Burros *see* Animals — donkeys

Bus drivers *see* Careers — bus drivers

Buses

Cole, Joanna. *The magic school bus and the science fair expedition*

Dale, Penny. *The boy on the bus*
Moore, Mary-Alice. *The wheels on the school bus*
Stoeke, Janet Morgan. *The bus stop*

Butterflies *see* Insects — butterflies, caterpillars

Cafés *see* Restaurants

Caldecott award books

Juster, Norton. *The hello, goodbye window*
Selznick, Brian. *The invention of Hugo Cabret*
Wiesner, David. *Flotsam*

Caldecott award honor books

Giovanni, Nikki. *Rosa*
Levine, Ellen. *Henry's freedom box*
McLimans, David. *Gone wild*
Muth, Jon J. *Zen shorts*
Priceman, Marjorie. *Hot air*
Seeger, Laura Vaccaro. *First the egg*
Sidman, Joyce. *Song of the water boatman*
Sís, Peter. *The wall*
Weatherford, Carole Boston. *Moses*
Willems, Mo. *Knuffle Bunny*
    Knuffle Bunny too

Calendars

Frasier, Debra. *A birthday cake is no ordinary cake*
Livingston, Myra Cohn. *Calendar*

Camels *see* Animals — camels

Camouflages *see* Disguises

Camps, camping

Bateman, Teresa. *Hamster Camp*
Nolen, Jerdine. *Plantzilla goes to camp*
Sauer, Tammi. *Cowboy camp*
Wilson, Karma. *Sweet Briar goes to camp*

Canada *see* Foreign lands — Canada

Cancer *see* Illness — cancer

Cards *see* Letters, cards

Careers

Catalanotto, Peter. *Kitten red, yellow, blue*
Cordsen, Carol Foskett. *The milkman*
Ericsson, Jennifer A. *Home to me, home to you*
Hartland, Jessie. *Night shift*
McNaughton, Colin. *When I grow up*
Reed, Lynn Rowe. *Please don't upset P.U. Zorilla!*
Reiser, Lynn. *Hardworking puppies*
Ziefert, Harriet. *The biggest job of all*

Careers — actors

Bell, Cece. *Sock Monkey boogie-woogie*
    Sock Monkey rides again
Francis, Pauline. *Sam stars at Shakespeare's Globe*
Schwartz, Amy. *Starring Miss Darlene*

Careers — airplane pilots

Johnson, Angela. *Wind flyers*

Careers — architects

Beaty, Andrea. *Iggy Peck, architect*

Careers — artists *see also* Activities — painting

Arrigan, Mary. *Mario's angels*
Christelow, Eileen. *Letters from a desperate dog*
Demi. *The boy who painted dragons*
Hong, Chen Jiang. *The magic horse of Han Gan*
Jahn-Clough, Lisa. *Little dog*
Kitamura, Satoshi. *Pablo the artist*
Rodríguez, Rachel Victoria. *Through Georgia's eyes*
Sís, Peter. *The wall*

Careers — astronauts

Aldrin, Buzz. *Reaching for the moon*
Brett, Jan. *Hedgie blasts off!*
Hilliard, Richard. *Godspeed, John Glenn*

Careers — authors

Kanninen, Barbara. *A story with pictures*
Kirk, David. *Library mouse*
Pulver, Robin. *Author day for room 3T*

Careers — bakers

Holt, Kimberly Willis. *Skinny brown dog*
Ogburn, Jacqueline K. *The bake shop ghost*
Simmonds, Posy. *Baker cat*
Wellington, Monica. *Mr. Cookie Baker*
Willard, Nancy. *The flying bed*

Careers — beekeepers

Kessler, Cristina. *The best beekeeper of Lalibela*

Careers — bus drivers

Pulver, Robin. *Axle Annie and the speed grump*

Careers — chefs, cooks

Barasch, Lynne. *Hiromi's hands*
Stowell, Penelope. *The greatest potatoes*
Wellington, Monica. *Pizza at Sally's*

Careers — construction workers

Hudson, Cheryl Willis. *Construction zone*
McMullan, Kate. *I'm dirty!*
Nevius, Carol. *Building with Dad*
Skultety, Nancy. *From here to there*

Careers — cooks *see* Careers — chefs, cooks

Careers — custodians, janitors

Brett, Jan. *Hedgie blasts off!*

Careers — dentists

Cousins, Lucy. *Maisy, Charley, and the wobbly tooth*

Careers — detectives

Pinkwater, Daniel Manus. *Bad bear detectives*
Yee, Wong Herbert. *Detective Small in the amazing banana caper*

Careers — doctors

Cole, Joanna. *My friend the doctor*
Murphy, Liz. *ABC doctor*

Careers — explorers

St. George, Judith. *So you want to be an explorer?*

Careers — farmers

Barbour, Karen. *Mr. Williams*
Carter, Don. *Old MacDonald drives a tractor*
Cronin, Doreen. *Dooby dooby moo*
Fitz-Gibbon, Sally. *On Uncle John's farm*
Palatini, Margie. *The cheese*
Pelletier, Andrew T. *The toy farmer*
Purmwell, Ann. *Christmas tree farm*
Sillifant, Alec. *Farmer Ham*
Spinelli, Eileen. *The best time of day*
Stock, Catherine. *A porc in New York*

Careers — firefighters

Armstrong, Jennifer. *Magnus at the fire*
Butler, Dori Hillestad. *F is for firefighting*
Frampton, David. *Mr. Ferlinghetti's poem*
Grambling, Lois G. *My mom is a firefighter*
Greene, Rhonda Gowler. *Firebears*
Hamilton, Kersten. *Firefighters to the rescue!*
Hubbell, Patricia. *Firefighters!*
Mammano, Julie. *Rhinos who rescue*
Martin, Bill, Jr. (William Ivan). *"Fire! Fire!" Said Mrs. McGuire*
Slater, Dashka. *Firefighters in the dark*
Wood, Audrey. *Alphabet rescue*
Zimmerman, Andrea Griffing. *Fire engine man*

Careers — fishermen

LaMarche, Jim. *Up*
Pennypacker, Sara. *Pierre in love*

Careers — fur traders

Pendziwol, Jean. *The red sash*

Careers — garbage collectors *see* Careers — sanitation workers

Careers — illustrators

Kanninen, Barbara. *A story with pictures*

Careers — inventors

Milgrim, David. *Young MacDonald*
Pelley, Kathleen T. *Inventor McGregor*
Priceman, Marjorie. *Hot air*

Careers — janitors *see* Careers — custodians, janitors

Careers — jockeys

Trollinger, Patsi B. *Perfect timing*

Careers — librarians

Morris, Carla. *The boy who was raised by librarians*

Careers — magicians

Baynton, Martin. *Jane and the magician*
Cate, Annette LeBlanc. *The magic rabbit*

Careers — mail carriers *see* Careers — postal workers

Careers — meteorologists

Schmidt, Karen Lee. *Carl's nose*

Careers — migrant workers

Stanton, Karen. *Papi's gift*

Careers — military

Andersen, H. C. (Hans Christian). *The tinderbox*
Bunting, Eve (Anne Evelyn). *My red balloon*
Demarest, Chris L. *Alpha Bravo Charlie*
McElroy, Lisa Tucker. *Love, Lizzie*
Nelson, S. D. *Quiet hero*
Seeger, Pete. *Some friends to feed*
Tomp, Sarah Wones. *Red, white, and blue goodbye*

Careers — miners

Addy, Sharon Hart. *Lucky Jake*
Provensen, Alice. *Klondike gold*

Careers — musicians

Dillon, Leo. *Jazz on a Saturday night*
Grimm, Jacob. *The Bremen town musicians*
   Musicians of Bremen
   Musicians of Bremen / Los musicos de Bremner
Seeger, Pete. *The deaf musicians*
Sís, Peter. *Play, Mozart, play*
Winter, Jonah. *Dizzy*

Careers — painters *see also* Activities — painting; Careers — artists

Careers — physicians *see* Careers — doctors

Careers — police officers

Niemann, Christoph. *The police cloud*
Whitehead, Kathy. *Looking for Uncle Louie on the Fourth of July*

Careers — postal workers

Bottner, Barbara. *Raymond and Nelda*
Steffensmeier, Alexander. *Millie waits for the mail*

Careers — principals *see* Careers — school principals

Careers — ranchers

Urbigkit, Cat. *A young shepherd*

Careers — salesmen

Rozen, Anna. *The merchant of noises*

Careers — sanitation workers

Odanaka, Barbara. *Smash! Mash! Crash! There goes the trash!*

Careers — school principals

Cocca-Leffler, Maryann. *Mr. Tanen's ties rule!*

Careers — scientists

McCully, Emily Arnold. *Marvelous Mattie*
Pettenati, Jeanne K. *Galileo's journal, 1609–1610*

Careers — sculptors

Stanley, Diane. *The trouble with wishes*

Careers — shepherds

Urbigkit, Cat. *A young shepherd*

Careers — sheriffs

Crummel, Susan Stevens. *Ten-gallon Bart*
Rumford, James. *Don't touch my hat!*
Sneed, Brad. *Deputy Harvey and the ant cow caper*

Careers — shoemakers

Bateman, Teresa. *Keeper of soles*
Grimm, Jacob. *The elves and the shoemaker*

Careers — singers

Sciurba, Katie. *Oye, Celia!*

Careers — soldiers *see* Careers — military

Careers — tailors

Charles, Veronika Martenova. *The birdman*
Oddino, Licia. *Finn and the fairies*

Careers — teachers

Brisson, Pat. *I remember Miss Perry*
Cole, Joanna. *The magic school bus and the science fair expedition*
Cuyler, Margery. *Kindness is cooler, Mrs. Ruler*
Danneberg, Julie. *Last day blues*
deGroat, Diane. *No more pencils, no more books, no more teacher's dirty looks!*
Dodds, Dayle Ann. *Teacher's pets*
Edwards, Pamela Duncan. *Ms. Bitsy Bat's kindergarten*
Finchler, Judy. *Miss Malarkey leaves no reader behind*
Garland, Michael. *Miss Smith reads again!*
Harper, Jamie. *Miss Mingo and the first day of school*
Henkes, Kevin. *Lilly's big day*
Hennessy, B. G. (Barbara G.). *Mr. Ouchy's first day*
Laminack, Lester L. *Snow day!*
Layne, Steven L. *T is for teachers*
McNaughton, Colin. *Once upon an ordinary school day*
Montanari, Eva. *A very full morning*
Pattou, Edith. *Mrs. Spitzer's garden*
Polacco, Patricia. *The lemonade club*
Puttock, Simon. *Miss Fox*
Rosen, Michael. *Totally wonderful Miss Plumberry*
Slate, Joseph. *Miss Bindergarten celebrates the last day of kindergarten*
   Miss Bindergarten has a wild day in kindergarten

Careers — truck drivers

Coffelt, Nancy. *Pug in a truck*
Wellington, Monica. *Truck driver Tom*

Careers — veterinarians

Carris, Joan. *Welcome to the bed and biscuit*

Careers — waiters, waitresses

Downey, Lynn. *Matilda's humdinger*

Careers — weather reporters *see* Careers — meteorologists

Caribbean Islands *see* Foreign lands — Caribbean Islands

Carnivals *see* Fairs, festivals

Carousels *see* Merry-go-rounds

Cars *see* Automobiles

Caterpillars *see* Insects — butterflies, caterpillars

Cats *see* Animals — cats

Cerebral palsy *see* Handicaps — cerebral palsy

Chairs *see* Furniture — chairs

Chameleons *see* Reptiles — chameleons

Change *see* Concepts — change

Character traits

Rosenthal, Amy Krouse. *Cookies*

Character traits — ambition

Aska, Warabe. *Tapicero tap tap*

Character traits — appearance

Allen, Jonathan. *"I'm not cute!"*
Andersen, H. C. (Hans Christian). *The ugly duckling*
Azore, Barbara. *Wanda and the wild hair*
Boelts, Maribeth. *Those shoes*
Brisson, Pat. *Melissa Parkington's beautiful, beautiful hair*
Brown, Jeff. *Flat Stanley*
Carlson, Nancy L. *Think big!*
Chen, Chih-Yuan. *The featherless chicken*
Choldenko, Gennifer. *How to make friends with a giant*
Crocker, Nancy. *Betty Lou Blue*
Ditchfield, Christin. *Cowlick!*
Duke, Shirley Smith. *No bows!*
Hogg, Gary. *Beautiful Buehla and the zany zoo makeover*
Hume, Lachie. *Clancy the courageous cow*
Johnson, Rebecca. *The proud pelican's secret*
Krensky, Stephen. *Milo and the really big bunny*
LaReau, Kara. *Ugly fish*
MacDonald, Margaret Read. *The great smelly, slobbery small-toothed dog*
Meddaugh, Susan. *Just Teenie*
Montserrat, Pep. *Ms. Rubinstein's beauty*
Napoli, Donna Jo. *Bobby the bold*
Pichon, Liz. *The very ugly bug*
Schwartz, Amy. *A beautiful girl*
Ziefert, Harriet. *There was a little girl who had a little curl*

Character traits — assertiveness

Henkes, Kevin. *Lilly's big day*

Character traits — being different

Andersen, H. C. (Hans Christian). *The ugly duckling*
Baryshnikov, Mikhail. *Because . . .*
Bradley, Kimberly Brubaker. *Ballerino Nate*
Brown, Peter. *Chowder*
Chen, Chih-Yuan. *The featherless chicken*
Edwards, Pamela Duncan. *The mixed-up rooster*
Le Neouanic, Lionel. *Little smudge*
Levert, Mireille. *Eddie Longpants*
Napoli, Donna Jo. *Bobby the bold*
Saltzberg, Barney. *Star of the week*
Schaefer, Lola M. *Frankie Stein*

Character traits — bravery

Bailey, Linda. *The farm team*
Demi. *The boy who painted dragons*
Giovanni, Nikki. *Rosa*
McDonald, Megan. *Beetle McGrady eats bugs!*
McGhee, Alison. *A very brave witch*
McKissack, Patricia C. *Precious and the Boo Hag*
Simon, Charnan. *Big bad Buzz*
Spinelli, Eileen. *Hero cat*
Stein, Mathilde. *Brave Ben*
Stohner, Anu. *Brave Charlotte*
Stryer, Andrea Stenn. *Kami and the yaks*
Watt, Melanie. *Scaredy Squirrel*

Character traits — cleanliness

Child, Lauren. *Say cheese!*
Church, Caroline Jayne. *One smart goose*

Ehrlich, Fred. *Does an elephant take a bath?*
Elschner, Geraldine. *Mark's messy room*
Ernst, Lisa Campbell. *This is the van that Dad cleaned*
Funke, Cornelia. *Princess Pigsty*
Harris, Robie H. *I love messes!*
Kroll, Virginia L. *Really rabbits*
Lichtenheld, Tom. *What's with this room?*
McElligott, Matthew. *Backbeard and the birthday suit*
Nelson, Robin. *Staying clean*
Sayre, April Pulley. *Stars beneath your bed*
Schertle, Alice. *The adventures of old Bo Bear*
Sloat, Teri. *This is the house that was tidy and neat*
Stewart, Amber. *Rabbit ears*
Teckentrup, Britta. *Big smelly bear*

Character traits — cleverness

Cole, Brock. *Good enough to eat*
Compestine, Ying Chang. *The real story of stone soup*
Geisert, Arthur. *Lights out*
Isaacs, Anne. *Pancakes for supper!*
Johnson, Rebecca. *Sea turtle's clever plan*
Johnson-Davies, Denys. *Goha, the wise fool*
Kimmel, Eric A. *The three cabritos*
McMillan, Bruce. *The problem with chickens*
Rozen, Anna. *The merchant of noises*
Seeger, Pete. *Some friends to feed*
Stewart, Joel. *Dexter Bexley and the big blue beastie*
The three little pigs. *The three little pigs / Los tres cerditos*

Character traits — clumsiness

Simon, Charnan. *Jeremy Jones, clumsy guy*

Character traits — confidence

Hillenbrand, Jane. *What a treasure!*
Latifah, Queen. *Queen of the scene*
Shea, Bob. *New socks*

Character traits — cooperation

Aliki. *A play's the thing*
Dorros, Alex. *Número uno*
Hester, Denia Lewis. *Grandma Lena's big ol' turnip*
Singer, Marilyn. *Let's build a clubhouse*
Vail, Rachel. *Righty and Lefty*
Willems, Mo. *Today I will fly!*

Character traits — courage *see* Character traits — bravery

Character traits — cruelty to animals *see* Character traits — kindness to animals

Character traits — curiosity

Cecka, Melanie. *Violet goes to the country*
Curtis, Jamie Lee. *Is there really a human race?*
Gorbachev, Valeri. *Red red red*
Hapka, Cathy. *Margret and H. A. Rey's Merry Christmas, Curious George*
Loupy, Christophe. *Wiggles*

Character traits — foolishness

Hurston, Zora Neale. *The six fools*
Johnson-Davies, Denys. *Goha, the wise fool*
Souhami, Jessica. *Sausages*

Character traits — fortune *see* Character traits — luck

Character traits — freedom

Grifalconi, Ann. *Ain't nobody a stranger to me*
Levine, Ellen. *Henry's freedom box*
Nadimi, Suzan. *The rich man and the parrot*

Character traits — generosity

Brisson, Pat. *Melissa Parkington's beautiful, beautiful hair*
Chamberlin, Mary. *Mama Panya's pancakes*
Frazee, Marla. *Hush, little baby*
Gibfried, Diane. *Brother Juniper*
Kromhout, Rindert. *Little Donkey and the birthday present*
Pinkney, J. Brian. *Hush, little baby*
Ziefert, Harriet. *Surprise!*

Character traits — helpfulness

Ancona, George. *Mis quehaceres / My chores*
Anderson, Derek. *How the Easter Bunny saved Christmas*
D'Amico, Carmela. *Ella takes the cake*
DiCamillo, Kate. *Great joy*
Grambling, Lois G. *Here comes T. Rex Cottontail*
Grimm, Jacob. *The elves and the shoemaker*
Heide, Iris van der. *A strange day*
Himmelman, John. *Chickens to the rescue*
Jenkins, Emily. *Up, up, up!*
Keller, Holly. *Nosy Rosie*
Knudsen, Michelle. *Library lion*
Kroll, Virginia L. *Good citizen Sarah*
    Makayla cares about others
Krosoczka, Jarrett J. *Giddy up, Cowgirl*
Mahoney, Daniel J. *A really good snowman*
Manning, Mick. *Cock-a-doodle hooooooo!*
Manzano, Sonia. *A box full of kittens*
Nolen, Jerdine. *Pitching in for Eubie*
Petrillo, Genevieve. *Keep your ear on the ball*
Ries, Lori. *Fix it, Sam*
Schubert, Leda. *Here comes Darrell*
Scotton, Rob. *Russell's Christmas magic*
Thomas, Shelley Moore. *Take care, Good Knight*
Toten, Teresa. *Bright red kisses*

Character traits — honesty

Abercrombie, Barbara. *The show-and-tell lion*
Kroll, Virginia L. *Honest Ashley*
Rankin, Laura. *Ruthie and the (not so) teeny tiny lie*
Robberecht, Thierry. *Sam tells stories*

Character traits — incentive *see* Character traits — ambition

Character traits — individuality

Dolenz, Micky. *Gakky Two-Feet*
Duke, Shirley Smith. *No bows!*
Harris, Robie H. *I'm all dressed!*
Himmelman, John. *Tudley didn't know*
Horacek, Petr. *Silly Suzy Goose*
Hughes, Susan. *Earth to Audrey*
Hume, Lachie. *Clancy the courageous cow*
Jenkins, Emily. *Daffodil*
    Daffodil, crocodile
McBratney, Sam. *Yes we can!*
Montserrat, Pep. *Ms. Rubinstein's beauty*
Pham, LeUyen. *Big sister, little sister*
Prelutsky, Jack. *Me I am!*
Saltzberg, Barney. *Star of the week*
Sauer, Tammi. *Cowboy camp*
Savadier, Elivia. *Time to get dressed!*
Urbanovic, Jackie. *Duck at the door*

Character traits — kindness

Andreasen, Dan. *The giant of Seville*
Butler, M. Christina. *One winter's day*
Cuyler, Margery. *Kindness is cooler, Mrs. Ruler*
Hasler, Eveline. *A tale of two brothers*
Hennessy, B. G. (Barbara G.). *Because of you*
Jules, Jacqueline. *No English*
Kroll, Virginia L. *Good neighbor Nicholas*

Rylant, Cynthia. *If you'll be my Valentine*
Wallace, Nancy Elizabeth. *The kindness quilt*

Character traits — kindness to animals

Chichester Clark, Emma. *Piper*
Church, Caroline Jayne. *Digby takes charge*
Federspiel, Jurg. *Alligator Mike*
Mora, Pat. *The song of Francis and the animals*
Pericoli, Matteo. *The true story of Stellina*
Soule, Jean Conder. *Never tease a weasel*

Character traits — laziness

Egan, Tim. *The pink refrigerator*
Hogg, Gary. *Look what the cat dragged in!*
Johnson, D. B. (Donald B.). *Four legs bad, two legs good!*
The little red hen. *The little red hen*
    The little red hen: an old fable
McGrath, Barbara Barbieri. *The little green witch*
Murphy, Jim. *Fergus and the Night-Demon*
Paul, Ann Whitford. *Mañana Iguana*
Stampler, Ann Redisch. *Shlemazel and the remarkable spoon of Pohost*

Character traits — luck

Addy, Sharon Hart. *Lucky Jake*
Bateman, Teresa. *Fiona's luck*
Christian, Mary Blount. *If not for the calico cat*
Friday, Mary Ellen. *It's a bad day*
Sasso, Sandy Eisenberg. *Butterflies under our hats*
Seki, Sunny. *The tale of the lucky cat*
Stampler, Ann Redisch. *Shlemazel and the remarkable spoon of Pohost*
Sutton, Jane. *The trouble with cauliflower*

Character traits — meanness

Hasler, Eveline. *A tale of two brothers*

Character traits — orderliness

Blankenship, Lee Ann. *Mr. Tuggle's troubles*
Harris, Robie H. *I love messes!*
Simon, Charnan. *Messy Molly*

Character traits — ostracism *see* Character traits — being different

Character traits — patience

Horowitz, Dave. *Soon, Baboon, soon*
Train, Mary. *Time for the fair*

Character traits — perfectionism

Fearnley, Jan. *The search for the perfect child*

Character traits — perseverance

Barber, Tiki. *Teammates*
Best, Cari. *Sally Jean, the Bicycle Queen*
Braver, Vanita. *Madison and the two wheeler*
Garland, Michael. *Hooray José!*
Hodge, Deborah. *Lily and the mixed-up letters*
Hubbard, Crystal. *Catching the moon*
Isadora, Rachel. *Luke goes to bat*
Kessler, Cristina. *The best beekeeper of Lalibela*
Kinerk, Robert. *Clorinda takes flight*
    Timothy Cox will not change his socks
Kurtz, Jane. *In the small, small night*
Piper, Watty. *The little engine that could*
Wild, Margaret. *Bobbie Dazzler*
Ziefert, Harriet. *Murphy jumps a hurdle*

Character traits — persistence

Jordan, Deloris. *Michael's golden rules*
Keller, Holly. *Pearl's new skates*

Murphy, Stuart J. *Same old horse*
O'Connor, Jane. *Ready, set, skip!*
Penner, Fred. *The cat came back*
Rodriguez, Alex. *Out of the ballpark*

Character traits — pride

Hillenbrand, Jane. *What a treasure!*
Johnson, Rebecca. *The proud pelican's secret*
Quattlebaum, Mary. *Sparks fly high*

Character traits — questioning

Carter, David A. *Whoo? Whoo?*
Coyle, Carmela LaVigna. *Do princesses really kiss frogs?*
Crumpacker, Bunny. *Alexander's pretending day*
Erlbruch, Wolf. *The big question*
Hornsey, Chris. *Why do I have to eat off the floor?*
Kuskin, Karla. *Green as a bean*
Menchin, Scott. *Taking a bath with the dog and other things that make me happy*
Phillips, Christopher. *Ceci Ann's day of why*
Raab, Brigitte. *Where does pepper come from?*
Walsh, Melanie. *Do lions live on lily pads?*
Wheeler, Valerie. *Yes, please! No, thank you!*

Character traits — resourcefulness

McAllister, Angela. *Trust me, Mom!*

Character traits — responsibility

Kroll, Virginia L. *Cristina keeps a promise*
    Jason takes responsibility

Character traits — selfishness

Davidson, Ellen Dee. *Princess Justina Albertina*
Meserve, Adria. *No room for Napoleon*
Stein, Mathilde. *Mine!*

Character traits — shyness

Bunge, Daniela. *Cherry time*
Choldenko, Gennifer. *Louder, Lili*
D'Amico, Carmela. *Ella sets the stage*
Graham, Bob. *Dimity Dumpty*
Haseley, Dennis. *The invisible moose*
Kirk, David. *Library mouse*
Lin, Grace. *Lissy's friends*
Morgan, Michaela. *Dear bunny*
Paraskevas, Betty. *Chocolate at the Four Seasons*
Pearson, Susan. *Slugs in love*

Character traits — smallness

Alborough, Jez. *Tall*
Andersen, H. C. (Hans Christian). *Thumbelina*
Carlson, Nancy L. *Think big!*
Clark, Katie. *Seagull Sam*
Emmett, Jonathan. *Ruby in her own time*
    This way, Ruby!
LaMarche, Jim. *Up*
McGrory, Anik. *Kidogo*
Masurel, Claire. *Domino*
Meserve, Jessica. *Small sister*
Nolen, Jerdine. *Hewitt Anderson's great big life*
O'Leary, Sara. *When you were small*
Palatini, Margie. *Shelly*

Character traits — stubbornness

Chaconas, Dori. *Dori the contrary hen*
Tyler, Anne. *Timothy Tugbottom says no!*

Character traits — willfulness

Carlson, Nancy L. *Loudmouth George earns his allowance*

Davidson, Ellen Dee. *Princess Justina Albertina*

Cheating *see* Behavior — cheating

Chefs *see* Careers — chefs, cooks

Cherokee Indians *see* Indians of North America — Cherokee

Cherubs *see* Angels

Chickens *see* Birds — chickens

Child abuse

Riggs, Shannon. *Not in Room 204*

Chile *see* Foreign lands — Chile

Chimpanzees *see* Animals — chimpanzees

China *see* Foreign lands — China

Chinese Americans *see* Ethnic groups in the U.S. — Chinese Americans

Chinese New Year *see* Holidays — Chinese New Year

Choctaw Indians *see* Indians of North America — Choctaw

Christmas *see* Holidays — Christmas

Cinco de Mayo *see* Holidays — Cinco de Mayo

Circular tales

Numeroff, Laura Joffe. *If you give a pig a party*

Circus

Alsenas, Linas. *Peanut*
Andreasen, Dan. *The giant of Seville*
Downs, Mike. *You see a circus, I see—*
Graham, Bob. *Dimity Dumpty*
Littlesugar, Amy. *Clown child*
Lobel, Anita. *Animal antics*
Montserrat, Pep. *Ms. Rubinstein's beauty*
Munro, Roxie. *Circus*
Weis, Carol. *When the cows got loose*
Ziefert, Harriet. *Circus parade*

Cities, towns

Cole, Henry. *On Meadowview Street*
Curlee, Lynn. *Skyscraper*
Dugan, Joanne. *ABC NYC*
Joel, Billy. *New York state of mind*
Melmed, Laura Krauss. *New York, New York!*
Neubecker, Robert. *Wow! City!*
Pearson, Debora. *Big city song*
Raschka, Chris. *New York is English, Chattanooga is Creek*
Singer, Marilyn. *City lullaby*
Smith, Marie. *N is for our nation's capital*
Spinelli, Eileen. *City angel*
Tauss, Marc. *Superhero*
Watts, Leslie Elizabeth. *The Baabaasheep Quartet*

Cleanliness *see* Character traits — cleanliness

Cleverness *see* Character traits — cleverness

Clocks, watches

Baker, Keith. *Hickory dickory dock*
Fraser, Mary Ann. *I.Q., it's time*
Murphy, Stuart J. *It's about time!*
Pilegard, Virginia Walton. *The warlord's alarm*

Clothing

Bae, Hyun-Joo. *New clothes for New Year's day*
Beaton, Clare. *Daisy gets dressed*
Blankenship, Lee Ann. *Mr. Tuggle's troubles*
Dodds, Dayle Ann. *Hello, sun!*
Ehrlich, Fred. *Does a chimp wear clothes?*
Harris, Robie H. *I'm all dressed!*
Lester, Helen. *The sheep in wolf's clothing*
Lunge-Larsen, Lise. *Noah's mittens*
MacDonald, Margaret Read. *Little Rooster's diamond button*
McElligott, Matthew. *Backbeard and the birthday suit*
Makhijani, Pooja. *Mama's saris*
Moss, Miriam. *Bare bear*
Müller, Birte. *I can dress myself!*
O'Connor, Jane. *Fancy Nancy*
Rao, Sandhya. *My mother's sari*
Savadier, Elivia. *Time to get dressed!*
Sheth, Kashmira. *My Dadima wears a sari*
Tafolla, Carmen. *What can you do with a rebozo?*

Clothing — coats

David, Ryan. *The magic raincoat*

Clothing — costumes

Bollinger, Peter. *Algernon Graeves is scary enough*
Chess, Victoria. *The costume party*
Ernst, Lisa Campbell. *Sylvia Jean, drama queen*
Kovalski, Maryann. *Omar's Halloween*
McDonald, Megan. *Ant and Honey Bee, what a pair!*
McGuirk, Leslie. *Tucker's spooky Halloween*
Neitzel, Shirley. *Who will I be?*

Clothing — dresses

Jenkins, Emily. *Daffodil*
Schaefer, Carole Lexa. *The Bora-Bora dress*

Clothing — gloves, mittens

Plourde, Lynn. *A mountain of mittens*
Quattlebaum, Mary. *Winter friends*

Clothing — hats

Chaconas, Dori. *Virginnie's hat*
Lamb, Albert. *Sam's winter hat*
Lear, Edward. *The Quangle Wangle's hat*
Rumford, James. *Don't touch my hat!*
Slingsby, Janet. *Hetty's 100 hats*
Ziefert, Harriet. *Grandma, it's for you!*

Clothing — neckties

Cocca-Leffler, Maryann. *Mr. Tanen's ties rule!*

Clothing — pajamas

Hayles, Marsha. *Pajamas anytime*
Plourde, Lynn. *Pajama day*

Clothing — scarves

Bunge, Daniela. *The scarves*

Clothing — shoes

Bateman, Teresa. *Keeper of soles*
Boelts, Maribeth. *Those shoes*
Daly, Niki. *Happy birthday, Jamela!*
Dunbar, Joyce. *Shoe baby*
Meunier, Brian. *Bravo, Tavo!*
Novak, Matt. *Flip flop bop*
Slater, Dashka. *Baby shoes*
Thermes, Jennifer. *Sam Bennett's new shoes*
Young, Amy. *Belinda in Paris*

Clothing — socks

Dunbar, Joyce. *Where's my sock?*
Evans, Cambria. *Martha moth makes socks*
Kinerk, Robert. *Timothy Cox will not change his socks*
Shea, Bob. *New socks*
Valckx, Catharina. *Lizette's green sock*

Clothing — sweaters

Larsen, Andrew. *Bella and the bunny*
Olsen, Sylvia. *Yetsa's sweater*
Waterton, Betty. *A bumblebee sweater*

Clouds *see* Weather — clouds

Clowns, jesters

Baynton, Martin. *Jane and the dragon*
Littlesugar, Amy. *Clown child*

Clubs, gangs

San Souci, Daniel. *The Mighty Pigeon Club*
Shannon, George. *The Secret Chicken Club*
Singer, Marilyn. *Let's build a clubhouse*

Clumsiness *see* Character traits — clumsiness

Coats *see* Clothing — coats

Cockroaches *see* Insects — cockroaches

Cold *see* Concepts — cold & heat; Weather — cold

Cold (disease) *see* Illness — cold (disease)

Collecting things *see* Behavior — collecting things

Color *see* Concepts — color

Communication

Ehrlich, Fred. *Does a seal smile?*

Communities, neighborhoods

Cooper, Elisha. *A good night walk*
Cupiano, Ina. *Quinito's neighborhood / El vecindario de Quinito*
Forman, Ruth. *Young Cornrows callin out the moon*
Harshman, Marc. *Only one neighborhood*
Isadora, Rachel. *Yo, Jo!*
Johnson, D. B. (Donald B.). *Eddie's kingdom*
Rockwell, Anne F. *Backyard bear*
Schubert, Leda. *Here comes Darrell*
Stevens, April. *Waking up Wendell*
Wong, Janet S. *The dumpster diver*

Competition *see* Sibling rivalry; Sports; Sportsmanship

Computers

Collins, Suzanne. *When Charlie McButton lost power*

Concepts

Dunn, Todd. *We go together*
Goldstone, Bruce. *Great estimations*

Hays, Anna Jane. *Ready, set, preschool!*
McCarthy, Mary. *A closer look*

Concepts — change

Seeger, Laura Vaccaro. *First the egg*

Concepts — cold & heat

Floyd, Madeleine. *Cold paws, warm heart*

Concepts — color

Catalanotto, Peter. *Kitten red, yellow, blue*
Ericsson, Jennifer A. *A piece of chalk*
Feiffer, Kate. *Double pink*
Ficocelli, Elizabeth. *Kid tea*
Fontes, Justine Korman. *Black meets White*
Freymann, Saxton. *Food for thought*
Gorbachev, Valeri. *Red red red*
Gravett, Emily. *Orange Pear Apple Bear*
Gregory, Nan. *Pink*
Hicks, Barbara Jean. *I like black and white*
Horacek, Petr. *Butterfly butterfly*
Jenkins, Steve. *Living color*
Kann, Victoria. *Pinkalicious*
Larios, Julie Hofstrand. *Yellow elephant*
Mockford, Caroline. *Cleo's color book*
Neubecker, Robert. *Courage of the blue boy*
Park, Linda Sue. *What does Bunny see?*
Seeger, Laura Vaccaro. *Lemons are not red*
Shannon, George. *White is for blueberry*
Slater, Dashka. *Baby shoes*
Sweet, Melissa. *Carmine*
Thomas, Valerie. *Winnie the witch*
Weeks, Sarah. *Counting Ovejas*
Wood, Audrey. *The deep blue sea*
Yolen, Jane. *How do dinosaurs learn their colors?*

Concepts — counting *see* Counting, numbers

Concepts — measurement

Murphy, Stuart J. *Polly's pen pal*

Concepts — motion

Ehrlich, Fred. *Does a giraffe drive?*
Jenkins, Steve. *Move!*
Lillegard, Dee. *Go!*
Rau, Dana Meachen. *Rolling*
Ziefert, Harriet. *Beach party!*

Concepts — opposites

Child, Lauren. *Charlie and Lola's opposites*
Cousins, Lucy. *Maisy big, Maisy small*
Crowther, Robert. *Opposites*
Freymann, Saxton. *Food for thought*
Guy, Ginger Foglesong. *Perros! Perros! Dogs! Dogs!*
Lewis, J. Patrick. *Big is big and little little*
Seeger, Laura Vaccaro. *Black? White! Day? Night!*

Concepts — patterns

Beaton, Clare. *Daisy gets dressed*
Olson, Nathan. *Animal patterns*

Concepts — perspective

Berry, Matt. *Up on Daddy's shoulders*

Concepts — self *see* Self-concept

Concepts — shape

Blackstone, Stella. *Ship shapes*

Falwell, Cathryn. *Shape capers*
Freymann, Saxton. *Food for thought*
Gravett, Emily. *Orange Pear Apple Bear*
Le Neouanic, Lionel. *Little smudge*
The Metropolitan Museum of Art, NY. *Museum shapes*
Rau, Dana Meachen. *Rectangles*
Reisberg, Joanne A. *Zachary Zormer shape transformer*
Walsh, Ellen Stoll. *Mouse shapes*

Concepts — size

Alborough, Jez. *Tall*
Brownlow, Mike. *Mickey Moonbeam*
Carlson, Nancy L. *Think big!*
Chaconas, Dori. *Cork and Fuzz*
Choldenko, Gennifer. *How to make friends with a giant*
Garland, Michael. *Hooray José!*
Jenkins, Steve. *Prehistoric actual size*
MacDonald, Ross. *Bad baby*
McGrory, Anik. *Kidogo*
Marks, Jennifer L. *Sorting by size*
Meddaugh, Susan. *Just Teenie*
Nolen, Jerdine. *Hewitt Anderson's great big life*
O'Leary, Sara. *When you were small*
Schotter, Roni. *When the Wizzy Foot goes walking*
Sherry, Kevin. *I'm the biggest thing in the ocean*
Ziefert, Harriet. *Bigger than Daddy*

Concepts — up & down

George, Kristine O'Connell. *Up!*
Redding, Sue. *Up above and down below*

Confidence *see* Character traits — confidence

Conservation *see* Ecology

Construction workers *see* Careers — construction workers

Contests

Arnold, Tedd. *The twin princes*
Clayton, Elaine. *A blue ribbon for Sugar*
Cole, Barbara Hancock. *Anna and Natalie*
Dorros, Alex. *Número uno*
Durango, Julia. *Pest fest*
Heide, Iris van der. *A strange day*
Leedy, Loreen. *The great graph contest*
Mahoney, Daniel J. *A really good snowman*
Polacco, Patricia. *Rotten Richie and the ultimate dare*
Quattlebaum, Mary. *Sparks fly high*
Spinelli, Eileen. *Callie Cat, ice skater*
Yamada, Utako. *The story of Cherry the pig*

Cooking *see* Activities — baking, cooking

Cooks *see* Careers — bakers; Careers — chefs, cooks

Cooperation *see* Character traits — cooperation

Costumes *see* Clothing — costumes

Couches, sofas *see* Furniture — couches, sofas

Cougars *see* Animals — cougars

Counting, numbers

Bailey, Linda. *Goodnight, sweet pig*
Barry, Frances. *Duckie's ducklings*
Bateman, Donna M. *Deep in the swamp*
Bates, Ivan. *Five little ducks*
Berkes, Marianne Collins. *Over in the jungle*
Bowen, Anne. *The great math tattle battle*

Brown, Margaret Wise. *Goodnight moon 123*
Bruel, Nick. *Poor puppy*
Butler, John. *Ten in the den*
Cabrera, Jane. *Ten in the bed*
Carlson, Nancy L. *Henry's 100 days of kindergarten*
Carter, David A. *One red dot*
Chae, In Seon. *How do you count a dozen ducklings?*
Child, Lauren. *Charlie and Lola's numbers*
Christelow, Eileen. *Five little monkeys go shopping*
Clements, Andrew. *A million dots*
Cronin, Doreen. *Click, clack, splish, splash*
Delessert, Etienne. *Hungry for numbers*
Denise, Anika. *Pigs love potatoes*
DiTerlizzi, Tony. *G is for one gzonk!*
Donaldson, Julia. *One Ted falls out of bed*
Downing, Johnette. *Down in Louisiana*
Durango, Julia. *Cha-cha chimps*
Elliott, David. *One little chicken*
Fisher, Aileen Lucia. *Know what I saw?*
Fisher, Doris. *My even day*
   One odd day
Fisher, Valorie. *How high can a dinosaur count?*
Fleming, Denise. *The first day of winter*
Franco, Betsy. *Birdsongs*
Freymann, Saxton. *Food for thought*
Fromental, Jean-Luc. *365 penguins*
Garland, Michael. *How many mice?*
Giganti, Paul. *How many blue birds flew away?*
Gillham, Bill. *How many sharks in the bath?*
Ginkel, Anne. *I've got an elephant*
Giogas, Valarie. *In my backyard*
Goldstone, Bruce. *Great estimations*
Harper, Charise Mericle. *Amy and Ivan*
Harris, Trudy. *Jenny found a penny*
   Twenty hungry piggies
Harshman, Marc. *Only one neighborhood*
Haskins, Jim (James). *Count your way through Afghanistan*
   Count your way through Iran
Hays, Anna Jane. *Kindergarten countdown*
Hennessy, B. G. (Barbara G.). *Mr. Ouchy's first day*
Imai, Ayano. *The 108th sheep*
Jay, Alison. *1 2 3*
Katz, Karen. *Ten tiny tickles*
Keller, Laurie. *Grandpa Gazillion's number yard*
Kimmelman, Leslie. *How do I love you?*
Kroll, Virginia L. *Equal shmequal*
   Uno, dos, tres, posada!
Laminack, Lester L. *Jake's 100th day of school*
Law, Diane. *Come out and play*
Leedy, Loreen. *The great graph contest*
Lessac, Frané. *Island Counting 123*
Lewison, Wendy Cheyette. *Two is for twins*
Ljungkvist, Laura. *Follow the line*
MacDonald, Margaret Read. *A hen, a chick, and a string guitar*
MacDonald, Suse. *Fish, swish! Splash, dash!*
McElligott, Matthew. *Bean thirteen*
McFarland, Lyn Rossiter. *Mouse went out to get a snack*
McMullan, Kate. *I'm dirty!*
McNamara, Margaret. *How many seeds in a pumpkin?*
Mother Goose. *Mother Goose numbers on the loose*
Murphy, Stuart J. *Jack the builder*
   Leaping lizards
   Mall mania
   Same old horse
Napoli, Donna Jo. *The wishing club*
Nickle, John. *Alphabet explosion!*
Numeroff, Laura Joffe. *Merry Christmas, Mouse!*
   When sheep sleep
Orozco, Jose-Luis. *Rin, rin, rin / do, re, mi*
Pallotta, Jerry. *Ocean counting*
Parenteau, Shirley. *One frog sang*
Parker, Kim. *Counting in the garden*
Perl, Erica S. *Ninety-three in my family*
Philpot, Lorna. *Find Anthony Ant*
Pierce, Terry. *Counting your way*
Raschka, Chris. *Five for a little one*
Reisberg, Joanne A. *Zachary Zormer shape transformer*

Reiser, Lynn. *Hardworking puppies*
Rose, Deborah Lee. *The twelve days of winter*
Schroeder, Lisa. *Baby can't sleep*
Schulman, Janet. *Ten trick-or-treaters*
Scotton, Rob. *Russell the sheep*
Shahan, Sherry. *Cool cats counting*
Singer, Marilyn. *City lullaby*
Slingsby, Janet. *Hetty's 100 hats*
Smith, Maggie (Margaret C.). *One naked baby*
Stevens, April. *Waking up Wendell*
Tang, Greg. *Math fables*
   Math fables too
Thompson, Lauren. *Little Quack*
   Little Quack's hide and seek
Ward, Jennifer. *Way up in the Arctic*
Weeks, Sarah. *Counting Ovejas*
Wells, Rosemary. *Max counts his chickens*
Weston, Carrie. *If a chicken stayed for supper*
Williams, Suzanne. *Ten naughty little monkeys*
Wong, Janet S. *Hide and seek*
Ziefert, Harriet. *Knick-knack paddywhack*

Countries, foreign *see* Foreign lands

Country

Cecka, Melanie. *Violet goes to the country*
Davies, Jacqueline. *The night is singing*

Courage *see* Character traits — bravery

Cousins *see* Family life — cousins

Cowboys, cowgirls

Bell, Cece. *Sock Monkey rides again*
Danneberg, Julie. *Cowboy Slim*
Elya, Susan Middleton. *Cowboy Jose*
The gingerbread boy. *The Gingerbread Cowboy*
McClements, George. *Ridin' dinos with Buck Bronco*
Sauer, Tammi. *Cowboy camp*
Scieszka, Jon. *Cowboy and Octopus*
Stein, David Ezra. *Cowboy Ned and Andy*
   Ned's new friend

Cows *see* Animals — bulls, cows

Coyotes *see* Animals — coyotes

Crabs *see* Crustaceans — crabs

Crafts *see* Activities — making things

Cranes (birds) *see* Birds — cranes

Creation

Bible. Old Testament. Genesis. *The Genesis of it all*
Wood, Nancy C. *Mr. and Mrs. God in the creation kitchen*

Creatures *see* Monsters; Mythical creatures

Cree Indians *see* Indians of North America — Cree

Crickets *see* Insects — crickets

Crime

Delessert, Etienne. *Alert!*
DiFiori, Lawrence. *Jackie and the Shadow Snatcher*
Grey, Mini. *The adventures of the dish and the spoon*
Grimm, Jacob. *The Bremen town musicians*
   Musicians of Bremen
   Musicians of Bremen / Los musicos de Bremner

Sneed, Brad. *Deputy Harvey and the ant cow caper*
Yee, Wong Herbert. *Detective Small in the amazing banana caper*

Criminals *see* Crime

Crippled *see* Handicaps — physical handicaps

Crocodiles *see* Reptiles — alligators, crocodiles

Crows *see* Birds — crows

Cruelty to animals *see* Character traits — kindness to animals

Crustaceans — crabs

Galloway, Ruth. *Clumsy crab*

Crustaceans — lobsters

Schwarz, Viviane. *Shark and Lobster's amazing undersea adventure*

Crustaceans

Tokuda, Yukihisa. *I'm a pill bug*

Crying *see* Emotions

Cuba *see* Foreign lands — Cuba

Cumulative tales

Bond, Rebecca. *The great doughnut parade*
Chicken Little. *Henny Penny*
Edwards, David. *The pen that Pa built*
Frazee, Marla. *Hush, little baby*
The gingerbread boy. *The Gingerbread Cowboy*
   The gingerbread girl
The gingerbread man. *Can't catch me*
Hatch, Elizabeth. *Halloween night*
Hester, Denia Lewis. *Grandma Lena's big ol' turnip*
The little red hen. *The little red hen*
   The little red hen: an old fable
Long, Kathy. *The runaway shopping cart*
MacDonald, Margaret Read. *A hen, a chick, and a string guitar*
   The squeaky door
   Teeny Weeny Bop
Martin, Bill, Jr. (William Ivan). *Baby bear, baby bear, what do you see?*
The old woman and her pig. *The old woman and her pig*
Pinkney, J. Brian. *Hush, little baby*
Rosenthal, Marc. *Phooey!*
Thompson, Lauren. *The apple pie that Papa baked*
Wood, Audrey. *Silly Sally*
Ziefert, Harriet. *Knick-knack paddywhack*

Curiosity *see* Character traits — curiosity

Currency *see* Money

Custodians *see* Careers — custodians, janitors

Cycles *see* Motorcycles; Sports — bicycling

Dancing *see* Activities — dancing; Ballet

Daniel *see* Religion — Daniel

Dark *see* Night

Darkness — fear *see* Emotions — fear

Daughters *see* Family life — daughters

Day

Charlip, Remy. *A perfect day*
Freedman, Claire. *One magical day*
Jenkins, Emily. *What happens on Wednesdays*
Murphy, Stuart J. *It's about time!*

Day care *see* School — nursery

Days of the week, months of the year

Downing, Johnette. *Today is Monday in Louisiana*
Ficocelli, Elizabeth. *Kid tea*
Gershator, Phillis. *This is the day!*
Harness, Cheryl. *Our colonial year*
Hayles, Marsha. *Pajamas anytime*
Hewitt, Kathryn. *No dogs here!*
Katz, Bobbi. *Once around the sun*
Livingston, Myra Cohn. *Calendar*
Spinelli, Eileen. *Heat wave*
Wang, Xiaohong. *One year in Beijing*

Deafness *see* Handicaps — deafness

Death

Anholt, Laurence. *Seven for a secret*
Bateman, Teresa. *Keeper of soles*
Bley, Anette. *And what comes after a thousand?*
Brisson, Pat. *I remember Miss Perry*
Cochran, Bill. *The forever dog*
Jeffs, Stephanie. *Jenny*
   Josh
Krishnaswami, Uma. *Remembering Grandpa*
Raschka, Chris. *The purple balloon*

Deer *see* Animals — deer

Demons *see* Devil; Monsters

Dentists *see* Careers — dentists

Department stores *see* Shopping; Stores

Desert

Arnosky, Jim. *Coyote raid in Cactus Canyon*
Moss, Miriam. *This is the oasis*
Paul, Ann Whitford. *Fiesta fiasco*
   Mañana Iguana

Detective stories *see* Mystery stories; Problem solving

Detectives *see* Careers — detectives

Devil

Quattlebaum, Mary. *Sparks fly high*

Diggers *see* Careers — construction workers; Machines

Diners *see* Restaurants

Dinosaurs

Andreae, Giles. *Captain Flinn and the pirate dinosaurs*
   Dinosaurs galore!

Bardhan-Quallen, Sudipta. *The Mine-o-saur*
Blackstone, Stella. *I dreamt I was a dinosaur*
Broach, Elise. *When dinosaurs came with everything*
Clarke, Jane. *Dippy's sleepover*
dePaola, Tomie. *Little Grunt and the big egg*
DiPucchio, Kelly S. *Dinosnores*
Edwards, Wallace. *The extinct files*
Fox, Diane. *Tyson the terrible*
Garland, Michael. *Miss Smith reads again!*
Gibbons, Gail. *Dinosaur discoveries*
Grambling, Lois G. *Here comes T. Rex Cottontail*
　　T. Rex trick-or-treats
Hort, Lenny. *Did dinosaurs eat pizza?*
Kudlinski, Kathleen V. *Boy, were we wrong about dinosaurs!*
Lewis, Kevin. *Dinosaur dinosaur*
Lund, Deb. *All aboard the dinotrain*
McClements, George. *Ridin' dinos with Buck Bronco*
Manning, Mick. *Dino-dinners*
O'Malley, Kevin. *Captain Raptor and the moon mystery*
　　Captain Raptor and the space pirates
Plourde, Lynn. *Dino pets*
Sabuda, Robert. *Encyclopedia prehistorica*
Schachner, Judith Byron. *Skippyjon Jones and the big bones*
Sharkey, Niamh. *Santasaurus*
Wallace, Karen. *I am an ankylosaurus*
Wheeler, Lisa. *Dino-hockey*
Whybrow, Ian. *Harry and the dinosaurs at the museum*
　　Harry and the dinosaurs go to school
Willems, Mo. *Edwina, the dinosaur who didn't know she was extinct*
Wilson, Karma. *Dinos in the snow!*
Yolen, Jane. *How do dinosaurs eat their food?*
　　How do dinosaurs go to school?
　　How do dinosaurs learn their colors?
　　How do dinosaurs play with their friends?
Zoehfeld, Kathleen Weidner. *Dinosaur tracks*

Disabilities *see* Handicaps

Diseases *see* Illness

Disguises

Lester, Helen. *The sheep in wolf's clothing*
Oliver, Narelle. *Twilight hunt*
Onishi, Satoru. *Who's hiding*
Schwartz, David M. *Where in the wild*
Weigelt, Udo. *Super Guinea Pig to the rescue*

Dissatisfaction *see* Behavior — dissatisfaction

Divorce

Bunting, Eve (Anne Evelyn). *My mom's wedding*
Clarke, Jane. *The best of both nests*
Coffelt, Nancy. *Fred stays with me!*
Moore-Mallinos, Jennifer. *When my parents forgot how to be friends*

Doctors *see* Careers — doctors

Dogs *see* Animals — dogs

Dolls *see* Toys — dolls

Donkeys *see* Animals — donkeys

Doves *see* Birds — doves

Down & up *see* Concepts — up & down

Dragonflies *see* Insects — dragonflies

Dragons

Baynton, Martin. *Jane and the dragon*
　　Jane and the magician

Beck, Scott. *Happy birthday, Monster!*
Berkeley, Jon. *Chopsticks*
Demi. *The boy who painted dragons*
Ellery, Amanda. *If I had a dragon*
Mayhew, James. *The knight who took all day*
Moore, Lilian. *Beware, take care*
Pendziwol, Jean. *The tale of Sir Dragon*
Robertson, M. P. *The dragon snatcher*
Schaefer, Carole Lexa. *Dragon dancing*
Thomas, Shelley Moore. *Happy birthday, Good Knight*
　　Take care, Good Knight
Yarrow, Peter. *Puff, the magic dragon*
Ziefert, Harriet. *William and the dragon*

Drawing *see* Activities — drawing

Dreams *see also* Nightmares
Blackstone, Stella. *I dreamt I was a dinosaur*
Durango, Julia. *Dream hop*
Gorbachev, Valeri. *When someone is afraid*
Jay, Alison. *1 2 3*
Johnson, Lindan Lee. *The dream jar*
McPhail, David. *Boy on the brink*
Milgrim, David. *Another day in the Milky Way*
Owens, Mary Beth. *Panda whispers*
Sayles, Elizabeth. *The goldfish yawned*
Slater, Dashka. *Firefighters in the dark*

Dresses *see* Clothing — dresses

Driving *see* Activities — driving

Droughts *see* Weather — droughts

Drums *see* Musical instruments — drums

Ducks *see* Birds — ducks

Dwarfs, midgets

Grimm, Jacob. *Snow White*

Dwellings *see* Buildings; Homes, houses

Dying *see* Death

Dyslexia *see* Handicaps — dyslexia

Ears *see* Handicaps — deafness

Earth

Karas, G. Brian. *On Earth*
Martin, Bill, Jr. (William Ivan). *I love our Earth*

East Africa *see* Foreign lands — East Africa

East Indian Americans *see* Ethnic groups in the U.S. —
　　East Indian Americans

Easter *see* Holidays — Easter

Eating *see* Food

Ecology

Appelt, Kathi. *Miss Lady Bird's wildflowers*
Bateman, Donna M. *Deep in the swamp*
Brown, Ruth. *The old tree*
Cole, Henry. *On Meadowview Street*
Corr, Christopher. *Whole world*
DePalma, Mary Newell. *A grand old tree*
Gibbons, Gail. *Coral reefs*
Himmelman, John. *Mouse in a meadow*
Jackson, Ellen B. *Earth Mother*
Kudlinski, Kathleen V. *The seaside switch*
Kurtz, Kevin. *A day in the salt marsh*
Rowe, John A. *Moondog*
St. Pierre, Stephanie. *What the sea saw*
Toft, Kim Michelle. *The world that we want*
Wong, Janet S. *The dumpster diver*

Education *see* School

Eggs

Aston, Dianna Hutts. *An egg is quiet*
Burg, Sarah Emmanuelle. *One more egg*
Fox, Mem. *Hunwick's egg*
Friend, Catherine. *The perfect nest*
Graham, Bob. *Dimity Dumpty*
Grambling, Lois G. *Here comes T. Rex Cottontail*
Kangas, Juli. *The surprise visitor*
Polhemus, Coleman. *The crocodile blues*
Posada, Mia. *Guess what is growing inside this egg*
Robertson, M. P. *The dragon snatcher*
Stoeke, Janet Morgan. *Minerva Louise and the colorful eggs*
Tafuri, Nancy. *Whose chick are you?*

Egypt *see* Foreign lands — Egypt

Elderly *see* Old age

Elections

Cronin, Doreen. *Duck for President*

Elephant seals *see* Animals — seals

Elephants *see* Animals — elephants

Elves *see* Mythical creatures — elves

Embarrassment *see* Emotions — embarrassment

Emotions

Berkner, Laurie. *The story of my feelings*
Dewdney, Anna. *Grumpy Gloria*
DiCamillo, Kate. *Great joy*
Freymann, Saxton. *How are you peeling?*
Klise, Kate. *Why do you cry?*
Konnecke, Ole. *Anthony and the girls*
Krosoczka, Jarrett J. *My buddy, Slug*
Seeger, Laura Vaccaro. *Walter was worried*
Spinelli, Eileen. *When you are happy*
Tankard, Jeremy. *Grumpy Bird*
Willems, Mo. *The Pigeon has feelings, too!*

Emotions — anger

Dewdney, Anna. *Llama Llama mad at mama*
Henkes, Kevin. *Lilly's big day*
Landa, Norbert. *Little Bear and the wishing tree*
Lyon, George Ella. *No dessert forever!*
Moroney, Trace. *When I'm feeling angry*
Shea, Pegi Deitz. *The boy and the spell*

Emotions — embarrassment

Baryshnikov, Mikhail. *Because . . .*

Emotions — envy, jealousy

Dierssen, Andreas. *The old red tractor*
Enderle, Judith Ross. *Smile, Principessa!*
Grimm, Jacob. *Snow White*
Hamilton, Arlene. *Only a cow*
Harper, Anita. *It's not fair!*
Layne, Steven L. *Love the baby*
Lindenbaum, Pija. *Mini Mia and her darling uncle*
Reynolds, Peter H. *The best kid in the world*
Robberecht, Thierry. *Back into Mommy's tummy*
Stein, David Ezra. *Ned's new friend*
Umansky, Kaye. *I don't like Gloria!*

Emotions — fear

Allen, Jonathan. *"I'm not scared!"*
Baker, Roberta. *Olive's first sleepover*
Baum, Louis. *The mouse who braved bedtime*
Bergman, Mara. *Snip snap!*
Bonnett-Rampersaud, Louise. *Bubble and Squeak*
Capucilli, Alyssa Satin. *Katy Duck*
Chaconas, Dori. *Pennies in a jar*
Davis, Katie. *Kindergarten rocks!*
Demi. *The boy who painted dragons*
Ellis, Sarah. *Ben over night*
Fore, S. J. *Tiger can't sleep*
Fox, Diane. *Tyson the terrible*
Funke, Cornelia. *The wildest brother*
Geisert, Arthur. *Lights out*
Gorbachev, Valeri. *When someone is afraid*
Helakoski, Leslie. *Big chickens*
Hicks, Barbara Jean. *Jitterbug jam*
Keller, Holly. *Help!*
    Sophie's window
Kroll, Virginia L. *Makayla cares about others*
Lin, Grace. *Olvina swims*
McAllister, Angela. *Trust me, Mom!*
MacDonald, Margaret Read. *The squeaky door*
McPhail, David. *Water boy*
Mayer, Mercer. *There are monsters everywhere*
Michelson, Richard. *Oh no, not ghosts!*
Moore, Lilian. *Beware, take care*
Moroney, Trace. *When I'm feeling scared*
Murphy, Jim. *Fergus and the Night-Demon*
Paul, Alison. *The crow (a not so scary story)*
Pitzer, Susanna. *Not afraid of dogs*
Riggs, Shannon. *Not in Room 204*
Robberecht, Thierry. *Sam is never scared*
Savadier, Elivia. *No haircut today!*
Schwarz, Viviane. *Shark and Lobster's amazing undersea adventure*
Simon, Charnan. *Big bad Buzz*
Stein, Mathilde. *Brave Ben*
Thach, James Otis. *A child's guide to common household monsters*
Waechter, Phillip. *Rosie and the nightmares*
Watt, Melanie. *Scaredy Squirrel*
    Scaredy Squirrel makes a friend

Emotions — grief

Bley, Anette. *And what comes after a thousand?*
Brisson, Pat. *I remember Miss Perry*
Charles, Veronika Martenova. *The birdman*
Cochran, Bill. *The forever dog*
Jeffs, Stephanie. *Jenny*
    Josh
Krishnaswami, Uma. *Remembering Grandpa*
Raschka, Chris. *The purple balloon*

Emotions — happiness

Cabrera, Jane. *If you're happy and you know it*
Menchin, Scott. *Taking a bath with the dog and other things that make me happy*

Moroney, Trace. *When I'm feeling happy*
Rayner, Catherine. *Augustus and his smile*
Warhola, James. *If you're happy and you know it*
Willis, Jeanne. *Misery Moo*
Wood, Douglas. *The secret of saying thanks*

Emotions — jealousy *see* Emotions — envy, jealousy

Emotions — loneliness

Chichester Clark, Emma. *Melrose and Croc*
Daly, Niki. *Welcome to Zanzibar Road*
Floyd, Madeleine. *Cold paws, warm heart*
Ginkel, Anne. *I've got an elephant*
Grey, Mini. *Ginger bear*
Haas, Irene. *Bess and Bella*
Jeffers, Oliver. *Lost and found*
Jules, Jacqueline. *No English*
Lacombe, Benjamin. *Cherry and Olive*
LaReau, Kara. *Snowbaby could not sleep*
    Ugly fish
Le Neouanic, Lionel. *Little smudge*
McElroy, Lisa Tucker. *Love, Lizzie*
Morison, Toby. *Little Louie takes off*
Rowe, John A. *I want a hug*
Segal, John. *The lonely moose*
Swaim, Jessica. *The hound from the pound*
Taback, Simms. *I miss you every day*
Teevin, Toni. *What to do? What to do?*
Waddell, Martin. *Sleep tight, Little Bear*
Watt, Melanie. *Scaredy Squirrel makes a friend*
Wilson, Karma. *Sweet Briar goes to camp*
Winter, Jeanette. *Angelina's island*

Emotions — love

Anholt, Laurence. *Seven for a secret*
Ashman, Linda. *What could be better than this*
Bang, Molly. *In my heart*
Bedford, David. *The way I love you*
Bunting, Eve (Anne Evelyn). *Baby can*
Clements, Andrew. *Because your daddy loves you*
Conway, David. *The most important gift of all*
Cruise, Robin. *Only you*
Duncan, Alice Faye. *Honey baby sugar child*
Durant, Alan. *I love you, little monkey*
Emmett, Jonathan. *I love you always and forever*
George, Lindsay Barrett. *The secret*
Hample, Stoo. *I will kiss you (lots & lots & lots!)*
Jacobs, Julie. *My heart is a magic house*
Jenkins, Emily. *Love you when you whine*
Joosse, Barbara M. *Papa do you love me?*
Katz, Karen. *Daddy hugs 1 2 3*
Kimmelman, Leslie. *How do I love you?*
Kindermans, Martine. *You and me*
Kuklin, Susan. *Families*
Lawler, Janet. *A father's song*
McAllister, Angela. *Mama and Little Joe*
MacDonald, Margaret Read. *The great smelly, slobbery small-toothed dog*
Milord, Susan. *Love that baby*
Morgan, Michaela. *Dear bunny*
Newman, Leslea. *Daddy's song*
Otsuka, Yuzo. *Suho's white horse*
Pearson, Susan. *Slugs in love*
Pennypacker, Sara. *Pierre in love*
Ritchie, Alison. *Me and my dad!*
Rossetti-Shustak, Bernadette. *I love you through and through*
Ryder, Joanne. *Bear of my heart*
Rylant, Cynthia. *If you'll be my Valentine*
Shapiro, Jody Fickes. *Family lullaby*
Taback, Simms. *I miss you every day*
Thomas, Eliza. *The red blanket*
Tinkham, Kelly A. *Hair for Mama*
Trotter, Deborah W. *How do you know?*
van Lieshout, Elle. *The wish*
Vischer, Phil. *Sidney and Norman*

Wells, Rosemary. *Carry me!*
Wild, Margaret. *Piglet and Mama*
    Piglet and Papa
Williams, Sam. *That's love*
Xinran, Xue. *Motherbridge of love*
Young, Ed. *My Mei Mei*
Zuckerman, Linda. *I will hold you 'til you sleep*

Emotions — sadness

Medina, Sarah. *Sad*
Moroney, Trace. *When I'm feeling sad*
Willems, Mo. *My friend is sad*
Willis, Jeanne. *Misery Moo*

Emotions — unhappiness *see* Emotions — happiness;
    Emotions — sadness

Emperors *see* Royalty — emperors

Endangered animals *see* Animals — endangered animals

Engineered books *see* Format, unusual — toy & movable
    books

England *see* Foreign lands — England

Environment *see* Ecology

Envy *see* Emotions — envy, jealousy

Eskimos *see also* Indians of North America — Inuit

Ethiopia *see* Foreign lands — Ethiopia

Ethnic groups in the U.S. — African Americans

Adler, David A. *Campy*
    Joe Louis
    Satchel Paige
Asim, Jabari. *Daddy goes to work*
Baicker, Karen. *You can do it too!*
Barber, Tiki. *Game day*
    Teammates
Barbour, Karen. *Mr. Williams*
Birtha, Becky. *Grandmama's pride*
Boelts, Maribeth. *Those shoes*
Brooks, Gwendolyn. *Bronzeville boys and girls*
Burleigh, Robert. *Stealing home*
Clinton, Catherine. *When Harriet met Sojourner*
Dawes, Kwame Senu Neville. *I saw your face*
Deans, Karen. *Playing to win*
Duncan, Alice Faye. *Honey baby sugar child*
Edwards, Pamela Duncan. *The bus ride that changed history*
Ehrhardt, Karen. *This jazz man*
English, Karen. *The baby on the way*
Forman, Ruth. *Young Cornrows callin out the moon*
Giovanni, Nikki. *Rosa*
Grifalconi, Ann. *Ain't nobody a stranger to me*
Grimes, Nikki. *Danitra Brown, class clown*
    Welcome, Precious
    When Gorilla goes walking
Harrington, Janice N. *The chicken-chasing queen of Lamar County*
Haskins, Jim (James). *Delivering justice*
Hester, Denia Lewis. *Grandma Lena's big ol' turnip*
Hubbard, Crystal. *Catching the moon*
Hurston, Zora Neale. *The six fools*
Isadora, Rachel. *Luke goes to bat*
    Yo, Jo!
Johnson, Angela. *Lily Brown's paintings*
    Wind flyers
Johnson, James Weldon. *Lift every voice and sing*
Jordan, Deloris. *Michael's golden rules*
Latifah, Queen. *Queen of the scene*
Lee, Spike. *Please, puppy, please*

Levine, Ellen. *Henry's freedom box*
Lorbiecki, Marybeth. *Jackie's bat*
Lyons, Kelly Starling. *One million men and me*
McKissack, Patricia C. *Precious and the Boo Hag*
McQuinn, Anna. *Lola at the library*
Michelson, Richard. *Across the alley*
Nolen, Jerdine. *Pitching in for Eubie*
Perry, Elizabeth. *Think cool thoughts*
Phillips, Christopher. *Ceci Ann's day of why*
Piernas-Davenport, Gail. *Shanté Keys and the New Year's peas*
Pinkney, Sandra L. *Read and rise*
Rappaport, Doreen. *The school is not white!*
Raven, Margot Theis. *Night boat to freedom*
Richards, Beah E. *Keep climbing, girls*
Robbins, Jacqui. *The new girl . . . and me*
Rodman, Mary Ann. *My best friend*
Sanders, Nancy. *D is for drinking gourd*
Seskin, Steve. *A chance to shine*
Shore, Diane Z. *This is the dream*
Smalls, Irene. *My Nana and me*
  My Pop Pop and me
Tauss, Marc. *Superhero*
This little light of mine
Tinkham, Kelly A. *Hair for Mama*
Trice, Linda. *Kenya's word*
Trollinger, Patsi B. *Perfect timing*
Turner, Glennette Tilley. *An apple for Harriet Tubman*
Uhlberg, Myron. *Dad, Jackie, and me*
Weatherford, Carole Boston. *Champions on the bench*
  Freedom on the menu
  Moses
Winter, Jonah. *Dizzy*
Winthrop, Elizabeth. *Squashed in the middle*
Woodson, Jacqueline. *Show way*
Ziefert, Harriet. *Bigger than Daddy*
Zolotow, Charlotte (Shapiro). *A father like that*

Ethnic groups in the U.S. — Arab Americans

Bunting, Eve (Anne Evelyn). *One green apple*

Ethnic groups in the U.S. — Asian Americans

Carlson, Nancy L. *My family is forever*
Yee, Wong Herbert. *Who likes rain?*
Yoo, Paula. *Sixteen years in sixteen seconds*

Ethnic groups in the U.S. — Chinese Americans

Lee, Milly. *Landed*
Lewis, Rose A. *Every year on your birthday*
Look, Lenore. *Uncle Peter's amazing Chinese wedding*
McMahon, Patricia. *Just add one Chinese sister*
Mochizuki, Ken. *Be water, my friend*
Thomas, Eliza. *The red blanket*
Thong, Roseanne. *Gai see*
Yin. *Brothers*
Young, Ed. *My Mei Mei*

Ethnic groups in the U.S. — East Indian Americans

Krishnaswami, Uma. *Bringing Asha home*
  The happiest tree
Makhijani, Pooja. *Mama's saris*
Rao, Sandhya. *My mother's sari*
Sheth, Kashmira. *My Dadima wears a sari*

Ethnic groups in the U.S. — Hispanic Americans

Ancona, George. *Mi música / My music*
  Mis abuelos / My grandparents
  Mis comidas / My foods
  Mis fiestas / My celebrations
  Mis juegos / My games
  Mis quehaceres / My chores
Chapra, Mimi. *Sparky's bark / El ladrido de Sparky*
Cupiano, Ina. *Quinito's neighborhood / El vecindario de Quinito*

Griessman, Annette. *The fire*
Kroll, Virginia L. *Uno, dos, tres, posada!*
Pinkney, Sandra L. *I am Latino*

Ethnic groups in the U.S. — Jamaican Americans

Winter, Jeanette. *Angelina's island*

Ethnic groups in the U.S. — Japanese Americans

Barasch, Lynne. *Hiromi's hands*
Lee-Tai, Amy. *A place where sunflowers grow / Sabaku ni saita himawari*

Ethnic groups in the U.S. — Jewish Americans

McDonough, Yona Zeldis. *Hammerin' Hank*

Ethnic groups in the U.S. — Korean Americans

Choi, Yangsook. *Behind the mask*
Park, Frances. *The Have a Good Day Cafe*
Patz, Nancy. *Babies can't eat kimchee!*
Recorvits, Helen. *Yoon and the Christmas mitten*
Williams, Laura E. *The best winds*

Ethnic groups in the U.S. — Mexican Americans

Cruise, Robin. *Little Mama forgets*
da Costa, Deborah. *Hanukkah moon*
Soto, Gary. *Chato goes cruisin'*
  My little car / Mi carrito
Tafolla, Carmen. *What can you do with a rebozo?*

Ethnic groups in the U.S. — Puerto Rican Americans

Manzano, Sonia. *A box full of kittens*

Ethnic groups in the U.S. — Racially mixed

Graham, Bob. *Oscar's half birthday*
Stowell, Penelope. *The greatest potatoes*

Etiquette

Best, Cari. *Are you going to be good?*
Dutton, Sandra. *Dear Miss Perfect*
Goldberg, Whoopi. *Whoopi's big book of manners*
Greenberg, David (David T.). *Don't forget your etiquette!*
Hamilton, Martha. *The hidden feast*
Joosse, Barbara M. *Please is a good word to say*
Katz, Alan. *Don't say that word!*
Keller, Laurie. *Do unto otters*
Melling, David. *The Scallywags*
Morris, Jennifer E. *May I please have a cookie?*
Post, Peggy. *Emily's everyday manners*
Rosenthal, Amy Krouse. *Cookies*
Sierra, Judy. *Mind your manners, B. B. Wolf*
Wheeler, Valerie. *Yes, please! No, thank you!*
Willems, Mo. *Time to say "please"!*
Yolen, Jane. *How do dinosaurs eat their food?*

Exercise *see* Health & fitness — exercise

Explorers *see* Careers — explorers

Extraterrestrial beings *see* Aliens

Eye glasses *see* Glasses

Eyes *see* Handicaps — blindness; Senses — sight

Fables *see* Folk & fairy tales

Faces *see* Anatomy — faces

Fairies

Bar-el, Dan. *Such a prince*
Bowen, Anne. *Tooth Fairy's first night*
Garland, Michael. *King Puck*
Oddino, Licia. *Finn and the fairies*
Rose, Marion. *The Christmas tree fairy*
Ward, Helen. *Little Moon Dog*

Fairs, festivals

Colato Laínez, René. *Playing lotería / El juego de la lotería*
Hamilton, Arlene. *Only a cow*
Reynolds, Jan. *Celebrate!*
Train, Mary. *Time for the fair*

Fairy tales *see* Folk & fairy tales

Falcons *see* Birds — falcons

Fall *see* Seasons — fall

Family life

Alcott, Louisa May. *An old-fashioned Thanksgiving*
Ashman, Linda. *To the beach!*
Bang, Molly. *In my heart*
Birtha, Becky. *Grandmama's pride*
Brown, Jeff. *Flat Stanley*
Carlson, Nancy L. *My family is forever*
Charlip, Remy. *A perfect day*
Clements, Andrew. *Slippers loves to run*
Coffelt, Nancy. *Fred stays with me!*
Coste, Marion. *Finding Joy*
Cruise, Robin. *Only you*
da Costa, Deborah. *Hanukkah moon*
Downs, Mike. *You see a circus, I see—*
Elvgren, Jennifer Riesmeyer. *Josias, hold the book*
Elya, Susan Middleton. *N is for Navidad*
Eschbacher, Roger. *Road trip*
Foreman, George. *Let George do it!*
Friedrich, Molly. *You're not my real mother!*
Graham, Bob. *Oscar's half birthday*
Gregory, Nan. *Pink*
Griessman, Annette. *The fire*
Guy, Ginger Foglesong. *My grandma / Mi abuelita*
Hazen, Barbara Shook. *Who is your favorite monster, mama?*
Helmer, Marilyn. *One splendid tree*
Isadora, Rachel. *What a family!*
Jenkins, Emily. *What happens on Wednesdays*
Joyce, William. *A day with Wilbur Robinson*
Kimmelman, Leslie. *How do I love you?*
Kinkade, Sheila. *My family*
Kirwan, Wednesday. *Nobody notices Minerva*
Kosofsky, Chaim. *Much, much better*
Krishnaswami, Uma. *Bringing Asha home*
Lears, Laurie. *Megan's birthday tree*
Lobel, Gillian. *Too small for honey cake*
Lyon, George Ella. *No dessert forever!*
Markle, Sandra. *A mother's journey*
Martín, Hugo C. *Pablo's Christmas*
Mauner, Claudia. *Zoe Sophia in New York*

Messinger, Carla. *When the shadbush blooms*
Modesitt, Jeanne. *Little Mouse's happy birthday*
Moore-Mallinos, Jennifer. *When my parents forgot how to be friends*
Nolen, Jerdine. *Hewitt Anderson's great big life*
   Pitching in for Eubie
O'Connor, Jane. *Fancy Nancy*
   Fancy Nancy and the posh puppy
   The snow globe family
Ohi, Ruth. *And you can come too*
O'Keefe, Susan Heyboer. *Baby day*
Orona-Ramirez, Kristy. *Kiki's journey*
Parr, Todd. *We belong together*
Paterson, Diane. *Hurricane wolf*
Pelley, Kathleen T. *Inventor McGregor*
Perkins, Lynne Rae. *Pictures from our vacation*
Perl, Erica S. *Ninety-three in my family*
Piernas-Davenport, Gail. *Shanté Keys and the New Year's peas*
Reynolds, Peter H. *My very big little world*
Riggs, Shannon. *Not in Room 204*
Rosen, Michael J. (1954[EN]). *A drive in the country*
Santiago, Esmeralda. *A doll for Navidades*
Schaefer, Lola M. *Frankie Stein*
Shapiro, Jody Fickes. *Family lullaby*
Spinelli, Eileen. *When you are happy*
Sugarman, Brynn Olenberg. *Rebecca's journey home*
Thermes, Jennifer. *Sam Bennett's new shoes*
Van Leeuwen, Jean. *Papa and the pioneer quilt*
Van Steenwyk, Elizabeth. *Prairie Christmas*
Wells, Rosemary. *Carry me!*
Winthrop, Elizabeth. *Squashed in the middle*
Woodruff, Elvira. *Small beauties*
Ziefert, Harriet. *Families have together*
Zolotow, Charlotte (Shapiro). *If it weren't for you*
Zuckerman, Linda. *I will hold you 'til you sleep*
Zweibel, Alan. *Our tree named Steve*

Family life — aunts, uncles

Baker, Roberta. *Olive's pirate party*
Beake, Lesley. *Home now*
Bevis, Mary. *Wolf song*
Jordan, Deloris. *Michael's golden rules*
Lindenbaum, Pija. *Mini Mia and her darling uncle*
Look, Lenore. *Uncle Peter's amazing Chinese wedding*
Major, Kevin. *Aunt Olga's Christmas postcards*
Perry, Elizabeth. *Think cool thoughts*
Whitehead, Kathy. *Looking for Uncle Louie on the Fourth of July*

Family life — brothers *see* Family life; Family life — brothers & sisters; Sibling rivalry

Family life — brothers & sisters

Archer, Peggy. *Turkey surprise*
Baicker, Karen. *You can do it too!*
Barber, Tiki. *Game day*
   Teammates
Bergman, Mara. *Snip snap!*
Bonnett-Rampersaud, Louise. *Bubble and Squeak*
Broach, Elise. *What the no-good baby is good for*
Browne, Anthony. *My brother*
Capucilli, Alyssa Satin. *Katy Duck, big sister*
Chaconas, Dori. *Dancing with Katya*
Cheng, Andrea. *The lemon sisters*
Chessa, Francesca. *The mysterious package*
Child, Lauren. *But, excuse me, that is my book*
   Charlie and Lola's I will never not ever eat a tomato
   Charlie and Lola's numbers
   Charlie and Lola's opposites
   Say cheese!
   Snow is my favorite and my best
Clark, Katie. *Seagull Sam*
Collins, Suzanne. *When Charlie McButton lost power*
Cuyler, Margery. *The bumpy little pumpkin*
Downey, Lynn. *The tattletale*
Duke, Kate. *The tale of Pip and Squeak*
Ellery, Amanda. *If I had a dragon*

Elliott, Laura Malone. *Hunter's big sister*
Elya, Susan Middleton. *Sophie's trophy*
Freedman, Deborah. *Scribble*
Funke, Cornelia. *The wildest brother*
Gay, Marie-Louise. *What are you doing, Sam?*
Graham, Bob. *Dimity Dumpty*
Grindley, Sally. *It's my school*
Gutierrez, Akemi. *The mummy and other adventures of Sam and Alice*
Guy, Ginger Foglesong. *Siesta*
Harper, Anita. *It's not fair!*
Harper, Jamie. *Me too!*
Hasler, Eveline. *A tale of two brothers*
Isadora, Rachel. *Yo, Jo!*
Jeffs, Stephanie. *Jenny*
Jenkins, Emily. *Daffodil*
　　Daffodil, crocodile
Johnson, Lindan Lee. *The dream jar*
Knudsen, Michelle. *A moldy mystery*
Koch, Ed. *Eddie's little sister makes a splash*
Kortepeter, Paul. *Oliver's red toboggan*
Kurtz, Jane. *In the small, small night*
LaMarche, Jim. *Up*
Landa, Norbert. *Little Bear and the wishing tree*
Lloyd-Jones, Sally. *How to be a baby — by me, the big sister*
McClintock, Barbara. *Adele and Simon*
McDonald, Rae A. *A fishing surprise*
MacDonald, Ross. *Bad baby*
McKissack, Patricia C. *The all-I'll-ever-want Christmas doll*
McKy, Katie. *Pumpkin town!*
Mahoney, Daniel J. *A really good snowman*
Meade, Holly. *Inside, inside, inside*
Meng, Cece. *The wonderful thing about hiccups*
Meserve, Jessica. *Small sister*
Michelson, Richard. *Oh no, not ghosts!*
Morrissey, Dean. *The crimson comet*
Muth, Jon J. *Zen shorts*
Napoli, Donna Jo. *The wishing club*
Newman, Marjorie. *Just like me*
Ohi, Ruth. *The couch was a castle*
　　Me and my brother
　　Me and my sister
　　A trip with Grandma
Patz, Nancy. *Babies can't eat kimchee!*
Pham, LeUyen. *Big sister, little sister*
Polacco, Patricia. *Rotten Richie and the ultimate dare*
Reynolds, Peter H. *The best kid in the world*
　　Ish
Ries, Lori. *Fix it, Sam*
Robertson, M. P. *Hieronymous Betts and his unusual pets*
Rockwell, Anne F. *Brendan and Belinda and the slam dunk!*
Rubel, Nicole. *Ham and Pickles*
Samuels, Barbara. *Dolores meets her match*
　　Happy Valentine's Day, Dolores
Schneider, Josh. *You'll be sorry*
Sheldon, Annette. *Big sister now*
Stoeke, Janet Morgan. *Waiting for May*
Sullivan, Sarah. *Dear Baby*
Voake, Charlotte. *Hello twins*
Ward, Nick. *Don't eat the babysitter!*
Whybrow, Ian. *Badness for beginners*
Wishinsky, Frieda. *Please, Louise!*
Wynne-Jones, Tim. *The boat in the tree*
Yin. *Brothers*
Yolen, Jane. *Soft house*
Young, Ed. *My Mei Mei*
Zemach, Margot. *Eating up Gladys*
Zimmerman, Andrea Griffing. *Fire engine man*

Family life — cousins

Buehner, Caralyn. *Would I ever lie to you?*
deGroat, Diane. *Last one in is a rotten egg!*
Holt, Kimberly Willis. *Waiting for Gregory*

Family life — daughters

Gray, Kes. *006 and a half*

Krosoczka, Jarrett J. *Giddy up, Cowgirl*
Makhijani, Pooja. *Mama's saris*
Rao, Sandhya. *My mother's sari*

Family life — fathers

Asim, Jabari. *Daddy goes to work*
Bee, William. *Whatever*
Berry, Matt. *Up on Daddy's shoulders*
Bildner, Phil. *The greatest game ever played*
Bluemle, Elizabeth. *My father the dog*
Briant, Ed. *A day at the beach*
Bunting, Eve (Anne Evelyn). *My red balloon*
Clements, Andrew. *Because your daddy loves you*
Coyle, Carmela LaVigna. *Do princesses really kiss frogs?*
Demers, Dominique. *Every single night*
Ehrlich, Fred. *Does a duck have a daddy?*
Ernst, Lisa Campbell. *This is the van that Dad cleaned*
Farmer, Nancy. *Clever Ali*
George, Kristine O'Connell. *Up!*
Hunter, Jana Novotny. *When Daddy's truck picks me up*
Ichikawa, Satomi. *My father's shop*
Joosse, Barbara M. *Papa do you love me?*
Kanevsky, Polly. *Sleepy boy*
Katz, Karen. *Daddy hugs 1 2 3*
Keillor, Garrison. *Daddy's girl*
Lawler, Janet. *A father's song*
Leuck, Laura. *I love my pirate papa*
London, Jonathan. *Do your ABC's, Little Brown Bear*
Loomis, Christine. *The best Father's Day present ever*
McCaughrean, Geraldine. *Father and son*
Mallat, Kathy. *Papa pride*
Many, Paul. *Dad's bald head*
Mazer, Norma Fox. *Has anyone seen my Emily Greene?*
Murphy, Jill. *Mr. Large in charge*
Newman, Leslea. *Daddy's song*
Nolan, Janet. *A Father's Day thank you*
O'Leary, Sara. *When you were small*
Paradis, Susan. *Snow princess*
Plourde, Lynn. *Dad, aren't you glad?*
Prap, Lila. *Daddies*
Rex, Michael. *You can do anything, Daddy!*
Ritchie, Alison. *Me and my dad!*
Savadier, Elivia. *Time to get dressed!*
Schaefer, Lola M. *Toolbox twins*
Shahan, Sherry. *That's not how you play soccer, Daddy*
Sockabasin, Allen. *Thanks to the animals*
Stanton, Karen. *Papi's gift*
Tellis, Annabel. *If my dad were a dog*
Thompson, Lauren. *Mouse's first snow*
Tomp, Sarah Wones. *Red, white, and blue goodbye*
Uhlberg, Myron. *Dad, Jackie, and me*
Wild, Margaret. *Piglet and Papa*
Yaccarino, Dan. *Every Friday*
Yolen, Jane. *Baby Bear's chairs*
Ziefert, Harriet. *Bigger than Daddy*
Zolotow, Charlotte (Shapiro). *A father like that*

Family life — grandfathers

Anholt, Laurence. *Seven for a secret*
Asher, Sandy. *What a party!*
Aska, Warabe. *Tapicero tap tap*
Balouch, Kristen. *Mystery bottle*
Briggs, Raymond. *The puddleman*
Butler, Dori Hillestad. *My grandpa had a stroke*
Choi, Yangsook. *Behind the mask*
Cohen, Deborah Bodin. *Papa Jethro*
Cumberbatch, Judy. *Can you hear the sea?*
Davies, Nicola. *White owl, barn owl*
Gower, Catherine. *Long-Long's new year*
Grifalconi, Ann. *Ain't nobody a stranger to me*
Hurst, Carol Otis. *Terrible storm*
Hutchins, Pat. *Bumpety bump*
Isadora, Rachel. *Yo, Jo!*
McKenna, Sharon. *Good morning, sunshine*
Moser, Lisa. *Watermelon wishes*

Murphy, Yannick. *Ahwooooooo!*
Parr, Todd. *The grandpa book*
Quigley, Mary. *Granddad's fishing buddy*
Rosenberry, Vera. *Vera's baby sister*
Smalls, Irene. *My Pop Pop and me*
Soto, Gary. *My little car / Mi carrito*
Williams, Laura E. *The best winds*
Ziefert, Harriet. *That's what grandpas are for*

Family life — grandmothers

Abeele, Veronique van den. *Still my Grandma*
Alcott, Louisa May. *An old-fashioned Thanksgiving*
Anderson, Peggy Perry. *Joe on the go*
Baryshnikov, Mikhail. *Because . . .*
Bootman, Colin. *Fish for the Grand Lady*
Borgo, Lacy. *Big Mama's baby*
Bouchard, Dave. *Nokum is my teacher*
Browne, Anthony. *Silly Billy*
Busse, Sarah Martin. *Banjo granny*
Caseley, Judith. *In style with Grandma Antoinette*
Colato Laínez, René. *Playing lotería / El juego de la lotería*
Cruise, Robin. *Little Mama forgets*
English, Karen. *The baby on the way*
Eriksson, Eva. *A crash course for Molly*
Griessman, Annette. *Like a hundred drums*
Isadora, Rachel. *Luke goes to bat*
Knister. *Sophie's dance*
Kroll, Virginia L. *Jason takes responsibility*
  The Thanksgiving bowl
Lindbergh, Reeve. *My little grandmother often forgets*
Lord, Janet. *Here comes Grandma!*
MacDonald, Margaret Read. *The squeaky door*
Mayer, Pamela. *The Grandma cure*
Ohi, Ruth. *A trip with Grandma*
Park, Frances. *The Have a Good Day Cafe*
Parr, Todd. *The grandma book*
Sheth, Kashmira. *My Dadima wears a sari*
Shulman, Lisa. *The moon might be milk*
Smalls, Irene. *My Nana and me*
Sweet, Melissa. *Carmine*
Wigersma, Tanneke. *Baby brother*
Williams, Barbara. *Albert's gift for grandmother*
Wood, Douglas. *What Grandmas can't do*
Yolen, Jane. *Grandma's hurrying child*
Ziefert, Harriet. *Grandma, it's for you!*
  That's what grandmas are for

Family life — grandparents

Ancona, George. *Mis abuelos / My grandparents*
Bunge, Daniela. *The scarves*
Hoberman, Mary Ann. *I'm going to Grandma's*
Juster, Norton. *The hello, goodbye window*
Kinsey-Warnock, Natalie. *Nora's ark*
Krishnaswami, Uma. *Remembering Grandpa*

Family life — mothers

Ashman, Linda. *Mama's day*
Aston, Dianna Hutts. *Mama outside, Mama inside*
Bauer, Marion Dane. *A mama for Owen*
Bedford, David. *Little Otter's big journey*
Breathed, Berkeley. *Mars needs moms!*
Brown, Susan Taylor. *Oliver's must-do list*
Browne, Anthony. *My Mom*
Bunting, Eve (Anne Evelyn). *My mom's wedding*
Cabrera, Jane. *Mommy, carry me please!*
Chaconas, Dori. *Christmas mouseling*
Côté, Geneviève. *With you always, Little Monday*
Cousins, Lucy. *Hooray for fish!*
Crumpacker, Bunny. *Alexander's pretending day*
Dewdney, Anna. *Llama Llama mad at mama*
  Llama, Llama red pajama
Duncan, Alice Faye. *Honey baby sugar child*
Ehrlich, Fred. *Does a mouse have a mommy?*
Ericsson, Jennifer A. *Home to me, home to you*

Freedman, Claire. *One magical morning*
Garden, Nancy. *Molly's family*
Gershator, Phillis. *This is the day!*
Gerstein, Mordicai. *Leaving the nest*
Goode, Diane. *The most perfect spot*
Grambling, Lois G. *My mom is a firefighter*
Gray, Kes. *006 and a half*
Hample, Stoo. *I will kiss you (lots & lots & lots!)*
Jenkins, Emily. *Love you when you whine*
Katz, Karen. *Mommy hugs*
Kindermans, Martine. *You and me*
Kono, Erin Eitter. *Hula lullaby*
Krosoczka, Jarrett J. *Giddy up, Cowgirl*
Lee, Tae-Jun. *Waiting for Mama*
Lobel, Gillian. *Little Honey Bear and the smiley moon*
McAllister, Angela. *Trust me, Mom!*
McCourt, Lisa. *Happy Halloween, Stinky Face*
McElroy, Lisa Tucker. *Love, Lizzie*
McGhee, Alison. *Someday*
McGinty, Alice B. *Eliza's kindergarten surprise*
Makhijani, Pooja. *Mama's saris*
Manushkin, Fran. *How Mama brought the spring*
Morrow, Tara Jaye. *Panda goes to school*
Norac, Carl. *My mommy is magic*
Parker, Marjorie. *Your kind of mommy*
Polacco, Patricia. *Mommies say shhh!*
Rao, Sandhya. *My mother's sari*
Robberecht, Thierry. *Back into Mommy's tummy*
Robbins, Maria Polushkin. *Mother, Mother, I want another*
Ross, Michael Elsohn. *Mama's milk*
Ryder, Joanne. *Bear of my heart*
Schotter, Roni. *Mama, I'll give you the world*
Tafuri, Nancy. *Whose chick are you?*
Thompson, Lauren. *Little Quack's hide and seek*
  Mouse's first spring
Toten, Teresa. *Bright red kisses*
Trotter, Deborah W. *How do you know?*
Watters, Debbie. *Where's Mom's hair?*
Weninger, Brigitte. *"Mom, wake up and play!"*
  "No bath! No way!"
Wild, Margaret. *Piglet and Mama*
Wilson, Karma. *Mama always comes home*
Winter, Jeanette. *Mama*
Woodson, Jacqueline. *Show way*
Xinran, Xue. *Motherbridge of love*
Yang, Belle. *Always come home to me*
Ziefert, Harriet. *The biggest job of all*
  Mommy, I want to sleep in your bed!
  Surprise!

Family life — new sibling

Broach, Elise. *What the no-good baby is good for*
Bunting, Eve (Anne Evelyn). *Baby can*
Conway, David. *The most important gift of all*
Cote, Nancy. *It's all about me!*
Dyer, Jane. *Little Brown Bear and the bundle of joy*
Enderle, Judith Ross. *Smile, Principessa!*
Gliori, Debi. *Where did that baby come from?*
Harper, Anita. *It's not fair!*
Jacobs, Julie. *My heart is a magic house*
Layne, Steven L. *Love the baby*
MacDonald, Ross. *Bad baby*
Newman, Marjorie. *Just like me*
Patz, Nancy. *Babies can't eat kimchee!*
Robberecht, Thierry. *Back into Mommy's tummy*
Rosenberry, Vera. *Vera's baby sister*
Sheldon, Annette. *Big sister now*
Van Leeuwen, Jean. *Benny and beautiful baby Delilah*
Wigersma, Tanneke. *Baby brother*

Family life — only child

Best, Cari. *What's so bad about being an only child?*

Family life — parents

Ashman, Linda. *What could be better than this*
Harper, Jo. *I could eat you up!*
Kerley, Barbara. *You and me together*
Mitchard, Jacquelyn. *Ready, set, school!*
Modarressi, Mitra. *Stay awake, Sally*
Ransom, Jeanie Franz. *What do parents do? (. . . When you're not home)*

Family life — single-parent families

Polacco, Patricia. *Something about Hensley's*
Schotter, Roni. *Mama, I'll give you the world*
Thomas, Eliza. *The red blanket*
Zolotow, Charlotte (Shapiro). *A father like that*

Family life — sisters *see* Family life; Family life — brothers & sisters; Sibling rivalry

Family life — step families

Perrault, Charles. *Cinderella*
Cinderella: a pop-up fairy tale

Family life — stepchildren *see* Divorce; Family life — step families

Family life — stepparents *see* Divorce; Family life — step families

Farmers *see* Careers — farmers

Farms

Baddiel, Ivor. *Cock-a-doodle quack! Quack!*
Bailey, Linda. *The farm team*
Barbour, Karen. *Mr. Williams*
Bunting, Eve (Anne Evelyn). *Hurry! Hurry!*
Burg, Sarah Emmanuelle. *One more egg*
Carter, Don. *Old MacDonald drives a tractor*
Chaconas, Dori. *Dori the contrary hen*
Church, Caroline Jayne. *Digby takes charge*
One smart goose
Cowley, Joy. *Mrs. Wishy-Washy's Christmas*
Cronin, Doreen. *Click clack, quackity-quack*
Click, clack, splish, splash
Dooby dooby moo
Edwards, David. *The pen that Pa built*
Fitz-Gibbon, Sally. *On Uncle John's farm*
Friend, Catherine. *The perfect nest*
Hamilton, Martha. *The hidden feast*
Harper, Jessica. *A place called Kindergarten*
Harrington, Janice N. *The chicken-chasing queen of Lamar County*
Hayward, Linda. *The King's chorus*
Heinz, Brian J. *Red Fox at McCloskey's farm*
Helakoski, Leslie. *Big chickens*
Hester, Denia Lewis. *Grandma Lena's big ol' turnip*
Himmelman, John. *Chickens to the rescue*
Hutchins, Pat. *Barn dance!*
Bumpety bump
Johnson, D. B. (Donald B.). *Four legs bad, two legs good!*
Kelly, Mij. *Where's my darling daughter?*
Kinsey-Warnock, Natalie. *Nora's ark*
Krosoczka, Jarrett J. *Punk Farm*
Punk Farm on tour
Krupinski, Loretta. *Pirate treasure*
Lee, Huy Voun. *In the leaves*
The little red hen. *The little red hen*
Loupy, Christophe. *Wiggles*
Manning, Mick. *Cock-a-doodle hooooooo!*
Martin, Jacqueline Briggs. *Chicken joy on Redbean Road*
Martín, Hugo C. *Pablo's Christmas*
Milgrim, David. *Young MacDonald*
Mortensen, Denise Dowling. *Ohio thunder*
Palatini, Margie. *The cheese*

Oink?
Pelletier, Andrew T. *The toy farmer*
Peterson, Cris. *Fantastic farm machines*
Pipe, Jim. *Farm animals*
Purmwell, Ann. *Christmas tree farm*
Ransom, Candice F. *Tractor day*
Reed, Lynn Rowe. *Thelonius Turkey lives!*
Reynolds, Aaron. *Chicks and salsa*
Ryder, Joanne. *Dance by the light of the moon*
Santoro, Scott. *Farm-fresh cats*
Sillifant, Alec. *Farmer Ham*
Spinelli, Eileen. *The best time of day*
Steffensmeier, Alexander. *Millie waits for the mail*
Thermes, Jennifer. *Sam Bennett's new shoes*
Whybrow, Ian. *Faraway farm*
Wild, Margaret. *Piglet and Mama*
Piglet and Papa

Father's Day *see* Holidays — Father's Day

Fathers *see* Family life — fathers; Family life — parents; Family life — single-parent families; Family life — step families

Fear *see* Emotions — fear

Feelings *see* Emotions

Feet *see* Anatomy — feet

Ferrets *see* Animals — ferrets

Fighting *see* Behavior — fighting, arguing

Finches *see* Birds — Finches

Fire

Beaver steals fire
Griessman, Annette. *The fire*
Hoberman, Mary Ann. *Mrs. O'Leary's cow*
Martin, Bill, Jr. (William Ivan). *"Fire! Fire!" Said Mrs. McGuire*
Nez, John. *One smart Cookie*
Spinelli, Eileen. *Hero cat*

Fire engines *see* Careers — firefighters; Trucks

Firefighters *see* Careers — firefighters

Fireflies *see* Insects — fireflies

Fish

Buckingham, Matt. *Bright Stanley*
Cousins, Lucy. *Hooray for fish!*
Elschner, Geraldine. *Fritz's fish*
Geist, Ken. *The three little fish and the big bad shark*
Grant, Joan. *Cat and Fish*
Krykorka, Ian. *Carl, the Christmas carp*
LaReau, Kara. *Ugly fish*
MacDonald, Suse. *Fish, swish! Splash, dash!*
Rohmann, Eric. *Clara and Asha*
Schwartz, Amy. *A beautiful girl*
Simeon, Jean-Pierre. *This is a poem that heals fish*
Yaccarino, Dan. *The birthday fish*
Yoo, Taeeun. *The little red fish*

Fish — seahorses

Butterworth, Chris. *Sea horse*

Fish — sharks

Geist, Ken. *The three little fish and the big bad shark*
Rockwell, Anne F. *Little shark*

Sabuda, Robert. *Encyclopedia prehistorica*
Schwarz, Viviane. *Shark and Lobster's amazing undersea adventure*
Ward, Nick. *Don't eat the babysitter!*

Fishermen *see* Careers — fishermen

Fishing *see* Sports — fishing

Fitness *see* Health & fitness

Flags

Cohan, George M. *You're a grand old flag*

Flamingos *see* Birds — flamingos

Flies *see* Insects — flies

Floods *see* Weather — floods

Flowers

Appelt, Kathi. *Miss Lady Bird's wildflowers*
Elschner, Geraldine. *Max's magic seeds*
Foreman, Michael. *Mia's story*
Lee-Tai, Amy. *A place where sunflowers grow / Sabaku ni saita himawari*
Noda, Takayo. *Song of the flowers*
Park, Linda Sue. *What does Bunny see?*
Wellington, Monica. *Zinnia's flower garden*

Flowers — roses

Valentina, Marina. *Lost in the roses*

Flying *see* Activities — flying

Fog *see* Weather — fog

Fold-out books *see* Format, unusual — toy & movable books

Folk & fairy tales

Aesop. *The hare and the tortoise / La liebre y la tortuga*
Ahlberg, Allan. *Previously*
Ahmed, Said Salah. *The lion's share / Qayb Libaax*
Andersen, H. C. (Hans Christian). *The princess and the pea*, ill. by Rachel Isadora
    The princess and the pea, retold by John Cech; ill. by Bernhard Oberdieck
    The princess and the pea in miniature
    Thumbelina
    The tinderbox
    The ugly duckling
    The wild swans
Auch, Mary Jane. *Chickerella*
Bar-el, Dan. *Such a prince*
Bateman, Teresa. *Traveling Tom and the leprechaun*
Beaver steals fire
Begin, Mary Jane. *The sorcerer's apprentice*
Brett, Jan. *The three snow bears*
Briant, Ed. *Seven stories*
Casey, Dawn. *The great race*
Catalanotto, Peter. *Ivan the terrier*
Chicken Little. *Henny Penny*
Compestine, Ying Chang. *The real story of stone soup*
Daly, Niki. *Pretty Salma*
Deedy, Carmen Agra. *Martina the beautiful cockroach*
dePaola, Tomie. *Little Grunt and the big egg*
Diakité, Baba Wagué. *Mee-an and the magic serpent*
Dick Whittington and his cat. *Dick Whittington and his cat*
Duvall, Deborah L. *The opossum's tale*
Fleischman, Paul. *Glass slipper, gold sandal*
The gingerbread boy. *The Gingerbread Cowboy*

The gingerbread girl
Grimm, Jacob. *The Bremen town musicians*
    The elves and the shoemaker
    The frog prince
    Hansel and Gretel
    Hansel and Gretel / Hansel y Gretel
    Jorinda and Jorindel
    Little Red Riding Hood, retold & ill. by Andrea Wisnewski
    Little Red Riding Hood, retold & ill. by Jerry Pinkney
    Musicians of Bremen
    Musicians of Bremen / Los musicos de Bremner
    Rapunzel
    Snow White
    The twelve dancing princesses
Hamilton, Martha. *The hidden feast*
    Priceless gifts
Hasler, Eveline. *A tale of two brothers*
Hennessy, B. G. (Barbara G.). *The boy who cried wolf*
Hong, Chen Jiang. *The magic horse of Han Gan*
Hopkins, Jackie Mims. *The gold miner's daughter*
Hurston, Zora Neale. *The six fools*
Jack and the beanstalk. *Jack and the beanstalk*
Jay, Alison. *1 2 3*
Johnson-Davies, Denys. *Goha, the wise fool*
Ketteman, Helen. *Waynetta and the cornstalk*
Kilaka, John. *True friends*
Kimmel, Eric A. *The frog princess*
    Rip Van Winkle's return
    The three cabritos
Kloske, Geoffrey. *Once upon a time, the end (asleep in 60 seconds)*
Kosofsky, Chaim. *Much, much better*
Krensky, Stephen. *Too many leprechauns*
Kurtz, Jane. *In the small, small night*
Langton, Jane. *Saint Francis and the wolf*
LaRochelle, David. *The end*
Lendler, Ian. *An undone fairy tale*
Lin, Grace. *The red thread*
The little red hen. *The little red hen*
    The little red hen: an old fable
McAlister, Caroline. *Holy Molé!*
MacDonald, Margaret Read. *Conejito*
    The great smelly, slobbery small-toothed dog
    A hen, a chick, and a string guitar
    Little Rooster's diamond button
    The squeaky door
    Teeny Weeny Bop
    Tunjur! Tunjur! Tunjur!
Matthews, Tina. *Out of the egg*
Muth, Jon J. *Zen shorts*
Nadimi, Suzan. *The rich man and the parrot*
Newman, Marlene. *Myron's magic cow*
The old woman and her pig. *The old woman and her pig*
Osborne, Mary Pope. *Sleeping Bobby*
Otsuka, Yuzo. *Suho's white horse*
Perrault, Charles. *Cinderella*
    Cinderella: a pop-up fairy tale
Poole, Amy Lowry. *The pea blossom*
Quattlebaum, Mary. *Sparks fly high*
Rocco, John. *Wolf! Wolf!*
Ryan, Pam Muñoz. *Nacho and Lolita*
Salley, Coleen. *Epossumondas saves the day*
Scott, Nathan Kumar. *Mangoes and bananas*
Seeger, Pete. *Some friends to feed*
Seki, Sunny. *The tale of the lucky cat*
Shah, Idries. *Fatima the spinner and the tent*
Shannon, George. *Rabbit's gift*
Shepard, Aaron. *One-eye! Two-eyes! Three-eyes!*
Sierra, Judy. *Mind your manners, B. B. Wolf*
Souhami, Jessica. *The little, little house*
    Sausages
Stampler, Ann Redisch. *Shlemazel and the remarkable spoon of Pohost*
Sweet, Melissa. *Carmine*
Taback, Simms. *Kibitzers and fools*
The three bears. *Goldilocks and the three bears*
The three little pigs. *The three little pigs / Los tres cerditos*
Tingle, Tim. *When turtle grew feathers*

Vallverdu, Josep. *Aladdin and the magic lamp / Aldino y la lampara maravillosa*
Waldman, Debby. *A sack full of feathers*
Wick, Walter. *Can you see what I see?*
Yee, Paul. *Bamboo*

Food

Ahlberg, Allan. *The runaway dinner*
Alcott, Louisa May. *An old-fashioned Thanksgiving*
Ancona, George. *Mis comidas / My foods*
Anderson, Derek. *Gladys goes out to lunch*
Armstrong, Jennifer. *Once upon a banana*
Aston, Dianna Hutts. *An orange in January*
Barasch, Lynne. *Hiromi's hands*
Baum, Maxie. *I have a little dreidel*
Bond, Rebecca. *The great doughnut parade*
Bruel, Nick. *Bad Kitty*
Bunting, Eve (Anne Evelyn). *One green apple*
Catalanotto, Peter. *The secret lunch special*
Cazet, Denys. *The perfect pumpkin pie*
Chamberlin, Mary. *Mama Panya's pancakes*
Child, Lauren. *Charlie and Lola's I will never not ever eat a tomato*
Church, Caroline Jayne. *Little Apple Goat*
Compestine, Ying Chang. *The real story of stone soup*
Cordsen, Carol Foskett. *The milkman*
DeFelice, Cynthia C. *One potato, two potato*
Delessert, Etienne. *Hungry for numbers*
Denise, Anika. *Pigs love potatoes*
Donnio, Sylviane. *I'd really like to eat a child*
Downing, Johnette. *Today is Monday in Louisiana*
Drescher, Henrik. *Hubert the Pudge*
Durant, Alan. *Burger boy*
Eaton, Maxwell. *Best buds*
Ehrlich, Fred. *Does a camel cook?*
Elliott, George. *The boy who loved bananas*
Elvgren, Jennifer Riesmeyer. *Josias, hold the book*
Evans, Lezlie. *The bunnies' picnic*
Fitzgerald, Joanne. *Yum! Yum!*
Flaherty, A. W. *The luck of the Loch Ness monster*
Freymann, Saxton. *Baby food*
    Dog food
    Fast Food
    Food for thought
    Food play
    How are you peeling?
Gibbons, Gail. *Ice cream*
    The vegetables we eat
The gingerbread boy. *The Gingerbread Cowboy*
    The gingerbread girl
Grey, Mini. *Ginger bear*
Hester, Denia Lewis. *Grandma Lena's big ol' turnip*
Horowitz, Dave. *The ugly pumpkin*
Isaacs, Anne. *Pancakes for supper!*
Jeffers, Oliver. *The incredible book eating boy*
Jocelyn, Marthe. *Eats*
Johnson, Paul Brett. *On top of spaghetti*
Kann, Victoria. *Pinkalicious*
Kasza, Keiko. *Badger's fancy meal*
Khing, T. T. *Where is the cake?*
Kleven, Elisa. *The apple doll*
Koster, Gloria. *The peanut-free cafe*
Leedy, Loreen. *The edible pyramid*
Lendler, Ian. *An undone fairy tale*
Lewis, Paeony. *No more cookies!*
McAlister, Caroline. *Holy Molé!*
McDonald, Megan. *Beetle McGrady eats bugs!*
McDonald, Rae A. *A fishing surprise*
McFarland, Lyn Rossiter. *Mouse went out to get a snack*
McNamara, Margaret. *How many seeds in a pumpkin?*
Madison, Alan. *The littlest grape stomper*
Manning, Mick. *Snap!*
Manushkin, Fran. *How Mama brought the spring*
Marino, Gianna. *Zoopa*
Martin, David. *All for pie, pie for all*
Martin, Jacqueline Briggs. *Chicken joy on Redbean Road*
Michelin, Linda (Donald B.). *Zuzu's wishing cake*

Mora, Pat. *Yum! Mmmm! Que rico!*
Morris, Jennifer E. *May I please have a cookie?*
Moser, Lisa. *Watermelon wishes*
Mozelle, Shirley. *The kitchen talks*
Näslund, Gorel Kristina. *Our apple tree*
Newgarden, Mark. *Bow-Wow orders lunch*
Norac, Carl. *Monster, don't eat me!*
Ogburn, Jacqueline K. *The bake shop ghost*
Palatini, Margie. *Bad boys get cookie!*
Park, Linda Sue. *Bee-bim bop!*
Patz, Nancy. *Babies can't eat kimchee!*
Piernas-Davenport, Gail. *Shanté Keys and the New Year's peas*
Reynolds, Aaron. *Buffalo wings*
    Chicks and salsa
Rosenthal, Amy Krouse. *Cookies*
    Little Pea
Rotner, Shelley. *Where does food come from?*
Sage, James. *Mr. Beast*
Santore, Charles. *Three hungry pigs and the wolf who came to dinner*
Seeger, Pete. *Some friends to feed*
Segal, John. *Carrot soup*
Shulman, Goldie. *Way too much challah dough*
Shulman, Lisa. *The moon might be milk*
Sierra, Judy. *Thelonius Monster's sky-high fly pie*
Souhami, Jessica. *Sausages*
Sperring, Mark. *The fairytale cake*
Stadler, Alexander. *Beverly Billingsly takes the cake*
Stainton, Sue. *The chocolate cat*
Stowell, Penelope. *The greatest potatoes*
Sutton, Jane. *The trouble with cauliflower*
Thompson, Lauren. *The apple pie that Papa baked*
Wellington, Monica. *Mr. Cookie Baker*
    Pizza at Sally's
Willems, Mo. *The Pigeon finds a hot dog!*
Wilson, Karma. *Whopper cake*
Wolff, Nancy. *Tallulah in the kitchen*
Yolen, Jane. *How do dinosaurs eat their food?*

Foolishness *see* Character traits — foolishness

Football *see* Sports — football

Foreign lands

Fleischman, Paul. *Glass slipper, gold sandal*
Frank, John. *How to catch a fish*
Kinkade, Sheila. *My family*
Reynolds, Jan. *Celebrate!*
Shah, Idries. *Fatima the spinner and the tent*

Foreign lands — Afghanistan

Haskins, Jim (James). *Count your way through Afghanistan*

Foreign lands — Africa

Beake, Lesley. *Home now*
Brett, Jan. *Honey, honey — lion!*
Conway, David. *The most important gift of all*
Daly, Niki. *Pretty Salma*
    Welcome to Zanzibar Road
Dawes, Kwame Senu Neville. *I saw your face*
Grimm, Jacob. *The twelve dancing princesses*
Joosse, Barbara M. *Papa do you love me?*
Landstrom, Lena. *A hippo's tale*
McGrory, Anik. *Kidogo*
Markham, Beryl. *The good lion*
Moss, Miriam. *This is the oasis*
Onyefulu, Ifeoma. *An African Christmas*
Pritchett, Dylan. *The first music*
Schaefer, Carole Lexa. *Cool time song*

Foreign lands — Antarctica

Jeffers, Oliver. *Lost and found*

Foreign lands — Arabia

Vallverdu, Josep. *Aladdin and the magic lamp / Aldino y la lampara maravillosa*

Foreign lands — Arctic

Blaikie, Lynn. *Beyond the northern lights*
Brett, Jan. *The three snow bears*
Crawford, Laura. *In arctic waters*
Spinelli, Eileen. *Polar bear, arctic hare*
Votaw, Carol. *Good morning, little polar bear*
Ward, Jennifer. *Way up in the Arctic*

Foreign lands — Australia

French, Jackie. *Josephine wants to dance*
Votaw, Carol. *Waking up down under*
Wild, Margaret. *Bobbie Dazzler*

Foreign lands — Belarus

Manushkin, Fran. *How Mama brought the spring*

Foreign lands — Brazil

Cline-Ransome, Lesa. *Young Pelé*

Foreign lands — British Columbia

Olsen, Sylvia. *Yetsa's sweater*

Foreign lands — Canada

Brebeuf, Jean de. *The Huron carol*
Downie, Mary Alice. *A pioneer ABC*
Miles, Victoria. *Old mother bear*
Pendziwol, Jean. *The red sash*
Perkins, Lynne Rae. *Pictures from our vacation*

Foreign lands — Caribbean Islands

Lessac, Frané. *Island Counting 123*

Foreign lands — Chile

Foreman, Michael. *Mia's story*
Rand, Gloria. *A pen pal for Max*

Foreign lands — China

Berkeley, Jon. *Chopsticks*
Compestine, Ying Chang. *D is for dragon dance*
  The real story of stone soup
Coste, Marion. *Finding Joy*
Crane, Carol. *D is for dancing dragon*
Hong, Chen Jiang. *The magic horse of Han Gan*
Krebs, Laurie. *We're riding on a caravan*
Lin, Grace. *The red thread*
Louis, Catherine. *Liu and the bird*
Pilegard, Virginia Walton. *The warlord's alarm*
Poole, Amy Lowry. *The pea blossom*
Rocco, John. *Wolf! Wolf!*
So, Sungwan. *Shanyi goes to China*
Stoeke, Janet Morgan. *Waiting for May*
Wang, Xiaohong. *One year in Beijing*
Yang, Belle. *Always come home to me*
Yee, Paul. *Bamboo*
Yi, Hu Yong. *Good morning China*

Foreign lands — Cuba

Deedy, Carmen Agra. *Martina the beautiful cockroach*
Sciurba, Katie. *Oye, Celia!*

Foreign lands — Czechoslovakia

Krykorka, Ian. *Carl, the Christmas carp*

Sís, Peter. *The wall*

Foreign lands — East Africa

Andersen, H. C. (Hans Christian). *The princess and the pea*

Foreign lands — Egypt

Farmer, Nancy. *Clever Ali*
Krebs, Laurie. *We're sailing down the Nile*

Foreign lands — England

Dick Whittington and his cat. *Dick Whittington and his cat*
Francis, Pauline. *Sam stars at Shakespeare's Globe*
MacDonald, Alan. *Wilfred to the rescue*
Rogers, Gregory. *The boy, the bear, the baron, the bard*
  Midsummer knight

Foreign lands — Ethiopia

Kessler, Cristina. *The best beekeeper of Lalibela*

Foreign lands — France

McClintock, Barbara. *Adele and Simon*
Magoon, Scott. *Hugo and Miles in I've painted everything!*
Palatini, Margie. *Three French hens*
Selznick, Brian. *The invention of Hugo Cabret*
Wells, Rosemary. *The miraculous tale of the two Maries*
Young, Amy. *Belinda in Paris*

Foreign lands — Galapagos Islands

Krebs, Laurie. *We're sailing to Galapagos*

Foreign lands — Germany

Grimm, Jacob. *The elves and the shoemaker*
Seeger, Pete. *Some friends to feed*

Foreign lands — Ghana

Cumberbatch, Judy. *Can you hear the sea?*
Kurtz, Jane. *In the small, small night*

Foreign lands — Haiti

Elvgren, Jennifer Riesmeyer. *Josias, hold the book*

Foreign lands — Hungary

MacDonald, Margaret Read. *Little Rooster's diamond button*

Foreign lands — Iceland

McMillan, Bruce. *How the ladies stopped the wind*
  The problem with chickens

Foreign lands — India

Charles, Veronika Martenova. *The birdman*
Kroll, Virginia L. *Selvakumar knew better*
Noyes, Deborah. *When I met the wolf girls*

Foreign lands — Indonesia

Scott, Nathan Kumar. *Mangoes and bananas*

Foreign lands — Iran

Balouch, Kristen. *Mystery bottle*
Haskins, Jim (James). *Count your way through Iran*

Foreign lands — Iraq

Kosofsky, Chaim. *Much, much better*

Foreign lands — Ireland

Bateman, Teresa. *Fiona's luck*
    Traveling Tom and the leprechaun
Garland, Michael. *King Puck*
Krensky, Stephen. *Too many leprechauns*
Murphy, Jim. *Fergus and the Night-Demon*
Woodruff, Elvira. *Small beauties*

Foreign lands — Israel

Abraham, Michelle Shapiro. *My cousin Tamar lives in Israel*

Foreign lands — Italy

Egielski, Richard. *St. Francis and the wolf*
Gibfried, Diane. *Brother Juniper*
Hamilton, Martha. *Priceless gifts*
Willard, Nancy. *The flying bed*

Foreign lands — Japan

Christian, Mary Blount. *If not for the calico cat*
Gershator, Phillis. *Sky sweeper*
Issa, Kobayashi. *Today and today*
Say, Allen. *Kamishibai man*
Seki, Sunny. *The tale of the lucky cat*
Yamada, Utako. *The story of Cherry the pig*

Foreign lands — Kenya

Chamberlin, Mary. *Mama Panya's pancakes*
Cunnane, Kelly. *For you are a Kenyan child*

Foreign lands — Korea

Bae, Hyun-Joo. *New clothes for New Year's day*
Lee, Tae-Jun. *Waiting for Mama*
Park, Linda Sue. *Bee-bim bop!*

Foreign lands — Latin America

Stanton, Karen. *Papi's gift*

Foreign lands — Mali

Diakité, Baba Wagué. *Mee-an and the magic serpent*
Diakité, Penda. *I lost my tooth in Africa*

Foreign lands — Mexico

Colato Laínez, René. *Playing lotería / El juego de la lotería*
Elya, Susan Middleton. *N is for Navidad*
Krebs, Laurie. *Off we go to Mexico*
Levy, Janice. *Celebrate! It's cinco de mayo! / Celebremos! Es el cinco de mayo!*
McAlister, Caroline. *Holy Molé!*
Martín, Hugo C. *Pablo's Christmas*
Meunier, Brian. *Bravo, Tavo!*
Tafolla, Carmen. *What can you do with a rebozo?*

Foreign lands — Middle East

Johnson-Davies, Denys. *Goha, the wise fool*

Foreign lands — Mongolia

Otsuka, Yuzo. *Suho's white horse*

Foreign lands — Morocco

Ichikawa, Satomi. *My father's shop*

Foreign lands — Nepal

Stryer, Andrea Stenn. *Kami and the yaks*

Foreign lands — Palestine

MacDonald, Margaret Read. *Tunjur! Tunjur! Tunjur!*

Foreign lands — Panama

MacDonald, Margaret Read. *Conejito*

Foreign lands — Persia

Nadimi, Suzan. *The rich man and the parrot*

Foreign lands — Poland

Sasso, Sandy Eisenberg. *Butterflies under our hats*

Foreign lands — Puerto Rico

Santiago, Esmeralda. *A doll for Navidades*

Foreign lands — Russia

Joosse, Barbara M. *Nikolai, the only bear*
Spirin, Gennady. *Martha*

Foreign lands — Siam *see* Foreign lands — Thailand

Foreign lands — Somalia

Ahmed, Said Salah. *The lion's share / Qayb Libaax*

Foreign lands — South Africa

Daly, Niki. *Happy birthday, Jamela!*

Foreign lands — Spain

Aska, Warabe. *Tapicero tap tap*

Foreign lands — Switzerland

Hasler, Eveline. *A tale of two brothers*

Foreign lands — Tanzania

Kilaka, John. *True friends*

Foreign lands — Thailand

Arnold, Katya. *Elephants can paint, too!*

Foreign lands — Trinidad

Bootman, Colin. *Fish for the Grand Lady*

Foreign lands — Venezuela

Nazoa, Aquiles. *A small Nativity*

Foreign lands — Vietnam

Alberti, Theresa Jarosz. *Vietnam ABCs*
Sugarman, Brynn Olenberg. *Rebecca's journey home*

Foreign lands — Yukon Territory

Provensen, Alice. *Klondike gold*

Foreign languages

Aesop. *The hare and the tortoise / La liebre y la tortuga*
Ahmed, Said Salah. *The lion's share / Qayb Libaax*
Ancona, George. *Mi música / My music*
    Mis abuelos / My grandparents
    Mis comidas / My foods
    Mis fiestas / My celebrations
    Mis juegos / My games
    Mis quehaceres / My chores
Argueta, Jorge. *Moony Luna / Luna, Lunita Lunera*

Bouchard, Dave. *Nokum is my teacher*
Chapra, Mimi. *Sparky's bark / El ladrido de Sparky*
Colato Laínez, René. *Playing lotería / El juego de la lotería*
Cupiano, Ina. *Quinito's neighborhood / El vecindario de Quinito*
Elya, Susan Middleton. *Bebe goes shopping*
   Cowboy Jose
   F is for fiesta
   Fairy trails
   N is for Navidad
   Oh no, gotta go #2
   Sophie's trophy
Evans, Lezlie. *Can you greet the whole wide world?*
Grimm, Jacob. *Hansel and Gretel / Hansel y Gretel*
   Musicians of Bremen / Los musicos de Bremner
Groner, Judyth Saypol. *My first Hebrew word book*
Guy, Ginger Foglesong. *My grandma / Mi abuelita*
   My school / Mi escuela
   Perros! Perros! Dogs! Dogs!
   Siesta
Haskins, Jim (James). *Count your way through Afghanistan*
   Count your way through Iran
Jocelyn, Marthe. *ABC x 3*
Katz, Karen. *Can you say peace?*
Krebs, Laurie. *Off we go to Mexico*
Law, Diane. *Come out and play*
Lee, Huy Voun. *In the leaves*
Lee-Tai, Amy. *A place where sunflowers grow / Sabaku ni saita himawari*
Levy, Janice. *Celebrate! It's cinco de mayo! / Celebremos! Es el cinco de mayo!*
Lujan, Jorge. *Sky blue accident / Accidente celeste*
MacDonald, Margaret Read. *Conejito*
Montes, Marissa. *Los gatos black on Halloween*
Mora, Pat. *Marimba!*
Orozco, Jose-Luis. *Rin, rin, rin / do, re, mi*
Park, Linda Sue. *Yum! Yuck!*
Paul, Ann Whitford. *Fiesta fiasco*
   Mañana Iguana
Prap, Lila. *Animals speak*
Reiser, Lynn. *My way / A mi manera*
Soto, Gary. *Chato goes cruisin'*
   My little car / Mi carrito
The three little pigs. *The three little pigs / Los tres cerditos*
Vallverdu, Josep. *Aladdin and the magic lamp / Aldino y la lampara maravillosa*
Weeks, Sarah. *Counting Ovejas*

Forest, woods

Grimm, Jacob. *Hansel and Gretel*
   Hansel and Gretel / Hansel y Gretel
Serfozo, Mary. *Whooo's there?*
Ward, Jennifer. *Forest bright, forest night*

Forgetfulness *see* Behavior — forgetfulness

Forgiving *see* Behavior — forgiving

Format, unusual

Behrens, Janice. *Let's find rain forest animals*
Horacek, Petr. *Butterfly butterfly*
Jenkins, Steve. *Dogs and cats*
MacDonald, Suse. *Fish, swish! Splash, dash!*
Pfister, Marcus. *Charlie at the zoo*
Rasmussen, Halfdan. *The ladder*
Toft, Kim Michelle. *The world that we want*
Ziefert, Harriet. *Messy Bessie*

Format, unusual — board books

Alborough, Jez. *Tall*
Ashman, Linda. *Babies on the go*
Capucilli, Alyssa Satin. *Katy Duck*
   Katy Duck, big sister
Child, Lauren. *Charlie and Lola's numbers*
   Charlie and Lola's opposites

Cousins, Lucy. *Happy Easter, Maisy!*
Ford, Bernette G. *No more diapers for Ducky!*
Frazee, Marla. *Hush, little baby*
Freymann, Saxton. *Baby food*
   Dog food
   Food for thought
Fuge, Charles. *Where to, Little Wombat?*
Harper, Jamie. *Night night, baby bundt*
   Splish splash, baby bundt
Jenkins, Emily. *Num, num, num!*
   Plonk, plonk, plonk!
   Up, up, up!
Meade, Holly. *John Willy and Freddy McGee*
Mother Goose. *Little Miss Muffet*
   Pat-a-cake
Newgarden, Mark. *Bow-Wow orders lunch*
Patricelli, Leslie. *Binky*
   Blankie
Pearson, Tracey Campbell. *Diddle diddle dumpling*
Rossetti-Shustak, Bernadette. *I love you through and through*
Saltzberg, Barney. *I love dogs*
Scotton, Rob. *Go to sleep, Russell the sheep*
Shannon, David. *David smells*
   Oh, David!
   Oops!
Thompson, Lauren. *Little Quack*
   Little Quack's hide and seek
Verdick, Elizabeth. *Tails are not for pulling*
Wallace, Nancy Elizabeth. *Snow*
Wheeler, Valerie. *Yes, please! No, thank you!*
Willems, Mo. *The Pigeon has feelings, too!*
   The Pigeon loves things that go!
Wilson, Karma. *Hello, Calico!*
Wood, Audrey. *Silly Sally*
Wright, Cliff. *Bear and ball*
   Bear and kite
Ziefert, Harriet. *Beach party!*
   Knick-knack paddywhack

Format, unusual — toy & movable books

Alborough, Jez. *Duck's key where can it be?*
Bauer, Marion Dane. *Christmas lights*
   I'm not afraid of Halloween!
Berenstain, Jan. *The Berenstain bears trim the tree*
Bernhard, Durga. *In the fiddle is a song*
Brown, Ruth. *The old tree*
Carter, David A. *Blue 2*
   One red dot
   600 black spots
   Whoo? Whoo?
Cheshire, Marc. *Merry Christmas, Eloise!*
Child, Lauren. *Charlie and Lola's I will never not ever eat a tomato*
Ciboul, Adele. *The five senses*
Cousins, Lucy. *Ha ha, Maisy!*
   Maisy's amazing big book of words
   Maisy's wonderful weather book
   More fun with Maisy!
   Stop and go, Maisy
   With love from Maisy
Crowther, Robert. *Opposites*
Denchfield, Nick. *Charlie Chick*
Dunrea, Olivier. *Gossie's busy day*
Emberley, Ed (Edward Randolph). *Ed Emberley's bye-bye, big bad bullybug!*
Fischer, Scott M. *Twinkle*
Fontes, Justine Korman. *Black meets White*
Fox, Diane. *Tyson the terrible*
Harper, Charise Mericle. *Amy and Ivan*
Janovitz, Marilyn. *A, B, see!*
Kaner, Etta. *Who likes the sun?*
Katz, Karen. *A potty for me!*
Munro, Roxie. *Circus*
Novak, Matt. *Too many bunnies*
Park, Linda Sue. *Yum! Yuck!*
Perrault, Charles. *Cinderella*
Reiser, Lynn. *Play ball with me!*

Sabuda, Robert. *Encyclopedia prehistorica: dinosaurs*
  Encyclopedia prehistorica: mega-beasts
  Encyclopedia prehistorica: sharks and other seamonsters
  Winter in white
  Winter's tale
Saltzberg, Barney. *Hi, Blueberry!*
Schwartz, David M. *Where in the wild*
Seeger, Laura Vaccaro. *Black? White! Day? Night!*
  First the egg
  Lemons are not red
Sendak, Maurice. *Mommy?*
Smee, Nicola. *No bed without Ted*
Smith, Lois T. *Carrie and Carl play*
Stadler, John. *Take me out to the ball game*
Thompson, Lauren. *Little Quack*
Tildes, Phyllis Limbacher. *Eye guess*
Weeks, Sarah. *Be mine, be mine, sweet valentine*
Willems, Mo. *Time to say "please"!*

Fortune *see* Character traits — luck

Fossils

Sabuda, Robert. *Encyclopedia prehistorica: mega-beasts*
  Encyclopedia prehistorica: sharks and other seamonsters
Zoehfeld, Kathleen Weidner. *Dinosaur tracks*

Fourth of July *see* Holidays — Fourth of July

Foxes *see* Animals — foxes

France *see* Foreign lands — France

Freedom *see* Character traits — freedom

Friendship

Amado, Elisa. *Tricycle*
Anderson, Derek. *Romeo and Lou blast off*
Baker, Roberta. *Olive's first sleepover*
Bardhan-Quallen, Sudipta. *The Mine-o-saur*
Bloom, Suzanne. *A splendid friend, indeed*
Bosca, Francesca. *The three grasshoppers*
Bottner, Barbara. *Raymond and Nelda*
Brooks, Erik. *Slow days, fast friends*
Bruel, Robert O. *Bob and Otto*
Buckingham, Matt. *Bright Stanley*
Bunge, Daniela. *Cherry time*
Butler, M. Christina. *Snow friends*
Bynum, Janie. *Nutmeg and Barley*
Calmenson, Stephanie. *May I pet your dog?*
Catalanotto, Peter. *The secret lunch special*
Chaconas, Dori. *Cork and Fuzz*
  Cork and Fuzz: good sports
  Cork and Fuzz: short and tall
Chichester Clark, Emma. *Melrose and Croc*
  Will and Squill
Chodos-Irvine, Margaret. *Best best friends*
Choldenko, Gennifer. *How to make friends with a giant*
  Louder, Lili
Cohen, Miriam. *First grade takes a test*
Consentino, Ralph. *The story of Honk-Honk-Ashoo and Swella-Bow-Wow*
Cooper, Helen (Helen F.). *Delicious!*
  A pipkin of pepper
deGroat, Diane. *No more pencils, no more books, no more teacher's dirty looks!*
Donofrio, Beverly. *Mary and the mouse, the mouse and Mary*
Eaton, Maxwell. *Best buds*
  Superheroes
Edwards, Pamela Duncan. *The old house*
Egan, Tim. *Roasted peanuts*
Elliott, Laura Malone. *Hunter and Stripe and the soccer showdown*
Floyd, Madeleine. *Cold paws, warm heart*
Foley, Greg. *Thank you, Bear*
Fox, Diane. *Tyson the terrible*

Fox, Mem. *Hunwick's egg*
Fuge, Charles. *Swim, Little Wombat, swim!*
Gleeson, Libby. *Half a world away*
Gorbachev, Valeri. *Heron and Turtle*
  That's what friends are for
Grant, Joan. *Cat and Fish*
Gretz, Susanna. *Riley and Rose in the picture*
Grey, Mini. *Ginger bear*
Grimes, Nikki. *Danitra Brown, class clown*
  When Gorilla goes walking
Haas, Irene. *Bess and Bella*
Harper, Charise Mericle. *When Randolph turned rotten*
Hills, Tad. *Duck and Goose*
  Duck, Duck, Goose
Himmelman, John. *Tudley didn't know*
Hobbie, Holly. *Toot and Puddle: let it snow*
  Toot and Puddle: wish you were here
Howe, James. *Houndsley and Catina*
  Houndsley and Catina and the birthday surprise
Hughes, Susan. *Earth to Audrey*
Jeffers, Oliver. *Lost and found*
Jeffs, Stephanie. *Josh*
Jenkins, Emily. *Num, num, num!*
  Plonk, plonk, plonk!
  Up, up, up!
Johansen, Hanna. *The duck and the owl*
Jules, Jacqueline. *No English*
Keller, Holly. *Help!*
  Sophie's window
Kilaka, John. *True friends*
Kitamura, Satoshi. *Pablo the artist*
Kroll, Virginia L. *Forgiving a friend*
Krosoczka, Jarrett J. *My buddy, Slug*
Le Neouanic, Lionel. *Little smudge*
Lewis, Kim. *Hooray for Harry*
Lin, Grace. *Lissy's friends*
Livingston, Irene. *Finklehopper Frog cheers*
Luthardt, Kevin. *You're weird!*
McBratney, Sam. *Yes we can!*
McDonnell, Patrick. *The gift of nothing*
McPhail, David. *Big Brown Bear goes to town*
  Big Brown Bear's birthday surprise
  Sylvie and True
Meserve, Adria. *No room for Napoleon*
Metz, Lorijo. *Floridius Bloom and the planet of Gloom*
Michelin, Linda (Donald B.). *Zuzu's wishing cake*
Michelson, Richard. *Across the alley*
Moore, Julianne. *Freckleface Strawberry*
Morgan, Michaela. *Bunny wishes*
  Dear bunny
Murphy, Mary. *Panda Foo and the new friend*
Newman, Leslea. *Skunk's spring surprise*
O'Connor, George. *Sally and the Some-Thing*
Ohi, Ruth. *Clara and the Bossy*
Petz, Moritz. *Wish you were here*
Polacco, Patricia. *Emma Kate*
Puttock, Simon. *Goat and Donkey in strawberry sunglasses*
  Goat and Donkey in the great outdoors
Quattlebaum, Mary. *Winter friends*
Rand, Gloria. *A pen pal for Max*
Rankin, Laura. *Fluffy and Baron*
Reiser, Lynn. *My way / A mi manera*
Ritchie, Alison. *What Bear likes best!*
Robberecht, Thierry. *Sam tells stories*
Robbins, Jacqui. *The new girl . . . and me*
Rodman, Mary Ann. *My best friend*
Rosen, Michael. *Bear's day out*
Sakai, Komako. *Emily's balloon*
Schwartz, Corey Rosen. *Hop! Plop!*
Scieszka, Jon. *Cowboy and Octopus*
Seeger, Laura Vaccaro. *Dog and Bear*
Segal, John. *The lonely moose*
Shannon, George. *Rabbit's gift*
Sidjanski, Brigitte. *Little Chicken and Little Duck*
Simmons, Jane. *Together*
Slonim, David. *He came with the couch*
Smallman, Steve. *The lamb who came for dinner*

Stein, David Ezra. *Cowboy Ned and Andy*
  Ned's new friend
Stewart, Joel. *Dexter Bexley and the big blue beastie*
Straaten, Harmen van. *Duck's tale*
  For me?
Sutton, Jane. *The trouble with cauliflower*
Tarlow, Ellen. *Pinwheel days*
Thomas, Shelley Moore. *Happy birthday, Good Knight*
Thompson, Lauren. *Little Quack's new friend*
Varon, Sara. *Chicken and Cat*
Walton, Rick. *The remarkable friendship of Mr. Cat and Mr. Rat*
Ward, Helen. *Little Moon Dog*
Watt, Melanie. *Scaredy Squirrel makes a friend*
Weninger, Brigitte. *Miko goes on vacation*
Wheeler, Lisa. *Hokey pokey*
Willems, Mo. *I am invited to a party!*
  Leonardo the terrible monster
  My friend is sad
  There is a bird on your head!
  Today I will fly!
Willis, Jeanne. *Misery Moo*
Wilson, Karma. *Bear feels sick*
Winget, Susan. *Tucker's four-carrot school day*
Winstead, Rosie. *Ruby and Bubbles*
Yin. *Brothers*
Yolen, Jane. *Dimity Duck*
  How do dinosaurs play with their friends?
Ziefert, Harriet. *Fun Land fun!*

Frogs & toads

Anderson, Peggy Perry. *Joe on the go*
Asher, Sandy. *Too many frogs!*
  What a party!
Azore, Barbara. *Wanda and the frogs*
Bonning, Tony. *Snog the frog*
Breen, Steve. *Stick*
Carlson, Nancy L. *Think big!*
Elya, Susan Middleton. *Sophie's trophy*
Ferri, Giuliano. *Little Tad grows up*
A frog he would a-wooing go (folk-song). *Froggy went a-courtin'*
Grimm, Jacob. *The frog prince*
Johnson, Rebecca. *Tree frog hears a sound*
Kimmel, Eric A. *The frog princess*
Leedy, Loreen. *The great graph contest*
Livingston, Irene. *Finklehopper Frog cheers*
London, Jonathan. *Froggy plays T-ball*
  Froggy rides a bike
Parenteau, Shirley. *One frog sang*
Ryder, Joanne. *Toad by the road*
Straaten, Harmen van. *Duck's tale*
  For me?
Tashiro, Chisato. *Five nice mice*
Thompson, Lauren. *Little Quack's new friend*
Tripp, Paul. *Tubby the tuba*
Waddell, Martin. *Bee frog*
Willis, Jeanne. *Tadpole's promise*
Yolen, Jane. *Dimity Duck*

Frontier life *see* U.S. history — frontier & pioneer life

Fur traders *see* Careers — fur traders

Furniture — beds

Ferreri, Della Ross. *How will I ever sleep in this bed?*
Willard, Nancy. *The flying bed*

Furniture — chairs

Mahy, Margaret. *Down the back of the chair*
Manuel, Lynn. *The trouble with Tilly Trumble*

Furniture — couches, sofas

Slonim, David. *He came with the couch*

Galapagos Islands *see* Foreign lands — Galapagos Islands

Games

Ancona, George. *Mis juegos / My games*
Behrens, Janice. *Let's find rain forest animals*
Butler, John. *Ten in the meadow*
Carter, David A. *Whoo? Whoo?*
Hays, Anna Jane. *Ready, set, preschool!*
Meade, Holly. *Inside, inside, inside*
Mother Goose. *Pat-a-cake*
Palatini, Margie. *The cheese*
Petrillo, Genevieve. *Keep your ear on the ball*
Root, Phyllis. *Looking for a moose*
Rueda, Claudia. *Let's play in the forest while the wolf is not around*
Thompson, Lauren. *Little Quack's hide and seek*
Yee, Wong Herbert. *Who likes rain?*

Gangs *see* Clubs, gangs

Garbage collectors *see* Careers — sanitation workers

Gardens, gardening

Ayres, Katherine. *Up, down, and around*
Elvgren, Jennifer Riesmeyer. *Josias, hold the book*
George, Lindsay Barrett. *In the garden*
Gershator, Phillis. *Sky sweeper*
Park, Linda Sue. *What does Bunny see?*
Parker, Kim. *Counting in the garden*
Pattou, Edith. *Mrs. Spitzer's garden*
Robbins, Ken. *Pumpkins*
Segal, John. *Carrot soup*
Shannon, George. *Busy in the garden*
Trapani, Iza. *Here we go 'round the mulberry bush*
Wellington, Monica. *Zinnia's flower garden*

Geese *see* Birds — geese

Gender roles

Baguley, Elizabeth. *Meggie moon*
Hill, Susanna Leonard. *Punxsutawney Phyllis*
Kessler, Cristina. *The best beekeeper of Lalibela*
Milgrim, David. *Time to get up, time to go*
Smith, Jada Pinkett. *Girls hold up this world*

Generosity *see* Character traits — generosity

Genies *see* Mythical creatures — genies

Geography

Cuyler, Margery. *That's good! That's bad! In Washington, D.C.*

Germany *see* Foreign lands — Germany

Ghana *see* Foreign lands — Ghana

Ghosts

Cazet, Denys. *The perfect pumpkin pie*
Clark, Mary Higgins. *Ghost ship*
Goodhart, Pippa. *Three little ghosties*
Moore, Lilian. *Beware, take care*

Murphy, Jim. *Fergus and the Night-Demon*
Ogburn, Jacqueline K. *The bake shop ghost*
Robberecht, Thierry. *Sarah's little ghosts*
Stein, Mathilde. *Mine!*

Giants

Andreasen, Dan. *The giant of Seville*
Beaty, Andrea. *When giants come to play*
Bertrand, Lynne. *Granite baby*
Hawkes, Kevin. *The wicked big toddlah*
Ivey, Randall. *Jay and the bounty of books*
Jack and the beanstalk. *Jack and the beanstalk*
Kennedy, Kim. *Pirate Pete's giant adventure*
Ketteman, Helen. *Waynetta and the cornstalk*
Mora, Pat. *Doña Flor*
Nolen, Jerdine. *Hewitt Anderson's great big life*
O'Malley, Kevin. *Once upon a cool motorcycle dude*
Schotter, Roni. *When the Wizzy Foot goes walking*

Gifts

Buehner, Caralyn. *Snowmen at Christmas*
Bunting, Eve (Anne Evelyn). *The baby shower*
Calmenson, Stephanie. *Birthday at the Panda Palace*
Chen, Chih-Yuan. *The best Christmas ever*
Conway, David. *The most important gift of all*
Cousins, Lucy. *With love from Maisy*
Danneberg, Julie. *Last day blues*
Evans, Cambria. *Martha moth makes socks*
Foley, Greg. *Thank you, Bear*
Frazee, Marla. *Santa Claus*
Friedman, Laurie. *Love, Ruby Valentine*
Hamilton, Martha. *Priceless gifts*
Harper, Charise Mericle. *Amy and Ivan*
Hobbie, Holly. *Toot and Puddle*
Kromhout, Rindert. *Little Donkey and the birthday present*
McDonnell, Patrick. *The gift of nothing*
Montanari, Eva. *My first . . .*
Nolan, Janet. *A Father's Day thank you*
Ommen, Sylvia van. *The surprise*
Paul, Ann Whitford. *Fiesta fiasco*
Pilgrim, Elza. *The china doll*
Rempt, Fiona. *Snail's birthday wish*
Santiago, Esmeralda. *A doll for Navidades*
Stanton, Karen. *Papi's gift*
Thomas, Shelley Moore. *Happy birthday, Good Knight*
Walton, Rick. *The remarkable friendship of Mr. Cat and Mr. Rat*
Weeks, Sarah. *Be mine, be mine, sweet valentine*
Weninger, Brigitte. *Double birthday*
Williams, Barbara. *Albert's gift for grandmother*
Ziefert, Harriet. *Grandma, it's for you!*

Giraffes *see* Animals — giraffes

Glasses

Headley, Justina Chen. *The patch*
Scillian, Devin. *Brewster the rooster*

Gloves *see* Clothing — gloves, mittens

Goats *see* Animals — goats

Gorillas *see* Animals — gorillas

Gossip *see* Behavior — gossip

Grammar *see* Language

Grandfathers *see* Family life — grandfathers; Family life — grandparents

Grandmothers *see* Family life — grandmothers; Family life — grandparents

Grandparents *see* Family life — grandfathers; Family life — grandmothers; Family life — grandparents

Grasshoppers *see* Insects — grasshoppers

Greed *see* Behavior — greed

Grief *see* Emotions — grief

Grocery stores *see* Shopping; Stores

Groundhog Day *see* Holidays — Groundhog Day

Groundhogs *see* Animals — groundhogs

Growing up *see* Behavior — growing up

Guinea pigs *see* Animals — guinea pigs

Gymnastics *see* Sports — gymnastics

Hair

Azore, Barbara. *Wanda and the wild hair*
Brisson, Pat. *Melissa Parkington's beautiful, beautiful hair*
Ditchfield, Christin. *Cowlick!*
Fisher, Jeff. *The hair scare*
Graves, Keith. *The unexpectedly bad hair of Barcelona Smith*
Grimm, Jacob. *Rapunzel*
Lubner, Susan. *Ruthie Bon Bair, do not go to bed with wringing wet hair!*
McElligott, Matthew. *Backbeard and the birthday suit*
Many, Paul. *Dad's bald head*
Napoli, Donna Jo. *Bobby the bold*
Savadier, Elivia. *No haircut today!*
Tinkham, Kelly A. *Hair for Mama*
Watters, Debbie. *Where's Mom's hair?*
Ziefert, Harriet. *There was a little girl who had a little curl*

Haiti *see* Foreign lands — Haiti

Halloween *see* Holidays — Halloween

Hamsters *see* Animals — hamsters

Handicaps

Niner, Holly L. *I can't stop!*

Handicaps — blindness

Cole, Barbara Hancock. *Anna and Natalie*
Liao, Jimmy. *The sound of colors*
Petrillo, Genevieve. *Keep your ear on the ball*

Handicaps — cerebral palsy

Lears, Laurie. *Nathan's wish*
Thompson, Lauren. *Ballerina dreams*

Handicaps — deafness

Seeger, Pete. *The deaf musicians*
Stryer, Andrea Stenn. *Kami and the yaks*
Uhlberg, Myron. *Dad, Jackie, and me*

Handicaps — dyslexia

Hodge, Deborah. *Lily and the mixed-up letters*

Handicaps — physical handicaps

Adler, David A. *Campy*
Moore-Mallinos, Jennifer. *It's ok to be me!*

Hanukkah *see* Holidays — Hanukkah

Happiness *see* Emotions — happiness

Hares *see* Animals — rabbits

Hats *see* Clothing — hats

Hawaii

Kono, Erin Eitter. *Hula lullaby*
Lin, Grace. *Olvina swims*

Hawks *see* Birds — hawks

Health & fitness

Cole, Joanna. *My friend the doctor*
Drescher, Henrik. *Hubert the Pudge*
Fraser, Mary Ann. *I.Q. gets fit*
Harper, Charise Mericle. *Flush!*
Krishnaswami, Uma. *The happiest tree*
Leedy, Loreen. *The edible pyramid*
Murphy, Liz. *ABC doctor*
Nelson, Robin. *Staying clean*
Wells, Rosemary. *The gulps*
Whitford, Rebecca. *Little yoga*
    Sleepy little yoga

Health & fitness — exercise

Bateman, Teresa. *Hamster Camp*
Carlson, Nancy L. *Get up and go!*
McKinlay, Penny. *Flabby Tabby*
Wells, Rosemary. *The gulps*

Hearing *see* Handicaps — deafness

Heat *see* Concepts — cold & heat

Heavy equipment *see* Machines

Hedgehogs *see* Animals — hedgehogs

Helpfulness *see* Character traits — helpfulness

Hens *see* Birds — chickens

Herons *see* Birds — herons

Hibernation

Cooper, Elisha. *Bear dreams*
Cuyler, Margery. *Groundhog stays up late*
Schertle, Alice. *Very hairy bear*
Stein, David Ezra. *Leaves*
Yolen, Jane. *Sleep, black bear, sleep*

Hiccups

Meng, Cece. *The wonderful thing about hiccups*

Hiding *see* Behavior — hiding

Hiking *see* Sports — hiking

Hippopotamuses *see* Animals — hippopotamuses

Hispanic Americans *see* Ethnic groups in the U.S. — Hispanic Americans

Hockey *see* Sports — hockey

Hogs *see* Animals — pigs

Holidays

Ancona, George. *Mis fiestas / My celebrations*
Mobin-Uddin, Asma. *The best Eid holiday ever*
Reynolds, Jan. *Celebrate!*

Holidays — Chanukah *see* Holidays — Hanukkah

Holidays — Chinese New Year

Compestine, Ying Chang. *D is for dragon dance*
Gower, Catherine. *Long-Long's new year*

Holidays — Christmas

Alsenas, Linas. *Mrs. Claus takes a vacation*
Anderson, Derek. *How the Easter Bunny saved Christmas*
Appelt, Kathi. *Merry Christmas, merry crow*
Bauer, Marion Dane. *Christmas lights*
Bedford, David. *I've seen Santa!*
Berenstain, Jan. *The Berenstain bears trim the tree*
Bond, Rebecca. *A city Christmas tree*
Bowen, Anne. *Christmas is coming*
Brebeuf, Jean de. *The Huron carol*
Brown, Margaret Wise. *The little fir tree*
Buehner, Caralyn. *Snowmen at Christmas*
Chaconas, Dori. *Christmas mouseling*
    When cows come home for Christmas
Chen, Chih-Yuan. *The best Christmas ever*
Cheshire, Marc. *Merry Christmas, Eloise!*
Chichester Clark, Emma. *Melrose and Croc*
Conahan, Carolyn. *The twelve days of Christmas dogs*
Cowley, Joy. *Mrs. Wishy-Washy's Christmas*
Deacon, Alexis. *While you are sleeping*
Demas, Corinne. *Two Christmas mice*
DePalma, Mary Newell. *The Nutcracker doll*
DiCamillo, Kate. *Great joy*
Duval, Kathy. *The Three Bears' Christmas*
Elschner, Geraldine. *Pashmina the little Christmas goat*
Elya, Susan Middleton. *N is for Navidad*
Engelbreit, Mary. *Mary Engelbreit's A merry little Christmas*
Farber, Norma. *How the hibernators came to Bethlehem*
Fisher, Aileen Lucia. *Do rabbits have Christmas?*
Frazee, Marla. *Santa Claus*
Godden, Rumer. *The story of Holly and Ivy*
Hapka, Cathy. *Margret and H. A. Rey's Merry Christmas, Curious George*
Harley, Bill. *Dear Santa*
Hassett, Ann. *The finest Christmas tree*
Helmer, Marilyn. *One splendid tree*
Hobbie, Holly. *Toot and Puddle*
Holabird, Katharine. *Christmas in Mouseland*
Johnson, David. *Snow sounds*
Johnston, Tony. *Noel*
Joslin, Mary. *On that Christmas night*
Kidslabel. *Spot 7*
Kroll, Steven. *Pooch on the loose*
Kroll, Virginia L. *Uno, dos, tres, posada!*
Krykorka, Ian. *Carl, the Christmas carp*
McCaughrean, Geraldine. *Father and son*
McKissack, Patricia C. *The all-I'll-ever-want Christmas doll*
Major, Kevin. *Aunt Olga's Christmas postcards*
Martín, Hugo C. *Pablo's Christmas*
Mayer, Mercer. *The little drummer mouse*
Minor, Wendell. *Christmas tree!*
Moore, Clement Clarke. *A creature was stirring*
    The night before Christmas, ill. by Lisbeth Zwerger

The night before Christmas, ill. by Richard Jesse Watson
The night before Christmas, ill. by Will Moses
The night before Christmas, ill. by Gennady Spirin
Morpurgo, Michael. *On angel wings*
Nazoa, Aquiles. *A small Nativity*
Numeroff, Laura Joffe. *Merry Christmas, Mouse!*
Onyefulu, Ifeoma. *An African Christmas*
Pasquali, Elena. *Ituku's Christmas journey*
Purmwell, Ann. *Christmas tree farm*
Recorvits, Helen. *Yoon and the Christmas mitten*
Reiss, Mike. *Merry un-Christmas*
Roberts, Bethany. *Cookie angel*
Rose, Marion. *The Christmas tree fairy*
Rox, John. *I want a hippopotamus for Christmas*
Ryan, Pam Muñoz. *There was no snow on Christmas Eve*
Santiago, Esmeralda. *A doll for Navidades*
Scotton, Rob. *Russell's Christmas magic*
Sharkey, Niamh. *Santasaurus*
Smith, Cynthia Leitich. *Santa knows*
Spirin, Gennady. *We three kings*
Stoeke, Janet Morgan. *Minerva Louise on Christmas Eve*
Trapani, Iza. *Jingle bells*
Van Steenwyk, Elizabeth. *Prairie Christmas*
Willey, Margaret. *A Clever Beatrice Christmas*
Wilson, Karma. *Mortimer's Christmas manger*

Holidays — Cinco de Mayo

Levy, Janice. *Celebrate! It's cinco de mayo! / Celebremos! Es el cinco de mayo!*

Holidays — Day of the Dead

Montes, Marissa. *Los gatos black on Halloween*

Holidays — Easter

Burg, Sarah Emmanuelle. *One more egg*
Cousins, Lucy. *Happy Easter, Maisy!*
deGroat, Diane. *Last one in is a rotten egg!*
Garland, Michael. *The great Easter egg hunt*
Grambling, Lois G. *Here comes T. Rex Cottontail*
Krensky, Stephen. *Milo and the really big bunny*
Stoeke, Janet Morgan. *Minerva Louise and the colorful eggs*
Wells, Rosemary. *Max counts his chickens*

Holidays — Father's Day

Loomis, Christine. *The best Father's Day present ever*
Nolan, Janet. *A Father's Day thank you*

Holidays — Fourth of July

Whitehead, Kathy. *Looking for Uncle Louie on the Fourth of July*

Holidays — Groundhog Day

Cuyler, Margery. *Groundhog stays up late*
Gibbons, Gail. *Groundhog Day*
Hill, Susanna Leonard. *Punxsutawney Phyllis*
Miller, Pat. *Substitute groundhog*
Swallow, Pamela Curtis. *Groundhog gets a say*

Holidays — Halloween

Bauer, Marion Dane. *I'm not afraid of Halloween!*
Bollinger, Peter. *Algernon Graeves is scary enough*
Cazet, Denys. *The perfect pumpkin pie*
Choi, Yangsook. *Behind the mask*
Cuyler, Margery. *The bumpy little pumpkin*
Duval, Kathy. *The Three Bears' Halloween*
Grambling, Lois G. *T. Rex trick-or-treats*
Hatch, Elizabeth. *Halloween night*
Horowitz, Dave. *The ugly pumpkin*
Kovalski, Maryann. *Omar's Halloween*
Krieb, Mr. *We're off to find the witch's house*
McCourt, Lisa. *Happy Halloween, Stinky Face*
McGhee, Alison. *A very brave witch*

McGuirk, Leslie. *Tucker's spooky Halloween*
Montes, Marissa. *Los gatos black on Halloween*
Neitzel, Shirley. *Who will I be?*
Schulman, Janet. *Ten trick-or-treaters*
Spurr, Elizabeth. *Pumpkin hill*

Holidays — Hanukkah

Baum, Maxie. *I have a little dreidel*
Chwast, Seymour. *The miracle of Hanukkah*
Cleary, Brian P. *Eight wild nights*
da Costa, Deborah. *Hanukkah moon*
Krensky, Stephen. *Hanukkah at Valley Forge*
Newman, Leslea. *The eight nights of Chanukah*

Holidays — Independence Day *see* Holidays — Fourth of July

Holidays — New Year's

Bae, Hyun-Joo. *New clothes for New Year's day*
Fromental, Jean-Luc. *365 penguins*
Piernas-Davenport, Gail. *Shanté Keys and the New Year's peas*

Holidays — Passover

Hanft, Josh. *The miracles of Passover*
Levine, Abby. *This is the matzah*
Schotter, Roni. *Passover!*

Holidays — Ramadan

Katz, Karen. *My first Ramadan*

Holidays — Rosh Hashanah

Kropf, Latifa Berry. *It's Shofar time!*

Holidays — Rosh Kodesh

da Costa, Deborah. *Hanukkah moon*

Holidays — Seder

Levine, Abby. *This is the matzah*

Holidays — Thanksgiving

Alcott, Louisa May. *An old-fashioned Thanksgiving*
Anderson, Derek. *Over the river*
Archer, Peggy. *Turkey surprise*
Auch, Mary Jane. *Beauty and the beaks*
Horowitz, Dave. *The ugly pumpkin*
Kroll, Virginia L. *The Thanksgiving bowl*
Mayr, Diane. *Run, Turkey, run*
Reed, Lynn Rowe. *Thelonius Turkey lives!*

Holidays — Valentine's Day

Friedman, Laurie. *Love, Ruby Valentine*
Gibbons, Gail. *Valentine's Day is—*
Rylant, Cynthia. *If you'll be my Valentine*
Samuels, Barbara. *Happy Valentine's Day, Dolores*
Weeks, Sarah. *Be mine, be mine, sweet valentine*

Homeless

Cole, Brock. *Good enough to eat*
DiCamillo, Kate. *Great joy*
King, Stephen Michael. *Mutt dog!*
Seskin, Steve. *A chance to shine*

Homes, houses

Banks, Kate (Katherine A.). *The great blue house*
Cecka, Melanie. *Violet comes to stay*
Crum, Shutta. *A family for Old Mill Farm*
Daly, Niki. *Welcome to Zanzibar Road*

Davies, Jacqueline. *The house takes a vacation*
Edwards, Pamela Duncan. *The old house*
Fuge, Charles. *Where to, Little Wombat?*
Johnson, D. B. (Donald B.). *Eddie's kingdom*
Ljungkvist, Laura. *Follow the line through the house*
Meserve, Adria. *No room for Napoleon*
Mozelle, Shirley. *The kitchen talks*
Raye, Rebekah. *The very best bed*
Sturges, Philemon. *I love tools!*
Veit, Barbara. *Who stole my house?*
Walsh, Melanie. *Do lions live on lily pads?*
Williams, Brenda. *Home for a tiger, home for a bear*
Zalben, Jane Breskin. *Hey, Mama Goose*

Homework

Kroll, Virginia L. *Honest Ashley*

Homosexuality

Richardson, Justin. *And Tango makes three*

Honesty *see* Character traits — honesty

Honey bees *see* Insects — bees

Hope

Sasso, Sandy Eisenberg. *Butterflies under our hats*

Horses *see* Animals — horses, ponies

Hospitals

Cousins, Lucy. *Maisy goes to the hospital*
Hapka, Cathy. *Margret and H. A. Rey's Merry Christmas, Curious George*

Hotels

Kovacs, Deborah. *Katie Copley*
Paraskevas, Betty. *Chocolate at the Four Seasons*

Houses *see* Homes, houses

Hugging

Cabrera, Jane. *Kitty's cuddles*
Clements, Andrew. *Slippers loves to run*
Crandall, Court. *Hugville*
Katz, Karen. *Daddy hugs 1 2 3*
    Mommy hugs
Rowe, John A. *I want a hug*
Ryder, Joanne. *Won't you be my hugaroo?*
Saltzberg, Barney. *Cornelius P. Mud, are you ready for bed?*
Stein, David Ezra. *Monster hug!*

Humorous stories

Agee, Jon. *Nothing*
Armstrong, Jennifer. *Once upon a banana*
Ashman, Linda. *To the beach!*
Auch, Mary Jane. *Chickerella*
Azore, Barbara. *Wanda and the frogs*
Bachelet, Gilles. *My cat, the silliest cat in the world*
    When the silliest cat was small
Broach, Elise. *When dinosaurs came with everything*
Brown, Jeff. *Flat Stanley*
Carroll, Lewis. *Jabberwocky*
Christelow, Eileen. *Letters from a desperate dog*
Cosentino, Ralph. *The marvelous misadventures of — Fun-Boy*
Crimi, Carolyn. *The Louds move in!*
DeFelice, Cynthia C. *One potato, two potato*
Ditchfield, Christin. *Cowlick!*
Dorros, Alex. *Número uno*
Durant, Alan. *Burger boy*
Edwards, Wallace. *The extinct files*

Egan, Tim. *Dodsworth in New York*
Foreman, George. *Let George do it!*
Fox, Mem. *A particular cow*
French, Jackie. *Pete the sheep-sheep*
Gravett, Emily. *Wolves*
Grey, Mini. *The adventures of the dish and the spoon*
Hapka, Cathy. *Margret and H. A. Rey's Merry Christmas, Curious George*
Hawkes, Kevin. *The wicked big toddlah*
Hicks, Barbara Jean. *The secret life of Walter Kitty*
Hornsey, Chris. *Why do I have to eat off the floor?*
Katz, Alan. *Don't say that word!*
Keller, Laurie. *Grandpa Gazillion's number yard*
Kelley, Ellen A. *My life as a chicken*
Landstrom, Lena. *Boo and Baa have company*
LaRochelle, David. *The end*
Lear, Edward. *The Quangle Wangle's hat*
Lendler, Ian. *An undone fairy tale*
Lewis, J. Patrick. *Tulip at the bat*
Lichtenheld, Tom. *What's with this room?*
Lubner, Susan. *Ruthie Bon Bair, do not go to bed with wringing wet hair!*
McElmurry, Jill. *I'm not a baby!*
Madison, Alan. *Pecorino plays ball*
    Pecorino's first concert
Melling, David. *The Scallywags*
Miranda, Anne. *To market, to market*
Muntean, Michaela. *Do not open this book!*
Newman, Jeff. *Hippo! No, rhino!*
Nolen, Jerdine. *Plantzilla goes to camp*
O'Malley, Kevin. *Gimme cracked corn and I will share*
Palatini, Margie. *Oink?*
    Three French hens
    The three silly billies
Pinkwater, Daniel Manus. *Bad bear detectives*
    Bad bears go visiting
    Dancing Larry
    Sleepover Larry
Prince, Joshua. *I saw an ant in a parking lot*
    I saw an ant on the railroad track
Ransom, Jeanie Franz. *What do parents do? (. . . When you're not home)*
Reiss, Mike. *Merry un-Christmas*
Rex, Michael. *You can do anything, Daddy!*
Rosenthal, Marc. *Phooey!*
Salley, Coleen. *Epossumondas saves the day*
Samuels, Barbara. *Dolores meets her match*
    Happy Valentine's Day, Dolores
Sierra, Judy. *Mind your manners, B. B. Wolf*
Smith, Lane. *John, Paul, George & Ben*
Souhami, Jessica. *The little, little house*
Soule, Jean Conder. *Never tease a weasel*
Tellis, Annabel. *If my dad were a dog*
Walton, Rick. *Just me and 6,000 rats*
Why did the chicken cross the road?
Willems, Mo. *Don't let the pigeon stay up late!*
    The Pigeon finds a hot dog!
    The Pigeon has feelings, too!

Hungary *see* Foreign lands — Hungary

Hurricanes *see* Weather — hurricanes

Hygiene *see* Character traits — cleanliness; Health & fitness

Ice skating *see* Sports — ice skating

Iceland *see* Foreign lands — Iceland

Identity *see* Self-concept

Iguanas *see* Reptiles — iguanas

Illness

Butler, Dori Hillestad. *My grandpa had a stroke*
Hobbie, Holly. *Toot and Puddle*
Jeffs, Stephanie. *Jenny*
McKissack, Patricia C. *Precious and the Boo Hag*
Martin, Jacqueline Briggs. *Chicken joy on Redbean Road*
Miller, Pat. *Substitute groundhog*
Murphy, Jill. *Mr. Large in charge*
Raschka, Chris. *The purple balloon*
Soto, Gary. *Chato goes cruisin'*
Wilson, Karma. *Bear feels sick*

Illness — AIDS

Beake, Lesley. *Home now*

Illness — allergies

Koster, Gloria. *The peanut-free cafe*

Illness — Alzheimer's

Abeele, Veronique van den. *Still my Grandma*

Illness — cancer

Lin, Grace. *Robert's snowflakes*
Polacco, Patricia. *The lemonade club*
Tinkham, Kelly A. *Hair for Mama*
Watters, Debbie. *Where's Mom's hair?*

Illness — cold (disease)

Mayer, Pamela. *The Grandma cure*

Illness — poliomyelitis

Chaconas, Dori. *Dancing with Katya*

Illustrators *see* Careers — illustrators

Imaginary friends *see* Imagination — imaginary friends

Imagination

Abercrombie, Barbara. *The show-and-tell lion*
Ahlberg, Allan. *The shopping expedition*
Almond, David. *Kate, the cat and the moon*
Andreae, Giles. *Captain Flinn and the pirate dinosaurs*
Baguley, Elizabeth. *Meggie moon*
Becker, Shari. *Maxwell's mountain*
Bergman, Mara. *Oliver who would not sleep!*
Brown, Lisa. *How to be*
Chessa, Francesca. *The mysterious package*
Cosentino, Ralph. *The marvelous misadventures of — Fun-Boy*
Crews, Nina. *Below*
Crumpacker, Bunny. *Alexander's pretending day*
Dubosarsky, Ursula. *Rex*
Ellery, Amanda. *If I had a dragon*
Faller, Regis. *The adventures of Polo*
    Polo
Fancher, Lou. *Star climbing*
Freedman, Deborah. *Scribble*
Gay, Marie-Louise. *Caramba*
Greenfield, Eloise. *The friendly four*
Harris, Robie H. *Maybe a bear ate it!*
Hughes, Susan. *Earth to Audrey*
Jenkins, Emily. *Daffodil, crocodile*
Jennings, Sharon. *The happily ever afternoon*
Johnson, Angela. *Lily Brown's paintings*

Johnson, Crockett. *Magic beach*
Jones, Sylvie. *Who's in the tub?*
Kanninen, Barbara. *A story with pictures*
Kwon, Yoon-duck. *My cat copies me*
Lehman, Barbara. *Museum trip*
    Rainstorm
Liao, Jimmy. *The sound of colors*
Ljungkvist, Laura. *Follow the line*
    Follow the line through the house
London, Jonathan. *My big rig*
Lucas, David. *Nutmeg*
McCarty, Peter. *Moon plane*
McCourt, Lisa. *Happy Halloween, Stinky Face*
McPhail, David. *Boy on the brink*
    Emma in charge
Manushkin, Fran. *The shivers in the fridge*
Mayer, Mercer. *The bravest knight*
Merz, Jennifer J. *Playground day*
Murphy, Stuart J. *Jack the builder*
Neubecker, Robert. *Beasty bath*
O'Connor, George. *Ker-splash!*
Ohi, Ruth. *The couch was a castle*
O'Leary, Sara. *When you were small*
Paradis, Susan. *Snow princess*
Patricelli, Leslie. *The birthday box*
Peck, Jan. *Way up high in a tall green tree*
Polacco, Patricia. *Emma Kate*
Portis, Antoinette. *Not a box*
Prelutsky, Jack. *Behold the bold umbrellaphant and other poems*
Rasmussen, Halfdan. *The ladder*
Reed, Neil. *The midnight unicorn*
Rymond, Lynda Gene. *Oscar and the mooncats*
Schaefer, Carole Lexa. *Dragon dancing*
Shulevitz, Uri. *So sleepy story*
Smith, Dana Kessimakis. *A brave spaceboy*
Spinelli, Eileen. *Someday*
Stadler, Alexander. *Beverly Billingsly takes the cake*
Stevenson, Robert Louis. *Block city*
Tanaka, Shinsuke. *Wings*
Van Allsburg, Chris. *Probuditi!*
Waddell, Martin. *Bee frog*
Wiesner, David. *Flotsam*
Willems, Mo. *Leonardo the terrible monster*
Willis, Jeanne. *Delilah D. at the library*
Wilson, Karma. *Princess me*
Wing, Natasha. *Go to bed, monster!*

Imagination — imaginary friends

Klise, Kate. *Imagine Harry*
Rohmann, Eric. *Clara and Asha*

Imitation *see* Behavior — imitation

Immigrants

Bunting, Eve (Anne Evelyn). *One green apple*
Hyde, Heidi Smith. *Mendel's accordion*
Jules, Jacqueline. *No English*
Kurtz, Jane. *In the small, small night*
Lee, Milly. *Landed*
Park, Frances. *The Have a Good Day Cafe*
Recorvits, Helen. *Yoon and the Christmas mitten*
Winter, Jeanette. *Angelina's island*
Woodruff, Elvira. *Small beauties*
Yin. *Brothers*

Incentive *see* Character traits — ambition

Independence Day *see* Holidays — Fourth of July

India *see* Foreign lands — India

Indians, American *see* Indians of North America

Indians of North America

Beaver steals fire
Brown, Don. *Bright path*
Olsen, Sylvia. *Yetsa's sweater*
Shoulders, Michael. *D is for drum*

Indians of North America — Cherokee

Duvall, Deborah L. *The opossum's tale*

Indians of North America — Choctaw

Tingle, Tim. *When turtle grew feathers*

Indians of North America — Cree

Bouchard, Dave. *Nokum is my teacher*

Indians of North America — Inuit

Pasquali, Elena. *Ituku's Christmas journey*

Indians of North America — Lenape

Messinger, Carla. *When the shadbush blooms*

Indians of North America — Metis

Pendziwol, Jean. *The red sash*

Indians of North America — Passamaquoddy

Sockabasin, Allen. *Thanks to the animals*

Indians of North America — Pima

Nelson, S. D. *Quiet hero*

Indians of North America — Powhatan

Krull, Kathleen. *Pocahontas*

Indians of North America — Tiwa

Orona-Ramirez, Kristy. *Kiki's journey*

Indians of North America — Tlingit

Kimmel, Eric A. *The frog princess*

Indifference *see* Behavior — indifference

Individuality *see* Character traits — individuality

Indonesia *see* Foreign lands — Indonesia

Insects

Durango, Julia. *Pest fest*
Gran, Julia. *Big bug surprise*
Green, Emily K. *Walkingsticks*
McDonald, Megan. *Beetle McGrady eats bugs!*
McElligott, Matthew. *Bean thirteen*
Newgarden, Mark. *Bow-Wow bugs a bug*
Peters, Lisa Westberg. *Sleepyhead bear*
Pichon, Liz. *The very ugly bug*

Insects — ants

McDonald, Megan. *Ant and Honey Bee, what a pair!*
Martin, David. *All for pie, pie for all*
Philpot, Lorna. *Find Anthony Ant*
Prince, Joshua. *I saw an ant in a parking lot*
　I saw an ant on the railroad track
Sneed, Brad. *Deputy Harvey and the ant cow caper*

Insects — bees

Gran, Julia. *Big bug surprise*
Green, Emily K. *Bumblebees*
Kessler, Cristina. *The best beekeeper of Lalibela*
McDonald, Megan. *Ant and Honey Bee, what a pair!*
Sayre, April Pulley. *The bumblebee queen*
Smallman, Steve. *The very greedy bee*

Insects — beetles

Fleming, Denise. *Beetle bop*

Insects — butterflies, caterpillars

Bruel, Robert O. *Bob and Otto*
Kelly, Irene. *It's a butterfly's life*
Madison, Alan. *Velma Gratch and the way cool butterfly*
Willis, Jeanne. *Tadpole's promise*

Insects — cockroaches

Deedy, Carmen Agra. *Martina the beautiful cockroach*
Schneider, Howie. *Wilky the White House cockroach*

Insects — crickets

Green, Emily K. *Crickets*

Insects — dragonflies

Breen, Steve. *Stick*

Insects — fireflies

Thomas, Patricia. *Firefly mountain*

Insects — flies

Cronin, Doreen. *Diary of a fly*
Schwartz, Amy. *A beautiful girl*
Sierra, Judy. *Thelonius Monster's sky-high fly pie*

Insects — grasshoppers

Bosca, Francesca. *The three grasshoppers*
Green, Emily K. *Grasshoppers*

Insects — lightning bugs *see* Insects — fireflies

Insects — moths

Evans, Cambria. *Martha moth makes socks*

Inuit Indians *see* Indians of North America — Inuit

Inventions

Geisert, Arthur. *Lights out*
McCully, Emily Arnold. *Marvelous Mattie*
Milgrim, David. *Young MacDonald*
Priceman, Marjorie. *Hot air*
Varela, Barry. *Gizmo*

Inventors *see* Careers — inventors

Iran *see* Foreign lands — Iran

Iraq *see* Foreign lands — Iraq

Ireland *see* Foreign lands — Ireland

Irish Americans *see* Ethnic groups in the U.S. — Irish Americans

Islam *see* Religion — Islam

Islands

Field, Rachel Lyman. *Grace for an island meal*
Godkin, Celia. *Wolf island*
Schaefer, Lola M. *An island grows*

Israel *see* Foreign lands — Israel

Italy *see* Foreign lands — Italy

Jamaican Americans *see* Ethnic groups in the U.S. — Jamaican Americans

Janitors *see* Careers — custodians, janitors

Japan *see* Foreign lands — Japan

Japanese Americans *see* Ethnic groups in the U.S. — Japanese Americans

Jealousy *see* Emotions — envy, jealousy

Jesters *see* Clowns, jesters

Jewish Americans *see* Ethnic groups in the U.S. — Jewish Americans

Jewish culture

Abraham, Michelle Shapiro. *My cousin Tamar lives in Israel*
Chwast, Seymour. *The miracle of Hanukkah*
Cohen, Deborah Bodin. *Papa Jethro*
Gadot, A. S. *The first gift*
Groner, Judyth Saypol. *My first Hebrew word book*
Hanft, Josh. *The miracles of Passover*
Hyde, Heidi Smith. *Mendel's accordion*
Kosofsky, Chaim. *Much, much better*
Kropf, Latifa Berry. *It's Shofar time!*
Levine, Abby. *This is the matzah*
Meltzer, Amy. *A mezuzah on the door*
Michelson, Richard. *Across the alley*
Newman, Leslea. *The eight nights of Chanukah*
Sasso, Sandy Eisenberg. *Butterflies under our hats*
Schotter, Roni. *Passover!*
Shulman, Goldie. *Way too much challah dough*
Stampler, Ann Redisch. *Shlemazel and the remarkable spoon of Pohost*
Sugarman, Brynn Olenberg. *Rebecca's journey home*
Taback, Simms. *Kibitzers and fools*
Waldman, Debby. *A sack full of feathers*

Jobs *see* Careers

Jockeys *see* Careers — Jockeys

Jokes *see* Riddles & jokes

Jumping *see* Activities — jumping

Jungles

Alborough, Jez. *Tall*
Ashman, Linda. *Starry safari*
Behrens, Janice. *Let's find rain forest animals*
Berkes, Marianne Collins. *Over in the jungle*
Derrick, Patricia. *Riley the rhinoceros*

Duquette, Keith. *Little Monkey lost*
Johnson, Rebecca. *Tree frog hears a sound*
Kroll, Steven. *Jungle bullies*
Mitchell, Susan K. *The rainforest grew all around*
Peck, Jan. *Way up high in a tall green tree*
Pritchett, Dylan. *The first music*
Warhola, James. *If you're happy and you know it*

Kangaroos *see* Animals — kangaroos

Karate *see* Sports — karate

Kenya *see* Foreign lands — Kenya

Kindness *see* Character traits — kindness

Kindness to animals *see* Character traits — kindness to animals

Kings *see* Royalty — kings

Kissing

Grimm, Jacob. *The frog prince*
Hample, Stoo. *I will kiss you (lots & lots & lots!)*
McAllister, Angela. *Take a kiss to school*
Plourde, Lynn. *Dad, aren't you glad?*
Robbins, Maria Polushkin. *Mother, Mother, I want another*
Saltzberg, Barney. *Cornelius P. Mud, are you ready for school?*

Kites

Clark, Katie. *Seagull Sam*
Williams, Laura E. *The best winds*
Wright, Cliff. *Bear and kite*

Knights

Adkins, Jan. *What if you met a knight?*
Baynton, Martin. *Jane and the dragon*
Mayer, Mercer. *The bravest knight*
Mayhew, James. *The knight who took all day*
Melling, David. *Good knight sleep tight*
Rogers, Gregory. *The boy, the bear, the baron, the bard*
    Midsummer knight
Thomas, Shelley Moore. *Happy birthday, Good Knight*
    Take care, Good Knight

Knitting *see* Activities — knitting

Koalas *see* Animals — koalas

Korea *see* Foreign lands — Korea

Korean Americans *see* Ethnic groups in the U.S. — Korean Americans

Lakes, ponds

Sidman, Joyce. *Song of the water boatman*
Thompson, Lauren. *Little Quack's new friend*

Lambs *see* Animals — babies; Animals — sheep

Language

Alda, Arlene. *Did you say pears?*
Ayres, Katherine. *Up, down, and around*
Banks, Kate (Katherine A.). *Max's words*
Barretta, Gene. *Dear deer*
Brennan-Nelson, Denise. *My grandma likes to say*
Carr, Jan. *Greedy apostrophe*
Cleary, Brian P. *A lime, a mime, a pool of slime*
    Peanut butter and jellyfishes
Cousins, Lucy. *Maisy's amazing big book of words*
Dahl, Michael. *If you were an adjective*
Donohue, Moira Rose. *Alfie the apostrophe*
Feiffer, Kate. *Henry, the dog with no tail*
Groner, Judyth Saypol. *My first Hebrew word book*
Hambleton, Laura. *Monkey business*
Harper, Jo. *I could eat you up!*
Heidbreder, Robert. *Lickety-split*
Isadora, Rachel. *Yo, Jo!*
Jenkins, Steve. *Move!*
Keller, Laurie. *Do unto otters*
Kubler, Annie. *My first signs*
Lee, Tae-Jun. *Waiting for Mama*
Lewis, J. Patrick. *Big is big and little little*
Mora, Pat. *Yum! Mmmm! Que rico!*
Paul, Alison. *The crow (a not so scary story)*
Pulver, Robin. *Nouns and verbs have a field day*
Schotter, Roni. *The boy who loved words*
Seeger, Laura Vaccaro. *Walter was worried*
Shannon, David. *Oops!*
Trice, Linda. *Kenya's word*
Truss, Lynne. *Eats, shoots & leaves*
Walton, Rick. *Just me and 6,000 rats*
Wise, William. *Zany zoo*

Language — sign language *see* Sign language

Languages, foreign *see* Foreign languages

Latin America *see* Foreign lands — Latin America

Laundry

Willems, Mo. *Knuffle Bunny*

Law *see* Careers — police officers; Crime

Laziness *see* Character traits — laziness

Legends *see* Folk & fairy tales

Lenape Indians *see* Indians of North America — Lenape

Leopards *see* Animals — leopards

Leprechauns *see* Mythical creatures — leprechauns

Letters, cards

Anholt, Laurence. *Seven for a secret*
Christelow, Eileen. *Letters from a desperate dog*
Cole, Barbara Hancock. *Anna and Natalie*
Harley, Bill. *Dear Santa*
Heide, Iris van der. *A strange day*
Kempter, Christa. *Dear Little Lamb*
McElroy, Lisa Tucker. *Love, Lizzie*
Major, Kevin. *Aunt Olga's Christmas postcards*
Nolen, Jerdine. *Plantzilla goes to camp*
Pattison, Darcy. *Searching for Oliver K. Woodman*
Rand, Gloria. *A pen pal for Max*
Rylant, Cynthia. *If you'll be my Valentine*
Steffensmeier, Alexander. *Millie waits for the mail*
Straaten, Harmen van. *For me?*
Sullivan, Sarah. *Dear Baby*
Taback, Simms. *I miss you every day*
Wallace, Nancy Elizabeth. *Look! Look! Look!*
Wigersma, Tanneke. *Baby brother*
Zweibel, Alan. *Our tree named Steve*

Librarians *see* Careers — librarians

Libraries

Child, Lauren. *But, excuse me, that is my book*
Cousins, Lucy. *Maisy goes to the library*
Ivey, Randall. *Jay and the bounty of books*
Kirk, David. *Library mouse*
Knudsen, Michelle. *Library lion*
Lakin, Patricia. *Rainy day*
McDonald, Megan. *When the library lights go out*
McGee, Marni. *Winston the book wolf*
McQuinn, Anna. *Lola at the library*
Meng, Cece. *The wonderful thing about hiccups*
Morris, Carla. *The boy who was raised by librarians*
Sierra, Judy. *Mind your manners, B. B. Wolf*
Willis, Jeanne. *Delilah D. at the library*
Yoo, Taeeun. *The little red fish*

Light, lights

McDonald, Megan. *When the library lights go out*

Lightning *see* Weather — lightning, thunder

Lightning bugs *see* Insects — fireflies

Lions *see* Animals — lions

Littleness *see* Character traits — smallness

Lizards *see* Reptiles — lizards

Llamas *see* Animals — llamas

Lobsters *see* Crustaceans — lobsters

Loneliness *see* Emotions — loneliness

Losing things *see* Behavior — lost & found possessions

Lost *see* Behavior — lost

Love *see* Emotions — love

Luck *see* Character traits — luck

Lullabies

Davies, Jacqueline. *The night is singing*
Frazee, Marla. *Hush, little baby*
Kono, Erin Eitter. *Hula lullaby*
Newman, Leslea. *Daddy's song*
Noda, Takayo. *Song of the flowers*
Pinkney, J. Brian. *Hush, little baby*
Prap, Lila. *Animal lullabies*
Withrow, Sarah. *Be a baby*
Yolen, Jane. *Sleep, black bear, sleep*

Lying *see* Behavior — lying

Machines

Hudson, Cheryl Willis. *Construction zone*
Olson-Brown, Ellen. *Hush little digger*
Pallotta, Jerry. *The construction alphabet book*
Peterson, Cris. *Fantastic farm machines*
Rockwell, Anne F. *Good morning, Digger*
Schubert, Leda. *Here comes Darrell*
Varela, Barry. *Gizmo*

Magic

Andersen, H. C. (Hans Christian). *The tinderbox*
   The wild swans
Bateman, Teresa. *Hamster Camp*
Baynton, Martin. *Jane and the magician*
Begin, Mary Jane. *The sorcerer's apprentice*
Briggs, Raymond. *The puddleman*
Carmody, Isobelle. *Magic night*
Cate, Annette LeBlanc. *The magic rabbit*
Cole, Joanna. *The magic school bus and the science fair expedition*
David, Ryan. *The magic raincoat*
DeFelice, Cynthia C. *One potato, two potato*
Diakité, Baba Wagué. *Mee-an and the magic serpent*
Elschner, Geraldine. *Max's magic seeds*
Franson, Scott E. *Un-brella*
Garland, Michael. *King Puck*
   Miss Smith reads again!
Grimm, Jacob. *Snow White*
Hong, Chen Jiang. *The magic horse of Han Gan*
Kennedy, Kim. *Pirate Pete's giant adventure*
Kimmel, Eric A. *The three cabritos*
LaMarche, Jim. *Up*
Lucas, David. *Nutmeg*
MacDonald, Margaret Read. *The great smelly, slobbery small-toothed dog*
McPhail, David. *Water boy*
Meddaugh, Susan. *The witch's walking stick*
Newman, Marlene. *Myron's magic cow*
Norac, Carl. *My mommy is magic*
Pelletier, Andrew T. *The toy farmer*
Prelutsky, Jack. *The wizard*
Shepard, Aaron. *One-eye! Two-eyes! Three-eyes!*
Stainton, Sue. *The chocolate cat*
Vallverdu, Josep. *Aladdin and the magic lamp / Aldino y la lampara maravillosa*
Van Allsburg, Chris. *Probuditi!*
Willard, Nancy. *The flying bed*
Yoo, Taeeun. *The little red fish*

Magicians *see* Careers — magicians

Mail *see* Letters, cards

Mail carriers *see* Careers — postal workers; Letters, cards

Making things *see* Activities — making things

Mali *see* Foreign lands — Mali

Manners *see* Etiquette

Marionettes *see* Puppets

Markets *see* Stores

Marriages *see* Weddings

Mars *see* Planets

Marsupials *see* Animals — marsupials

Masks

Choi, Yangsook. *Behind the mask*

Math *see* Counting, numbers

Mazes

Philpot, Lorna. *Find Anthony Ant*

Meanness *see* Character traits — meanness

Measurement *see* Concepts — measurement

Meerkats *see* Animals — meerkats

Memories, memory

Cheng, Andrea. *The lemon sisters*
Cruise, Robin. *Little Mama forgets*
Lindbergh, Reeve. *My little grandmother often forgets*

Mermaids *see* Mythical creatures — mermaids, mermen

Merry-go-rounds

Cecil, Randy. *Gator*
Selick, Henry. *Moongirl*

Messy *see* Behavior — messy

Metamorphosis

Willis, Jeanne. *Tadpole's promise*

Meteorologists *see* Careers — meteorologists

Metis Indians *see* Indians of North America — Metis

Mexican Americans *see* Ethnic groups in the U.S. — Mexican Americans

Mexico *see* Foreign lands — Mexico

Mice *see* Animals — mice

Middle Ages

Adkins, Jan. *What if you met a knight?*
Dick Whittington and his cat. *Dick Whittington and his cat*
Nikola-Lisa, W. *Magic in the margins*

Middle East *see* Foreign lands — Middle East

Migrant workers *see* Careers — migrant workers

Migration

George, Jean Craighead. *Luck*
Madison, Alan. *Velma Gratch and the way cool butterfly*
Willis, Nancy Carol. *Red knot*

Military *see* Careers — military

Miners *see* Careers — miners

Minorities *see* Ethnic groups in the U.S.

Misbehavior *see* Behavior — misbehavior

Missions

Ryan, Pam Muñoz. *Nacho and Lolita*

Mist *see* Weather — fog

Mistakes *see* Behavior — mistakes

Misunderstanding *see* Behavior — misunderstanding

Mittens *see* Clothing — gloves, mittens

Moles *see* Animals — moles

Money

Harris, Trudy. *Jenny found a penny*
Marks, Jennifer L. *Sorting money*

Mongolia *see* Foreign lands — Mongolia

Monkeys *see* Animals — monkeys

Monsters

Bauer, Marion Dane. *I'm not afraid of Halloween!*
Baum, Louis. *The mouse who braved bedtime*
Beck, Scott. *Happy birthday, Monster!*
Emberley, Ed (Edward Randolph). *Ed Emberley's bye-bye, big bad bullybug!*
Flaherty, A. W. *The luck of the Loch Ness monster*
Funke, Cornelia. *The wildest brother*
Hazen, Barbara Shook. *Who is your favorite monster, mama?*
Hicks, Barbara Jean. *Jitterbug jam*
Kimmel, Eric A. *The three cabritos*
Kutner, Merrily. *The Zombie Nite Cafe*
McAllister, Angela. *Trust me, Mom!*
McKissack, Patricia C. *Precious and the Boo Hag*
Mayer, Mercer. *The bravest knight*
　There are monsters everywhere
Metz, Lorijo. *Floridius Bloom and the planet of Gloom*
Montes, Marisa. *Los gatos black on Halloween*
Moore, Lilian. *Beware, take care*
Neubecker, Robert. *Beasty bath*
Norac, Carl. *Monster, don't eat me!*
O'Connor, George. *Sally and the Some-Thing*
O'Keefe, Susan Heyboer. *Hungry monster ABC*
Pickering, Jimmy. *Skelly the skeleton girl*
Sage, James. *Mr. Beast*
Schaefer, Lola M. *Frankie Stein*
Selick, Henry. *Moongirl*
Sendak, Maurice. *Mommy?*
Sierra, Judy. *Thelonius Monster's sky-high fly pie*
Stein, David Ezra. *Monster hug!*
Stein, Mathilde. *Monstersong*
Stewart, Joel. *Dexter Bexley and the big blue beastie*
Taylor, Sean. *When a monster is born*
Thach, James Otis. *A child's guide to common household monsters*
Vestergaard, Hope. *What do you do when a monster says boo?*
Waechter, Phillip. *Rosie and the nightmares*
Willems, Mo. *Leonardo the terrible monster*
Wing, Natasha. *Go to bed, monster!*

Months of the year *see* Days of the week, months of the year

Moon

Aldrin, Buzz. *Reaching for the moon*
Brown, Margaret Wise. *Goodnight moon 123*
Cain, Sheridan. *By the light of the moon*

Côté, Geneviève. *With you always, Little Monday*
Florian, Douglas. *Comets, stars, the moon, and Mars*
Goldberg, Myla. *Catching the moon*
Lobel, Gillian. *Little Honey Bear and the smiley moon*
McCarty, Peter. *Moon plane*
McNulty, Faith. *If you decide to go to the moon*
Morrissey, Dean. *The crimson comet*
Nishimura, Kae. *Bunny Lune*
Rowe, John A. *Moondog*
Rymond, Lynda Gene. *Oscar and the mooncats*
Selick, Henry. *Moongirl*
Shulman, Lisa. *The moon might be milk*
Stevenson, Robert Louis. *The moon*
Ward, Helen. *Little Moon Dog*

Moose *see* Animals — moose

Morning

Freedman, Claire. *One magical morning*
Hayward, Linda. *The King's chorus*
Mortensen, Denise Dowling. *Wake up engines*
Stevens, April. *Waking up Wendell*
Votaw, Carol. *Good morning, little polar bear*
Weninger, Brigitte. *"Mom, wake up and play!"*
Yi, Hu Yong. *Good morning China*

Morocco *see* Foreign lands — Morocco

Moses *see* Religion — Moses

Mothers *see* Family life — mothers; Family life — parents; Family life — single-parent families; Family life — step families

Moths *see* Insects — moths

Motion *see* Concepts — motion

Motorcycles

O'Malley, Kevin. *Once upon a cool motorcycle dude*
Whitehead, Kathy. *Looking for Uncle Louie on the Fourth of July*

Mountain climbing *see* Sports — mountain climbing

Mountain lions *see* Animals — cougars

Mountains

Gill, Shelley. *Up on Denali*
Schmidt, Karen Lee. *Carl's nose*

Moving

Beake, Lesley. *Home now*
Crum, Shutta. *A family for Old Mill Farm*
Gleeson, Libby. *Half a world away*
Lears, Laurie. *Megan's birthday tree*
Lobel, Anita. *Nini here and there*
Meltzer, Amy. *A mezuzah on the door*
Michelin, Linda (Donald B.). *Zuzu's wishing cake*
Smith, Dana Kessimakis. *A brave spaceboy*

Multiple births — triplets

Jenkins, Emily. *Daffodil*
　Daffodil, crocodile

Multiple births — twins

Arnold, Tedd. *The twin princes*
Barber, Tiki. *Game day*
　Teammates
LaReau, Kara. *Rocko and Spanky have company*
Lewison, Wendy Cheyette. *Two is for twins*

Rockwell, Anne F. *Brendan and Belinda and the slam dunk!*
Ryder, Joanne. *A pair of polar bears*
Voake, Charlotte. *Hello twins*
Yang, Belle. *Always come home to me*

Mummies

Schachner, Judith Byron. *Skippyjon Jones in mummy trouble*

Museums

Hooper, Meredith. *Celebrity cat*
Hopkins, Lee Bennett. *Behind the museum door*
Lehman, Barbara. *Museum trip*
Mauner, Claudia. *Zoe Sophia in New York*
The Metropolitan Museum of Art, NY. *Museum shapes*
Ruzzier, Sergio. *The room of wonders*
Whybrow, Ian. *Harry and the dinosaurs at the museum*

Music

Ancona, George. *Mi música / My music*
Bateman, Teresa. *Traveling Tom and the leprechaun*
Berkner, Laurie. *The story of my feelings*
Bosca, Francesca. *The three grasshoppers*
Cabrera, Jane. *If you're happy and you know it*
Chernaik, Judith. *Carnival of the animals*
Daly, Niki. *Ruby sings the blues*
Dillon, Leo. *Jazz on a Saturday night*
Ehrhardt, Karen. *This jazz man*
Falconer, Ian. *Olivia forms a band*
Frazee, Marla. *Hush, little baby*
Here we go round the mulberry bush
High, Linda Oatman. *Cool Bopper's choppers*
Horowitz, Dave. *Soon, Baboon, soon*
Hyde, Heidi Smith. *Mendel's accordion*
Jenkins, Emily. *Plonk, plonk, plonk!*
Johnson, James Weldon. *Lift every voice and sing*
Kimmel, Eric A. *The three cabritos*
Krosoczka, Jarrett J. *Punk Farm*
Madison, Alan. *Pecorino's first concert*
Martin, Jacqueline Briggs. *Chicken joy on Redbean Road*
Mayer, Mercer. *The little drummer mouse*
Michelson, Richard. *Across the alley*
Milgrim, David. *Young MacDonald*
Moore, Mary-Alice. *The wheels on the school bus*
Olson-Brown, Ellen. *Hush little digger*
Palatini, Margie. *The cheese*
Pinkney, Gloria Jean. *Music from our Lord's holy heaven*
Pinkney, J. Brian. *Hush, little baby*
Pritchett, Dylan. *The first music*
Roth, Susan L. *Do re mi*
Sciurba, Katie. *Oye, Celia!*
Seeger, Pete. *The deaf musicians*
Shea, Pegi Deitz. *The boy and the spell*
Shulevitz, Uri. *So sleepy story*
Sís, Peter. *Play, Mozart, play*
Tashiro, Chisato. *Five nice mice*
Trapani, Iza. *Jingle bells*
Watts, Leslie Elizabeth. *The Baabaasheep Quartet*
Wheeler, Lisa. *Jazz baby*
Winter, Jonah. *Dizzy*
Yarrow, Peter. *Puff, the magic dragon*

Musical instruments

Horowitz, Dave. *Soon, Baboon, soon*
Madison, Alan. *Pecorino's first concert*

Musical instruments — accordions

Hyde, Heidi Smith. *Mendel's accordion*

Musical instruments — banjos

Busse, Sarah Martin. *Banjo granny*

Musical instruments — drums

Mayer, Mercer. *The little drummer mouse*
Protopopescu, Orel. *Two sticks*

Musical instruments — fiddles *see* Musical instruments — violins

Musical instruments — orchestras

Tripp, Paul. *Tubby the tuba*

Musical instruments — saxophones

High, Linda Oatman. *Cool Bopper's choppers*

Musical instruments — tubas

Tripp, Paul. *Tubby the tuba*

Musical instruments — violins

Otsuka, Yuzo. *Suho's white horse*

Musicians *see* Careers — musicians

Muskrats *see* Animals — muskrats

Mystery stories

Mauner, Claudia. *Zoe Sophia in New York*
Selznick, Brian. *The invention of Hugo Cabret*
Sneed, Brad. *Deputy Harvey and the ant cow caper*
Wick, Walter. *I spy treasure hunt*

Mythical creatures

Carmody, Isobelle. *Magic night*
Carroll, Lewis. *Jabberwocky*
Mayer, Mercer. *The bravest knight*

Mythical creatures — elves

Grimm, Jacob. *The elves and the shoemaker*
Kimmel, Eric A. *Rip Van Winkle's return*

Mythical creatures — genies

Lucas, David. *Nutmeg*

Mythical creatures — leprechauns

Bateman, Teresa. *Fiona's luck*
  Traveling Tom and the leprechaun
Bunting, Eve (Anne Evelyn). *That's what leprechauns do*
Krensky, Stephen. *Too many leprechauns*

Mythical creatures — mermaids, mermen

Sperring, Mark. *Mermaid dreams*

Mythical creatures — ogres

Cole, Brock. *Good enough to eat*

Mythical creatures — trolls

Bolliger, Max. *The happy troll*
Mayer, Mercer. *The bravest knight*
Palatini, Margie. *The three silly billies*
Root, Phyllis. *Lucia and the light*

Mythical creatures — unicorns

Reed, Neil. *The midnight unicorn*

Name calling *see* Behavior — name calling

Names

Foreman, George. *Let George do it!*
Gadot, A. S. *The first gift*
Raschka, Chris. *New York is English, Chattanooga is Creek*

Napping *see* Sleep

Native Americans *see* Indians of North America

Nativity *see* Religion — Nativity

Nature

Appelt, Kathi. *My father's house*
Arnosky, Jim. *Babies in the bayou*
    Parrotfish and sunken ships
Bevis, Mary. *Wolf song*
Blaikie, Lynn. *Beyond the northern lights*
Chrustowski, Rick. *Turtle crossing*
Cole, Henry. *On Meadowview Street*
Corr, Christopher. *Whole world*
DePalma, Mary Newell. *A grand old tree*
Ehlert, Lois. *Leaf man*
Ferri, Giuliano. *Little Tad grows up*
Fisher, Aileen Lucia. *Do rabbits have Christmas?*
    The story goes on
George, Lindsay Barrett. *In the garden*
Gershator, Phillis. *Listen, listen*
Giogas, Valarie. *In my backyard*
Guiberson, Brenda Z. *Mud city*
Horacek, Petr. *Butterfly butterfly*
Issa, Kobayashi. *Today and today*
Jackson, Ellen B. *Earth Mother*
Johnston, Tony. *The whole green world*
Jolivet, Joëlle. *Almost everything*
Kurtz, Kevin. *A day in the salt marsh*
McCarthy, Mary. *A closer look*
MacLachlan, Patricia. *Fiona loves the night*
McNamara, Margaret. *Fall leaf project*
Markle, Sandra. *Little lost bat*
Martin, Bill, Jr. (William Ivan). *I love our Earth*
Miles, Victoria. *Old mother bear*
Oliver, Narelle. *Twilight hunt*
Poppenhäger, Nicole. *Snow leopards*
Powell, Consie. *The first day of winter*
Raczka, Bob. *Spring things*
Rotner, Shelley. *Every season*
Ruurs, Margriet. *In my backyard*
Rylant, Cynthia. *The stars will still shine*
Schwartz, Roslyn. *Tales from Parc la Fontaine*
Shannon, George. *White is for blueberry*
Sidman, Joyce. *Butterfly eyes and other secrets of the meadow*
    Song of the water boatman
Walsh, Melanie. *Do lions live on lily pads?*
Wood, Douglas. *The secret of saying thanks*

Naughty *see* Behavior — misbehavior

Neckties *see* Clothing — neckties

Negotiation *see* Activities — trading

Neighborhoods *see* Communities, neighborhoods

Nepal *see* Foreign lands — Nepal

New Year's *see* Holidays — New Year's

Night

Almond, David. *Kate, the cat and the moon*
Bean, Jonathan. *At night*
Brunelle, Nicholas. *Snow Moon*
Davies, Jacqueline. *The night is singing*
Davies, Nicola. *White owl, barn owl*
Deacon, Alexis. *While you are sleeping*
Ford, Bernette G. *First snow*
Harris, Peter. *The night pirates*
Hartland, Jessie. *Night shift*
Hoberman, Mary Ann. *I'm going to Grandma's*
Kudlinski, Kathleen V. *The sunset switch*
MacLachlan, Patricia. *Fiona loves the night*
Morales, Yuyi. *Little night*
Murphy, Stuart J. *It's about time!*
Rockwell, Anne F. *Here comes the night*
Serfozo, Mary. *Whooo's there?*
Shulevitz, Uri. *So sleepy story*
Thomas, Patricia. *Firefly mountain*
Tillman, Nancy. *On the night you were born*
Waddell, Martin. *Sleep tight, Little Bear*
Weston, Carrie. *If a chicken stayed for supper*

Nightmares

Durango, Julia. *Dream hop*
Johnson, Lindan Lee. *The dream jar*
Waechter, Phillip. *Rosie and the nightmares*

No text *see* Wordless

Noah *see* Religion — Noah

Noise, sounds

Arnold, Marsha Diane. *Roar of a snore*
Baddiel, Ivor. *Cock-a-doodle quack! Quack!*
Bee, William. *And the train goes . . .*
Butler, John. *Can you growl like a bear?*
Crimi, Carolyn. *The Louds move in!*
Cumberbatch, Judy. *Can you hear the sea?*
Daly, Niki. *Ruby sings the blues*
Davies, Jacqueline. *The night is singing*
DiPucchio, Kelly S. *Dinosnores*
Fleming, Denise. *The cow who clucked*
Gershator, Phillis. *Listen, listen*
Glass, Beth Raisner. *Noises at night*
Johnson, David. *Snow sounds*
London, Jonathan. *A train goes clickety-clack*
    A truck goes rattley-bumpa
MacDonald, Margaret Read. *The squeaky door*
Mayo, Margaret. *Choo choo clickety-clack!*
Mozelle, Shirley. *The bear upstairs*
Murphy, Yannick. *Ahwooooooo!*
Park, Linda Sue. *Yum! Yuck!*
Pearson, Debora. *Big city song*
Polacco, Patricia. *Mommies say shhh!*
Rozen, Anna. *The merchant of noises*
Schwartz, Corey Rosen. *Hop! Plop!*
Singer, Marilyn. *City lullaby*
Stevens, April. *Waking up Wendell*
Wolff, Ferida. *It is the wind*

North Pole *see* Foreign lands — Arctic

Noses *see* Senses — smell

Numbers *see* Counting, numbers

Nursery rhymes

Butler, John. *Ten in the den*
Delessert, Etienne. *A was an apple pie*
Edwards, Pamela Duncan. *The neat line*
Fitzgerald, Joanne. *Yum! Yum!*
Grey, Mini. *The adventures of the dish and the spoon*
Harris, Trudy. *Twenty hungry piggies*
Martin, Bill, Jr. (William Ivan). *"Fire! Fire!" Said Mrs. McGuire*
Mother Goose. *Little Miss Muffet*
    Mother Goose numbers on the loose
    Pat-a-cake
Pearson, Tracey Campbell. *Diddle diddle dumpling*
Pierce, Terry. *Counting your way*
Spirin, Gennady. *A apple pie*
Zalben, Jane Breskin. *Hey, Mama Goose*

Nursery school *see* School — nursery

Occupations *see* Careers

Oceans *see* Sea & seashore

Octopuses

Scieszka, Jon. *Cowboy and Octopus*

Odors *see* Senses — smell

Ogres *see* Mythical creatures — ogres

Old age

Alsenas, Linas. *Peanut*
Arnosky, Jim. *Grandfather Buffalo*
Barbour, Karen. *Mr. Williams*
Best, Cari. *Are you going to be good?*
Bley, Anette. *And what comes after a thousand?*
Cheng, Andrea. *The lemon sisters*
Cruise, Robin. *Little Mama forgets*
Grimm, Jacob. *The Bremen town musicians*
    Musicians of Bremen
    Musicians of Bremen / Los musicos de Bremner
Lindbergh, Reeve. *My little grandmother often forgets*

Olympics *see* Sports — Olympics

Only child *see* Family life — only child

Opossums *see* Animals — possums

Opposites *see* Concepts — opposites

Orangutans *see* Animals — orangutans

Orchestras *see* Musical instruments — orchestras

Orderliness *see* Character traits — orderliness

Orphans

Beake, Lesley. *Home now*
Godden, Rumer. *The story of Holly and Ivy*
Joosse, Barbara M. *Nikolai, the only bear*
Noyes, Deborah. *When I met the wolf girls*

Odone, Jamison. *Honey badgers*
Selznick, Brian. *The invention of Hugo Cabret*

Otters *see* Animals — otters

Outer space *see* Space & space ships

Owls *see* Birds — owls

Pack rats *see* Animals — pack rats

Painters *see* Activities — painting; Careers — painters

Painting *see* Activities — painting

Pajamas *see* Clothing — pajamas

Palestine *see* Foreign lands — Palestine

Panama *see* Foreign lands — Panama

Pandas *see* Animals — pandas

Panthers *see* Animals — leopards

Parades

Bond, Rebecca. *The great doughnut parade*
Whitehead, Kathy. *Looking for Uncle Louie on the Fourth of July*
Ziefert, Harriet. *Circus parade*

Parks

Becker, Shari. *Maxwell's mountain*
Schwartz, Roslyn. *Tales from Parc la Fontaine*

Parks — amusement

Cecil, Randy. *Gator*
Gavril, David. *Penelope Nuthatch and the big surprise*
Rogalski, Mark. *Tickets to ride*
Ziefert, Harriet. *Fun Land fun!*

Parrots *see* Birds — parrots

Parties

Anholt, Catherine. *Happy birthday, Chimp and Zee*
Asher, Sandy. *What a party!*
Baker, Roberta. *Olive's pirate party*
Beck, Scott. *Happy birthday, Monster!*
Berry, Lynne. *The curious demise of a contrary cat*
Best, Cari. *Are you going to be good?*
Buehner, Caralyn. *Snowmen at Christmas*
Chess, Victoria. *The costume party*
Elya, Susan Middleton. *F is for fiesta*
Evans, Cambria. *Martha moth makes socks*
Ford, Bernette G. *No more bottles for Bunny!*
Foreman, George. *Let George do it!*
Harper, Charise Mericle. *When Randolph turned rotten*
Howe, James. *Houndsley and Catina and the birthday surprise*
McDonald, Megan. *Ant and Honey Bee, what a pair!*
McElligott, Matthew. *Backbeard and the birthday suit*
Mora, Pat. *Marimba!*
Numeroff, Laura Joffe. *If you give a pig a party*
Paul, Ann Whitford. *Mañana Iguana*

Raschka, Chris. *New York is English, Chattanooga is Creek*
Schaefer, Carole Lexa. *The Bora-Bora dress*
Schotter, Roni. *Mama, I'll give you the world*
Stadler, Alexander. *Beverly Billingsly takes the cake*
Sturges, Philemon. *This little pirate*
Willems, Mo. *I am invited to a party!*

Passamaquoddy Indians *see* Indians of North America
— Passamaquoddy

Passover *see* Holidays — Passover

Patience *see* Character traits — patience

Patterns *see* Concepts — patterns

Pelicans *see* Birds — pelicans

Pen pals

Brownlow, Mike. *Mickey Moonbeam*
Kempter, Christa. *Dear Little Lamb*
Murphy, Stuart J. *Polly's pen pal*
Rand, Gloria. *A pen pal for Max*

Penguins *see* Birds — penguins

Perfectionism *see* Character traits — perfectionism

Perseverance *see* Character traits — perseverance

Persia *see* Foreign lands — Persia

Persistence *see* Character traits — persistence

Perspective *see* Concepts — perspective

Pets

Alsenas, Linas. *Peanut*
Bachelet, Gilles. *My cat, the silliest cat in the world*
    When the silliest cat was small
Bedford, David. *The way I love you*
Berenzy, Alix. *Sammy*
Boelts, Maribeth. *Before you were mine*
Bunting, Eve (Anne Evelyn). *Emma's turtle*
Calmenson, Stephanie. *May I pet your dog?*
Chichester Clark, Emma. *Will and Squill*
Clements, Andrew. *Dogku*
    Slippers loves to run
Cochran, Bill. *The forever dog*
Davidson, Ellen Dee. *Princess Justina Albertina*
dePaola, Tomie. *Little Grunt and the big egg*
Dodds, Dayle Ann. *Teacher's pets*
Dubosarsky, Ursula. *Rex*
Elschner, Geraldine. *Fritz's fish*
Fraser, Mary Ann. *I.Q. gets fit*
    I.Q., it's time
Gay, Marie-Louise. *What are you doing, Sam?*
Goldfinger, Jennifer P. *My dog Lyle*
Graham, Bob. *"The trouble with dogs," said Dad*
Grimes, Nikki. *When Gorilla goes walking*
Heide, Florence Parry. *A promise is a promise*
Heiligman, Deborah. *Fun dog, sun dog*
Hogg, Gary. *Look what the cat dragged in!*
Imai, Ayano. *Chester*
Katz, Susan. *Oh, Theodore!*
Kroll, Virginia L. *Really rabbits*
Kwon, Yoon-duck. *My cat copies me*
Lee, Spike. *Please, puppy, please*
Lewis, Kim. *A puppy for Annie*
Perret, Delphine. *The Big Bad Wolf and me*
Plourde, Lynn. *Dino pets*
Polacco, Patricia. *Ginger and Petunia*
Ries, Lori. *Aggie and Ben*

Robbins, Jacqui. *The new girl . . . and me*
Robertson, M. P. *Hieronymous Betts and his unusual pets*
Samuels, Barbara. *Dolores meets her match*
Schwartz, Amy. *Oscar*
Simeon, Jean-Pierre. *This is a poem that heals fish*
Smath, Jerry. *Sammy Salami*
Swaim, Jessica. *The hound from the pound*
Umansky, Kaye. *I don't like Gloria!*
Urbanovic, Jackie. *Duck at the door*
Verdick, Elizabeth. *Tails are not for pulling*
Weigelt, Udo. *Super Guinea Pig to the rescue*
Weninger, Brigitte. *Miko wants a dog*
Winstead, Rosie. *Ruby and Bubbles*
Yaccarino, Dan. *The birthday fish*

Photography *see* Activities — photographing

Physical handicaps *see* Handicaps — physical handicaps

Physicians *see* Careers — doctors

Picnics *see* Activities — picnicking

Picture puzzles

Behrens, Janice. *Let's find rain forest animals*
Carter, David A. *Blue 2*
    One red dot
    600 black spots
    Whoo? Whoo?
Cleary, Brian P. *Peanut butter and jellyfishes*
Gannij, Joan. *Elusive moose*
Garland, Michael. *The great Easter egg hunt*
Kamm, Katja. *Invisible*
Khing, T. T. *Where is the cake?*
Kidslabel. *Spot 7: Christmas*
    Spot 7: School
Ljungkvist, Laura. *Follow the line*
    Follow the line through the house
Munro, Roxie. *Amazement Park*
    Circus
    Mazeways
Nickle, John. *Alphabet explosion!*
Oliver, Narelle. *Twilight hunt*
Onishi, Satoru. *Who's hiding*
Philpot, Lorna. *Find Anthony Ant*
Whybrow, Ian. *Faraway farm*
Wick, Walter. *Can you see what I see? Once upon a time*
    Can you see what I see? Seymour makes new friends: a search and find storybook
    I spy treasure hunt
Ziefert, Harriet. *Messy Bessie*

Pigeons *see* Birds — pigeons

Pigs *see* Animals — pigs

Pilots *see* Careers — airplane pilots

Pima Indians *see* Indians of North America — Pima

Pioneer life *see* U.S. history — frontier & pioneer life

Pirates

Andreae, Giles. *Captain Flinn and the pirate dinosaurs*
Baker, Roberta. *Olive's pirate party*
Crimi, Carolyn. *Henry and the Buccaneer Bunnies*
Funke, Cornelia. *Pirate girl*
Harris, Peter. *The night pirates*
Kennedy, Kim. *Pirate Pete's giant adventure*
Krupinski, Loretta. *Pirate treasure*
Lasky, Kathryn. *Pirate Bob*
Leuck, Laura. *I love my pirate papa*
Long, Melinda. *Pirates don't change diapers*

McElligott, Matthew. *Backbeard and the birthday suit*
McNaughton, Colin. *Captain Abdul's little treasure*
O'Malley, Kevin. *Captain Raptor and the space pirates*
Sobel, June. *Shiver me letters*
Sturges, Philemon. *This little pirate*
Wick, Walter. *I spy treasure hunt*

Planes *see* Airplanes, airports

Planets

Florian, Douglas. *Comets, stars, the moon, and Mars*
Gibbons, Gail. *The planets*

Plants

Gibbons, Gail. *The vegetables we eat*
Henkes, Kevin. *So happy!*
Hester, Denia Lewis. *Grandma Lena's big ol' turnip*
Himmelman, John. *Mouse in a meadow*
Hobbie, Holly. *Toot and Puddle*
Jack and the beanstalk. *Jack and the beanstalk*
Ketteman, Helen. *Waynetta and the cornstalk*
Kudlinski, Kathleen V. *What do roots do?*
The little red hen. *The little red hen*
    The little red hen: an old fable
McGrath, Barbara Barbieri. *The little green witch*
McKy, Katie. *Pumpkin town!*
Meddaugh, Susan. *Just Teenie*
Mitchell, Susan K. *The rainforest grew all around*
Nolen, Jerdine. *Plantzilla goes to camp*
Poole, Amy Lowry. *The pea blossom*

Platypuses *see* Animals — platypuses

Playing *see* Activities — playing

Plays *see* Theater

Poetry

Andreae, Giles. *Dinosaurs galore!*
Appelt, Kathi. *My father's house*
Archer, Peggy. *From dawn to dreams*
Bagert, Brod. *Shout!*
Belle, Jennifer. *Animal stackers*
Brooks, Gwendolyn. *Bronzeville boys and girls*
Brown, Margaret Wise. *Nibble, nibble*
Carroll, Lewis. *Jabberwocky*
Chernaik, Judith. *Carnival of the animals*
Clements, Andrew. *Dogku*
Crawley, Dave. *Cat poems*
Creech, Sharon. *Who's that baby?*
Danneberg, Julie. *Cowboy Slim*
Dawes, Kwame Senu Neville. *I saw your face*
Dotlich, Rebecca Kai. *What is science?*
Downes, Belinda. *Baby days*
Farber, Norma. *How the hibernators came to Bethlehem*
Field, Rachel Lyman. *Grace for an island meal*
Fischer, Scott M. *Twinkle*
Fisher, Aileen Lucia. *Do rabbits have Christmas?*
    The story goes on
Florian, Douglas. *Comets, stars, the moon, and Mars*
    Handsprings
    Zoo's who
Forman, Ruth. *Young Cornrows callin out the moon*
Frampton, David. *Mr. Ferlinghetti's poem*
Frank, John. *How to catch a fish*
Gilchrist, Jan Spivey. *My America*
Greenberg, David (David T.). *Don't forget your etiquette!*
Greenfield, Eloise. *The friendly four*
Grimes, Nikki. *Danitra Brown, class clown*
    When Gorilla goes walking
Gutman, Dan. *Casey back at bat*
Hague, Michael. *Animal friends*
Hopkins, Lee Bennett. *Behind the museum door*

Horton, Joan. *Hippopotamus stew*
Issa, Kobayashi. *Today and today*
Katz, Bobbi. *Once around the sun*
Katz, Susan. *Oh, Theodore!*
Krauss, Ruth. *Bears*
Kumin, Maxine W. *Mites to astodons*
Kuskin, Karla. *Toots the cat*
Larios, Julie Hofstrand. *Yellow elephant*
Lear, Edward. *The owl and the pussycat*
    The Quangle Wangle's hat
Lillegard, Dee. *Go!*
Lin, Grace. *Robert's snowflakes*
Livingston, Myra Cohn. *Calendar*
MacDonald, Suse. *Edward Lear's A was once an apple pie*
Moore, Clement Clarke. *A creature was stirring*
    The night before Christmas, ill. by Lisbeth Zwerger
    The night before Christmas, ill. by Richard Jesse Watson
    The night before Christmas, ill. by Will Moses
    The night before Christmas, ill. by Gennady Spirin
Moore, Lilian. *Beware, take care*
Mora, Pat. *Yum! Mmmm! Que rico!*
Mozelle, Shirley. *The kitchen talks*
Pearson, Susan. *Slugs in love*
Prelutsky, Jack. *Behold the bold umbrellaphant and other poems*
    Good sports
    It's snowing! It's snowing!
    Me I am!
    What a day it was at school!
Quattlebaum, Mary. *Winter friends*
Richards, Beah E. *Keep climbing, girls*
Ruddell, Deborah. *Today at the bluebird cafe*
Ryder, Joanne. *Toad by the road*
Schertle, Alice. *We*
Schwartz, David M. *Where in the wild*
Shannon, George. *Busy in the garden*
Sidman, Joyce. *Butterfly eyes and other secrets of the meadow*
    Meow ruff
    Song of the water boatman
Silvano, Wendi. *What does the wind say?*
Simeon, Jean-Pierre. *This is a poem that heals fish*
Spinelli, Eileen. *Polar bear, arctic hare*
Stevenson, Robert Louis. *Block city*
    The moon
Wells, Rosemary. *Carry me!*
Wood, Audrey. *Silly Sally*
Xinran, Xue. *Motherbridge of love*

Poland *see* Foreign lands — Poland

Polar bears *see* Animals — polar bears

Police officers *see* Careers — police officers

Polio *see* Illness — poliomyelitis

Ponds *see* Lakes, ponds

Ponies *see* Animals — horses, ponies

Poor *see* Homeless; Poverty

Pop-up books *see* Format, unusual — toy & movable books

Porcupines *see* Animals — porcupines

Possums *see* Animals — possums

Postal workers *see* Careers — postal workers

Potty training *see* Toilet training

Poverty

Mahy, Margaret. *Down the back of the chair*

Powhatan Indians *see* Indians of North America —
    Powhatan

Prairie dogs *see* Animals — prairie dogs

Prehistory

Dolenz, Micky. *Gakky Two-Feet*
Jenkins, Steve. *Prehistoric actual size*
Roth, Susan L. *Great big guinea pigs*
Sabuda, Robert. *Encyclopedia prehistorica: dinosaurs*
    Encyclopedia prehistorica: mega-beasts
    Encyclopedia prehistorica: sharks and other seamonsters

Prejudice

Amado, Elisa. *Tricycle*
Barbour, Karen. *Mr. Williams*
Birtha, Becky. *Grandmama's pride*
Edwards, Pamela Duncan. *The bus ride that changed history*
Giovanni, Nikki. *Rosa*
Gruska, Denise. *The only boy in ballet class*
Haskins, Jim (James). *Delivering justice*
Hume, Lachie. *Clancy the courageous cow*
Lorbiecki, Marybeth. *Jackie's bat*
Michelson, Richard. *Across the alley*
Rappaport, Doreen. *The school is not white!*
Shore, Diane Z. *This is the dream*
Sidjanski, Brigitte. *Little Chicken and Little Duck*
Weatherford, Carole Boston. *Champions on the bench*
    Freedom on the menu

Preschool *see* School — nursery

Pride *see* Character traits — pride

Princes *see* Royalty — princes

Princesses *see* Royalty — princesses

Problem solving

Brown, Jeff. *Flat Stanley*
Dierssen, Andreas. *The old red tractor*
George, Lindsay Barrett. *In the garden*
Harvey, Damian. *Just the thing!*
Hester, Denia Lewis. *Grandma Lena's big ol' turnip*
McCully, Emily Arnold. *Marvelous Mattie*
Souhami, Jessica. *The little, little house*
Tauss, Marc. *Superhero*
Weeks, Sarah. *Ella, of course!*

Puerto Ricans *see* Ethnic groups in the U.S. — Puerto
    Rican Americans

Puerto Rico *see* Foreign lands — Puerto Rico

Puffins *see* Birds — puffins

Pumas *see* Animals — cougars

Puppets

McDonald, Megan. *When the library lights go out*

Puzzles *see also* Picture puzzles; Rebuses; Riddles &
    jokes
Fisher, Valorie. *How high can a dinosaur count?*
Philpot, Lorna. *Find Anthony Ant*

Queens *see* Royalty — queens

Questioning *see* Character traits — questioning

Quilts

Hoberman, Mary Ann. *I'm going to Grandma's*
Van Leeuwen, Jean. *Papa and the pioneer quilt*
Wallace, Nancy Elizabeth. *The kindness quilt*
Woodson, Jacqueline. *Show way*

Rabbits *see* Animals — rabbits

Raccoons *see* Animals — raccoons

Race relations *see* Prejudice

Racially mixed *see* Ethnic groups in the U.S. — Racially
    mixed

Racing *see* Sports — racing

Railroads *see* Trains

Rain *see* Weather — rain

Ramadan *see* Holidays — Ramadan

Ranchers *see* Careers — ranchers

Rats *see* Animals — rats

Reading *see* Books, reading

Rebuses

Neitzel, Shirley. *Who will I be?*
Rau, Dana Meachen. *Flying*
    Riding
    Rolling

Religion

Appelt, Kathi. *My father's house*
Bible. Old Testament. Ecclesiastes. *To everything there is a season*
Bible. Old Testament. Genesis. *The Genesis of it all*
Bible. Old Testament. Psalms. *The Lord is my shepherd*
Bible. Old Testament. Psalms. *I will rejoice*
Bible. Old Testament. Ruth. *Ruth and Naomi*
A children's treasury of prayers
Cohen, Deborah Bodin. *Papa Jethro*
Egielski, Richard. *St. Francis and the wolf*
Farber, Norma. *How the hibernators came to Bethlehem*
Field, Rachel Lyman. *Grace for an island meal*
Gadot, A. S. *The first gift*

Gibfried, Diane. *Brother Juniper*
Gold, August. *Does God hear my prayer?*
Jeffs, Stephanie. *Jenny*
　　Josh
Jules, Jacqueline. *Abraham's search for God*
Katz, Karen. *My first Ramadan*
Kimmel, Eric A. *The lady in the blue cloak*
Kropf, Latifa Berry. *It's Shofar time!*
Langton, Jane. *Saint Francis and the wolf*
Let it shine
Mora, Pat. *The song of Francis and the animals*
Nelson, Kadir. *He's got the whole world in His hands*
Pinkney, Gloria Jean. *Music from our Lord's holy heaven*
Rock, Lois. *A child's book of graces*
Schotter, Roni. *Passover!*
Thomas, Joyce Carol. *Shouting*
Vischer, Phil. *Sidney and Norman*
Wells, Rosemary. *The miraculous tale of the two Maries*
Wood, Nancy C. *Mr. and Mrs. God in the creation kitchen*

Religion — Daniel

Hartman, Bob. *Dinner in the lions' den*

Religion — Islam

Mobin-Uddin, Asma. *The best Eid holiday ever*

Religion — Moses

Hodges, Margaret. *Moses*
Topek, Susan Remick. *Ten good rules*

Religion — Nativity

Brebeuf, Jean de. *The Huron carol*
Chaconas, Dori. *Christmas mouseling*
Cotten, Cynthia. *This is the stable*
Crisp, Marty. *The most precious gift*
Joslin, Mary. *On that Christmas night*
McCaughrean, Geraldine. *Father and son*
Mayer, Mercer. *The little drummer mouse*
Morpurgo, Michael. *On angel wings*
Nazoa, Aquiles. *A small Nativity*
Pasquali, Elena. *Ituku's Christmas journey*
Ryan, Pam Muñoz. *There was no snow on Christmas Eve*
Slate, Joseph. *What star is this?*
Spirin, Gennady. *We three kings*
Wilson, Karma. *Mortimer's Christmas manger*

Religion — Noah

Greene, Rhonda Gowler. *Noah and the mighty ark*
Lunge-Larsen, Lise. *Noah's mittens*
Mitton, Tony. *All afloat on Noah's boat!*
Stewig, John Warren. *The animals watched*

Remembering *see* Memories, memory

Repetitive stories *see* Cumulative tales

Reptiles — alligators, crocodiles

Bergman, Mara. *Snip snap!*
Cecil, Randy. *Gator*
Chichester Clark, Emma. *Melrose and Croc*
Cousins, Lucy. *Maisy, Charley, and the wobbly tooth*
Donnio, Sylviane. *I'd really like to eat a child*
Federspiel, Jurg. *Alligator Mike*
Huggins, Peter. *Trosclair and the alligator*
Kimmelman, Leslie. *How do I love you?*
Kleven, Elisa. *The wishing ball*
Lakin, Patricia. *Rainy day*
Morris, Jennifer E. *May I please have a cookie?*
Palatini, Margie. *No biting, Louise*
Polhemus, Coleman. *The crocodile blues*
Protopopescu, Orel. *Two sticks*

Rowe, John A. *I want a hug*
Rylant, Cynthia. *Alligator boy*
Schubert, Ingrid. *There's a crocodile under my bed!*
Tourville, Amanda Doering. *A crocodile grows up*

Reptiles — chameleons

Cowley, Joy. *Chameleon, chameleon*
Dubosarsky, Ursula. *Rex*

Reptiles — crocodiles *see* Reptiles — alligators, crocodiles

Reptiles — iguanas

Paul, Ann Whitford. *Mañana Iguana*
Robbins, Jacqui. *The new girl . . . and me*

Reptiles — lizards

Leedy, Loreen. *The great graph contest*
Murphy, Stuart J. *Leaping lizards*

Reptiles — snakes

Arnosky, Jim. *Coyote raid in Cactus Canyon*
Aruego, Jose. *The last laugh*
Diakité, Baba Wagué. *Mee-an and the magic serpent*
Hayes, Joe. *The gum-chewing rattler*
Jarman, Julia. *Class Two at the zoo*
Keller, Holly. *Help!*
McPhail, David. *Sylvie and True*

Reptiles — turtles, tortoises

Aesop. *The hare and the tortoise / La liebre y la tortuga*
Bauer, Marion Dane. *A mama for Owen*
Bunting, Eve (Anne Evelyn). *Emma's turtle*
Chrustowski, Rick. *Turtle crossing*
Fleming, Candace. *Sunny Boy!*
George, Margaret. *Lucille lost*
Gorbachev, Valeri. *Heron and Turtle*
　　Red red red
Himmelman, John. *Tudley didn't know*
Johnson, Rebecca. *Sea turtle's clever plan*
Luthardt, Kevin. *You're weird!*
Swinburne, Stephen R. *Turtle tide*
Tingle, Tim. *When turtle grew feathers*
Williams, Barbara. *Albert's gift for grandmother*
Winter, Jeanette. *Mama*

Resourcefulness *see* Behavior — resourcefulness; Character traits — resourcefulness

Responsibility *see* Character traits — responsibility

Restaurants

Downey, Lynn. *Matilda's humdinger*
Kutner, Merrily. *The Zombie Nite Cafe*
Park, Frances. *The Have a Good Day Cafe*
Stowell, Penelope. *The greatest potatoes*
Weatherford, Carole Boston. *Freedom on the menu*
Wellington, Monica. *Pizza at Sally's*

Rhinoceros *see* Animals — rhinoceros

Rhyming text

Alborough, Jez. *Duck's key where can it be?*
　　Hit the ball duck
　　Tall
Anderson, Lena. *The hedgehog, the pig, and their little friend*
Anderson, Peggy Perry. *Chuck's truck*
Anholt, Catherine. *Happy birthday, Chimp and Zee*
Appelt, Kathi. *Merry Christmas, merry crow*
Arnold, Marsha Diane. *Roar of a snore*

Ashman, Linda. *Mama's day*
 Starry safari
 To the beach!
Asim, Jabari. *Daddy goes to work*
Aylesworth, Jim. *Little Bitty Mousie*
Ayres, Katherine. *Up, down, and around*
Baicker, Karen. *You can do it too!*
Bailey, Linda. *Goodnight, sweet pig*
Barner, Bob. *Penguins, penguins, everywhere!*
Bateman, Donna M. *Deep in the swamp*
Bateman, Teresa. *Hamster Camp*
Beaton, Clare. *Daisy gets dressed*
Beaty, Andrea. *Iggy Peck, architect*
Beaumont, Karen. *I ain't gonna paint no more!*
 Move over, Rover
Berkes, Marianne Collins. *Over in the jungle*
Bernhard, Durga. *In the fiddle is a song*
Berry, Lynne. *Duck skates*
Bertram, Debbie. *The best time to read*
Bible. Old Testament. Psalms. *I will rejoice*
Blackstone, Stella. *Alligator alphabet*
 I dreamt I was a dinosaur
 Ship shapes
Blaikie, Lynn. *Beyond the northern lights*
Bonnett-Rampersaud, Louise. *How do you sleep?*
Brennan-Nelson, Denise. *My grandma likes to say*
Bryan, Sean. *A bear and his boy*
Buehner, Caralyn. *Snowmen at Christmas*
 Would I ever lie to you?
Bunting, Eve (Anne Evelyn). *The baby shower*
Butler, John. *Can you growl like a bear?*
Calmenson, Stephanie. *Birthday at the Panda Palace*
Carter, Don. *Old MacDonald drives a tractor*
Cartwright, Reg. *What we do*
Chaconas, Dori. *Virginnie's hat*
 When cows come home for Christmas
Cleary, Brian P. *Eight wild nights*
 A lime, a mime, a pool of slime
 Peanut butter and jellyfishes
Collins, Suzanne. *When Charlie McButton lost power*
Cordsen, Carol Foskett. *The milkman*
Cousins, Lucy. *Hooray for fish!*
Cowley, Joy. *Mrs. Wishy-Washy's Christmas*
Crandall, Court. *Hugville*
Crawford, Laura. *In arctic waters*
Crocker, Nancy. *Betty Lou Blue*
Cronin, Doreen. *Bounce*
 Click, clack, splish, splash
Cruise, Robin. *Only you*
Crum, Shutta. *A family for Old Mill Farm*
Curtis, Jamie Lee. *Is there really a human race?*
Davies, Jacqueline. *The night is singing*
Davies, Sarah. *Happy to be girls*
Denise, Anika. *Pigs love potatoes*
Dewdney, Anna. *Grumpy Gloria*
DiPucchio, Kelly S. *Dinosnores*
DiTerlizzi, Tony. *G is for one gzonk!*
Dodds, Dayle Ann. *Hello, sun!*
 The prince won't go to bed
Donaldson, Julia. *Charlie Cook's favorite book*
Downs, Mike. *You see a circus, I see—*
Doyle, Charlotte Lackner. *The bouncing, dancing, galloping ABC*
Dunbar, Joyce. *Shoe baby*
Dunn, Todd. *We go together*
Durango, Julia. *Cha-cha chimps*
Edwards, David. *The pen that Pa built*
Ehrhardt, Karen. *This jazz man*
Elliott, David. *One little chicken*
Elya, Susan Middleton. *Bebe goes shopping*
 Cowboy Jose
 F is for fiesta
 Oh no, gotta go #2
Engelbreit, Mary. *Mary Engelbreit's A merry little Christmas*
Ernst, Lisa Campbell. *This is the van that Dad cleaned*
Esbaum, Jill. *Estelle takes a bath*
Eschbacher, Roger. *Road trip*
Estefan, Gloria. *Noelle's treasure tale*

Evans, Lezlie. *The bunnies' picnic*
Fallon, Jimmy. *Snowball fight!*
Falwell, Cathryn. *Shape capers*
Ferreri, Della Ross. *How will I ever sleep in this bed?*
Ficocelli, Elizabeth. *Kid tea*
Fisher, Aileen Lucia. *Know what I saw?*
Fisher, Doris. *My even day*
 One odd day
Fleming, Denise. *Beetle bop*
 The first day of winter
Fox, Mem. *Where the giant sleeps*
Freedman, Claire. *One magical day*
 One magical morning
 Snuggle up, sleepy ones
Garland, Michael. *The great Easter egg hunt*
 Hooray José!
George, Kristine O'Connell. *Up!*
Gershator, Phillis. *Listen, listen*
 Summer is summer
Ginkel, Anne. *I've got an elephant*
Giogas, Valarie. *In my backyard*
Glass, Beth Raisner. *Noises at night*
Gliori, Debi. *Where did that baby come from?*
Gray, Rita. *The wild little horse*
Hächler, Bruno. *What does my teddy bear do all night?*
Hager, Sarah. *Dancing Matilda*
Hamilton, Richard. *Let's take over the kindergarten*
Hample, Stoo. *I will kiss you (lots & lots & lots!)*
Harris, Trudy. *Jenny found a penny*
 Twenty hungry piggies
Harrison, David Lee. *Piggy Wiglet*
Hatch, Elizabeth. *Halloween night*
Hayles, Marsha. *Pajamas anytime*
Hays, Anna Jane. *Kindergarten countdown*
Heidbreder, Robert. *A sea-wishing day*
Heinz, Brian J. *Red Fox at McCloskey's farm*
Hicks, Barbara Jean. *I like black and white*
Hindley, Judy. *Baby talk*
 Sleepy places
Hoberman, Mary Ann. *I'm going to Grandma's*
 Mrs. O'Leary's cow
Horowitz, Dave. *Soon, Baboon, soon*
 The ugly pumpkin
Hubbell, Patricia. *Cars*
 Firefighters!
 Hurray for spring!
 Trains
Hunter, Jana Novotny. *When Daddy's truck picks me up*
Hutchins, Pat. *Bumpety bump*
Inches, Alison. *The stuffed animals get ready for bed*
Janovitz, Marilyn. *We love school!*
Jarman, Julia. *Class Two at the zoo*
Johnston, Tony. *Chicken in the kitchen*
 Off to kindergarten
 The whole green world
Jones, Sylvie. *Who's in the tub?*
Katz, Alan. *Don't say that word!*
Keillor, Garrison. *Daddy's girl*
Keller, Laurie. *Grandpa Gazillion's number yard*
Kelley, Marty. *Winter woes*
Kelly, Mij. *One more sheep*
 Where's my darling daughter?
Kimmelman, Leslie. *How do I love you?*
Kindermans, Martine. *You and me*
Kinerk, Robert. *Clorinda takes flight*
 Timothy Cox will not change his socks
Kono, Erin Eitter. *Hula lullaby*
Krebs, Laurie. *Off we go to Mexico*
 We're sailing down the Nile
 We're sailing to Galapagos
Krieb, Mr. *We're off to find the witch's house*
Kroll, Virginia L. *Everybody has a teddy*
 On the way to kindergarten
 Uno, dos, tres, posada!
Kurtz, Kevin. *A day in the salt marsh*
Kuskin, Karla. *Green as a bean*
 So, what's it like to be a cat?

Kutner, Merrily. *The Zombie Nite Cafe*
Latifah, Queen. *Queen of the scene*
Lawler, Janet. *A father's song*
Lessac, Frané. *Island Counting 123*
Leuck, Laura. *I love my pirate papa*
Levine, Abby. *This is the matzah*
Lewis, J. Patrick. *Big is big and little little*
    Tulip at the bat
Lewis, Kevin. *Dinosaur dinosaur*
Lewison, Wendy Cheyette. *Two is for twins*
Lies, Brian. *Bats at the beach*
Lillegard, Dee. *Balloons, balloons, balloons*
Lithgow, John. *Mahalia Mouse goes to college*
The little red hen. *The little red hen*
Livingston, Irene. *Finklehopper Frog cheers*
Ljungkvist, Laura. *Follow the line through the house*
Lloyd-Jones, Sally. *Time to say goodnight*
London, Jonathan. *A train goes clickety-clack*
    A truck goes rattley-bumpa
Lubner, Susan. *Ruthie Bon Bair, do not go to bed with wringing wet hair!*
Lund, Deb. *All aboard the dinotrain*
Lyon, George Ella. *Trucks roll!*
McDonald, Rae A. *A fishing surprise*
McDonnell, Patrick. *Art*
McGinty, Alice B. *Thank you, world*
MacLennan, Cathy. *Chicky Chicky Chook Chook*
McNaughton, Colin. *When I grow up*
Mahy, Margaret. *Down the back of the chair*
Mallat, Kathy. *Papa pride*
Markes, Julie. *Shhhhh! Everybody's sleeping*
Martin, Bill, Jr. (William Ivan). *Baby bear, baby bear, what do you see?*
Mazer, Norma Fox. *Has anyone seen my Emily Greene?*
Merz, Jennifer J. *Playground day*
Meyers, Susan. *Kittens! Kittens! Kittens!*
    Puppies! Puppies! Puppies!
    This is the way a baby rides
Michelson, Richard. *Oh no, not ghosts!*
Minor, Wendell. *Christmas tree!*
Mitton, Tony. *All afloat on Noah's boat!*
    Cool cars
    Playful little penguins
Mizzoni, Chris. *Clancy with the puck*
Mockford, Caroline. *Cleo's color book*
Modarressi, Mitra. *Stay awake, Sally*
Montes, Marissa. *Los gatos black on Halloween*
Mora, Pat. *Marimba!*
Mortensen, Denise Dowling. *Wake up engines*
Morton-Shaw, Christine. *Wake up, sleepy bear!*
Moss, Miriam. *Bare bear*
Munro, Roxie. *Circus*
Murphy, Stuart J. *Same old horse*
Neitzel, Shirley. *Who will I be?*
Neubecker, Robert. *Beasty bath*
Nevius, Carol. *Building with Dad*
    Karate hour
Newman, Leslea. *Daddy's song*
    Skunk's spring surprise
Novak, Matt. *Flip flop bop*
Numeroff, Laura Joffe. *When sheep sleep*
O'Connor, Jane. *Ready, set, skip!*
Odanaka, Barbara. *Smash! Mash! Crash! There goes the trash!*
O'Hair, Margaret. *Star baby*
Ohi, Ruth. *Me and my brother*
    Me and my sister
O'Keefe, Susan Heyboer. *Baby day*
    Hungry monster ABC
Olson, David J. *The thunderstruck stork*
Owens, Mary Beth. *Panda whispers*
Oxenbury, Helen. *Pig tale*
Park, Linda Sue. *Bee-bim bop!*
    What does Bunny see?
Parker, Marjorie. *Your kind of mommy*
Pearson, Debora. *Big city song*
Pearson, Susan. *Hooray for feet!*
Peck, Jan. *Way up high in a tall green tree*
Peddicord, Jane Ann. *That special little baby*

Pendziwol, Jean. *The tale of Sir Dragon*
Perl, Erica S. *Ninety-three in my family*
Peters, Lisa Westberg. *Sleepyhead bear*
Phillips, Christopher. *Ceci Ann's day of why*
Plourde, Lynn. *Dino pets*
Postgate, Daniel. *Smelly Bill*
Prap, Lila. *Animal lullabies*
    Daddies
Prelutsky, Jack. *The wizard*
Prince, April Jones. *What do wheels do all day?*
Prince, Joshua. *I saw an ant in a parking lot*
    I saw an ant on the railroad track
Protopopescu, Orel. *Two sticks*
Raczka, Bob. *Spring things*
    Who loves the fall?
Ransom, Candice F. *Tractor day*
Rasmussen, Halfdan. *The ladder*
Redding, Sue. *Up above and down below*
Rex, Michael. *Dunk skunk*
Ritchie, Alison. *Me and my dad!*
Roemer, Heidi Bee. *What kind of seeds are these?*
Ross, Michael Elsohn. *Mama's milk*
Rossetti-Shustak, Bernadette. *I love you through and through*
Ryan, Pam Muñoz. *There was no snow on Christmas Eve*
Ryder, Joanne. *Bear of my heart*
    Dance by the light of the moon
    Won't you be my hugaroo?
Rylant, Cynthia. *Alligator boy*
    If you'll be my Valentine
    The stars will still shine
Sabuda, Robert. *Winter in white*
Saltzberg, Barney. *I love cats*
    I love dogs
Sayles, Elizabeth. *The goldfish yawned*
Sayre, April Pulley. *Hush, little puppy*
    Vulture view
Schaefer, Lola M. *An island grows*
    Toolbox twins
Schotter, Roni. *When the Wizzy Foot goes walking*
Schroeder, Lisa. *Baby can't sleep*
Schulman, Janet. *Ten trick-or-treaters*
Scillian, Devin. *Brewster the rooster*
Serfozo, Mary. *Whooo's there?*
Shindler, Ramon. *Found alphabet*
Shore, Diane Z. *Look both ways*
    This is the dream
Shulman, Lisa. *Over in the meadow at the big ballet*
Sierra, Judy. *The secret science project that almost ate school*
    Thelonius Monster's sky-high fly pie
Silvano, Wendi. *What does the wind say?*
Singer, Marilyn. *City lullaby*
    Let's build a clubhouse
Skalak, Barbara Anne. *Waddle, waddle, quack, quack, quack*
Slate, Joseph. *Miss Bindergarten celebrates the last day of kindergarten*
    Miss Bindergarten has a wild day in kindergarten
    What star is this?
Slater, Dashka. *Baby shoes*
Sloat, Teri. *This is the house that was tidy and neat*
Smalls, Irene. *My Pop Pop and me*
Smith, Jada Pinkett. *Girls hold up this world*
Smith, Maggie (Margaret C.). *One naked baby*
Smith, Stu. *The bubble gum kid*
Sobel, June. *The goodnight train*
    Shiver me letters
Soule, Jean Conder. *Never tease a weasel*
Sperring, Mark. *The fairytale cake*
Spinelli, Eileen. *The best time of day*
    City angel
Stein, Mathilde. *Monstersong*
Stoeke, Janet Morgan. *The bus stop*
Sturges, Philemon. *How do you make a baby smile?*
    I love tools!
    This little pirate
    Waggers
Swaim, Jessica. *The hound from the pound*
Taback, Simms. *I miss you every day*
Tang, Greg. *Math fables*

Math fables too
Tellis, Annabel. *If my dad were a dog*
Thach, James Otis. *A child's guide to common household monsters*
Thong, Roseanne. *Gai see*
    Tummy girl
Tyler, Michael. *The skin you live in*
Varela, Barry. *Gizmo*
Vestergaard, Hope. *Hillside lullaby*
    What do you do when a monster says boo?
Votaw, Carol. *Waking up down under*
Walton, Rick. *Bunny school*
Ward, Jennifer. *Way up in the Arctic*
Weeks, Sarah. *Be mine, be mine, sweet valentine*
    I'm a pig
    Overboard!
Wheeler, Lisa. *Castaway cats*
    Dino-hockey
    Jazz baby
    Mammoths on the move
Whybrow, Ian. *Faraway farm*
Wick, Walter. *Can you see what I see?*
    I spy treasure hunt
Williams, Brenda. *Home for a tiger, home for a bear*
Williams, Sam. *That's love*
Williams, Suzanne. *Ten naughty little monkeys*
Wilson, Karma. *Animal strike at the zoo, it's true!*
    Dinos in the snow!
    How to bake an American pie
    Mama always comes home
    Moose tracks!
    Princess me
    Sakes alive!
    Sleepyhead
    Whopper cake
Wong, Janet S. *Hide and seek*
Wood, Audrey. *A dog needs a bone*
Wright, Cliff. *Bear and ball*
    Bear and kite
Wright, Michael. *Jake stays awake*
Yee, Wong Herbert. *Detective Small in the amazing banana caper*
    Who likes rain?
Yolen, Jane. *Baby Bear's big dreams*
    Baby Bear's books
    Baby Bear's chairs
    Dimity Duck
    How do dinosaurs eat their food?
    How do dinosaurs go to school?
    How do dinosaurs learn their colors?
    How do dinosaurs play with their friends?
Zalben, Jane Breskin. *Hey, Mama Goose*
Ziefert, Harriet. *Beach party!*
    Families have together
    From Kalamazoo to Timbuktu!
    Messy Bessie
    William and the dragon

Riddles & jokes

Fisher, Doris. *Happy birthday to whooo?*
Granfield, Linda. *What am I?*
Sidman, Joyce. *Butterfly eyes and other secrets of the meadow*
Wick, Walter. *I spy treasure hunt*

Roads

Skultety, Nancy. *From here to there*

Robbers *see* Crime

Robins *see* Birds — robins

Robots

Selznick, Brian. *The invention of Hugo Cabret*
Tauss, Marc. *Superhero*

Rockets *see* Space & space ships

Rocking chairs *see* Furniture — chairs

Rocks

Bertrand, Lynne. *Granite baby*

Rodeos

Elya, Susan Middleton. *Cowboy Jose*
Munro, Roxie. *Rodeo*
Murphy, Stuart J. *Rodeo time*

Roosters *see* Birds — chickens

Rosh Hashanah *see* Holidays — Rosh Hashanah

Rosh Kodesh *see* Holidays — Rosh Kodesh

Royalty

Fleischman, Paul. *Glass slipper, gold sandal*
Lin, Grace. *The red thread*

Royalty — kings

Fisher, Jeff. *The hair scare*
MacDonald, Margaret Read. *Little Rooster's diamond button*

Royalty — princes

Arnold, Tedd. *The twin princes*
Dodds, Dayle Ann. *The prince won't go to bed*
Grimm, Jacob. *The frog prince*
    Rapunzel
Osborne, Mary Pope. *Sleeping Bobby*
Perrault, Charles. *Cinderella*
    Cinderella: a pop-up fairy tale
Shepard, Aaron. *One-eye! Two-eyes! Three-eyes!*

Royalty — princesses

Andersen, H. C. (Hans Christian). *The princess and the pea*, retold by John Cech; ill. by Bernhard Oberdieck
    The princess and the pea, ill. by Rachel Isadora
    The princess and the pea in miniature
Bar-el, Dan. *Such a prince*
Bonning, Tony. *Snog the frog*
Coyle, Carmela LaVigna. *Do princesses really kiss frogs?*
Davidson, Ellen Dee. *Princess Justina Albertina*
Funke, Cornelia. *Princess Pigsty*
Grimm, Jacob. *The frog prince*
    The twelve dancing princesses
Holabird, Katharine. *Angelina at the palace*
Kimmel, Eric A. *The frog princess*
LaRochelle, David. *The end*
Lendler, Ian. *An undone fairy tale*
Melling, David. *Good knight sleep tight*
O'Malley, Kevin. *Once upon a cool motorcycle dude*
Osborne, Mary Pope. *Sleeping Bobby*
Ross, Tony. *I want my tooth*
Wilson, Karma. *Princess me*

Royalty — queens

Cullen, Lynn. *Moi and Marie Antoinette*
Ellis, Sarah. *The queen's feet*

Royalty — sultans

Farmer, Nancy. *Clever Ali*

Running *see* Sports — racing

Running away *see* Behavior — running away

Russia *see* Foreign lands — Russia

Sadness *see* Emotions — sadness

Safety

Calmenson, Stephanie. *May I pet your dog?*
Cuyler, Margery. *Please play safe!*
Kurtz, Jane. *Do kangaroos wear seat belts?*
Shore, Diane Z. *Look both ways*

Sailing *see* Sports — sailing

Salesmen *see* Careers — salesmen

Sandpipers *see* Birds — sandpipers

Sanitation workers *see* Careers — sanitation workers

Santa Claus

Alsenas, Linas. *Mrs. Claus takes a vacation*
Anderson, Derek. *How the Easter Bunny saved Christmas*
Bedford, David. *I've seen Santa!*
Duval, Kathy. *The Three Bears' Christmas*
Frazee, Marla. *Santa Claus*
Harley, Bill. *Dear Santa*
Hassett, Ann. *The finest Christmas tree*
Moore, Clement Clarke. *A creature was stirring*
    The night before Christmas, ill. by Lisbeth Zwerger
    The night before Christmas, ill. by Richard Jesse Watson
    The night before Christmas, ill. by Will Moses
    The night before Christmas, ill. by Gennady Spirin
Scotton, Rob. *Russell's Christmas magic*
Sharkey, Niamh. *Santasaurus*
Smith, Cynthia Leitich. *Santa knows*
Stoeke, Janet Morgan. *Minerva Louise on Christmas Eve*
Willey, Margaret. *A Clever Beatrice Christmas*

Saxophones *see* Musical instruments — saxophones

School

Aliki. *A play's the thing*
Andreae, Giles. *Captain Flinn and the pirate dinosaurs*
Berenzy, Alix. *Sammy*
Bowen, Anne. *The great math tattle battle*
Brisson, Pat. *I remember Miss Perry*
Carlson, Nancy L. *Henry's 100 days of kindergarten*
    I don't like to read!
    Think big!
Catalanotto, Peter. *The secret lunch special*
Child, Lauren. *Say cheese!*
Choldenko, Gennifer. *How to make friends with a giant*
    Louder, Lili
Clements, Andrew. *Slippers at School*
Cocca-Leffler, Maryann. *Mr. Tanen's ties rule!*
Cohen, Miriam. *First grade takes a test*
Cole, Barbara Hancock. *Anna and Natalie*
Cuyler, Margery. *Kindness is cooler, Mrs. Ruler*
D'Amico, Carmela. *Ella sets the stage*
Danneberg, Julie. *Last day blues*
deGroat, Diane. *No more pencils, no more books, no more teacher's dirty looks!*
Derby, Sally. *Whoosh went the wind!*
Dodds, Dayle Ann. *Teacher's pets*
Dubosarsky, Ursula. *Rex*
Edwards, Pamela Duncan. *Ms. Bitsy Bat's kindergarten*

Elschner, Geraldine. *Max's magic seeds*
Elvgren, Jennifer Riesmeyer. *Josias, hold the book*
Finchler, Judy. *Miss Malarkey leaves no reader behind*
Fraser, Mary Ann. *I.Q. gets fit*
    I.Q., it's time
Garden, Nancy. *Molly's family*
Garland, Michael. *Miss Smith reads again!*
Gran, Julia. *Big bug surprise*
Grimes, Nikki. *Danitra Brown, class clown*
Guy, Ginger Foglesong. *My school / Mi escuela*
Hamilton, Richard. *Let's take over the kindergarten*
Hays, Anna Jane. *Ready, set, preschool!*
Heck, Ed. *Monkey lost*
Hodge, Deborah. *Lily and the mixed-up letters*
Janovitz, Marilyn. *We love school!*
Katz, Alan. *Don't say that word!*
Kidslabel. *Spot 7*
Kleven, Elisa. *The apple doll*
Koster, Gloria. *The peanut-free cafe*
Krensky, Stephen. *Big bad wolves at school*
Kroll, Virginia L. *Ryan respects*
Laminack, Lester L. *Jake's 100th day of school*
Layne, Steven L. *T is for teachers*
Lin, Grace. *Lissy's friends*
Lithgow, John. *Mahalia Mouse goes to college*
McAllister, Angela. *Take a kiss to school*
McCully, Emily Arnold. *School*
McDonald, Megan. *Beetle McGrady eats bugs!*
McNaughton, Colin. *Once upon an ordinary school day*
    When I grow up
Madison, Alan. *Velma Gratch and the way cool butterfly*
Mills, Claudia. *Ziggy's blue-ribbon day*
Moore, Mary-Alice. *The wheels on the school bus*
Nevius, Carol. *Building with Dad*
Nez, John. *One smart Cookie*
Pattou, Edith. *Mrs. Spitzer's garden*
Petrillo, Genevieve. *Keep your ear on the ball*
Pinkwater, Daniel Manus. *Yo-yo man*
Plourde, Lynn. *Book Fair Day*
    Pajama day
Polacco, Patricia. *The lemonade club*
Poydar, Nancy. *The bad-news report card*
    The biggest test in the universe
Prelutsky, Jack. *What a day it was at school!*
Pulver, Robin. *Author day for room 3T*
    Axle Annie and the speed grump
    Nouns and verbs have a field day
Puttock, Simon. *Miss Fox*
Rankin, Laura. *Ruthie and the (not so) teeny tiny lie*
Rappaport, Doreen. *The school is not white!*
Robberecht, Thierry. *Sam tells stories*
Robbins, Jacqui. *The new girl . . . and me*
Rosen, Michael. *Totally wonderful Miss Plumberry*
Saltzberg, Barney. *Cornelius P. Mud, are you ready for school?*
    Star of the week
Schwartz, Amy. *Oscar*
Sierra, Judy. *The secret science project that almost ate school*
Slate, Joseph. *Miss Bindergarten celebrates the last day of kindergarten*
    Miss Bindergarten has a wild day in kindergarten
Stoeke, Janet Morgan. *The bus stop*
Walton, Rick. *Bunny school*
Wolff, Nancy. *It's time for school with Tallulah*
Yolen, Jane. *How do dinosaurs go to school?*
Ziefert, Harriet. *Buzzy had a little lamb*
    Messy Bessie

School — field trips

Beaty, Andrea. *Iggy Peck, architect*
Bunting, Eve (Anne Evelyn). *One green apple*
Cole, Joanna. *The magic school bus and the science fair expedition*
Cuyler, Margery. *That's good! That's bad! In Washington, D.C.*
Jarman, Julia. *Class Two at the zoo*

School — first day

Argueta, Jorge. *Moony Luna / Luna, Lunita Lunera*

Carlson, Nancy L. *First grade, here I come!*
Cocca-Leffler, Maryann. *Jack's talent*
Davis, Katie. *Kindergarten rocks!*
deGroat, Diane. *Brand-new pencils, brand-new books*
Grindley, Sally. *It's my school*
Hale, Nathan. *Yellowbelly and Plum go to school*
Harper, Jamie. *Miss Mingo and the first day of school*
Harper, Jessica. *A place called Kindergarten*
Hays, Anna Jane. *Kindergarten countdown*
Hennessy, B. G. (Barbara G.). *Mr. Ouchy's first day*
Johnston, Tony. *Off to kindergarten*
Kroll, Virginia L. *On the way to kindergarten*
McGinty, Alice B. *Eliza's kindergarten surprise*
Mitchard, Jacquelyn. *Ready, set, school!*
Montanari, Eva. *A very full morning*
Morrow, Tara Jaye. *Panda goes to school*
Neubecker, Robert. *Wow! School!*
Ormerod, Jan. *When an elephant comes to school*
Parr, Todd. *Otto goes to school*
Rodman, Mary Ann. *First grade stinks!*
Rubel, Nicole. *Ham and Pickles*
Whybrow, Ian. *Harry and the dinosaurs go to school*
Winget, Susan. *Tucker's four-carrot school day*

School — nursery

Chodos-Irvine, Margaret. *Best best friends*
Kroll, Virginia L. *Everybody has a teddy*
Larsen, Andrew. *Bella and the bunny*
Willems, Mo. *Knuffle Bunny too*

School principals *see* Careers — school principals

School teachers *see* Careers — teachers

Science

Boothroyd, Jennifer. *What is a gas?*
Cole, Joanna. *The magic school bus and the science fair expedition*
Dotlich, Rebecca Kai. *What is science?*
Edwards, Wallace. *The extinct files*
Ferri, Giuliano. *Little Tad grows up*
Gibbons, Gail. *Dinosaur discoveries*
    Galaxies, galaxies!
Hort, Lenny. *Did dinosaurs eat pizza?*
Jolivet, Joëlle. *Almost everything*
Knudsen, Michelle. *A moldy mystery*
Kudlinski, Kathleen V. *Boy, were we wrong about dinosaurs!*
Lunde, Darrin. *Hello, bumblebee bat*
McNamara, Margaret. *How many seeds in a pumpkin?*
Manning, Mick. *Snap!*
Morrison, Gordon. *A drop of water*
Pettenati, Jeanne K. *Galileo's journal, 1609–1610*
Posada, Mia. *Guess what is growing inside this egg*
Raab, Brigitte. *Where does pepper come from?*
Sabuda, Robert. *Encyclopedia prehistorica: mega-beasts*
    Encyclopedia prehistorica: sharks and other seamonsters
Sierra, Judy. *The secret science project that almost ate school*
Tang, Greg. *Math fables too*
Wells, Robert E. *Did a dinosaur drink this water?*

Scientists *see* Careers — scientists

Sculptors *see* Careers — sculptors

Sea & seashore

Arnosky, Jim. *Parrotfish and sunken ships*
Buckingham, Matt. *Bright Stanley*
Butterworth, Chris. *Sea horse*
Cousins, Lucy. *Hooray for fish!*
Cumberbatch, Judy. *Can you hear the sea?*
Davies, Jacqueline. *The house takes a vacation*
Geist, Ken. *The three little fish and the big bad shark*
Gibbons, Gail. *Coral reefs*
Heidbreder, Robert. *A sea-wishing day*

Hodgkins, Fran. *Between the tides*
Kudlinski, Kathleen V. *The seaside switch*
O'Connor, George. *Ker-splash!*
Pallotta, Jerry. *Ocean counting*
Rose, Deborah Lee. *Ocean babies*
Sabuda, Robert. *Encyclopedia prehistorica*
St. Pierre, Stephanie. *What the sea saw*
Schwarz, Viviane. *Shark and Lobster's amazing undersea adventure*
Sherry, Kevin. *I'm the biggest thing in the ocean*
Sperring, Mark. *Mermaid dreams*
Stevenson, Robert Louis. *Block city*
Taylor, Eleanor. *Beep, beep, let's go!*
Wood, Audrey. *The deep blue sea*
Ziefert, Harriet. *Beach party!*

Sea & seashore — beaches

Ashman, Linda. *To the beach!*
Briant, Ed. *A day at the beach*
Clements, Andrew. *Because your daddy loves you*
Cooper, Elisha. *Beach*
Estefan, Gloria. *Noelle's treasure tale*
Johnson, Crockett. *Magic beach*
Lies, Brian. *Bats at the beach*
Rotner, Shelley. *Senses at the seashore*
Thaler, Mike. *Pig Little*
Wallace, Nancy Elizabeth. *Shells! Shells! Shells!*
Weninger, Brigitte. *Miko goes on vacation*
Wiesner, David. *Flotsam*

Seagulls *see* Birds — seagulls

Seahorses *see* Fish — seahorses

Seals *see* Animals — seals

Seashore *see* Sea & seashore — beaches

Seasons

Banks, Kate (Katherine A.). *The great blue house*
Gershator, Phillis. *Listen, listen*
Glaser, Linda. *Hello, squirrels!*
Hubery, Julia. *A friend for all seasons*
Issa, Kobayashi. *Today and today*
Katz, Bobbi. *Once around the sun*
Krauss, Ruth. *The growing story*
Lin, Grace. *Our seasons*
Livingston, Myra Cohn. *Calendar*
Martin, Bill, Jr. (William Ivan). *I love our Earth*
Messinger, Carla. *When the shadbush blooms*
Näslund, Gorel Kristina. *Our apple tree*
Rotner, Shelley. *Every season*
Ryder, Joanne. *Toad by the road*
Schertle, Alice. *Very hairy bear*
Schubert, Leda. *Here comes Darrell*
Stein, David Ezra. *Leaves*
Thong, Roseanne. *Gai see*
Train, Mary. *Time for the fair*

Seasons — fall

Ehlert, Lois. *Leaf man*
Gerritsen, Paula. *Nuts*
Lee, Huy Voun. *In the leaves*
McNamara, Margaret. *Fall leaf project*
Raczka, Bob. *Who loves the fall?*
Rawlinson, Julia. *Fletcher and the falling leaves*
Robbins, Ken. *Pumpkins*
Tafuri, Nancy. *The busy little squirrel*
Thompson, Lauren. *Mouse's first fall*

Seasons — spring

Florian, Douglas. *Handsprings*
Hubbell, Patricia. *Hurray for spring!*

Newman, Leslea. *Skunk's spring surprise*
Raczka, Bob. *Spring things*
Thompson, Lauren. *Mouse's first spring*
Yee, Wong Herbert. *Who likes rain?*

Seasons — summer

Broach, Elise. *Wet dog!*
Frampton, David. *Mr. Ferlinghetti's poem*
Franco, Betsy. *Summer beat*
Freedman, Claire. *One magical day*
Gershator, Phillis. *Summer is summer*
Hughes, Susan. *Earth to Audrey*
Novak, Matt. *Flip flop bop*
Payne, Nina. *Summertime waltz*
Perry, Elizabeth. *Think cool thoughts*
Thomas, Patricia. *Firefly mountain*

Seasons — winter

Berry, Lynne. *Duck skates*
Brett, Jan. *The three snow bears*
Brunelle, Nicholas. *Snow Moon*
Butler, M. Christina. *One winter's day*
    Snow friends
Child, Lauren. *Snow is my favorite and my best*
Cooper, Elisha. *Bear dreams*
Denslow, Sharon Phillips. *In the snow*
Emmett, Jonathan. *Diamond in the snow*
Fisher, Aileen Lucia. *Do rabbits have Christmas?*
Fleming, Denise. *The first day of winter*
Ford, Bernette G. *First snow*
Gore, Leonid. *Danny's first snow*
Hayes, Karel. *The winter visitors*
Huneck, Stephen. *Sally's snow adventure*
Hurst, Carol Otis. *Terrible storm*
Kelley, Marty. *Winter woes*
Laminack, Lester L. *Snow day!*
Lester, Helen. *Tacky and the Winter Games*
Lobel, Gillian. *Little Honey Bear and the smiley moon*
McDaniels, Preston. *A perfect snowman*
Manushkin, Fran. *How Mama brought the spring*
Morgan, Michaela. *Bunny wishes*
Plourde, Lynn. *A mountain of mittens*
Powell, Consie. *The first day of winter*
Prelutsky, Jack. *It's snowing! It's snowing!*
Quattlebaum, Mary. *Winter friends*
Root, Phyllis. *Lucia and the light*
Rose, Deborah Lee. *The twelve days of winter*
Sabuda, Robert. *Winter in white*
    Winter's tale
Stringer, Lauren. *Winter is the warmest season*
Thompson, Lauren. *Mouse's first snow*
Wallace, Nancy Elizabeth. *Snow*
Whybrow, Ian. *Bella gets her skates on*
Wilson, Karma. *Dinos in the snow!*
Yolen, Jane. *Sleep, black bear, sleep*

Secrets *see* Behavior — secrets

Seder *see* Holidays — Seder

Seeds

Aston, Dianna Hutts. *A seed is sleepy*
Henkes, Kevin. *So happy!*
Roemer, Heidi Bee. *What kind of seeds are these?*

Seeing *see* Glasses; Handicaps — blindness; Senses — sight

Seeing eye dogs *see* Animals — service animals

Self-concept

Baryshnikov, Mikhail. *Because . . .*

Brown, Lisa. *How to be*
Bunting, Eve (Anne Evelyn). *One green apple*
Carlson, Nancy L. *Think big!*
Cazet, Denys. *Will you read to me?*
Chen, Chih-Yuan. *The featherless chicken*
Cocca-Leffler, Maryann. *Jack's talent*
Cote, Nancy. *It's all about me!*
Danneberg, Julie. *Cowboy Slim*
Davies, Sarah. *Happy to be girls*
Dijkstra, Lida. *Cute*
Elya, Susan Middleton. *Sophie's trophy*
Erlbruch, Wolf. *The big question*
Ernst, Lisa Campbell. *Sylvia Jean, drama queen*
Feiffer, Kate. *Henry, the dog with no tail*
Frazee, Marla. *Walk on!*
Friedrich, Molly. *You're not my real mother!*
Funke, Cornelia. *Princess Pigsty*
Galloway, Ruth. *Clumsy crab*
Gershator, Phillis. *Sky sweeper*
Gerstein, Mordicai. *Leaving the nest*
Harper, Charise Mericle. *When Randolph turned rotten*
Headley, Justina Chen. *The patch*
Hodge, Deborah. *Lily and the mixed-up letters*
Horacek, Petr. *Silly Suzy Goose*
Kasza, Keiko. *The dog who cried wolf*
Krishnaswami, Uma. *The happiest tree*
LaMarche, Jim. *Up*
Latifah, Queen. *Queen of the scene*
Meserve, Jessica. *Small sister*
Mills, Claudia. *Ziggy's blue-ribbon day*
Moore, Julianne. *Freckleface Strawberry*
Neubecker, Robert. *Courage of the blue boy*
O'Connor, Jane. *Fancy Nancy*
    Fancy Nancy and the posh puppy
    Ready, set, skip!
Pinkney, Sandra L. *I am Latino*
Prelutsky, Jack. *Me I am!*
Reynolds, Peter H. *Ish*
    My very big little world
Richards, Beah E. *Keep climbing, girls*
Rosenthal, Amy Krouse. *The OK book*
Rossetti-Shustak, Bernadette. *I love you through and through*
Saltzberg, Barney. *Star of the week*
Schotter, Roni. *The boy who loved words*
Schwartz, Amy. *Starring Miss Darlene*
Shea, Bob. *New socks*
Smith, Jada Pinkett. *Girls hold up this world*
Tyler, Michael. *The skin you live in*
Waddell, Martin. *Bee frog*
Weeks, Sarah. *I'm a pig*
Wells, Rosemary. *The gulps*
Willems, Mo. *Edwina, the dinosaur who didn't know she was extinct*
Winthrop, Elizabeth. *Squashed in the middle*

Self-esteem *see* Self-concept

Self-image *see* Self-concept

Self-reliance *see* Character traits — confidence

Selfishness *see* Character traits — selfishness

Senses

Ciboul, Adele. *The five senses*
Henderson, Kathy. *Look at you!*
Raschka, Chris. *Five for a little one*
Rotner, Shelley. *Senses at the seashore*
Shannon, David. *David smells*

Senses — sight

McCarthy, Mary. *A closer look*
Shannon, George. *White is for blueberry*

Senses — smell

Keller, Holly. *Nosy Rosie*
Kinerk, Robert. *Timothy Cox will not change his socks*

Service animals *see* Animals — service animals

Sewing *see* Activities — sewing

Sex instruction

Saltz, Gail. *Amazing you*

Sex roles *see* Gender roles

Shadows

DiFiori, Lawrence. *Jackie and the Shadow Snatcher*

Shape *see* Concepts — shape

Sharing *see* Behavior — sharing

Sharks *see* Fish — sharks

Sheep *see* Animals — sheep

Shepherds *see* Careers — shepherds

Sheriffs *see* Careers — sheriffs

Ships *see* Boats, ships

Shoemakers *see* Careers — shoemakers

Shoes *see* Clothing — shoes

Shopping

Agee, Jon. *Nothing*
Ahlberg, Allan. *The shopping expedition*
Christelow, Eileen. *Five little monkeys go shopping*
Dewdney, Anna. *Llama Llama mad at mama*
Elya, Susan Middleton. *Bebe goes shopping*
Ichikawa, Satomi. *My father's shop*
Korchek, Lori. *Adventures of Cow, too*
Long, Kathy. *The runaway shopping cart*
McAllister, Angela. *Trust me, Mom!*
Miranda, Anne. *To market, to market*
Puttock, Simon. *Goat and Donkey in strawberry sunglasses*

Shops *see* Stores

Shows *see* Theater

Shyness *see* Character traits — shyness

Siam *see* Foreign lands — Thailand

Sibling rivalry

Broach, Elise. *What the no-good baby is good for*
Bunting, Eve (Anne Evelyn). *Baby can*
Capucilli, Alyssa Satin. *Katy Duck, big sister*
Cote, Nancy. *It's all about me!*
Duke, Kate. *The tale of Pip and Squeak*
Hazen, Barbara Shook. *Who is your favorite monster, mama?*
Lobel, Gillian. *Too small for honey cake*
Perrault, Charles. *Cinderella*
    Cinderella: a pop-up fairy tale
Reynolds, Peter H. *The best kid in the world*
Robberecht, Thierry. *Back into Mommy's tummy*
Rosenberry, Vera. *Vera's baby sister*
Wells, Rosemary. *Max counts his chickens*

Wynne-Jones, Tim. *The boat in the tree*
Young, Ed. *My Mei Mei*
Zolotow, Charlotte (Shapiro). *If it weren't for you*

Siblings *see* Family life — brothers & sisters; Family life — step families

Sickness *see* Health & fitness; Illness

Sight *see* Glasses; Handicaps — blindness; Senses — sight

Sign language

Kubler, Annie. *My first signs*

Singers *see* Careers — singers

Singing *see* Activities — singing

Single-parent families *see* Family life — single-parent families

Sisters *see* Family life; Family life — brothers & sisters; Sibling rivalry

Size *see* Concepts — size

Skating *see* Sports — ice skating

Skeletons *see* Anatomy — skeletons

Skiing *see* Sports — skiing

Skin *see* Anatomy — skin

Skunks *see* Animals — skunks

Sky

Berger, Barbara. *Thunder Bunny*
Lujan, Jorge. *Sky blue accident / Accidente celeste*

Slavery

Grifalconi, Ann. *Ain't nobody a stranger to me*
Levine, Ellen. *Henry's freedom box*
Raven, Margot Theis. *Night boat to freedom*
Sanders, Nancy. *D is for drinking gourd*
Turner, Glennette Tilley. *An apple for Harriet Tubman*
Weatherford, Carole Boston. *Moses*
Woodson, Jacqueline. *Show way*

Sledding *see* Sports — sledding

Sleep

Andersen, H. C. (Hans Christian). *The princess and the pea*, retold by John Cech; ill. by Bernhard Oberdieck
    The princess and the pea, ill. by Rachel Isadora
    The princess and the pea in miniature
Baker, Roberta. *Olive's first sleepover*
Bean, Jonathan. *At night*
Bergman, Mara. *Oliver who would not sleep!*
Bonnett-Rampersaud, Louise. *How do you sleep?*
Capucilli, Alyssa Satin. *Little spotted cat*
Clements, Andrew. *Naptime for Slippers*
Deacon, Alexis. *While you are sleeping*
Demers, Dominique. *Every single night*
Durango, Julia. *Dream hop*
Ehrlich, Fred. *Does a baboon sleep in a bed?*
Fox, Mem. *Where the giant sleeps*
Freedman, Claire. *Snuggle up, sleepy ones*
Guy, Ginger Foglesong. *Siesta*

Hindley, Judy. *Sleepy places*
Hurd, Thacher. *Sleepy Cadillac*
Kanevsky, Polly. *Sleepy boy*
Kimmel, Eric A. *Rip Van Winkle's return*
Lewis, Kim. *Hooray for Harry*
Markes, Julie. *Shhhh! Everybody's sleeping*
Osborne, Mary Pope. *Sleeping Bobby*
Peters, Lisa Westberg. *Sleepyhead bear*
Robbins, Maria Polushkin. *Mother, Mother, I want another*
Scotton, Rob. *Go to sleep, Russell the sheep*
    Russell the sheep
Shulevitz, Uri. *So sleepy story*
Waddell, Martin. *Sleep tight, Little Bear*
Wolff, Ferida. *It is the wind*
Wright, Michael. *Jake stays awake*
Ziefert, Harriet. *Mommy, I want to sleep in your bed!*

Sleep — snoring

Arnold, Marsha Diane. *Roar of a snore*
DiPucchio, Kelly S. *Dinosnores*

Sleepovers

Clarke, Jane. *Dippy's sleepover*
Ellis, Sarah. *Ben over night*
Harper, Charise Mericle. *When Randolph turned rotten*
Mitchard, Jacquelyn. *Ready, set, school!*
Pinkwater, Daniel Manus. *Sleepover Larry*
Tyler, Anne. *Timothy Tugbottom says no!*
Winthrop, Elizabeth. *Squashed in the middle*

Sleight-of-hand *see* Magic

Slugs *see* Animals — slugs

Smallness *see* Character traits — smallness

Smell *see* Senses — smell

Smiles, smiling *see* Anatomy — faces

Snails *see* Animals — snails

Snakes *see* Reptiles — snakes

Snoring *see* Sleep — snoring

Snow *see* Weather — blizzards; Weather — snow

Snowmen

Buehner, Caralyn. *Snowmen at Christmas*
Fleming, Denise. *The first day of winter*
LaReau, Kara. *Snowbaby could not sleep*
McDaniels, Preston. *A perfect snowman*
Mahoney, Daniel J. *A really good snowman*

Soccer *see* Sports — soccer

Socks *see* Clothing — socks

Sofas *see* Furniture — couches, sofas

Soldiers *see* Careers — military

Solitude *see* Behavior — solitude

Somalia *see* Foreign lands — Somalia

Songs

Anderson, Derek. *Over the river*
Bates, Ivan. *Five little ducks*

Baum, Maxie. *I have a little dreidel*
Brebeuf, Jean de. *The Huron carol*
Busse, Sarah Martin. *Banjo granny*
Cabrera, Jane. *If you're happy and you know it*
Cohan, George M. *You're a grand old flag*
Conahan, Carolyn. *The twelve days of Christmas dogs*
Corr, Christopher. *Whole world*
Creech, Sharon. *Who's that baby?*
Dale, Penny. *The boy on the bus*
Downes, Belinda. *Baby days*
Downing, Johnette. *Down in Louisiana*
    Today is Monday in Louisiana
Durango, Julia. *Angels watching over me*
Ehrhardt, Karen. *This jazz man*
Emmett, Jonathan. *She'll be coming 'round the mountain*
A frog he would a-wooing go (folk-song). *Froggy went a-courtin'*
Gershator, Phillis. *This is the day!*
Here we go round the mulberry bush
Joel, Billy. *New York state of mind*
Johnson, James Weldon. *Lift every voice and sing*
Johnson, Paul Brett. *On top of spaghetti*
Krosoczka, Jarrett J. *Punk Farm on tour*
Let it shine
MacDonald, Margaret Read. *A hen, a chick, and a string guitar*
Milgrim, David. *Young MacDonald*
Mitchell, Susan K. *The rainforest grew all around*
Moore, Mary-Alice. *The wheels on the school bus*
Nelson, Kadir. *He's got the whole world in His hands*
Newman, Leslea. *The eight nights of Chanukah*
Norworth, Jack. *Take me out to the ballgame*
Palatini, Margie. *The cheese*
    Three French hens
Penner, Fred. *The cat came back*
Pinkney, Gloria Jean. *Music from our Lord's holy heaven*
Rox, John. *I want a hippopotamus for Christmas*
Rueda, Claudia. *Let's play in the forest while the wolf is not around*
Ryder, Joanne. *Dance by the light of the moon*
Seskin, Steve. *A chance to shine*
Spirin, Gennady. *We three kings*
Stadler, John. *Take me out to the ball game*
This little light of mine
Trapani, Iza. *Here we go 'round the mulberry bush*
    Jingle bells
Warhola, James. *If you're happy and you know it*
Yarrow, Peter. *Puff, the magic dragon*
Zane, Alexander. *The wheels on the race car*
Ziefert, Harriet. *Knick-knack paddywhack*

Sorcerers *see* Wizards

Sounds *see* Noise, sounds

South Africa *see* Foreign lands — South Africa

South Pole *see* Foreign lands — Antarctica

Space & space ships

Aldrin, Buzz. *Reaching for the moon*
Anderson, Derek. *Romeo and Lou blast off*
Brett, Jan. *Hedgie blasts off!*
Brownlow, Mike. *Mickey Moonbeam*
Collicutt, Paul. *This rocket*
Fischer, Scott M. *Twinkle*
Gibbons, Gail. *Galaxies, galaxies!*
Landry, Leo. *Space boy*
McNulty, Faith. *If you decide to go to the moon*
Milgrim, David. *Another day in the Milky Way*
Morrissey, Dean. *The crimson comet*
O'Malley, Kevin. *Captain Raptor and the moon mystery*
    Captain Raptor and the space pirates
Rowe, John A. *Moondog*
Schories, Pat. *Jack and the night visitors*
Wakeman, Daniel. *Ben's bunny trouble*

Spain *see* Foreign lands — Spain

Spectacles *see* Glasses

Spiders

Cronin, Doreen. *Diary of a spider*
Mother Goose. *Little Miss Muffet*
Williams, Brenda. *Home for a tiger, home for a bear*

Sports

Adler, David A. *Joe Louis*
Brown, Don. *Bright path*
Chaconas, Dori. *Cork and Fuzz*
Clayton, Elaine. *A blue ribbon for Sugar*
Deans, Karen. *Playing to win*
Hammerle, Susa. *Let's try horseback riding*
Lester, Helen. *Tacky and the Winter Games*
Mills, Claudia. *Ziggy's blue-ribbon day*
Mochizuki, Ken. *Be water, my friend*
Prelutsky, Jack. *Good sports*
Reiser, Lynn. *Play ball with me!*
Rex, Michael. *Dunk skunk*
Ziefert, Harriet. *Murphy jumps a hurdle*

Sports — baseball

Adler, David A. *Campy*
   Satchel Paige
Alborough, Jez. *Hit the ball duck*
Bildner, Phil. *The shot heard 'round the world*
Burleigh, Robert. *Stealing home*
Egan, Tim. *Roasted peanuts*
Gutman, Dan. *Casey back at bat*
Hubbard, Crystal. *Catching the moon*
Isadora, Rachel. *Luke goes to bat*
Jordan, Deloris. *Michael's golden rules*
Lester, Helen. *Batter up Wombat*
Lewis, J. Patrick. *Tulip at the bat*
Lorbiecki, Marybeth. *Jackie's bat*
McDonough, Yona Zeldis. *Hammerin' Hank*
Madison, Alan. *Pecorino plays ball*
Michelson, Richard. *Across the alley*
Norworth, Jack. *Take me out to the ballgame*
Rodriguez, Alex. *Out of the ballpark*
Stadler, John. *Take me out to the ball game*
Uhlberg, Myron. *Dad, Jackie, and me*
Weatherford, Carole Boston. *Champions on the bench*

Sports — basketball

Garland, Michael. *Hooray José!*
Meunier, Brian. *Bravo, Tavo!*
Rockwell, Anne F. *Brendan and Belinda and the slam dunk!*

Sports — bicycling

Best, Cari. *Sally Jean, the Bicycle Queen*
Braver, Vanita. *Madison and the two wheeler*
Eriksson, Eva. *A crash course for Molly*
London, Jonathan. *Froggy rides a bike*

Sports — boxing

Adler, David A. *Joe Louis*
Lewin, Ted. *At Gleason's gym*

Sports — fishing

Bootman, Colin. *Fish for the Grand Lady*
Cronin, Doreen. *Click, clack, splish, splash*
Frank, John. *How to catch a fish*
McDonald, Rae A. *A fishing surprise*
Quigley, Mary. *Granddad's fishing buddy*
Selick, Henry. *Moongirl*

Sports — football

Barber, Tiki. *Game day*

Teammates
Bildner, Phil. *The greatest game ever played*
Gruska, Denise. *The only boy in ballet class*
Reynolds, Aaron. *Buffalo wings*

Sports — gymnastics

Lasky, Kathryn. *Tumble bunnies*

Sports — hiking

Coyle, Carmela LaVigna. *Do princesses really kiss frogs?*

Sports — hockey

Bailey, Linda. *The farm team*
Leonetti, Mike. *Gretzky's game*
Mizzoni, Chris. *Clancy with the puck*
Polacco, Patricia. *Rotten Richie and the ultimate dare*
Wheeler, Lisa. *Dino-hockey*

Sports — ice skating

Berry, Lynne. *Duck skates*
Bunge, Daniela. *The scarves*
Keller, Holly. *Pearl's new skates*
Spinelli, Eileen. *Callie Cat, ice skater*
Whybrow, Ian. *Bella gets her skates on*

Sports — karate

Mayer, Mercer. *There are monsters everywhere*
Nevius, Carol. *Karate hour*

Sports — mountain climbing

Becker, Shari. *Maxwell's mountain*

Sports — Olympics

Yoo, Paula. *Sixteen years in sixteen seconds*

Sports — racing

Aesop. *The hare and the tortoise / La liebre y la tortuga*
Herzog, Brad. *R is for race*
London, Jonathan. *Sled dogs run*
Tingle, Tim. *When turtle grew feathers*
Trollinger, Patsi B. *Perfect timing*
Zane, Alexander. *The wheels on the race car*

Sports — sailing

Heidbreder, Robert. *A sea-wishing day*

Sports — skiing

Huneck, Stephen. *Sally's snow adventure*

Sports — sledding

Kortepeter, Paul. *Oliver's red toboggan*
London, Jonathan. *Sled dogs run*

Sports — soccer

Cline-Ransome, Lesa. *Young Pelé*
Elliott, Laura Malone. *Hunter and Stripe and the soccer showdown*
Fox, Diane. *Tyson the terrible*
Shahan, Sherry. *That's not how you play soccer, Daddy*

Sports — swimming

Fuge, Charles. *Swim, Little Wombat, swim!*
Harper, Jamie. *Me too!*
Koch, Ed. *Eddie's little sister makes a splash*
Lin, Grace. *Olvina swims*
Reiser, Lynn. *Two dogs swimming*

Webster, Christine. *Otter everywhere*
Weninger, Brigitte. *Miko goes on vacation*

Sports — T-ball

London, Jonathan. *Froggy plays T-ball*

Sports — tennis

McG, Shane. *Tennis, anyone?*

Sportsmanship

Chaconas, Dori. *Cork and Fuzz*
Elliott, Laura Malone. *Hunter and Stripe and the soccer showdown*
Jordan, Deloris. *Michael's golden rules*
Lasky, Kathryn. *Tumble bunnies*
Rockwell, Anne F. *Brendan and Belinda and the slam dunk!*

Spring *see* Seasons — spring

Squid

Sherry, Kevin. *I'm the biggest thing in the ocean*

Squirrels *see* Animals — squirrels

Stage *see* Theater

Stars

Fancher, Lou. *Star climbing*
Fischer, Scott M. *Twinkle*
Florian, Douglas. *Comets, stars, the moon, and Mars*
Mackall, Dandi Daley. *Seeing stars*
Marzollo, Jean. *Little Bear, you're a star!*
Pettenati, Jeanne K. *Galileo's journal, 1609–1610*

Stealing *see* Behavior — stealing; Crime

Step families *see* Divorce; Family life — step families

Stepchildren *see* Divorce; Family life — step families

Stepparents *see* Divorce; Family life — step families

Stones *see* Rocks

Stores

Agee, Jon. *Nothing*
Egan, Tim. *The pink refrigerator*
Elya, Susan Middleton. *Bebe goes shopping*
Korchek, Lori. *Adventures of Cow, too*
Lewin, Ted. *How much?*
Murphy, Stuart J. *Mall mania*
Polacco, Patricia. *Something about Hensley's*
Thong, Roseanne. *Gai see*
Yin. *Brothers*

Stories in rhyme *see* Rhyming text

Storks *see* Birds — storks

Storms *see* Weather — storms

Storytelling *see* Activities — storytelling

Strangers *see* Behavior — talking to strangers

Streets *see* Roads

Stubbornness *see* Character traits — stubbornness

Sultans *see* Royalty — sultans

Summer *see* Seasons — summer

Sun

Kaner, Etta. *Who likes the sun?*
Root, Phyllis. *Lucia and the light*

Superstition

Rumford, James. *Don't touch my hat!*
Sutton, Jane. *The trouble with cauliflower*

Surfing *see* Sports — surfing

Swallows *see* Birds — swallows

Swamps

Bateman, Donna M. *Deep in the swamp*
Chaconas, Dori. *Virginnie's hat*
Downing, Johnette. *Down in Louisiana*
Huggins, Peter. *Trosclair and the alligator*

Swans *see* Birds — swans

Swapping *see* Activities — trading

Sweaters *see* Clothing — sweaters

Swimming *see* Sports — swimming

Switzerland *see* Foreign lands — Switzerland

T-ball *see* Sports — T-ball

Tailors *see* Careers — tailors

Tails *see* Anatomy — tails

Talking *see* Activities — talking

Talking to strangers *see* Behavior — talking to strangers

Tall tales

Andreasen, Dan. *The giant of Seville*
Bertrand, Lynne. *Granite baby*
Crunk, Tony. *Railroad John and the Red Rock run*
Derby, Sally. *Whoosh went the wind!*
Hayes, Joe. *The gum-chewing rattler*
Isaacs, Anne. *Pancakes for supper!*
Kimmel, Eric A. *The great Texas hamster drive*
Madison, Alan. *The littlest grape stomper*
Mora, Pat. *Doña Flor*
Pinkney, Andrea Davis. *Peggony-Po*
Wilson, Karma. *Whopper cake*

Tanzania *see* Foreign lands — Tanzania

Teachers *see* Careers — teachers

Teasing *see* Behavior — bullying

Teddy bears *see* Toys — bears

Teeth

Bowen, Anne. *Tooth Fairy's first night*
Cousins, Lucy. *Maisy, Charley, and the wobbly tooth*
Diakité, Penda. *I lost my tooth in Africa*
High, Linda Oatman. *Cool Bopper's choppers*
Palatini, Margie. *No biting, Louise*
Ross, Tony. *I want my tooth*

Television

Weigelt, Udo. *Super Guinea Pig to the rescue*

Telling stories *see* Activities — storytelling

Telling time *see* Clocks, watches; Time

Temper tantrums *see* Emotions — anger

Tennis *see* Sports — tennis

Texas

Borgo, Lacy. *Big Mama's baby*
Ketteman, Helen. *Waynetta and the cornstalk*
Kimmel, Eric A. *The great Texas hamster drive*
　　The lady in the blue cloak
　　The three cabritos

Thailand *see* Foreign lands — Thailand

Thanksgiving *see* Holidays — Thanksgiving

Theater

Aliki. *A play's the thing*
Cronin, Doreen. *Dooby dooby moo*
D'Amico, Carmela. *Ella sets the stage*
DePalma, Mary Newell. *The Nutcracker doll*
Francis, Pauline. *Sam stars at Shakespeare's Globe*
McNaughton, Colin. *When I grow up*
Say, Allen. *Kamishibai man*
Schwartz, Amy. *Starring Miss Darlene*
Waterton, Betty. *A bumblebee sweater*

Thunder *see* Weather — lightning, thunder; Weather — storms

Tigers *see* Animals — tigers

Time

Baker, Keith. *Hickory dickory dock*
Fraser, Mary Ann. *I.Q., it's time*
Hennessy, B. G. (Barbara G.). *Mr. Ouchy's first day*
Hutchins, Hazel (Hazel J.). *A second is a hiccup*
Murphy, Stuart J. *It's about time!*
　　Rodeo time
Pilegard, Virginia Walton. *The warlord's alarm*
Skinner, Daphne. *All aboard!*

Tiwa Indians *see* Indians of North America — Tiwa

Tlingit Indians *see* Indians of North America — Tlingit

Toads *see* Frogs & toads

Toes *see* Anatomy — toes

Toilet training

Elya, Susan Middleton. *Oh no, gotta go #2*

Ford, Bernette G. *No more diapers for Ducky!*
Katz, Karen. *A potty for me!*

Toilets

Harper, Charise Mericle. *Flush!*

Tools

Miura, Taro. *Tools*
Schaefer, Lola M. *Toolbox twins*
Singer, Marilyn. *Let's build a clubhouse*
Sturges, Philemon. *I love tools!*

Tornadoes *see* Weather — tornadoes

Tortoises *see* Reptiles — turtles, tortoises

Towns *see* Cities, towns

Toy & movable books *see* Format, unusual — toy & movable books

Toys

Ayres, Katherine. *Matthew's truck*
Bardhan-Quallen, Sudipta. *The Mine-o-saur*
Bell, Cece. *Sock Monkey boogie-woogie*
　　Sock Monkey rides again
Cabrera, Jane. *Ten in the bed*
Cowell, Cressida. *That rabbit belongs to Emily Brown*
Crews, Nina. *Below*
Deacon, Alexis. *While you are sleeping*
DeSeve, Randall. *Toy boat*
Dierssen, Andreas. *The old red tractor*
Donaldson, Julia. *One Ted falls out of bed*
Dunbar, Polly. *Penguin*
Ferreri, Della Ross. *How will I ever sleep in this bed?*
Frazee, Marla. *Santa Claus*
Heck, Ed. *Monkey lost*
Herman, R. A. (Ronnie Ann). *Gomer and Little Gomer*
Ichikawa, Satomi. *I am Pangoo the penguin*
Inches, Alison. *The stuffed animals get ready for bed*
Korchek, Lori. *Adventures of Cow, too*
LaReau, Kara. *Rocko and Spanky have company*
Lewis, Kim. *Hooray for Harry*
Lewis, Paeony. *No more cookies!*
London, Jonathan. *My big rig*
McAllister, Angela. *Mama and Little Joe*
Marks, Jennifer L. *Sorting toys*
Patricelli, Leslie. *Binky*
Pelletier, Andrew T. *The amazing adventures of Bathman!*
　　The toy farmer
Pinkney, Andrea Davis. *Peggony-Po*
Pinkwater, Daniel Manus. *Yo-yo man*
Roberts, Bethany. *Cookie angel*
Schwartz, Amy. *Oscar*
Soto, Gary. *My little car / Mi carrito*
Stevenson, Robert Louis. *Block city*
Weninger, Brigitte. *Double birthday*
　　Miko goes on vacation
Whybrow, Ian. *Harry and the dinosaurs at the museum*
　　Harry and the dinosaurs go to school
Wick, Walter. *Can you see what I see?*
Willems, Mo. *Knuffle Bunny*
　　Knuffle Bunny too
Wilson, Karma. *Princess me*
Ziefert, Harriet. *Buzzy had a little lamb*

Toys — balloons

Lillegard, Dee. *Balloons, balloons, balloons*

Toys — balls

Cronin, Doreen. *Bounce*

Hills, Tad. *Duck and Goose*
Stevens, Janet. *The great fuzz frenzy*
Wright, Cliff. *Bear and ball*

Toys — bears

Donaldson, Julia. *One Ted falls out of bed*
Guy, Ginger Foglesong. *Siesta*
Hächler, Bruno. *What does my teddy bear do all night?*
Hale, Nathan. *Yellowbelly and Plum go to school*
Kroll, Virginia L. *Everybody has a teddy*
Schertle, Alice. *The adventures of old Bo Bear*
Schneider, Christine M. *I'm bored!*
Seeger, Laura Vaccaro. *Dog and Bear*
Simon, Charnan. *Messy Molly*
Smee, Nicola. *No bed without Ted*
Wilson, Karma. *Sleepyhead*

Toys — dolls

Browne, Anthony. *Silly Billy*
Godden, Rumer. *The story of Holly and Ivy*
McKissack, Patricia C. *The all-I'll-ever-want Christmas doll*
McPhail, David. *Emma in charge*
Milgrim, David. *Time to get up, time to go*
Montanari, Eva. *My first . . .*
Pattison, Darcy. *Searching for Oliver K. Woodman*
Pilgrim, Elza. *The china doll*
Santiago, Esmeralda. *A doll for Navidades*

Toys — pandas *see* Toys — bears

Toys — teddy bears *see* Toys — bears

Tractors

Carter, Don. *Old MacDonald drives a tractor*
Dierssen, Andreas. *The old red tractor*
Pallotta, Jerry. *The construction alphabet book*
Peterson, Cris. *Fantastic farm machines*
Ransom, Candice F. *Tractor day*
Schubert, Leda. *Here comes Darrell*
van Lieshout, Elle. *The wish*

Trading *see* Activities — trading

Trains

Bee, William. *And the train goes . . .*
C is for caboose
Crunk, Tony. *Railroad John and the Red Rock run*
Hubbell, Patricia. *Trains*
London, Jonathan. *A train goes clickety-clack*
Lund, Deb. *All aboard the dinotrain*
Piper, Watty. *The little engine that could*
Prince, Joshua. *I saw an ant on the railroad track*
Skinner, Daphne. *All aboard!*
Sobel, June. *The goodnight train*

Transportation

Cousins, Lucy. *Stop and go, Maisy*
Freymann, Saxton. *Fast Food*
Lillegard, Dee. *Go!*
London, Jonathan. *My big rig*
Lord, Janet. *Here comes Grandma!*
Mayo, Margaret. *Choo choo clickety-clack!*
Mitton, Tony. *Cool cars*
Mortensen, Denise Dowling. *Wake up engines*
Rau, Dana Meachen. *Riding*
Wellington, Monica. *Truck driver Tom*
Willems, Mo. *The Pigeon loves things that go!*
Ziefert, Harriet. *From Kalamazoo to Timbuktu!*

Traveling *see* Activities — traveling

Trees

Aston, Dianna Hutts. *An orange in January*
Atwood, Margaret. *Up in the tree*
Bond, Rebecca. *A city Christmas tree*
Brown, Margaret Wise. *The little fir tree*
Brown, Ruth. *The old tree*
Demas, Corinne. *Two Christmas mice*
DePalma, Mary Newell. *A grand old tree*
Hassett, Ann. *The finest Christmas tree*
Helmer, Marilyn. *One splendid tree*
Hubery, Julia. *A friend for all seasons*
Landa, Norbert. *Little Bear and the wishing tree*
Lears, Laurie. *Megan's birthday tree*
Minor, Wendell. *Christmas tree!*
Näslund, Gorel Kristina. *Our apple tree*
Purmwell, Ann. *Christmas tree farm*
Rawlinson, Julia. *Fletcher and the falling leaves*
Stein, David Ezra. *Leaves*
Thompson, Lauren. *The apple pie that Papa baked*
Zweibel, Alan. *Our tree named Steve*

Trickery *see* Behavior — trickery

Tricks *see* Magic

Trinidad *see* Foreign lands — Trinidad

Trolls *see* Mythical creatures — trolls

Truck drivers *see* Careers — truck drivers

Trucks

Anderson, Peggy Perry. *Chuck's truck*
Armstrong, Jennifer. *Magnus at the fire*
Ayres, Katherine. *Matthew's truck*
Coffelt, Nancy. *Pug in a truck*
Garcia, Emma. *Tip tip dig dig*
Hunter, Jana Novotny. *When Daddy's truck picks me up*
London, Jonathan. *My big rig*
    A truck goes rattley-bumpa
Lyon, George Ella. *Trucks roll!*
Maass, Robert. *Little trucks with big jobs*
McMullan, Kate. *I'm dirty!*
Moore, Patrick. *The mighty street sweeper*
Odanaka, Barbara. *Smash! Mash! Crash! There goes the trash!*
Olson-Brown, Ellen. *Hush little digger*
Pallotta, Jerry. *The construction alphabet book*
Roberts, Cynthia. *Tow trucks*
Rockwell, Anne F. *Good morning, Digger*
Schubert, Leda. *Here comes Darrell*
Skultety, Nancy. *From here to there*
Timmers, Leo. *Who is driving?*
Wellington, Monica. *Truck driver Tom*
Wood, Audrey. *Alphabet rescue*

Tsunamis

Bauer, Marion Dane. *A mama for Owen*
Kroll, Virginia L. *Selvakumar knew better*
Lucas, David. *Whale*
Winter, Jeanette. *Mama*

Tubas *see* Musical instruments — tubas

Turkeys *see* Birds — turkeys

Turtles *see* Reptiles — turtles, tortoises

TV *see* Television

Twins *see* Multiple births — twins

U.S. history

Adler, David A. *A picture book of John Hancock*
　A picture book of Samuel Adams
Allen, Kathy. *The U.S. Constitution*
Appelt, Kathi. *Miss Lady Bird's wildflowers*
Barbour, Karen. *Mr. Williams*
Bildner, Phil. *The greatest game ever played*
Birtha, Becky. *Grandmama's pride*
Burleigh, Robert. *Stealing home*
Chaconas, Dori. *Pennies in a jar*
Clinton, Catherine. *When Harriet met Sojourner*
Cohan, George M. *You're a grand old flag*
Cole, Barbara Hancock. *Anna and Natalie*
Cotten, Cynthia. *Abbie in stitches*
Edwards, David. *The pen that Pa built*
Edwards, Pamela Duncan. *The bus ride that changed history*
FitzGerald, Dawn. *Vinnie and Abraham*
Floca, Brian. *Lightship*
Gilchrist, Jan Spivey. *My America*
Giovanni, Nikki. *Rosa*
Grifalconi, Ann. *Ain't nobody a stranger to me*
Harness, Cheryl. *Our colonial year*
Haskins, Jim (James). *Delivering justice*
Heinz, Brian J. *Nathan of yesteryear and Michael of today*
Helmer, Marilyn. *One splendid tree*
Hilliard, Richard. *Godspeed, John Glenn*
Hubbard, Crystal. *Catching the moon*
Johnson, Angela. *Wind flyers*
Kinsey-Warnock, Natalie. *Nora's ark*
Krensky, Stephen. *Hanukkah at Valley Forge*
Krull, Kathleen. *Pocahontas*
Lee-Tai, Amy. *A place where sunflowers grow / Sabaku ni saita himawari*
Levine, Ellen. *Henry's freedom box*
Lyons, Kelly Starling. *One million men and me*
McKissack, Patricia C. *The all-I'll-ever-want Christmas doll*
Messinger, Carla. *When the shadbush blooms*
Minor, Wendell. *Yankee Doodle America*
Nelson, S. D. *Quiet hero*
Neubecker, Robert. *Wow! America!*
Raschka, Chris. *New York is English, Chattanooga is Creek*
Raven, Margot Theis. *Night boat to freedom*
Sanders, Nancy. *D is for drinking gourd*
Shore, Diane Z. *This is the dream*
Smith, Lane. *John, Paul, George & Ben*
Smith, Marie. *N is for our nation's capital*
Thermes, Jennifer. *Sam Bennett's new shoes*
Turner, Glennette Tilley. *An apple for Harriet Tubman*
Weatherford, Carole Boston. *Champions on the bench*
　Freedom on the menu
　Moses
Wilson, Karma. *How to bake an American pie*
Woodruff, Elvira. *Small beauties*
Woodson, Jacqueline. *Show way*
Yin. *Brothers*

U.S. history — frontier & pioneer life

Crunk, Tony. *Railroad John and the Red Rock run*
Emmett, Jonathan. *She'll be coming 'round the mountain*
Hopkins, Jackie Mims. *The gold miner's daughter*
Kimmel, Eric A. *The great Texas hamster drive*
Rumford, James. *Don't touch my hat!*
Sneed, Brad. *Deputy Harvey and the ant cow caper*
Stein, David Ezra. *Cowboy Ned and Andy*
　Ned's new friend

Van Leeuwen, Jean. *Papa and the pioneer quilt*
Van Steenwyk, Elizabeth. *Prairie Christmas*

Umbrellas

Franson, Scott E. *Un-brella*
Weeks, Sarah. *Ella, of course!*

Uncles *see* Family life — aunts, uncles

Unhappiness *see* Emotions — happiness; Emotions — sadness

Unicorns *see* Mythical creatures — unicorns

Unusual format *see* Format, unusual

Up & down *see* Concepts — up & down

Vacationing *see* Activities — vacationing

Valentine's Day *see* Holidays — Valentine's Day

Venezuela *see* Foreign lands — Venezuela

Veterinarians *see* Careers — veterinarians

Vietnam *see* Foreign lands — Vietnam

Violins *see* Musical instruments — violins

Volcanoes

Schaefer, Lola M. *An island grows*

Vultures *see* Birds — vultures

Waiters *see* Careers — waiters, waitresses

Waitresses *see* Careers — waiters, waitresses

Walking *see* Activities — walking

Wallabies *see* Animals — wallabies

War

Chaconas, Dori. *Pennies in a jar*
Helmer, Marilyn. *One splendid tree*
Johnson, Angela. *Wind flyers*
Lee-Tai, Amy. *A place where sunflowers grow / Sabaku ni saita himawari*
McElroy, Lisa Tucker. *Love, Lizzie*

Watches *see* Clocks, watches

Water

McPhail, David. *Water boy*
Morrison, Gordon. *A drop of water*
Strauss, Rochelle. *One well*
Wells, Robert E. *Did a dinosaur drink this water?*

Weasels *see* Animals — weasels

Weather

Bauer, Marion Dane. *If frogs made the weather*
Cousins, Lucy. *Maisy's wonderful weather book*
Dodds, Dayle Ann. *Hello, sun!*
Krupinski, Loretta. *Pirate treasure*
MacLennan, Cathy. *Chicky Chicky Chook Chook*
Michaels, Pat. *W is for wind*
Ryan, Pam Muñoz. *There was no snow on Christmas Eve*
Schmidt, Karen Lee. *Carl's nose*
Spinelli, Eileen. *Heat wave*

Weather — blizzards

Hurst, Carol Otis. *Terrible storm*

Weather — clouds

Niemann, Christoph. *The police cloud*

Weather — cold

Aillaud, Cindy Lou. *Recess at 20 below*
Powell, Consie. *The first day of winter*

Weather — droughts

Meunier, Brian. *Bravo, Tavo!*

Weather — floods

Kinsey-Warnock, Natalie. *Nora's ark*
MacDonald, Alan. *Wilfred to the rescue*
Schneider, Josh. *You'll be sorry*
Stewig, John Warren. *The animals watched*

Weather — fog

McDonnell, Patrick. *Just like Heaven*
Trotter, Deborah W. *How do you know?*

Weather — hurricanes

Paterson, Diane. *Hurricane wolf*

Weather — lightning, thunder

Griessman, Annette. *Like a hundred drums*
Mortensen, Denise Dowling. *Ohio thunder*

Weather — mist *see* Weather — fog

Weather — rain

Beaumont, Karen. *Move over, Rover*
Bridges, Margaret Park. *I love the rain*
Lakin, Patricia. *Rainy day*
Lehman, Barbara. *Rainstorm*
Stewig, John Warren. *The animals watched*
Yee, Wong Herbert. *Who likes rain?*

Weather — snow

Aillaud, Cindy Lou. *Recess at 20 below*
Berry, Lynne. *Duck skates*
Brett, Jan. *The three snow bears*
Brunelle, Nicholas. *Snow Moon*
Butler, M. Christina. *Snow friends*
Child, Lauren. *Snow is my favorite and my best*

Denslow, Sharon Phillips. *In the snow*
Emmett, Jonathan. *Diamond in the snow*
Fallon, Jimmy. *Snowball fight!*
Fleming, Denise. *The first day of winter*
Ford, Bernette G. *First snow*
Gore, Leonid. *Danny's first snow*
Hobbie, Holly. *Toot and Puddle*
Huneck, Stephen. *Sally's snow adventure*
Kroll, Virginia L. *Good citizen Sarah*
Laminack, Lester L. *Snow day!*
Lin, Grace. *Robert's snowflakes*
Mahoney, Daniel J. *A really good snowman*
Paradis, Susan. *Snow princess*
Sabuda, Robert. *Winter's tale*
Schoenherr, Ian. *Pip and Squeak*
Thompson, Lauren. *Mouse's first snow*
Wallace, Nancy Elizabeth. *Snow*
Wilson, Karma. *Dinos in the snow!*

Weather — storms

Berger, Barbara. *Thunder Bunny*
Emmett, Jonathan. *This way, Ruby!*
Gerritsen, Paula. *Nuts*
Griessman, Annette. *Like a hundred drums*
Krensky, Stephen. *Milo and the really big bunny*
Mortensen, Denise Dowling. *Ohio thunder*
Seeger, Laura Vaccaro. *Walter was worried*
Sidman, Joyce. *Meow ruff*

Weather — thunder *see* Weather — lightning, thunder

Weather — tornadoes

Lester, Helen. *Batter up Wombat*

Weather — wind

Derby, Sally. *Whoosh went the wind!*
Ehlert, Lois. *Leaf man*
Kaner, Etta. *Who likes the wind?*
McMillan, Bruce. *How the ladies stopped the wind*
Thompson, Lauren. *Mouse's first spring*

Weather reporters *see* Careers — meteorologists

Weaving *see* Activities — weaving

Weddings

Broach, Elise. *Wet dog!*
Bunting, Eve (Anne Evelyn). *My mom's wedding*
Crunk, Tony. *Railroad John and the Red Rock run*
A frog he would a-wooing go (folk-song). *Froggy went a-courtin'*
Henkes, Kevin. *Lilly's big day*
Look, Lenore. *Uncle Peter's amazing Chinese wedding*
Stanley, Mandy. *Lettice the flower girl*

Weekdays *see* Days of the week, months of the year

West *see* U.S. history — frontier & pioneer life

Whales *see* Animals — whales

Wheels

Pearson, Debora. *Sophie's wheels*
Prince, April Jones. *What do wheels do all day?*

Willfulness *see* Character traits — willfulness

Wind *see* Weather — wind

Wings *see* Anatomy — wings

Winter *see* Seasons — winter

Wishing *see* Behavior — wishing

Witches

Berry, Lynne. *The curious demise of a contrary cat*
Grimm, Jacob. *Hansel and Gretel*
    Hansel and Gretel / Hansel y Gretel
    Jorinda and Jorindel
    Rapunzel
    Snow White
McGhee, Alison. *A very brave witch*
McGrath, Barbara Barbieri. *The little green witch*
Meddaugh, Susan. *The witch's walking stick*
Thomas, Valerie. *Winnie the witch*

Wizards

Prelutsky, Jack. *The wizard*
Robertson, M. P. *The dragon snatcher*

Wolves *see* Animals — wolves

Wombats *see* Animals — wombats

Woodcarving *see* Activities — wood carving

Woodchucks *see* Animals — groundhogs

Woods *see* Forest, woods

Wooly mammoths *see* Animals — wooly mammoths

Word games *see* Language

Wordless

Cosentino, Ralph. *The marvelous misadventures of — Fun-Boy*
Faller, Regis. *The adventures of Polo*
    Polo
Franson, Scott E. *Un-brella*
Geisert, Arthur. *Oops*
Kamm, Katja. *Invisible*
Khing, T. T. *Where is the cake?*
Lehman, Barbara. *Museum trip*
    Rainstorm
Newgarden, Mark. *Bow-Wow bugs a bug*
Nickle, John. *Alphabet explosion!*
Ommen, Sylvia van. *The surprise*
Polhemus, Coleman. *The crocodile blues*
Rogers, Gregory. *The boy, the bear, the baron, the bard*
    Midsummer knight
Schories, Pat. *Jack and the night visitors*
Tanaka, Shinsuke. *Wings*
Varon, Sara. *Chicken and Cat*
Wakeman, Daniel. *Ben's bunny trouble*

Working *see* Activities — working; Careers

World

Brunhoff, Laurent de. *Babar's world tour*
Carney-Nunes, Charisse. *I dream for you a world*
Corr, Christopher. *Whole world*

Frank, John. *How to catch a fish*
    Here we go round the mulberry bush
Jackson, Ellen B. *Earth Mother*
Katz, Karen. *Can you say peace?*
Kerley, Barbara. *You and me together*
Lewin, Ted. *How much?*
McGinty, Alice B. *Thank you, world*
Reynolds, Jan. *Celebrate!*
Rylant, Cynthia. *The stars will still shine*
Schertle, Alice. *We*
Willis, Jeanne. *Gorilla! Gorilla!*

Worms *see* Animals — worms

Worrying *see* Behavior — worrying

Writing *see* Activities — writing

Writing letters *see* Letters, cards

Yaks *see* Animals — yaks

Yukon Territory *see* Foreign lands — Yukon Territory

Zodiac

Casey, Dawn. *The great race*

Zoos

Elliott, George. *The boy who loved bananas*
Hogg, Gary. *Beautiful Buehla and the zany zoo makeover*
Ichikawa, Satomi. *I am Pangoo the penguin*
Jarman, Julia. *Class Two at the zoo*
Kurtz, Jane. *Do kangaroos wear seat belts?*
Mora, Pat. *Marimba!*
Napoli, Donna Jo. *Bobby the bold*
Pfister, Marcus. *Charlie at the zoo*
Pinkwater, Daniel Manus. *Bad bears go visiting*
Rex, Adam. *Pssst!*
Richardson, Justin. *And Tango makes three*
Ryder, Joanne. *A pair of polar bears*
Smith, Marie. *Z is for zookeeper*
Wilson, Karma. *Animal strike at the zoo, it's true!*
Wise, William. *Zany zoo*

Bibliographic Guide

Arranged alphabetically by author's name in boldface (or by title, if author is unknown), each entry includes title, illustrator, publisher, publication date, and subjects. Joint authors and their titles appear as short entries, with the main author name (in parentheses after the title) citing where the complete entry will be found. Where only an author and title are given, complete information is listed under the title as the main entry.

Abeele, Veronique van den. *Still my Grandma* ill. by Claude K. Dubois. Eerdmans, 2007. ISBN 978-0-8028-5323-3 Subj: Family life — grandmothers. Illness — Alzheimer's.

Abercrombie, Barbara. *The show-and-tell lion* ill. by Lynne Cravath. Simon & Schuster, 2006. ISBN 0-689-86408-6 Subj: Behavior — lying. Character traits — honesty. Imagination.

Abeya, Elisabet. *Hansel and Gretel / Hansel y Gretel* (Grimm, Jacob)

Abraham, Michelle Shapiro. *My cousin Tamar lives in Israel* ill. by Ann D. Koffsky. URJ Press, 2007. ISBN 978-0-8074-0989-3 Subj: Foreign lands — Israel. Jewish culture.

Addy, Sharon Hart. *Lucky Jake* ill. by Wade Zahares. Houghton Mifflin, 2007. ISBN 978-0-618-47286-4 Subj: Animals — pigs. Careers — miners. Character traits — luck.

Adkins, Jan. *What if you met a knight?* ill. by author. Macmillan, 2006. ISBN 1-59643-148-2 Subj: Knights. Middle Ages.

Adler, David A. *Campy: the story of Roy Campanella* ill. by Gordon C. James. Penguin, 2007. ISBN 0-670-06041-0 Subj: Ethnic groups in the U.S. — African Americans. Handicaps — physical handicaps. Sports — baseball.

Joe Louis: America's fighter ill. by Terry Widener. Harcourt, 2005. ISBN 0-15-216480-4 Subj: Ethnic groups in the U.S. — African Americans. Sports. Sports — boxing.

A picture book of John Hancock ill. by Ronald Himler. Holiday House, 2007. ISBN 978-0-8234-2005-6 Subj: U.S. history.

A picture book of Samuel Adams by David A. & Michael S. Adler; ill. by Ronald Himler. Holiday House, 2005. ISBN 0-8234-1846-4 Subj: U.S. history.

Satchel Paige: don't look back ill. by Terry Widener. Harcourt, 2007. ISBN 0-15-205585-1 Subj: Ethnic groups in the U.S. — African Americans. Sports — baseball.

Adler, Michael S. *A picture book of Samuel Adams* (Adler, David A.)

Aesop. *The hare and the tortoise / La liebre y la tortuga* adapt. by Maria Eulalia Valeri; ill. by Max. Chronicle, 2006. ISBN 0-8118-5057-9 Subj: Animals — rabbits. Folk & fairy tales. Foreign languages. Reptiles — turtles, tortoises. Sports — racing.

Agee, Jon. *Nothing* ill. by author. Hyperion, 2007. ISBN 978-0-7868-3694-9 Subj: Humorous stories. Shopping. Stores.

Terrific ill. by author. Hyperion, 2005. ISBN 0-7868-5184-8 Subj: Behavior — bad day. Behavior — dissatisfaction. Birds — parrots.

Ahlberg, Allan. *Previously* ill. by Bruce Ingman. Candlewick, 2007. ISBN 978-0-7636-3542-8 Subj: Folk & fairy tales.

The runaway dinner ill. by Bruce Ingman. Candlewick, 2006. ISBN 0-7636-3142-6 Subj: Behavior — running away. Food.

The shopping expedition ill. by André Amstutz. Candlewick, 2005. ISBN 0-7636-2586-8 Subj: Imagination. Shopping.

Ahmed, Said Salah. *The lion's share / Qayb Libaax: a Somali folktale* ill. by Kelly Dupre. Minnesota Humanities Commission, 2006. ISBN 1-931016-12-7 Subj: Behavior — greed. Folk & fairy tales. Foreign lands — Somalia. Foreign languages.

Aillaud, Cindy Lou. *Recess at 20 below* photos by author. Alaska Northwest/Graphic Arts Center Publishing, 2005. ISBN 0-88540-609-4 Subj: Alaska. Weather — cold. Weather — snow.

Alberti, Theresa Jarosz. *Vietnam ABCs: a book about the people and places of Vietnam* ill. by Natascha Alex Blanks. Picture Window, 2007. ISBN 978-1-4048-2251-1 Subj: ABC books. Foreign lands — Vietnam.

Alborough, Jez. *Duck's key where can it be?* ill. by author. Kane/Miller, 2005. ISBN 1-929132-72-7 Subj: Behavior — lost & found possessions. Birds — ducks. Format, unusual — toy & movable books. Rhyming text.

Hit the ball duck ill. by author. Kane/Miller, 2006. ISBN 1-929132-96-4 Subj: Birds — ducks. Rhyming text. Sports — baseball.

Tall ill. by author. Candlewick, 2005. ISBN 0-7636-2784-4 Subj: Animals. Animals — monkeys. Character traits — smallness. Concepts — size. Format, unusual — board books. Jungles. Rhyming text.

Yes ill. by author. Candlewick, 2006. ISBN 0-7636-3183-3 Subj: Animals — chimpanzees. Bedtime. Behavior — fighting, arguing.

Alcott, Louisa May. *An old-fashioned Thanksgiving* ill. by James Bernardin. HarperCollins, 2005. ISBN 0-06-000451-7 Subj: Family life. Family life — grandmothers. Food. Holidays — Thanksgiving.

Alda, Arlene. *Did you say pears?* photos by author. Tundra, 2006. ISBN 0-88776-739-7 Subj: Language.

Aldrin, Buzz. *Reaching for the moon* ill. by Wendell Minor. HarperCollins, 2005. ISBN 0-06-055446-0 Subj: Careers — astronauts. Moon. Space & space ships.

Alexander, Jessica. *Look both ways: a cautionary tale* (Shore, Diane Z.)

This is the dream (Shore, Diane Z.)

Aliki. *A play's the thing* ill. by author. HarperCollins, 2005. ISBN 0-06-074356-5 Subj: Character traits — cooperation. School. Theater.

Allen, Jonathan. *"I'm not cute!"* ill. by author. Hyperion, 2006. ISBN 0-7868-3720-9 Subj: Animals. Birds — owls. Character traits — appearance.

"I'm not scared!" ill. by author. Hyperion, 2007. ISBN 978-0-7868-3722-9 Subj: Birds — owls. Emotions — fear.

Allen, Kathy. *The U.S. Constitution.* Capstone, 2006. ISBN 0-7368-9594-9 Subj: U.S. history.

Almond, David. *Kate, the cat and the moon* ill. by Stephen Lambert. Random House, 2005. ISBN 0-385-90929-2 Subj: Animals — cats. Imagination. Night.

Alsenas, Linas. *Mrs. Claus takes a vacation* ill. by author. Scholastic, 2006. ISBN 0-439-77978-2 Subj: Activities — traveling. Activities — vacationing. Holidays — Christmas. Santa Claus.

Peanut ill. by author. Scholastic, 2007. ISBN 978-0-439-77980-7 Subj: Animals — camels. Animals — elephants. Circus. Old age. Pets.

Amado, Elisa. *Monster, don't eat me!* (Norac, Carl)

Sky blue accident / Accidente celeste (Lujan, Jorge)

Tricycle ill. by Alfonso Ruano. Groundwood, 2007. ISBN 978-0-88899-614-5 Subj: Behavior — stealing. Friendship. Prejudice.

Ancona, George. *Mi música / My music* photos by author. Scholastic, 2005. ISBN 0-516-25295-X Subj: Ethnic groups in the U.S. — Hispanic Americans. Foreign languages. Music.

Mis abuelos / My grandparents photos by author. Scholastic, 2005. ISBN 0-516-25294-1 Subj: Ethnic groups in the U.S. — Hispanic Americans. Family life — grandparents. Foreign languages.

Mis comidas / My foods photos by author. Scholastic, 2005. ISBN 0-516-25292-5 Subj: Ethnic groups in the U.S. — Hispanic Americans. Food. Foreign languages.

Mis fiestas / My celebrations photos by author. Scholastic, 2005. ISBN 0-516-25290-9 Subj: Ethnic groups in the U.S. — Hispanic Americans. Foreign languages. Holidays.

Mis juegos / My games photos by author. Scholastic, 2005. ISBN 0-516-25293-3 Subj: Ethnic groups in the U.S. — Hispanic Americans. Foreign languages. Games.

Mis quehaceres / My chores photos by author. Scholastic, 2005. ISBN 0-516-25291-7 Subj: Activities — working. Character traits — helpfulness. Ethnic groups in the U.S. — Hispanic Americans. Foreign languages.

Andersen, H. C. (Hans Christian). *The princess and the pea* ill. by Rachel Isadora. Penguin, 2007. ISBN 978-0-399-24611-1 Subj: Folk & fairy tales. Foreign lands — East Africa. Royalty — princesses. Sleep.

The princess and the pea retold by John Cech; ill. by Bernhard Oberdieck. Sterling, 2007. ISBN 978-1-4027-3065-8 Subj: Folk & fairy tales. Royalty — princesses. Sleep.

The princess and the pea in miniature: after the fairy tale by Hans Christian Andersen adapt. by Lauren Child; photos by Polly Borland. Hyperion, 2006. ISBN 0-7868-3886-8 Subj: Folk & fairy tales. Royalty — princesses. Sleep.

Thumbelina retold & ill. by Lauren A. Mills. Little, Brown, 2005. ISBN 0-316-57359-0 Subj: Character traits — smallness. Folk & fairy tales.

The tinderbox retold by Stephen Mitchell; ill. by Bagram Ibatoulline. Candlewick, 2007. ISBN 978-0-7636-2078-3 Subj: Careers — military. Folk & fairy tales. Magic.

The ugly duckling ill. by Robert Ingpen. Minedition, 2005. ISBN 0-698-40010-0 Subj: Birds — ducks. Birds — swans. Character traits — appearance. Character traits — being different. Folk & fairy tales.

The wild swans ill. by Anne Yvonne Gilbert. Barefoot, 2005. ISBN 1-84148-164-5 Subj: Birds — swans. Folk & fairy tales. Magic.

Anderson, Christine. *Bedtime!* ill. by Steven Salerno. Penguin, 2005. ISBN 0-399-24004-7 Subj: Bedtime.

Anderson, Derek. *Gladys goes out to lunch* ill. by author. Simon & Schuster, 2005. ISBN 0-689-85688-1 Subj: Animals — gorillas. Food.

How the Easter Bunny saved Christmas ill. by author. Simon & Schuster, 2006. ISBN 0-689-87634-3 Subj: Animals — rabbits. Character traits — helpfulness. Holidays — Christmas. Santa Claus.

Over the river: a turkey's tale ill. by author. Simon & Schuster, 2005. ISBN 0-689-87635-1 Subj: Birds — turkeys. Holidays — Thanksgiving. Songs.

Romeo and Lou blast off ill. by author. Simon & Schuster, 2007. ISBN 978-1-4169-3784-5 Subj: Animals — polar bears. Birds — penguins. Friendship. Space & space ships.

Anderson, Lena. *The hedgehog, the pig, and their little friend* trans. from Swedish by Joan Sandin; ill. by Lena Anderson. Farrar, Straus & Giroux, 2007. ISBN 978-91-29-66742-4 Subj: Animals — hedgehogs. Animals — pigs. Behavior — lost. Rhyming text.

Anderson, Peggy Perry. *Chuck's truck* ill. by author. Houghton Mifflin, 2006. ISBN 0-618-66836-5 Subj: Animals. Rhyming text. Trucks.

Joe on the go ill. by author. Houghton Mifflin, 2007. ISBN 978-0-618-77331-2 Subj: Activities — playing. Family life — grandmothers. Frogs & toads.

Andreae, Giles. *Captain Flinn and the pirate dinosaurs* ill. by Russell Ayto. Simon & Schuster, 2005. ISBN 1-4169-0713-0 Subj: Dinosaurs. Imagination. Pirates. School.

Dinosaurs galore! ill. by David Wojtowycz. Tiger Tales, 2005. ISBN 1-58925-044-3 Subj: Dinosaurs. Poetry.

Andreasen, Dan. *The giant of Seville: A "tall" tale based on a true story* ill. by author. Abrams, 2007. ISBN 978-0-8109-0988-5 Subj: Character traits — kindness. Circus. Giants. Tall tales.

Angelou, Maya. *Read and rise* (Pinkney, Sandra L.)

Anholt, Catherine. *Happy birthday, Chimp and Zee* by Catherine & Laurence Anholt; ill. by authors. Frances Lincoln, 2006. ISBN 1-84507-507-2 Subj: Animals — chimpanzees. Birthdays. Parties. Rhyming text.

Anholt, Laurence. *Happy birthday, Chimp and Zee* (Anholt, Catherine)

Seven for a secret ill. by Jim Coplestone. Frances Lincoln, 2006. ISBN 1-84507-300-2 Subj: Death. Emotions — love. Family life — grandfathers. Letters, cards.

Appelt, Kathi. *Merry Christmas, merry crow* ill. by Jon Goodell. Harcourt, 2005. ISBN 0-15-202651-7 Subj: Birds — crows. Holidays — Christmas. Rhyming text.

Miss Lady Bird's wildflowers: how a first lady changed America ill. by Joy Fisher Hein. HarperCollins, 2005. ISBN 0-06-001108-4 Subj: Ecology. Flowers. U.S. history.

My father's house ill. by Raúl Colón. Penguin, 2007. ISBN 978-0-670-03669-1 Subj: Nature. Poetry. Religion.

Archer, Peggy. *From dawn to dreams: poems for busy babies* ill. by Hanako Wakiyama. Candlewick, 2007. ISBN 978-0-7636-2467-5 Subj: Babies. Poetry.

Turkey surprise ill. by Thor Wickstrom. Penguin, 2005. ISBN 0-8037-2969-3 Subj: Birds — turkeys. Family life — brothers & sisters. Holidays — Thanksgiving.

Argueta, Jorge. *Moony Luna / Luna, Lunita Lunera* ill. by Elizabeth Gomez. Children's Book Press, 2005. ISBN 0-89239-205-3 Subj: Foreign languages. School — first day.

Arisa, Miguel. *Celebrate! It's cinco de mayo! / Celebremos! Es el cinco de mayo!* (Levy, Janice)

Armstrong, Jennifer. *Magnus at the fire* ill. by Owen Smith. Simon & Schuster, 2005. ISBN 0-689-83922-7 Subj: Animals — horses, ponies. Careers — firefighters. Trucks.

Once upon a banana ill. by David Small. Simon & Schuster, 2006. ISBN 978-0-689-84251 Subj: Food. Humorous stories.

Arnold, Caroline. *A penguin's world* ill. by author. Picture Window, 2006. ISBN 1-4048-1323-3 Subj: Birds — penguins.

Arnold, Katya. *Elephants can paint, too!* photos by author. Simon & Schuster, 2005. ISBN 0-689-86985-1 Subj: Activities — painting. Animals — elephants. Foreign lands — Thailand.

Arnold, Marsha Diane. *Roar of a snore* ill. by Pierre Pratt. Penguin, 2006. ISBN 0-8037-2936-7 Subj: Bedtime. Noise, sounds. Rhyming text. Sleep — snoring.

Arnold, Tedd. *The twin princes* ill. by author. Penguin, 2007. ISBN 978-0-8037-2696-3 Subj: Birds — chickens. Contests. Multiple births — twins. Royalty — princes.

Arnosky, Jim. *Babies in the bayou* ill. by author. Penguin, 2007. ISBN 0-399-22653-2 Subj: Animals. Babies. Nature.

Coyote raid in Cactus Canyon ill. by author. Penguin, 2005. ISBN 0-399-23413-6 Subj: Animals — coyotes. Desert. Reptiles — snakes.

Grandfather Buffalo ill. by author. Penguin, 2006. ISBN 0-399-24169-8 Subj: Animals — buffaloes. Old age.

Parrotfish and sunken ships: exploring a tropical reef ill. by author. HarperCollins, 2007. ISBN 978-0-688-17123-0 Subj: Boats, ships. Nature. Sea & seashore.

Arrigan, Mary. *Mario's angels: a story about the artist Giotto* ill. by Gillian McClure. Frances Lincoln, 2006. ISBN 1-84507-404-1 Subj: Angels. Art. Careers — artists.

Aruego, Jose. *The last laugh* by Jose Aruego & Ariane Dewey; ill. by authors. Penguin, 2006. ISBN 0-8037-3093-4 Subj: Behavior — bullying. Birds — ducks. Reptiles — snakes.

Asch, Frank. *Mrs. Marlowe's mice* ill. by Devin Asch. Kids Can, 2007. ISBN 978-1-55453-022-9 Subj: Animals — cats. Animals — mice. Behavior — secrets.

Asher, Sandy. *Too many frogs!* ill. by Keith Graves. Penguin, 2005. ISBN 0-399-23978-2 Subj: Animals — rabbits. Behavior — solitude. Frogs & toads.

What a party! ill. by Keith Graves. Penguin, 2007. ISBN 978-0-399-24496-4 Subj: Birthdays. Family life — grandfathers. Frogs & toads. Parties.

Ashman, Linda. *Babies on the go* ill. by Jane Dyer. Harcourt, 2007. ISBN 978-0-15-205886-9 Subj: Animals. Babies. Format, unusual — board books.

Desmond and the naughtybugs ill. by Anik McCrory. Penguin, 2006. ISBN 978-0-525-47203-2 Subj: Behavior — misbehavior.

Mama's day ill. by Jan Ormerod. Simon & Schuster, 2006. ISBN 0-689-83475-6 Subj: Babies. Family life — mothers. Rhyming text.

Starry safari ill. by Jeff Mack. Harcourt, 2005. ISBN 0-15-204766-2 Subj: Bedtime. Jungles. Rhyming text.

To the beach! ill. by Nadine Bernard Westcott. Harcourt, 2005. ISBN 0-15-216490-1 Subj: Behavior — forgetfulness. Family life. Humorous stories. Rhyming text. Sea & seashore — beaches.

What could be better than this ill. by Linda S. Wingerter. Penguin, 2006. ISBN 0-525-46954-0 Subj: Emotions — love. Family life — parents.

Asim, Jabari. *Daddy goes to work* ill. by Aaron Boyd. Little, Brown, 2006. ISBN 0-316-73575-2 Subj: Activities — working. Ethnic groups in the U.S. — African Americans. Family life — fathers. Rhyming text.

Aska, Warabe. *Tapicero tap tap* ill. by author. Tundra, 2006. ISBN 0-88776-760-5 Subj: Activities — storytelling. Character traits — ambition. Family life — grandfathers. Foreign lands — Spain.

Aston, Dianna Hutts. *An egg is quiet* ill. by Sylvia Long. Chronicle, 2006. ISBN 0-8118-4428-5 Subj: Eggs.

Mama outside, Mama inside ill. by Susan Gaber. Henry Holt, 2006. ISBN 0-8050-7716-2 Subj: Babies. Birds. Birth. Family life — mothers.

An orange in January ill. by Julie Maren. Penguin, 2007. ISBN 978-0-8037-3146-2 Subj: Food. Trees.

A seed is sleepy ill. by Sylvia Long. Chronicle, 2007. ISBN 978-0-8118-5520-4 Subj: Seeds.

Atwood, Margaret. *Up in the tree* ill. by author. Groundwood, 2006. ISBN 0-88899-729-9 Subj: Trees.

Auch, Herm. *Beauty and the beaks: a turkey's cautionary tale* (Auch, Mary Jane)

Chickerella (Auch, Mary Jane)

Auch, Mary Jane. *Beauty and the beaks: a turkey's cautionary tale* by Mary Jane & Herm Auch; ill. by authors. Holiday House, 2007. ISBN 978-0-8234-1990-6 Subj: Behavior — boasting. Birds — chickens. Birds — turkeys. Holidays — Thanksgiving.

Chickerella by Mary Jane & Herm Auch; ill. by authors. Holiday House, 2005. ISBN 0-8234-1804-9 Subj: Birds — chickens. Folk & fairy tales. Humorous stories.

Aylesworth, Jim. *Little Bitty Mousie* ill. by Michael Hague. Walker & Company, 2007. ISBN 978-0-8027-9637-0 Subj: ABC books. Animals — mice. Rhyming text.

Ayres, Katherine. *Matthew's truck* ill. by Hideko Takahashi. Candlewick, 2005. ISBN 0-7636-2269-9 Subj: Activities — playing. Toys. Trucks.

Up, down, and around ill. by Nadine Bernard Westcott. Candlewick, 2007. ISBN 978-0-7636-2378-4 Subj: Gardens, gardening. Language. Rhyming text.

Azore, Barbara. *Wanda and the frogs* ill. by Georgia Graham. Tundra, 2007. ISBN 978-0-88776-761-6 Subj: Frogs & toads. Humorous stories.

Wanda and the wild hair ill. by Georgia Graham. Tundra, 2005. ISBN 0-88776-717-6 Subj: Character traits — appearance. Hair.

Bachelet, Gilles. *My cat, the silliest cat in the world* ill. by author. Abrams, 2006. ISBN 0-8109-4913-X Subj: Animals — elephants. Humorous stories. Pets.

When the silliest cat was small ill. by author. Abrams, 2007. ISBN 978-0-8109-9415-7 Subj: Animals — elephants. Humorous stories. Pets.

Baddiel, Ivor. *Cock-a-doodle quack! Quack!* by Ivor Baddiel & Sophie Jubb; ill. by Ailie Busby. Random House, 2007. ISBN 978-0-385-75104-9 Subj: Animals. Animals — babies. Birds — chickens. Farms. Noise, sounds.

Bae, Hyun-Joo. *New clothes for New Year's day* ill. by author. Kane/Miller, 2007. ISBN 978-1-933605-29-6 Subj: Clothing. Foreign lands — Korea. Holidays — New Year's.

Bagert, Brod. *Shout! Little poems that roar* ill. by Sachiko Yoshikawa. Penguin, 2007. ISBN 978-0-8037-2972-8 Subj: Poetry.

Baguley, Elizabeth. *Meggie moon* ill. by Gregoire Mabire. Good Books, 2005. ISBN 1-56148-474-1 Subj: Activities — playing. Gender roles. Imagination.

Baicker, Karen. *You can do it too!* ill. by Ken Wilson-Max. Handprint, 2005. ISBN 1-59354-080-9 Subj: Ethnic groups in the U.S. — African Americans. Family life — brothers & sisters. Rhyming text.

Bailey, Linda. *The farm team* ill. by Bill Slavin. Kids Can, 2006. ISBN 1-55337-850-4 Subj: Animals. Behavior — cheating. Character traits — bravery. Farms. Sports — hockey.

Goodnight, sweet pig ill. by Josée Masse. Kids Can, 2006. ISBN 978-1-55337-844-0 Subj: Animals — pigs. Bedtime. Counting, numbers. Rhyming text.

Stanley's wild ride ill. by Bill Slavin. Kids Can, 2006. ISBN 1-55337-960-8 Subj: Animals — dogs. Behavior — running away.

Baillie, Marilyn. *Small wonders: baby animals in the wild* ill. by Romi Caron. Maple Tree, 2006. ISBN 978-1-987066-72-0 Subj: Animals — babies.

Baker, Keith. *Hickory dickory dock* ill. by author. Harcourt, 2007. ISBN 978-0-15-205818-0 Subj: Animals — mice. Clocks, watches. Time.

Baker, Roberta. *Olive's first sleepover* ill. by Debbie Tilley. Little, Brown, 2007. ISBN 978-0-316-73418-9 Subj: Bedtime. Emotions — fear. Friendship. Sleep.

Olive's pirate party ill. by Debbie Tilley. Little, Brown, 2005. ISBN 978-0-316-16792-5 Subj: Birthdays. Family life — aunts, uncles. Parties. Pirates.

Balouch, Kristen. *Mystery bottle* ill. by author. Hyperion, 2006. ISBN 0-7868-0999-X Subj: Family life — grandfathers. Foreign lands — Iran.

Bang, Molly. *In my heart* ill. by author. Little, Brown, 2006. ISBN 0-316-79617-4 Subj: Emotions — love. Family life.

Banks, Kate (Katherine A.). *Fox* ill. by Georg Hallensleben. Farrar, Straus & Giroux, 2007. ISBN 978-0-374-39967-2 Subj: Animals — foxes. Behavior — growing up.

The great blue house ill. by Georg Hallensleben. Farrar, Straus & Giroux, 2005. ISBN 0-374-32769-6 Subj: Homes, houses. Seasons.

Max's words ill. by Boris Kulikov. Farrar, Straus & Giroux, 2006. ISBN 0-374-39949-2 Subj: Activities — storytelling. Behavior — collecting things. Language.

Banks, Merry. *N is for Navidad* (Elya, Susan Middleton)

Bar-el, Dan. *Such a prince* ill. by John Manders. Houghton Mifflin, 2007. ISBN 978-0-618-71468-1 Subj: Fairies. Folk & fairy tales. Royalty — princesses.

Barasch, Lynne. *Hiromi's hands* ill. by author. Lee & Low, 2007. ISBN 978-1-58430-275-9 Subj: Careers — chefs, cooks. Ethnic groups in the U.S. — Japanese Americans. Food.

Barber, Ronde. *Game day* (Barber, Tiki)

Teammates (Barber, Tiki)

Barber, Tiki. *Game day* by Tiki & Ronde Barber; ill. by Barry Root. Simon & Schuster, 2005. ISBN 1-4169-0093-4 Subj: Ethnic groups in the U.S. — African Americans. Family life — brothers & sisters. Multiple births — twins. Sports — football.

Teammates by Tiki & Ronde Barber; with Robert Burleigh; ill. by Barry Root. Simon & Schuster, 2006. ISBN 1-4169-2489-2 Subj: Character traits — perseverance. Ethnic groups in the U.S. — African Americans. Family life — brothers & sisters. Multiple births — twins. Sports — football.

Barbour, Karen. *Mr. Williams* ill. by author. Henry Holt, 2005. ISBN 0-8050-6773-6 Subj: Careers — farmers. Ethnic groups in the U.S. — African Americans. Farms. Old age. Prejudice. U.S. history.

Bardhan-Quallen, Sudipta. *The Mine-o-saur* ill. by David Clard. Penguin, 2007. ISBN 978-0-399-24642-5 Subj: Behavior — greed. Behavior — sharing. Dinosaurs. Friendship. Toys.

Barner, Bob. *Penguins, penguins, everywhere!* ill. by author. Chronicle, 2007. ISBN 978-0-8118-5664-5 Subj: Birds — penguins. Rhyming text.

Barrett, John S. *The duck and the owl* (Johansen, Hanna)

Barretta, Gene. *Dear deer: a book of homophones* ill. by author. Henry Holt, 2007. ISBN 978-0-8050-8104-6 Subj: Animals. Language.

Barry, Frances. *Duckie's ducklings: a one-to-ten counting Book* ill. by author. Candlewick, 2005. ISBN 0-7636-2514-0 Subj: Birds — ducks. Counting, numbers.

Bartoletti, Susan Campbell. *Nobody's diggier than a dog* ill. by Beppe Giacobbe. Hyperion, 2005. ISBN 0-7868-1824-7 Subj: Animals — dogs.

Baryshnikov, Mikhail. *Because . . .* by Mikhail Baryshnikov & Vladimir Radunsky; ill. by Vladimir Radunsky. Simon & Schuster/Atheneum, 2007. ISBN 978-0-689-87582-3 Subj: Activities — dancing. Character traits — being different. Emotions — embarrassment. Family life — grandmothers. Self-concept.

Bateman, Donna M. *Deep in the swamp* ill. by Brian Lies. Charlesbridge, 2007. ISBN 978-1-57091-596-3 Subj: Counting, numbers. Ecology. Rhyming text. Swamps.

Bateman, Teresa. *Fiona's luck* ill. by Kelly Murphy. Charlesbridge, 2007. ISBN 978-1-57091-651-9 Subj: Character traits — luck. Foreign lands — Ireland. Mythical creatures — leprechauns.

Hamster Camp: how Harry got fit ill. by Nancy Cote. Albert Whitman, 2005. ISBN 0-8075-3139-1 Subj: Animals — hamsters. Camps, camping. Health & fitness — exercise. Magic. Rhyming text.

Keeper of soles ill. by Yayo. Holiday House, 2006. ISBN 0-8234-1734-4 Subj: Behavior — trickery. Careers — shoemakers. Clothing — shoes. Death.

Traveling Tom and the leprechaun ill. by Mélisande Potter. Holiday House, 2007. ISBN 978-0-8234-1976-0 Subj: Folk & fairy tales. Foreign lands — Ireland. Music. Mythical creatures — leprechauns.

Bates, Ivan. *Five little ducks* adapt. & ill. by Ivan Bates. Scholastic, 2006. ISBN 0-439-74693-0 Subj: Birds — ducks. Counting, numbers. Songs.

Bauer, Marion Dane. *Christmas lights* ill. by Susan K. Mitchell. Simon & Schuster/Little Simon, 2006. ISBN 0-689-86942-8 Subj: Format, unusual — toy & movable books. Holidays — Christmas.

If frogs made the weather ill. by Dorothy Donohue. Holiday House, 2005. ISBN 0-8234-1622-4 Subj: Animals. Weather.

I'm not afraid of Halloween! a pop-up and flap book ill. by Rusty Fletcher. Simon & Schuster/Little Simon, 2006. ISBN 0-689-85050-6 Subj: Format, unusual — toy & movable books. Holidays — Halloween. Monsters.

A mama for Owen ill. by John Butler. Simon & Schuster, 2007. ISBN 0-689-85787-X Subj: Animals — hippopotamuses. Behavior — lost. Family life — mothers. Reptiles — turtles, tortoises. Tsunamis.

Baum, Louis. *The mouse who braved bedtime* ill. by Sue Hellard. Bloomsbury, 2006. ISBN 1-58234-691-7 Subj: Animals — mice. Bedtime. Emotions — fear. Monsters.

Baum, Maxie. *I have a little dreidel* ill. by Julie Paschkis. Scholastic, 2006. ISBN 0-439-64997-8 Subj: Food. Holidays — Hanukkah. Songs.

Baynton, Martin. *Jane and the dragon* ill. by author. Candlewick, 2007. ISBN 978-0-7636-3570-1 Subj: Clowns, jesters. Dragons. Knights.

Jane and the magician ill. by author. Candlewick, 2007. ISBN 978-0-7636-3571-8 Subj: Careers — magicians. Dragons. Magic.

Beake, Lesley. *Home now* ill. by Karin Littlewood. Charlesbridge, 2007. ISBN 978-1-58089-162-2 Subj: Animals — elephants. Family life — aunts, uncles. Foreign lands — Africa. Illness — AIDS. Moving. Orphans.

Bean, Jonathan. *At night* ill. by author. Farrar, Straus & Giroux, 2007. ISBN 978-0-374-30446-1 Subj: Bedtime. Night. Sleep.

Beaton, Clare. *Daisy gets dressed* ill. by author. Barefoot, 2005. ISBN 1-84148-794-5 Subj: Clothing. Concepts — patterns. Rhyming text.

Beaty, Andrea. *Iggy Peck, architect* ill. by David Roberts. Abrams, 2007. ISBN 978-0-8109-1106-2 Subj: Buildings. Careers — architects. Rhyming text. School — field trips.

When giants come to play ill. by Kevin Hawkes. Abrams, 2006. ISBN 0-8109-5759-0 Subj: Activities — playing. Giants.

Beaumont, Karen. *I ain't gonna paint no more!* ill. by David Catrow. Harcourt, 2005. ISBN 0-15-202488-3 Subj: Activities — painting. Rhyming text.

Move over, Rover ill. by Jane Dyer. Harcourt, 2006. ISBN 0-15-201979-0 Subj: Animals — dogs. Behavior — sharing. Rhyming text. Weather — rain.

Beaver steals fire: a Salish Coyote story ill. by Sam Sandoval. Univ. of Nebraska, 2005. ISBN 0-8032-4323-5 Subj: Animals. Animals — coyotes. Behavior — stealing. Behavior — trickery. Fire. Folk & fairy tales. Indians of North America.

Beck, Scott. *Happy birthday, Monster!* ill. by author. Abrams, 2007. ISBN 978-0-8109-9363-1 Subj: Birthdays. Dragons. Monsters. Parties.

Becker, Shari. *Maxwell's mountain* ill. by Nicole Wong. Charlesbridge, 2006. ISBN 1-58089-047-4 Subj: Imagination. Parks. Sports — mountain climbing.

Becker, Suzy. *Manny's cows: the Niagara Falls tale* ill. by author. HarperCollins, 2006. ISBN 0-06-054152-0 Subj: Activities — vacationing. Animals — bulls, cows.

Bedford, David. *I've seen Santa!* ill. by Tim Warnes. Tiger Tales, 2006. ISBN 1-58925-058-3 Subj: Animals — bears. Holidays — Christmas. Santa Claus.

Little Otter's big journey ill. by Susan Winter. Good Books, 2006. ISBN 1-56148-548-9 Subj: Animals — otters. Behavior — lost. Family life — mothers.

The way I love you ill. by Ann James. Simon & Schuster, 2005. ISBN 0-689-87625-4 Subj: Animals — dogs. Emotions — love. Pets.

Bedrick, Claudia Zoe. *The magic horse of Han Gan* (Hong, Chen Jiang)

This is a poem that heals fish (Simeon, Jean-Pierre)

Bee, William. *And the train goes . . .* ill. by author. Candlewick, 2007. ISBN 978-0-7636-3248-9 Subj: Birds — parrots. Noise, sounds. Trains.

Whatever ill. by author. Candlewick, 2005. ISBN 0-7636-2886-7 Subj: Animals — tigers. Behavior — indifference. Family life — fathers.

Begin, Mary Jane. *The sorcerer's apprentice* ill. by author. Little, Brown, 2005. ISBN 0-316-73611-2 Subj: Folk & fairy tales. Magic.

Behrens, Janice. *Let's find rain forest animals: up, down, around* ill. with photos. Scholastic, 2007. ISBN 0-531-14874-2 Subj: Animals. Format, unusual. Games. Jungles. Picture puzzles.

Bell, Anthea. *The Bremen town musicians* (Grimm, Jacob)

The five senses (Ciboul, Adele)

Bell, Cece. *Sock Monkey boogie-woogie: a friend is made* ill. by author. Candlewick, 2004. ISBN 0-7636-2392-X Subj: Activities — dancing. Animals — monkeys. Careers — actors. Toys.

Sock Monkey rides again ill. by author. Candlewick, 2007. ISBN 0-7636-3089-6 Subj: Animals — monkeys. Careers — actors. Cowboys, cowgirls. Toys.

Belle, Jennifer. *Animal stackers* ill. by David McPhail. Hyperion, 2005. ISBN 0-7868-1834-4 Subj: ABC books. Animals. Poetry.

Benson, Kathleen. *Count your way through Afghanistan* (Haskins, Jim (James))

Count your way through Iran (Haskins, Jim (James))

Berenstain, Jan. *The Berenstain bears trim the tree* by Jan & Michael Berenstain; ill. by authors. HarperCollins, 2007. ISBN 978-0-06-057417-8 Subj: Animals — bears. Format, unusual — toy & movable books. Holidays — Christmas.

Berenstain, Michael. *The Berenstain bears trim the tree* (Berenstain, Jan)

Berenzy, Alix. *Sammy: the classroom guinea pig* ill. by author. Henry Holt, 2005. ISBN 0-8050-4024-2 Subj: Animals — guinea pigs. Pets. School.

Berger, Barbara. *Thunder Bunny* ill. by author. Penguin, 2007. ISBN 978-0-399-22035-7 Subj: Animals — rabbits. Sky. Weather — storms.

Bergman, Mara. *Oliver who would not sleep!* ill. by Nick Naland. Scholastic, 2007. ISBN 978-0-439-92826-7 Subj: Bedtime. Imagination. Sleep.

Snip snap! What's that? ill. by Nick Maland. HarperCollins, 2005. ISBN 0-06-077754-0 Subj: Emotions — fear. Family life — brothers & sisters. Reptiles — alligators, crocodiles.

Berkeley, Jon. *Chopsticks* ill. by author. Random House, 2005. ISBN 0-375-83309-9 Subj: Activities — flying. Animals — mice. Dragons. Foreign lands — China.

Berkes, Marianne Collins. *Over in the jungle: a rainforest rhyme* ill. by Jeanette Canyon. Dawn, 2007. ISBN 978-1-5846-9091 Subj: Animals. Counting, numbers. Jungles. Rhyming text.

Berkner, Laurie. *The story of my feelings* ill. by Caroline Jayne Church. Scholastic, 2007. ISBN 978-0-439-42915-3 Subj: Emotions. Music.

Bernhard, Durga. *In the fiddle is a song: a lift-the-flap book of hidden potential* ill. by author. Chronicle, 2006. ISBN 0-8118-4951-1 Subj: Format, unusual — toy & movable books. Rhyming text.

Berry, Lynne. *The curious demise of a contrary cat* ill. by Luke LaMarca. Simon & Schuster, 2006. ISBN 1-4169-0211-2 Subj: Animals — cats. Parties. Witches.

Duck skates ill. by Hiroe Nakata. Henry Holt, 2005. ISBN 0-8050-7219-5 Subj: Birds — ducks. Rhyming text. Seasons — winter. Sports — ice skating. Weather — snow.

Berry, Matt. *Up on Daddy's shoulders* ill. by Lucy Corvino. Scholastic/Cartwheel, 2006. ISBN 0-439-67045-4 Subj: Concepts — perspective. Family life — fathers.

Bertram, Debbie. *The best time to read* by Debbie Bertram & Susan Bloom; ill. by Michael Bloom. Random House, 2005. ISBN 0-375-93025-6 Subj: Books, reading. Rhyming text.

Bertrand, Lynne. *Granite baby* ill. by Kevin Hawkes. Farrar, Straus & Giroux, 2005. ISBN 0-374-32761-0 Subj: Babies. Giants. Rocks. Tall tales.

Best, Cari. *Are you going to be good?* ill. by G. Brian Karas. Farrar, Straus & Giroux, 2005. ISBN 0-374-30394-0 Subj: Etiquette. Old age. Parties.

Sally Jean, the Bicycle Queen ill. by Christine Davenier. Farrar, Straus & Giroux, 2006. ISBN 0-374-36386-2 Subj: Behavior — growing up. Character traits — perseverance. Sports — bicycling.

What's so bad about being an only child? ill. by Sophie Blackall. Farrar, Straus & Giroux, 2007. ISBN 978-0-374-39943-6 Subj: Family life — only child.

Bevis, Mary. *Wolf song* ill. by Consie Powell. Raven, 2007. ISBN 978-0-979420-20-7 Subj: Animals — wolves. Family life — aunts, uncles. Nature.

Bible. Old Testament. Ecclesiastes. *To everything there is a season* ill. by Jude Daly. Eerdmans, 2006. ISBN 0-8028-5286-6 Subj: Religion.

Bible. Old Testament. Genesis. *The Genesis of it all* retold by Luci Shaw; ill. by Huai-Kuang Miao. Paraclete, 2006. ISBN 1-55725-480-X Subj: Creation. Religion.

Bible. Old Testament. Psalms. *The Lord is my shepherd* ill. by Regolo Ricci. Tundra, 2007. ISBN 978-0-88776-776-0 Subj: Religion.

I will rejoice: celebrating Psalm 118 by Karma Wilson; ill. by Amy June Bates. Zondervan, 2007. ISBN 0-310-71117-7 Subj: Religion. Rhyming text.

Bible. Old Testament. Ruth. *Ruth and Naomi: a Bible story* retold & ill. by Jean Marzollo. Little, Brown, 2005. ISBN 0-316-74139-6 Subj: Religion.

Bildner, Phil. *The greatest game ever played: a football story* ill. by Zachary Pullen. Penguin, 2006. ISBN 0-399-24171-X Subj: Family life — fathers. Sports — football. U.S. history.

The shot heard 'round the world ill. by C. F. Payne. Simon & Schuster, 2005. ISBN 0-689-86273-3 Subj: Sports — baseball.

Birtha, Becky. *Grandmama's pride* ill. by Colin Bootman. Albert Whitman, 2005. ISBN 0-8075-3028-X Subj: Ethnic groups in the U.S. — African Americans. Family life. Prejudice. U.S. history.

Bishop, Kathryn. *Bye-bye, Binky* (Weninger, Brigitte)

Cherry time (Bunge, Daniela)

Fritz's fish (Elschner, Geraldine)

Good night, Nori (Weninger, Brigitte)

The scarves (Bunge, Daniela)

Sophie's dance (Knister)

Blackford, Harriet. *Tiger's story* ill. by Manya Stojic. Sterling, 2007. ISBN 978-1-905417-39-1 Subj: Animals — tigers. Behavior — growing up.

Blackstone, Stella. *Alligator alphabet* ill. by Stephanie Bauer. Barefoot, 2005. ISBN 1-84148-494-6 Subj: ABC books. Animals. Rhyming text.

Cleo's color book (Mockford, Caroline)

I dreamt I was a dinosaur ill. by Clare Beaton. Barefoot, 2005. ISBN 1-84148-238-2 Subj: Dinosaurs. Dreams. Rhyming text.

Ship shapes ill. by Siobhan Bell. Barefoot, 2006. ISBN 1-905236-34-4 Subj: Boats, ships. Concepts — shape. Rhyming text.

Blaikie, Lynn. *Beyond the northern lights* ill. by author. Fitzhenry & Whiteside, 2006. ISBN 1-55041-123-7 Subj: Foreign lands — Arctic. Nature. Rhyming text.

Blankenship, Lee Ann. *Mr. Tuggle's troubles* ill. by Karen Dugan. Boyds Mills, 2005. ISBN 1-59078-196-1 Subj: Behavior — lost & found possessions. Behavior — messy. Character traits — orderliness. Clothing.

Bley, Anette. *And what comes after a thousand?* ill. by author. Kane/Miller, 2007. ISBN 978-1-933605-27-2 Subj: Death. Emotions — grief. Old age.

Bloom, Susan (Susan Lynn). *The best time to read* (Bertram, Debbie)

Bloom, Suzanne. *A splendid friend, indeed* ill. by author. Boyds Mills, 2005. ISBN 1-59078-286-0 Subj: Animals — polar bears. Birds — geese. Friendship.

Bluemle, Elizabeth. *My father the dog* ill. by Randy Cecil. Candlewick, 2006. ISBN 0-7636-2222-2 Subj: Animals — dogs. Family life — fathers.

Boelts, Maribeth. *Before you were mine* ill. by David Walker. Penguin, 2007. ISBN 978-0-399-24526-8 Subj: Animals — dogs. Pets.

Those shoes ill. by Noah Z. Jones. Candlewick, 2007. ISBN 978-0-7636-2499-6 Subj: Character traits — appearance. Clothing — shoes. Ethnic groups in the U.S. — African Americans.

Bofill, Francesc. *Rapunzel* (Grimm, Jacob)

Bogue, Gary. *There's an opossum in my backyard* ill. by Chuck Todd. Heyday Books, 2007. ISBN 978-1-59714-059-1 Subj: Animals — babies. Animals — possums.

Bolliger, Max. *The happy troll* ill. by Peter Sís. Henry Holt, 2005. ISBN 0-8050-6982-8 Subj: Activities — singing. Behavior — greed. Mythical creatures — trolls.

Bollinger, Peter. *Algernon Graeves is scary enough* ill. by author. HarperCollins, 2005. ISBN 0-06-052269-0 Subj: Clothing — costumes. Holidays — Halloween.

Bond, Rebecca. *A city Christmas tree* ill. by author. Little, Brown, 2005. ISBN 0-316-53731-4 Subj: Holidays — Christmas. Trees.

The great doughnut parade ill. by author. Houghton Mifflin, 2007. ISBN 978-0-618-77705-1 Subj: Cumulative tales. Food. Parades.

Bonnett-Rampersaud, Louise. *Bubble and Squeak* ill. by Susan Banta. Marshall Cavendish, 2006. ISBN 0-7614-5310-5 Subj: Animals — mice. Bedtime. Emotions — fear. Family life — brothers & sisters.

How do you sleep? ill. by Kristin Kest. Marshall Cavendish, 2005. ISBN 0-7614-5231-1 Subj: Animals. Rhyming text. Sleep.

Bonning, Tony. *Snog the frog* ill. by Rosalind Beardshaw. Barron's, 2005. ISBN 0-7641-5824-4 Subj: Frogs & toads. Royalty — princesses.

Boothroyd, Jennifer. *What is a gas?* ill. with photos. Lerner, 2007. ISBN 978-0-8225-6818-6 Subj: Science.

Bootman, Colin. *Fish for the Grand Lady* ill. by author. Holiday House, 2006. ISBN 0-8234-1898-7 Subj: Family life — grandmothers. Foreign lands — Trinidad. Sports — fishing.

Borgo, Lacy. *Big Mama's baby* ill. by Nancy Cote. Boyds Mills, 2007. ISBN 978-1-59078-187-6 Subj: Animals — bulls, cows. Family life — grandmothers. Texas.

Bosca, Francesca. *The three grasshoppers* ill. by Giuliano Ferri. Purple Bear, 2006. ISBN 1-933327-13-8 Subj: Friendship. Insects — grasshoppers. Music.

Bottner, Barbara. *Raymond and Nelda* ill. by Nancy Hayashi. Peachtree, 2007. ISBN 978-1-56145-394-8 Subj: Animals — rabbits. Animals — squirrels. Careers — postal workers. Friendship.

Bouchard, Dave. *Nokum is my teacher* ill. by Allen Sapp. Fitzhenry & Whiteside, 2007. ISBN 978-0-88995-367-3 Subj: Family life — grandmothers. Foreign languages. Indians of North America — Cree.

Bowen, Anne. *Christmas is coming* ill. by Tomek Bogacki. Lerner, 2007. ISBN 978-1-57505-934-1 Subj: Holidays — Christmas.

The great math tattle battle ill. by Jaime Zollars. Albert Whitman, 2006. ISBN 0-8075-3163-4 Subj: Behavior — gossip. Counting, numbers. School.

Tooth Fairy's first night ill. by Jon Berkeley. Carolrhoda, 2005. ISBN 1-57505753-0 Subj: Fairies. Teeth.

Bradley, Kimberly Brubaker. *Ballerino Nate* ill. by R. W. Alley. Penguin, 2006. ISBN 0-8037-2954-5 Subj: Activities — dancing. Animals — dogs. Ballet. Character traits — being different.

The perfect pony ill. by Shelagh McNicholas. Penguin, 2007. ISBN 978-0-8037-2851-6 Subj: Animals — horses, ponies.

Braver, Vanita. *Madison and the two wheeler* ill. by Carl DiRocco. Star Bright, 2007. ISBN 978-1-59572-110-5 Subj: Character traits — perseverance. Sports — bicycling.

Breathed, Berkeley. *Mars needs moms!* ill. by author. Penguin, 2007. ISBN 978-0-399-24736-1 Subj: Aliens. Family life — mothers.

Brebeuf, Jean de. *The Huron carol* English lyrics by Jesse Edgar Middleton; ill. by Ian Wallace. Groundwood, 2006. ISBN 0-88899-711-6 Subj: Foreign lands — Canada. Holidays — Christmas. Religion — Nativity. Songs.

Breen, Steve. *Stick* ill. by author. Penguin, 2007. ISBN 0-8037-3124-8 Subj: Frogs & toads. Insects — dragonflies.

Brennan-Nelson, Denise. *Grady the goose* ill. by Michael Glenn Monroe. Sleeping Bear, 2006. ISBN 1-58536-282-4 Subj: Behavior — lost. Birds — geese.

My grandma likes to say ill. by Jane Monroe Donovan. Sleeping Bear, 2007. ISBN 978-1-58536-284-4 Subj: Language. Rhyming text.

Brett, Jan. *Hedgie blasts off!* ill. by author. Penguin, 2006. ISBN 0-399-24621-5 Subj: Animals — hedgehogs. Careers — astronauts. Careers — custodians, janitors. Space & space ships.

Honey, honey — lion! A story from Africa ill. by author. Penguin, 2005. ISBN 0-399-24463-8 Subj: Animals — badgers. Behavior — greed. Birds. Foreign lands — Africa.

The three snow bears ill. by author. Penguin, 2007. ISBN 978-0-399-24792-7 Subj: Animals — polar bears. Folk & fairy tales. Foreign lands — Arctic. Seasons — winter. Weather — snow.

Briant, Ed. *A day at the beach* ill. by author. HarperCollins, 2005. ISBN 0-06-079982-X Subj: Animals — pandas. Family life — fathers. Sea & seashore — beaches.

Seven stories ill. by author. Macmillan, 2005. ISBN 1-59643-056-7 Subj: Books, reading. Folk & fairy tales.

Bridges, Margaret Park. *I love the rain* ill. by Christine Davenier. Chronicle, 2005. ISBN 1-58717-208-9 Subj: Weather — rain.

Briggs, Raymond. *The puddleman* ill. by author. Red Fox, 2006. ISBN 0-09-945642-7 Subj: Activities — walking. Family life — grandfathers. Magic.

Brisson, Pat. *I remember Miss Perry* ill. by Stephane Jorisch. Penguin, 2006. ISBN 0-8037-2981-2 Subj: Careers — teachers. Death. Emotions — grief. School.

Melissa Parkington's beautiful, beautiful hair ill. by Suzanne Bloom. Boyds Mills, 2006. ISBN 1-59078-409-X Subj: Character traits — appearance. Character traits — generosity. Hair.

Broach, Elise. *Wet dog!* ill. by David Catrow. Penguin, 2005. ISBN 0-8037-2809-3 Subj: Animals — dogs. Seasons — summer. Weddings.

What the no-good baby is good for ill. by Abby Carter. Penguin, 2005. ISBN 0-399-23877-8 Subj: Babies. Family life — brothers & sisters. Family life — new sibling. Sibling rivalry.

When dinosaurs came with everything ill. by David Small. Simon & Schuster/Atheneum, 2007. ISBN 978-0-689-86922-8 Subj: Dinosaurs. Humorous stories.

Brooks, Erik. *Slow days, fast friends* ill. by author. Albert Whitman, 2005. ISBN 0-8075-7437-6 Subj: Animals. Friendship.

Brooks, Gwendolyn. *Bronzeville boys and girls* ill. by Faith Ringgold. HarperCollins, 2007. ISBN 978-0-06-029505-9 Subj: Ethnic groups in the U.S. — African Americans. Poetry.

Brown, Don. *Bright path: young Jim Thorpe* ill. by author. Macmillan, 2006. ISBN 1-59643-041-9 Subj: Indians of North America. Sports.

Brown, Jeff. *Flat Stanley* ill. by Scott Nash. HarperCollins, 2006. ISBN 0-06-112904-6 Subj: Character traits — appearance. Family life. Humorous stories. Problem solving.

Brown, Jo. *Hoppity skip Little Chick* ill. by author. Tiger Tales, 2005. ISBN 1-58925-045-1 Subj: Activities — playing. Birds — chickens.

Brown, Lisa. *How to be* ill. by author. HarperCollins, 2006. ISBN 0-06-054636-0 Subj: Animals. Behavior — imitation. Imagination. Self-concept.

Brown, Margaret Wise. *Goodnight moon 123: a counting book* ill. by Clement Hurd. HarperCollins, 2007. ISBN 978-0-06-112593-5 Subj: Animals — rabbits. Bedtime. Counting, numbers. Moon.

The little fir tree ill. by Jim LaMarche. HarperCollins, 2005. ISBN 0-06-028190-1 Subj: Holidays — Christmas. Trees.

Nibble, nibble ill. by Wendell Minor. HarperCollins, 2007. ISBN 978-0-06-059208-0 Subj: Poetry.

Brown, Peter. *Chowder* ill. by author. Little, Brown, 2006. ISBN 0-316-01180-0 Subj: Animals — dogs. Character traits — being different.

Brown, Ruth. *The old tree: an environmental fable* ill. by author. Candlewick, 2007. ISBN 978-0-7636-3461-2 Subj: Ecology. Format, unusual — toy & movable books. Trees.

Brown, Susan Taylor. *Oliver's must-do list* ill. by Mary Sullivan. Boyds Mills, 2005. ISBN 1-59078-198-8 Subj: Activities — playing. Animals — rhinoceros. Family life — mothers.

Browne, Anthony. *My brother* ill. by author. Farrar, Straus & Giroux, 2007. ISBN 978-0-374-35120-5 Subj: Family life — brothers & sisters.

My Mom ill. by author. Farrar, Straus & Giroux, 2005. ISBN 0-374-35098-1 Subj: Family life — mothers.

Silly Billy ill. by author. Candlewick, 2006. ISBN 0-7636-3124-8 Subj: Behavior — worrying. Family life — grandmothers. Toys — dolls.

Brownlow, Mike. *Mickey Moonbeam* ill. by author. Bloomsbury, 2006. ISBN 1-58234-704-2 Subj: Concepts — size. Pen pals. Space & space ships.

Bruel, Nick. *Bad Kitty* ill. by author. Macmillan, 2005. ISBN 1-59643-069-9 Subj: ABC books. Animals — cats. Behavior — misbehavior. Food.

Poor puppy ill. by author. Macmillan, 2007. ISBN 978-1-59643-270-3 Subj: ABC books. Animals — cats. Animals — dogs. Counting, numbers.

Bruel, Robert O. *Bob and Otto* ill. by Nick Bruel. Macmillan, 2007. ISBN 978-1-59643-203-1 Subj: Animals — worms. Friendship. Insects — butterflies, caterpillars.

Brunelle, Nicholas. *Snow Moon* ill. by author. Penguin, 2005. ISBN 0-670-06024-0 Subj: Bedtime. Birds — owls. Night. Seasons — winter. Weather — snow.

Brunhoff, Laurent de. *Babar's world tour* ill. by author. Abrams, 2005. ISBN 0-8109-5780-9 Subj: Activities — traveling. Animals — elephants. World.

Bryan, Sean. *A bear and his boy* ill. by Tom Murphy. Arcade, 2007. ISBN 978-1-55970-838-8 Subj: Animals — bears. Rhyming text.

Buckingham, Matt. *Bright Stanley* ill. by author. Tiger Tales, 2006. ISBN 1-58925-059-1 Subj: Behavior — lost. Fish. Friendship. Sea & seashore.

Buehner, Caralyn. *Snowmen at Christmas* ill. by Mark Buehner. Penguin, 2005. ISBN 0-8037-2995-2 Subj: Gifts. Holidays — Christmas. Parties. Rhyming text. Snowmen.

Would I ever lie to you? ill. by Jack E. Davis. Penguin, 2007. ISBN 978-0-8037-2793-9 Subj: Behavior — bullying. Behavior — lying. Family life — cousins. Rhyming text.

Bunge, Daniela. *Cherry time* trans. from German by Kathryn Bishop; ill. by Daniela Bunge. Minedition, 2007. ISBN 978-0-698-40057-3 Subj: Animals — dogs. Character traits — shyness. Friendship.

The scarves trans. from German by Kathryn Bishop; ill. by Daniela Bunge. Minedition, 2006. ISBN 0-698-40045-3 Subj: Activities — knitting. Clothing — scarves. Family life — grandparents. Sports — ice skating.

Bunting, Eve (Anne Evelyn). *Baby can* ill. by Maxie Chambliss. Boyds Mills, 2007. ISBN 978-1-59078-322-1 Subj: Babies. Emotions — love. Family life — new sibling. Sibling rivalry.

The baby shower ill. by Judy Love. Charlesbridge, 2007. ISBN 978-1-58089-139-4 Subj: Animals — babies. Animals — bulls, cows. Gifts. Rhyming text.

Emma's turtle ill. by Marsha Winborn. Boyds Mills, 2007. ISBN 978-1-59078-350-4 Subj: Behavior — running away. Pets. Reptiles — turtles, tortoises.

Hurry! Hurry! ill. by Jeff Mack. Harcourt, 2007. ISBN 978-0-15-205410-6 Subj: Animals. Birds — chickens. Farms.

My mom's wedding ill. by Lisa Papp. Sleeping Bear, 2006. ISBN 1-58536-288-3 Subj: Divorce. Family life — mothers. Weddings.

My red balloon ill. by Kay Life. Boyds Mills, 2005. ISBN 1-59078-263-1 Subj: Careers — military. Family life — fathers.

One green apple ill. by Ted Lewin. Houghton Mifflin, 2006. ISBN 0-618-43477-1 Subj: Ethnic groups in the U.S. — Arab Americans. Food. Immigrants. School — field trips. Self-concept.

That's what leprechauns do ill. by Emily Arnold McCully. Houghton Mifflin, 2006. ISBN 0-618-35410-7 Subj: Mythical creatures — leprechauns.

Burg, Sarah Emmanuelle. *One more egg* ill. by author. NorthSouth, 2006. ISBN 0-7358-2001-5 Subj: Animals — rabbits. Birds — chickens. Eggs. Farms. Holidays — Easter.

Burleigh, Robert. *Stealing home: Jackie Robinson against the odds* ill. by Mike Wimmer. Simon & Schuster, 2007. ISBN 0-689-86276-8 Subj: Ethnic groups in the U.S. — African Americans. Sports — baseball. U.S. history.

Teammates (Barber, Tiki)

Burningham, John. *Edwardo: the horriblest boy in the whole world* ill. by author. Random House, 2007. ISBN 0-375-84053-1 Subj: Behavior — misbehavior.

Busse, Sarah Martin. *Banjo granny* by Sarah Martin Busse & Jacqueline Briggs Martin; ill. by Barry Root. Houghton Mifflin, 2006. ISBN 0-618-33603-6 Subj: Family life — grandmothers. Musical instruments — banjos. Songs.

Butler, Dori Hillestad. *F is for firefighting* ill. by Joan Waites. Pelican, 2007. ISBN 978-1-58980-420-3 Subj: ABC books. Careers — firefighters.

My grandpa had a stroke ill. by Nicole Wong. Magination, 2007. ISBN 978-1-59147-806-5 Subj: Family life — grandfathers. Illness.

Butler, John. *Can you growl like a bear?* ill. by author. Peachtree, 2007. ISBN 978-1-56145-396-2 Subj: Animals. Bedtime. Noise, sounds. Rhyming text.

Ten in the den ill. by author. Peachtree, 2005. ISBN 1-56145-344-7 Subj: Animals. Counting, numbers. Nursery rhymes.

Ten in the meadow ill. by author. Peachtree, 2006. ISBN 1-56145-372-2 Subj: Activities — playing. Animals. Behavior — hiding. Games.

Butler, M. Christina. *One winter's day* ill. by Tina Macnaughton. Good Books, 2006. ISBN 1-56148-532-2 Subj: Animals. Animals — hedgehogs. Character traits — kindness. Seasons — winter.

Snow friends ill. by Tina Macnaughton. Good Books, 2005. ISBN 1-56148-485-7 Subj: Animals — bears. Friendship. Seasons — winter. Weather — snow.

Butterworth, Chris. *Sea horse: the shyest fish in the sea* ill. by John Lawrence. Candlewick, 2006. ISBN 978-0-7636-2989-2 Subj: Fish — seahorses. Sea & seashore.

Bynum, Janie. *Nutmeg and Barley: a budding friendship* ill. by author. Candlewick, 2006. ISBN 0-7636-2382-2 Subj: Animals — mice. Animals — squirrels. Friendship.

C is for caboose: riding the rails from A to Z illus. Chronicle, 2007. ISBN 0-8118-5643-7 Subj: ABC books. Trains.

Cabrera, Jane. *If you're happy and you know it* ill. by author. Holiday House, 2005. ISBN 0-8234-1881-2 Subj: Animals. Emotions — happiness. Music. Songs.

Kitty's cuddles ill. by author. Holiday House, 2007. ISBN 978-0-8234-2066-7 Subj: Animals — cats. Hugging.

Mommy, carry me please! ill. by author. Holiday House, 2006. ISBN 0-8234-1935-5 Subj: Animals — babies. Family life — mothers.

Ten in the bed ill. by author. Holiday House, 2006. ISBN 0-8234-2027-2 Subj: Bedtime. Counting, numbers. Toys.

Cain, Sheridan. *By the light of the moon* ill. by Gaby Hansen. Tiger Tales, 2007. ISBN 978-1-58925-062-8 Subj: Animals — mice. Bedtime. Moon.

Calmenson, Stephanie. *Birthday at the Panda Palace* ill. by Doug Cushman. HarperCollins, 2007. ISBN 978-0-06-052663-4 Subj: Animals. Animals — mice. Animals — pandas. Birthdays. Gifts. Rhyming text.

May I pet your dog? The how-to guide for kids meeting dogs (and dogs meeting kids) ill. by Jan Ormerod. Houghton Mifflin, 2007. ISBN 978-0-618-51034-4 Subj: Animals — dogs. Friendship. Pets. Safety.

Capucilli, Alyssa Satin. *Katy Duck* ill. by Henry Cole. Simon & Schuster/Little Simon, 2007. ISBN 978-1-4169-1901-8 Subj: Activities — dancing. Birds — ducks. Emotions — fear. Format, unusual — board books.

Katy Duck, big sister ill. by Henry Cole. Simon & Schuster/Little Simon, 2007. ISBN 978-1-4169-4209-2 Subj: Activities — dancing. Birds — ducks. Family life — brothers & sisters. Format, unusual — board books. Sibling rivalry.

Little spotted cat ill. by Dan Andreasen. Penguin, 2005. ISBN 0-8037-2692-9 Subj: Activities — playing. Animals — cats. Sleep.

Carlson, Nancy L. *First grade, here I come!* ill. by author. Penguin, 2006. ISBN 0-670-06127-1 Subj: Animals — mice. School — first day.

Get up and go! ill. by author. Penguin, 2006. ISBN 0-670-05981-1 Subj: Animals. Animals — pigs. Health & fitness — exercise.

Henry's 100 days of kindergarten ill. by author. Penguin, 2005. ISBN 0-670-05977-3 Subj: Animals — mice. Counting, numbers. School.

I don't like to read! ill. by author. Penguin, 2007. ISBN 978-0-670-06191-4 Subj: Animals — mice. Books, reading. School.

Loudmouth George earns his allowance ill. by author. CarolRhoda, 2007. ISBN 978-0-8225-6550-4 Subj: Animals — rabbits. Behavior — misbehavior. Character traits — willfulness.

My family is forever ill. by author. Penguin, 2004. ISBN 0-670-03650-1 Subj: Adoption. Ethnic groups in the U.S. — Asian Americans. Family life.

Think big! ill. by author. Carolrhoda, 2005. ISBN 1-57505-622-4 Subj: Character traits — appearance. Character traits — smallness. Concepts — size. Frogs & toads. School. Self-concept.

Carmody, Isobelle. *Magic night* ill. by Declan Lee. Random House, 2007. ISBN 978-0-375-83918-4 Subj: Animals — cats. Magic. Mythical creatures.

Carney-Nunes, Charisse. *I dream for you a world: a covenant for our children* ill. by Ann Marie Williams. Brand Nu Words, 2007. ISBN 978-0-9748142-3-0 Subj: World.

Carr, Jan. *Greedy apostrophe: a cautionary tale* ill. by Ethan Long. Holiday House, 2007. ISBN 978-0-8234-2006-3 Subj: Behavior — greed. Language.

Carris, Joan. *Welcome to the bed and biscuit* ill. by Noah Z. Jones. Candlewick, 2006. ISBN 0-7636-2151-X Subj: Animals. Careers — veterinarians.

Carroll, Lewis. *Jabberwocky* ill. by Christopher Myers. Hyperion, 2007. ISBN 978-1-4231-0372-1 Subj: Humorous stories. Mythical creatures. Poetry.

Carter, David A. *Blue 2: a pop-up book for children of all ages* ill. by author. Simon & Schuster/Little Simon, 2007. ISBN 1-4169-1781-0 Subj: Format, unusual — toy & movable books. Picture puzzles.

One red dot: a pop-up book for children of all ages ill. by author. Simon & Schuster/Little Simon, 2005. ISBN 0-689-87769-2 Subj: Counting, numbers. Format, unusual — toy & movable books. Picture puzzles.

600 black spots: a pop-up book for children of all ages ill. by author. Simon & Schuster/Little Simon, 2007. ISBN 978-1-4169-4092-0 Subj: Format, unusual — toy & movable books. Picture puzzles.

Whoo? Whoo? ill. by author. Simon & Schuster/Little Simon, 2007. ISBN 978-1-4169-3816-3 Subj: Animals. Character traits — questioning. Format, unusual — toy & movable books. Games. Picture puzzles.

Carter, Don. *Old MacDonald drives a tractor* ill. by author. Macmillan, 2007. ISBN 978-1-59643-023-5 Subj: Careers — farmers. Farms. Rhyming text. Tractors.

Cartwright, Reg. *What we do* ill. by author. Henry Holt, 2005. ISBN 0-8050-7671-9 Subj: Animals. Rhyming text.

Casanova, Mary. *Some dog!* ill. by Ard Hoyt. Farrar, Straus & Giroux, 2007. ISBN 978-0-347-37133-3 Subj: Animals — dogs.

Caseley, Judith. *In style with Grandma Antoinette* ill. by author. Tanglewood, 2005. ISBN 0-9749303-4-2 Subj: Beauty shops. Family life — grandmothers.

Casey, Dawn. *The great race: the story of the Chinese zodiac* ill. by Anne Wilson. Barefoot, 2006. ISBN 1-905236-77-8 Subj: Animals. Folk & fairy tales. Zodiac.

Cash, Megan Montague. *Bow-Wow bugs a bug* (Newgarden, Mark)

Bow-Wow orders lunch (Newgarden, Mark)

Catalanotto, Peter. *Ivan the terrier* ill. by author. Simon & Schuster, 2007. ISBN 978-1-4169-1247-7 Subj: Animals — dogs. Behavior — misbehavior. Folk & fairy tales.

Kitten red, yellow, blue ill. by author. Simon & Schuster, 2005. ISBN 0-689-86562-7 Subj: Animals — cats. Careers. Concepts — color.

The secret lunch special by Peter Catalanotto & Pamela Schembri; ill. by Peter Catalanotto. Henry Holt, 2006. ISBN 0-8050-7838-X Subj: Food. Friendship. School.

Cate, Annette LeBlanc. *The magic rabbit* ill. by author. Candlewick, 2007. ISBN 978-0-7636-2672-3 Subj: Animals — rabbits. Behavior — lost & found possessions. Careers — magicians. Magic.

Cazet, Denys. *The perfect pumpkin pie* ill. by author. Simon & Schuster/Atheneum, 2005. ISBN 0-689-86467-1 Subj: Activities — baking, cooking. Food. Ghosts. Holidays — Halloween.

Will you read to me? ill. by author. Simon & Schuster/Atheneum, 2007. ISBN 978-1-4169-0935-4 Subj: Animals — pigs. Books, reading. Self-concept.

Cech, John. *The elves and the shoemaker* (Grimm, Jacob)

The princess and the pea (Andersen, H. C. (Hans Christian))

Cecil, Randy. *Gator* ill. by author. Candlewick, 2007. ISBN 978-0-7636-2952-6 Subj: Merry-go-rounds. Parks — amusement. Reptiles — alligators, crocodiles.

Cecka, Melanie. *Violet comes to stay* ill. by Emily Arnold McCully. Penguin, 2006. ISBN 0-670-06073-9 Subj: Animals — cats. Behavior — misbehavior. Homes, houses.

Violet goes to the country ill. by Emily Arnold McCully. Penguin, 2007. ISBN 978-0-670-06181-5 Subj: Animals — cats. Character traits — curiosity. Country.

Chaconas, Dori. *Christmas mouseling* ill. by Susan Kathleen Hartung. Penguin, 2005. ISBN 0-670-05984-6 Subj: Animals — babies. Animals — mice. Family life — mothers. Holidays — Christmas. Religion — Nativity.

Cork and Fuzz ill. by Lisa McCue. Penguin, 2005. ISBN 0-670-03602-1 Subj: Animals — muskrats. Animals — possums. Friendship.

Cork and Fuzz: good sports ill. by Lisa McCue. Penguin, 2007. ISBN 0-670-06145-X Subj: Animals — muskrats. Animals — possums. Friendship. Sports. Sportsmanship.

Cork and Fuzz: short and tall ill. by Lisa McCue. Penguin, 2006. ISBN 0-670-05985-4 Subj: Animals — muskrats. Animals — possums. Concepts — size. Friendship.

Dancing with Katya ill. by Constance R. Bergum. Peachtree, 2006. ISBN 1-56145-376-5 Subj: Activities — dancing. Ballet. Family life — brothers & sisters. Illness — poliomyelitis.

Dori the contrary hen ill. by Marsha Gray Carrington. Carolrhoda, 2007. ISBN 978-1-57505-749-1 Subj: Birds — chickens. Character traits — stubbornness. Farms.

Pennies in a jar ill. by Ted Lewin. Peachtree, 2007. ISBN 1-56145-422-2 Subj: Emotions — fear. U.S. history. War.

Virginnie's hat ill. by Holly Meade. Candlewick, 2007. ISBN 978-0-7636-2397-5 Subj: Clothing — hats. Rhyming text. Swamps.

When cows come home for Christmas ill. by Lynne Chapman. Albert Whitman, 2005. ISBN 0-8075-8877-6 Subj: Animals — bulls, cows. Holidays — Christmas. Rhyming text.

Chae, In Seon. *How do you count a dozen ducklings?* ill. by Seung Ha Rew. Albert Whitman, 2006. ISBN 0-8075-1718-6 Subj: Birds — ducks. Counting, numbers.

Chamberlin, Mary. *Mama Panya's pancakes: a village tale from Kenya* by Mary & Rich Chamberlin; ill. by Julia Cairns. Barefoot, 2005. ISBN 1-84148-139-4 Subj: Character traits — generosity. Food. Foreign lands — Kenya.

Chamberlin, Rich. *Mama Panya's pancakes: a village tale from Kenya* (Chamberlin, Mary)

Chapra, Mimi. *Sparky's bark / El ladrido de Sparky* ill. by Vivi Escriva. HarperCollins, 2006. ISBN 0-06-053172-X Subj: Activities — vacationing. Animals — dogs. Ethnic groups in the U.S. — Hispanic Americans. Foreign languages.

Charest, Emily MacLachlan. *Fiona loves the night* (MacLachlan, Patricia)

Charles, Veronika Martenova. *The birdman* ill. by Annouchka Gravel Galouchko. Tundra, 2006. ISBN 0-88776-740-0 Subj: Birds. Careers — tailors. Emotions — grief. Foreign lands — India.

Charlip, Remy. *A perfect day* ill. by author. HarperCollins, 2007. ISBN 978-0-06-051972-8 Subj: Day. Family life.

Chen, Chih-Yuan. *The best Christmas ever* ill. by author. Heryin, 2005. ISBN 0-976205-62-9 Subj: Animals — bears. Gifts. Holidays — Christmas.

The featherless chicken ill. by author. Heryin, 2006. ISBN 0-9762-0569-6 Subj: Birds — chickens. Character traits — appearance. Character traits — being different. Self-concept.

Cheng, Andrea. *The lemon sisters* ill. by Tatjana Mai-Wyss. Penguin, 2006. ISBN 0-399-24023-3 Subj: Birthdays. Family life — brothers & sisters. Memories, memory. Old age.

Chernaik, Judith. *Carnival of the animals: poems inspired by Saint-Saëns' music* ed. by Judith Chernaik; ill. by Satoshi Kitamura. Candlewick, 2006. ISBN 0-76362960-X Subj: Animals. Music. Poetry.

Cheshire, Marc. *Merry Christmas, Eloise! A lift-the-flap book* ill. by Carolyn Bracken. Simon & Schuster/Little Simon, 2006. ISBN 0-689-87155-4 Subj: Format, unusual — toy & movable books. Holidays — Christmas.

Chess, Victoria. *The costume party* ill. by author. Kane/Miller, 2005. ISBN 1-929132-87-5 Subj: Animals — dogs. Clothing — costumes. Parties.

Chessa, Francesca. *The mysterious package* ill. by author. Bloomsbury, 2007. ISBN 978-1-59990-028-5 Subj: Family life — brothers & sisters. Imagination.

Chichester Clark, Emma. *Melrose and Croc: a Christmas to remember* ill. by author. Walker & Company, 2006. ISBN 0-8027-9597-8 Subj: Animals — dogs. Emotions — loneliness. Friendship. Holidays — Christmas. Reptiles — alligators, crocodiles.

Piper ill. by author. Eerdmans, 2007. ISBN 978-0-902853-14-1 Subj: Animals — dogs. Behavior — running away. Character traits — kindness to animals.

Will and Squill ill. by author. Carolrhoda, 2006. ISBN 1-57505-936-3 Subj: Animals — cats. Animals — squirrels. Babies. Friendship. Pets.

Chicken Little. *Henny Penny* retold by Vivian French; ill. by Sophie Windham. Bloomsbury, 2006. ISBN 1-58234-706-9 Subj: Animals. Behavior — gossip. Behavior — trickery. Birds — chickens. Cumulative tales. Folk & fairy tales.

Child, Lauren. *But, excuse me, that is my book* ill. by author. Penguin, 2005. ISBN 978-0-8037-3096-0 Subj: Books, reading. Family life — brothers & sisters. Libraries.

Charlie and Lola's I will never not ever eat a tomato ill. by author. Candlewick, 2007. ISBN 978-0-7636-3708-8 Subj: Family life — brothers & sisters. Food. Format, unusual — toy & movable books.

Charlie and Lola's numbers ill. by author. Candlewick, 2007. ISBN 978-0-7636-3534-3 Subj: Counting, numbers. Family life — brothers & sisters. Format, unusual — board books.

Charlie and Lola's opposites ill. by author. Candlewick, 2007. ISBN 978-0-7636-3535-0 Subj: Concepts — opposites. Family life — brothers & sisters. Format, unusual — board books.

The princess and the pea in miniature: after the fairy tale by Hans Christian Andersen (Andersen, H. C. (Hans Christian))

Say cheese! ill. by author. Penguin, 2007. ISBN 978-0-8037-3095-3 Subj: Character traits — cleanliness. Family life — brothers & sisters. School.

Snow is my favorite and my best ill. by author. Penguin, 2006. ISBN 0-8037-3174-4 Subj: Family life — brothers & sisters. Seasons — winter. Weather — snow.

A children's treasury of prayers ill. by Linda Bleck. Sterling, 2006. ISBN 1-4027-2982-0 Subj: Religion.

Chin, Eun Hee. *Waiting for Mama: a bilingual picture book* (Lee, Tae-Jun)

Chodos-Irvine, Margaret. *Best best friends* ill. by author. Harcourt, 2006. ISBN 0-15-205694-7 Subj: Birthdays. Friendship. School — nursery.

Choi, Yangsook. *Behind the mask* ill. by author. Farrar, Straus & Giroux, 2006. ISBN 0-374-30522-6 Subj: Ethnic groups in the U.S. — Korean Americans. Family life — grandfathers. Holidays — Halloween. Masks.

Choldenko, Gennifer. *How to make friends with a giant* ill. by Amy Walrod. Penguin, 2006. ISBN 0-399-23779-8 Subj: Character traits — appearance. Concepts — size. Friendship. School.

Louder, Lili ill. by S. D. Schindler. Penguin, 2007. ISBN 978-0-399-24252-6 Subj: Behavior — bossy. Character traits — shyness. Friendship. School.

Christelow, Eileen. *Five little monkeys go shopping* ill. by author. Houghton Mifflin, 2007. ISBN 978-0-618-82161-7 Subj: Animals — monkeys. Counting, numbers. Shopping.

Letters from a desperate dog ill. by author. Houghton Mifflin, 2006. ISBN 0-618-51003-6 Subj: Activities — writing. Animals — dogs. Behavior — misbehavior. Careers — artists. Humorous stories. Letters, cards.

Christian, Mary Blount. *If not for the calico cat* ill. by Sebastia Serra. Penguin, 2007. ISBN 0-525-47779-9 Subj: Animals — cats. Boats, ships. Character traits — luck. Foreign lands — Japan.

Chrustowski, Rick. *Turtle crossing* ill. by author. Henry Holt, 2006. ISBN 0-8050-7498-8 Subj: Nature. Reptiles — turtles, tortoises.

Church, Caroline Jayne. *Digby takes charge* ill. by author. Simon & Schuster, 2007. ISBN 978-1-4169-3441-7 Subj: Animals — dogs. Animals — sheep. Behavior — misbehavior. Character traits — kindness to animals. Farms.

Little Apple Goat ill. by author. Eerdmans, 2007. ISBN 978-0-8028-5320-2 Subj: Animals — goats. Food.

One smart goose ill. by author. Scholastic/Orchard, 2005. ISBN 0-439-68765-9 Subj: Animals — foxes. Behavior — bullying. Birds — geese. Character traits — cleanliness. Farms.

Chwast, Seymour. *The miracle of Hanukkah* ill. by author. Blue Apple, 2006. ISBN 1-59354-157-0 Subj: Holidays — Hanukkah. Jewish culture.

Ciboul, Adele. *The five senses* trans. by Anthea Bell; ill. by Clementine Collinet, Benoit Debecker, & Frankie Merlier. Firefly, 2006. ISBN 1-55407-007-4 Subj: Format, unusual — toy & movable books. Senses.

Clark, Emma Chichester. *see* Chichester Clark, Emma

Clark, Katie. *Seagull Sam* ill. by Amy Huntington. Down East, 2007. ISBN 978-0-89272-715-5 Subj: Birds — seagulls. Character traits — smallness. Family life — brothers & sisters. Kites.

Clark, Mary Higgins. *Ghost ship: a Cape Cod story* ill. by Wendell Minor. Simon & Schuster, 2007. ISBN 978-1-4169-3514-8 Subj: Boats, ships. Ghosts.

Clarke, Jane. *The best of both nests* ill. by Anne Kennedy. Albert Whitman, 2007. ISBN 978-0-8075-0668-4 Subj: Behavior — worrying. Birds — storks. Divorce.

Dippy's sleepover ill. by Mary McQuillan. Barron's, 2006. ISBN 0-7641-3425-6 Subj: Behavior — bedwetting. Dinosaurs. Sleepovers.

Clayton, Elaine. *A blue ribbon for Sugar* ill. by author. Macmillan, 2006. ISBN 1-59643-157-1 Subj: Animals — horses, ponies. Contests. Sports.

Cleary, Brian P. *Eight wild nights: a family Hanukkah tale* ill. by David Udovic. Lerner, 2006. ISBN 1-58013-152-2 Subj: Holidays — Hanukkah. Rhyming text.

A lime, a mime, a pool of slime: more about nouns ill. by Brian Gable. Lerner, 2006. ISBN 1-57505-937-1 Subj: Language. Rhyming text.

Peanut butter and jellyfishes: a very silly alphabet book ill. by Betsy E. Snyder. Lerner, 2007. ISBN 978-0-8225-6188-0 Subj: ABC books. Language. Picture puzzles. Rhyming text.

Clements, Andrew. *Because your daddy loves you* ill. by R. W. Alley. Houghton Mifflin, 2005. ISBN 0-618-00361-4 Subj: Emotions — love. Family life — fathers. Sea & seashore — beaches.

Dogku ill. by Tim Bowers. Simon & Schuster, 2007. ISBN 978-0-689-85823-9 Subj: Animals — dogs. Pets. Poetry.

A million dots ill. by Mike Reed. Simon & Schuster, 2006. ISBN 0-689-85824-8 Subj: Counting, numbers.

Naptime for Slippers ill. by Janie Bynum. Penguin, 2005. ISBN 0-525-47287-8 Subj: Animals — dogs. Sleep.

Slippers at School ill. by Janie Bynum. Penguin, 2005. ISBN 0-525-47189-8 Subj: Animals — dogs. School.

Slippers loves to run ill. by Janie Bynum. Penguin, 2006. ISBN 0-525-47648-2 Subj: Animals — dogs. Family life. Hugging. Pets.

Cline-Ransome, Lesa. *Young Pelé: soccer's first star* ill. by James Ransome. Random House, 2007. ISBN 978-0-375-83599-5 Subj: Foreign lands — Brazil. Sports — soccer.

Clinton, Catherine. *When Harriet met Sojourner* ill. by Shane W. Evans. HarperCollins, 2007. ISBN 978-0-06-050425-0 Subj: Ethnic groups in the U.S. — African Americans. U.S. history.

Cocca-Leffler, Maryann. *Jack's talent* ill. by author. Farrar, Straus & Giroux, 2007. ISBN 978-0-374-33681-3 Subj: Behavior — worrying. School — first day. Self-concept.

Mr. Tanen's ties rule! ill. by author. Albert Whitman, 2005. ISBN 0-8075-5308-5 Subj: Careers — school principals. Clothing — neckties. School.

Cochran, Bill. *The forever dog* ill. by Dan Andreasen. HarperCollins, 2007. ISBN 0-06-053939-9 Subj: Animals — dogs. Death. Emotions — grief. Pets.

Coffelt, Nancy. *Fred stays with me!* ill. by Tricia Tusa. Little, Brown, 2007. ISBN 978-0-316-88269-9 Subj: Animals — dogs. Divorce. Family life.

Pug in a truck ill. by author. Houghton Mifflin, 2006. ISBN 0-618-56319-9 Subj: Animals — dogs. Careers — truck drivers. Trucks.

Cohan, George M. *You're a grand old flag* ill. by Warren Kimble. Walker & Company, 2007. ISBN 978-0-8027-9575-5 Subj: Flags. Songs. U.S. history.

Cohen, Deborah Bodin. *Papa Jethro* ill. by author. Kar-Ben, 2007. ISBN 978-1-58013-250-3 Subj: Family life — grandfathers. Jewish culture. Religion.

Cohen, Miriam. *First grade takes a test* ill. by Ronald Himler. Star Bright, 2006. ISBN 1-59572-054-5 Subj: Friendship. School.

Colato Laínez, René. *Playing lotería / El juego de la lotería* ill. by Jill Arena. Luna Rising, 2005. ISBN 0-87358-881-9 Subj: Fairs, festivals. Family life — grandmothers. Foreign lands — Mexico. Foreign languages.

Cole, Barbara Hancock. *Anna and Natalie* ill. by Ronald Himler. Star Bright, 2007. ISBN 978-1-59572-105-1 Subj: Animals — dogs. Contests. Handicaps — blindness. Letters, cards. School. U.S. history.

Cole, Brock. *Good enough to eat* ill. by author. Farrar, Straus & Giroux, 2007. ISBN 978-0-374-32737-8 Subj: Character traits — cleverness. Homeless. Mythical creatures — ogres.

Cole, Henry. *On Meadowview Street* ill. by author. HarperCollins, 2007. ISBN 978-0-06-056481-0 Subj: Cities, towns. Ecology. Nature.

Cole, Joanna. *The magic school bus and the science fair expedition* ill. by Bruce Degen. Scholastic, 2006. ISBN 0-590-10824-7 Subj: Buses. Careers — teachers. Magic. School — field trips. Science.

My friend the doctor ill. by Maxie Chambliss. HarperCollins, 2005. ISBN 0-06-050500-1 Subj: Careers — doctors. Health & fitness.

Collard, Sneed B. *A platypus, probably* ill. by Andrew Plant. Charlesbridge, 2005. ISBN 1-57091-583-0 Subj: Animals — platypuses.

Collicutt, Paul. *This rocket* ill. by author. Farrar, Straus & Giroux, 2005. ISBN 0-374-37484-8 Subj: Space & space ships.

Collins, Suzanne. *When Charlie McButton lost power* ill. by Mike Lester. Penguin, 2005. ISBN 0-399-24000-4 Subj: Computers. Family life — brothers & sisters. Rhyming text.

Compestine, Ying Chang. *D is for dragon dance* ill. by YongSheng Xuan. Holiday House, 2006. ISBN 0-8234-1887-1 Subj: ABC books. Foreign lands — China. Holidays — Chinese New Year.

The real story of stone soup ill. by Stephane Jorisch. Penguin, 2007. ISBN 0-525-47493-5 Subj: Character traits — cleverness. Folk & fairy tales. Food. Foreign lands — China.

Conahan, Carolyn. *The twelve days of Christmas dogs* ill. by author. Penguin, 2005. ISBN 0-525-47486-2 Subj: Animals — dogs. Holidays — Christmas. Songs.

Consentino, Ralph. *The story of Honk-Honk-Ashoo and Swella-Bow-Wow* ill. by author. Penguin, 2005. ISBN 0-670-05997-8 Subj: Animals — dogs. Friendship.

Conway, David. *The most important gift of all* ill. by Karin Littlewood. School Specialty/Gingham Dog, 2006. ISBN 0-7696-4618-2 Subj: Animals. Emotions — love. Family life — new sibling. Foreign lands — Africa. Gifts.

Coombs, Kate. *The secret-keeper* ill. by Heather M. Solomon. Simon & Schuster/Atheneum, 2006. ISBN 0-689-83963-4 Subj: Behavior — secrets.

Cooper, Elisha. *Beach* ill. by author. Scholastic, 2006. ISBN 0-439-68785-3 Subj: Sea & seashore — beaches.

Bear dreams ill. by author. HarperCollins, 2006. ISBN 0-06-087428-7 Subj: Animals — bears. Hibernation. Seasons — winter.

A good night walk ill. by author. Scholastic/Orchard, 2005. ISBN 0-439-68783-7 Subj: Activities — walking. Communities, neighborhoods.

Cooper, Helen (Helen F.). *Delicious! A pumpkin soup story* ill. by author. Farrar, Straus & Giroux, 2007. ISBN 978-0-374-31756-0 Subj: Activities — baking, cooking. Animals. Animals — cats. Animals — squirrels. Birds — ducks. Friendship.

A pipkin of pepper ill. by author. Farrar, Straus & Giroux, 2005. ISBN 978-0-374-35953-9 Subj: Activities — baking, cooking. Animals. Animals — cats. Animals — squirrels. Birds — ducks. Friendship.

Cooper, Ilene. *The golden rule* ill. by Gabi Swiatkowska. Abrams, 2007. ISBN 978-0-8109-0960-1 Subj: Behavior.

Copper, Melinda. *Snow White* (Grimm, Jacob)

Cordsen, Carol Foskett. *The milkman* ill. by Douglas B. Jones. Penguin, 2005. ISBN 0-525-47208-8 Subj: Activities — working. Careers. Food. Rhyming text.

Corr, Christopher. *Whole world* ill. by author. Barefoot, 2007. ISBN 978-1-84686-043-0 Subj: Ecology. Nature. Songs. World.

Cosentino, Ralph. *The marvelous misadventures of — Fun-Boy* ill. by author. Penguin, 2006. ISBN 0-670-05961-7 Subj: Humorous stories. Imagination. Wordless.

Coste, Marion. *Finding Joy* ill. by Yong Chen. Boyds Mills, 2006. ISBN 1-59078-192-0 Subj: Adoption. Family life. Foreign lands — China.

Cote, Nancy. *It's all about me!* ill. by author. Penguin, 2005. ISBN 0-399-24280-5 Subj: Family life — new sibling. Self-concept. Sibling rivalry.

Côté, Geneviève. *What elephant?* ill. by author. Kids Can, 2006. ISBN 1-55337-875-X Subj: Animals — elephants.

With you always, Little Monday ill. by author. Harcourt, 2007. ISBN 978-0-15-205997-2 Subj: Animals. Animals — rabbits. Behavior — lost. Family life — mothers. Moon.

Cotten, Cynthia. *Abbie in stitches* ill. by Beth Peck. Farrar, Straus & Giroux, 2006. ISBN 0-374-30004-6 Subj: Activities — sewing. U.S. history.

This is the stable ill. by Delana Bettoli. Henry Holt, 2006. ISBN 0-8050-7556-9 Subj: Religion — Nativity.

Cousins, Lucy. *Ha ha, Maisy!* ill. by author. Candlewick, 2005. ISBN 0-7636-2633-3 Subj: Animals — mice. Format, unusual — toy & movable books.

Happy Easter, Maisy! ill. by author. Candlewick, 2007. ISBN 978-0-7636-3230-4 Subj: Animals — mice. Format, unusual — board books. Holidays — Easter.

Hooray for fish! ill. by author. Candlewick, 2005. ISBN 0-7636-2741-0 Subj: Family life — mothers. Fish. Rhyming text. Sea & seashore.

Maisy big, Maisy small ill. by author. Candlewick, 2007. ISBN 978-0-7636-3406-3 Subj: Animals — mice. Concepts — opposites.

Maisy, Charley, and the wobbly tooth ill. by author. Candlewick, 2006. ISBN 0-7636-2904-9 Subj: Animals. Animals — mice. Careers — dentists. Reptiles — alligators, crocodiles. Teeth.

Maisy goes to the hospital ill. by author. Candlewick, 2007. ISBN 978-0-7636-3377-6 Subj: Animals — mice. Hospitals.

Maisy goes to the library ill. by author. Candlewick, 2005. ISBN 0-7636-2669-4 Subj: Animals — mice. Books, reading. Libraries.

Maisy's amazing big book of words ill. by author. Candlewick, 2007. ISBN 978-0-7636-0794-4 Subj: Animals — mice. Format, unusual — toy & movable books. Language.

Maisy's wonderful weather book ill. by author. Candlewick, 2006. ISBN 0-7636-2987-1 Subj: Animals — mice. Format, unusual — toy & movable books. Weather.

More fun with Maisy! ill. by author. Candlewick, 2005. ISBN 0-7636-2632-5 Subj: Animals — mice. Format, unusual — toy & movable books.

Stop and go, Maisy ill. by author. Candlewick, 2005. ISBN 0-7636-2668-6 Subj: Animals — mice. Format, unusual — toy & movable books. Transportation.

Sweet dreams, Maisy ill. by author. Candlewick, 2005. ISBN 0-7636-2874-3 Subj: Animals — mice. Bedtime.

With love from Maisy ill. by author. Candlewick, 2005. ISBN 0-7636-2513-2 Subj: Animals — mice. Format, unusual — toy & movable books. Gifts.

Cowell, Cressida. *That rabbit belongs to Emily Brown* ill. by Neal Layton. Hyperion, 2007. ISBN 978-1-4231-0645-6 Subj: Animals — rabbits. Toys.

Cowley, Joy. *Chameleon, chameleon* photos by Nic Bishop. Scholastic, 2005. ISBN 0-439-66653-8 Subj: Reptiles — chameleons.

Mrs. Wishy-Washy's Christmas ill. by Elizabeth Fuller. Penguin, 2005. ISBN 0-399-24344-5 Subj: Animals. Farms. Holidays — Christmas. Rhyming text.

Coyle, Carmela LaVigna. *Do princesses really kiss frogs?* ill. by Mike & Carl Gordon. Rising Moon, 2005. ISBN 0-8735-8880-0 Subj: Character traits — questioning. Family life — fathers. Royalty — princesses. Sports — hiking.

Crandall, Court. *Hugville* ill. by Joe Murray. Random House, 2005. ISBN 0-375-82418-9 Subj: Hugging. Rhyming text.

Crane, Carol. *D is for dancing dragon: a China alphabet* ill. by Zong-Zhou Wang. Sleeping Bear, 2006. ISBN 1-58536-273-5 Subj: ABC books. Foreign lands — China.

Crawford, Laura. *In arctic waters* ill. by Ben Hodson. Random House, 2007. ISBN 978-0-9768823-4-3 Subj: Animals. Foreign lands — Arctic. Rhyming text.

Crawley, Dave. *Cat poems* ill. by Tamara Petrosino. Boyds Mills, 2005. ISBN 1-59078-287-9 Subj: Animals — cats. Poetry.

Creech, Sharon. *Who's that baby? New-baby songs* ill. by David Diaz. HarperCollins, 2005. ISBN 0-06-052940-7 Subj: Babies. Poetry. Songs.

Crews, Nina. *Below* photos by author. Henry Holt, 2006. ISBN 0-8050-7728-6 Subj: Activities — playing. Imagination. Toys.

Crimi, Carolyn. *Henry and the Buccaneer Bunnies* ill. by John Manders. Candlewick, 2005. ISBN 0-7636-2449-7 Subj: Animals — rabbits. Books, reading. Pirates.

The Louds move in! ill. by Regan Dunnick. Marshall Cavendish, 2006. ISBN 0-7614-5221-4 Subj: Humorous stories. Noise, sounds.

Crisp, Marty. *The most precious gift: a story of the Nativity* ill. by Floyd Cooper. Penguin, 2006. ISBN 0-399-24296-1 Subj: Animals — dogs. Religion — Nativity.

Crocker, Nancy. *Betty Lou Blue* ill. by Boris Kulikov. Penguin, 2006. ISBN 0-8037-2937-5 Subj: Anatomy — feet. Behavior — bullying. Character traits — appearance. Rhyming text.

Cronin, Doreen. *Bounce* ill. by Scott Menchin. Simon & Schuster/Atheneum, 2007. ISBN 978-1-4169-1627-7 Subj: Activities — jumping. Activities – playing. Animals — dogs. Rhyming text. Toys — balls.

Click clack, quackity-quack: an alphabetical adventure ill. by Betsy Lewin. Simon & Schuster, 2005. ISBN 0-689-87715-3 Subj: ABC books. Activities — picnicking. Activities — writing. Animals. Birds — ducks. Farms.

Click, clack, splish, splash: a counting adventure ill. by Betsy Lewin. Simon & Schuster, 2006. ISBN 0-689-87716-1 Subj: Animals. Counting, numbers. Farms. Rhyming text. Sports — fishing.

Diary of a fly ill. by Harry Bliss. HarperCollins, 2007. ISBN 978-0-06-000156-8 Subj: Activities — writing. Insects — flies.

Diary of a spider ill. by Harry Bliss. HarperCollins, 2005. ISBN 0-06-000154-2 Subj: Activities — writing. Spiders.

Dooby dooby moo ill. by Betsy Lewin. Simon & Schuster/Atheneum, 2006. ISBN 0-689-84507-3 Subj: Animals. Careers — farmers. Farms. Theater.

Duck for President ill. by Betsy Lewin. Simon & Schuster, 2004. ISBN 0-689-86377-2 Subj: Birds — ducks. Elections.

Crowther, Robert. *Opposites* ill. by author. Candlewick, 2005. ISBN 0-76362783-6 Subj: Concepts — opposites. Format, unusual — toy & movable books.

Cruise, Robin. *Little Mama forgets* ill. by Stacey Dressen-McQueen. Farrar, Straus & Giroux, 2006. ISBN 978-0-374-34613-3 Subj: Behavior — forgetfulness. Ethnic groups in the U.S. — Mexican Americans. Family life — grandmothers. Memories, memory. Old age.

Only you ill. by Margaret Chodos-Irvine. Harcourt, 2007. ISBN 978-0-15-216604-5 Subj: Emotions — love. Family life. Rhyming text.

Crum, Shutta. *A family for Old Mill Farm* ill. by Niki Daly. Houghton Mifflin, 2007. ISBN 978-0-618-42846-5 Subj: Animals. Homes, houses. Moving. Rhyming text.

Crummel, Susan Stevens. *The great fuzz frenzy* (Stevens, Janet)

Ten-gallon Bart ill. by Dorothy Donohue. Marshall Cavendish, 2006. ISBN 0-7614-5246-X Subj: Animals — dogs. Animals — goats. Careers — sheriffs.

Crumpacker, Bunny. *Alexander's pretending day* ill. by Dan Andreasen. Penguin, 2005. ISBN 0-525-46936-2 Subj: Character traits — questioning. Family life — mothers. Imagination.

Crunk, Tony. *Railroad John and the Red Rock run* ill. by Michael Austin. Peachtree, 2006. ISBN 1-56145-363-3 Subj: Tall tales. Trains. U.S. history — frontier & pioneer life. Weddings.

Cullen, Lynn. *Moi and Marie Antoinette* ill. by Amy Young. Bloomsbury, 2006. ISBN 1-58234-958-4 Subj: Animals — dogs. Royalty — queens.

Cumberbatch, Judy. *Can you hear the sea?* ill. by Ken Wilson-Max. Bloomsbury, 2006. ISBN 1-58234-703-4 Subj: Family life — grandfathers. Foreign lands — Ghana. Noise, sounds. Sea & seashore.

Cunnane, Kelly. *For you are a Kenyan child* ill. by Ana Juan. Simon & Schuster/Atheneum, 2006. ISBN 978-0-689-86194-9 Subj: Foreign lands — Kenya.

Cupiano, Ina. *Quinito's neighborhood / El vecindario de Quinito* ill. by Jose Ramirez. Children's Book Press, 2005. ISBN 0-89239-209-6 Subj: Communities, neighborhoods. Ethnic groups in the U.S. — Hispanic Americans. Foreign languages.

Curlee, Lynn. *Skyscraper* ill. by author. Simon & Schuster/Atheneum, 2007. ISBN 0-689-84489-1 Subj: Buildings. Cities, towns.

Curtis, Jamie Lee. *Is there really a human race?* ill. by Laura Cornell. HarperCollins, 2006. ISBN 0-06-075346-3 Subj: Character traits — curiosity. Rhyming text.

Cuyler, Margery. *The bumpy little pumpkin* ill. by Will Hillenbrand. Scholastic, 2005. ISBN 0-439-52835-6 Subj: Family life — brothers & sisters. Holidays — Halloween.

Groundhog stays up late ill. by Jean Cassels. Walker & Company, 2005. ISBN 0-8027-8939-0 Subj: Animals — groundhogs. Hibernation. Holidays — Groundhog Day.

Kindness is cooler, Mrs. Ruler ill. by Sachiko Yohikawa. Simon & Schuster, 2007. ISBN 978-0-689-87344-7 Subj: Careers — teachers. Character traits — kindness. School.

Please play safe! Penguin's guide to playground safety ill. by Will Hillenbrand. Scholastic, 2006. ISBN 0-439-52832-1 Subj: Activities — playing. Birds — penguins. Safety.

That's good! That's bad! In Washington, D.C. ill. by Michael Garland. Henry Holt, 2007. ISBN 978-0-8050-7727-8 Subj: Geography. School — field trips.

da Costa, Deborah. *Hanukkah moon* ill. by Gosia Mosz. Kar-Ben, 2007. ISBN 978-1-58013-244-2 Subj: Ethnic groups in the U.S. — Mexican Americans. Family life. Holidays — Hanukkah. Holidays — Rosh Kodesh.

Daddo, Andrew. *Goodnight, me* ill. by Emma Quay. Bloomsbury, 2007. ISBN 978-1-59990-153-4 Subj: Animals — orangutans. Bedtime.

Dahl, Michael. *If you were an adjective* ill. by Sara Gray. Picture Window, 2006. ISBN 1-4048-1356-X Subj: Language.

Dale, Penny. *The boy on the bus* ill. by author. Candlewick, 2007. ISBN 978-0-7636-3381-3 Subj: Animals. Buses. Songs.

Daly, Niki. *Happy birthday, Jamela!* ill. by author. Farrar, Straus & Giroux, 2006. ISBN 0-374-32842-0 Subj: Birthdays. Clothing — shoes. Foreign lands — South Africa.

Pretty Salma: a Little Red Riding Hood story from Africa ill. by author. Houghton Mifflin, 2007. ISBN 978-0-618-72345-4 Subj: Animals — dogs. Behavior — trickery. Folk & fairy tales. Foreign lands — Africa.

Ruby sings the blues ill. by author. Bloomsbury, 2005. ISBN 1-58234-995-9 Subj: Activities — singing. Music. Noise, sounds.

Welcome to Zanzibar Road ill. by author. Houghton Mifflin, 2006. ISBN 0-618-64926-3 Subj: Animals. Animals — elephants. Birds — chickens. Emotions — loneliness. Foreign lands — Africa. Homes, houses.

D'Amico, Carmela. *Ella sets the stage* by Carmela & Steve D'Amico; ill. by Steve D'Amico. Scholastic, 2006. ISBN 0-439-83152-0 Subj: Animals — elephants. Character traits — shyness. School. Theater.

Ella takes the cake by Carmela & Steve D'Amico; ill. by Steve D'Amico. Arthur A. Levine, 2005. ISBN 0-439-62794-X Subj: Animals — elephants. Character traits — helpfulness.

D'Amico, Steve. *Ella sets the stage* (D'Amico, Carmela)

Ella takes the cake (D'Amico, Carmela)

Danneberg, Julie. *Cowboy Slim* ill. by Margot Apple. Charlesbridge, 2006. ISBN 1-58089-045-8 Subj: Activities — writing. Cowboys, cowgirls. Poetry. Self-concept.

Last day blues ill. by Judy Love. Charlesbridge, 2006. ISBN 1-58089-046-6 Subj: Careers — teachers. Gifts. School.

David, Ryan. *The magic raincoat* ill. by Sibylla Benatova. Boyds Mills, 2007. ISBN 978-1-932425-68-0 Subj: Clothing — coats. Magic.

Davidson, Ellen Dee. *Princess Justina Albertina: a cautionary tale* ill. by Michael Chesworth. Charlesbridge, 2007. ISBN 978-1-57091-652-6 Subj: Character traits — selfishness. Character traits — willfulness. Pets. Royalty — princesses.

Davies, Jacqueline. *The house takes a vacation* ill. by Lee White. Marshall Cavendish, 2007. ISBN 978-0-7314-5331-4 Subj: Activities — vacationing. Homes, houses. Sea & seashore.

The night is singing ill. by Kyrsten Brooker. Penguin, 2006. ISBN 0-8037-3004-7 Subj: Bedtime. Country. Lullabies. Night. Noise, sounds. Rhyming text.

Davies, Nicola. *Ice bear: in the steps of the polar bear* ill. by Gary Blythe. Candlewick, 2005. ISBN 0-7636-2759-3 Subj: Animals — polar bears.

White owl, barn owl ill. by Michael Foreman. Candlewick, 2007. ISBN 978-0-7636-3364-6 Subj: Birds — owls. Family life — grandfathers. Night.

Davies, Sarah. *Happy to be girls* ill. by Jenny Mattheson. Penguin, 2005. ISBN 0-399-23983-9 Subj: Rhyming text. Self-concept.

Davis, Katie. *Kindergarten rocks!* ill. by author. Harcourt, 2005. ISBN 0-15-204932-0 Subj: Emotions — fear. School — first day.

Dawes, Kwame Senu Neville. *I saw your face* ill. by Tom Feelings. Penguin, 2005. ISBN 0-8037-1894-2 Subj: Art. Ethnic groups in the U.S. — African Americans. Foreign lands — Africa. Poetry.

Day, Alexandra. *Carl's sleepy afternoon* ill. by author. Farrar, Straus & Giroux, 2005. ISBN 0-374-31088-2 Subj: Activities. Animals — dogs.

Deacon, Alexis. *While you are sleeping* ill. by author. Farrar, Straus & Giroux, 2006. ISBN 0-374-38330-8 Subj: Holidays — Christmas. Night. Sleep. Toys.

Deans, Karen. *Playing to win: the story of Althea Gibson* ill. by Elbrite Brown. Holiday House, 2007. ISBN 978-0-8234-1926-5 Subj: Ethnic groups in the U.S. — African Americans. Sports.

De Brunhoff, Laurent. *see* Brunhoff, Laurent de

Deedy, Carmen Agra. *Martina the beautiful cockroach: a Cuban folktale* ill. by Michael Austin. Peachtree, 2007. ISBN 978-1-56145-399-3 Subj: Animals — mice. Folk & fairy tales. Foreign lands — Cuba. Insects — cockroaches.

DeFelice, Cynthia C. *One potato, two potato* ill. by Andrea U'Ren. Farrar, Straus & Giroux, 2006. ISBN 0-374-35640-8 Subj: Food. Humorous stories. Magic.

deGroat, Diane. *Brand-new pencils, brand-new books* ill. by author. HarperCollins, 2005. ISBN 0-06-072615-6 Subj: Animals — possums. School — first day.

Last one in is a rotten egg! ill. by author. HarperCollins, 2007. ISBN 0-06-089294-3 Subj: Animals — possums. Behavior — bossy. Behavior — sharing. Family life — cousins. Holidays — Easter.

No more pencils, no more books, no more teacher's dirty looks! ill. by author. HarperCollins, 2006. ISBN 0-06-079114-4 Subj: Careers — teachers. Friendship. School.

Delessert, Etienne. *A was an apple pie: an English nursery rhyme* ill. by author. Creative Editions, 2005. ISBN 1-56846-196-8 Subj: ABC books. Nursery rhymes.

Alert! ill. by author. Houghton Mifflin, 2007. ISBN 978-0-618-73474-0 Subj: Animals — moles. Behavior — collecting things. Crime.

Hungry for numbers ill. by author. Creative Editions, 2006. ISBN 1-56846-198-4 Subj: Counting, numbers. Food.

Demarest, Chris L. *Alpha Bravo Charlie: the military alphabet* ill. by author. Simon & Schuster, 2005. ISBN 0-689-86928-2 Subj: ABC books. Careers — military.

Demas, Corinne. *Two Christmas mice* ill. by Stephanie Roth. Holiday House, 2005. ISBN 0-8234-1785-9 Subj: Animals — mice. Holidays — Christmas. Trees.

Demers, Dominique. *Every single night* trans. from French by Sarah Quinn; ill. by Nicolas Debon. Groundwood, 2006. ISBN 0-88899-699-3 Subj: Animals. Bedtime. Family life — fathers. Sleep.

Demi. *The boy who painted dragons* ill. by author. Simon & Schuster, 2007. ISBN 978-1-4169-2469-2 Subj: Activities — painting. Careers — artists. Character traits — bravery. Dragons. Emotions — fear.

Denchfield, Nick. *Charlie Chick* ill. by Ant Parker. Harcourt, 2007. ISBN 978-0-15-206013-8 Subj: Birds — chickens. Format, unusual — toy & movable books.

Denise, Anika. *Pigs love potatoes* ill. by Christopher Denise. Penguin, 2007. ISBN 978-0-399-24036-2 Subj: Activities — baking, cooking. Animals — pigs. Counting, numbers. Food. Rhyming text.

Denslow, Sharon Phillips. *In the snow* ill. by Nancy Tafuri. HarperCollins, 2005. ISBN 0-06-059684-8 Subj: Animals. Seasons — winter. Weather — snow.

DePalma, Mary Newell. *A grand old tree* ill. by author. Scholastic, 2005. ISBN 0-439-62334-0 Subj: Ecology. Nature. Trees.

The Nutcracker doll ill. by author. Scholastic, 2007. ISBN 0-439-80242-3 Subj: Activities — dancing. Ballet. Holidays — Christmas. Theater.

dePaola, Tomie. *Angels, Angels everywhere* ill. by author. Penguin, 2005. ISBN 0-399-24370-4 Subj: Angels.

Little Grunt and the big egg: a prehistoric fairy tale ill. by author. Penguin, 2006. ISBN 0-399-24529-4 Subj: Dinosaurs. Folk & fairy tales. Pets.

Derby, Sally. *Whoosh went the wind!* ill. by Vincent Nguyen. Marshall Cavendish, 2006. ISBN 0-7614-5309-1 Subj: School. Tall tales. Weather — wind.

Derrick, Patricia. *Riley the rhinoceros* ill. by J-P Loppo Martinez. KSB Promotions, 2007. ISBN 978-1-933818-15-3 Subj: Animals. Animals — rhinoceros. Jungles.

DeSeve, Randall. *Toy boat* ill. by Loren Long. Penguin, 2007. ISBN 978-0-399-24374-5 Subj: Behavior — lost & found possessions. Toys.

Dewdney, Anna. *Grumpy Gloria* ill. by author. Penguin, 2006. ISBN 0-670-06123-9 Subj: Animals — dogs. Emotions. Rhyming text.

Llama Llama mad at mama ill. by author. Penguin, 2007. ISBN 978-0-670-06240-9 Subj: Animals — llamas. Emotions — anger. Family life — mothers. Shopping.

Llama, Llama red pajama ill. by author. Penguin, 2005. ISBN 0-670-05983-8 Subj: Animals — llamas. Bedtime. Family life — mothers.

Dewey, Ariane. *The last laugh* (Aruego, Jose)

Diakité, Baba Wagué. *Mee-an and the magic serpent: a folktale from Mali* ill. by author. Groundwood, 2007. ISBN 978-0-88899-719-7 Subj: Folk & fairy tales. Foreign lands — Mali. Magic. Reptiles — snakes.

Diakité, Penda. *I lost my tooth in Africa* ill. by Baba Wagué Diakité. Scholastic, 2006. ISBN 0-439-66226-5 Subj: Birds — chickens. Foreign lands — Mali. Teeth.

Díaz, Katacha. *Badger at Sandy Ridge Road* ill. by Kristin Kest. Soundprints, 2005. ISBN 1-59249-420-X Subj: Animals. Animals — badgers.

DiCamillo, Kate. *Great joy* ill. by Bagram Ibatoulline. Candlewick, 2007. ISBN 978-0-7636-2920-5 Subj: Animals — monkeys. Character traits — helpfulness. Emotions. Holidays — Christmas. Homeless.

Dick Whittington and his cat. *Dick Whittington and his cat* retold by Margaret Hodges; ill. by Mélisande Potter. Holiday House, 2006. ISBN 0-8234-1987-8 Subj: Animals — cats. Folk & fairy tales. Foreign lands — England. Middle Ages.

Dierssen, Andreas. *The old red tractor* trans. from German by Marianne Martens; ill. by Daniel Sohr. NorthSouth, 2006. ISBN 0-7358-2088-0 Subj: Emotions — envy, jealousy. Problem solving. Toys. Tractors.

DiFiori, Lawrence. *Jackie and the Shadow Snatcher* ill. by author. Random House, 2006. ISBN 0-375-97515-2 Subj: Behavior — lost & found possessions. Crime. Shadows.

Dijkstra, Lida. *Cute* ill. by Marije Tolman. Boyds Mills, 2007. ISBN 978-1-59078-505-8 Subj: Animals — rabbits. Self-concept.

Dillon, Diane. *Jazz on a Saturday night* (Dillon, Leo)

Mother Goose numbers on the loose (Dillon, Leo)

Dillon, Leo. *Jazz on a Saturday night* by Leo & Diane Dillon; ill. by authors. Scholastic, 2007. ISBN 978-0-590-47893-9 Subj: Careers — musicians. Music.

DiPucchio, Kelly S. *Dinosnores* ill. by Ponder Goembel. HarperCollins, 2005. ISBN 0-06-051578-3 Subj: Dinosaurs. Noise, sounds. Rhyming text. Sleep — snoring.

Ditchfield, Christin. *Cowlick!* ill. by Rosalind Beardshaw. Random House, 2007. ISBN 0-375-83540-7 Subj: Animals — bulls, cows. Character traits — appearance. Hair. Humorous stories.

DiTerlizzi, Tony. *G is for one gzonk! An alpha-number-bet book* ill. by author. Simon & Schuster, 2006. ISBN 0-689-85290-8 Subj: ABC books. Counting, numbers. Rhyming text.

Dodds, Dayle Ann. *Hello, sun!* ill. by Sachiko Yoshikawa. Penguin, 2005. ISBN 0-8037-2895-6 Subj: Clothing. Rhyming text. Weather.

The prince won't go to bed ill. by Kyrsten Brooker. Farrar, Straus & Giroux, 2007. ISBN 978-0-374-36108-2 Subj: Bedtime. Behavior — misbehavior. Rhyming text. Royalty — princes.

Teacher's pets ill. by Marylin Hafner. Candlewick, 2006. ISBN 0-7636-2252-4 Subj: Careers — teachers. Pets. School.

Dolenz, Micky. *Gakky Two-Feet* ill. by David Clark. Penguin, 2006. ISBN 0-399-24468-9 Subj: Behavior — bullying. Character traits — individuality. Prehistory.

Domeniconi, David. *M is for masterpiece: an art alphabet* ill. by Will Bullas. Sleeping Bear, 2006. ISBN 1-58536-276-X Subj: ABC books. Art.

Donaldson, Julia. *Charlie Cook's favorite book* ill. by Axel Scheffler. Penguin, 2006. ISBN 0-8037-3142-6 Subj: Books, reading. Rhyming text.

One Ted falls out of bed ill. by Anna Currey. Henry Holt, 2006. ISBN 0-8050-7787-1 Subj: Bedtime. Counting, numbers. Toys. Toys — bears.

Donnio, Sylviane. *I'd really like to eat a child* trans. from French by Leslie Martin; ill. by Dorothée de Monfreid. Random House, 2007. ISBN 978-0-375-83761-6 Subj: Food. Reptiles — alligators, crocodiles.

Donofrio, Beverly. *Mary and the mouse, the mouse and Mary* ill. by Barbara McClintock. Random House, 2007. ISBN 978-0-375-83609-1 Subj: Animals — mice. Friendship.

Donohue, Moira Rose. *Alfie the apostrophe* ill. by JoAnn Adinolfi. Albert Whitman, 2006. ISBN 0-8075-0255-3 Subj: Language.

Dorros, Alex. *Número uno* by Alex & Arthur Dorros; ill. by Susan Guevara. Abrams, 2007. ISBN 978-0-8109-5764-0 Subj: Behavior — fighting, arguing. Character traits — cooperation. Contests. Humorous stories.

Dorros, Arthur. *Número uno* (Dorros, Alex)

Dotlich, Rebecca Kai. *What is science?* ill. by Sachiko Yoshikawa. Henry Holt, 2006. ISBN 0-8050-7394-9 Subj: Poetry. Science.

Downes, Belinda. *Baby days: a quilt of rhymes and pictures* ill. by author. Candlewick, 2006. ISBN 0-7636-2786-0 Subj: Babies. Poetry. Songs.

Downey, Lynn. *Matilda's humdinger* ill. by Tim Bowers. Random House, 2006. ISBN 0-375-92403-5 Subj: Activities — storytelling. Animals. Animals — cats. Careers — waiters, waitresses. Restaurants.

The tattletale ill. by Pam Paparone. Henry Holt, 2006. ISBN 0-8050-7152-0 Subj: Animals — pigs. Behavior — gossip. Family life — brothers & sisters.

Downie, Mary Alice. *A pioneer ABC* ill. by Mary Jane Gerber. Tundra, 2005. ISBN 0-88776-688-9 Subj: ABC books. Foreign lands — Canada.

Downing, Johnette. *Down in Louisiana: traditional song* adapt. by Johnette Downing; ill. by Deborah Ousley Kadair. Pelican, 2007. ISBN 978-1-58980-451-7 Subj: Animals. Counting, numbers. Songs. Swamps.

Today is Monday in Louisiana ill. by Deborah Ousley Kadair. Pelican, 2006. ISBN 1-58980-406-6 Subj: Days of the week, months of the year. Food. Songs.

Downs, Mike. *You see a circus, I see—* ill. by Anik McGrory. Charlesbridge, 2005. ISBN 1-58089-097-0 Subj: Circus. Family life. Rhyming text.

Dowson, Nick. *Tracks of a panda* ill. by Yu Rong. Candlewick, 2007. ISBN 978-0-7636-3146-8 Subj: Animals — pandas.

Doyle, Charlotte Lackner. *The bouncing, dancing, galloping ABC* ill. by Julia Gorton. Penguin, 2006. ISBN 0-399-23778-X Subj: ABC books. Activities — playing. Rhyming text.

Drescher, Henrik. *Hubert the Pudge: a vegetarian tale* ill. by author. Candlewick, 2006. ISBN 0-7636-1992-2 Subj: Food. Health & fitness.

Dubosarsky, Ursula. *Rex* ill. by David Mackintosh. Macmillan, 2006. ISBN 1-59643-186-5 Subj: Activities — writing. Imagination. Pets. Reptiles — chameleons. School.

Dugan, Joanne. *ABC NYC: a book about seeing New York City* photos by author. Abrams, 2005. ISBN 0-8109-5854-6 Subj: ABC books. Cities, towns.

Duke, Kate. *The tale of Pip and Squeak* ill. by author. Penguin, 2007. ISBN 978-0-525-47777-8 Subj: Animals — mice. Family life — brothers & sisters. Sibling rivalry.

Duke, Shirley Smith. *No bows!* ill. by Jenny Mattheson. Peachtree, 2006. ISBN 1-56145-356-0 Subj: Character traits — appearance. Character traits — individuality.

Dunbar, Joyce. *Shoe baby* ill. by Polly Dunbar. Candlewick, 2005. ISBN 0-7636-2779-8 Subj: Activities — traveling. Babies. Clothing — shoes. Rhyming text.

Where's my sock? ill. by Sanja Rescek. Scholastic, 2006. ISBN 0-439-74831-3 Subj: Behavior — lost & found possessions. Clothing — socks.

Dunbar, Polly. *Penguin* ill. by author. Candlewick, 2007. ISBN 978-0-7636-3404-9 Subj: Birds — penguins. Toys.

Duncan, Alice Faye. *Honey baby sugar child* ill. by Susan Keeter. Simon & Schuster, 2005. ISBN 0-689-84678-9 Subj: Emotions — love. Ethnic groups in the U.S. — African Americans. Family life — mothers.

Dunn, Todd. *We go together* ill. by Miki Sakamoto. Sterling, 2007. ISBN 978-1-4027-3260-7 Subj: Concepts. Rhyming text.

Dunrea, Olivier. *Gossie's busy day: a first tab book* ill. by author. Houghton Mifflin, 2007. ISBN 978-0-618-82148-8 Subj: Birds — geese. Format, unusual — toy & movable books.

Duquette, Keith. *Little Monkey lost* ill. by author. Penguin, 2007. ISBN 978-0-399-24294-6 Subj: Animals — monkeys. Behavior — lost. Jungles.

Durango, Julia. *Angels watching over me* ill. by Elisa Kleven. Simon & Schuster, 2007. ISBN 978-0-689-86252-6 Subj: Angels. Songs.

Cha-cha chimps ill. by Eleanor Taylor. Simon & Schuster, 2006. ISBN 978-0-689-86456-8 Subj: Activities — dancing. Animals — chimpanzees. Counting, numbers. Rhyming text.

Dream hop ill. by Jared Lee. Simon & Schuster, 2005. ISBN 0-689-87163-5 Subj: Bedtime. Dreams. Nightmares. Sleep.

Pest fest ill. by Kurt Cyrus. Simon & Schuster, 2007. ISBN 978-0-689-85569-6 Subj: Contests. Insects.

Yum! Yuck! A foldout book of people sounds (Park, Linda Sue)

Durant, Alan. *Burger boy* ill. by Mei Matsuoka. Houghton Mifflin, 2006. ISBN 0-618-71466-9 Subj: Food. Humorous stories.

I love you, little monkey ill. by Katharine McEwen. Simon & Schuster, 2007. ISBN 978-1-4169-2481-4 Subj: Animals — monkeys. Emotions — love.

Dutton, Sandra. *Dear Miss Perfect: a beast's guide to proper behavior* ill. by author. Houghton Mifflin, 2007. ISBN 978-0-618-67717-7 Subj: Animals. Behavior. Etiquette.

Duval, Kathy. *The Three Bears' Christmas* ill. by Paul Meisel. Holiday House, 2005. ISBN 0-8234-1871-5 Subj: Animals — bears. Holidays — Christmas. Santa Claus.

The Three Bears' Halloween ill. by Paul Meisel. Holiday House, 2007. ISBN 978-0-8234-2032-2 Subj: Animals — bears. Holidays — Halloween.

Duvall, Deborah L. *The opossum's tale: a grandmother story* ill. by Murv Jacob. Univ. of New Mexico, 2005. ISBN 0-8263-3694-9 Subj: Anatomy — tails. Animals — possums. Folk & fairy tales. Indians of North America — Cherokee.

Dyer, Jane. *Little Brown Bear and the bundle of joy* ill. by author. Little, Brown, 2005. ISBN 0-316-17469-6 Subj: Animals — bears. Babies. Family life — new sibling.

Dyssegaard, Elisabeth Kallick. *Mini Mia and her darling uncle* (Lindenbaum, Pija)

Eaton, Maxwell. *Best buds* ill. by author. Random House, 2006. ISBN 0-375-93803-6 Subj: Animals — pigs. Food. Friendship.

Superheroes ill. by author. Random House, 2007. ISBN 978-0-375-83805-7 Subj: Activities — playing. Animals — pigs. Friendship.

Edwards, David. *The pen that Pa built* ill. by Ashley Wolff. Ten Speed, 2007. ISBN 978-1-58246-153-3 Subj: Animals — sheep. Cumulative tales. Farms. Rhyming text. U.S. history.

Edwards, Pamela Duncan. *The bus ride that changed history: the story of Rosa Parks* ill. by Danny Shanahan. Houghton Mifflin, 2005. ISBN 0-618-44911-6 Subj: Ethnic groups in the U.S. — African Americans. Prejudice. U.S. history.

The mixed-up rooster ill. by Megan Lloyd. HarperCollins, 2006. ISBN 0-06-028999-6 Subj: Birds — chickens. Character traits — being different.

Ms. Bitsy Bat's kindergarten ill. by Henry Cole. Hyperion, 2005. ISBN 0-7868-0669-9 Subj: Animals. Animals — bats. Careers — teachers. School.

The neat line: scribbling through Mother Goose ill. by Diana Cain Bluthenthal. HarperCollins, 2005. ISBN 0-06-623971-0 Subj: Activities — drawing. Books, reading. Nursery rhymes.

The old house ill. by Henry Cole. Penguin, 2007. ISBN 978-0-525-47796-9 Subj: Friendship. Homes, houses.

Edwards, Wallace. *The extinct files: my science project* ill. by author. Kids Can, 2006. ISBN 1-55337-971-3 Subj: Dinosaurs. Humorous stories. Science.

Egan, Tim. *Dodsworth in New York* ill. by author. Houghton Mifflin, 2007. ISBN 978-0-618-77708-2 Subj: Activities — traveling. Animals. Behavior — hiding. Birds — ducks. Humorous stories.

The pink refrigerator ill. by author. Houghton Mifflin, 2007. ISBN 978-0-618-63154-4 Subj: Animals. Character traits — laziness. Stores.

Roasted peanuts ill. by author. Houghton Mifflin, 2006. ISBN 0-618-33718-0 Subj: Animals — cats. Animals — horses, ponies. Friendship. Sports — baseball.

Egielski, Richard. *St. Francis and the wolf* ill. by author. Harper-Collins, 2005. ISBN 0-06-623870-6 Subj: Animals — wolves. Foreign lands — Italy. Religion.

Ehlert, Lois. *Leaf man* ill. by author. Harcourt, 2005. ISBN 0-15-205304-2 Subj: Nature. Seasons — fall. Weather — wind.

Wag a tail ill. by author. Harcourt, 2007. ISBN 978-0-15-205843-2 Subj: Animals — dogs.

Ehrhardt, Karen. *This jazz man* ill. by R. G. Roth. Harcourt, 2006. ISBN 0-15-205307-7 Subj: Ethnic groups in the U.S. — African Americans. Music. Rhyming text. Songs.

Ehrlich, Fred. *Does a baboon sleep in a bed?* ill. by Emily Bolam. Blue Apple, 2006. ISBN 1-59354-142-2 Subj: Animals. Sleep.

Does a camel cook? ill. by Emily Bolam. Blue Apple, 2007. ISBN 978-1-59354-588-8 Subj: Animals. Food.

Does a chimp wear clothes? ill. by Emily Bolam. Blue Apple, 2005. ISBN 978-1-59354-110-1 Subj: Animals. Clothing.

Does a duck have a daddy? ill. by Emily Bolam. Blue Apple, 2004. ISBN 1-59354-032-9 Subj: Animals. Family life — fathers.

Does a giraffe drive? ill. by Emily Bolam. Blue Apple, 2007. ISBN 978-1-59354-614-4 Subj: Animals. Concepts — motion.

Does a mouse have a mommy? ill. by Emily Bolam. Blue Apple, 2004. ISBN 1-59354-034-5 Subj: Animals. Family life — mothers.

Does a seal smile? ill. by Emily Bolam. Blue Apple, 2006. ISBN 1-59354-168-6 Subj: Anatomy — faces. Animals. Communication.

Does an elephant take a bath? ill. by Emily Bolam. Blue Apple, 2005. ISBN 978-1-59354-111-8 Subj: Activities — bathing. Animals. Character traits — cleanliness.

Elffers, Joost. *Baby food* (Freymann, Saxton)

Dog food (Freymann, Saxton)

Fast Food (Freymann, Saxton)

Food for thought: the complete book of concepts for growing minds (Freymann, Saxton)

Food play (Freymann, Saxton)

How are you peeling? Foods with moods (Freymann, Saxton)

Ellery, Amanda. *If I had a dragon* ill. by Tom Ellery. Simon & Schuster, 2006. ISBN 1-4169-0924-9 Subj: Activities — playing. Dragons. Family life — brothers & sisters. Imagination.

Elliott, David. *One little chicken: a counting book* ill. by Ethan Long. Holiday House, 2007. ISBN 978-0-8234-1983-8 Subj: Activities — dancing. Birds — chickens. Counting, numbers. Rhyming text.

Elliott, George. *The boy who loved bananas* ill. by Andrej Krystoforski. Kids Can, 2005. ISBN 1-55337-744-3 Subj: Animals — monkeys. Food. Zoos.

Elliott, Laura Malone. *Hunter and Stripe and the soccer showdown* ill. by Lynn Munsinger. HarperCollins, 2005. ISBN 0-06-052759-5 Subj: Animals — raccoons. Friendship. Sports — soccer. Sportsmanship.

Hunter's big sister ill. by Lynn Munsinger. HarperCollins, 2007. ISBN 978-0-06-000233-6 Subj: Animals — raccoons. Family life — brothers & sisters.

Ellis, Sarah. *Ben over night* ill. by Kim LaFave. Fitzhenry & Whiteside, 2005. ISBN 1-55041-807-6 Subj: Emotions — fear. Sleepovers.

The queen's feet ill. by Dusan Petricic. Red Deer, 2006. ISBN 0-88995-320-1 Subj: Anatomy — feet. Royalty — queens.

Elschner, Geraldine. *Fritz's fish* trans. from German by Kathryn Bishop; ill. by Daniela Bunge. Penguin, 2006. ISBN 0-698-40028-3 Subj: Fish. Pets.

Mark's messy room trans. from German by Charise Myngheer; ill. by Alexandra Junge. Minedition, 2006. ISBN 0-698-40047-X Subj: Animals — cats. Behavior — messy. Character traits — cleanliness.

Max's magic seeds trans. from German by Charise Myngheer; ill. by Jean-Pierre Corderoch. Penguin, 2007. ISBN 978-0-698-40059-7 Subj: Behavior — boredom. Flowers. Magic. School.

Pashmina the little Christmas goat ill. by Angela Kehlenbeck. Penguin, 2006. ISBN 0-698-40046-1 Subj: Animals — goats. Holidays — Christmas.

Elvgren, Jennifer Riesmeyer. *Josias, hold the book* ill. by Nicole Tadgell. Boyds Mills, 2006. ISBN 1-59078-318-2 Subj: Family life. Food. Foreign lands — Haiti. Gardens, gardening. School.

Elya, Susan Middleton. *Bebe goes shopping* ill. by Steven Salerno. Harcourt, 2006. ISBN 0-15-205426-X Subj: Babies. Foreign languages. Rhyming text. Shopping. Stores.

Cowboy Jose ill. by Tim Raglin. Penguin, 2005. ISBN 0-399-23570-1 Subj: Cowboys, cowgirls. Foreign languages. Rhyming text. Rodeos.

F is for fiesta ill. by G. Brian Karas. Penguin, 2006. ISBN 0-399-24225-2 Subj: ABC books. Birthdays. Foreign languages. Parties. Rhyming text.

Fairy trails: a story told in English and Spanish ill. by Mercedes McDonald. Bloomsbury, 2005. ISBN 1-58234-927-4 Subj: Books, reading. Foreign languages.

N is for Navidad by Susan Middleton Elya & Merry Banks; ill. by Joe Cepeda. Chronicle, 2007. ISBN 0-8118-5205-9 Subj: ABC books. Family life. Foreign lands — Mexico. Foreign languages. Holidays — Christmas.

Oh no, gotta go #2 ill. by Lynne Avril. Penguin, 2007. ISBN 978-0-399-24308-0 Subj: Activities — picnicking. Foreign languages. Rhyming text. Toilet training.

Sophie's trophy ill. by Viviana Garofoli. Penguin, 2006. ISBN 0-399-24199-X Subj: Activities — singing. Family life — brothers & sisters. Foreign languages. Frogs & toads. Self-concept.

Emberley, Ed (Edward Randolph). *Ed Emberley's bye-bye, big bad bullybug!* ill. by Ed Emberley. Little, Brown, 2007. ISBN 978-0-316-01762-6 Subj: Behavior — bullying. Format, unusual — toy & movable books. Monsters.

Emmett, Jonathan. *Diamond in the snow* ill. by Vanessa Cabban. Candlewick, 2007. ISBN 978-0-7636-3117-8 Subj: Animals — moles. Seasons — winter. Weather — snow.

I love you always and forever ill. by Daniel Howarth. Scholastic, 2007. ISBN 978-0-439-91654-7 Subj: Animals — mice. Behavior — growing up. Emotions — love.

Ruby in her own time ill. by Rebecca Harry. Scholastic, 2004. ISBN 0-439-57915-5 Subj: Birds — ducks. Character traits — smallness.

She'll be coming 'round the mountain ill. by Deborah Allwright. Simon & Schuster, 2007. ISBN 1-4169-3652-1 Subj: Songs. U.S. history — frontier & pioneer life.

This way, Ruby! ill. by Rebecca Harry. Scholastic, 2007. ISBN 978-0-439-87992-7 Subj: Behavior — lost. Birds — ducks. Character traits — smallness. Weather — storms.

Enderle, Judith Ross. *Smile, Principessa!* by Judith Ross Enderle & Stephanie Jacob Gordon; ill. by Serena Curmi. Simon & Schuster, 2007. ISBN 978-1-4169-1004-6 Subj: Emotions — envy, jealousy. Family life — new sibling.

Engelbreit, Mary. *Mary Engelbreit's A merry little Christmas: celebrate from a to z* ill. by author. HarperCollins, 2006. ISBN 0-06-074159-7 Subj: ABC books. Animals — mice. Holidays — Christmas. Rhyming text.

English, Karen. *The baby on the way* ill. by Sean Qualls. Farrar, Straus & Giroux, 2005. ISBN 0-374-37361-2 Subj: Babies. Ethnic groups in the U.S. — African Americans. Family life — grandmothers.

Ericsson, Jennifer A. *Home to me, home to you* ill. by Ashley Wolff. Little, Brown, 2005. ISBN 0-316-60922-6 Subj: Activities — working. Careers. Family life — mothers.

A piece of chalk ill. by Michelle Shapiro. Macmillan, 2007. ISBN 978-1-59643-057-0 Subj: Activities — drawing. Concepts — color.

Eriksson, Eva. *A crash course for Molly* ill. by author. Farrar, Straus & Giroux, 2005. ISBN 91-29-66156-0 Subj: Animals. Family life — grandmothers. Sports — bicycling.

Erlbruch, Wolf. *The big question* by Wolf Erlbruch & Michael Reynolds; ill. by Wolf Erlbruch. Europa, 2005. ISBN 1-933372-03-6 Subj: Character traits — questioning. Self-concept.

Ernst, Lisa Campbell. *Sylvia Jean, drama queen* ill. by author. Penguin, 2005. ISBN 0-525-46962-1 Subj: Animals — pigs. Clothing — costumes. Self-concept.

This is the van that Dad cleaned ill. by author. Simon & Schuster, 2005. ISBN 0-689-86190-7 Subj: Automobiles. Character traits — cleanliness. Family life — fathers. Rhyming text.

Esbaum, Jill. *Estelle takes a bath* ill. by Mary Newell. Henry Holt, 2006. ISBN 0-8050-7741-3 Subj: Activities — bathing. Animals — mice. Rhyming text.

Eschbacher, Roger. *Road trip* ill. by Thor Wickstrom. Penguin, 2006. ISBN 0-8037-2927-8 Subj: Activities — traveling. Family life. Rhyming text.

Estefan, Gloria. *Noelle's treasure tale: a new magically mysterious adventure* ill. by Michael Garland. HarperCollins, 2006. ISBN 978-0-06-112614-7 Subj: Animals — dogs. Rhyming text. Sea & seashore — beaches.

Evans, Cambria. *Martha moth makes socks* ill. by author. Houghton Mifflin, 2006. ISBN 0-618-55745-8 Subj: Birthdays. Clothing — socks. Gifts. Insects — moths. Parties.

Evans, Lezlie. *The bunnies' picnic* ill. by Kay Chorao. Hyperion, 2007. ISBN 0-7868-1612-0 Subj: Activities — baking, cooking. Activities — picnicking. Animals — rabbits. Food. Rhyming text.

Can you greet the whole wide world? Twelve common phrases in twelve different languages ill. by Denis Roche. Houghton Mifflin, 2006. ISBN 0-618-56327-X Subj: Foreign languages.

Falconer, Ian. *Olivia forms a band* ill. by author. Simon & Schuster/Atheneum, 2006. ISBN 978-1-4169-2454-8 Subj: Animals — pigs. Music.

Faller, Regis. *The adventures of Polo* ill. by author. Macmillan, 2006. ISBN 1-59643-160-1 Subj: Activities — traveling. Animals — dogs. Imagination. Wordless.

Polo: the runaway book ill. by author. Macmillan, 2007. ISBN 1-59643-189-8 Subj: Activities — traveling. Animals — dogs. Imagination. Wordless.

Fallon, Jimmy. *Snowball fight!* ill. by Adam Stower. Penguin, 2005. ISBN 0-525-47456-0 Subj: Rhyming text. Weather — snow.

Falwell, Cathryn. *Shape capers* ill. by author. HarperCollins, 2007. ISBN 978-0-06-123700-3 Subj: Concepts — shape. Rhyming text.

Fancher, Lou. *Star climbing* ill. by Steve Johnson. HarperCollins, 2006. ISBN 0-06-073902-9 Subj: Bedtime. Imagination. Stars.

Farber, Norma. *How the hibernators came to Bethlehem* ill. by Barbara Cooney. Walker & Company, 2006. ISBN 0-8027-9610-9 Subj: Animals. Holidays — Christmas. Poetry. Religion.

Farmer, Nancy. *Clever Ali* ill. by Gail De Marcken. Scholastic/Orchard, 2006. ISBN 0-439-37014-0 Subj: Birds — pigeons. Family life — fathers. Foreign lands — Egypt. Royalty — sultans.

Fearnley, Jan. *The search for the perfect child* ill. by author. Candlewick, 2006. ISBN 0-7636-3231-7 Subj: Animals — dogs. Behavior. Character traits — perfectionism.

Federspiel, Jurg. *Alligator Mike* ill. by Petra Rappo. NorthSouth, 2007. ISBN 978-0-7358-2124-8 Subj: Character traits — kindness to animals. Reptiles — alligators, crocodiles.

Feiffer, Kate. *Double pink* ill. by Bruce Ingman. Simon & Schuster, 2005. ISBN 0-689-87190-2 Subj: Concepts — color.

Henry, the dog with no tail ill. by Jules Feiffer. Simon & Schuster, 2007. ISBN 978-1-4169-1614-7 Subj: Anatomy — tails. Animals — dogs. Language. Self-concept.

Ferreri, Della Ross. *How will I ever sleep in this bed?* ill. by Capucine Mazille. Sterling, 2005. ISBN 1-4027-1492-0 Subj: Bedtime. Furniture — beds. Rhyming text. Toys.

Ferri, Giuliano. *Little Tad grows up* ill. by author. Penguin, 2007. ISBN 978-0-698-40060-3 Subj: Behavior — growing up. Frogs & toads. Nature. Science.

Ficocelli, Elizabeth. *Kid tea* ill. by Glin Dibley. Marshall Cavendish, 2007. ISBN 978-0-7614-5333-8 Subj: Activities — bathing. Concepts — color. Days of the week, months of the year. Rhyming text.

Field, Rachel Lyman. *Grace for an island meal* ill. by Cynthia Jabar. Farrar, Straus & Giroux, 2006. ISBN 0-374-32759-9 Subj: Islands. Poetry. Religion.

Finchler, Judy. *Miss Malarkey leaves no reader behind* by Judy Finchler & Kevin O'Malley; ill. by Kevin O'Malley. Walker & Company, 2006. ISBN 0-8027-8084-9 Subj: Books, reading. Careers — teachers. School.

Fischer, Scott M. *Twinkle* ill. by author. Simon & Schuster, 2007. ISBN 978-1-4169-3980-1 Subj: Format, unusual — toy & movable books. Poetry. Space & space ships. Stars.

Fisher, Aileen Lucia. *Do rabbits have Christmas?* ill. by Sarah Fox-Davies. Henry Holt, 2007. ISBN 0-8050-7491-0 Subj: Animals. Holidays — Christmas. Nature. Poetry. Seasons — winter.

Know what I saw? ill. by Deborah Durland DeSaix. Macmillan, 2005. ISBN 1-59643-055-9 Subj: Animals. Counting, numbers. Rhyming text.

The story goes on ill. by Mique Moriuchi. Macmillan, 2005. ISBN 1-59643-037-0 Subj: Nature. Poetry.

Fisher, Doris. *Happy birthday to whooo? A baby animal riddle book* ill. by Lisa Downey. Sylvan Dell, 2006. ISBN 0-9768823-1-0 Subj: Animals — babies. Riddles & jokes.

My even day by Doris Fisher & Dani Sneed; ill. by Karen Lee. Sylvan Dell, 2007. ISBN 978-0-977742-33-2 Subj: Counting, numbers. Rhyming text.

One odd day by Doris Fisher & Dani Sneed; ill. by Karen Lee. Sylvan Dell, 2006. ISBN 978-0-976882-33-6 Subj: Counting, numbers. Rhyming text.

Fisher, Jeff. *The hair scare* ill. by author. Bloomsbury, 2005. ISBN 1-58234-672-0 Subj: Hair. Royalty — kings.

Fisher, Valorie. *How high can a dinosaur count? And other math mysteries* ill. by author. Random House, 2006. ISBN 0-375-83608-X Subj: Counting, numbers. Puzzles.

Fitz-Gibbon, Sally. *On Uncle John's farm* ill. by Brian Deines. Fitzhenry & Whiteside, 2005. ISBN 1-55041-691-X Subj: Careers — farmers. Farms.

FitzGerald, Dawn. *Vinnie and Abraham* ill. by Catherine Stock. Charlesbridge, 2007. ISBN 978-1-57091-658-8 Subj: Art. U.S. history.

Fitzgerald, Joanne. *Yum! Yum! Delicious nursery rhymes* ill. by author. Fitzhenry & Whiteside, 2007. ISBN 978-1-55041-888-0 Subj: Animals. Food. Nursery rhymes.

Flaherty, A. W. *The luck of the Loch Ness monster: a tale of picky eating* ill. by Scott Magoon. Houghton Mifflin, 2007. ISBN 978-0-618-55644-1 Subj: Food. Monsters.

Fleischman, Paul. *Glass slipper, gold sandal: a worldwide Cinderella* ill. by Julie Paschkis. Henry Holt, 2007. ISBN 978-0-8050-7953-1 Subj: Folk & fairy tales. Foreign lands. Royalty.

Fleming, Candace. *Sunny Boy! The life and times of a tortoise* ill. by Anne Wilsdorf. Farrar, Straus & Giroux, 2005. ISBN 0-374-37297-7 Subj: Reptiles — turtles, tortoises.

Tippy-tippy-tippy, hide! ill. by G. Brian Karas. Simon & Schuster, 2007. ISBN 0-689-87479-0 Subj: Animals — rabbits. Behavior — hiding.

Fleming, Denise. *Beetle bop* ill. by author. Harcourt, 2007. ISBN 978-0-15-205936-1 Subj: Insects — beetles. Rhyming text.

The cow who clucked ill. by author. Henry Holt, 2006. ISBN 0-8050-7365-9 Subj: Animals. Animals — bulls, cows. Noise, sounds.

The first day of winter ill. by author. Henry Holt, 2005. ISBN 0-8050-7384-1 Subj: Counting, numbers. Rhyming text. Seasons — winter. Snowmen. Weather — snow.

Floca, Brian. *Lightship* ill. by author. Simon & Schuster, 2007. ISBN 978-1-4169-2436-4 Subj: Boats, ships. U.S. history.

Florian, Douglas. *Comets, stars, the moon, and Mars: space poems and paintings* ill. by author. Harcourt, 2007. ISBN 978-0-15-205372-7 Subj: Moon. Planets. Poetry. Stars.

Handsprings ill. by author. HarperCollins, 2006. ISBN 0-06-009281-5 Subj: Poetry. Seasons — spring.

Zoo's who: poems and paintings ill. by author. Harcourt, 2005. ISBN 0-15-204639-9 Subj: Animals. Poetry.

Floyd, Madeleine. *Cold paws, warm heart* ill. by author. Candlewick, 2005. ISBN 0-7636-2761-5 Subj: Animals — polar bears. Concepts — cold & heat. Emotions — loneliness. Friendship.

Foley, Greg. *Thank you, Bear* ill. by author. Penguin, 2007. ISBN 0-670-06165-4 Subj: Animals. Animals — bears. Animals — mice. Friendship. Gifts.

Fontes, Justine Korman. *Black meets White* ill. by Geoff Waring. Candlewick, 2005. ISBN 0-7636-1933-7 Subj: Concepts — color. Format, unusual — toy & movable books.

Ford, Bernette G. *Ballet Kitty* ill. by Sam Williams. Boxer, 2007. ISBN 978-1-905417-56-8 Subj: Animals — cats. Ballet.

First snow ill. by Sebastien Braun. Holiday House, 2005. 32p. ISBN 0-8234-1937-1 Subj: Animals — rabbits. Night. Seasons — winter. Weather — snow.

No more bottles for Bunny! ill. by Sam Williams. Boxer, 2007. ISBN 978-1-905417-34-6 Subj: Animals — rabbits. Behavior — growing up. Parties.

No more diapers for Ducky! ill. by Sam Williams. Sterling, 2007. ISBN 978-1-905417-38-4 Subj: Birds — ducks. Format, unusual — board books. Toilet training.

Fore, S. J. *Tiger can't sleep* ill. by R. W. Alley. Penguin, 2006. ISBN 0-670-06078-X Subj: Animals — tigers. Bedtime. Emotions — fear.

Foreman, George. *Let George do it!* by George Foreman & Fran Manushkin; ill. by Whitney Martin. Simon & Schuster, 2005. ISBN 0-689-87807-9 Subj: Birthdays. Family life. Humorous stories. Names. Parties.

Foreman, Michael. *Mia's story: a sketchbook of hopes and dreams* ill. by author. Candlewick, 2006. ISBN 0-7636-3063-2 Subj: Animals — dogs. Flowers. Foreign lands — Chile.

Forman, Ruth. *Young Cornrows callin out the moon: poem* ill. by Cbabi Bayoc. Children's Book Press, 2007. ISBN 978-0-89239-218-6 Subj: Communities, neighborhoods. Ethnic groups in the U.S. — African Americans. Poetry.

Fox, Christyan. *Tyson the terrible* (Fox, Diane)

Fox, Diane. *Tyson the terrible* by Diane & Christyan Fox; ill. by authors. Bloomsbury, 2007. ISBN 978-1-58234-734-9 Subj: Dinosaurs. Emotions — fear. Format, unusual — toy & movable books. Friendship. Sports — soccer.

Fox, Mem. *Hunwick's egg* ill. by Pamela Lofts. Harcourt, 2005. ISBN 0-15-216318-2 Subj: Animals — bandicoots. Eggs. Friendship.

A particular cow ill. by Terry Denton. Harcourt, 2006. ISBN 0-15-200250-2 Subj: Animals — bulls, cows. Humorous stories.

Where the giant sleeps ill. by Vladimir Radunsky. Harcourt, 2007. ISBN 978-0-15-205785-5 Subj: Bedtime. Rhyming text. Sleep.

Frampton, David. *Mr. Ferlinghetti's poem* ill. by author. Eerdmans, 2006. ISBN 0-8028-5290-4 Subj: Careers — firefighters. Poetry. Seasons — summer.

Francis, Pauline. *Sam stars at Shakespeare's Globe* ill. by Jane Tattersfield. Frances Lincoln, 2006. ISBN 1-84507-406-8 Subj: Careers — actors. Foreign lands — England. Theater.

Franco, Betsy. *Birdsongs* ill. by Steve Jenkins. Simon & Schuster, 2007. ISBN 0-689-87777-3 Subj: Birds. Counting, numbers.

Summer beat ill. by Charlotte Middleton. Simon & Schuster, 2007. ISBN 978-1-4169-1237-8 Subj: Activities. Seasons — summer.

Frank, John. *How to catch a fish* ill. by Peter Sylvada. Macmillan, 2007. ISBN 978-1-59643-163-8 Subj: Foreign lands. Poetry. Sports — fishing. World.

Franson, Scott E. *Un-brella* ill. by author. Macmillan, 2007. ISBN 978-1-59643-179-9 Subj: Magic. Umbrellas. Wordless.

Fraser, Mary Ann. *I.Q. gets fit* ill. by author. Walker & Company, 2007. ISBN 978-0-8027-9558-8 Subj: Animals — mice. Health & fitness. Pets. School.

I.Q., it's time ill. by author. Walker & Company, 2005. ISBN 0-8027-8978-1 Subj: Animals — mice. Clocks, watches. Pets. School. Time.

Frasier, Debra. *A birthday cake is no ordinary cake* ill. by author. Harcourt, 2006. ISBN 0-15-205742-0 Subj: Birthdays. Calendars.

Frazee, Marla. *Hush, little baby: a folk song with pictures* ill. by author. Harcourt, 2007. ISBN 978-0-15-205887-6 Subj: Babies. Character traits — generosity. Cumulative tales. Format, unusual — board books. Lullabies. Music.

Santa Claus: the world's number one toy expert ill. by author. Harcourt, 2005. ISBN 0-15-204970-3 Subj: Gifts. Holidays — Christmas. Santa Claus. Toys.

Walk on! A guide for babies of all ages ill. by author. Harcourt, 2006. ISBN 0-15-205573-8 Subj: Activities — walking. Babies. Behavior — growing up. Self-concept.

Freedman, Claire. *One magical day* ill. by Tina Macnaughton. Good Books, 2007. ISBN 978-1-56148-567-3 Subj: Animals. Day. Rhyming text. Seasons — summer.

One magical morning ill. by Louise Ho. Good Books, 2005. ISBN 1-56148-472-5 Subj: Animals. Animals — bears. Family life — mothers. Morning. Rhyming text.

Snuggle up, sleepy ones ill. by Tina Macnaughton. Good Books, 2005. ISBN 1-56148-475-X Subj: Animals. Bedtime. Rhyming text. Sleep.

Freedman, Deborah. *Scribble* ill. by author. Random House, 2007. ISBN 978-0-375-83966-5 Subj: Activities — drawing. Family life — brothers & sisters. Imagination.

Freeman, Don. *Earl the squirrel* ill. by author. Penguin, 2005. ISBN 0-670-06019-4 Subj: Animals — squirrels.

French, Jackie. *Josephine wants to dance* ill. by Bruce Whatley. Abrams, 2007. ISBN 0-8109-9431-3 Subj: Activities — dancing. Animals — kangaroos. Ballet. Foreign lands — Australia.

Pete the sheep-sheep ill. by Bruce Whatley. Houghton Mifflin, 2005. ISBN 0-618-56862-X Subj: Animals — dogs. Animals — sheep. Humorous stories.

Freymann, Saxton. *Baby food* by Saxton Freymann & Joost Elffers; ill. by Saxton Freymann. Arthur A. Levine, 2006. ISBN 0-439-11021-1 Subj: Animals — babies. Food. Format, unusual — board books.

Dog food by Saxton Freymann & Joost Elffers; ill. by Saxton Freymann. Arthur A. Levine, 2006. ISBN 0-439-11020-3 Subj: Animals — dogs. Food. Format, unusual — board books.

Fast Food by Saxton Freymann & Joost Elffers; ill. by Saxton Freymann. Scholastic, 2006. ISBN 0-439-11019-X Subj: Food. Transportation.

Food for thought: the complete book of concepts for growing minds by Saxton Freymann & Joost Elffers; ill. by Saxton Freymann. Arthur A. Levine, 2005. ISBN 978-0-439-11018-1 Subj: ABC books. Concepts — color. Concepts — opposites. Concepts — shape. Counting, numbers. Food. Format, unusual — board books.

Food play by Saxton Freymann & Joost Elffers; ill. by Saxton Freymann. Chronicle, 2006. ISBN 978-0-81185-705-5 Subj: Food.

How are you peeling? Foods with moods by Saxton Freymann & Joost Elffers; ill. by Saxton Freymann. Scholastic, 2004. ISBN 0-439-59841-9 Subj: Emotions. Food.

Friday, Mary Ellen. *It's a bad day* ill. by Glin Dibley. Rising Moon, 2006. ISBN 0-8735-8904-1 Subj: Behavior — bad day. Character traits — luck.

Friedlaender, Linda K. *Look! Look! Look!* (Wallace, Nancy Elizabeth)

Friedman, Laurie. *Love, Ruby Valentine* ill. by Lynne Cravath. Carolrhoda, 2006. ISBN 1-57505-899-5 Subj: Gifts. Holidays — Valentine's Day.

Friedrich, Molly. *You're not my real mother!* ill. by Christy Hale. Little, Brown, 2004. ISBN 978-0-316-60553-3 Subj: Adoption. Family life. Self-concept.

Friend, Catherine. *The perfect nest* ill. by John Manders. Candlewick, 2007. ISBN 978-0-7636-2430-9 Subj: Animals — cats. Behavior — trickery. Birds. Eggs. Farms.

A frog he would a-wooing go (folk-song). *Froggy went a-courtin'* adapt. & ill. by Gillian Tyler. Candlewick, 2005. ISBN 0-7636-2306-7 Subj: Animals. Frogs & toads. Songs. Weddings.

Fromental, Jean-Luc. *365 penguins* by Jean-Luc Fromental & Joëlle Jolivet; ill. by authors. Abrams, 2006. ISBN 0-8109-4460-X Subj: Birds — penguins. Counting, numbers. Holidays — New Year's.

Fuge, Charles. *Swim, Little Wombat, swim!* ill. by author. Sterling, 2005. ISBN 1-4027-2375-X Subj: Animals — platypuses. Animals — wombats. Friendship. Sports — swimming.

Where to, Little Wombat? ill. by author. Sterling, 2006. ISBN 1-4027-3698-3 Subj: Animals — wombats. Format, unusual — board books. Homes, houses.

Funke, Cornelia. *Pirate girl* ill. by Kerstin Meyer. Scholastic/Chicken House, 2005. ISBN 0-439-71672-1 Subj: Pirates.

Princess Pigsty trans. by Chantal Wright; ill. by Kerstin Meyer. Scholastic, 2007. ISBN 0-439-98855-4 Subj: Behavior — misbehavior. Character traits — cleanliness. Royalty — princesses. Self-concept.

The wildest brother ill. by Kerstin Meyer. Scholastic, 2006. ISBN 0-439-82862-7 Subj: Emotions — fear. Family life — brothers & sisters. Monsters.

Furrow, Eva. *Bobby the bold* (Napoli, Donna Jo)

Gadot, A. S. *The first gift* ill. by Marie Lafrance. Lerner, 2006. ISBN 1-58013-146-8 Subj: Jewish culture. Names. Religion.

Galloway, Ruth. *Clumsy crab* ill. by author. Tiger Tales, 2005. ISBN 1-58925-050-8 Subj: Crustaceans — crabs. Self-concept.

Gannij, Joan. *Elusive moose* ill. by Clare Beaton. Barefoot, 2006. ISBN 1-905236-75-1 Subj: Animals — moose. Picture puzzles.

Garcia, Emma. *Tip tip dig dig* ill. by author. Boxer, 2007. ISBN 978-1-905417-59-9 Subj: Trucks.

Garden, Nancy. *Molly's family* ill. by Sharon Wooding. Farrar, Straus & Giroux, 2004. ISBN 0-374-35002-7 Subj: Adoption. Behavior — bullying. Family life — mothers. School.

Garland, Michael. *The great Easter egg hunt* ill. by author. Penguin, 2005. ISBN 0-525-47357-2 Subj: Holidays — Easter. Picture puzzles. Rhyming text.

Hooray José! ill. by author. Marshall Cavendish, 2007. ISBN 978-0-7614-5345-1 Subj: Animals — mice. Character traits — perseverance. Concepts — size. Rhyming text. Sports — basketball.

How many mice? ill. by author. Penguin, 2007. ISBN 978-0-525-47833-1 Subj: Animals — mice. Counting, numbers.

King Puck ill. by author. HarperCollins, 2007. ISBN 978-0-06-084809-5 Subj: Animals — goats. Books, reading. Fairies. Foreign lands — Ireland. Magic.

Miss Smith reads again! ill. by author. Penguin, 2006. ISBN 0-525-47722-5 Subj: Books, reading. Careers — teachers. Dinosaurs. Magic. School.

Gavril, David. *Penelope Nuthatch and the big surprise* ill. by author. Abrams, 2006. ISBN 0-8109-5762-0 Subj: Behavior — worrying. Birds. Parks — amusement.

Gay, Marie-Louise. *Caramba* ill. by author. Groundwood, 2005. ISBN 0-88899-667-5 Subj: Animals — cats. Imagination.

What are you doing, Sam? ill. by author. Groundwood, 2006. ISBN 0-88899-734-5 Subj: Animals — dogs. Behavior — messy. Family life — brothers & sisters. Pets.

Geisert, Arthur. *Lights out* ill. by author. Houghton Mifflin, 2005. ISBN 0-618-47892-2 Subj: Animals — pigs. Bedtime. Character traits — cleverness. Emotions — fear. Inventions.

Oops ill. by author. Houghton Mifflin, 2006. ISBN 0-618-60904-0 Subj: Animals — pigs. Wordless.

Geist, Ken. *The three little fish and the big bad shark* ill. by Julia Gorton. Scholastic, 2007. ISBN 978-0-439-71962-9 Subj: Fish. Fish — sharks. Sea & seashore.

George, Jean Craighead. *Frightful's daughter meets the Baron Weasel* ill. by Daniel San Souci. Penguin, 2007. ISBN 978-0-525-47202-5 Subj: Animals — weasels. Birds — falcons.

Luck ill. by Wendell Minor. HarperCollins, 2006. ISBN 0-06-008201-1 Subj: Birds — cranes. Migration.

George, Kristine O'Connell. *Up!* ill. by Hiroe Nakata. Houghton Mifflin, 2005. ISBN 0-618-06489-3 Subj: Concepts — up & down. Family life — fathers. Rhyming text.

George, Lindsay Barrett. *In the garden: who's been here?* ill. by author. HarperCollins, 2006. ISBN 0-06-078762-7 Subj: Animals. Gardens, gardening. Nature. Problem solving.

The secret ill. by author. HarperCollins, 2005. ISBN 0-06-029600-3 Subj: Animals. Behavior — secrets. Emotions — love.

George, Margaret. *Lucille lost: a true adventure* by Margaret George & Christopher J. Murphy; ill. by Debra Bandelin & Bob Dacey. Penguin, 2006. ISBN 0-670-06093-3 Subj: Behavior — lost & found possessions. Reptiles — turtles, tortoises.

Gerritsen, Paula. *Nuts* ill. by author. Boyds Mills, 2006. ISBN 1-932425-66-7 Subj: Animals — mice. Seasons — fall. Weather — storms.

Gershator, David. *Summer is summer* (Gershator, Phillis)

Gershator, Phillis. *Listen, listen* ill. by Alison Jay. Barefoot, 2007. ISBN 978-1-84686-084-3 Subj: Nature. Noise, sounds. Rhyming text. Seasons.

Sky sweeper ill. by Holly Meade. Farrar, Straus & Giroux, 2007. ISBN 978-0-374-37007-7 Subj: Activities — working. Foreign lands — Japan. Gardens, gardening. Self-concept.

Summer is summer by Phillis & David Gershator; ill. by Sophie Blackall. Henry Holt, 2006. ISBN 0-8050-7444-9 Subj: Rhyming text. Seasons — summer.

This is the day! adapt. by Phillis Gershator; ill. by Marjorie Priceman. Houghton Mifflin, 2007. ISBN 978-0-618-49746-1 Subj: Babies. Days of the week, months of the year. Family life — mothers. Songs.

Gerstein, Mordicai. *Leaving the nest* ill. by author. Farrar, Straus & Giroux, 2007. ISBN 978-0-374-34369-9 Subj: Animals. Behavior — growing up. Family life — mothers. Self-concept.

Gibbons, Gail. *Coral reefs* ill. by author. Holiday House, 2007. ISBN 978-0-8234-2080-3 Subj: Ecology. Sea & seashore.

Dinosaur discoveries ill. by author. Holiday House, 2005. ISBN 0-8234-1971-1 Subj: Dinosaurs. Science.

Galaxies, galaxies! ill. by author. Holiday House, 2006. ISBN 0-8234-2002-7 Subj: Science. Space & space ships.

Groundhog Day ill. by author. Holiday House, 2007. ISBN 978-0-8234-2003-2 Subj: Holidays — Groundhog Day.

Ice cream: the full scoop ill. by author. Holiday House, 2006. ISBN 0-8234-2000-0 Subj: Food.

Owls ill. by author. Holiday House, 2005. ISBN 0-8234-1880-4 Subj: Birds — owls.

The planets ill. by author. rev. ed. Holiday House, 2005. ISBN 0-8234-1957-6 Subj: Astronomy. Planets.

Valentine's Day is— ill. by author. Holiday House, 2006. ISBN 0-8234-1852-9 Subj: Holidays — Valentine's Day.

The vegetables we eat ill. by author. Holiday House, 2007. ISBN 978-0-8234-2001-8 Subj: Food. Plants.

Gibfried, Diane. *Brother Juniper* ill. by Meilo So. Houghton Mifflin, 2006. ISBN 0-618-54361-9 Subj: Character traits — generosity. Foreign lands — Italy. Religion.

Giganti, Paul. *How many blue birds flew away? A counting book with a difference* ill. by Donald Crews. HarperCollins, 2005. ISBN 0-06-000763-X Subj: Counting, numbers.

Gilchrist, Jan Spivey. *My America* ill. by Ashley Bryan & Jan Spivey Gilchrist. HarperCollins, 2007. ISBN 978-0-06-079105-6 Subj: Poetry. U.S. history.

Gill, Shelley. *Up on Denali* ill. by Shannon Cartwright. Sasquatch, 2006. ISBN 1-57061-366-4 Subj: Alaska. Mountains.

Gillham, Bill. *How many sharks in the bath?* ill. by Christyan Fox. Frances Lincoln, 2005. ISBN 1-84507-288-X Subj: Animals. Counting, numbers.

The gingerbread boy. *The Gingerbread Cowboy* by Janet Squires; ill. by Holly Berry. HarperCollins, 2006. ISBN 0-06-077863-6 Subj: Animals — coyotes. Behavior — running away. Cowboys, cowgirls. Cumulative tales. Folk & fairy tales. Food.

The gingerbread girl by Lisa Campbell Ernst; ill. by author. Penguin, 2006. ISBN 0-525-47667-9 Subj: Behavior — running away. Cumulative tales. Folk & fairy tales. Food.

The gingerbread man. *Can't catch me* by John & Ann Hassett; ill. by authors. Houghton Mifflin, 2006. ISBN 0-618-70490-6 Subj: Behavior — running away. Cumulative tales.

Ginkel, Anne. *I've got an elephant* ill. by Janie Bynum. Peachtree, 2006. ISBN 1-56145-373-0 Subj: Animals — elephants. Counting, numbers. Emotions — loneliness. Rhyming text.

Giogas, Valarie. *In my backyard* ill. by Katherine Zecca. Sylvan Dell, 2007. ISBN 978-0-977742-31-8 Subj: Animals. Counting, numbers. Nature. Rhyming text.

Giovanni, Nikki. *Rosa* ill. by Bryan Collier. Henry Holt, 2005. ISBN 0-8050-7106-7 Subj: Caldecott award honor books. Character traits — bravery. Ethnic groups in the U.S. — African Americans. Prejudice. U.S. history.

Glaser, Linda. *Hello, squirrels! Scampering through the seasons* ill. by Gay W. Holland. Lerner, 2006. ISBN 0-7613-2887-4 Subj: Animals — squirrels. Seasons.

Glass, Beth Raisner. *Noises at night* by Beth Raisner Glass & Susan Lubner; ill. by Bruce Whatley. Abrams, 2005. ISBN 0-8109-5750-7 Subj: Bedtime. Noise, sounds. Rhyming text.

Glazer, Tom. *On top of spaghetti* (Johnson, Paul Brett)

Gleeson, Libby. *Half a world away* ill. by Freya Blackwood. Scholastic, 2007. ISBN 978-0-439-88977-3 Subj: Friendship. Moving.

Gliori, Debi. *Where did that baby come from?* ill. by author. Harcourt, 2005. ISBN 0-15-205373-5 Subj: Animals — tigers. Babies. Family life — new sibling. Rhyming text.

Godden, Rumer. *The story of Holly and Ivy* ill. by Barbara Cooney. Penguin, 2006. ISBN 0-670-06219-7 Subj: Holidays — Christmas. Orphans. Toys — dolls.

Godkin, Celia. *Wolf island* ill. by author. Fitzhenry & Whiteside, 2006. ISBN 978-1-55455-007-4 Subj: Animals — wolves. Islands.

Gold, August. *Does God hear my prayer?* ill. by Diane Hardy Waller. SkyLight Paths, 2005. ISBN 1-59473-102-0 Subj: Religion.

Goldberg, Myla. *Catching the moon* ill. by Chris Sheban. Scholastic, 2007. ISBN 978-0-439-57686-4 Subj: Moon.

Goldberg, Whoopi. *Whoopi's big book of manners* ill. by Olo. Hyperion, 2006. ISBN 0-7868-5295-X Subj: Etiquette.

Goldfinger, Jennifer P. *My dog Lyle* ill. by author. Houghton Mifflin, 2007. ISBN 978-0-618-63983-0 Subj: Animals — dogs. Pets.

Goldstone, Bruce. *Great estimations* ill. with photos. Henry Holt, 2006. ISBN 0-8050-7446-5 Subj: Concepts. Counting, numbers.

Goode, Diane. *The most perfect spot* ill. by author. HarperCollins, 2006. ISBN 0-06-072697-0 Subj: Activities — picnicking. Animals — dogs. Family life — mothers.

Goodhart, Pippa. *Three little ghosties* ill. by AnnaLaura Cantone. Bloomsbury, 2007. ISBN 978-1-58234-711-0 Subj: Ghosts.

Goodrich, Carter. *A creature was stirring: one boy's night before Christmas* (Moore, Clement Clarke)

Gorbachev, Valeri. *Heron and Turtle* ill. by author. Penguin, 2006. ISBN 0-399-24321-6 Subj: Birds — herons. Friendship. Reptiles — turtles, tortoises.

Red red red ill. by author. Penguin, 2007. ISBN 978-0-399-24628-9 Subj: Animals. Character traits — curiosity. Concepts — color. Reptiles — turtles, tortoises.

That's what friends are for ill. by author. Penguin, 2005. ISBN 0-399-23966-9 Subj: Animals — goats. Animals — pigs. Friendship.

When someone is afraid ill. by Kostya Gorbachev. Star Bright, 2005. ISBN 1-932065-99-7 Subj: Dreams. Emotions — fear.

Gordon, Stephanie Jacob. *Smile, Principessa!* (Enderle, Judith Ross)

Gore, Leonid. *Danny's first snow* ill. by author. Simon & Schuster/Atheneum, 2007. ISBN 978-1-4169-1330-6 Subj: Animals — rabbits. Seasons — winter. Weather — snow.

Goss, Gary. *Where does food come from?* (Rotner, Shelley)

Gower, Catherine. *Long-Long's new year: a story about the Chinese spring festival* ill. by He Zhihong. Periplus/Tuttle, 2005. ISBN 0-8048-3666-3 Subj: Family life — grandfathers. Holidays — Chinese New Year.

Graham, Bob. *Dimity Dumpty: the story of Humpty's little sister* ill. by author. Candlewick, 2007. ISBN 978-0-7636-3078-2 Subj: Character traits — shyness. Circus. Eggs. Family life — brothers & sisters.

Oscar's half birthday ill. by author. Candlewick, 2005. ISBN 0-7636-2699-6 Subj: Activities — picnicking. Birthdays. Ethnic groups in the U.S. — Racially mixed. Family life.

"The trouble with dogs," said Dad ill. by author. Candlewick, 2007. ISBN 978-0-7636-3316-5 Subj: Animals — dogs. Pets.

Grambling, Lois G. *Here comes T. Rex Cottontail* ill. by Jack E. Davis. HarperCollins, 2007. ISBN 978-0-06-053129-4 Subj: Animals — rabbits. Character traits — helpfulness. Dinosaurs. Eggs. Holidays — Easter.

My mom is a firefighter ill. by Jane Manning. HarperCollins, 2007. ISBN 978-0-06-058640-9 Subj: Careers — firefighters. Family life — mothers.

T. Rex trick-or-treats ill. by Jack E. Davis. HarperCollins, 2005. ISBN 0-06-050253-3 Subj: Dinosaurs. Holidays — Halloween.

Gran, Julia. *Big bug surprise* ill. by author. Scholastic, 2007. ISBN 978-0-439-67609-0 Subj: Insects. Insects — bees. School.

Granfield, Linda. *What am I?* ill. by Jennifer Herbert. Tundra, 2007. ISBN 978-0-88776-812-5 Subj: Riddles & jokes.

Graniczewski, Wojciech. *Found alphabet* (Shindler, Ramon)

Granström, Brita. *Snap!* (Manning, Mick)

Grant, Joan. *Cat and Fish* ill. by Neil Curtis. Simply Read, 2005. ISBN 1-894965-14-0 Subj: Animals — cats. Fish. Friendship.

Graves, Keith. *The unexpectedly bad hair of Barcelona Smith* ill. by author. Penguin, 2006. ISBN 0-399-24273-2 Subj: Behavior — worrying. Hair.

Gravett, Emily. *Orange Pear Apple Bear* ill. by author. Simon & Schuster, 2007. ISBN 978-1-4169-3999-3 Subj: Animals — bears. Concepts — color. Concepts — shape.

Wolves ill. by author. Simon & Schuster, 2006. ISBN 978-1-4169-1491-4 Subj: Animals — rabbits. Animals — wolves. Humorous stories.

Gray, Kes. *006 and a half* ill. by Nick Sharratt. Abrams, 2007. ISBN 978-0-8109-1719-4 Subj: Behavior — secrets. Family life — daughters. Family life — mothers.

Gray, Rita. *The wild little horse* ill. by Ashley Wolff. Penguin, 2005. ISBN 0-525-47455-2 Subj: Animals — horses, ponies. Rhyming text.

Green, Emily K. *Bumblebees* ill. with photos. Scholastic, 2006. ISBN 978-0-531-17859-1 Subj: Insects — bees.

Crickets ill. with photos. Scholastic, 2006. ISBN 978-0-531-17861-4 Subj: Insects — crickets.

Grasshoppers ill. with photos. Scholastic, 2006. ISBN 978-0-531-17864-5 Subj: Insects — grasshoppers.

Walkingsticks ill. with photos. Scholastic, 2006. ISBN 978-0-531-17865-2 Subj: Insects.

Greenberg, David (David T.). *Don't forget your etiquette! The essential guide to misbehavior* ill. by Nadine Bernard Westcott. Farrar, Straus & Giroux, 2006. ISBN 0-374-34990-8 Subj: Etiquette. Poetry.

Greene, Rhonda Gowler. *Firebears: the rescue team* ill. by Dan Andreasen. Henry Holt, 2005. ISBN 0-8050-7010-9 Subj: Animals — bears. Careers — firefighters.

Noah and the mighty ark ill. by Santiago Cohen. Zondervan, 2007. ISBN 978-0-310-71097-4 Subj: Animals. Boats, ships. Religion — Noah.

Greenfield, Eloise. *The friendly four* ill. by Jan Spivey Gilchrist. HarperCollins, 2006. ISBN 0-06-000760-5 Subj: Activities — playing. Imagination. Poetry.

Gregory, Nan. *Pink* ill. by author. Groundwood, 2007. ISBN 978-0-88899-781-4 Subj: Behavior — greed. Concepts — color. Family life.

Gretz, Susanna. *Riley and Rose in the picture* ill. by author. Candlewick, 2005. ISBN 0-7636-2681-3 Subj: Activities — drawing. Animals — cats. Animals — dogs. Behavior — fighting, arguing. Friendship.

Grey, Mini. *The adventures of the dish and the spoon* ill. by author. Random House, 2006. ISBN 0-375-93691-2 Subj: Crime. Humorous stories. Nursery rhymes.

Ginger bear ill. by author. Random House, 2007. ISBN 978-0-375-84253-5 Subj: Activities — baking, cooking. Emotions — loneliness. Food. Friendship.

Griessman, Annette. *The fire* ill. by Leonid Gore. Penguin, 2005. ISBN 0-399-24019-5 Subj: Ethnic groups in the U.S. — Hispanic Americans. Family life. Fire.

Like a hundred drums ill. by Julie Monks. Houghton Mifflin, 2006. ISBN 0-618-55878-0 Subj: Animals. Family life — grandmothers. Weather — lightning, thunder. Weather — storms.

Grifalconi, Ann. *Ain't nobody a stranger to me* ill. by Jerry Pinkney. Hyperion, 2007. ISBN 978-0-7868-1857-0 Subj: Character traits — freedom. Ethnic groups in the U.S. — African Americans. Family life — grandfathers. Slavery. U.S. history.

Grimes, Nikki. *Danitra Brown, class clown* ill. by E. B. Lewis. HarperCollins, 2005. ISBN 0-68-817290-3 Subj: Ethnic groups in the U.S. — African Americans. Friendship. Poetry. School.

Welcome, Precious ill. by Bryan Collier. Scholastic/Orchard, 2006. ISBN 0-439-55702-X Subj: Babies. Ethnic groups in the U.S. — African Americans.

When Gorilla goes walking ill. by Shane W. Evans. Scholastic, 2007. ISBN 978-0-439-31770-2 Subj: Animals — cats. Ethnic groups in the U.S. — African Americans. Friendship. Pets. Poetry.

Grimm, Jacob. *The Bremen town musicians* by Jacob & Wilhelm Grimm; trans. from German by Anthea Bell; ill. by Lisbeth Zwerger. Penguin, 2007. ISBN 978-0-698-40042-9 Subj: Animals. Careers — musicians. Crime. Folk & fairy tales. Old age.

The elves and the shoemaker by Jacob & Wilhelm Grimm; retold by John Cech; ill. by Kirill Chelushkin. Sterling, 2007. ISBN 978-1-4027-3067-2 Subj: Careers — shoemakers. Character traits — helpfulness. Folk & fairy tales. Foreign lands — Germany. Mythical creatures — elves.

The frog prince by Jacob & Wilhelm Grimm; retold by Kathy-Jo Wargin; ill. by Anne Yvonne Gilbert. Mitten, 2007. ISBN 978-1-58726-279-1 Subj: Folk & fairy tales. Frogs & toads. Kissing. Royalty — princes. Royalty — princesses.

Hansel and Gretel: a retelling from the original tale by the Brothers Grimm by Jacob & Wilhelm Grimm; retold & ill. by Will Moses. Penguin, 2006. ISBN 0-399-24234-1 Subj: Behavior — lost. Folk & fairy tales. Forest, woods. Witches.

Hansel and Gretel / Hansel y Gretel by Jacob & Wilhelm Grimm; adapt. by Elisabet Abeya; ill. by Cristina Losantos. Chronicle, 2005. ISBN 0-8118-4793-4 Subj: Behavior — lost. Folk & fairy tales. Foreign languages. Forest, woods. Witches.

Jorinda and Jorindel by Jacob & Wilhelm Grimm; retold & ill. by Bernadette Watts. NorthSouth, 2005. ISBN 0-7358-1987-4 Subj: Folk & fairy tales. Witches.

Little Red Riding Hood by Jacob & Wilhelm Grimm; retold & ill. by Andrea Wisnewski. Godine, 2007. ISBN 978-1-56792-303-2 Subj: Animals — wolves. Behavior — talking to strangers. Folk & fairy tales.

Little Red Riding Hood by Jacob & Wilhelm Grimm; retold & ill. by Jerry Pinkney. Little, Brown, 2007. ISBN 978-0-316-01355-0 Subj: Animals — wolves. Behavior — talking to strangers. Folk & fairy tales.

Musicians of Bremen by Jacob & Wilhelm Grimm; retold & ill. by Niroot Puttapipat. Candlewick, 2005. ISBN 0-7636-2758-5 Subj: Animals. Careers — musicians. Crime. Folk & fairy tales. Old age.

Musicians of Bremen / Los musicos de Bremner: a bilingual book by Jacob & Wilhelm Grimm; adapt. by Roser Ros; ill. by Pep Montserrat. Chronicle, 2005. ISBN 0-8118-4795-0 Subj: Animals. Careers — musicians. Crime. Folk & fairy tales. Foreign languages. Old age.

Rapunzel by Jacob & Wilhelm Grimm; adapt. by Francesc Bofill; ill. by Joma. Chronicle, 2006. ISBN 0-8118-5059-5 Subj: Folk & fairy tales. Hair. Royalty — princes. Witches.

Snow White by Jacob & Wilhelm Grimm; retold & ill. by Melinda Copper. Penguin, 2005. ISBN 0-525-47474-9 Subj: Animals. Dwarfs, midgets. Emotions — envy, jealousy. Folk & fairy tales. Magic. Witches.

The twelve dancing princesses by Jacob & Wilhelm Grimm; ill. by Rachel Isadora. Penguin, 2007. ISBN 978-0-399-24744-6 Subj: Activities — dancing. Folk & fairy tales. Foreign lands — Africa. Royalty — princesses.

Grimm, Wilhelm. *The Bremen town musicians* (Grimm, Jacob)

The elves and the shoemaker (Grimm, Jacob)

The frog prince (Grimm, Jacob)

Hansel and Gretel: a retelling from the original tale by the Brothers Grimm (Grimm, Jacob)

Hansel and Gretel / Hansel y Gretel (Grimm, Jacob)

Jorinda and Jorindel (Grimm, Jacob)

Little Red Riding Hood (Grimm, Jacob)

Little Red Riding Hood (Grimm, Jacob)

Musicians of Bremen (Grimm, Jacob)

Musicians of Bremen / Los musicos de Bremner: a bilingual book (Grimm, Jacob)

Rapunzel (Grimm, Jacob)

Snow White (Grimm, Jacob)

The twelve dancing princesses (Grimm, Jacob)

Grindley, Sally. *It's my school* ill. by Margaret Chamberlain. Walker & Company, 2006. ISBN 0-8027-8086-5 Subj: Family life — brothers & sisters. School — first day.

Grogan, John. *Bad dog, Marley!* ill. by Richard Cowdrey. HarperCollins, 2007. ISBN 978-0-06-117114-7 Subj: Animals — dogs. Behavior — misbehavior.

Groner, Judyth Saypol. *My first Hebrew word book* ill. by Pepi Marzel. Kar-Ben, 2005. ISBN 1-58013-126-3 Subj: Foreign languages. Jewish culture. Language.

Gruska, Denise. *The only boy in ballet class* ill. by Amy Wummer. Gibbs Smith, 2007. ISBN 978-1-4236-0220-0 Subj: Activities — dancing. Ballet. Prejudice. Sports — football.

Guiberson, Brenda Z. *Mud city: a flamingo story* ill. by author. Henry Holt, 2005. ISBN 0-8050-7177-6 Subj: Birds — flamingos. Nature.

Gutierrez, Akemi. *The mummy and other adventures of Sam and Alice* ill. by author. Houghton Mifflin, 2005. ISBN 0-618-50761-2 Subj: Activities — playing. Family life — brothers & sisters.

Gutman, Dan. *Casey back at bat* ill. by Steve Johnson & Lou Francher. HarperCollins, 2007. ISBN 0-06-056025-8 Subj: Poetry. Sports — baseball.

Guy, Ginger Foglesong. *My grandma / Mi abuelita* ill. by Vivi Escriva. HarperCollins, 2007. ISBN 0-06-079098-9 Subj: Family life. Foreign languages.

My school / Mi escuela ill. by Vivi Escriva. HarperCollins, 2006. ISBN 0-06-079101-2 Subj: Foreign languages. School.

Perros! Perros! Dogs! Dogs! A story in English and Spanish ill. by Sharon Glick. HarperCollins, 2006. ISBN 0-06-083574-5 Subj: Animals — dogs. Concepts — opposites. Foreign languages.

Siesta ill. by René King Moreno. HarperCollins, 2005. ISBN 0-06-056063-0 Subj: Family life — brothers & sisters. Foreign languages. Sleep. Toys — bears.

Haas, Irene. *Bess and Bella* ill. by author. Simon & Schuster, 2006. ISBN 978-1-4169-0013-9 Subj: Birds. Emotions — loneliness. Friendship.

Hächler, Bruno. *What does my teddy bear do all night?* ill. by Birte Müller. Minedition, 2005. ISBN 0-698-40029-1 Subj: Bedtime. Rhyming text. Toys — bears.

Hager, Sarah. *Dancing Matilda* ill. by Kelly Murphy. HarperCollins, 2005. ISBN 0-06-051453-1 Subj: Activities — dancing. Rhyming text.

Hague, Michael. *Animal friends: a collection of poems for children* comp. & ill. by Michael Hague. Henry Holt, 2007. ISBN 0-8050-3817-5 Subj: Animals. Poetry.

Hale, Nathan. *Yellowbelly and Plum go to school* ill. by author. Penguin, 2007. ISBN 978-0-399-24624-1 Subj: School — first day. Toys — bears.

Hambleton, Laura. *Monkey business: fun with idioms* by Laura Hambleton & Sedat Turhan; ill. by Herve Tullet. Milet, 2007. ISBN 978-1-84059-499-7 Subj: Language.

Hamilton, Arlene. *Only a cow* ill. by Dean Griffiths. Fitzhenry & Whiteside, 2006. ISBN 1-55041-871-8 Subj: Animals — bulls, cows. Animals — horses, ponies. Emotions — envy, jealousy. Fairs, festivals.

Hamilton, Kersten. *Firefighters to the rescue!* ill. by Rich Davis. Penguin, 2005. ISBN 0-670-03503-3 Subj: Careers — firefighters.

Hamilton, Martha. *The hidden feast: a folktale from the American South* by Martha Hamilton & Mitch Weiss; ill. by Don Tate. August House, 2006. ISBN 0-87483-758-8 Subj: Animals. Etiquette. Farms. Folk & fairy tales.

Priceless gifts: a folktale from Italy by Martha Hamilton & Mitch Weiss; ill. by John Kanzler. August House, 2007. ISBN 978-0-87483-788-9 Subj: Animals — cats. Animals — rats. Folk & fairy tales. Foreign lands — Italy. Gifts.

Hamilton, Richard. *Let's take over the kindergarten* ill. by Sue Heap. Bloomsbury, 2007. ISBN 978-1-58234-707-3 Subj: Rhyming text. School.

Hammerle, Susa. *Let's try horseback riding* trans. by Marisa Miller; ill. by Kyrima Trapp. NorthSouth, 2006. ISBN 0-7358-2093-7 Subj: Animals — horses, ponies. Sports.

Hample, Stoo. *I will kiss you (lots & lots & lots!)* ill. by author. Candlewick, 2005. ISBN 0-7636-2787-9 Subj: Animals — rabbits. Emotions — love. Family life — mothers. Kissing. Rhyming text.

Hanft, Josh. *The miracles of Passover* ill. by Seymour Chwast. Blue Apple, 2007. ISBN 978-1-59354-600-7 Subj: Holidays — Passover. Jewish culture.

Hapka, Cathy. *Margret and H. A. Rey's Merry Christmas, Curious George* ill. in the style of H. A. Rey by Mary O'Keefe Young. Houghton Mifflin, 2006. ISBN 0-618-69237-1 Subj: Animals — monkeys. Character traits — curiosity. Holidays — Christmas. Hospitals. Humorous stories.

Harley, Bill. *Dear Santa: the letters of James B. Dobbins* ill. by R. W. Alley. HarperCollins, 2005. ISBN 0-06-623779-3 Subj: Behavior. Holidays — Christmas. Letters, cards. Santa Claus.

Harness, Cheryl. *Our colonial year* ill. by author. Simon & Schuster, 2005. ISBN 0-689-83479-9 Subj: Days of the week, months of the year. U.S. history.

Harper, Anita. *It's not fair!* ill. by Mary McQuillan. Holiday House, 2007. ISBN 978-0-8234-2094-0 Subj: Animals — cats. Emotions — envy, jealousy. Family life — brothers & sisters. Family life — new sibling.

Harper, Charise Mericle. *Amy and Ivan* ill. by author. Ten Speed, 2006. ISBN 1-58246-134-1 Subj: Birds. Counting, numbers. Format, unusual — toy & movable books. Gifts.

Flush! The scoop on poop throughout the ages ill. by author. Little, Brown, 2007. ISBN 0-316-01064-2 Subj: Health & fitness. Toilets.

When Randolph turned rotten ill. by author. Random House, 2007. ISBN 978-0-375-84071-5 Subj: Animals — beavers. Birds — geese. Birthdays. Friendship. Parties. Self-concept. Sleepovers.

Harper, Jamie. *Me too!* ill. by author. Little, Brown, 2005. ISBN 0-316-60552-2 Subj: Behavior — imitation. Family life — brothers & sisters. Sports — swimming.

Miss Mingo and the first day of school ill. by author. Candlewick, 2006. ISBN 0-7636-2410-1 Subj: Animals. Birds — flamingos. Careers — teachers. School — first day.

Night night, baby bundt ill. by author. Candlewick, 2007. ISBN 978-0-7636-3239-7 Subj: Bedtime. Format, unusual — board books.

Splish splash, baby bundt ill. by author. Candlewick, 2007. ISBN 978-0-7636-3240-3 Subj: Activities — bathing. Format, unusual — board books.

Harper, Jessica. *A place called Kindergarten* ill. by G. Brian Karas. Penguin, 2006. ISBN 0-399-24226-0 Subj: Animals. Farms. School — first day.

Harper, Jo. *I could eat you up!* ill. by Kay Chorao. Holiday House, 2007. ISBN 978-0-8234-1733-9 Subj: Animals. Family life — parents. Language.

Harrington, Janice N. *The chicken-chasing queen of Lamar County* ill. by Shelley Jackson. Farrar, Straus & Giroux, 2007. ISBN 978-0-374-31251-0 Subj: Birds — chickens. Ethnic groups in the U.S. — African Americans. Farms.

Harris, Peter. *The night pirates* ill. by Deborah Allwright. Scholastic, 2006. ISBN 0-439-79959-7 Subj: Bedtime. Night. Pirates.

Harris, Robie H. *I love messes!* ill. by Nicole Hollander. Little, Brown, 2005. ISBN 0-316-10946-0 Subj: Behavior — messy. Character traits — cleanliness. Character traits — orderliness.

I'm all dressed! ill. by Nicole Hollander. Little, Brown, 2005. ISBN 0-316-10948-7 Subj: Character traits — individuality. Clothing.

Maybe a bear ate it! ill. by Michael Emberley. Scholastic/Orchard, 2007. ISBN 978-0-439-92961-5 Subj: Animals. Bedtime. Books, reading. Imagination.

Harris, Trudy. *Jenny found a penny* ill. by John Hovell. Lerner, 2007. ISBN 978-0-8225-6725-7 Subj: Counting, numbers. Money. Rhyming text.

Twenty hungry piggies ill. by Andrew N. Harris. Lerner, 2007. ISBN 978-0-8225-6370-9 Subj: Animals — pigs. Counting, numbers. Nursery rhymes. Rhyming text.

Harrison, David Lee. *Piggy Wiglet* ill. by Karen Stormer Brooks. Boyds Mills, 2007. ISBN 978-1-59078-386-3 Subj: Animals — pigs. Behavior — running away. Rhyming text.

Harshman, Marc. *Only one neighborhood* ill. by Barbara Garrison. Penguin, 2007. ISBN 978-0-525-47468-5 Subj: Communities, neighborhoods. Counting, numbers.

Hartland, Jessie. *Night shift* ill. by author. Bloomsbury, 2007. ISBN 978-1-59990-025-4 Subj: Activities — working. Careers. Night.

Hartman, Bob. *Dinner in the lions' den* ill. by Tim Raglin. Penguin, 2007. ISBN 978-0-399-24674-6 Subj: Animals — lions. Religion — Daniel.

Harvey, Damian. *Just the thing!* ill. by Lynne Chapman. School Specialty/Gingham Dog, 2005. ISBN 0-7696-4300-0 Subj: Animals — gorillas. Problem solving.

Haseley, Dennis. *The invisible moose* ill. by Steven Kellogg. Penguin, 2006. ISBN 0-8037-2892-1 Subj: Animals — moose. Character traits — shyness.

Haskins, Jim (James). *Count your way through Afghanistan* by Jim Haskins & Kathleen Benson; ill. by Megan Moore. Lerner, 2006. ISBN 1-57505-880-4 Subj: Counting, numbers. Foreign lands — Afghanistan. Foreign languages.

Count your way through Iran by Jim Haskins & Kathleen Benson; ill. by Farida Zaman. Lerner, 2006. ISBN 1-57505-881-2 Subj: Counting, numbers. Foreign lands — Iran. Foreign languages.

Delivering justice: W. W. Law and the fight for civil rights ill. by Benny Andrews. Candlewick, 2006. ISBN 0-7636-2592-2 Subj: Ethnic groups in the U.S. — African Americans. Prejudice. U.S. history.

Hasler, Eveline. *A tale of two brothers* trans. from German by Marianne Martens; ill. by Kathi Bhend. NorthSouth, 2006. ISBN 0-7358-2102-X Subj: Character traits — kindness. Character traits — meanness. Family life — brothers & sisters. Folk & fairy tales. Foreign lands — Switzerland.

Hassett, Ann. *Can't catch me* (Hassett, John)

The finest Christmas tree by Ann & John Hassett; ill. by authors. Houghton Mifflin, 2005. ISBN 0-618-50901-1 Subj: Holidays — Christmas. Santa Claus. Trees.

Hassett, John. *The finest Christmas tree* (Hassett, Ann)

Hatch, Elizabeth. *Halloween night* ill. by Jimmy Pickering. Random House, 2005. ISBN 0-385-90887-3 Subj: Cumulative tales. Holidays — Halloween. Rhyming text.

Hawkes, Kevin. *The wicked big toddlah* ill. by author. Random House, 2007. ISBN 978-0-375-82427-2 Subj: Babies. Giants. Humorous stories.

Hayes, Joe. *The gum-chewing rattler* ill. by Antonio Castro Lopez. Cinco Puntos, 2006. ISBN 0-9383179-9-7 Subj: Reptiles — snakes. Tall tales.

Hayes, Karel. *The winter visitors* ill. by author. Down East, 2007. ISBN 978-0-89272-750-6 Subj: Animals — bears. Seasons — winter.

Hayles, Marsha. *Pajamas anytime* ill. by Hiroe Nakata. Penguin, 2005. ISBN 0-399-23871-9 Subj: Clothing — pajamas. Days of the week, months of the year. Rhyming text.

Hays, Anna Jane. *Kindergarten countdown* ill. by Linda Davick. Random House, 2007. ISBN 978-0-375-84252-8 Subj: Counting, numbers. Rhyming text. School — first day.

Ready, set, preschool! Stories, poems, and picture games, with an educational guide for parents ill. by True Kelley. Random House, 2005. ISBN 0-375-92519-8 Subj: Concepts. Games. School.

Hayward, Linda. *I am a book* ill. by Carol Nicklaus. Lerner, 2005. ISBN 0-7613-1826-7 Subj: Books, reading.

The King's chorus ill. by Jennifer P. Goldfinger. Houghton Mifflin, 2006. ISBN 0-618-51618-2 Subj: Animals. Birds — chickens. Farms. Morning.

Hazelton, Hugh. *A small Nativity* (Nazoa, Aquiles)

Hazen, Barbara Shook. *Who is your favorite monster, mama?* ill. by Maryann Kovalski. Hyperion, 2006. ISBN 0-7868-1810-7 Subj: Family life. Monsters. Sibling rivalry.

Headley, Justina Chen. *The patch* ill. by Mitch Vane. Charlesbridge, 2006. ISBN 1-58089-049-0 Subj: Activities — dancing. Ballet. Glasses. Self-concept.

Heck, Ed. *Monkey lost* ill. by author. Simon & Schuster, 2005. ISBN 0-689-04633-2 Subj: Animals — monkeys. Behavior — lost. School. Toys.

Heidbreder, Robert. *Lickety-split* ill. by Dusan Petricic. Kids Can, 2007. ISBN 978-1-55337-710-8 Subj: Language.

A sea-wishing day ill. by Kady MacDonald Denton. Kids Can, 2007. ISBN 978-1-55337-707-8 Subj: Rhyming text. Sea & seashore. Sports — sailing.

Heide, Florence Parry. *A promise is a promise* ill. by Tony Auth. Candlewick, 2007. ISBN 978-0-7636-2285-5 Subj: Pets.

Heide, Iris van der. *The red chalk* ill. by Marije Tolman. Boyds Mills, 2006. ISBN 1-932425-79-9 Subj: Activities — playing. Activities — trading. Behavior — boredom.

A strange day ill. by Marijke ten Cate. Boyds Mills, 2007. ISBN 978-1-932425-94-9 Subj: Character traits — helpfulness. Contests. Letters, cards.

Heiligman, Deborah. *Fun dog, sun dog* ill. by Tim Bowers. Marshall Cavendish, 2005. ISBN 0-7614-5162-5 Subj: Animals — dogs. Pets.

Heinz, Brian J. *Nathan of yesteryear and Michael of today* ill. by Joanne Friar. Lerner, 2006. ISBN 0-7613-2893-9 Subj: U.S. history.

Red Fox at McCloskey's farm ill. by Chris Sheban. Creative Editions, 2006. ISBN 1-56846-195-X Subj: Animals — foxes. Farms. Rhyming text.

Helakoski, Leslie. *Big chickens* ill. by Henry Cole. Penguin, 2006. ISBN 0-525-47575-3 Subj: Animals — wolves. Birds — chickens. Emotions — fear. Farms.

Helmer, Marilyn. *One splendid tree* ill. by Dianne Eastman. Kids Can, 2005. ISBN 1-55337-683-8 Subj: Family life. Holidays — Christmas. Trees. U.S. history. War.

Henderson, Kathy. *Look at you! A baby body book* ill. by Paul Howard. Candlewick, 2006. ISBN 978-0-7636-2745-4 Subj: Anatomy. Babies. Senses.

Henkes, Kevin. *A good day* ill. by author. HarperCollins, 2007. ISBN 978-0-06-114019-8 Subj: Animals. Behavior — bad day.

Lilly's big day ill. by author. HarperCollins, 2006. ISBN 0-06-074236-4 Subj: Animals — mice. Careers — teachers. Character traits — assertiveness. Emotions — anger. Weddings.

So happy! ill. by Anita Lobel. HarperCollins, 2005. ISBN 0-06-056484-9 Subj: Animals — rabbits. Plants. Seeds.

Hennessy, B. G. (Barbara G.). *Because of you: a book of kindness* ill. by Hiroe Nakata. Candlewick, 2005. ISBN 0-7636-1926-4 Subj: Character traits — kindness.

The boy who cried wolf ill. by Boris Kulikov. Simon & Schuster, 2006. ISBN 0-689-87433-2 Subj: Animals — wolves. Behavior — lying. Behavior — trickery. Folk & fairy tales.

Mr. Ouchy's first day ill. by Paul Meisel. Penguin, 2006. ISBN 0-399-24248-1 Subj: Careers — teachers. Counting, numbers. School — first day. Time.

Here we go round the mulberry bush ill. by Sophie Fatus. Barefoot, 2007. ISBN 978-1-84686-035-5 Subj: Music. Songs. World.

Herman, R. A. (Ronnie Ann). *Gomer and Little Gomer* ill. by Steve Haskamp. Penguin, 2005. ISBN 0-525-47359-9 Subj: Animals — dogs. Toys.

Herzog, Brad. *R is for race: a stock car alphabet* ill. by Jane Gilltrap Bready. Sleeping Bear, 2006. ISBN 1-58536-272-7 Subj: ABC books. Automobiles. Sports — racing.

Hester, Denia Lewis. *Grandma Lena's big ol' turnip* ill. by Jackie Urbanovic. Albert Whitman, 2005. ISBN 0-8075-3027-1 Subj: Character traits — cooperation. Cumulative tales. Ethnic groups in the U.S. — African Americans. Farms. Food. Plants. Problem solving.

Hewitt, Kathryn. *No dogs here!* ill. by author. Penguin, 2005. ISBN 0-525-47200-2 Subj: Animals — dogs. Days of the week, months of the year.

Hicks, Barbara Jean. *I like black and white* ill. by Lila Prap. Tiger Tales, 2006. ISBN 1-58925-057-5 Subj: Concepts — color. Rhyming text.

Jitterbug jam: a monster tale ill. by Alexis Deacon. Farrar, Straus & Giroux, 2005. ISBN 0-374-33685-7 Subj: Bedtime. Emotions — fear. Monsters.

The secret life of Walter Kitty ill. by Dan Santat. Random House, 2007. ISBN 978-0-375-83196-6 Subj: Animals — cats. Humorous stories.

High, Linda Oatman. *Cool Bopper's choppers* ill. by John O'Brien. Boyds Mills, 2007. ISBN 978-1-59078-379-5 Subj: Music. Musical instruments — saxophones. Teeth.

Hill, Ros. *Shamoo: a whale of a cow* ill. by author. Simon & Schuster, 2005. ISBN 0-689-04634-0 Subj: Animals — bulls, cows. Animals — whales.

Hill, Susanna Leonard. *Punxsutawney Phyllis* ill. by Jeffrey Ebbeler. Holiday House, 2005. ISBN 0-8234-1872-3 Subj: Animals — groundhogs. Gender roles. Holidays — Groundhog Day.

Hillenbrand, Jane. *What a treasure!* ill. by Will Hillenbrand. Holiday House, 2006. ISBN 0-8234-1896-0 Subj: Animals — moles. Character traits — confidence. Character traits — pride.

Hillenbrand, Will. *My book box* ill. by author. Harcourt, 2006. ISBN 0-15-202029-2 Subj: Animals — elephants. Books, reading.

Hilliard, Richard. *Godspeed, John Glenn* ill. by author. Boyds Mills, 2006. ISBN 1-59078-384-0 Subj: Careers — astronauts. U.S. history.

Hills, Tad. *Duck and Goose* ill. by author. Random House, 2006. ISBN 0-375-93611-4 Subj: Birds — ducks. Birds — geese. Friendship. Toys — balls.

Duck, Duck, Goose ill. by author. Random House, 2007. ISBN 978-0-375-84068-5 Subj: Birds — ducks. Birds — geese. Friendship.

Himmelman, John. *Chickens to the rescue* ill. by author. Henry Holt, 2006. ISBN 0-8050-7951-3 Subj: Birds — chickens. Character traits — helpfulness. Farms.

Mouse in a meadow ill. by author. Charlesbridge, 2005. ISBN 1-57091-520-2 Subj: Animals. Ecology. Plants.

Tudley didn't know ill. by author. Sylvan Dell, 2006. ISBN 0-9764943-6-1 Subj: Character traits — individuality. Friendship. Reptiles — turtles, tortoises.

Hindley, Judy. *Baby talk* ill. by Brita Granström. Candlewick, 2006. ISBN 0-7636-2971-5 Subj: Activities — talking. Babies. Rhyming text.

Sleepy places ill. by Tor Freeman. Candlewick, 2006. ISBN 0-7636-2983-9 Subj: Animals. Bedtime. Rhyming text. Sleep.

Hobbie, Holly. *Toot and Puddle: let it snow* ill. by author. Little, Brown, 2007. ISBN 978-0-316-16686-7 Subj: Animals — pigs. Friendship. Gifts. Holidays — Christmas. Weather — snow.

Toot and Puddle: wish you were here ill. by author. Little, Brown, 2005. ISBN 0-316-36602-1 Subj: Activities — traveling. Animals — pigs. Friendship. Illness. Plants.

Hoberman, Mary Ann. *I'm going to Grandma's* ill. by Tiphanie Beeke. Harcourt, 2007. ISBN 978-0-15-216592-5 Subj: Family life — grandparents. Night. Quilts. Rhyming text.

Mrs. O'Leary's cow ill. by Jenny Mattheson. Little, Brown, 2007. ISBN 978-0-316-14840-5 Subj: Animals — bulls, cows. Fire. Rhyming text.

Hodge, Deborah. *Lily and the mixed-up letters* ill. by France Brassard. Tundra, 2007. ISBN 978-0-88776-757-9 Subj: Books, reading. Character traits — perseverance. Handicaps — dyslexia. School. Self-concept.

Hodge, Marie. *Are you sleepy yet, Petey?* ill. by Renée Graef. Sterling, 2005. ISBN 1-4027-1265-0 Subj: Animals — dogs. Bedtime.

Hodges, Margaret. *Moses* ill. by Barry Moser. Harcourt, 2006. ISBN 0-15-200946-9 Subj: Religion — Moses.

Hodgkins, Fran. *Between the tides* ill. by Jim Sollers. Down East, 2007. ISBN 978-0-89272-727-8 Subj: Sea & seashore.

The cat of Strawberry Hill: a true story ill. by Lesia Sochor. Down East, 2005. ISBN 0-89272-684-9 Subj: Animals — cats. Behavior — lost.

How people learned to fly ill. by True Kelley. HarperCollins, 2007. ISBN 978-0-06-029558-5 Subj: Activities — flying. Airplanes, airports.

Hogg, Gary. *Beautiful Buehla and the zany zoo makeover* ill. by Victoria Chess. HarperCollins, 2006. ISBN 0-06-009420-6 Subj: Animals. Character traits — appearance. Zoos.

Look what the cat dragged in! ill. by Mike Wohnoutka. Penguin, 2005. ISBN 0-525-46984-2 Subj: Animals — cats. Character traits — laziness. Pets.

Holabird, Katharine. *Angelina at the palace* ill. by Helen Craig. Penguin, 2005. ISBN 0-670-06048-8 Subj: Animals — mice. Ballet. Royalty — princesses.

Christmas in Mouseland based on the illustrations of Helen Craig. Penguin, 2007. Based on the stories of Katharine Holabird. ISBN 978-0-448-44663-9 Subj: Activities — dancing. Animals — mice. Ballet. Holidays — Christmas.

Holt, Kimberly Willis. *Skinny brown dog* ill. by Donald Saaf. Henry Holt, 2007. ISBN 978-0-8050-7587-8 Subj: Animals — dogs. Careers — bakers.

Waiting for Gregory ill. by Gabi Swiatkowska. Henry Holt, 2006. ISBN 0-8050-7388-4 Subj: Babies. Birth. Family life — cousins.

Hong, Chen Jiang. *The magic horse of Han Gan* trans. by Claudia Zoe Bedrick; ill. by Chen Jiang Hong. Enchanted Lion, 2006. ISBN 1-59270-063-2 Subj: Activities — painting. Animals — horses, ponies. Art. Careers — artists. Folk & fairy tales. Foreign lands — China. Magic.

Hooper, Meredith. *Celebrity cat* ill. by Bee Willey. Frances Lincoln, 2006. ISBN 1-84507-290-1 Subj: Animals — cats. Art. Museums.

Hopkins, Jackie Mims. *The gold miner's daughter: a melodramatic fairytale* ill. by Jon Goodell. Peachtree, 2006. ISBN 1-56145-362-5 Subj: Folk & fairy tales. U.S. history — frontier & pioneer life.

Hopkins, Lee Bennett. *Behind the museum door* ed. by Lee Bennett Hopkins; ill. by Stacey Dressen-McQueen. Abrams, 2007. ISBN 0-8109-1204-X Subj: Art. Museums. Poetry.

Horacek, Petr. *Butterfly butterfly: a book of colors* ill. by author. Candlewick, 2007. ISBN 978-0-7636-3343-1 Subj: Concepts — color. Format, unusual. Nature.

Silly Suzy Goose ill. by author. Candlewick, 2006. ISBN 0-7636-3040-3 Subj: Animals. Animals — lions. Birds — geese. Character traits — individuality. Self-concept.

Hornsey, Chris. *Why do I have to eat off the floor?* ill. by Gwen Perkins. Walker & Company, 2007. ISBN 0-8027-9617-6 Subj: Animals — dogs. Character traits — questioning. Humorous stories.

Horowitz, Dave. *Soon, Baboon, soon* ill. by author. Penguin, 2005. ISBN 0-399-24268-6 Subj: Animals. Animals — baboons. Character traits — patience. Music. Musical instruments. Rhyming text.

The ugly pumpkin ill. by author. Penguin, 2005. ISBN 0-399-24267-8 Subj: Food. Holidays — Halloween. Holidays — Thanksgiving. Rhyming text.

Horse, Harry. *Little Rabbit runaway* ill. by author. Peachtree, 2005. ISBN 1-56145-343-9 Subj: Animals — rabbits. Behavior — running away.

Hort, Lenny. *Did dinosaurs eat pizza? Mysteries science hasn't solved* ill. by John O'Brien. Henry Holt, 2006. ISBN 0-8050-6757-4 Subj: Dinosaurs. Science.

Horton, Joan. *Hippopotamus stew: and other silly animal poems* ill. by JoAnn Adinolfi. Henry Holt, 2006. ISBN 0-8050-7350-7 Subj: Animals. Poetry.

Horvath, David. *Bossy bear* ill. by author. Hyperion, 2007. ISBN 978-1-4231-0336-3 Subj: Animals — bears. Behavior — bossy.

Howe, James. *Houndsley and Catina* ill. by Marie-Louise Gay. Candlewick, 2006. ISBN 0-7636-2404-7 Subj: Activities — baking, cooking. Activities — writing. Animals — cats. Animals — dogs. Friendship.

Houndsley and Catina and the birthday surprise ill. by Marie-Louise Gay. Candlewick, 2006. ISBN 0-7636-2405-5 Subj: Animals — cats. Animals — dogs. Birthdays. Friendship. Parties.

Howlett, Peter. *Suho's white horse: a Mongolian legend* (Otsuka, Yuzo)

Hubbard, Crystal. *Catching the moon: the story of a young girl's baseball dream* ill. by Randy DuBurke. Lee & Low, 2005. ISBN 1-58430-243-7 Subj: Character traits — perseverance. Ethnic groups in the U.S. — African Americans. Sports — baseball. U.S. history.

Hubbell, Patricia. *Cars: Rushing! Honking! Zooming!* ill. by Megan Halsey. Marshall Cavendish, 2006. ISBN 0-7614-5296-6 Subj: Automobiles. Rhyming text.

Firefighters! Speeding! Spraying! Saving! ill. by Viviana Garofoli. Marshall Cavendish, 2007. ISBN 978-0-7614-5337-6 Subj: Careers — firefighters. Rhyming text.

Hurray for spring! ill. by Taia Morley. NorthWord, 2005. ISBN 1-55971-913-3 Subj: Rhyming text. Seasons — spring.

Trains: Steaming! Pulling! Huffing! ill. by Megan Halsey & Sean Addy. Marshall Cavendish, 2005. ISBN 0-7614-5194-3 Subj: Rhyming text. Trains.

Hubery, Julia. *A friend for all seasons* ill. by Mei Matsuoka. Simon & Schuster/Atheneum, 2007. ISBN 978-1-4169-2685-6 Subj: Animals — raccoons. Seasons. Trees.

Hudson, Cheryl Willis. *Construction zone* photos by Richard Sobol. Candlewick, 2006. ISBN 0-7636-2684-8 Subj: Buildings. Careers — construction workers. Machines.

Huggins, Peter. *Trosclair and the alligator* ill. by Lindsey Gardiner. Star Bright, 2006. ISBN 1-932065-98-9 Subj: Reptiles — alligators, crocodiles. Swamps.

Hughes, Susan. *Earth to Audrey* ill. by Stéphane Poulin. Kids Can, 2005. ISBN 1-55337-843-1 Subj: Character traits — individuality. Friendship. Imagination. Seasons — summer.

Hume, Lachie. *Clancy the courageous cow* ill. by author. HarperCollins, 2007. ISBN 978-0-06-117249-6 Subj: Animals — bulls, cows. Character traits — appearance. Character traits — individuality. Prejudice.

Huneck, Stephen. *Sally's snow adventure* ill. by author. Abrams, 2006. ISBN 0-8109-7061-9 Subj: Animals — dogs. Behavior — lost. Seasons — winter. Sports — skiing. Weather — snow.

Hunter, Jana Novotny. *When Daddy's truck picks me up* ill. by Carol Thompson. Albert Whitman, 2006. ISBN 0-8075-8914-4 Subj: Family life — fathers. Rhyming text. Trucks.

Hurd, Thacher. *Sleepy Cadillac: a bedtime drive* ill. by author. HarperCollins, 2005. ISBN 0-06-073021-8 Subj: Automobiles. Bedtime. Sleep.

Hurst, Carol Otis. *Terrible storm* ill. by S. D. Schindler. HarperCollins, 2007. ISBN 0-06-009001-4 Subj: Family life — grandfathers. Seasons — winter. Weather — blizzards.

Hurston, Zora Neale. *The six fools* coll. by Zora Neale Hurston; adapt. by Joyce Carol Thomas; ill. by Ann Tanksley. HarperCollins, 2006. ISBN 0-06-000647-1 Subj: Character traits — foolishness. Ethnic groups in the U.S. — African Americans. Folk & fairy tales.

Hutchins, Hazel (Hazel J.). *A second is a hiccup: a child's book of time* ill. by Kady MacDonald Denton. Scholastic, 2007. ISBN 0-439-83106-7 Subj: Time.

Hutchins, Pat. *Barn dance!* ill. by author. HarperCollins, 2007. ISBN 978-0-089122-0 Subj: Activities — dancing. Animals. Farms.

Bumpety bump ill. by author. HarperCollins, 2006. ISBN 0-06-056000-2 Subj: Birds — chickens. Family life — grandfathers. Farms. Rhyming text.

Hyde, Heidi Smith. *Mendel's accordion* ill. by Johanna van der Sterre. Lerner, 2007. ISBN 978-1-58013-212-1 Subj: Immigrants. Jewish culture. Music. Musical instruments — accordions.

Ichikawa, Satomi. *I am Pangoo the penguin* ill. by author. Penguin, 2006. ISBN 0-399-23313-X Subj: Behavior — running away. Birds — penguins. Toys. Zoos.

My father's shop ill. by author. Kane/Miller, 2006. ISBN 1-929132-99-9 Subj: Family life — fathers. Foreign lands — Morocco. Shopping.

Imai, Ayano. *Chester* ill. by author. Minedition, 2007. ISBN 0-698-40062-3 Subj: Animals — dogs. Behavior — running away. Pets.

The 108th sheep ill. by author. Tiger Tales, 2007. ISBN 978-1-58925-063-5 Subj: Animals — sheep. Bedtime. Counting, numbers.

Inches, Alison. *The stuffed animals get ready for bed* ill. by Bryan Langdo. Harcourt, 2006. ISBN 0-15-216466-9 Subj: Bedtime. Rhyming text. Toys.

Isaacs, Anne. *Pancakes for supper!* ill. by Mark Teague. Scholastic, 2006. ISBN 0-439-64483-6 Subj: Animals. Character traits — cleverness. Food. Tall tales.

Isadora, Rachel. *Luke goes to bat* ill. by author. Penguin, 2005. ISBN 0-399-23604-X Subj: Character traits — perseverance. Ethnic groups in the U.S. — African Americans. Family life — grandmothers. Sports — baseball.

What a family! ill. by author. Penguin, 2006. ISBN 0-399-24254-6 Subj: Family life.

Yo, Jo! ill. by author. Harcourt, 2007. ISBN 978-0-15-205783-1 Subj: Communities, neighborhoods. Ethnic groups in the U.S. — African Americans. Family life — brothers & sisters. Family life — grandfathers. Language.

Issa, Kobayashi. *Today and today* ill. by G. Brian Karas. Scholastic, 2007. ISBN 0-439-59078-7 Subj: Foreign lands — Japan. Nature. Poetry. Seasons.

Ives, Penny. *Rabbit pie* ill. by author. Penguin, 2006. ISBN 0-670-05951-X Subj: Animals — rabbits. Bedtime.

Ivey, Randall. *Jay and the bounty of books* ill. by Chuck Galey. Pelican, 2007. ISBN 978-1-58980-372-5 Subj: Books, reading. Giants. Libraries.

Jack and the beanstalk. *Jack and the beanstalk* retold by E. Nesbit; ill. by Matt Tavares. Candlewick, 2006. ISBN 0-7636-2124-2 Subj: Folk & fairy tales. Giants. Plants.

Jackson, Ellen B. *Earth Mother* ill. by Leo & Diane Dillon. Walker & Company, 2005. ISBN 0-8027-8993-5 Subj: Ecology. Nature. World.

Jacobs, Julie. *My heart is a magic house* ill. by Bernadette Pons. Albert Whitman, 2007. ISBN 978-0-8075-5335-0 Subj: Behavior — worrying. Emotions — love. Family life — new sibling.

Jacobs, Paul DuBois. *The deaf musicians* (Seeger, Pete)

Some friends to feed: the story of Stone Soup (Seeger, Pete)

Jahn-Clough, Lisa. *Little dog* ill. by author. Houghton Mifflin, 2006. ISBN 0-618-57405-0 Subj: Animals — dogs. Careers — artists.

James, J. Alison. *Charlie at the zoo* (Pfister, Marcus)

Where does pepper come from? And other fun facts (Raab, Brigitte)

Janovitz, Marilyn. *A, B, see!* ill. by author. Chronicle, 2005. ISBN 0-8118-4673-3 Subj: ABC books. Animals. Format, unusual — toy & movable books.

We love school! ill. by author. NorthSouth, 2007. ISBN 978-0-7358-2112-5 Subj: Animals — cats. Rhyming text. School.

Jarman, Julia. *Class Two at the zoo* ill. by Lynne Chapman. Carolrhoda, 2007. ISBN 978-0-8225-7132-2 Subj: Reptiles — snakes. Rhyming text. School — field trips. Zoos.

Jay, Alison. *1 2 3: a child's first counting book* ill. by author. Penguin, 2007. ISBN 978-0-525-47836-2 Subj: Counting, numbers. Dreams. Folk & fairy tales.

Jeffers, Oliver. *The incredible book eating boy* ill. by author. Penguin, 2007. ISBN 978-0-399-24749-1 Subj: Food. Books, reading.

Lost and found ill. by author. Penguin, 2006. ISBN 0-399-24503-0 Subj: Behavior — lost. Birds — penguins. Emotions — loneliness. Foreign lands — Antarctica. Friendship.

Jeffs, Stephanie. *Jenny: coming to terms with the death of a sibling* ill. by Jacqui Thomas. Abingdon, 2006. ISBN 0-687-49709-4 Subj: Death. Emotions — grief. Family life — brothers & sisters. Illness. Religion.

Josh: coming to terms with the death of a friend ill. by Jacqui Thomas. Abingdon, 2006. ISBN 0-687-49719-1 Subj: Death. Emotions — grief. Friendship. Religion.

Jenkins, Emily. *Daffodil* ill. by Tomek Bogacki. Farrar, Straus & Giroux, 2004. ISBN 0-374-31676-7 Subj: Character traits — individuality. Clothing — dresses. Family life — brothers & sisters. Multiple births — triplets.

Daffodil, crocodile ill. by Tomek Bogacki. Farrar, Straus & Giroux, 2007. ISBN 978-0-374-39944-3 Subj: Character traits — individuality. Family life — brothers & sisters. Imagination. Multiple births — triplets.

Love you when you whine ill. by Sergio Ruzzier. Farrar, Straus & Giroux, 2006. ISBN 0-374-34652-6 Subj: Animals — cats. Behavior — misbehavior. Emotions — love. Family life — mothers.

Num, num, num! A Bea and Haha book ill. by Tomek Bogacki. Farrar, Straus & Giroux, 2006. ISBN 0-374-30583-8 Subj: Animals — ferrets. Animals — hippopotamuses. Format, unusual — board books. Friendship.

Plonk, plonk, plonk! A Bea and Haha book ill. by Tomek Bogacki. Farrar, Straus & Giroux, 2006. ISBN 0-374-30585-4 Subj: Animals — ferrets. Animals — hippopotamuses. Format, unusual — board books. Friendship. Music.

That new animal ill. by Pierre Pratt. Farrar, Straus & Giroux, 2005. ISBN 0-374-37443-0 Subj: Animals — dogs. Babies.

Up, up, up! A Bea and Haha book ill. by Tomek Bogacki. Farrar, Straus & Giroux, 2006. ISBN 0-374-30584-6 Subj: Animals — ferrets. Animals — hippopotamuses. Character traits — helpfulness. Format, unusual — board books. Friendship.

What happens on Wednesdays ill. by Lauren Castillo. Farrar, Straus & Giroux, 2007. ISBN 978-0-374-38303-9 Subj: Day. Family life.

Jenkins, Steve. *Almost gone: the world's rarest animals* ill. by author. HarperCollins, 2006. ISBN 0-06-053600-4 Subj: Animals — endangered animals.

Dogs and cats ill. by author. Houghton Mifflin, 2007. ISBN 978-0-618-50767-2 Subj: Animals — cats. Animals — dogs. Format, unusual.

Living color ill. by author. Houghton Mifflin, 2007. ISBN 978-0-618-70897-0 Subj: Animals. Concepts — color.

Move! by Steve Jenkins & Robin Page; ill. by Steve Jenkins. Houghton Mifflin, 2006. ISBN 0-618-64637-X Subj: Animals. Concepts — motion. Language.

Prehistoric actual size ill. by author. Houghton Mifflin, 2005. ISBN 0-618-53578-0 Subj: Anatomy. Animals. Concepts — size. Prehistory.

Jennings, Sharon. *The happily ever afternoon* ill. by Ron Lightburn. Annick, 2006. ISBN 1-55037-945-3 Subj: Imagination.

Jocelyn, Marthe. *ABC x 3: english, espanol, francais* ill. by Tom Slaughter. Tundra, 2005. ISBN 0-88776-707-9 Subj: ABC books. Foreign languages.

Eats ill. by Tom Slaughter. Tundra, 2007. ISBN 978-0-88776-820-0 Subj: Animals. Food.

Joel, Billy. *New York state of mind* ill. by Izak. Scholastic, 2005. ISBN 0-439-55382-2 Subj: Cities, towns. Songs.

Johansen, Hanna. *The duck and the owl* trans. from German by John S. Barrett; ill. by Kathi Bhend. Godine, 2005. ISBN 1-56792-285-6 Subj: Birds — ducks. Birds — owls. Friendship.

Johnson, Angela. *Lily Brown's paintings* ill. by E. B. Lewis. Scholastic/Orchard, 2007. ISBN 978-0-439-78225-8 Subj: Activities — painting. Ethnic groups in the U.S. — African Americans. Imagination.

Wind flyers ill. by Loren Long. Simon & Schuster, 2007. ISBN 0-689-84879-X Subj: Activities — flying. Careers — airplane pilots. Ethnic groups in the U.S. — African Americans. U.S. history. War.

Johnson, Crockett. *Magic beach* ill. by author. Boyds Mills, 2005. ISBN 1-932425-27-6 Subj: Imagination. Sea & seashore — beaches.

Johnson, D. B. (Donald B.). *Eddie's kingdom* ill. by author. Houghton Mifflin, 2005. ISBN 0-618-56299-0 Subj: Activities — drawing. Behavior — fighting, arguing. Communities, neighborhoods. Homes, houses.

Four legs bad, two legs good! ill. by author. Houghton Mifflin, 2007. ISBN 978-0-618-80909-7 Subj: Animals. Character traits — laziness. Farms.

Johnson, David. *Snow sounds: an onomatopoeic story* ill. by author. Houghton Mifflin, 2006. ISBN 0-618-47310-6 Subj: Holidays — Christmas. Noise, sounds.

Johnson, James Weldon. *Lift every voice and sing* ill. by Bryan Collier. HarperCollins, 2007. ISBN 978-0-06-054147-7 Subj: Ethnic groups in the U.S. — African Americans. Music. Songs.

Johnson, Lindan Lee. *The dream jar* ill. by Serena Curmi. Houghton Mifflin, 2005. ISBN 0-618-17698-5 Subj: Bedtime. Dreams. Family life — brothers & sisters. Nightmares.

Johnson, Paul Brett. *On top of spaghetti* lyrics by Tom Glazer; ill. by Paul Brett Johnson. Scholastic, 2006. ISBN 0-439-74944-1 Subj: Animals. Food. Songs.

Johnson, Rebecca. *The proud pelican's secret* photos by Steve Parish. Gareth Stevens, 2005. ISBN 0-8368-5974-X Subj: Birds — pelicans. Character traits — appearance. Character traits — pride.

Sea turtle's clever plan photos by Steve Parish. Gareth Stevens, 2005. ISBN 0-8368-5975-8 Subj: Character traits — cleverness. Reptiles — turtles, tortoises.

Tree frog hears a sound photos by Steve Parish. Gareth Stevens, 2005. ISBN 0-8368-5976-6 Subj: Frogs & toads. Jungles.

Johnson-Davies, Denys. *Goha, the wise fool* ill. by Hany el Saed Ahmed & Hag Hamdy Mohamed Fattouh. Penguin, 2005. ISBN 0-399-24222-8 Subj: Character traits — cleverness. Character traits — foolishness. Folk & fairy tales. Foreign lands — Middle East.

Johnston, Tony. *Chicken in the kitchen* ill. by Eleanor Taylor. Simon & Schuster, 2005. ISBN 0-689-85641-5 Subj: Birds — chickens. Rhyming text.

Noel ill. by Cheng-Khee Chee. Carolrhoda, 2005. ISBN 1-57505-752-2 Subj: Holidays — Christmas.

Off to kindergarten ill. by Melissa Sweet. Houghton Mifflin, 2007. ISBN 0-439-73090-2 Subj: Rhyming text. School — first day.

The whole green world ill. by Elisa Kleven. Farrar, Straus & Giroux, 2005. ISBN 0-374-38400-2 Subj: Nature. Rhyming text.

Jolivet, Joëlle. *Almost everything* ill. by author. Macmillan, 2005. ISBN 1-59643-090-7 Subj: Nature. Science.

365 penguins (Fromental, Jean-Luc)

Jones, Sylvie. *Who's in the tub?* ill. by Pascale Constantin. Blue Apple, 2007. ISBN 978-1-59354-612-0 Subj: Activities — bathing. Animals. Imagination. Rhyming text.

Joosse, Barbara M. *Nikolai, the only bear* ill. by Renata Liwska. Penguin, 2005. ISBN 0-399-23884-0 Subj: Adoption. Animals — bears. Foreign lands — Russia. Orphans.

Papa do you love me? ill. by Barbara Lavallee. Chronicle, 2005. ISBN 0-8118-4265-7 Subj: Emotions — love. Family life — fathers. Foreign lands — Africa.

Please is a good word to say ill. by Jennifer Plecas. Penguin, 2007. ISBN 978-0-399-24217-5 Subj: Behavior — misbehavior. Etiquette.

Wind-wild dog ill. by Kate Kiesler. Henry Holt, 2006. ISBN 0-8050-7053-2 Subj: Alaska. Animals — dogs.

Jordan, Deloris. *Michael's golden rules* by Deloris & Roslyn M. Jordan; intro. by Michael Jordan; ill. by Kadir Nelson. Simon & Schuster, 2007. ISBN 978-0-689-87016-3 Subj: Character traits — persistence. Ethnic groups in the U.S. — African Americans. Family life — aunts, uncles. Sports — baseball. Sportsmanship.

Jordan, Michael. *Michael's golden rules* (Jordan, Deloris)

Jordan, Roslyn M. *Michael's golden rules* (Jordan, Deloris)

Joslin, Mary. *On that Christmas night* ill. by Helen Cann. Good Books, 2005. ISBN 1-56148-494-6 Subj: Holidays — Christmas. Religion — Nativity.

Joyce, William. *A day with Wilbur Robinson* ill. by author. HarperCollins, 2006. ISBN 0-06-089098-3 Subj: Family life.

Jubb, Sophie. *Cock-a-doodle quack! Quack!* (Baddiel, Ivor)

Jules, Jacqueline. *Abraham's search for God* ill. by Natascia Ugliano. Kar-Ben, 2007. ISBN 978-1-58013-243-5 Subj: Religion.

No English ill. by Amy Huntington. Mitten, 2007. ISBN 1-58726-474-9 Subj: Character traits — kindness. Emotions — loneliness. Friendship. Immigrants.

Juster, Norton. *The hello, goodbye window* ill. by Chris Raschka. Hyperion, 2005. ISBN 0-7868-0914-0 Subj: Caldecott award books. Family life — grandparents.

Kamm, Katja. *Invisible* ill. by author. NorthSouth, 2006. ISBN 0-7358-2052-X Subj: Art. Picture puzzles. Wordless.

Kaner, Etta. *Who likes the sun?* ill. by Marie Lafrance. Kids Can, 2007. ISBN 978-1-55337-840-2 Subj: Format, unusual — toy & movable books. Sun.

Who likes the wind? ill. by Marie Lafrance. Kids Can, 2006. ISBN 1-55337-839-3 Subj: Weather — wind.

Kanevsky, Polly. *Sleepy boy* ill. by Stephanie Anderson. Simon & Schuster/Atheneum, 2006. ISBN 978-0-689-86735-4 Subj: Animals — lions. Bedtime. Family life — fathers. Sleep.

Kangas, Juli. *The surprise visitor* ill. by author. Penguin, 2005. ISBN 0-8037-2989-8 Subj: Animals. Animals — mice. Eggs.

Kann, Elizabeth. *Pinkalicious* (Kann, Victoria)

Kann, Victoria. *Pinkalicious* by Victoria & Elizabeth Kann; ill. by Victoria Kann. HarperCollins, 2006. ISBN 0-06-077639-0 Subj: Concepts — color. Food.

Kanninen, Barbara. *A story with pictures* ill. by Lynn Rowe Reed. Holiday House, 2007. ISBN 978-0-8234-2049-0 Subj: Books, reading. Careers — authors. Careers — illustrators. Imagination.

Karas, G. Brian. *On Earth* ill. by author. Penguin, 2005. ISBN 0-399-24025-X Subj: Earth.

Kasza, Keiko. *Badger's fancy meal* ill. by author. Penguin, 2007. ISBN 978-0-399-24603-6 Subj: Animals — badgers. Food.

The dog who cried wolf ill. by author. Penguin, 2005. ISBN 0-399-24247-3 Subj: Animals — dogs. Animals — wolves. Self-concept.

Katz, Alan. *Don't say that word!* ill. by David Catrow. Simon & Schuster, 2007. ISBN 978-0-689-86971-6 Subj: Etiquette. Humorous stories. Rhyming text. School.

Katz, Bobbi. *Once around the sun* ill. by LeUyen Pham. Harcourt, 2006. ISBN 0-15-216397-2 Subj: Days of the week, months of the year. Poetry. Seasons.

Katz, Karen. *Can you say peace?* ill. by author. Henry Holt, 2006. ISBN 0-8050-7893-2 Subj: Foreign languages. World.

Daddy hugs 1 2 3 ill. by author. Simon & Schuster, 2005. ISBN 0-689-87771-4 Subj: Emotions — love. Family life — fathers. Hugging.

Mommy hugs ill. by author. Simon & Schuster, 2006. ISBN 0-689-87772-2 Subj: Family life — mothers. Hugging.

My first Ramadan ill. by author. Henry Holt, 2007. ISBN 978-0-8050-7894-7 Subj: Holidays — Ramadan. Religion.

A potty for me! A lift-the-flap instruction manual ill. by author. Simon & Schuster/Little Simon, 2005. ISBN 0-689-87423-5 Subj: Format, unusual — toy & movable books. Toilet training.

Ten tiny tickles ill. by author. Simon & Schuster, 2005. ISBN 0-689-85976-7 Subj: Babies. Counting, numbers.

Katz, Susan. *Oh, Theodore! Guinea pig poems* ill. by Stacey Schuett. Houghton Mifflin, 2007. ISBN 978-0-618-70222-0 Subj: Animals — guinea pigs. Pets. Poetry.

When the shadbush blooms (Messinger, Carla)

Kazeroid, Sibylle. *Liu and the bird: a journey in Chinese calligraphy* (Louis, Catherine)

Keillor, Garrison. *Daddy's girl* ill. by Robin Preiss Glasser. Hyperion, 2005. ISBN 0-7868-1986-3 Subj: Family life — fathers. Rhyming text.

Keller, Holly. *Help! A story of friendship* ill. by author. HarperCollins, 2007. ISBN 978-0-06-123913-7 Subj: Animals. Animals — mice. Behavior — resourcefulness. Emotions — fear. Friendship. Reptiles — snakes.

Nosy Rosie ill. by author. HarperCollins, 2006. ISBN 0-06-078758-9 Subj: Animals — foxes. Behavior — bullying. Character traits — helpfulness. Senses — smell.

Pearl's new skates ill. by author. HarperCollins, 2005. ISBN 0-06-056281-1 Subj: Animals — rabbits. Character traits — persistence. Sports — ice skating.

Sophie's window ill. by author. HarperCollins, 2005. ISBN 0-06-056283-8 Subj: Animals — dogs. Birds — pigeons. Emotions — fear. Friendship.

Keller, Laurie. *Do unto otters: a book about manners* ill. by author. Henry Holt, 2007. ISBN 978-0-8050-7996-8 Subj: Animals. Behavior. Etiquette. Language.

Grandpa Gazillion's number yard ill. by author. Henry Holt, 2005. ISBN 0-8050-6282-3 Subj: Counting, numbers. Humorous stories. Rhyming text.

Kelley, Ellen A. *My life as a chicken* ill. by Michael Slack. Harcourt, 2007. ISBN 978-0-15-205306-2 Subj: Birds — chickens. Humorous stories.

Kelley, Marty. *Winter woes* ill. by author. Zino, 2005. ISBN 1-55933-306-5 Subj: Behavior — worrying. Rhyming text. Seasons — winter.

Kelly, Irene. *It's a butterfly's life* ill. by author. Holiday House, 2007. ISBN 978-0-8234-1860-2 Subj: Insects — butterflies, caterpillars.

Kelly, Mij. *One more sheep* ill. by Russell Ayto. Peachtree, 2006. ISBN 1-56145-378-1 Subj: Animals — sheep. Animals — wolves. Behavior — trickery. Rhyming text.

Where's my darling daughter? ill. by Katharine McEwen. Good Books, 2006. ISBN 1-56148-537-3 Subj: Animals. Behavior — lost. Farms. Rhyming text.

Kempter, Christa. *Dear Little Lamb* ill. by Frauke Weldin. North-South, 2006. ISBN 0-7358-2086-4 Subj: Activities — writing. Animals — sheep. Animals — wolves. Letters, cards. Pen pals.

Kennedy, Kim. *Pirate Pete's giant adventure* ill. by Doug Kennedy. Abrams, 2006. ISBN 0-8109-5965-8 Subj: Birds — parrots. Giants. Magic. Pirates.

Kerley, Barbara. *You and me together: moms, dads, and kids around the world* ill. with photos. National Geographic, 2005. ISBN 0-7922-8298-1 Subj: Family life — parents. World.

Kessler, Cristina. *The best beekeeper of Lalibela: a tale from Africa* ill. by Leonard Jenkins. Holiday House, 2006. ISBN 0-8234-1858-8 Subj: Careers — beekeepers. Character traits — perseverance. Foreign lands — Ethiopia. Gender roles. Insects — bees.

Ketteman, Helen. *Waynetta and the cornstalk: a Texas fairy tale* ill. by Diane Greenseid. Albert Whitman, 2007. ISBN 978-0-8075-8687-7 Subj: Folk & fairy tales. Giants. Plants. Texas.

Khing, T. T. *Where is the cake?* ill. by author. Abrams, 2007. ISBN 978-0-8109-1798-9 Subj: Animals. Behavior — stealing. Food. Picture puzzles. Wordless.

Kidslabel. *Spot 7: Christmas* ill. with photos. Chronicle, 2006. ISBN 0-8118-5323-3 Subj: Holidays — Christmas. Picture puzzles.

Spot 7: School ill. with photos. Chronicle, 2006. ISBN 0-8118-5324-1 Subj: Picture puzzles. School.

Kilaka, John. *True friends: a tale from Tanzania* trans. by Shelley Tanaka; ill. by John Kilaka. Groundwood, 2006. ISBN 0-88899-698-5 Subj: Animals — elephants. Animals — rats. Folk & fairy tales. Foreign lands — Tanzania. Friendship.

Kimmel, Eric A. *The frog princess: a Tlingit legend from Alaska* retold by Eric A. Kimmel; ill. by Rosanne Litzinger. Holiday House, 2006. ISBN 0-8234-1618-6 Subj: Folk & fairy tales. Frogs & toads. Indians of North America — Tlingit. Royalty — princesses.

The great Texas hamster drive ill. by Bruce Whatley. Marshall Cavendish, 2007. ISBN 978-0-7614-5357-4 Subj: Animals — hamsters. Tall tales. Texas. U.S. history — frontier & pioneer life.

The lady in the blue cloak: legends from the Texas missions ill. by Susan Guevara. Holiday House, 2006. ISBN 0-8234-1738-7 Subj: Religion. Texas.

Rip Van Winkle's return adapt. & retold by Eric A. Kimmel; ill. by Leonard Everett Fisher. Farrar, Straus & Giroux, 2007. ISBN 978-0-374-36308-6 Subj: Behavior — lost. Folk & fairy tales. Mythical creatures — elves. Sleep.

The three cabritos adapt. by Eric A. Kimmel; ill. by Stephen Gilpin. Marshall Cavendish, 2007. ISBN 978-0-7614-5343-7 Subj: Animals — goats. Character traits — cleverness. Folk & fairy tales. Magic. Monsters. Music. Texas.

Kimmelman, Leslie. *How do I love you?* ill. by Lisa McCue. Harper-Collins, 2005. ISBN 0-06-001200-5 Subj: Counting, numbers. Emotions — love. Family life. Reptiles — alligators, crocodiles. Rhyming text.

Kindermans, Martine. *You and me* by Martine Kindermans & Sasha Quinton; ill. by Martine Kindermans. Penguin, 2006. ISBN 0-399-24471-9 Subj: Birds — geese. Emotions — love. Family life — mothers. Rhyming text.

Kinerk, Robert. *Clorinda takes flight* ill. by Steven Kellogg. Simon & Schuster, 2007. ISBN 978-0-689-86864-1 Subj: Activities — flying. Animals. Animals — bulls, cows. Character traits — perseverance. Rhyming text.

Timothy Cox will not change his socks ill. by Stephen Gammell. Simon & Schuster, 2005. ISBN 0-689-87181-3 Subj: Animals — dogs. Character traits — perseverance. Clothing — socks. Rhyming text. Senses — smell.

King, Stephen Michael. *Mutt dog!* ill. by author. Harcourt, 2005. ISBN 0-15-205561-4 Subj: Animals — dogs. Homeless.

Kinkade, Sheila. *My family* photos by Elaine Little. Charlesbridge, 2006. ISBN 1-57091-662-4 Subj: Family life. Foreign lands.

Kinsey-Warnock, Natalie. *Nora's ark* ill. by Emily Arnold McCully. HarperCollins, 2005. ISBN 0-06-029517-1 Subj: Family life — grandparents. Farms. U.S. history. Weather — floods.

Kirk, David. *Library mouse* ill. by author. Abrams, 2007. ISBN 978-0-8109-9346-4 Subj: Activities — writing. Animals — mice. Books, reading. Careers — authors. Character traits — shyness. Libraries.

Kirwan, Wednesday. *Nobody notices Minerva* ill. by author. Sterling, 2007. ISBN 978-1-4027-4728-1 Subj: Animals — dogs. Behavior — misbehavior. Family life.

Kitamura, Satoshi. *Pablo the artist* ill. by author. Farrar, Straus & Giroux, 2006. ISBN 0-374-35687-4 Subj: Animals — elephants. Art. Careers — artists. Friendship.

Klein, Tali. *Hop! Plop!* (Schwartz, Corey Rosen)

Kleven, Elisa. *The apple doll* ill. by author. Farrar, Straus & Giroux, 2007. ISBN 978-0-374-30380-8 Subj: Activities — making things. Food. School.

The wishing ball ill. by author. Farrar, Straus & Giroux, 2006. ISBN 0-374-38449-5 Subj: Animals — cats. Behavior — wishing. Birds — crows. Reptiles — alligators, crocodiles.

Klinting, Lars. *What do you want?* trans. from Swedish by Maria Lundin; ill. by Lars Klinting. Groundwood, 2006. ISBN 0-88899-636-5 Subj: Behavior — wishing.

Klise, Kate. *Imagine Harry* ill. by M. Sarah Klise. Harcourt, 2007. ISBN 978-0-15-205704-6 Subj: Animals — rabbits. Imagination — imaginary friends.

Why do you cry? Not a sob story ill. by M. Sarah Klise. Henry Holt, 2006. ISBN 0-8050-7319-1 Subj: Animals. Animals — rabbits. Emotions.

Kloske, Geoffrey. *Once upon a time, the end (asleep in 60 seconds)* ill. by Barry Blitt. Simon & Schuster, 2005. ISBN 0-689-86619-4 Subj: Bedtime. Books, reading. Folk & fairy tales.

Knister. *Sophie's dance* trans. from German by Kathryn Bishop; ill. by Mandy Schlunt. Minedition, 2007. ISBN 978-0-698-40056-6 Subj: Activities — dancing. Family life — grandmothers.

Knudsen, Michelle. *Library lion* ill. by Kevin Hawkes. Candlewick, 2006. ISBN 0-7636-2262-1 Subj: Animals — lions. Character traits — helpfulness. Libraries.

A moldy mystery ill. by Barry Gott. Kane, 2006. ISBN 1-57565-167-X Subj: Family life — brothers & sisters. Science.

Koch, Ed. *Eddie's little sister makes a splash* by Ed & Pat Koch; ill. by James Warhola. Penguin, 2007. ISBN 978-0-399-24310-3 Subj: Activities — vacationing. Family life — brothers & sisters. Sports — swimming.

Koch, Pat. *Eddie's little sister makes a splash* (Koch, Ed)

Konnecke, Ole. *Anthony and the girls* ill. by author. Farrar, Straus & Giroux, 2006. ISBN 0-374-30376-2 Subj: Activities — playing. Behavior — indifference. Emotions.

Kono, Erin Eitter. *Hula lullaby* ill. by author. Little, Brown, 2005. ISBN 0-316-73591-4 Subj: Bedtime. Family life — mothers. Hawaii. Lullabies. Rhyming text.

Kontis, Alethea. *Alpha oops! The day Z went first* ill. by Bob Kolar. Candlewick, 2006. ISBN 0-7636-2728-3 Subj: ABC books.

Korchek, Lori. *Adventures of Cow, too* photos by Marshall Taylor. Ten Speed, 2007. ISBN 978-1-58246-189-2 Subj: Animals — bulls, cows. Shopping. Stores. Toys.

Kortepeter, Paul. *Oliver's red toboggan* ill. by Susan Wheeler. Penguin, 2006. ISBN 0-525-47752-7 Subj: Animals — rabbits. Behavior — fighting, arguing. Behavior — sharing. Family life — brothers & sisters. Sports — sledding.

Kosofsky, Chaim. *Much, much better* ill. by Jessica Schiffman. Hachai, 2006. ISBN 978-1-929628-22-3 Subj: Family life. Folk & fairy tales. Foreign lands — Iraq. Jewish culture.

Koster, Gloria. *The peanut-free cafe* ill. by Maryann Cocca-Leffler. Albert Whitman, 2006. ISBN 0-8075-6386-2 Subj: Food. Illness — allergies. School.

Kovacs, Deborah. *Katie Copley* ill. by Jared T. Williams. Godine, 2007. ISBN 978-1-56792-332-2 Subj: Animals — dogs. Animals — service animals. Behavior — lost & found possessions. Hotels.

Kovalski, Maryann. *Omar's Halloween* ill. by author. Fitzhenry & Whiteside, 2006. ISBN 1-55041-559-X Subj: Clothing — costumes. Holidays — Halloween.

Krauss, Ruth. *Bears* ill. by Maurice Sendak. HarperCollins, 2005. ISBN 0-06-075716-7 Subj: Animals — bears. Poetry.

The growing story ill. by Helen Oxenbury. HarperCollins, 2007. ISBN 0-06-024716-9 Subj: Animals — babies. Behavior — growing up. Seasons.

Krebs, Laurie. *Off we go to Mexico: an adventure in the sun* ill. by Christopher Corr. Barefoot, 2006. ISBN 1-905236-40-9 Subj: Activities — traveling. Foreign lands — Mexico. Foreign languages. Rhyming text.

We're riding on a caravan: an adventure on the Silk Road ill. by Helen Cann. Barefoot, 2005. ISBN 1-84148-343-5 Subj: Activities — traveling. Foreign lands — China.

We're sailing down the Nile: a journey through Egypt ill. by Anne Wilson. Barefoot, 2007. ISBN 978-1-84686-040-9 Subj: Activities — traveling. Foreign lands — Egypt. Rhyming text.

We're sailing to Galapagos: a week in the Pacific ill. by Grazia Restelli. Barefoot, 2005. ISBN 978-1-84148-902-5 Subj: Activities — traveling. Animals. Foreign lands — Galapagos Islands. Rhyming text.

Krensky, Stephen. *Big bad wolves at school* ill. by Brad Sneed. Simon & Schuster, 2007. ISBN 978-0-689-38799-9 Subj: Animals — wolves. School.

The crimson comet (Morrissey, Dean)

Hanukkah at Valley Forge ill. by Greg Harlin. Penguin, 2006. ISBN 0-525-47738-1 Subj: Holidays — Hanukkah. U.S. history.

Milo and the really big bunny ill. by Melissa Suber. Simon & Schuster, 2006. ISBN 0-689-87345-X Subj: Animals — rabbits. Character traits — appearance. Holidays — Easter. Weather — storms.

Too many leprechauns: or how that pot o' gold got to the end of the rainbow ill. by Dan Andreasen. Simon & Schuster, 2007. ISBN 978-0-689-85112-4 Subj: Folk & fairy tales. Foreign lands — Ireland. Mythical creatures — leprechauns.

Krieb, Mr. *We're off to find the witch's house* ill. by R. W. Alley. Penguin, 2005. ISBN 0-525-47003-4 Subj: Holidays — Halloween. Rhyming text.

Krishnaswami, Uma. *Bringing Asha home* ill. by Jamel Akib. Lee & Low, 2006. ISBN 1-58430-259-3 Subj: Adoption. Babies. Ethnic groups in the U.S. — East Indian Americans. Family life.

The happiest tree: a yoga story ill. by Ruth Jeyaveeran. Lee & Low, 2005. ISBN 1-58430-237-2 Subj: Ethnic groups in the U.S. — East Indian Americans. Health & fitness. Self-concept.

Remembering Grandpa ill. by Layne Johnson. Boyds Mills, 2007. ISBN 978-1-59078-424-2 Subj: Animals — rabbits. Death. Emotions — grief. Family life — grandparents.

Kroll, Steven. *Jungle bullies* ill. by Vincent Nguyen. Marshall Cavendish, 2006. ISBN 0-7614-5297-4 Subj: Animals. Behavior — bullying. Behavior — sharing. Jungles.

Pooch on the loose: a Christmas adventure ill. by Michael Garland. Marshall Cavendish, 2005. ISBN 0-7614-5239-7 Subj: Animals — dogs. Behavior — lost. Holidays — Christmas.

Kroll, Virginia L. *Cristina keeps a promise* ill. by Enrique O. Sánchez. Albert Whitman, 2006. ISBN 0-8075-1350-4 Subj: Behavior. Character traits — responsibility.

Equal shmequal: a math adventure ill. by Philomena O'Neill. Charlesbridge, 2005. ISBN 1-57091-891-0 Subj: Counting, numbers.

Everybody has a teddy ill. by Sophie Allsopp. Sterling, 2007. ISBN 978-1-4027-3580-6 Subj: Rhyming text. School — nursery. Toys — bears.

Forgiving a friend ill. by Paige Billin-Frye. Albert Whitman, 2005. ISBN 0-8075-0618-4 Subj: Behavior — forgiving. Friendship.

Good citizen Sarah ill. by Nancy Cote. Albert Whitman, 2007. ISBN 978-0-8075-2992-8 Subj: Behavior. Character traits — helpfulness. Weather — snow.

Good neighbor Nicholas ill. by Nancy Cote. Albert Whitman, 2006. ISBN 0-8075-2998-2 Subj: Behavior. Character traits — kindness.

Honest Ashley ill. by Nancy Cote. Albert Whitman, 2006. ISBN 0-8075-3371-8 Subj: Character traits — honesty. Homework.

Jason takes responsibility ill. by Nancy Cote. Albert Whitman, 2005. ISBN 0-8075-2537-5 Subj: Birthdays. Character traits — responsibility. Family life — grandmothers.

Makayla cares about others ill. by Nancy Cote. Albert Whitman, 2007. ISBN 978-0-8075-4945-2 Subj: Character traits — helpfulness. Emotions — fear.

On the way to kindergarten ill. by Elisabeth Schlossberg. Penguin, 2006. ISBN 0-399-24168-X Subj: Animals — bears. Behavior — growing up. Rhyming text. School — first day.

Really rabbits ill. by Philomena O'Neill. Charlesbridge, 2006. ISBN 1-57091-897-X Subj: Animals — rabbits. Character traits — cleanliness. Pets.

Ryan respects ill. by Paige Billin-Frye. Albert Whitman, 2006. ISBN 0-8075-6946-1 Subj: Behavior — bullying. School.

Selvakumar knew better ill. by Xiaojun Li. Shen's, 2006. ISBN 1-88500-829-5 Subj: Animals — dogs. Foreign lands — India. Tsunamis.

The Thanksgiving bowl ill. by Philomena O'Neill. Pelican, 2007. ISBN 978-1-58980-365-7 Subj: Family life — grandmothers. Holidays — Thanksgiving.

Uno, dos, tres, posada! Let's celebrate Christmas ill. by Loretta Lopez. Penguin, 2006. ISBN 0-670-05923-3 Subj: Counting, numbers. Ethnic groups in the U.S. — Hispanic Americans. Holidays — Christmas. Rhyming text.

Kromhout, Rindert. *Little Donkey and the baby-sitter* ill. by Annemarie van Haeringen. NorthSouth, 2006. ISBN 0-7358-2057-0 Subj: Activities — babysitting. Animals — donkeys. Birds — chickens.

Little Donkey and the birthday present trans. from Dutch by Marianne Martens; ill. by Annemarie van Haeringen. NorthSouth, 2007. ISBN 978-0-7358-2132-3 Subj: Animals — donkeys. Animals — yaks. Birthdays. Character traits — generosity. Gifts.

Kropf, Latifa Berry. *It's Shofar time!* ill. by Tod Cohen. Kar-Ben, 2006. ISBN 1-58013-158-1 Subj: Holidays — Rosh Hashanah. Jewish culture. Religion.

Krosoczka, Jarrett J. *Giddy up, Cowgirl* ill. by author. Penguin, 2006. ISBN 0-670-06050-X Subj: Character traits — helpfulness. Family life — daughters. Family life — mothers.

My buddy, Slug ill. by author. Random House, 2006. ISBN 0-375-83342-0 Subj: Animals — slugs. Emotions. Friendship.

Punk Farm ill. by author. Random House, 2005. ISBN 0-375-92429-9 Subj: Animals. Farms. Music.

Punk Farm on tour ill. by author. Random House, 2007. ISBN 978-0-375-83343-4 Subj: Animals. Farms. Songs.

Krull, Kathleen. *Pocahontas: princess of the New World* ill. by David Diaz. Walker & Company, 2007. ISBN 978-0-8027-9555-7 Subj: Indians of North America — Powhatan. U.S. history.

Krupinski, Loretta. *Pirate treasure* ill. by author. Penguin, 2006. ISBN 0-525-47579-6 Subj: Animals — mice. Farms. Pirates. Weather.

Krykorka, Ian. *Carl, the Christmas carp* ill. by Vladyana Krykorka. Orca, 2006. ISBN 1-55143-329-X Subj: Fish. Foreign lands — Czechoslovakia. Holidays — Christmas.

Kubler, Annie. *My first signs* ill. by author. Child's Play, 2005. ISBN 1-904550-39-8 Subj: Language. Sign language.

Kudlinski, Kathleen V. *Boy, were we wrong about dinosaurs!* ill. by S. D. Schindler. Penguin, 2005. ISBN 0-525-46978-8 Subj: Dinosaurs. Science.

The seaside switch ill. by Lindy Burnett. NorthWord, 2007. ISBN 978-1-55971-964-3 Subj: Ecology. Sea & seashore.

The sunset switch ill. by Lindy Burnett. NorthWord, 2005. ISBN 1-55971-916-8 Subj: Animals. Night.

What do roots do? ill. by David Schuppert. NorthWord, 2005. ISBN 1-55971-896-X Subj: Plants.

Kuklin, Susan. *Families* photos by author. Hyperion, 2006. ISBN 0-7868-0822-5 Subj: Emotions — love. Family life.

Kulka, Joe. *Wolf's coming* ill. by author. Carolrhoda, 2007. ISBN 978-1-57505-930-3 Subj: Animals — wolves. Birthdays.

Kumin, Maxine W. *Mites to astodons: a book of animal poems* ill. by Pamela Zagarenski. Houghton Mifflin, 2006. ISBN 0-618-50753-1 Subj: Animals. Poetry.

Kurtz, Jane. *Do kangaroos wear seat belts?* ill. by Jane Manning. Penguin, 2005. ISBN 0-525-47358-0 Subj: Animals. Safety. Zoos.

In the small, small night ill. by Rachel Isadora. HarperCollins, 2005. ISBN 0-06-623813-7 Subj: Activities — storytelling. Bedtime. Character traits — perseverance. Family life — brothers & sisters. Folk & fairy tales. Foreign lands — Ghana. Immigrants.

Kurtz, Kevin. *A day in the salt marsh* ill. by Consie Powell. Sylvan Dell, 2007. ISBN 978-0-976882-35-0 Subj: Ecology. Nature. Rhyming text.

Kuskin, Karla. *Green as a bean* ill. by Melissa Iwai. HarperCollins, 2007. ISBN 978-0-06-075334-4 Subj: Character traits — questioning. Rhyming text.

So, what's it like to be a cat? ill. by Betsy Lewin. Simon & Schuster/Atheneum, 2005. ISBN 0-689-84733-5 Subj: Animals — cats. Rhyming text.

Toots the cat ill. by Lisze Bechtold. Henry Holt, 2005. ISBN 0-8050-6841-4 Subj: Animals — cats. Poetry.

Kutner, Merrily. *The Zombie Nite Cafe* ill. by Ethan Long. Holiday House, 2007. ISBN 978-0-8234-1963-0 Subj: Monsters. Restaurants. Rhyming text.

Kwon, Yoon-duck. *My cat copies me* ill. by author. Kane/Miller, 2007. ISBN 978-1-933605-26-5 Subj: Animals — cats. Imagination. Pets.

Lacombe, Benjamin. *Cherry and Olive* ill. by author. Walker & Company, 2007. ISBN 0-8027-9707-5 Subj: Animals — dogs. Behavior — bullying. Emotions — loneliness.

Lakin, Patricia. *Rainy day* ill. by Scott Nash. Penguin, 2007. ISBN 978-0-8037-3092-2 Subj: Activities — playing. Behavior — boredom. Books, reading. Libraries. Reptiles — alligators, crocodiles. Weather — rain.

LaMarche, Jim. *Up* ill. by author. Chronicle, 2006. ISBN 0-8118-4445-5 Subj: Careers — fishermen. Character traits — smallness. Family life — brothers & sisters. Magic. Self-concept.

Lamb, Albert. *Sam's winter hat* ill. by David McPhail. Scholastic/Cartwheel, 2006. ISBN 0-439-79304-1 Subj: Animals — bears. Behavior — lost & found possessions. Clothing — hats.

Laminack, Lester L. *Jake's 100th day of school* ill. by Judy Love. Peachtree, 2006. ISBN 1-56145-355-2 Subj: Counting, numbers. School.

Snow day! ill. by Adam Gustavson. Peachtree, 2007. ISBN 1-56145-418-4 Subj: Careers — teachers. Seasons — winter. Weather — snow.

Landa, Norbert. *Little Bear and the wishing tree* ill. by Simon Mendez. Good Books, 2007. ISBN 978-1-56148-566-6 Subj: Animals — bears. Behavior — sharing. Behavior — wishing. Emotions — anger. Family life — brothers & sisters. Trees.

Landry, Leo. *Space boy* ill. by author. Houghton Mifflin, 2007. ISBN 978-0-618-60568-2 Subj: Bedtime. Space & space ships.

Landstrom, Lena. *Boo and Baa have company* trans. from Swedish by Joan Sandin; ill. by Olof Landstrom. Farrar, Straus & Giroux, 2006. ISBN 91-29-66546-9 Subj: Animals — sheep. Humorous stories.

A hippo's tale trans. from Swedish by Joan Sandin; ill. by Lena Landstrom. Farrar, Straus & Giroux, 2007. ISBN 978-91-29-66603-8 Subj: Activities — bathing. Animals — hippopotamuses. Animals — monkeys. Foreign lands — Africa.

Langton, Jane. *Saint Francis and the wolf* ill. by Ilse Plume. Godine, 2007. ISBN 978-1-56792-320-9 Subj: Animals — wolves. Folk & fairy tales. Religion.

LaReau, Kara. *Rocko and Spanky have company* ill. by Jenna LaReau. Harcourt, 2006. ISBN 0-15-216618-1 Subj: Animals — monkeys. Multiple births — twins. Toys.

Snowbaby could not sleep ill. by Jim Ishikawa. Little, Brown, 2005. ISBN 0-316-60703-7 Subj: Bedtime. Emotions — loneliness. Snowmen.

Ugly fish ill. by Scott Magoon. Harcourt, 2006. ISBN 0-15-205082-5 Subj: Behavior — bullying. Behavior — sharing. Character traits — appearance. Emotions — loneliness. Fish.

Larios, Julie Hofstrand. *Yellow elephant: a bright bestiary* ill. by Julie Paschkis. Harcourt, 2006. ISBN 0-15-205422-7 Subj: Animals. Concepts — color. Poetry.

LaRochelle, David. *The end* ill. by Richard Egielski. Scholastic, 2007. ISBN 0-439-64011-3 Subj: Folk & fairy tales. Humorous stories. Royalty — princesses.

Larsen, Andrew. *Bella and the bunny* ill. by Kate Endle. Kids Can, 2007. ISBN 978-1-55337-970-6 Subj: Animals — rabbits. Clothing — sweaters. School — nursery.

Lasky, Kathryn. *Pirate Bob* ill. by David Clark. Charlesbridge, 2006. ISBN 1-57091-595-4 Subj: Behavior — greed. Pirates.

Tumble bunnies ill. by Marylin Hafner. Candlewick, 2005. ISBN 0-7636-2265-6 Subj: Animals — rabbits. Sports — gymnastics. Sportsmanship.

Latifah, Queen. *Queen of the scene* ill. by Frank Morrison. HarperCollins, 2006. ISBN 0-06-077857-1 Subj: Character traits — confidence. Ethnic groups in the U.S. — African Americans. Rhyming text. Self-concept.

Law, Diane. *Come out and play: count around the world in five languages* ill. by author. NorthSouth, 2006. ISBN 0-7358-2060-0 Subj: Counting, numbers. Foreign languages.

Lawler, Janet. *A father's song* ill. by Lucy Corvino. Sterling, 2006. ISBN 1-4027-2501-9 Subj: Activities — playing. Emotions — love. Family life — fathers. Rhyming text.

Layne, Deborah Dover. *T is for teachers: a school alphabet* (Layne, Steven L.)

Layne, Steven L. *Love the baby* ill. by Ard Hoyt. Pelican, 2007. ISBN 978-1-58980-392-3 Subj: Animals — rabbits. Babies. Emotions — envy, jealousy. Family life — new sibling.

T is for teachers: a school alphabet by Steven L. & Deborah Dover Layne; ill. by Doris Ettlinger. Sleeping Bear, 2005. ISBN 1-58536-159-3 Subj: ABC books. Careers — teachers. School.

Lear, Edward. *The owl and the pussycat* ill. by Anne Mortimer. HarperCollins, 2006. ISBN 0-06-027229-5 Subj: Animals — cats. Birds — owls. Poetry.

The Quangle Wangle's hat ill. by Louise Voce. Candlewick, 2005. ISBN 0-7636-1289-8 Subj: Clothing — hats. Humorous stories. Poetry.

Lears, Laurie. *Megan's birthday tree: a story about open adoption* ill. by Bill Farnsworth. Albert Whitman, 2005. ISBN 978-0-8075-5036-6 Subj: Adoption. Birthdays. Family life. Moving. Trees.

Nathan's wish: a story about cerebral palsy ill. by Stacey Schuett. Albert Whitman, 2005. ISBN 0-8075-7101-6 Subj: Birds — owls. Handicaps — cerebral palsy.

Lee, Huy Voun. *In the leaves* ill. by author. Henry Holt, 2005. ISBN 0-8050-6764-7 Subj: Farms. Foreign languages. Seasons — fall.

Lee, Milly. *Landed* ill. by Yangsook Choi. Farrar, Straus & Giroux, 2006. ISBN 978-0-374-34314-9 Subj: Ethnic groups in the U.S. — Chinese Americans. Immigrants.

Lee, Spike. *Please, puppy, please* by Spike & Tonya Lewis Lee; ill. by Kadir Nelson. Simon & Schuster, 2005. ISBN 0-689-86804-9 Subj: Animals — dogs. Ethnic groups in the U.S. — African Americans. Pets.

Lee, Tae-Jun. *Waiting for Mama: a bilingual picture book* trans. from Korean by Eun Hee Chin; ill. by Dong-Seong Kim. NorthSouth, 2007. ISBN 978-0-7358-2143-9 Subj: Family life — mothers. Foreign lands — Korea. Language.

Lee, Tonya Lewis. *Please, puppy, please* (Lee, Spike)

Lee-Tai, Amy. *A place where sunflowers grow / Sabaku ni saita himawari* ill. by Felicia Hoshino. Children's Book Press, 2006. ISBN 0-89239-215-0 Subj: Art. Ethnic groups in the U.S. — Japanese Americans. Flowers. Foreign languages. U.S. history. War.

Leedy, Loreen. *The edible pyramid: good eating every day* ill. by author. rev. ed. Holiday House, 2007. ISBN 978-0-8234-2074-2 Subj: Food. Health & fitness.

The great graph contest ill. by author. Holiday House, 2005. ISBN 0-8234-1710-7 Subj: Animals — snails. Contests. Counting, numbers. Frogs & toads. Reptiles — lizards.

It's probably penny ill. by author. Henry Holt, 2007. ISBN 978-0-8050-7389-8 Subj: Animals — dogs.

Lehman, Barbara. *Museum trip* ill. by author. Houghton Mifflin, 2006. ISBN 0-618-58125-1 Subj: Imagination. Museums. Wordless.

Rainstorm ill. by author. Houghton Mifflin, 2007. ISBN 978-0-618-75639-1 Subj: Imagination. Weather — rain. Wordless.

Lendler, Ian. *An undone fairy tale* ill. by Whitney Martin. Simon & Schuster, 2005. ISBN 0-689-86677-1 Subj: Folk & fairy tales. Food. Humorous stories. Royalty — princesses.

Le Neouanic, Lionel. *Little smudge* ill. by author. Boxer, 2006. ISBN 1-905417-22-5 Subj: Character traits — being different. Concepts — shape. Emotions — loneliness. Friendship.

Leonetti, Mike. *Gretzky's game* ill. by Greg Banning. Raincoast, 2006. ISBN 1-55192-851-5 Subj: Sports — hockey.

Lessac, Frané. *Island Counting 123* ill. by author. Candlewick, 2005. ISBN 0-7636-1960-4 Subj: Counting, numbers. Foreign lands — Caribbean Islands. Rhyming text.

Lester, Helen. *Batter up Wombat* ill. by Lynn Munsinger. Houghton Mifflin, 2006. ISBN 0-618-73784-7 Subj: Animals — wombats. Sports — baseball. Weather — tornadoes.

The sheep in wolf's clothing ill. by Lynn Munsinger. Houghton Mifflin, 2007. ISBN 978-0-618-86844-5 Subj: Animals — sheep. Animals — wolves. Clothing. Disguises.

Tacky and the Winter Games ill. by Lynn Munsinger. Houghton Mifflin, 2005. ISBN 0-618-55659-1 Subj: Birds — penguins. Seasons — winter. Sports.

Let it shine: three favorite spirituals ill. by Ashley Bryan. Simon & Schuster/Atheneum, 2007. ISBN 978-0-689-84732-5 Subj: Religion. Songs.

Leuck, Laura. *I love my pirate papa* ill. by Kyle M. Stone. Harcourt, 2007. ISBN 978-0-15-205664-3 Subj: Family life — fathers. Pirates. Rhyming text.

Levert, Mireille. *Eddie Longpants* ill. by author. Groundwood, 2005. ISBN 0-88899-671-3 Subj: Behavior — bullying. Character traits — being different.

Levine, Abby. *This is the matzah* ill. by Paige Billin-Frye. Albert Whitman, 2005. ISBN 0-8075-7885-1 Subj: Holidays — Passover. Holidays — Seder. Jewish culture. Rhyming text.

Levine, Ellen. *Henry's freedom box* ill. by Kadir Nelson. Scholastic, 2007. ISBN 978-0-439-77733-9 Subj: Caldecott award honor books. Character traits — freedom. Ethnic groups in the U.S. — African Americans. Slavery. U.S. history.

Levy, Janice. *Celebrate! It's cinco de mayo! / Celebremos! Es el cinco de mayo!* trans. from Spanish by Miguel Arisa; ill. by Loretta Lopez. Albert Whitman, 2007. ISBN 978-0-8075-1176-3 Subj: Foreign lands — Mexico. Foreign languages. Holidays — Cinco de Mayo.

Lewin, Ted. *At Gleason's gym* ill. by author. Macmillan, 2007. ISBN 978-1-59643-231-4 Subj: Sports — boxing.

How much? Visiting markets around the world ill. by author. HarperCollins, 2006. ISBN 0-688-17553-8 Subj: Stores. World.

Lewis, J. Patrick. *Big is big and little little: a book of contrasts* ill. by Bob Barner. Holiday House, 2007. ISBN 978-0-8234-1909-8 Subj: Concepts — opposites. Language. Rhyming text.

Tulip at the bat ill. by Amiko Hirao. Little, Brown, 2007. ISBN 978-0-316-61280-7 Subj: Animals. Humorous stories. Rhyming text. Sports — baseball.

Lewis, Kevin. *Dinosaur dinosaur* ill. by Daniel Kirk. Scholastic/Orchard, 2006. ISBN 0-439-60371-4 Subj: Dinosaurs. Rhyming text.

Lewis, Kim. *Hooray for Harry* ill. by author. Candlewick, 2006. ISBN 0-7636-2962-6 Subj: Animals — elephants. Behavior — lost & found possessions. Friendship. Sleep. Toys.

A puppy for Annie ill. by author. Candlewick, 2006. ISBN 0-7636-3200-7 Subj: Animals — dogs. Pets.

Lewis, Paeony. *No more cookies!* ill. by Brita Granström. Scholastic/Chicken House, 2005. ISBN 0-439-68332-7 Subj: Food. Toys.

Lewis, Rose A. *Every year on your birthday* ill. by Jane Dyer. Little, Brown, 2007. ISBN 978-0-316-52552-7 Subj: Adoption. Birthdays. Ethnic groups in the U.S. — Chinese Americans.

Lewison, Wendy Cheyette. *Two is for twins* ill. by Hiroe Nakata. Penguin, 2006. ISBN 0-670-06128-X Subj: Counting, numbers. Multiple births — twins. Rhyming text.

Liao, Jimmy. *The sound of colors: a journey of the imagination* ill. by author. Little, Brown, 2005. ISBN 0-316-93992-7 Subj: Handicaps — blindness. Imagination.

Lichtenheld, Tom. *What's with this room?* ill. by author. Little, Brown, 2005. ISBN 0-316-59286-2 Subj: Behavior — messy. Character traits — cleanliness. Humorous stories.

Lies, Brian. *Bats at the beach* ill. by author. Houghton Mifflin, 2006. ISBN 0-618-55744-X Subj: Activities — picnicking. Animals — bats. Rhyming text. Sea & seashore — beaches.

Lillegard, Dee. *Balloons, balloons, balloons* ill. by Bernadette Pons. Penguin, 2007. ISBN 978-0-525-45940-8 Subj: Animals — rabbits. Rhyming text. Toys — balloons.

Go! Poetry in motion: poems ill. by Valeri Gorbachev. Random House, 2006. ISBN 0-375-92387-X Subj: Concepts — motion. Poetry. Transportation.

Lin, Grace. *Lissy's friends* ill. by author. Penguin, 2007. ISBN 978-0-670-06072-6 Subj: Activities — making things. Character traits — shyness. Friendship. School.

Olvina swims ill. by author. Henry Holt, 2007. ISBN 978-0-8050-7661-5 Subj: Birds — chickens. Birds — penguins. Emotions — fear. Hawaii. Sports — swimming.

Our seasons by Grace Lin & Ranida T. McKneally; ill. by Grace Lin. Charlesbridge, 2006. ISBN 1-57091-360-9 Subj: Seasons.

The red thread: an adoption fairy tale ill. by author. Albert Whitman, 2007. ISBN 978-0-8075-6922-1 Subj: Adoption. Folk & fairy tales. Foreign lands — China. Royalty.

Robert's snowflakes: artists' snowflakes for cancer's cure comp. by Grace Lin & Robert Mercer; ill. by various. Penguin, 2005. ISBN 0-670-06044-5 Subj: Art. Illness — cancer. Poetry. Weather — snow.

Lindbergh, Reeve. My little grandmother often forgets ill. by Kathryn Brown. Candlewick, 2007. ISBN 978-0-7636-1989-3 Subj: Behavior — forgetfulness. Family life — grandmothers. Memories, memory. Old age.

Lindenbaum, Pija. Mini Mia and her darling uncle trans. from Swedish by Elisabeth Kallick Dyssegaard; ill. by Pija Lindenbaum. R&S Books, 2007. ISBN 978-91-29-66734-9 Subj: Emotions — envy, jealousy. Family life — aunts, uncles.

Lipton, Leonard. Puff, the magic dragon (Yarrow, Peter)

Lithgow, John. Mahalia Mouse goes to college ill. by Igor Oleynikov. Simon & Schuster, 2007. ISBN 978-1-4169-2715-0 Subj: Animals — mice. Rhyming text. School.

The little red hen. The little red hen retold & ill. by Jerry Pinkney. Penguin, 2006. ISBN 0-8037-2935-9 Subj: Activities — baking, cooking. Animals. Behavior — sharing. Birds — chickens. Character traits — laziness. Cumulative tales. Farms. Folk & fairy tales. Plants.

The little red hen: an old fable retold by Heather Forest; ill. by Susan Gaber. August House, 2006. ISBN 0-87483-795-2 Subj: Activities — baking, cooking. Animals. Behavior — sharing. Birds — chickens. Character traits — laziness. Cumulative tales. Folk & fairy tales. Plants. Rhyming text.

Littlesugar, Amy. Clown child ill. by Kimberly Bulcken Root. Penguin, 2006. ISBN 0-399-23106-4 Subj: Circus. Clowns, jesters.

Livingston, Irene. Finklehopper Frog cheers ill. by Brian Lies. Ten Speed, 2005. ISBN 1-58246-138-4 Subj: Activities — picnicking. Animals — rabbits. Friendship. Frogs & toads. Rhyming text.

Livingston, Myra Cohn. Calendar ill. by Will Hillenbrand. Holiday House, 2007. ISBN 978-0-8234-1725-4 Subj: Calendars. Days of the week, months of the year. Poetry. Seasons.

Ljungkvist, Laura. Follow the line ill. by author. Penguin, 2006. ISBN 0-670-06049-6 Subj: Counting, numbers. Imagination. Picture puzzles.

Follow the line through the house ill. by author. Penguin, 2007. ISBN 978-0-670-06225-6 Subj: Homes, houses. Imagination. Picture puzzles. Rhyming text.

Lloyd, Sam. Mr. Pusskins: a love story ill. by author. Simon & Schuster, 2006. ISBN 1-4169-2517-1 Subj: Animals — cats. Behavior — running away.

Lloyd-Jones, Sally. How to be a baby — by me, the big sister ill. by Sue Heap. Random House, 2007. ISBN 978-0-375-83843-9 Subj: Babies. Family life — brothers & sisters.

Time to say goodnight ill. by Jane Chapman. HarperCollins, 2006. ISBN 0-06-054328-0 Subj: Animals. Bedtime. Rhyming text.

Lobel, Anita. Animal antics: A to Z ill. by author. HarperCollins, 2005. ISBN 0-06-051815-4 Subj: ABC books. Animals. Circus.

Nini here and there ill. by author. HarperCollins, 2007. ISBN 978-0-06-078767-7 Subj: Animals — cats. Moving.

Lobel, Gillian. Little Honey Bear and the smiley moon ill. by Tim Warnes. Good Books, 2006. ISBN 1-56148-533-0 Subj: Animals.

Animals — bears. Behavior — lost. Family life — mothers. Moon. Seasons — winter.

Too small for honey cake ill. by Sebastien Braun. Harcourt, 2006. ISBN 0-15-206097-9 Subj: Animals — foxes. Babies. Family life. Sibling rivalry.

London, Jonathan. Do your ABC's, Little Brown Bear ill. by Margie Moore. Penguin, 2005. ISBN 0-525-47360-2 Subj: ABC books. Animals — bears. Family life — fathers.

Froggy plays T-ball ill. by Frank Remkiewicz. Penguin, 2007. ISBN 978-0-670-06187-7 Subj: Frogs & toads. Sports — T-ball.

Froggy rides a bike ill. by Frank Remkiewicz. Penguin, 2006. ISBN 0-670-06099-2 Subj: Frogs & toads. Sports — bicycling.

My big rig ill. by Viviana Garofoli. Marshall Cavendish, 2007. ISBN 978-0-7614-5346-8 Subj: Imagination. Toys. Transportation. Trucks.

Sled dogs run ill. by Jonathan Van Zyle. Walker & Company, 2005. ISBN 0-8027-8958-7 Subj: Alaska. Animals — dogs. Sports — racing. Sports — sledding.

A train goes clickety-clack ill. by Denis Roche. Henry Holt, 2007. ISBN 978-0-8050-7972-2 Subj: Noise, sounds. Rhyming text. Trains.

A truck goes rattley-bumpa ill. by Denis Roche. Henry Holt, 2005. ISBN 0-8050-7233-0 Subj: Noise, sounds. Rhyming text. Trucks.

Long, Kathy. The runaway shopping cart ill. by Susan Estelle Kwas. Penguin, 2007. ISBN 978-0-525-47187-5 Subj: Behavior — running away. Cumulative tales. Shopping.

Long, Melinda. Pirates don't change diapers ill. by David Shannon. Harcourt, 2007. ISBN 978-0-15-205353-6 Subj: Pirates.

Look, Lenore. Uncle Peter's amazing Chinese wedding ill. by Yumi Heo. Simon & Schuster/Atheneum, 2006. ISBN 978-0-689-84458-4 Subj: Ethnic groups in the U.S. — Chinese Americans. Family life — aunts, uncles. Weddings.

Loomis, Christine. The best Father's Day present ever ill. by Pam Paparone. Penguin, 2007. ISBN 978-0-399-24253-3 Subj: Animals — snails. Family life — fathers. Holidays — Father's Day.

Hattie hippo ill. by Robert Neubecker. Scholastic/Orchard, 2006. ISBN 978-0-439-54340-8 Subj: Animals — hippopotamuses.

Lorbiecki, Marybeth. Jackie's bat ill. by J. Brian Pinkney. Simon & Schuster, 2006. ISBN 0-689-84102-7 Subj: Ethnic groups in the U.S. — African Americans. Prejudice. Sports — baseball.

Lord, Janet. Here comes Grandma! ill. by Julie Paschkis. Henry Holt, 2005. ISBN 0-8050-7666-2 Subj: Family life — grandmothers. Transportation.

Louis, Catherine. Liu and the bird: a journey in Chinese calligraphy trans. from French by Sybille Kazeroid; ill. by Catherine Louis. NorthSouth, 2006. ISBN 0-7358-2050-3 Subj: Activities — traveling. Activities — writing. Foreign lands — China.

Louise, Tina. When I grow up ill. by Oliver Corwin. Abrams, 2007. ISBN 978-0-8109-3948-6 Subj: Animals. Behavior — growing up.

Loupy, Christophe. Wiggles ill. by Eve Tharlet. NorthSouth, 2005. ISBN 0-7358-1981-5 Subj: Animals — dogs. Character traits — curiosity. Farms.

Love, Pamela. A moose's morning ill. by Lesia Sochor. Down East, 2007. ISBN 978-0-89272-733-9 Subj: Animals — moose.

Lowell, Susan. Josefina javelina: a hairy tale ill. by Bruce MacPherson. Rising Moon, 2005. ISBN 0-8735-8790-1 Subj: Animals — coyotes. Animals — pigs. Ballet.

Lubner, Susan. Noises at night (Glass, Beth Raisner)

Ruthie Bon Bair, do not go to bed with wringing wet hair! ill. by Bruce Whatley. Abrams, 2006. ISBN 0-8109-5470-2 Subj: Behavior — bad day. Hair. Humorous stories. Rhyming text.

Lucas, David. *Nutmeg* ill. by author. Random House, 2006. ISBN 0-375-93519-3 Subj: Imagination. Magic. Mythical creatures — genies.

Whale ill. by author. Random House, 2007. ISBN 978-0-375-84338-9 Subj: Animals — whales. Tsunamis.

Lujan, Jorge. *Sky blue accident / Accidente celeste* trans. from Spanish by Elisa Amado; ill. by Piet Grobler. Groundwood, 2007. ISBN 978-0-88899-805-7 Subj: Accidents. Foreign languages. Sky.

Lund, Deb. *All aboard the dinotrain* ill. by Howard Fine. Harcourt, 2006. ISBN 0-15-205237-2 Subj: Dinosaurs. Rhyming text. Trains.

Lunde, Darrin. *Hello, bumblebee bat* ill. by Patricia J. Wynne. Charlesbridge, 2007. ISBN 978-1-57091-374-7 Subj: Animals — bats. Animals — endangered animals. Science.

Meet the meerkat ill. by Patricia J. Wynne. Charlesbridge, 2007. ISBN 978-1-58089-110-3 Subj: Animals — meerkats.

Lundin, Maria. *What do you want?* (Klinting, Lars)

Lunge-Larsen, Lise. *Noah's mittens: the story of felt* ill. by Matthew Trueman. Houghton Mifflin, 2006. ISBN 0-618-32950-1 Subj: Animals — sheep. Clothing. Religion — Noah.

Luthardt, Kevin. *You're weird!* ill. by author. Penguin, 2005. ISBN 0-8037-2986-3 Subj: Animals — rabbits. Behavior — name calling. Friendship. Reptiles — turtles, tortoises.

Lyon, George Ella. *No dessert forever!* ill. by Peter Catalanotto. Simon & Schuster, 2006. ISBN 1-4169-0385-2 Subj: Behavior — fighting, arguing. Emotions — anger. Family life.

Trucks roll! ill. by Craig Frazier. Simon & Schuster/Atheneum, 2007. ISBN 978-1-4169-2435-7 Subj: Rhyming text. Trucks.

Lyons, Kelly Starling. *One million men and me* ill. by Peter Ambush. Just Us, 2007. ISBN 978-1-933491-07-3 Subj: Ethnic groups in the U.S. — African Americans. U.S. history.

Maass, Robert. *Little trucks with big jobs* photos by author. Henry Holt, 2007. ISBN 978-0-8050-7748-3 Subj: Trucks.

McAlister, Caroline. *Holy Molé! A folktale from Mexico* ill. by Stefan Czernecki. August House, 2007. ISBN 978-0-87483-775-9 Subj: Activities — baking, cooking. Folk & fairy tales. Food. Foreign lands — Mexico.

McAllister, Angela. *Found you, Little Wombat!* ill. by Charles Fuge. Sterling, 2004. ISBN 1-4027-1599-4 Subj: Animals — wombats. Behavior — lost.

Mama and Little Joe ill. by Terry Milne. Simon & Schuster, 2007. ISBN 978-1-4169-1631-4 Subj: Animals — kangaroos. Behavior — lost. Emotions — love. Toys.

Take a kiss to school ill. by Sue Hellard. Bloomsbury, 2006. ISBN 1-58234-702-6 Subj: Animals — moles. Kissing. School.

Trust me, Mom! ill. by Ross Collins. Bloomsbury, 2005. ISBN 1-58234-955-X Subj: Character traits — resourcefulness. Emotions — fear. Family life — mothers. Monsters. Shopping.

McBratney, Sam. *Yes we can!* ill. by Charles Fuge. HarperCollins, 2007. ISBN 978-0-06-121515-5 Subj: Animals — kangaroos. Behavior — bullying. Character traits — individuality. Friendship.

McCarthy, Conor Clarke. *Just add one Chinese sister* (McMahon, Patricia)

McCarthy, Mary. *A closer look* ill. by author. HarperCollins, 2007. ISBN 978-0-06-124073-7 Subj: Concepts. Nature. Senses — sight.

McCarthy, Meghan. *City hawk: the story of pale male* ill. by author. Simon & Schuster, 2007. ISBN 978-1-4169-3359-5 Subj: Birds — hawks.

McCarty, Peter. *Fabian escapes* ill. by author. Henry Holt, 2007. ISBN 978-0-8050-7713-1 Subj: Animals — cats. Animals — dogs.

Moon plane ill. by author. Henry Holt, 2006. ISBN 0-8050-7943-2 Subj: Activities — flying. Airplanes, airports. Imagination. Moon.

McCaughrean, Geraldine. *Father and son: a nativity story* ill. by Fabian Negrin. Hyperion, 2006. ISBN 1-4231-0344-0 Subj: Family life — fathers. Holidays — Christmas. Religion — Nativity.

McClements, George. *Ridin' dinos with Buck Bronco* ill. by author. Harcourt, 2007. ISBN 978-0-15-205989-7 Subj: Cowboys, cowgirls. Dinosaurs.

McClintock, Barbara. *Adele and Simon* ill. by author. Farrar, Straus & Giroux, 2006. ISBN 0-374-38044-9 Subj: Behavior — lost & found possessions. Family life — brothers & sisters. Foreign lands — France.

Cinderella (Perrault, Charles)

McCourt, Lisa. *Happy Halloween, Stinky Face* ill. by Cyd Moore. Scholastic, 2007. ISBN 978-0-439-77977-7 Subj: Family life — mothers. Holidays — Halloween. Imagination.

McCully, Emily Arnold. *Marvelous Mattie: how Margaret E. Knight became an inventor* ill. by author. Farrar, Straus & Giroux, 2006. ISBN 0-374-34810-3 Subj: Careers — scientists. Inventions. Problem solving.

School ill. by author. HarperCollins, 2005. ISBN 0-06-623856-0 Subj: Animals — mice. School.

McDaniels, Preston. *A perfect snowman* ill. by author. Simon & Schuster, 2007. ISBN 978-1-4169-1026-8 Subj: Behavior — sharing. Seasons — winter. Snowmen.

MacDonald, Alan. *Wilfred to the rescue: stories from Brambly Hedge* ill. by Lizzie Sanders. Simon & Schuster/Atheneum, 2006. ISBN 1-4169-0901-X Subj: Animals. Animals — mice. Behavior — lost. Foreign lands — England. Weather — floods.

MacDonald, Margaret Read. *Conejito: a folktale from Panama* ill. by Geraldo Vaério. August House, 2006. ISBN 0-87483-779-0 Subj: Animals — rabbits. Behavior — trickery. Folk & fairy tales. Foreign lands — Panama. Foreign languages.

The great smelly, slobbery small-toothed dog ill. by Julie Paschkis. Random House, 2007. ISBN 0-87483-808-8 Subj: Animals — dogs. Character traits — appearance. Emotions — love. Folk & fairy tales. Magic.

A hen, a chick, and a string guitar retold by Margaret Read MacDonald; ill. by Sophie Fatus. Barefoot, 2005. ISBN 1-84148-796-1 Subj: Animals. Counting, numbers. Cumulative tales. Folk & fairy tales. Songs.

Little Rooster's diamond button retold by Margaret Read MacDonald; ill. by Will Terry. Albert Whitman, 2007. ISBN 978-0-8075-4644-4 Subj: Behavior — greed. Birds — chickens. Clothing. Folk & fairy tales. Foreign lands — Hungary. Royalty — kings.

The squeaky door ill. by Mary Newell DePalma. HarperCollins, 2006. ISBN 978-0-06-028373-5 Subj: Animals. Bedtime. Cumulative tales. Emotions — fear. Family life — grandmothers. Folk & fairy tales. Noise, sounds.

Teeny Weeny Bop ill. by Diane Greenseid. Albert Whitman, 2006. ISBN 0-8075-7992-0 Subj: Cumulative tales. Folk & fairy tales.

Tunjur! Tunjur! Tunjur! A Palestinian folktale retold by Margaret Read MacDonald; ill. by Alik Arzoumanian. Marshall Cavendish, 2006. ISBN 0-7614-5225-7 Subj: Behavior — stealing. Folk & fairy tales. Foreign lands — Palestine.

McDonald, Megan. *Ant and Honey Bee, what a pair!* ill. by G. Brian Karas. Candlewick, 2005. ISBN 0-7636-1265-0 Subj: Clothing — costumes. Insects — ants. Insects — bees. Parties.

Beetle McGrady eats bugs! ill. by Jane Manning. HarperCollins, 2005. ISBN 0-06-001355-9 Subj: Character traits — bravery. Food. Insects. School.

When the library lights go out ill. by Katherine Tillotson. Simon & Schuster, 2005. ISBN 0-689-86170-2 Subj: Animals. Behavior — lost. Libraries. Light, lights. Puppets.

McDonald, Rae A. *A fishing surprise* ill. by Kathleen Kemly. North-Word, 2007. ISBN 978-1-55971-977-3 Subj: Family life — brothers & sisters. Food. Rhyming text. Sports — fishing.

MacDonald, Ross. *Bad baby* ill. by author. Macmillan, 2005. ISBN 1-59643-064-8 Subj: Babies. Concepts — size. Family life — brothers & sisters. Family life — new sibling.

MacDonald, Suse. *Edward Lear's A was once an apple pie* adapt. & ill. by Suse MacDonald. Scholastic/Orchard, 2005. ISBN 0-439-66056-4 Subj: ABC books. Poetry.

Fish, swish! Splash, dash! Counting round and round ill. by author. Simon & Schuster, 2007. ISBN 978-1-4169-3605-3 Subj: Counting, numbers. Fish. Format, unusual.

McDonnell, Patrick. *Art* ill. by author. Little, Brown, 2006. ISBN 0-316-11491-X Subj: Activities — drawing. Art. Rhyming text.

The gift of nothing ill. by author. Little, Brown, 2005. ISBN 0-316-11488-X Subj: Animals — cats. Animals — dogs. Friendship. Gifts.

Just like Heaven ill. by author. Little, Brown, 2006. ISBN 0-316-11493-6 Subj: Animals — cats. Animals — dogs. Weather — fog.

McDonough, Yona Zeldis. *Hammerin' Hank: the life of Hank Greenberg* ill. by Malcah Zeldis. Walker & Company, 2006. ISBN 0-8027-8997-8 Subj: Ethnic groups in the U.S. — Jewish Americans. Sports — baseball.

McElligott, Matthew. *Backbeard and the birthday suit: the hairiest pirate who ever lived* ill. by author. Walker & Company, 2006. ISBN 0-8027-8065-2 Subj: Birthdays. Character traits — cleanliness. Clothing. Hair. Parties. Pirates.

Bean thirteen ill. by author. Penguin, 2007. ISBN 978-0-399-24535-0 Subj: Counting, numbers. Insects.

McElmurry, Jill. *I'm not a baby!* ill. by author. Random House, 2006. ISBN 0-375-93614-9 Subj: Babies. Behavior — growing up. Humorous stories.

McElroy, Lisa Tucker. *Love, Lizzie: letters to a military mom* ill. by Diane Paterson. Albert Whitman, 2005. ISBN 0-8075-4777-8 Subj: Careers — military. Emotions — loneliness. Family life — mothers. Letters, cards. War.

McFarland, Lyn Rossiter. *Mouse went out to get a snack* ill. by Jim McFarland. Farrar, Straus & Giroux, 2005. ISBN 0-374-37672-7 Subj: Animals — mice. Counting, numbers. Food.

McG, Shane. *Tennis, anyone?* ill. by author. Carolrhoda, 2007. ISBN 978-0-8225-6901-5 Subj: Sports — tennis.

McGee, Marni. *Winston the book wolf* ill. by Ian Beck. Walker & Company, 2006. ISBN 0-8027-9569-2 Subj: Animals — wolves. Books, reading. Libraries.

McGhee, Alison. *Someday* ill. by Peter H. Reynolds. Simon & Schuster/Atheneum, 2006. ISBN 978-1-4169-2811-9 Subj: Behavior — growing up. Family life — mothers.

A very brave witch ill. by Harry Bliss. Simon & Schuster, 2006. ISBN 0-689-86730-1 Subj: Character traits — bravery. Holidays — Halloween. Witches.

McGinty, Alice B. *Eliza's kindergarten surprise* ill. by Nancy Speir. Marshall Cavendish, 2007. ISBN 978-0-7614-5351-2 Subj: Behavior — collecting things. Family life — mothers. School — first day.

Thank you, world ill. by Wendy Anderson Halperin. Penguin, 2007. ISBN 978-0-8037-2705-2 Subj: Rhyming text. World.

McGrath, Barbara Barbieri. *The little green witch* ill. by Martha Alexander. Charlesbridge, 2005. ISBN 1-58089-042-3 Subj: Character traits — laziness. Plants. Witches.

McGrory, Anik. *Kidogo* ill. by author. Bloomsbury, 2005. ISBN 1-58234-974-6 Subj: Animals — elephants. Character traits — smallness. Concepts — size. Foreign lands — Africa.

McGuirk, Leslie. *Tucker's spooky Halloween* ill. by author. Candlewick, 2007. ISBN 978-0-7636-3181-9 Subj: Animals — dogs. Clothing — costumes. Holidays — Halloween.

McHenry, E. B. *Has anyone seen Winnie and Jean?* ill. by author. Bloomsbury, 2007. ISBN 978-1-58234-999-2 Subj: Animals — dogs. Behavior — lost. Behavior — running away.

Mackall, Dandi Daley. *Seeing stars* ill. by Claudine Gevry. Simon & Schuster/Little Simon, 2006. ISBN 1-4169-0361-5 Subj: Stars.

McKenna, Sharon. *Good morning, sunshine: a grandpa story* ill. by author. Red Cygnet, 2007. ISBN 1-60108-003-4 Subj: Family life — grandfathers.

McKinlay, Penny. *Flabby Tabby* ill. by Britta Teckentrup. Frances Lincoln, 2006. ISBN 1-84507-090-9 Subj: Animals — cats. Health & fitness — exercise.

McKissack, Patricia C. *The all-I'll-ever-want Christmas doll* ill. by Jerry Pinkney. Random House, 2007. ISBN 978-0-375-93759-0 Subj: Behavior — sharing. Family life — brothers & sisters. Holidays — Christmas. Toys — dolls. U.S. history.

Precious and the Boo Hag by Patricia C. McKissack & Onawumi Jean Moss; ill. by Kyrsten Brooker. Simon & Schuster/Atheneum, 2005. ISBN 0-689-85194-4 Subj: Character traits — bravery. Ethnic groups in the U.S. — African Americans. Illness. Monsters.

McKneally, Ranida T. *Our seasons* (Lin, Grace)

McKy, Katie. *Pumpkin town! (Or, nothing is better and worse than pumpkins)* ill. by Pablo Bernasconi. Houghton Mifflin, 2006. ISBN 0-618-60569-X Subj: Family life — brothers & sisters. Plants.

MacLachlan, Patricia. *Fiona loves the night* by Patricia MacLachlan & Emily MacLachlan Charest; ill. by Amanda Shepherd. HarperCollins, 2007. ISBN 978-0-06-057031-6 Subj: Nature. Night.

MacLennan, Cathy. *Chicky Chicky Chook Chook* ill. by author. Sterling, 2007. ISBN 978-1-905417-40-7 Subj: Activities — playing. Animals. Rhyming text. Weather.

McLeod, Bob. *Super hero ABC* ill. by author. HarperCollins, 2006. ISBN 0-06-074514-2 Subj: ABC books.

McLimans, David. *Gone wild* ill. by author. Walker & Company, 2006. ISBN 0-8027-9563-3 Subj: ABC books. Animals — endangered animals. Caldecott award honor books.

McMahon, Patricia. *Just add one Chinese sister* by Patricia McMahon & Conor Clarke McCarthy; ill. by Karen A. Jerome. Boyds Mills, 2005. ISBN 1-56397-989-6 Subj: Adoption. Ethnic groups in the U.S. — Chinese Americans.

McMillan, Bruce. *How the ladies stopped the wind* ill. by Gunnella. Houghton Mifflin, 2007. ISBN 978-0-618-77330-5 Subj: Behavior — resourcefulness. Foreign lands — Iceland. Weather — wind.

The problem with chickens ill. by Gunnella. Houghton Mifflin, 2005. ISBN 0-618-58581-8 Subj: Behavior — resourcefulness. Birds — chickens. Character traits — cleverness. Foreign lands — Iceland.

McMullan, Kate. *I'm dirty!* ill. by Jim McMullan. HarperCollins, 2006. ISBN 0-06-009294-7 Subj: Careers — construction workers. Counting, numbers. Trucks.

McNamara, Margaret. *Fall leaf project* ill. by Mike Gordon. Simon & Schuster, 2006. ISBN 1-4169-1538-9 Subj: Nature. Seasons — fall.

How many seeds in a pumpkin? ill. by G. Brian Karas. Random House, 2007. ISBN 978-0-375-84014-2 Subj: Counting, numbers. Food. Science.

McNamara, Richard. *Suho's white horse: a Mongolian legend* (Otsuka, Yuzo)

McNaughton, Colin. *Captain Abdul's little treasure* ill. by author. Candlewick, 2006. ISBN 0-7636-3045-4 Subj: Babies. Pirates.

Once upon an ordinary school day ill. by Satoshi Kitamura. Farrar, Straus & Giroux, 2005. ISBN 0-374-35634-3 Subj: Careers — teachers. School.

When I grow up ill. by author. Candlewick, 2005. ISBN 0-7636-2675-9 Subj: Careers. Rhyming text. School. Theater.

McNulty, Faith. *If you decide to go to the moon* ill. by Steven Kellogg. Scholastic, 2005. ISBN 0-590-48359-5 Subj: Moon. Space & space ships.

McPhail, David. *Big Brown Bear goes to town* ill. by author. Harcourt, 2006. ISBN 978-1-4156-7142-9 Subj: Animals — bears. Animals — rats. Friendship.

Big Brown Bear's birthday surprise ill. by author. Harcourt, 2007. ISBN 0-15-206098-5 Subj: Animals — bears. Animals — rats. Birthdays. Friendship.

Boy on the brink ill. by author. Henry Holt, 2006. ISBN 0-8050-7618-2 Subj: Dreams. Imagination.

Emma in charge ill. by author. Penguin, 2005. ISBN 0-525-47411-0 Subj: Activities — playing. Animals — bears. Imagination. Toys — dolls.

Sylvie and True ill. by author. Farrar, Straus & Giroux, 2007. ISBN 978-0-374-37364-1 Subj: Animals — rabbits. Friendship. Reptiles — snakes.

Water boy ill. by author. Abrams, 2007. ISBN 978-0-8109-1784-2 Subj: Emotions — fear. Magic. Water.

McQuinn, Anna. *Lola at the library* ill. by Rosalind Beardshaw. Charlesbridge, 2006. ISBN 1-58089-113-6 Subj: Books, reading. Ethnic groups in the U.S. — African Americans. Libraries.

Madison, Alan. *The littlest grape stomper* ill. by Giselle Potter. Random House, 2007. ISBN 978-0-375-83675-6 Subj: Anatomy — toes. Food. Tall tales.

Pecorino plays ball ill. by AnnaLaura Cantone. Simon & Schuster/Atheneum, 2006. ISBN 0-689-86522-8 Subj: Humorous stories. Sports — baseball.

Pecorino's first concert ill. by AnnaLaura Cantone. Simon & Schuster, 2005. ISBN 0-689-85952-X Subj: Humorous stories. Music. Musical instruments.

Velma Gratch and the way cool butterfly ill. by Kevin Hawkes. Random House, 2007. ISBN 978-0-375-83597-1 Subj: Insects — butterflies, caterpillars. Migration. School.

Magoon, Scott. *Hugo and Miles in I've painted everything!* ill. by author. Houghton Mifflin, 2007. ISBN 978-0-618-64638-8 Subj: Animals — dogs. Animals — elephants. Art. Foreign lands — France.

Mahoney, Daniel J. *A really good snowman* ill. by author. Houghton Mifflin, 2005. ISBN 0-618-47554-0 Subj: Animals — bears. Character traits — helpfulness. Contests. Family life — brothers & sisters. Snowmen. Weather — snow.

Mahy, Margaret. *Down the back of the chair* ill. by Polly Dunbar. Houghton Mifflin, 2006. ISBN 0-618-69395-5 Subj: Behavior — lost & found possessions. Furniture — chairs. Poverty. Rhyming text.

Major, Kevin. *Aunt Olga's Christmas postcards* ill. by Bruce Roberts. Groundwood, 2005. ISBN 0-88899-593-8 Subj: Behavior — collecting things. Family life — aunts, uncles. Holidays — Christmas. Letters, cards.

Makhijani, Pooja. *Mama's saris* ill. by Elena Gomez. Little, Brown, 2007. ISBN 0-316-01105-3 Subj: Clothing. Ethnic groups in the U.S. — East Indian Americans. Family life — daughters. Family life — mothers.

Mallat, Kathy. *Papa pride* ill. by author. Walker & Company, 2005. ISBN 0-8027-8964-1 Subj: Animals — wolves. Family life — fathers. Rhyming text.

Mammano, Julie. *Rhinos who rescue* ill. by author. Chronicle, 2007. ISBN 978-0-8118-5419-1 Subj: Animals — rhinoceros. Careers — firefighters.

Manning, Mick. *Cock-a-doodle hooooooo!* ill. by Brita Granström. Good Books, 2007. ISBN 978-1-56148-568-0 Subj: Birds — chickens. Birds — owls. Character traits — helpfulness. Farms.

Dino-dinners ill. by Brita Granström. Holiday House, 2007. ISBN 978-0-8234-2089-6 Subj: Dinosaurs.

Snap! by Mick Manning & Brita Granström; ill. by authors. Frances Lincoln, 2006. ISBN 1-84507-408-4 Subj: Food. Science.

Manuel, Lynn. *The trouble with Tilly Trumble* ill. by Diane Greenseid. Abrams, 2006. ISBN 0-8109-5972-0 Subj: Animals — dogs. Behavior — collecting things. Furniture — chairs.

Manushkin, Fran. *How Mama brought the spring* ill. by Holly Berry. Penguin, 2007. ISBN 978-0-525-42027-9 Subj: Activities — baking, cooking. Family life — mothers. Food. Foreign lands — Belarus. Seasons — winter.

Let George do it! (Foreman, George)

The shivers in the fridge ill. by Paul O. Zelinsky. Penguin, 2006. ISBN 0-525-46943-5 Subj: Imagination.

Many, Paul. *Dad's bald head* ill. by Kevin O'Malley. Walker & Company, 2007. ISBN 978-0-8027-9579-3 Subj: Family life — fathers. Hair.

Manzano, Sonia. *A box full of kittens* ill. by Matt Phelan. Simon & Schuster/Atheneum, 2007. ISBN 978-0-689-83089-1 Subj: Animals — cats. Babies. Character traits — helpfulness. Ethnic groups in the U.S. — Puerto Rican Americans.

Marcus, Leonard S. *Oscar: the big adventures of a little sock monkey* (Schwartz, Amy)

Marino, Gianna. *Zoopa: an animal alphabet* ill. by author. Chronicle, 2005. ISBN 0-8118-4789-6 Subj: ABC books. Animals. Food.

Markes, Julie. *Shhhhh! Everybody's sleeping* ill. by David Parkins. HarperCollins, 2005. ISBN 0-06-053791-4 Subj: Bedtime. Rhyming text. Sleep.

Markham, Beryl. *The good lion* ill. by Don Brown. Houghton Mifflin, 2005. ISBN 0-618-56306-7 Subj: Animals — lions. Foreign lands — Africa.

Markle, Sandra. *Little lost bat* ill. by Alan Marks. Charlesbridge, 2006. ISBN 1-57091-656-X Subj: Animals — bats. Nature.

A mother's journey ill. by Alan Marks. Charlesbridge, 2005. ISBN 1-57091-621-7 Subj: Birds — penguins. Family life.

Marks, Jennifer L. *Sorting by size* ill. with photos. Capstone, 2006. ISBN 978-0-7368-6740-5 Subj: Concepts — size.

Sorting money ill. with photos. Capstone, 2006. ISBN 978-0-7368-6738-2 Subj: Money.

Sorting toys ill. with photos. Capstone, 2006. ISBN 978-0-7368-6737-5 Subj: Toys.

Martens, Marianne. *Duck's tale* (Straaten, Harmen van)

I can dress myself! (Müller, Birte)

Little Donkey and the birthday present (Kromhout, Rindert)

The old red tractor (Dierssen, Andreas)

A tale of two brothers (Hasler, Eveline)

Who stole my house? (Veit, Barbara)

Martin, Bill, Jr. (William Ivan). *Baby bear, baby bear, what do you see?* ill. by Eric Carle. Henry Holt, 2007. ISBN 978-0-8050-8336-1 Subj: Animals. Animals — bears. Cumulative tales. Rhyming text.

"Fire! Fire!" Said Mrs. McGuire ill. by Vladimir Radunsky. Harcourt, 2006. ISBN 0-15-205725-0 Subj: Birthdays. Careers — firefighters. Fire. Nursery rhymes.

I love our Earth by Bill Martin & Michael R. Sampson; ill. by Dan Lipow. Charlesbridge, 2006. ISBN 1-58089-106-3 Subj: Earth. Nature. Seasons.

Martin, David. *All for pie, pie for all* ill. by Valeri Gorbachev. Candlewick, 2006. ISBN 0-7636-2393-8 Subj: Activities — baking, cooking. Animals — cats. Animals — mice. Behavior — sharing. Food. Insects — ants.

Martin, Jacqueline Briggs. *Banjo granny* (Busse, Sarah Martin)

Chicken joy on Redbean Road: a bayou country romp ill. by Melissa Sweet. Houghton Mifflin, 2007. ISBN 978-0-618-50759-7 Subj: Activities — singing. Birds — chickens. Farms. Food. Illness. Music.

Martin, Leslie. *I'd really like to eat a child* (Donnio, Sylviane)

Martín, Hugo C. *Pablo's Christmas* ill. by Lee Chapman. Sterling, 2006. ISBN 1-4027-2560-4 Subj: Activities — wood carving. Family life. Farms. Foreign lands — Mexico. Holidays — Christmas.

Marzollo, Jean. *I spy treasure hunt: a book of picture riddles* (Wick, Walter)

Little Bear, you're a star! A Greek myth about the constellations retold & ill. by Jean Marzollo. Little, Brown, 2005. ISBN 0-316-74135-3 Subj: Animals — bears. Stars.

Masurel, Claire. *Domino* ill. by David Walker. Candlewick, 2007. ISBN 978-0-7636-2862-8 Subj: Animals — dogs. Character traits — smallness.

Matthews, Tina. *Out of the egg* ill. by author. Houghton Mifflin, 2007. ISBN 978-0-618-73741-3 Subj: Birds — chickens. Folk & fairy tales.

Mauner, Claudia. *Zoe Sophia in New York: the mystery of the Pink Phoenix papers* by Claudia Mauner & Elisa Smalley; ill. by Claudia Mauner. Chronicle, 2006. ISBN 0-8118-4877-9 Subj: Family life. Museums. Mystery stories.

Mayer, Mercer. *The bravest knight* ill. by author. Penguin, 2007. ISBN 978-0-8037-3206-3 Subj: Imagination. Knights. Monsters. Mythical creatures. Mythical creatures — trolls.

The little drummer mouse: a Christmas story ill. by author. Penguin, 2006. ISBN 0-8037-3147-7 Subj: Animals — mice. Holidays — Christmas. Music. Musical instruments — drums. Religion — Nativity.

There are monsters everywhere ill. by author. Penguin, 2005. ISBN 0-8037-0621-9 Subj: Emotions — fear. Monsters. Sports — karate.

Mayer, Pamela. *The Grandma cure* ill. by John Nez. Penguin, 2005. ISBN 0-525-47559-1 Subj: Behavior — fighting, arguing. Family life — grandmothers. Illness — cold (disease).

Mayhew, James. *The knight who took all day* ill. by author. Scholastic/Chicken House, 2005. ISBN 0-439-74829-1 Subj: Dragons. Knights.

Mayo, Margaret. *Choo choo clickety-clack!* ill. by Alex Ayliffe. Carolrhoda, 2005. ISBN 1-57505-819-7 Subj: Noise, sounds. Transportation.

Roar! ill. by Alex Ayliffe. Carolrhoda, 2007. ISBN 978-0-7613-9473-0 Subj: Animals.

Mayr, Diane. *Run, Turkey, run* ill. by Laura Rader. Walker & Company, 2007. ISBN 978-0-8027-9630-1 Subj: Behavior — hiding. Birds — turkeys. Holidays — Thanksgiving.

Mazer, Norma Fox. *Has anyone seen my Emily Greene?* ill. by Christine Davenier. Candlewick, 2007. ISBN 978-0-7636-1384-6 Subj: Behavior — hiding. Family life — fathers. Rhyming text.

Meade, Holly. *Inside, inside, inside* ill. by author. Marshall Cavendish, 2005. ISBN 0-7614-5125-0 Subj: Family life — brothers & sisters. Games.

John Willy and Freddy McGee ill. by author. Marshall Cavendish, 2007. ISBN 978-0-7614-5363-5 Subj: Animals — guinea pigs. Format, unusual — board books.

Meddaugh, Susan. *Just Teenie* ill. by author. Houghton Mifflin, 2006. ISBN 0-618-68565-0 Subj: Character traits — appearance. Concepts — size. Plants.

The witch's walking stick ill. by author. Houghton Mifflin, 2005. ISBN 0-618-52948-9 Subj: Behavior — wishing. Magic. Witches.

Medina, Sarah. *Sad* ill. by Jo Brooker. Heinemann, 2007. ISBN 978-1-4034-9293-7 Subj: Emotions — sadness.

Melling, David. *Good knight sleep tight* ill. by author. Barron's, 2006. ISBN 0-7641-5878-3 Subj: Knights. Royalty — princesses.

The Scallywags ill. by author. Barron's, 2006. ISBN 978-0-7641-5991-6 Subj: Animals — wolves. Etiquette. Humorous stories.

Melmed, Laura Krauss. *New York, New York! The Big Apple from A to Z* ill. by Frané Lessac. HarperCollins, 2005. ISBN 0-06-054876-2 Subj: ABC books. Cities, towns.

Meltzer, Amy. *A mezuzah on the door* ill. by Janice Fried. Kar-Ben, 2007. ISBN 978-1-58013-249-7 Subj: Jewish culture. Moving.

Menchin, Scott. *Taking a bath with the dog and other things that make me happy* ill. by author. Candlewick, 2007. ISBN 978-0-7636-2919-9 Subj: Character traits — questioning. Emotions — happiness.

Meng, Cece. *The wonderful thing about hiccups* ill. by Janet Pedersen. Houghton Mifflin, 2007. ISBN 978-0-618-59544-0 Subj: Animals — hippopotamuses. Family life — brothers & sisters. Hiccups. Libraries.

Mercer, Robert. *Robert's snowflakes: artists' snowflakes for cancer's cure* (Lin, Grace)

Merz, Jennifer J. *Playground day* ill. by author. Houghton Mifflin, 2007. ISBN 978-0-618-81696-5 Subj: Activities — playing. Animals. Behavior — imitation. Imagination. Rhyming text.

Meserve, Adria. *No room for Napoleon* ill. by author. Farrar, Straus & Giroux, 2006. ISBN 0-374-35536-3 Subj: Animals — dogs. Behavior — sharing. Character traits — selfishness. Friendship. Homes, houses.

Meserve, Jessica. *Small sister* ill. by author. Houghton Mifflin, 2007. ISBN 978-0-618-77658-0 Subj: Character traits — smallness. Family life — brothers & sisters. Self-concept.

Messinger, Carla. *When the shadbush blooms* by Carla Messinger & Susan Katz; ill. by David Kanietakeron Fadden. Ten Speed, 2007. ISBN 978-1-58246-192-2 Subj: Family life. Indians of North America — Lenape. Seasons. U.S. history.

The Metropolitan Museum of Art, NY. *Museum shapes.* Little, Brown, 2005. ISBN 0-316-05698-7 Subj: Art. Concepts — shape. Museums.

Metz, Lorijo. *Floridius Bloom and the planet of Gloom* ill. by Matt Phelan. Penguin, 2007. ISBN 978-0-8037-3084-7 Subj: Behavior — greed. Friendship. Monsters.

Meunier, Brian. *Bravo, Tavo!* ill. by Perky Edgerton. Penguin, 2007. ISBN 978-0-525-47478-4 Subj: Clothing — shoes. Foreign lands — Mexico. Sports — basketball. Weather — droughts.

Meyers, Susan. *Kittens! Kittens! Kittens!* ill. by David Walker. Abrams, 2007. ISBN 978-0-8109-1218-2 Subj: Animals — cats. Rhyming text.

Puppies! Puppies! Puppies! ill. by David Walker. Abrams, 2005. ISBN 978-0-8109-5856-2 Subj: Animals — dogs. Rhyming text.

This is the way a baby rides ill. by Hiroe Nakata. Abrams, 2005. ISBN 0-8109-5763-9 Subj: Animals. Babies. Behavior — imitation. Rhyming text.

Michaels, Pat. *W is for wind: a weather alphabet* ill. by Melanie Rose. Sleeping Bear, 2005. ISBN 1-58536-237-9 Subj: ABC books. Weather.

Michelin, Linda (Donald B.). *Zuzu's wishing cake* ill. by D. B. Johnson. Houghton Mifflin, 2006. ISBN 0-618-64640-X Subj: Activities — making things. Behavior — wishing. Food. Friendship. Moving.

Michelson, Richard. *Across the alley* ill. by E. B. Lewis. Penguin, 2006. ISBN 0-399-23970-7 Subj: Ethnic groups in the U.S. — African Americans. Friendship. Jewish culture. Music. Prejudice. Sports — baseball.

Oh no, not ghosts! ill. by Adam McCauley. Harcourt, 2006. ISBN 0-15-205186-4 Subj: Emotions — fear. Family life — brothers & sisters. Rhyming text.

Middleton, Jesse Edgar. *The Huron carol* (Brebeuf, Jean de)

Miles, Victoria. *Old mother bear* ill. by Molly Bang. Chronicle, 2007. ISBN 978-0-8118-5033-9 Subj: Animals — bears. Foreign lands — Canada. Nature.

Milgrim, David. *Another day in the Milky Way* ill. by author. Penguin, 2007. ISBN 0-399-24548-0 Subj: Dreams. Space & space ships.

Time to get up, time to go ill. by author. Houghton Mifflin, 2006. ISBN 0-618-51998-X Subj: Activities — playing. Gender roles. Toys — dolls.

Young MacDonald ill. by author. Penguin, 2006. ISBN 0-525-47570-2 Subj: Animals. Careers — inventors. Farms. Inventions. Music. Songs.

Miller, Marisa. *Let's try horseback riding* (Hammerle, Susa)

Miller, Pat. *Substitute groundhog* ill. by Kathi Ember. Albert Whitman, 2006. ISBN 0-8075-7643-3 Subj: Animals. Animals — groundhogs. Holidays — Groundhog Day. Illness.

Mills, Claudia. *Ziggy's blue-ribbon day* ill. by R. W. Alley. Farrar, Straus & Giroux, 2005. ISBN 0-374-32352-6 Subj: Activities — drawing. School. Self-concept. Sports.

Mills, Lauren A. *Thumbelina* (Andersen, H. C. (Hans Christian))

Milord, Susan. *Love that baby* ill. by author. Houghton Mifflin, 2005. ISBN 0-618-56323-7 Subj: Babies. Emotions — love.

Minor, Florence. *Christmas tree!* (Minor, Wendell)

Minor, Wendell. *Christmas tree!* by Wendell & Florence Minor; ill. by authors. HarperCollins, 2005. ISBN 0-06-056035-5 Subj: Holidays — Christmas. Rhyming text. Trees.

Yankee Doodle America: the spirit of 1776 from A to Z ill. by author. Penguin, 2006. ISBN 0-399-24003-9 Subj: ABC books. U.S. history.

Miranda, Anne. *To market, to market* ill. by Janet Stevens. Harcourt, 2007. ISBN 978-0-15-205903-3 Subj: Animals. Humorous stories. Shopping.

Mitchard, Jacquelyn. *Ready, set, school!* ill. by Paul Ratz de Tagyos. HarperCollins, 2007. ISBN 978-0-06-050766-4 Subj: Animals — raccoons. Family life — parents. School — first day. Sleepovers.

Mitchell, Stephen. *The tinderbox* (Andersen, H. C. (Hans Christian))

Mitchell, Susan K. *The rainforest grew all around* ill. by Connie McLennan. Random House, 2007. ISBN 978-0-976882-36-7 Subj: Animals. Jungles. Plants. Songs.

Mitton, Tony. *All afloat on Noah's boat!* ill. by Guy Parker-Rees. Scholastic/Orchard, 2007. ISBN 978-0-439-87397-0 Subj: Animals. Boats, ships. Religion — Noah. Rhyming text.

Cool cars ill. by Ant Parker. Houghton Mifflin, 2005. ISBN 0-7534-5802-0 Subj: Automobiles. Rhyming text. Transportation.

Playful little penguins ill. by Guy Parker-Rees. Walker & Company, 2007. ISBN 978-0-8027-9710-0 Subj: Animals — seals. Behavior — lost. Birds — penguins. Rhyming text.

Miura, Taro. *Tools* ill. by author. Chronicle, 2006. ISBN 0-8118-5519-8 Subj: Tools.

Mizzoni, Chris. *Clancy with the puck* ill. by author. Raincoast, 2007. ISBN 978-1-55192-804-3 Subj: Rhyming text. Sports — hockey.

Mobin-Uddin, Asma. *The best Eid holiday ever* ill. by Laura Jacobsen. Boyds Mills, 2007. ISBN 978-1-59078-431-0 Subj: Holidays. Religion — Islam.

Mochizuki, Ken. *Be water, my friend: the early years of Bruce Lee* ill. by Dom Lee. Lee & Low, 2006. ISBN 1-58430-265-8 Subj: Ethnic groups in the U.S. — Chinese Americans. Sports.

Mockford, Caroline. *Cleo's color book* by Caroline Mockford & Stella Blackstone; ill. by Caroline Mockford. Barefoot, 2006. ISBN 1-905236-30-1 Subj: Animals — cats. Concepts — color. Rhyming text.

Modarressi, Mitra. *Stay awake, Sally* ill. by author. Penguin, 2007. ISBN 978-0-399-24545-9 Subj: Animals — raccoons. Bedtime. Family life — parents. Rhyming text.

Modesitt, Jeanne. *Little Mouse's happy birthday* ill. by Robin Spowart. Boyds Mills, 2007. ISBN 978-1-59078-272-9 Subj: Animals — mice. Birthdays. Family life.

Montanari, Eva. *My first . . .* ill. by author. Houghton Mifflin, 2007. ISBN 978-0-618-64644-9 Subj: Books, reading. Gifts. Toys — dolls.

A very full morning ill. by author. Houghton Mifflin, 2006. ISBN 0-618-56318-0 Subj: Animals — rabbits. Behavior — worrying. Careers — teachers. School — first day.

Montes, Marissa. *Los gatos black on Halloween* ill. by Yuyi Morales. Henry Holt, 2006. ISBN 0-8050-7429-5 Subj: Animals — cats. Foreign languages. Holidays — Day of the Dead. Holidays — Halloween. Monsters. Rhyming text.

Montserrat, Pep. *Ms. Rubinstein's beauty* ill. by author. Sterling, 2006. ISBN 1-4027-3063-2 Subj: Character traits — appearance. Character traits — individuality. Circus.

Moore, Clement Clarke. *A creature was stirring: one boy's night before Christmas* by Clement Clarke Moore & Carter Goodrich; ill. by Carter Goodrich. Simon & Schuster, 2006. ISBN 0-689-86399-3 Subj: Holidays — Christmas. Poetry. Santa Claus.

The night before Christmas ill. by Lisbeth Zwerger. Penguin, 2005. ISBN 0-698-40030-5 Subj: Holidays — Christmas. Poetry. Santa Claus.

The night before Christmas ill. by Richard Jesse Watson. Harper-Collins, 2006. ISBN 0-06-075742-6 Subj: Holidays — Christmas. Poetry. Santa Claus.

The night before Christmas ill. by Will Moses. Penguin, 2006. ISBN 0-399-23745-3 Subj: Holidays — Christmas. Poetry. Santa Claus.

The night before Christmas ill. by Gennady Spirin. Marshall Cavendish, 2006. ISBN 0-7614-5298-2 Subj: Holidays — Christmas. Poetry. Santa Claus.

Moore, Julianne. *Freckleface Strawberry* ill. by LeUyen Pham. Bloomsbury, 2007. ISBN 978-1-59990-107-7 Subj: Anatomy. Friendship. Self-concept.

Moore, Lilian. *Beware, take care: fun and spooky poems* ill. by Howard Fine. Henry Holt, 2006. ISBN 0-8050-6917-8 Subj: Dragons. Emotions — fear. Ghosts. Monsters. Poetry.

Moore, Mary-Alice. *The wheels on the school bus* ill. by Laura Huliska-Beith. HarperCollins, 2006. ISBN 0-06-059427-6 Subj: Buses. Music. School. Songs.

Moore, Patrick. *The mighty street sweeper* ill. by author. Henry Holt, 2006. ISBN 0-8050-7789-8 Subj: Trucks.

Moore-Mallinos, Jennifer. *It's ok to be me! Just like you, I can do almost anything!* ill. by Marta Fabrega. Barron's, 2007. ISBN 978-0-7641-3584-2 Subj: Handicaps — physical handicaps.

When my parents forgot how to be friends ill. by Marta Fabrega. Barron's, 2005. ISBN 0-7641-3172-9 Subj: Divorce. Family life.

Mora, Pat. *Doña Flor: a tall tale about a giant woman with a great big heart* ill. by Raúl Colón. Random House, 2005. ISBN 0-679-98002-4 Subj: Animals — cougars. Giants. Tall tales.

Marimba! Animales from A to Z ill. by Doug Cushman. Houghton Mifflin, 2006. ISBN 0-618-19453-3 Subj: ABC books. Animals. Foreign languages. Parties. Rhyming text. Zoos.

The song of Francis and the animals ill. by David Frampton. Eerdmans, 2005. ISBN 0-8028-5253-X Subj: Animals. Character traits — kindness to animals. Religion.

Yum! Mmmm! Que rico! Americas' sproutings ill. by Rafael López. Lee & Low, 2007. ISBN 978-1-58430-271-1 Subj: Food. Language. Poetry.

Morales, Yuyi. *Little night* ill. by author. Macmillan, 2007. ISBN 978-1-59643-088-4 Subj: Bedtime. Night.

Morgan, Michaela. *Bunny wishes* ill. by Caroline Jayne Church. Scholastic, 2007. ISBN 978-0-439-91812-1 Subj: Animals — mice. Animals — rabbits. Behavior — wishing. Friendship. Seasons — winter.

Dear bunny: a bunny love story ill. by Caroline Jayne Church. Scholastic/Chicken House, 2006. ISBN 0-439-74833-X Subj: Activities — writing. Animals — mice. Animals — rabbits. Character traits — shyness. Emotions — love. Friendship.

Morison, Toby. *Little Louie takes off* ill. by author. Walker & Company, 2007. ISBN 978-0-8027-9645-5 Subj: Activities — flying. Birds — penguins. Emotions — loneliness.

Moroney, Trace. *When I'm feeling angry* ill. by author. School Specialty/Gingham Dog, 2006. ISBN 0-7696-4424-4 Subj: Animals — rabbits. Emotions — anger.

When I'm feeling happy ill. by author. School Specialty/Gingham Dog, 2006. ISBN 0-7696-4425-2 Subj: Animals — rabbits. Emotions — happiness.

When I'm feeling sad ill. by author. School Specialty/Gingham Dog, 2006. ISBN 0-7696-4426-0 Subj: Animals — rabbits. Emotions — sadness.

When I'm feeling scared ill. by author. School Specialty/Gingham Dog, 2006. ISBN 0-7696-4427-9 Subj: Animals — rabbits. Emotions — fear.

Morpurgo, Michael. *On angel wings* ill. by Quentin Blake. Candlewick, 2007. ISBN 978-0-7636-3466-7 Subj: Angels. Holidays — Christmas. Religion — Nativity.

Morris, Carla. *The boy who was raised by librarians* ill. by Brad Sneed. Peachtree, 2007. ISBN 978-1-56145-391-7 Subj: Books, reading. Careers — librarians. Libraries.

Morris, Jennifer E. *May I please have a cookie?* ill. by author. Scholastic, 2005. ISBN 0-439-73819-9 Subj: Etiquette. Food. Reptiles — alligators, crocodiles.

Morrison, Gordon. *A drop of water* ill. by author. Houghton Mifflin, 2006. ISBN 0-618-58557-5 Subj: Science. Water.

Morrissey, Dean. *The crimson comet* by Dean Morrissey & Stephen Krensky; ill. by Dean Morrissey. HarperCollins, 2006. ISBN 0-06-008070-1 Subj: Bedtime. Family life — brothers & sisters. Moon. Space & space ships.

Morrow, Tara Jaye. *Panda goes to school* ill. by Aaron Boyd. Sterling, 2007. ISBN 978-1-4027-4313-9 Subj: Animals — pandas. Family life — mothers. School — first day.

Mortensen, Denise Dowling. *Ohio thunder* ill. by Kate Kiesler. Houghton Mifflin, 2006. ISBN 0-618-59542-2 Subj: Farms. Weather — lightning, thunder. Weather — storms.

Wake up engines ill. by Melissa Iwai. Houghton Mifflin, 2007. ISBN 978-0-618-51736-7 Subj: Morning. Rhyming text. Transportation.

Morton-Shaw, Christine. *Wake up, sleepy bear!* by Christine Morton-Shaw & Greg Shaw; ill. by John Butler. Penguin, 2006. ISBN 0-670-06175-1 Subj: Animals — babies. Rhyming text.

Moser, Lisa. *Watermelon wishes* ill. by Stacey Schuett. Houghton Mifflin, 2006. ISBN 0-618-56433-0 Subj: Behavior — wishing. Family life — grandfathers. Food.

Moses, Will. *Hansel and Gretel: a retelling from the original tale by the Brothers Grimm* (Grimm, Jacob)

Moss, Miriam. *Bare bear* ill. by Mary McQuillan. Holiday House, 2005. ISBN 0-8234-1934-7 Subj: Animals — bears. Behavior — lost & found possessions. Clothing. Rhyming text.

This is the oasis ill. by Adrienne Kennaway. Kane/Miller, 2005. ISBN 1-929132-76-X Subj: Desert. Foreign lands — Africa.

Moss, Onawumi Jean. *Precious and the Boo Hag* (McKissack, Patricia C.)

Mother Goose. *Little Miss Muffet* adapt. & ill. by Tracey Campbell Pearson. Farrar, Straus & Giroux, 2005. ISBN 0-374-30862-4 Subj: Format, unusual — board books. Nursery rhymes. Spiders.

Mother Goose numbers on the loose adapt. by Leo Dillon; by Diane Dillon. Harcourt, 2007. ISBN 978-0-15-205676-6 Subj: Counting, numbers. Nursery rhymes.

Pat-a-cake adapt. by R. A. Herman; ill. by Olga & Aleksey Ivanov. Handprint, 2005. ISBN 1-59354-039-6 Subj: Activities — baking, cooking. Format, unusual — board books. Games. Nursery rhymes.

Mozelle, Shirley. *The bear upstairs* ill. by Doug Cushman. Henry Holt, 2005. ISBN 0-8050-6820-1 Subj: Activities — baking, cooking. Animals — bears. Noise, sounds.

The kitchen talks ill. by Petra Mathers. Henry Holt, 2006. ISBN 0-8050-7143-1 Subj: Food. Homes, houses. Poetry.

Müller, Birte. *I can dress myself!* trans. from German by Marianne Martens; ill. by Birte Müller. NorthSouth, 2007. ISBN 978-0-7358-2128-6 Subj: Animals — rabbits. Clothing.

Munro, Roxie. *Amazement Park* ill. by author. Chronicle, 2005. ISBN 978-0-8118-4581-6 Subj: Picture puzzles.

Circus ill. by author. Chronicle, 2006. ISBN 0-8118-5209-1 Subj: Circus. Format, unusual — toy & movable books. Picture puzzles. Rhyming text.

Mazeways: A to Z ill. by author. Sterling, 2007. ISBN 978-1-4027-3774-9 Subj: Picture puzzles.

Rodeo ill. by author. Bright Sky, 2007. ISBN 978-1-933979-03-8 Subj: Rodeos.

Muntean, Michaela. *Do not open this book!* ill. by Pascal LeMaitre. Scholastic, 2006. ISBN 0-439-66037-4 Subj: Activities — writing. Animals — pigs. Books, reading. Humorous stories.

Murphy, Christopher J. *Lucille lost: a true adventure* (George, Margaret)

Murphy, Jill. *Mr. Large in charge* ill. by author. Candlewick, 2007. ISBN 978-0-7636-3504-6 Subj: Animals — elephants. Family life — fathers. Illness.

Murphy, Jim. *Fergus and the Night-Demon: an Irish ghost story* ill. by John Manders. Houghton Mifflin, 2006. ISBN 0-618-33955-8 Subj: Character traits — laziness. Emotions — fear. Foreign lands — Ireland. Ghosts.

Murphy, Liz. *ABC doctor: staying healthy from A to Z* ill. by author. Blue Apple, 2007. ISBN 978-1-59354-593-2 Subj: ABC books. Careers — doctors. Health & fitness.

Murphy, Mary. *Panda Foo and the new friend* ill. by author. Candlewick, 2007. ISBN 978-0-7636-3405-6 Subj: Activities — picnicking. Animals — pandas. Friendship.

Murphy, Stuart J. *It's about time!* ill. by John Speirs. HarperCollins, 2005. ISBN 0-06-055768-0 Subj: Clocks, watches. Day. Night. Time.

Jack the builder ill. by Michael Rex. HarperCollins, 2006. ISBN 0-06-055775-3 Subj: Counting, numbers. Imagination.

Leaping lizards ill. by JoAnn Adinolfi. HarperCollins, 2005. ISBN 0-06-000130-5 Subj: Counting, numbers. Reptiles — lizards.

Mall mania ill. by Renée Andriani. HarperCollins, 2006. ISBN 0-06-055776-1 Subj: Counting, numbers. Stores.

Polly's pen pal ill. by Remy Simard. HarperCollins, 2005. ISBN 0-06-053168-1 Subj: Concepts — measurement. Pen pals.

Rodeo time ill. by David T. Wenzel. HarperCollins, 2006. ISBN 0-06-055778-8 Subj: Rodeos. Time.

Same old horse ill. by Steve Bjorkman. HarperCollins, 2005. ISBN 0-06-055770-2 Subj: Animals — horses, ponies. Character traits — persistence. Counting, numbers. Rhyming text.

Murphy, Yannick. *Ahwoooooooo!* ill. by Claudio Muñoz. Houghton Mifflin, 2006. ISBN 0-618-11762-8 Subj: Animals — wolves. Family life — grandfathers. Noise, sounds.

Muth, Jon J. *Zen shorts* ill. by author. Scholastic, 2005. ISBN 0-439-33911-1 Subj: Activities — storytelling. Animals — pandas. Caldecott award honor books. Family life — brothers & sisters. Folk & fairy tales.

Myngheer, Charise. *Mark's messy room* (Elschner, Geraldine)

Max's magic seeds (Elschner, Geraldine)

Miko goes on vacation (Weninger, Brigitte)

Nadimi, Suzan. *The rich man and the parrot* ill. by Ande Cook. Albert Whitman, 2007. ISBN 978-0-8075-5059-5 Subj: Behavior — trickery. Birds — parrots. Character traits — freedom. Folk & fairy tales. Foreign lands — Persia.

Napoli, Donna Jo. *Bobby the bold* by Donna Jo Napoli & Eva Furrow; ill. by Ard Hoyt. Penguin, 2006. ISBN 0-8037-2990-1 Subj: Animals — bonobos. Animals — chimpanzees. Character traits — appearance. Character traits — being different. Hair. Zoos.

The wishing club: a story about fractions ill. by Anna Currey. Henry Holt, 2007. ISBN 978-0-8050-7665-3 Subj: Behavior — wishing. Counting, numbers. Family life — brothers & sisters.

Näslund, Gorel Kristina. *Our apple tree* ill. by Kristina Digman. Macmillan, 2005. ISBN 1-59643-052-4 Subj: Food. Seasons. Trees.

Nazoa, Aquiles. *A small Nativity* trans. by Hugh Hazelton; ill. by Ana Palmero Caceres. Groundwood, 2007. ISBN 0-88899-839-2 Subj: Foreign lands — Venezuela. Holidays — Christmas. Religion — Nativity.

Neitzel, Shirley. *Who will I be? A Halloween rebus story* ill. by Nancy Winslow Parker. HarperCollins, 2005. ISBN 0-06-056068-1 Subj: Clothing — costumes. Holidays — Halloween. Rebuses. Rhyming text.

Nelson, Kadir. *He's got the whole world in His hands* ill. by author. Penguin, 2005. ISBN 0-8037-2850-6 Subj: Religion. Songs.

Nelson, Marilyn. *The ladder* (Rasmussen, Halfdan)

Nelson, Robin. *Staying clean* ill. with photos. Lerner, 2005. ISBN 0-8225-2638-7 Subj: Character traits — cleanliness. Health & fitness.

Nelson, S. D. *Quiet hero: the Ira Hayes story* ill. by author. Lee & Low, 2006. ISBN 1-58430-263-1 Subj: Careers — military. Indians of North America — Pima. U.S. history.

Neubecker, Robert. *Beasty bath* ill. by author. Scholastic/Orchard, 2005. ISBN 0-439-64000-8 Subj: Activities — bathing. Imagination. Monsters. Rhyming text.

Courage of the blue boy ill. by author. Ten Speed, 2006. ISBN 1-58246-182-1 Subj: Activities — traveling. Animals — bulls, cows. Concepts — color. Self-concept.

Wow! America! ill. by author. Hyperion, 2006. ISBN 0-7868-3816-7 Subj: U.S. history.

Wow! City! ill. by author. Hyperion, 2004. ISBN 0-7868-0951-5 Subj: Cities, towns.

Wow! School! ill. by author. Hyperion, 2007. ISBN 978-0-7868-3896-7 Subj: School — first day.

Nevius, Carol. *Building with Dad* ill. by Bill Thomson. Marshall Cavendish, 2006. ISBN 0-7614-5312-1 Subj: Careers — construction workers. Rhyming text. School.

Karate hour ill. by Bill Thomson. Marshall Cavendish, 2004. ISBN 0-7614-5169-2 Subj: Rhyming text. Sports — karate.

Newgarden, Mark. *Bow-Wow bugs a bug* by Mark Newgarden & Megan Montague Cash; ill. by authors. Harcourt, 2007. ISBN 978-0-15-205813-5 Subj: Animals — dogs. Insects. Wordless.

Bow-Wow orders lunch by Mark Newgarden & Megan Montague Cash; ill. by authors. Harcourt, 2007. ISBN 978-0-15-205829 Subj: Animals — dogs. Food. Format, unusual — board books.

Newman, Jeff. *Hippo! No, rhino!* ill. by author. Little, Brown, 2006. ISBN 0-316-15573-X Subj: Animals — rhinoceros. Humorous stories.

Newman, Leslea. *Daddy's song* ill. by Karen Ritz. Henry Holt, 2007. ISBN 978-0-8050-6975-4 Subj: Bedtime. Emotions — love. Family life — fathers. Lullabies. Rhyming text.

The eight nights of Chanukah ill. by Elivia Savadier. Abrams, 2005. ISBN 0-8109-5785-X Subj: Holidays — Hanukkah. Jewish culture. Songs.

Skunk's spring surprise ill. by Valeri Gorbachev. Harcourt, 2007. ISBN 0-15-205683-1 Subj: Animals. Animals — skunks. Friendship. Rhyming text. Seasons — spring.

Newman, Marjorie. *Just like me* ill. by Ken Wilson-Max. Walker & Company, 2006. ISBN 0-8027-8080-6 Subj: Babies. Family life — brothers & sisters. Family life — new sibling.

Newman, Marlene. *Myron's magic cow* ill. by Jago. Barefoot, 2005. ISBN 1-84148-496-2 Subj: Animals — bulls, cows. Behavior — wishing. Folk & fairy tales. Magic.

Nez, John. *One smart Cookie* ill. by author. Albert Whitman, 2006. ISBN 0-8075-6099-5 Subj: Animals — dogs. Books, reading. Fire. School.

Nickle, John. *Alphabet explosion! Search and count from alien to zebra* ill. by author. Random House, 2006. ISBN 0-375-83598-9 Subj: ABC books. Counting, numbers. Picture puzzles. Wordless.

Niemann, Christoph. *The police cloud* ill. by author. Random House, 2007. ISBN 978-0-375-83963-4 Subj: Careers — police officers. Weather — clouds.

Nikola-Lisa, W. *Magic in the margins: a medieval tale of bookmaking* ill. by Bonne Christensen. Houghton Mifflin, 2007. ISBN 978-0-618-49642-6 Subj: Animals — mice. Art. Books, reading. Middle Ages.

Niner, Holly L. *I can't stop! A story about Tourette Syndrome* ill. by Meryl Treatner. Albert Whitman, 2005. ISBN 0-8075-3620-2 Subj: Handicaps.

Nishimura, Kae. *Bunny Lune* ill. by author. Houghton Mifflin, 2007. ISBN 978-0-618-71606-7 Subj: Animals — rabbits. Moon.

Noda, Takayo. *Song of the flowers* ill. by author. Penguin, 2006. ISBN 0-8037-2934-0 Subj: Flowers. Lullabies.

Nolan, Janet. *A Father's Day thank you* ill. by Kathi Ember. Albert Whitman, 2007. ISBN 978-0-8075-2291-2 Subj: Animals — bears. Art. Family life — fathers. Gifts. Holidays — Father's Day.

Nolen, Jerdine. *Hewitt Anderson's great big life* ill. by Kadir Nelson. Simon & Schuster, 2005. ISBN 0-689-86866-9 Subj: Character traits — smallness. Concepts — size. Family life. Giants.

Pitching in for Eubie ill. by E. B. Lewis. HarperCollins, 2007. ISBN 0-06-056960-3 Subj: Character traits — helpfulness. Ethnic groups in the U.S. — African Americans. Family life.

Plantzilla goes to camp ill. by David Catrow. Simon & Schuster, 2006. ISBN 0-689-86803-0 Subj: Behavior — bullying. Camps, camping. Humorous stories. Letters, cards. Plants.

Norac, Carl. *Monster, don't eat me!* trans. from Dutch by Elisa Amado; ill. by Carll Cneut. Groundwood, 2007. ISBN 978-0-88899-800-2 Subj: Animals — pigs. Behavior — greed. Food. Monsters.

My mommy is magic ill. by Ingrid Godon. Houghton Mifflin, 2007. ISBN 978-0-618-75766-4 Subj: Family life — mothers. Magic.

Norworth, Jack. *Take me out to the ballgame: the sensational baseball song* ill. by Jim Burke. Little, Brown, 2006. ISBN 978-0-316-75819-2 Subj: Songs. Sports — baseball.

Novak, Matt. *Flip flop bop* ill. by author. Macmillan, 2005. ISBN 1-59643049-4 Subj: Clothing — shoes. Rhyming text. Seasons — summer.

Too many bunnies ill. by author. Macmillan, 2005. ISBN 1-59643-038-9 Subj: Animals — rabbits. Format, unusual — toy & movable books.

Noyes, Deborah. *When I met the wolf girls* ill. by August Hall. Houghton Mifflin, 2007. ISBN 978-0-618-60567-5 Subj: Foreign lands — India. Orphans.

Numeroff, Laura Joffe. *If you give a pig a party* ill. by Felicia Bond. HarperCollins, 2005. ISBN 0-06-028327-0 Subj: Animals — pigs. Circular tales. Parties.

Merry Christmas, Mouse! ill. by Felicia Bond. HarperCollins, 2007. ISBN 978-0-06-134499-2 Subj: Animals — mice. Counting, numbers. Holidays — Christmas.

When sheep sleep ill. by David McPhail. Abrams, 2006. ISBN 0-8109-5469-9 Subj: Animals. Animals — sheep. Bedtime. Counting, numbers. Rhyming text.

O'Brien, Patrick. *Captain Raptor and the space pirates* (O'Malley, Kevin)

O'Connor, George. *Ker-splash!* ill. by author. Simon & Schuster, 2005. ISBN 0-689-87682-3 Subj: Activities — playing. Behavior — bullying. Imagination. Sea & seashore.

Sally and the Some-Thing ill. by author. Macmillan, 2006. ISBN 1-59643-141-5 Subj: Friendship. Monsters.

O'Connor, Jane. *Fancy Nancy* ill. by Robin Preiss Glasser. HarperCollins, 2006. ISBN 0-06-054209-8 Subj: Clothing. Family life. Self-concept.

Fancy Nancy and the posh puppy ill. by Robin Preiss Glasser. HarperCollins, 2007. ISBN 0-06-054213-6 Subj: Animals — dogs. Family life. Self-concept.

Ready, set, skip! ill. by Ann James. Penguin, 2007. ISBN 978-0-670-06216-4 Subj: Activities. Character traits — persistence. Rhyming text. Self-concept.

The snow globe family ill. by S. D. Schindler. Penguin, 2006. ISBN 0-399-24242-2 Subj: Family life.

Odanaka, Barbara. *Smash! Mash! Crash! There goes the trash!* ill. by Will Hillenbrand. Simon & Schuster, 2006. ISBN 0-689-85160-X Subj: Animals — pigs. Careers — sanitation workers. Rhyming text. Trucks.

Oddino, Licia. *Finn and the fairies* ill. by Alessandra Toni. Purple Bear, 2006. ISBN 1-933327-17-0 Subj: Careers — tailors. Fairies.

Odone, Jamison. *Honey badgers* ill. by author. Boyds Mills, 2007. ISBN 978-1-932425-51-2 Subj: Animals — badgers. Orphans.

Offill, Jenny. *17 things I'm not allowed to do anymore* ill. by Nancy Carpenter. Random House, 2006. ISBN 0-375-83596-2 Subj: Behavior — misbehavior.

Ogburn, Jacqueline K. *The bake shop ghost* ill. by Marjorie Priceman. Houghton Mifflin, 2005. ISBN 0-618-44557-9 Subj: Careers — bakers. Food. Ghosts.

O'Hair, Margaret. *Star baby* ill. by Erin Eitter Kono. Houghton Mifflin, 2005. ISBN 0-618-30668-4 Subj: Babies. Rhyming text.

Ohi, Ruth. *And you can come too* ill. by author. Annick, 2005. ISBN 1-55037-905-4 Subj: Activities — playing. Behavior — running away. Family life.

Clara and the Bossy ill. by author. Annick, 2006. ISBN 1-55037-943-7 Subj: Animals — guinea pigs. Behavior — bossy. Friendship.

The couch was a castle ill. by author. Annick, 2006. ISBN 1-55451-014-7 Subj: Animals — guinea pigs. Family life — brothers & sisters. Imagination.

Me and my brother ill. by author. Annick, 2007. ISBN 1-55451-091-0 Subj: Family life — brothers & sisters. Rhyming text.

Me and my sister ill. by author. Annick, 2005. ISBN 1-55037-892-9 Subj: Family life — brothers & sisters. Rhyming text.

A trip with Grandma ill. by author. Annick, 2007. ISBN 1-55451-072-4 Subj: Activities — traveling. Animals — guinea pigs. Behavior — worrying. Family life — brothers & sisters. Family life — grandmothers.

O'Keefe, Susan Heyboer. *Baby day* ill. by Robin Spowart. Boyds Mills, 2006. ISBN 1-59078-981-0 Subj: Activities — playing. Animals — bears. Babies. Family life. Rhyming text.

Hungry monster ABC ill. by Lynn Munsinger. Little, Brown, 2007. ISBN 978-0-316-15574-8 Subj: ABC books. Monsters. Rhyming text.

The old woman and her pig. *The old woman and her pig: an Appalachian folktale* retold by Margaret Read MacDonald; ill. by John Kanzler. HarperCollins, 2007. ISBN 0-06-028090-5 Subj: Cumulative tales. Folk & fairy tales.

O'Leary, Sara. *When you were small* ill. by Julie Morstad. Simply Read, 2006. ISBN 1-894965-36-1 Subj: Character traits — smallness. Concepts — size. Family life — fathers. Imagination.

Oliver, Narelle. *Twilight hunt: a seek-and-find book* ill. by author. Star Bright, 2007. ISBN 978-1-59572-107-5 Subj: Behavior — hiding. Birds — owls. Disguises. Nature. Picture puzzles.

Olsen, Sylvia. *Yetsa's sweater* ill. by Joan Larson. Sono Nis, 2006. ISBN 978-1-55039-155-8 Subj: Animals — sheep. Clothing — sweaters. Foreign lands — British Columbia. Indians of North America.

Olson, David J. *The thunderstruck stork* ill. by Lynn Munsinger. Albert Whitman, 2007. ISBN 978-0-8075-7910-7 Subj: Animals. Animals — babies. Birds — storks. Rhyming text.

Olson, Nathan. *Animal patterns* ill. with photos. Capstone, 2006. ISBN 978-0-7368-6728-3 Subj: Animals. Concepts — patterns.

Olson-Brown, Ellen. *Hush little digger* ill. by Lee White. Ten Speed, 2006. ISBN 1-58246-160-0 Subj: Machines. Music. Trucks.

O'Malley, Kevin. *Captain Raptor and the moon mystery* ill. by Patrick O'Brien. Walker & Company, 2005. ISBN 0-8027-8935-8 Subj: Aliens. Dinosaurs. Space & space ships.

Captain Raptor and the space pirates by Kevin O'Malley & Patrick O'Brien; ill. by Patrick O'Brien. Walker & Company, 2007. ISBN 978-0-8027-9571-7 Subj: Dinosaurs. Pirates. Space & space ships.

Gimme cracked corn and I will share ill. by author. Walker & Company, 2007. ISBN 978-0-8027-9684-4 Subj: Birds — chickens. Humorous stories.

Miss Malarkey leaves no reader behind (Finchler, Judy)

Once upon a cool motorcycle dude ill. by Kevin O'Malley, Carol Heyer, & Scott Goto. Walker & Company, 2005. ISBN 0-8027-8949-8 Subj: Activities — writing. Giants. Motorcycles. Royalty — princesses.

Ommen, Sylvia van. *The surprise* ill. by author. Boyds Mills, 2007. ISBN 978-1-932425-85-7 Subj: Animals — giraffes. Animals — sheep. Gifts. Wordless.

Onishi, Satoru. *Who's hiding* ill. by author. Kane/Miller, 2007. ISBN 978-1-933605-24-1 Subj: Animals. Disguises. Picture puzzles.

Onyefulu, Ifeoma. *An African Christmas* ill. with photos. Frances Lincoln, 2005. ISBN 1-84507-387-8 Subj: Foreign lands — Africa. Holidays — Christmas.

Ormerod, Jan. *When an elephant comes to school* ill. by author. Scholastic/Orchard, 2005. ISBN 0-439-73967-5 Subj: Animals — elephants. School — first day.

Orona-Ramirez, Kristy. *Kiki's journey* ill. by Jonathan Warm Day. Children's Book Press, 2006. ISBN 0-89239-214-2 Subj: Activities — traveling. Family life. Indians of North America — Tiwa.

Orozco, Jose-Luis. *Rin, rin, rin / do, re, mi: libro ilustrado en Español e Inglés = a picture book in Spanish and English* ill. by David Diaz. Scholastic/Orchard, 2005. ISBN 0-439-64941-2 Subj: Books, reading. Counting, numbers. Foreign languages.

Osborne, Mary Pope. *Sleeping Bobby* ill. by Giselle Potter. Simon & Schuster/Atheneum, 2005. ISBN 0-689-87668-8 Subj: Folk & fairy tales. Royalty — princes. Royalty — princesses. Sleep.

Otsuka, Yuzo. *Suho's white horse: a Mongolian legend* retold by Yuzo Otsuka; trans. by Richard McNamara & Peter Howlett; ill. by Suekichi Akaba. R.I.C., 2007. ISBN 1-74126-021-3 Subj: Animals — horses, ponies. Emotions — love. Folk & fairy tales. Foreign lands — Mongolia. Musical instruments — violins.

Owens, Mary Beth. *Panda whispers* ill. by author. Penguin, 2007. ISBN 978-0-525-47171-4 Subj: Animals. Bedtime. Dreams. Rhyming text.

Oxenbury, Helen. *Pig tale* ill. by author. Simon & Schuster, 2005. ISBN 1-4169-0277-5 Subj: Animals — pigs. Behavior — greed. Rhyming text.

Page, Robin. *Move!* (Jenkins, Steve)

Palatini, Margie. *Bad boys get cookie!* ill. by Henry Cole. HarperCollins, 2006. ISBN 0-06-074437-5 Subj: Animals — wolves. Food.

The cheese ill. by Steve Johnson & Lou Fancher. HarperCollins, 2007. ISBN 978-0-06-052630-6 Subj: Careers — farmers. Farms. Games. Music. Songs.

No biting, Louise ill. by Matthew Reinhart. HarperCollins, 2007. ISBN 978-0-06-052627-6 Subj: Reptiles — alligators, crocodiles. Teeth.

Oink? ill. by Henry Cole. Simon & Schuster, 2006. ISBN 0-689-86258-X Subj: Animals — pigs. Farms. Humorous stories.

Shelly ill. by Guy Francis. Penguin, 2006. ISBN 0-525-47565-6 Subj: Behavior — bossy. Birds — chickens. Character traits — smallness.

Three French hens ill. by Richard Egielski. Hyperion, 2005. ISBN 0-7868-5167-8 Subj: Animals — foxes. Birds — chickens. Foreign lands — France. Humorous stories. Songs.

The three silly billies ill. by Barry Moser. Simon & Schuster, 2005. ISBN 0-689-85862-0 Subj: Animals — goats. Books, reading. Humorous stories. Mythical creatures — trolls.

Pallotta, Jerry. *The construction alphabet book* ill. by Rob Bolster. Charlesbridge, 2006. ISBN 1-57091-437-0 Subj: ABC books. Machines. Tractors. Trucks.

Ocean counting: odd numbers ill. by Shennen Bersani. Charlesbridge, 2005. ISBN 0-88106-151-4 Subj: Animals. Counting, numbers. Sea & seashore.

Paradis, Susan. *Snow princess* ill. by author. Boyds Mills, 2005. ISBN 1-932425-31-4 Subj: Family life — fathers. Imagination. Weather — snow.

Paraskevas, Betty. *Chocolate at the Four Seasons* ill. by Mickey Paraskevas. Little, Brown, 2007. ISBN 978-0-306-01375-8 Subj: Animals — dogs. Character traits — shyness. Hotels.

Parenteau, Shirley. *One frog sang* ill. by Cynthia Jabar. Candlewick, 2006. ISBN 978-0-7636-2394-4 Subj: Counting, numbers. Frogs & toads.

Park, Frances. *The Have a Good Day Cafe* by Frances & Ginger Park; ill. by Katherine Potter. Lee & Low, 2005. ISBN 1-58430-171-6 Subj: Ethnic groups in the U.S. — Korean Americans. Family life — grandmothers. Immigrants. Restaurants.

Park, Ginger. *The Have a Good Day Cafe* (Park, Frances)

Park, Linda Sue. *Bee-bim bop!* ill. by Ho Baek Lee. Houghton Mifflin, 2005. ISBN 0-618-26511-2 Subj: Activities — baking, cooking. Food. Foreign lands — Korea. Rhyming text.

What does Bunny see? A book of colors and flowers ill. by Maggie Smith. Houghton Mifflin, 2005. ISBN 0-618-23485-3 Subj: Animals — rabbits. Concepts — color. Flowers. Gardens, gardening. Rhyming text.

Yum! Yuck! A foldout book of people sounds by Linda Sue Park & Julia Durango; ill. by Sue Ramá. Charlesbridge, 2005. ISBN 1-57091-659-4 Subj: Foreign languages. Format, unusual — toy & movable books. Noise, sounds.

Parker, Kim. *Counting in the garden* ill. by author. Scholastic/Orchard, 2005. ISBN 0-439-69452-3 Subj: Animals. Counting, numbers. Gardens, gardening.

Parker, Marjorie. *Your kind of mommy* ill. by Cyd Moore. Penguin, 2007. ISBN 978-0-525-46989-6 Subj: Animals. Family life — mothers. Rhyming text.

Parnell, Peter. *And Tango makes three* (Richardson, Justin)

Parr, Todd. *The grandma book* ill. by author. Little, Brown, 2006. ISBN 978-0-316-05802-5 Subj: Family life — grandmothers.

The grandpa book ill. by author. Little, Brown, 2006. ISBN 0-316-05801-7 Subj: Family life — grandfathers.

Otto goes to school ill. by author. Little, Brown, 2005. ISBN 0-316-83533-1 Subj: Animals — dogs. School — first day.

Reading makes you feel good ill. by author. Little, Brown, 2005. ISBN 0-316-16004-0 Subj: Books, reading.

We belong together: a book about adoption and families ill. by author. Little, Brown, 2005. ISBN 978-0-316-01668-1 Subj: Adoption. Family life.

Pasquali, Elena. *Ituku's Christmas journey* ill. by Dubravka Kolanovic. Good Books, 2005. ISBN 1-56148-495-4 Subj: Holidays — Christmas. Indians of North America — Inuit. Religion — Nativity.

Paterson, Diane. *Hurricane wolf* ill. by author. Albert Whitman, 2006. ISBN 0-8075-3438-2 Subj: Family life. Weather — hurricanes.

Patricelli, Leslie. *Binky* ill. by author. Candlewick, 2005. ISBN 0-76362364-4 Subj: Babies. Format, unusual — board books. Toys.

The birthday box ill. by author. Candlewick, 2007. ISBN 978-0-7636-2825-3 Subj: Birthdays. Imagination.

Blankie ill. by author. Candlewick, 2005. ISBN 0-7636-2363-6 Subj: Babies. Format, unusual — board books.

Pattison, Darcy. *Searching for Oliver K. Woodman* ill. by Joe Cepeda. Harcourt, 2005. ISBN 0-15-205184-8 Subj: Activities — traveling. Letters, cards. Toys — dolls.

Pattou, Edith. *Mrs. Spitzer's garden* ill. by Tricia Tusa. gift edition. Harcourt, 2007. ISBN 0-15-205802-8 Subj: Careers — teachers. Gardens, gardening. School.

Patz, Nancy. *Babies can't eat kimchee!* by Nancy Patz & Susan L. Roth; ill. by authors. Bloomsbury, 2007. ISBN 1-59990-017-3 Subj: Babies. Behavior — growing up. Ethnic groups in the U.S. — Korean Americans. Family life — brothers & sisters. Family life — new sibling. Food.

Paul, Alison. *The crow (a not so scary story)* ill. by author. Houghton Mifflin, 2007. ISBN 978-0-618-66380-4 Subj: Birds — crows. Emotions — fear. Language.

Paul, Ann Whitford. *Fiesta fiasco* ill. by Ethan Long. Holiday House, 2007. ISBN 978-0-8234-2037-7 Subj: Animals. Birthdays. Desert. Foreign languages. Gifts.

Mañana Iguana ill. by Ethan Long. Holiday House, 2004. ISBN 0-8234-1808-1 Subj: Character traits — laziness. Desert. Foreign languages. Parties. Reptiles — iguanas.

Payne, Nina. *Summertime waltz* ill. by Gabi Swiatkowska. Farrar, Straus & Giroux, 2005. ISBN 0-374-37291-8 Subj: Seasons — summer.

Pearson, Debora. *Big city song* ill. by Lynn Rowe Reed. Holiday House, 2006. ISBN 0-8234-1988-6 Subj: Cities, towns. Noise, sounds. Rhyming text.

Sophie's wheels ill. by Nora Hilb. Annick, 2006. ISBN 978-1-55451-038-2 Subj: Behavior — growing up. Wheels.

Pearson, Susan. *Hooray for feet!* ill. by Roxanna Baer-Block. Blue Apple, 2005. ISBN 1-59354-093-0 Subj: Anatomy — feet. Rhyming text.

Slugs in love ill. by Kevin O'Malley. Marshall Cavendish, 2006. ISBN 978-0-7614-5311-6 Subj: Activities — writing. Animals — slugs. Character traits — shyness. Emotions — love. Poetry.

Pearson, Tracey Campbell. *Diddle diddle dumpling* ill. by author. Farrar, Straus & Giroux, 2005. ISBN 0-374-30861-6 Subj: Format, unusual — board books. Nursery rhymes.

Peck, Jan. *Way up high in a tall green tree* ill. by Valeria Petrone. Simon & Schuster, 2005. ISBN 1-4169-0071-3 Subj: Animals. Bedtime. Imagination. Jungles. Rhyming text.

Peddicord, Jane Ann. *That special little baby* ill. by Meilo So. Harcourt, 2007. ISBN 978-0-15-205430-4 Subj: Babies. Rhyming text.

Pelletier, Andrew T. *The amazing adventures of Bathman!* ill. by Peter Elwell. Penguin, 2005. ISBN 0-525-47164-2 Subj: Activities — bathing. Toys.

The toy farmer ill. by Scott Nash. Penguin, 2007. ISBN 978-0-525-47649-8 Subj: Careers — farmers. Farms. Magic. Toys.

Pelley, Kathleen T. *Inventor McGregor* ill. by Michael Chesworth. Farrar, Straus & Giroux, 2006. ISBN 0-374-33606-7 Subj: Careers — inventors. Family life.

Pendziwol, Jean. *The red sash* ill. by Nicolas Debon. Groundwood, 2005. ISBN 0-88899-589-X Subj: Careers — fur traders. Foreign lands — Canada. Indians of North America — Metis.

The tale of Sir Dragon: dealing with bullies for kids (and dragons) ill. by Martine Gourbault. Kids Can, 2007. ISBN 978-1-55453-135-6 Subj: Behavior — bullying. Dragons. Rhyming text.

Penner, Fred. *The cat came back* ill. by Renee Reichert. Macmillan, 2005. ISBN 1-59643-030-3 Subj: Animals — cats. Character traits — persistence. Songs.

Pennypacker, Sara. *Pierre in love* ill. by Petra Mathers. Scholastic/Orchard, 2007. ISBN 0-439-51740-0 Subj: Animals — mice. Animals — rabbits. Ballet. Careers — fishermen. Emotions — love.

Pericoli, Matteo. *The true story of Stellina* ill. by author. Random House, 2006. ISBN 0-375-93273-9 Subj: Birds — finches. Character traits — kindness to animals.

Perkins, Lynne Rae. *Pictures from our vacation* ill. by author. HarperCollins, 2007. ISBN 978-0-06-085098-2 Subj: Activities — photographing. Activities — vacationing. Family life. Foreign lands — Canada.

Perl, Erica S. *Ninety-three in my family* ill. by Mike Lester. Abrams, 2006. ISBN 0-8109-5760-4 Subj: Counting, numbers. Family life. Rhyming text.

Perrault, Charles. *Cinderella* retold & ill. by Barbara McClintock. Scholastic, 2005. ISBN 0-439-56145-0 Subj: Family life — step families. Folk & fairy tales. Royalty — princes. Sibling rivalry.

Cinderella: a pop-up fairy tale retold & ill. by Matthew Reinhart. Simon & Schuster/Little Simon, 2005. ISBN 1-4169-0501-4 Subj: Family life — step families. Folk & fairy tales. Format, unusual — toy & movable books. Royalty — princes. Sibling rivalry.

Perret, Delphine. *The Big Bad Wolf and me* ill. by author. Sterling, 2006. ISBN 1-4027-3725-4 Subj: Animals — wolves. Pets.

Perry, Elizabeth. *Think cool thoughts* ill. by Linda Bronson. Houghton Mifflin, 2005. ISBN 0-618-23493-4 Subj: Ethnic groups in the U.S. — African Americans. Family life — aunts, uncles. Seasons — summer.

Peters, Lisa Westberg. *Sleepyhead bear* ill. by Ian Schoenherr. HarperCollins, 2006. ISBN 0-06-059675-9 Subj: Animals — bears. Insects. Rhyming text. Sleep.

Peterson, Cris. *Fantastic farm machines* ill. by David R. Lundquist. Boyds Mills, 2006. ISBN 1-59078-271-2 Subj: Farms. Machines. Tractors.

Petrillo, Genevieve. *Keep your ear on the ball* ill. by Lea Lyon. Tilbury House, 2007. ISBN 978-0-88448-296-3 Subj: Character traits — helpfulness. Games. Handicaps — blindness. School.

Pettenati, Jeanne K. *Galileo's journal, 1609–1610* ill. by Paolo Rui. Charlesbridge, 2006. ISBN 1-57091-879-1 Subj: Astronomy. Careers — scientists. Science. Stars.

Petz, Moritz. *Wish you were here* ill. by Quentin Greban. North-South, 2005. ISBN 0-7358-2005-8 Subj: Animals — hedgehogs. Animals — mice. Friendship.

Pfister, Marcus. *Charlie at the zoo* trans. from German by J. Alison James; ill. by Marcus Pfister. NorthSouth, 2004. ISBN 978-0-7358-2144-6 Subj: Animals. Birds — ducks. Format, unusual. Zoos.

Pham, LeUyen. *Big sister, little sister* ill. by author. Hyperion, 2005. ISBN 0-7868-5182-1 Subj: Character traits — individuality. Family life — brothers & sisters.

Phillips, Christopher. *Ceci Ann's day of why* ill. by Shino Arihara. Ten Speed, 2006. ISBN 1-58246-171-6 Subj: Character traits — questioning. Ethnic groups in the U.S. — African Americans. Rhyming text.

Philpot, Graham. *Find Anthony Ant* (Philpot, Lorna)

Philpot, Lorna. *Find Anthony Ant* by Lorna & Graham Philpot; ill. by Lorna Philpot. Sterling, 2006. ISBN 1-905417-10-1 Subj: Counting, numbers. Insects — ants. Mazes. Picture puzzles. Puzzles.

Pichon, Liz. *The very ugly bug* ill. by author. Tiger Tales, 2005. ISBN 1-58925-048-6 Subj: Character traits — appearance. Insects.

Pickering, Jimmy. *Skelly the skeleton girl* ill. by author. Simon & Schuster, 2007. ISBN 978-1-4169-1192-0 Subj: Anatomy — skeletons. Animals — dogs. Monsters.

Pierce, Terry. *Counting your way: number nursery rhymes* ed. by Terry Pierce; ill. by Andrea Petrlik Huseinovic. Picture Window, 2007. ISBN 978-1-4048-2346-4 Subj: Counting, numbers. Nursery rhymes.

Piernas-Davenport, Gail. *Shanté Keys and the New Year's peas* ill. by Marion Eldridge. Albert Whitman, 2007. ISBN 978-0-8075-7330-3 Subj: Ethnic groups in the U.S. — African Americans. Family life. Food. Holidays — New Year's.

Pilegard, Virginia Walton. *The warlord's alarm: a mathematical adventure* ill. by Nicolas Debon. Pelican, 2006. ISBN 1-58980-378-7 Subj: Clocks, watches. Foreign lands — China. Time.

Pilgrim, Elza. *The china doll* ill. by Carmen Segovia. Sterling, 2006. ISBN 1-4027-2223-0 Subj: Birthdays. Gifts. Toys — dolls.

Pinkney, Andrea Davis. *Peggony-Po: a whale of a tale* ill. by J. Brian Pinkney. Hyperion, 2006. ISBN 0-7868-1958-8 Subj: Animals — whales. Tall tales. Toys.

Pinkney, Gloria Jean. *Music from our Lord's holy heaven* comp. by Gloria Jean Pinkney; ill. by Jerry , J. Brian, & Myles C. Pinkney. HarperCollins, 2005. ISBN 0-06-000769-9 Subj: Music. Religion. Songs.

Pinkney, J. Brian. *Hush, little baby* adapt. & ill. by J. Brian Pinkney. HarperCollins, 2006. ISBN 0-06-055994-2 Subj: Babies. Character traits — generosity. Cumulative tales. Lullabies. Music.

Pinkney, Jerry. *Little Red Riding Hood* (Grimm, Jacob)

Pinkney, Sandra L. *I am Latino: the beauty in me* photos by Myles C. Pinkney. Little, Brown, 2007. ISBN 978-0-316-16009-4 Subj: Ethnic groups in the U.S. — Hispanic Americans. Self-concept.

Read and rise foreword by Maya Angelou; photos by Myles C. Pinkney. Scholastic/Cartwheel, 2006. ISBN 0-439-30929-8 Subj: Books, reading. Ethnic groups in the U.S. — African Americans.

Pinkwater, Daniel Manus. *Bad bear detectives: an Irving and Muktuk story* ill. by Jill Pinkwater. Houghton Mifflin, 2006. ISBN 0-618-43125-X Subj: Animals — polar bears. Behavior — stealing. Careers — detectives. Humorous stories.

Bad bears go visiting ill. by Jill Pinkwater. Houghton Mifflin, 2007. ISBN 978-0-618-43126-7 Subj: Animals — polar bears. Humorous stories. Zoos.

Dancing Larry ill. by Jill Pinkwater. Marshall Cavendish, 2006. ISBN 0-7614-5220-6 Subj: Activities — dancing. Animals — polar bears. Ballet. Humorous stories.

Sleepover Larry ill. by Jill Pinkwater. Marshall Cavendish, 2007. ISBN 978-0-7614-5314-7 Subj: Animals — polar bears. Humorous stories. Sleepovers.

Yo-yo man ill. by Jack E. Davis. HarperCollins, 2007. ISBN 978-0-06-055502-3 Subj: Behavior — bullying. School. Toys.

Pipe, Jim. *Baby animals* ill. with photos. Stargazer, 2007. ISBN 978-1-59604-111-0 Subj: Animals — babies.

Dogs ill. with photos. Stargazer, 2007. ISBN 978-1-59604-113-4 Subj: Animals — dogs.

Farm animals ill. with photos. Stargazer, 2007. ISBN 978-1-59604-112-7 Subj: Animals. Farms.

Horses ill. with photos. Stargazer, 2007. ISBN 978-1-59604-114-1 Subj: Animals — horses, ponies.

Piper, Watty. *The little engine that could* retold by Watty Piper; ill. by Loren Long. Penguin, 2005. ISBN 0-399-24467-0 Subj: Character traits — perseverance. Trains.

Pitzer, Susanna. *Not afraid of dogs* ill. by Larry Day. Walker & Company, 2006. ISBN 0-8027-8067-9 Subj: Animals — dogs. Behavior — animals, dislike of. Emotions — fear.

Plourde, Lynn. *Book Fair Day* ill. by Thor Wickstrom. Penguin, 2006. ISBN 0-525-47696-2 Subj: Books, reading. School.

Dad, aren't you glad? ill. by Amy Wummer. Penguin, 2005. ISBN 0-525-47362-9 Subj: Family life — fathers. Kissing.

Dino pets ill. by Gideon Kendall. Penguin, 2007. ISBN 978-0-525-47778-5 Subj: Dinosaurs. Pets. Rhyming text.

A mountain of mittens ill. by Mitch Vane. Charlesbridge, 2007. ISBN 978-1-57091-585-7 Subj: Behavior — lost & found possessions. Clothing — gloves, mittens. Seasons — winter.

Pajama day ill. by Thor Wickstrom. Penguin, 2005. ISBN 0-525-47355-6 Subj: Behavior — forgetfulness. Clothing — pajamas. School.

Polacco, Patricia. *Emma Kate* ill. by author. Penguin, 2005. ISBN 0-399-24452-2 Subj: Animals — elephants. Friendship. Imagination.

Ginger and Petunia ill. by author. Penguin, 2007. ISBN 978-0-399-24539-8 Subj: Animals — pigs. Pets.

The lemonade club ill. by author. Penguin, 2007. ISBN 978-0-399-24540-4 Subj: Careers — teachers. Illness — cancer. School.

Mommies say shhh! ill. by author. Penguin, 2005. ISBN 0-399-24341-0 Subj: Animals. Family life — mothers. Noise, sounds.

Rotten Richie and the ultimate dare ill. by author. Penguin, 2006. ISBN 0-399-24531-6 Subj: Ballet. Behavior — bullying. Contests. Family life — brothers & sisters. Sports — hockey.

Something about Hensley's ill. by author. Penguin, 2006. ISBN 0-399-24538-3 Subj: Family life — single-parent families. Stores.

Polhemus, Coleman. *The crocodile blues* ill. by author. Candlewick, 2007. ISBN 978-0-7636-3543-5 Subj: Eggs. Reptiles — alligators, crocodiles. Wordless.

Poole, Amy Lowry. *The pea blossom* retold & ill. by Amy Lowry Poole. Holiday House, 2005. Based on the Hans Christian Andersen story: Five peas in a pod. ISBN 0-8234-1864-2 Subj: Folk & fairy tales. Foreign lands — China. Plants.

Poppenhäger, Nicole. *Snow leopards* ill. by Ivan Gantschev. North-South, 2006. ISBN 0-7358-2087-2 Subj: Animals — leopards. Nature.

Portis, Antoinette. *Not a box* ill. by author. HarperCollins, 2006. ISBN 0-06-112322-6 Subj: Activities — playing. Animals — rabbits. Imagination.

Posada, Mia. *Guess what is growing inside this egg* ill. by author. Lerner, 2007. ISBN 978-0-8225-6192-7 Subj: Eggs. Science.

Post, Peggy. *Emily's everyday manners* by Peggy Post & Cindy Post Senning; ill. by Steve Bjorkman. HarperCollins, 2006. ISBN 0-06-076177-6 Subj: Etiquette.

Postgate, Daniel. *Smelly Bill* ill. by author. NorthSouth, 2007. ISBN 978-0-7358-2135-4 Subj: Animals — dogs. Rhyming text.

Powell, Consie. *The first day of winter* ill. by author. Albert Whitman, 2005. ISBN 0-8075-2450-6 Subj: Nature. Seasons — winter. Weather — cold.

Poydar, Nancy. *The bad-news report card* ill. by author. Holiday House, 2006. ISBN 0-8234-1992-4 Subj: Behavior — worrying. School.

The biggest test in the universe ill. by author. Holiday House, 2005. ISBN 0-8234-1944-4 Subj: Behavior — worrying. School.

Prap, Lila. *Animal lullabies* ill. by author. NorthSouth, 2006. ISBN 0-7358-2097-X Subj: Animals. Lullabies. Rhyming text.

Animals speak ill. by author. NorthSouth, 2006. ISBN 0-7358-2058-9 Subj: Animals. Foreign languages.

Daddies ill. by author. NorthSouth, 2007. ISBN 978-0-7358-2140-8 Subj: Animals. Bedtime. Family life — fathers. Rhyming text.

Prelutsky, Jack. *Behold the bold umbrellaphant and other poems* ill. by Carin Berger. HarperCollins, 2006. ISBN 0-06-054318-3 Subj: Animals. Imagination. Poetry.

Good sports: rhymes about running, jumping, throwing, and more ill. by Chris Raschka. Random House, 2007. ISBN 978-0-375-83700-5 Subj: Poetry. Sports.

It's snowing! It's snowing! Winter poems ill. by Yossi Abolafia. HarperCollins, 2006. ISBN 0-06-053715-9 Subj: Poetry. Seasons — winter.

Me I am! ill. by Christine Davenier. Farrar, Straus & Giroux, 2007. ISBN 0-374-64902-9 Subj: Character traits — individuality. Poetry. Self-concept.

What a day it was at school! ill. by Doug Cushman. HarperCollins, 2006. ISBN 0-06-082335-6 Subj: Poetry. School.

The wizard ill. by Brandon Dorman. HarperCollins, 2007. ISBN 978-0-06-124076-8 Subj: Magic. Rhyming text. Wizards.

Priceman, Marjorie. *Hot air: the (mostly) true story of the first hot-air balloon ride* ill. by author. Simon & Schuster/Atheneum, 2005. ISBN 0-689-82642-7 Subj: Activities — ballooning. Caldecott award honor books. Careers — inventors. Inventions.

Prince, April Jones. *Twenty-one elephants and still standing* ill. by Francois Roca. Houghton Mifflin, 2005. ISBN 0-618-44887-X Subj: Animals — elephants. Bridges.

What do wheels do all day? ill. by Giles Laroche. Houghton Mifflin, 2006. ISBN 0-618-56307-5 Subj: Rhyming text. Wheels.

Prince, Joshua. *I saw an ant in a parking lot* ill. by Macky Pamintuan. Sterling, 2007. ISBN 978-1-4027-3823-4 Subj: Humorous stories. Insects — ants. Rhyming text.

I saw an ant on the railroad track ill. by Macky Pamintuan. Sterling, 2006. ISBN 1-4027-2183-8 Subj: Humorous stories. Insects — ants. Rhyming text. Trains.

Pritchett, Dylan. *The first music* ill. by Erin Bennett Banks. August House, 2006. ISBN 0-87483-776-6 Subj: Foreign lands — Africa. Jungles. Music.

Protopopescu, Orel. *Two sticks* ill. by Anne Wilsdorf. Farrar, Straus & Giroux, 2007. ISBN 978-0-374-38022-9 Subj: Musical instruments — drums. Reptiles — alligators, crocodiles. Rhyming text.

Provensen, Alice. *Klondike gold* ill. by author. Simon & Schuster, 2005. ISBN 0-689-84885-4 Subj: Careers — miners. Foreign lands — Yukon Territory.

Pulver, Robin. *Author day for room 3T* ill. by Chuck Richards. Houghton Mifflin, 2005. ISBN 0-618-35406-9 Subj: Careers — authors. School.

Axle Annie and the speed grump ill. by Tedd Arnold. Penguin, 2005. ISBN 0-8037-2787-9 Subj: Accidents. Activities — driving. Careers — bus drivers. School.

Nouns and verbs have a field day ill. by Lynn Rowe Reed. Holiday House, 2006. ISBN 0-8234-1982-7 Subj: Language. School.

Purmwell, Ann. *Christmas tree farm* ill. by Jill Weber. Holiday House, 2006. ISBN 0-8234-1886-3 Subj: Activities — working. Careers — farmers. Farms. Holidays — Christmas. Trees.

Puttapipat, Niroot. *Musicians of Bremen* (Grimm, Jacob)

Puttock, Simon. *Goat and Donkey in strawberry sunglasses* ill. by Russell Julian. Good Books, 2007. ISBN 978-1-56148-572-7 Subj: Animals — donkeys. Animals — goats. Friendship. Shopping.

Goat and Donkey in the great outdoors ill. by Russell Julian. Good Books, 2007. ISBN 978-1-56148-573-4 Subj: Activities — vacationing. Animals — donkeys. Animals — goats. Friendship.

Miss Fox ill. by Holly Swain. Frances Lincoln, 2006. ISBN 1-84507-475-0 Subj: Animals — foxes. Animals — sheep. Careers — teachers. School.

Quattlebaum, Mary. *Sparks fly high: the legend of Dancing Point* ill. by Leonid Gore. Farrar, Straus & Giroux, 2006. ISBN 0-374-34452-3 Subj: Activities — dancing. Character traits — pride. Contests. Devil. Folk & fairy tales.

Winter friends ill. by Hiroe Nakata. Random House, 2005. ISBN 0-385-90868-7 Subj: Behavior — lost & found possessions. Clothing — gloves, mittens. Friendship. Poetry. Seasons — winter.

Quigley, Mary. *Granddad's fishing buddy* ill. by Stephane Jorisch. Penguin, 2007. ISBN 978-0-8037-2942-1 Subj: Birds — herons. Family life — grandfathers. Sports — fishing.

Quinn, Sarah. *Every single night* (Demers, Dominique)

Quinton, Sasha. *You and me* (Kindermans, Martine)

Raab, Brigitte. *Where does pepper come from? And other fun facts* trans. from German by J. Alison James; ill. by Manuela Olten. North-South, 2006. ISBN 0-7358-2070-8 Subj: Character traits — questioning. Science.

Raczka, Bob. *Spring things* ill. by Judy Stead. Albert Whitman, 2007. ISBN 978-0-8075-7596-3 Subj: Nature. Rhyming text. Seasons — spring.

3-D ABC: a sculptural alphabet ill. with photos. Lerner, 2006. ISBN 0-7613-9456-7 Subj: ABC books.

Who loves the fall? ill. by Judy Stead. Albert Whitman, 2007. ISBN 978-0-8075-9037-9 Subj: Rhyming text. Seasons — fall.

Radunsky, Vladimir. *Because . . .* (Baryshnikov, Mikhail)

Rand, Gloria. *A pen pal for Max* ill. by Ted Rand. Henry Holt, 2005. ISBN 0-8050-7586-0 Subj: Foreign lands — Chile. Friendship. Letters, cards. Pen pals.

Rankin, Laura. *Fluffy and Baron* ill. by author. Penguin, 2006. ISBN 0-8037-2953-7 Subj: Animals — dogs. Birds — ducks. Friendship.

Ruthie and the (not so) teeny tiny lie ill. by author. Bloomsbury, 2007. ISBN 978-1-59990-010-0 Subj: Animals — foxes. Behavior — lying. Character traits — honesty. School.

Ransom, Candice F. *Tractor day* ill. by Laura J. Bryant. Walker & Company, 2007. ISBN 0-8027-8090-3 Subj: Farms. Rhyming text. Tractors.

Ransom, Jeanie Franz. *Don't squeal unless it's a big deal: a tale of tattletales* ill. by Jackie Urbanovic. Magination, 2006. ISBN 1-59147-239-3 Subj: Animals — pigs. Behavior — fighting, arguing. Behavior — gossip.

What do parents do? (. . . When you're not home) ill. by Cyd Moore. Peachtree, 2007. ISBN 978-1-56145-409-9 Subj: Family life — parents. Humorous stories.

Rao, Sandhya. *My mother's sari* ill. by Nina Sabnani. NorthSouth, 2006. ISBN 0-7358-2101-1 Subj: Clothing. Ethnic groups in the U.S. — East Indian Americans. Family life — daughters. Family life — mothers.

Rappaport, Doreen. *The school is not white! A true story of the civil rights movement* ill. by Curtis James. Hyperion, 2005. ISBN 0-7868-1838-7 Subj: Ethnic groups in the U.S. — African Americans. Prejudice. School.

Raschka, Chris. *Five for a little one* ill. by author. Simon & Schuster/Atheneum, 2006. ISBN 978-0-689-84599-4 Subj: Animals — rabbits. Counting, numbers. Senses.

New York is English, Chattanooga is Creek ill. by author. Simon & Schuster, 2005. ISBN 0-689-84600-2 Subj: Cities, towns. Names. Parties. U.S. history.

The purple balloon ill. by author. Random House, 2007. ISBN 978-0-375-84146-0 Subj: Death. Emotions — grief. Illness.

Rasmussen, Halfdan. *The ladder* trans. by Marilyn Nelson; ill. by Pierre Pratt. Candlewick, 2006. ISBN 0-7636-2282-6 Subj: Format, unusual. Imagination. Rhyming text.

Rau, Dana Meachen. *Flying* ill. with photos. Benchmark, 2006. ISBN 978-0-7614-2319-5 Subj: Activities — flying. Rebuses.

Rectangles ill. with photos. Marshall Cavendish, 2006. ISBN 0-7614-2282-X Subj: Concepts — shape.

Riding ill. with photos. Benchmark, 2006. ISBN 978-0-7614-2317-1 Subj: Rebuses. Transportation.

Rolling ill. with photos. Benchmark, 2006. ISBN 978-0-7614-2314-0 Subj: Concepts — motion. Rebuses.

Raven, Margot Theis. *Night boat to freedom* ill. by E. B. Lewis. Farrar, Straus & Giroux, 2006. ISBN 0-374-31266-4 Subj: Ethnic groups in the U.S. — African Americans. Slavery. U.S. history.

Rawlinson, Julia. *Fletcher and the falling leaves* ill. by Tiphanie Beeke. HarperCollins, 2006. ISBN 0-06-113401-5 Subj: Animals — foxes. Seasons — fall. Trees.

A surprise for Rosie ill. by Tim Warnes. Tiger Tales, 2005. ISBN 1-58925-046-X Subj: Activities — ballooning. Animals — rabbits.

Rawson, Katherine. *If you were a parrot* ill. by Sherry Rogers. Sylvan Dell, 2006. ISBN 0-9764943-9-6 Subj: Birds — parrots.

Raye, Rebekah. *The very best bed* ill. by author. Tilbury House, 2006. ISBN 0-88448-284-7 Subj: Animals. Animals — squirrels. Bedtime. Homes, houses.

Rayner, Catherine. *Augustus and his smile* ill. by author. Good Books, 2006. ISBN 1-56148-510-1 Subj: Anatomy — faces. Animals — tigers. Emotions — happiness.

Recorvits, Helen. *Yoon and the Christmas mitten* ill. by Gabi Swiatkowska. Farrar, Straus & Giroux, 2006. ISBN 0-374-38688-9 Subj: Ethnic groups in the U.S. — Korean Americans. Holidays — Christmas. Immigrants.

Redding, Sue. *Up above and down below* ill. by author. Chronicle, 2006. ISBN 0-8118-4876-0 Subj: Concepts — up & down. Rhyming text.

Reed, Lynn Rowe. *Please don't upset P.U. Zorilla!* ill. by author. Random House, 2006. ISBN 0-375-93654-8 Subj: Animals — skunks. Careers.

Thelonius Turkey lives! (On Felicia Ferguson's farm) ill. by author. Random House, 2005. ISBN 0-375-93126-0 Subj: Birds — turkeys. Farms. Holidays — Thanksgiving.

Reed, Neil. *The midnight unicorn* ill. by author. Sterling, 2006. ISBN 1-4027-3218-X Subj: Imagination. Mythical creatures — unicorns.

Reinhart, Matthew. *Cinderella: a pop-up fairy tale* (Perrault, Charles)

Encyclopedia prehistorica: dinosaurs (Sabuda, Robert)

Encyclopedia prehistorica: mega-beasts (Sabuda, Robert)

Encyclopedia prehistorica: sharks and other seamonsters (Sabuda, Robert)

Reisberg, Joanne A. *Zachary Zormer shape transformer: a math adventure* ill. by David Hohn. Charlesbridge, 2006. ISBN 1-57091-875-9 Subj: Concepts — shape. Counting, numbers.

Reiser, Lynn. *Hardworking puppies* ill. by author. Harcourt, 2006. ISBN 0-15-205404-9 Subj: Animals — dogs. Careers. Counting, numbers.

My way / A mi manera: a Margaret and Margarita story / un cuento de Margarita y Margaret ill. by author. HarperCollins, 2007. ISBN 0-06-084101-X Subj: Foreign languages. Friendship.

Play ball with me! ill. by author. Random House, 2006. ISBN 0-375-83244-0 Subj: Format, unusual — toy & movable books. Sports.

Two dogs swimming ill. by author. HarperCollins, 2005. ISBN 0-06-008648-3 Subj: Animals — dogs. Sports — swimming.

Reiss, Mike. *Merry un-Christmas* ill. by David Catrow. HarperCollins, 2006. ISBN 0-06-059126-9 Subj: Holidays — Christmas. Humorous stories.

Rempt, Fiona. *Snail's birthday wish* ill. by Noelle Smit. Boxer, 2007. ISBN 978-1-905417-52-0 Subj: Animals. Animals — snails. Birthdays. Gifts.

Rex, Adam. *Pssst!* ill. by author. Harcourt, 2007. ISBN 978-0-15-205817-3 Subj: Zoos.

Rex, Michael. *Dunk skunk* ill. by author. Penguin, 2005. ISBN 0-399-24281-3 Subj: Animals. Rhyming text. Sports.

You can do anything, Daddy! ill. by author. Penguin, 2007. ISBN 978-0-399-24298-4 Subj: Bedtime. Family life — fathers. Humorous stories.

Reynolds, Aaron. *Buffalo wings* ill. by Paulette Bogan. Bloomsbury, 2007. ISBN 978-1-59990-062-9 Subj: Activities — baking, cooking. Animals. Birds — chickens. Food. Sports — football.

Chicks and salsa ill. by Paulette Bogan. Bloomsbury, 2005. ISBN 1-58234-972-X Subj: Activities — baking, cooking. Birds — chickens. Farms. Food.

Reynolds, Jan. *Celebrate! Connections among cultures* photos by author. Lee & Low, 2006. ISBN 1-58430-253-4 Subj: Fairs, festivals. Foreign lands. Holidays. World.

Reynolds, Michael. *The big question* (Erlbruch, Wolf)

Reynolds, Peter H. *The best kid in the world: a SugarLoaf book* ill. by author. Simon & Schuster/Atheneum, 2006. ISBN 0-689-87624-6 Subj: Emotions — envy, jealousy. Family life — brothers & sisters. Sibling rivalry.

Ish ill. by author. Candlewick, 2004. ISBN 0-7636-2344-X Subj: Art. Family life — brothers & sisters. Self-concept.

My very big little world: a SugarLoaf book ill. by author. Simon & Schuster/Atheneum, 2006. ISBN 0-689-87621-1 Subj: Family life. Self-concept.

Richards, Beah E. *Keep climbing, girls* ill. by R. Gregory Christie. Simon & Schuster, 2006. ISBN 1-4169-0264-3 Subj: Ethnic groups in the U.S. — African Americans. Poetry. Self-concept.

Richardson, Justin. *And Tango makes three* by Justin Richardson & Peter Parnell; ill. by Henry Cole. Simon & Schuster, 2005. ISBN 0-689-87845-1 Subj: Birds — penguins. Homosexuality. Zoos.

Ries, Lori. *Aggie and Ben: three stories* ill. by Frank W. Dormer. Charlesbridge, 2006. ISBN 1-57091-594-6 Subj: Animals — dogs. Pets.

Fix it, Sam ill. by Sue Ramá. Charlesbridge, 2007. ISBN 978-1-57091-598-7 Subj: Character traits — helpfulness. Family life — brothers & sisters.

Riggs, Shannon. *Not in Room 204* ill. by Jaime Zollars. Albert Whitman, 2007. ISBN 978-0-8075-5764-8 Subj: Child abuse. Emotions — fear. Family life.

Ritchie, Alison. *Me and my dad!* ill. by Alison Edgson. Good Books, 2007. ISBN 978-1-56148-565-9 Subj: Animals — bears. Emotions — love. Family life — fathers. Rhyming text.

What Bear likes best! ill. by Dubravka Kolanovic. Good Books, 2005. ISBN 1-56148-473-3 Subj: Activities — playing. Animals — bears. Friendship.

Robberecht, Thierry. *Back into Mommy's tummy* ill. by Philippe Goossens. Houghton Mifflin, 2005. ISBN 0-618-58106-5 Subj: Babies. Emotions — envy, jealousy. Family life — mothers. Family life — new sibling. Sibling rivalry.

Sam is never scared ill. by Philippe Goossens. Houghton Mifflin, 2006. ISBN 0-618-73278-0 Subj: Emotions — fear.

Sam tells stories ill. by Philippe Goossens. Houghton Mifflin, 2007. ISBN 978-0-618-73280-7 Subj: Activities — storytelling. Behavior — lying. Character traits — honesty. Friendship. School.

Sarah's little ghosts ill. by Philippe Goossens. Houghton Mifflin, 2007. ISBN 978-0-618-89210-5 Subj: Behavior — lying. Ghosts.

Robbins, Jacqui. *The new girl . . . and me* ill. by Matt Phelan. Simon & Schuster/Atheneum, 2006. ISBN 978-0-689-86468-1 Subj: Ethnic groups in the U.S. — African Americans. Friendship. Pets. Reptiles — iguanas. School.

Robbins, Ken. *Pumpkins* photos by author. Macmillan, 2006. ISBN 1-59643-184-9 Subj: Gardens, gardening. Seasons — fall.

Robbins, Maria Polushkin. *Mother, Mother, I want another* ill. by Jon Goodell. Random House, 2005. ISBN 0-375-92588-0 Subj: Bedtime. Family life — mothers. Kissing. Sleep.

Roberts, Bethany. *Cookie angel* ill. by Vladimir Vagin. Henry Holt, 2007. ISBN 0-8050-6974-7 Subj: Activities — baking, cooking. Angels. Holidays — Christmas. Toys.

Roberts, Cynthia. *Tow trucks* ill. with photos. Child's World, 2007. ISBN 1-59296-836-7 Subj: Trucks.

Robertson, M. P. *The dragon snatcher* ill. by author. Penguin, 2005. ISBN 0-8037-3103-5 Subj: Dragons. Eggs. Wizards.

Hieronymous Betts and his unusual pets ill. by author. Frances Lincoln, 2005. ISBN 1-84507-289-8 Subj: Family life — brothers & sisters. Pets.

Rocco, John. *Wolf! Wolf!* ill. by author. Hyperion, 2007. ISBN 1-4231-0012-3 Subj: Animals — wolves. Behavior — lying. Behavior — trickery. Folk & fairy tales. Foreign lands — China.

Rock, Lois. *A child's book of graces* ill. by Alison Jay. Good Books, 2006. ISBN 1-56148-514-4 Subj: Religion.

Rockwell, Anne F. *Backyard bear* ill. by Megan Halsey. Walker & Company, 2006. ISBN 0-8027-9573-0 Subj: Animals — bears. Communities, neighborhoods.

Brendan and Belinda and the slam dunk! ill. by Paul Meisel. HarperCollins, 2007. ISBN 978-0-06-028443-5 Subj: Animals — pigs. Family life — brothers & sisters. Multiple births — twins. Sports — basketball. Sportsmanship.

Good morning, Digger ill. by Melanie Hope Greenberg. Penguin, 2005. ISBN 0-670-05959-5 Subj: Machines. Trucks.

Here comes the night ill. by Anne Rockwell. Henry Holt, 2006. ISBN 0-8050-7663-8 Subj: Bedtime. Night.

Little shark ill. by Megan Halsey. Walker & Company, 2005. ISBN 0-8027-8955-2 Subj: Fish — sharks.

Rodman, Mary Ann. *First grade stinks!* ill. by Beth Spiegel. Peachtree, 2006. ISBN 1-56145-377-3 Subj: Behavior — bad day. School — first day.

My best friend ill. by E. B. Lewis. Penguin, 2005. ISBN 0-670-05989-7 Subj: Activities — playing. Ethnic groups in the U.S. — African Americans. Friendship.

Rodriguez, Alex. *Out of the ballpark* ill. by Frank Morrison. Harper-Collins, 2007. ISBN 978-0-06-115194-1 Subj: Character traits — persistence. Sports — baseball.

Rodríguez, Rachel Victoria. *Through Georgia's eyes* ill. by Julie Paschkis. Henry Holt, 2006. ISBN 0-8050-7740-5 Subj: Art. Careers — artists.

Roemer, Heidi Bee. *What kind of seeds are these?* ill. by Olena Kassian. NorthWord, 2006. ISBN 1-55971-955-9 Subj: Rhyming text. Seeds.

Rogalski, Mark. *Tickets to ride: an alphabetic amusement* ill. by author. Running Press, 2006. ISBN 0-7624-2782-5 Subj: ABC books. Parks — amusement.

Rogers, Gregory. *The boy, the bear, the baron, the bard* ill. by author. Macmillan, 2004. ISBN 1-59643-009-5 Subj: Animals — bears. Foreign lands — England. Knights. Wordless.

Midsummer knight ill. by author. Macmillan, 2007. ISBN 978-1-56943-183-6 Subj: Animals — bears. Foreign lands — England. Knights. Wordless.

Rohmann, Eric. *Clara and Asha* ill. by author. Macmillan, 2005. ISBN 1-59643-031-1 Subj: Bedtime. Fish. Imagination — imaginary friends.

Root, Phyllis. *Looking for a moose* ill. by Randy Cecil. Candlewick, 2006. ISBN 0-7636-2005-X Subj: Animals — moose. Games.

Lucia and the light ill. by Mary Grandpre. Candlewick, 2006. ISBN 0-7636-2296-6 Subj: Animals — cats. Mythical creatures — trolls. Seasons — winter. Sun.

Ros, Roser. *Musicians of Bremen / Los musicos de Bremner: a bilingual book* (Grimm, Jacob)

Rose, Deborah Lee. *Ocean babies* ill. by Hiroe Nakata. National Geographic, 2005. ISBN 0-7922-8312-0 Subj: Animals — babies. Sea & seashore.

The twelve days of winter: a school counting book ill. by Carey Armstrong-Ellis. Abrams, 2006. ISBN 0-8109-5472-9 Subj: Counting, numbers. Seasons — winter.

Rose, Marion. *The Christmas tree fairy* ill. by Jason Cockcroft. Bloomsbury, 2005. ISBN 1-58234-668-2 Subj: Behavior — wishing. Fairies. Holidays — Christmas.

Rosen, Michael. *Bear's day out* ill. by Adrian Reynolds. Bloomsbury, 2007. ISBN 978-1-59990-007-0 Subj: Animals — bears. Friendship.

Totally wonderful Miss Plumberry ill. by Chinlun Lee. Candlewick, 2006. ISBN 0-7636-2744-5 Subj: Behavior — bad day. Careers — teachers. School.

Rosen, Michael J. (1954[EN]). *A drive in the country* ill. by Marc Burckhardt. Candlewick, 2007. ISBN 978-0-7636-2140-7 Subj: Activities — traveling. Family life.

Rosenberry, Vera. *Vera's baby sister* ill. by author. Henry Holt, 2005. ISBN 0-8050-7126-1 Subj: Family life — grandfathers. Family life — new sibling. Sibling rivalry.

Rosenthal, Amy Krouse. *Cookies: bite-size life lessons* ill. by Jane Dyer. HarperCollins, 2006. ISBN 0-06-058081-X Subj: Activities — baking, cooking. Behavior. Character traits. Etiquette. Food.

Little Pea ill. by Jen Corace. Chronicle, 2005. ISBN 0-8118-4658-X Subj: Food.

The OK book ill. by Tom Lichtenheld. HarperCollins, 2007. ISBN 978-0-06-115255-9 Subj: Self-concept.

One of those days ill. by Rebecca Doughty. Penguin, 2006. ISBN 0-399-24365-8 Subj: Behavior — bad day.

Rosenthal, Marc. *Phooey!* ill. by author. HarperCollins, 2007. ISBN 978-0-06-075248-4 Subj: Behavior — boredom. Cumulative tales. Humorous stories.

Ross, Michael Elsohn. *Mama's milk* ill. by Ashley Wolff. Ten Speed, 2007. ISBN 978-1-58246-181-6 Subj: Animals. Babies. Family life — mothers. Rhyming text.

Ross, Tony. *I want my tooth* ill. by author. Kane/Miller, 2005. ISBN 1-929132-85-9 Subj: Royalty — princesses. Teeth.

Rossetti-Shustak, Bernadette. *I love you through and through* ill. by Caroline Jayne Church. Scholastic/Cartwheel, 2005. ISBN 0-439-67363-1 Subj: Emotions — love. Format, unusual — board books. Rhyming text. Self-concept.

Roth, Susan L. *Babies can't eat kimchee!* (Patz, Nancy)

Do re mi: if you can read music, thank Guido d'Arezzo ill. by author. Houghton Mifflin, 2007. ISBN 978-0-618-46572-9 Subj: Music.

Great big guinea pigs ill. by author. Bloomsbury, 2006. ISBN 1-58234-724-7 Subj: Animals — guinea pigs. Prehistory.

Rotner, Shelley. *Every season* by Shelley Rotner & Anne Love Woodhull; photos by Shelley Rotner. Macmillan, 2007. ISBN 978-1-59643-136-2 Subj: Nature. Seasons.

Senses at the seashore photos by author. Lerner, 2006. ISBN 0-7613-2897-1 Subj: Sea & seashore — beaches. Senses.

Where does food come from? by Shelley Rotner & Gary Goss; photos by Shelley Rotner. Lerner, 2006. ISBN 0-7613-2935-8 Subj: Food.

Rowe, John A. *I want a hug* ill. by author. Minedition, 2007. ISBN 978-0-698-40064-1 Subj: Animals — porcupines. Emotions — loneliness. Hugging. Reptiles — alligators, crocodiles.

Moondog ill. by author. Minedition, 2005. ISBN 0-698-40031-3 Subj: Animals — dogs. Ecology. Moon. Space & space ships.

Rox, John. *I want a hippopotamus for Christmas* ill. by Bruce Whatley. HarperCollins, 2005. ISBN 0-06-058549-8 Subj: Animals — hippopotamuses. Holidays — Christmas. Songs.

Rozen, Anna. *The merchant of noises* trans. from French by Carl W. Scarbrough; ill. by Francois Avril. Godine, 2006. ISBN 1-56792-321-6 Subj: Careers — salesmen. Character traits — cleverness. Noise, sounds.

Rubel, Nicole. *Ham and Pickles: first day of school* ill. by author. Harcourt, 2006. ISBN 0-15-205039-6 Subj: Animals — hamsters. Family life — brothers & sisters. School — first day.

Ruddell, Deborah. *Today at the bluebird cafe: a branchful of birds* ill. by Joan Rankin. Simon & Schuster, 2007. ISBN 0-689-87153-8 Subj: Birds. Poetry.

Rueda, Claudia. *Let's play in the forest while the wolf is not around* ill. by author. Scholastic, 2006. ISBN 0-439-82323-4 Subj: Animals. Animals — wolves. Games. Songs.

Rumford, James. *Don't touch my hat!* ill. by author. Random House, 2007. ISBN 978-0-375-93782-1 Subj: Careers — sheriffs. Clothing — hats. Superstition. U.S. history — frontier & pioneer life.

Russo, Marisabina. *The bunnies are not in their beds* ill. by author. Random House, 2007. ISBN 978-0-375-93961-7 Subj: Animals — rabbits. Bedtime. Behavior — misbehavior.

Ruurs, Margriet. *In my backyard* ill. by Ron Broda. Tundra, 2007. ISBN 978-0-88776-775-3 Subj: Animals. Nature.

Wake up, Henry Rooster! ill. by Sean Cassidy. Fitzhenry & Whiteside, 2006. ISBN 1-55041-952-8 Subj: Birds — chickens.

Ruzzier, Sergio. *The room of wonders* ill. by author. Farrar, Straus & Giroux, 2006. ISBN 0-374-36343-9 Subj: Animals — pack rats. Behavior — collecting things. Museums.

Ryan, Pam Muñoz. *Nacho and Lolita* ill. by Claudia Rueda. Scholastic, 2005. ISBN 0-439-26968-7 Subj: Birds — swallows. Folk & fairy tales. Missions.

There was no snow on Christmas Eve ill. by Dennis Nolan. Hyperion, 2005. ISBN 0-786-85492-8 Subj: Holidays — Christmas. Religion — Nativity. Rhyming text. Weather.

Ryder, Joanne. *Bear of my heart* ill. by Margie Moore. Simon & Schuster, 2007. ISBN 978-0-689-85947-2 Subj: Animals — bears. Emotions — love. Family life — mothers. Rhyming text.

Dance by the light of the moon ill. by Guy Francis. Hyperion, 2007. ISBN 0-7868-1820-4 Subj: Activities — dancing. Animals. Farms. Rhyming text. Songs.

A pair of polar bears: twin cubs find a home at the San Diego Zoo ill. with photos. Simon & Schuster, 2006. ISBN 0-689-85871-X Subj: Animals — polar bears. Multiple births — twins. Zoos.

Toad by the road: a year in the life of these amazing amphibians ill. by Maggie Kneen. Henry Holt, 2007. ISBN 978-0-8050-7354-6 Subj: Frogs & toads. Poetry. Seasons.

Won't you be my hugaroo? ill. by Melissa Sweet. Harcourt, 2006. ISBN 0-15-205778-1 Subj: Hugging. Rhyming text.

Rylant, Cynthia. *Alligator boy* ill. by Diane Goode. Harcourt, 2007. ISBN 978-0-15-206092-3 Subj: Reptiles — alligators, crocodiles. Rhyming text.

If you'll be my Valentine ill. by Fumi Kosaka. HarperCollins, 2005. ISBN 0-06-009270-X Subj: Activities — making things. Character traits — kindness. Emotions — love. Holidays — Valentine's Day. Letters, cards. Rhyming text.

The stars will still shine ill. by Tiphanie Beeke. HarperCollins, 2005. ISBN 0-06-054640-9 Subj: Nature. Rhyming text. World.

Rymond, Lynda Gene. *Oscar and the mooncats* ill. by Nicoletta Ceccoli. Houghton Mifflin, 2007. ISBN 978-0-618-56316-6 Subj: Animals — cats. Imagination. Moon.

Sabuda, Robert. *Encyclopedia prehistorica: dinosaurs* by Robert Sabuda & Matthew Reinhart; ill. by authors. Candlewick, 2005. ISBN 0-7636-2228-1 Subj: Dinosaurs. Format, unusual — toy & movable books. Prehistory.

Encyclopedia prehistorica: mega-beasts by Robert Sabuda & Matthew Reinhart; ill. by authors. Candlewick, 2007. ISBN 978-0-7636-2230-5 Subj: Format, unusual — toy & movable books. Fossils. Prehistory. Science.

Encyclopedia prehistorica: sharks and other seamonsters by Robert Sabuda & Matthew Reinhart; ill. by authors. Candlewick, 2006. ISBN 978-0-7636-2229-9 Subj: Fish — sharks. Format, unusual — toy & movable books. Fossils. Prehistory. Science. Sea & seashore.

Winter in white: a mini pop-up treat ill. by author. Simon & Schuster/Little Simon, 2007. ISBN 978-0-689-85365-4 Subj: Format, unusual — toy & movable books. Rhyming text. Seasons — winter.

Winter's tale: an original pop-up journey ill. by author. Simon & Schuster/Little Simon, 2005. ISBN 0-689-85363-7 Subj: Format, unusual — toy & movable books. Seasons — winter. Weather — snow.

Sage, James. *Mr. Beast: a monster fright in the night!* ill. by Russell Ayto. Henry Holt, 2005. ISBN 0-8050-7730-8 Subj: Food. Monsters.

St. George, Judith. *So you want to be an explorer?* ill. by David Small. Penguin, 2005. ISBN 0-399-23868-9 Subj: Careers — explorers.

St. Pierre, Stephanie. *What the sea saw* ill. by Beverly Doyle. Peachtree, 2006. ISBN 1-56145-359-5 Subj: Animals. Ecology. Sea & seashore.

Sakai, Komako. *Emily's balloon* ill. by author. Chronicle, 2006. ISBN 0-8118-5219-9 Subj: Activities — ballooning. Friendship.

Salley, Coleen. *Epossumondas saves the day* ill. by Janet Stevens. Harcourt, 2006. ISBN 0-15-205701-3 Subj: Animals. Animals — possums. Folk & fairy tales. Humorous stories.

Saltz, Gail. *Amazing you: getting smart about your private parts* ill. by Lynne Cravath. Button, 2005. ISBN 0-525-47389-0 Subj: Anatomy. Birth. Sex instruction.

Saltzberg, Barney. *Cornelius P. Mud, are you ready for bed?* ill. by author. Candlewick, 2005. ISBN 0-7636-2399-7 Subj: Animals — pigs. Bedtime. Hugging.

Cornelius P. Mud, are you ready for school? ill. by author. Candlewick, 2007. ISBN 978-0-7636-2913-7 Subj: Animals — pigs. Kissing. School.

Hi, Blueberry! ill. by author. Harcourt, 2007. ISBN 978-0-15-205984-2 Subj: Animals — rabbits. Birthdays. Format, unusual — toy & movable books.

I love cats ill. by author. Candlewick, 2005. ISBN 0-7636-2588-4 Subj: Animals — cats. Rhyming text.

I love dogs ill. by author. Candlewick, 2005. ISBN 0-7636-2587-6 Subj: Animals — dogs. Format, unusual — board books. Rhyming text.

Star of the week ill. by author. Candlewick, 2006. ISBN 0-7636-2914-6 Subj: Character traits — being different. Character traits — individuality. School. Self-concept.

Sampson, Michael R. *I love our Earth* (Martin, Bill (William Ivan))

Samuels, Barbara. *Dolores meets her match* ill. by author. Farrar, Straus & Giroux, 2007. ISBN 978-0-374-31758-4 Subj: Animals — cats. Family life — brothers & sisters. Humorous stories. Pets.

Happy Valentine's Day, Dolores ill. by author. Farrar, Straus & Giroux, 2006. ISBN 0-374-32844-7 Subj: Animals — cats. Family life — brothers & sisters. Holidays — Valentine's Day. Humorous stories.

Sanders, Nancy. *D is for drinking gourd: an African American alphabet* ill. by E. B. Lewis. Sleeping Bear, 2007. ISBN 978-1-58536-293-6 Subj: ABC books. Ethnic groups in the U.S. — African Americans. Slavery. U.S. history.

Sandin, Joan. *Boo and Baa have company* (Landstrom, Lena)

The hedgehog, the pig, and their little friend (Anderson, Lena)

A hippo's tale (Landstrom, Lena)

San Souci, Daniel. *The Mighty Pigeon Club* ill. by author. Ten Speed, 2007. ISBN 978-1-58246-213-4 Subj: Birds — pigeons. Clubs, gangs.

Santiago, Esmeralda. *A doll for Navidades* ill. by Enrique O. Sánchez. Scholastic, 2005. ISBN 0-439-55398-9 Subj: Family life. Foreign lands — Puerto Rico. Gifts. Holidays — Christmas. Toys — dolls.

Santore, Charles. *Three hungry pigs and the wolf who came to dinner* ill. by author. Random House, 2005. ISBN 0-375-92946-0 Subj: Animals — pigs. Animals — wolves. Food.

Santoro, Scott. *Farm-fresh cats* ill. by author. HarperCollins, 2006. ISBN 0-06-078179-3 Subj: Animals — cats. Farms.

Sasso, Sandy Eisenberg. *Butterflies under our hats* ill. by Joani Keller Rothenberg. Paraclete, 2006. ISBN 1-55725-474-5 Subj: Character traits — luck. Foreign lands — Poland. Hope. Jewish culture.

Sauer, Tammi. *Cowboy camp* ill. by Mike Reed. Sterling, 2005. ISBN 1-4027-2224-9 Subj: Behavior — bullying. Camps, camping. Character traits — individuality. Cowboys, cowgirls.

Savadier, Elivia. *No haircut today!* ill. by author. Macmillan, 2005. ISBN 1-59643-046-X Subj: Emotions — fear. Hair.

Time to get dressed! ill. by author. Macmillan, 2006. ISBN 1-59643-161-X Subj: Babies. Character traits — individuality. Clothing. Family life — fathers.

Say, Allen. *Kamishibai man* ill. by author. Houghton Mifflin, 2005. ISBN 0-618-47954-6 Subj: Activities — storytelling. Foreign lands — Japan. Theater.

Sayles, Elizabeth. *The goldfish yawned* ill. by author. Henry Holt, 2005. ISBN 0-8050-7624-7 Subj: Bedtime. Dreams. Rhyming text.

Sayre, April Pulley. *The bumblebee queen* ill. by Patricia J. Wynne. Charlesbridge, 2005. ISBN 1-57091-362-5 Subj: Insects — bees.

Hush, little puppy ill. by Susan Winter. Henry Holt, 2007. ISBN 978-0-8050-7102-3 Subj: Animals — dogs. Bedtime. Rhyming text.

Stars beneath your bed: the surprising story of dust ill. by Ann Jonas. HarperCollins, 2005. ISBN 0-06-057189-6 Subj: Character traits — cleanliness.

Vulture view ill. by Steve Jenkins. Henry Holt, 2007. ISBN 978-0-8050-7557-1 Subj: Birds — vultures. Rhyming text.

Scarbrough, Carl W. *The merchant of noises* (Rozen, Anna)

Schachner, Judith Byron. *Skippyjon Jones and the big bones* ill. by author. Penguin, 2007. ISBN 978-0-525-47884-3 Subj: Animals — cats. Animals — dogs. Dinosaurs.

Skippyjon Jones in mummy trouble ill. by author. Penguin, 2006. ISBN 0-525-47754-3 Subj: Animals — cats. Animals — dogs. Mummies.

Schaefer, Carole Lexa. *The Bora-Bora dress* ill. by Catherine Stock. Candlewick, 2005. ISBN 0-7636-1234-0 Subj: Clothing — dresses. Parties.

Cool time song ill. by Pierr Morgan. Penguin, 2005. ISBN 0-670-05928-5 Subj: Animals. Foreign lands — Africa.

Dragon dancing ill. by Pierr Morgan. Penguin, 2007. ISBN 0-670-06084-4 Subj: Activities — dancing. Dragons. Imagination.

Schaefer, Lola M. *Frankie Stein* ill. by Kevan Atteberry. Marshall Cavendish, 2007. ISBN 978-0-7614-5358-1 Subj: Character traits — being different. Family life. Monsters.

An island grows ill. by Cathie Felstead. HarperCollins, 2006. ISBN 0-06-623930-3 Subj: Islands. Rhyming text. Volcanoes.

Toolbox twins ill. by Melissa Iwai. Henry Holt, 2006. ISBN 0-8050-7733-2 Subj: Family life — fathers. Rhyming text. Tools.

Schembri, Pamela. *The secret lunch special* (Catalanotto, Peter)

Schertle, Alice. *The adventures of old Bo Bear* ill. by David Parkins. Chronicle, 2006. ISBN 0-8118-3476-X Subj: Activities — playing. Character traits — cleanliness. Toys — bears.

Very hairy bear ill. by Matt Phelan. Harcourt, 2007. ISBN 978-0-15-216568-0 Subj: Animals — bears. Hibernation. Seasons.

We ill. by Kenneth Addison. Lee & Low, 2007. ISBN 978-1-58430-060-1 Subj: Poetry. World.

Schmidt, Karen Lee. *Carl's nose* ill. by author. Harcourt, 2006. ISBN 0-15-205049-3 Subj: Animals — dogs. Careers — meteorologists. Mountains. Weather.

Schneider, Christine M. *I'm bored!* ill. by Herve Pinel. Houghton Mifflin, 2006. ISBN 0-618-65760-6 Subj: Animals — dogs. Behavior — boredom. Toys — bears.

Schneider, Howie. *Wilky the White House cockroach* ill. by author. Penguin, 2006. ISBN 0-399-24388-7 Subj: Insects — cockroaches.

Schneider, Josh. *You'll be sorry* ill. by author. Houghton Mifflin, 2007. ISBN 978-0-618-81932-4 Subj: Behavior — misbehavior. Family life — brothers & sisters. Weather — floods.

Schoenherr, Ian. *Pip and Squeak* ill. by author. HarperCollins, 2007. ISBN 0-06-087253-5 Subj: Animals — mice. Animals — rabbits. Birthdays. Weather — snow.

Schories, Pat. *Jack and the night visitors* ill. by author. Boyds Mills, 2006. ISBN 1-932425-33-0 Subj: Aliens. Animals — dogs. Space & space ships. Wordless.

Schotter, Roni. *The boy who loved words* ill. by Giselle Potter. Random House, 2006. ISBN 0-375-93601-7 Subj: Language. Self-concept.

Mama, I'll give you the world ill. by S. Saelig Gallagher. Random House, 2006. ISBN 0-375-93612-2 Subj: Beauty shops. Birthdays. Family life — mothers. Family life — single-parent families. Parties.

Passover! ill. by Erin Eitter Kono. Little, Brown, 2006. ISBN 0-316-93991-9 Subj: Holidays — Passover. Jewish culture. Religion.

When the Wizzy Foot goes walking ill. by Mike Wohnoutka. Penguin, 2007. ISBN 978-0-525-47791-4 Subj: Behavior — misbehavior. Concepts — size. Giants. Rhyming text.

Schroeder, Lisa. *Baby can't sleep* ill. by Viviana Garofoli. Sterling, 2005. ISBN 1-4027-2171-4 Subj: Animals — sheep. Babies. Bedtime. Counting, numbers. Rhyming text.

Schubert, Dieter. *There's a crocodile under my bed!* (Schubert, Ingrid)

Schubert, Ingrid. *There's a crocodile under my bed!* by Ingrid & Dieter Schubert; ill. by authors. Boyds Mills, 2005. ISBN 1-932425-48-9 Subj: Bedtime. Reptiles — alligators, crocodiles.

Schubert, Leda. *Ballet of the elephants* ill. by Robert Andrew Parker. Macmillan, 2006. ISBN 1-59643-075-3 Subj: Animals — elephants. Ballet.

Here comes Darrell ill. by Mary Azarian. Houghton Mifflin, 2005. ISBN 0-618-41605-6 Subj: Barns. Character traits — helpfulness. Communities, neighborhoods. Machines. Seasons. Tractors. Trucks.

Schulman, Janet. *Ten trick-or-treaters: a Halloween counting book* ill. by Linda Davick. Random House, 2005. ISBN 0-375-95225-9 Subj: Counting, numbers. Holidays — Halloween. Rhyming text.

Schwartz, Amy. *A beautiful girl* ill. by Amy Schartz. Macmillan, 2006. ISBN 1-59643-165-2 Subj: Anatomy. Animals. Animals — elephants. Birds — robins. Character traits — appearance. Fish. Insects — flies.

Begin at the beginning: a little artist learns about life ill. by author. HarperCollins, 2005. ISBN 0-06-000112-7 Subj: Behavior — growing up.

Oscar: the big adventures of a little sock monkey by Amy Schwartz & Leonard S. Marcus; ill. by Amy Schwartz. HarperCollins, 2006. ISBN 0-06-072622-9 Subj: Animals — monkeys. Animals — rabbits. Pets. School. Toys.

Starring Miss Darlene ill. by author. Macmillan, 2007. ISBN 978-1-59643-230-7 Subj: Animals. Animals — hippopotamuses. Behavior — mistakes. Careers — actors. Self-concept. Theater.

Schwartz, Corey Rosen. *Hop! Plop!* by Corey Rosen Schwartz & Tali Klein; ill. by Olivier Dunrea. Walker & Company, 2006. ISBN 0-8027-8056-3 Subj: Activities — playing. Animals — elephants. Animals — mice. Friendship. Noise, sounds.

Schwartz, David M. *Where in the wild: camouflaged animals concealed and revealed: ear-tickling poems* by David M. Schwartz & Yael Schy; photos by Dwight Kuhn. Ten Speed, 2007. ISBN 978-1-58246-207-

3 Subj: Animals. Disguises. Format, unusual — toy & movable books. Poetry.

Schwartz, Roslyn. *Tales from Parc la Fontaine* ill. by author. Firefly, 2006. ISBN 1-55451-044-9 Subj: Animals. Nature. Parks.

Schwarz, Viviane. *Shark and Lobster's amazing undersea adventure* ill. by author. Candlewick, 2006. ISBN 0-7636-2910-3 Subj: Crustaceans — lobsters. Emotions — fear. Fish — sharks. Sea & seashore.

Schy, Yael. *Where in the wild: camouflaged animals concealed and revealed: ear-tickling poems* (Schwartz, David M.)

Scieszka, Jon. *Cowboy and Octopus* ill. by Lane Smith. Penguin, 2007. ISBN 978-0-670-91058-8 Subj: Cowboys, cowgirls. Friendship. Octopuses.

Scillian, Devin. *Brewster the rooster* ill. by Lee White. Little, Brown, 2007. ISBN 978-1-58536-311-7 Subj: Birds — chickens. Glasses. Rhyming text.

Sciurba, Katie. *Oye, Celia! A song for Celia Cruz* ill. by Edel Rodriguez. Henry Holt, 2007. ISBN 0-8050-7468-6 Subj: Careers — singers. Foreign lands — Cuba. Music.

Scott, Nathan Kumar. *Mangoes and bananas* ill. by T. Balaji. Tara, 2006. ISBN 81-86211-06-3 Subj: Animals — deer. Animals — monkeys. Behavior — greed. Behavior — trickery. Folk & fairy tales. Foreign lands — Indonesia.

Scotton, Rob. *Go to sleep, Russell the sheep* ill. by author. HarperCollins, 2007. ISBN 978-0-06-128434-2 Subj: Animals — sheep. Bedtime. Format, unusual — board books. Sleep.

Russell and the lost treasure ill. by author. HarperCollins, 2006. ISBN 0-06-059851-4 Subj: Activities — photographing. Animals — sheep.

Russell the sheep ill. by author. HarperCollins, 2005. ISBN 0-06-059848-4 Subj: Animals — sheep. Bedtime. Counting, numbers. Sleep.

Russell's Christmas magic ill. by author. HarperCollins, 2007. ISBN 978-0-06-059854-9 Subj: Animals — sheep. Character traits — helpfulness. Holidays — Christmas. Santa Claus.

Seeger, Laura Vaccaro. *Black? White! Day? Night!* ill. by author. Macmillan, 2006. ISBN 1-59643-185-7 Subj: Concepts — opposites. Format, unusual — toy & movable books.

Dog and Bear: two friends, three stories ill. by author. Macmillan, 2007. ISBN 978-1-59643-053-2 Subj: Animals — dogs. Friendship. Toys — bears.

First the egg ill. by author. Macmillan, 2007. ISBN 978-1-59643-272-7 Subj: Caldecott award honor books. Concepts — change. Format, unusual — toy & movable books.

Lemons are not red ill. by author. Macmillan, 2004. ISBN 978-1-59643-008-2 Subj: Concepts — color. Format, unusual — toy & movable books.

Walter was worried ill. by author. Macmillan, 2005. ISBN 978-1-59643-068-6 Subj: ABC books. Emotions. Language. Weather — storms.

Seeger, Pete. *The deaf musicians* by Pete Seeger & Paul DuBois Jacobs; ill. by R. Gregory Christie. Penguin, 2006. ISBN 0-399-24316-X Subj: Careers — musicians. Handicaps — deafness. Music.

Some friends to feed: the story of Stone Soup by Pete Seeger & Paul DuBois Jacobs; ill. by Michael Hays. Penguin, 2005. ISBN 0-399-24017-9 Subj: Careers — military. Character traits — cleverness. Folk & fairy tales. Food. Foreign lands — Germany.

Segal, John. *Carrot soup* ill. by author. Simon & Schuster, 2006. ISBN 0-689-87702-1 Subj: Animals — rabbits. Food. Gardens, gardening.

The lonely moose ill. by author. Hyperion, 2007. ISBN 978-1-4231-0173-4 Subj: Animals — moose. Birds. Emotions — loneliness. Friendship.

Seki, Sunny. *The tale of the lucky cat* ill. by author. East West, 2007. ISBN 978-0-966943-75-7 Subj: Animals — cats. Character traits — luck. Folk & fairy tales. Foreign lands — Japan.

Selick, Henry. *Moongirl* ill. by Peter Chan. Candlewick, 2006. ISBN 0-7636-3068-3 Subj: Merry-go-rounds. Monsters. Moon. Sports — fishing.

Selznick, Brian. *The invention of Hugo Cabret: a novel in words and pictures* ill. by author. Scholastic, 2007. ISBN 978-0-439-81378-5 Subj: Caldecott award books. Foreign lands — France. Mystery stories. Orphans. Robots.

Sendak, Maurice. *Mommy?* ill. by Maurice Sendak; paper engineering by Matthew Reinhart. Scholastic, 2006. ISBN 0-439-88050-5 Subj: Format, unusual — toy & movable books. Monsters.

Senning, Cindy Post. *Emily's everyday manners* (Post, Peggy)

Serfozo, Mary. *Whooo's there?* ill. by Jeffrey Scherer. Random House, 2007. ISBN 978-0-375-84050-0 Subj: Animals. Birds — owls. Forest, woods. Night. Rhyming text.

Seskin, Steve. *A chance to shine* by Steve Seskin & Allen Shamblin; ill. by R. Gregory Christie. Ten Speed, 2006. ISBN 1-58246-167-0 Subj: Ethnic groups in the U.S. — African Americans. Homeless. Songs.

Shah, Idries. *Fatima the spinner and the tent* ill. by Natasha Delmar. Hoopoe, 2006. ISBN 1-883536-42-1 Subj: Activities — weaving. Folk & fairy tales. Foreign lands.

Shahan, Sherry. *Cool cats counting* ill. by Paula Barragán. August House, 2005. ISBN 0-87483-757-X Subj: Animals. Counting, numbers.

That's not how you play soccer, Daddy ill. by Tatjana Mai-Wyss. Peachtree, 2007. ISBN 978-1-56145-416-7 Subj: Family life — fathers. Sports — soccer.

Shamblin, Allen. *A chance to shine* (Seskin, Steve)

Shannon, David. *David smells: a diaper David book* ill. by author. Scholastic/Blue Sky, 2005. ISBN 0-439-69138-9 Subj: Babies. Format, unusual — board books. Senses.

Good boy, Fergus! ill. by author. Scholastic, 2006. ISBN 0-439-49027-8 Subj: Animals — dogs. Behavior — misbehavior.

Oh, David! A diaper David book ill. by author. Scholastic/Blue Sky, 2005. ISBN 0-439-68881-7 Subj: Babies. Behavior — misbehavior. Format, unusual — board books.

Oops! A diaper David book ill. by author. Scholastic/Blue Sky, 2005. ISBN 0-439-68882-5 Subj: Babies. Format, unusual — board books. Language.

Shannon, George. *Busy in the garden* ill. by Sam Williams. Harper-Collins, 2006. ISBN 0-06-000464-9 Subj: Gardens, gardening. Poetry.

Rabbit's gift ill. by Laura Dronzek. Harcourt, 2007. ISBN 978-0-15-206073-2 Subj: Animals. Animals — rabbits. Behavior — sharing. Folk & fairy tales. Friendship.

The Secret Chicken Club ill. by Deborah Zemke. Handprint, 2005. ISBN 1-59354-118-X Subj: Animals — bulls, cows. Birds — chickens. Clubs, gangs.

White is for blueberry ill. by Laura Dronzek. HarperCollins, 2005. ISBN 0-06-029275-X Subj: Concepts — color. Nature. Senses — sight.

Shapiro, Jody Fickes. *Family lullaby* ill. by Cathie Felstead. Harper-Collins, 2007. ISBN 978-0-06-051482-2 Subj: Babies. Emotions — love. Family life.

Sharkey, Niamh. *Santasaurus* ill. by author. Candlewick, 2005. ISBN 0-7636-2671-6 Subj: Dinosaurs. Holidays — Christmas. Santa Claus.

Shaw, Greg. *Wake up, sleepy bear!* (Morton-Shaw, Christine)

Shea, Bob. *New socks* ill. by author. Little, Brown, 2007. ISBN 978-0-316-01357-4 Subj: Behavior — growing up. Birds — chickens. Character traits — confidence. Clothing — socks. Self-concept.

Shea, Pegi Deitz. *The boy and the spell* ill. by Serena Riglietti. Pumpkin House, 2007. ISBN 978-0-964601-04-8 Subj: Emotions — anger. Music.

Sheldon, Annette. *Big sister now: a story about me and our new baby* ill. by Karen Maizel. Magination, 2006. ISBN 1-59147-243-1 Subj: Babies. Family life — brothers & sisters. Family life — new sibling.

Shepard, Aaron. *One-eye! Two-eyes! Three-eyes! A very Grimm fairy tale* ill. by Gary Clement. Simon & Schuster/Atheneum, 2006. ISBN 0-689-86740-9 Subj: Animals — goats. Folk & fairy tales. Magic. Royalty — princes.

Sherry, Kevin. *I'm the biggest thing in the ocean* ill. by author. Penguin, 2007. ISBN 978-0-8037-3192-9 Subj: Concepts — size. Sea & seashore. Squid.

Sheth, Kashmira. *My Dadima wears a sari* ill. by Yoshiko Jaeggi. Peachtree, 2007. ISBN 978-1-56145-392-4 Subj: Clothing. Ethnic groups in the U.S. — East Indian Americans. Family life — grandmothers.

Shindler, Ramon. *Found alphabet* by Ramon Shindler & Wojciech Graniczewski; ill. by Anita Andrzejewska & Andrzej Pilichowski-Ragno. Houghton Mifflin, 2005. ISBN 0-618-44232-4 Subj: ABC books. Rhyming text.

Shore, Diane Z. *Look both ways: a cautionary tale* by Diane Z. Shore & Jessica Alexander; ill. by Teri Weidner. Bloomsbury, 2005. ISBN 1-58234-968-1 Subj: Animals — squirrels. Rhyming text. Safety.

This is the dream by Diane Z. Shore & Jessica Alexander; ill. by James Ransome. HarperCollins, 2006. ISBN 0-06-055520-3 Subj: Ethnic groups in the U.S. — African Americans. Prejudice. Rhyming text. U.S. history.

Shoulders, Debbie. *D is for drum: a Native American alphabet* (Shoulders, Michael)

Shoulders, Michael. *D is for drum: a Native American alphabet* by Michael & Debbie Shoulders; ill. by Irving Toddy. Sleeping Bear, 2006. ISBN 1-58536-274-3 Subj: ABC books. Indians of North America.

Shulevitz, Uri. *So sleepy story* ill. by author. Farrar, Straus & Giroux, 2006. ISBN 0-374-37031-1 Subj: Imagination. Music. Night. Sleep.

Shulman, Goldie. *Way too much challah dough* ill. by Vitaliy Romanenko. Hachai, 2006. ISBN 1-929628-23-4 Subj: Behavior — running away. Food. Jewish culture.

Shulman, Lisa. *The moon might be milk* ill. by Will Hillenbrand. Penguin, 2007. ISBN 978-0-525-47647-4 Subj: Activities — baking, cooking. Animals. Family life — grandmothers. Food. Moon.

Over in the meadow at the big ballet ill. by Sarah Massini. Penguin, 2007. ISBN 978-0-399-24289-2 Subj: Ballet. Birds — swans. Rhyming text.

Shulman, Mark. *A is for zebra* ill. by Tamara Petrosino. Sterling, 2006. ISBN 1-4027-3494-8 Subj: ABC books.

Aa is for Aardvark ill. by author. Sterling, 2005. ISBN 1-4027-2871-9 Subj: ABC books.

Sidjanski, Brigitte. *Little Chicken and Little Duck* ill. by author. Minedition, 2007. ISBN 978-0-698-40055-9 Subj: Birds — chickens. Birds — ducks. Friendship. Prejudice.

Sidman, Joyce. *Butterfly eyes and other secrets of the meadow* ill. by Beth Krommes. Houghton Mifflin, 2006. ISBN 0-618-56313-X Subj: Nature. Poetry. Riddles & jokes.

Meow ruff: A story in concrete poetry ill. by Michelle Berg. Houghton Mifflin, 2006. ISBN 0-618-44894-2 Subj: Animals — cats. Animals — dogs. Poetry. Weather — storms.

Song of the water boatman: & other pond poems ill. by Beckie Prange. Houghton Mifflin, 2005. ISBN 0-618-13547-2 Subj: Caldecott award honor books. Lakes, ponds. Nature. Poetry.

Sierra, Judy. *Mind your manners, B. B. Wolf* ill. by J. Otto Seibold. Random House, 2007. ISBN 978-0-375-83532-2 Subj: Animals — wolves. Etiquette. Folk & fairy tales. Humorous stories. Libraries.

The secret science project that almost ate school ill. by Stephen Gammell. Simon & Schuster, 2006. ISBN 1-4169-1175-8 Subj: Rhyming text. School. Science.

Thelonius Monster's sky-high fly pie: a revolting rhyme ill. by Edward Koren. Random House, 2006. ISBN 0-375-93218-6 Subj: Food. Insects — flies. Monsters. Rhyming text.

Sill, Cathryn P. *About marsupials: a guide for children* ill. by John Sill. Peachtree, 2006. ISBN 1-56145-358-7 Subj: Animals — marsupials.

Sillifant, Alec. *Farmer Ham* ill. by Mike Spoor. NorthSouth, 2007. ISBN 978-0-7358-2134-7 Subj: Animals — pigs. Birds — crows. Careers — farmers. Farms.

Silvano, Wendi. *What does the wind say?* ill. by Joan M. Delehanty. NorthWord, 2006. ISBN 1-55971-954-0 Subj: Poetry. Rhyming text.

Simeon, Jean-Pierre. *This is a poem that heals fish* trans. by Claudia Zoe Bedrick; ill. by Olivier Tallec. Enchanted Lion, 2007. ISBN 978-1-59270-067-7 Subj: Fish. Pets. Poetry.

Simmonds, Posy. *Baker cat* ill. by author. Red Fox, 2006. ISBN 0-09-945596-X Subj: Activities — baking, cooking. Animals — cats. Animals — mice. Careers — bakers.

Simmons, Jane. *Together* ill. by author. Random House, 2007. ISBN 978-0-375-84339-6 Subj: Animals — dogs. Friendship.

Simon, Charnan. *Big bad Buzz* ill. by Len Epstein. Child's World, 2006. ISBN 1-59296-617-9 Subj: Animals — dogs. Behavior — animals, dislike of. Character traits — bravery. Emotions — fear.

A greedy little pig ill. by Marcy Ramsey. Child's World, 2006. ISBN 1-59296-622-5 Subj: Animals — pigs. Behavior — greed.

Jeremy Jones, clumsy guy ill. by Cari Pillo. Child's World, 2006. ISBN 1-59296-619-5 Subj: Character traits — clumsiness.

Messy Molly ill. by Mernie Gallagher-Cole. Child's World, 2006. ISBN 1-59296-625-X Subj: Behavior — lost & found possessions. Behavior — messy. Character traits — orderliness. Toys — bears.

Singer, Marilyn. *City lullaby* ill. by Carll Cneut. Houghton Mifflin, 2007. ISBN 978-0-618-60703-7 Subj: Babies. Cities, towns. Counting, numbers. Noise, sounds. Rhyming text.

Let's build a clubhouse ill. by Timothy Bush. Houghton Mifflin, 2006. ISBN 0-618-30670-6 Subj: Character traits — cooperation. Clubs, gangs. Rhyming text. Tools.

Sís, Peter. *Play, Mozart, play* ill. by author. HarperCollins, 2006. ISBN 0-06-112182-7 Subj: Careers — musicians. Music.

The wall: growing up behind the Iron Curtain ill. by author. Farrar, Straus & Giroux, 2007. ISBN 978-0-374-34701-7 Subj: Caldecott award honor books. Careers — artists. Foreign lands — Czechoslovakia.

Skalak, Barbara Anne. *Waddle, waddle, quack, quack, quack* ill. by Sylvia Long. Chronicle, 2005. ISBN 0-8118-4342-4 Subj: Behavior — lost. Birds — ducks. Rhyming text.

Skinner, Daphne. *All aboard!* ill. by Jerry Smath. Kane, 2007. ISBN 978-1-57565-239-9 Subj: Activities — traveling. Time. Trains.

Skultety, Nancy. *From here to there* ill. by Tammie Lyon. Boyds Mills, 2005. ISBN 1-59078-092-2 Subj: Careers — construction workers. Roads. Trucks.

Slate, Joseph. *Miss Bindergarten celebrates the last day of kindergarten* ill. by Ashley Wolff. Penguin, 2006. ISBN 0-525-47744-6 Subj: ABC books. Animals. Careers — teachers. Rhyming text. School.

Miss Bindergarten has a wild day in kindergarten ill. by Ashley Wolff. Penguin, 2005. ISBN 0-525-47084-0 Subj: ABC books. Animals. Behavior — bad day. Careers — teachers. Rhyming text. School.

What star is this? ill. by Alison Jay. Penguin, 2005. ISBN 0-399-24014-4 Subj: Religion — Nativity. Rhyming text.

Slater, Dashka. *Baby shoes* ill. by Hiroe Nakata. Bloomsbury, 2006. ISBN 1-58234-684-4 Subj: Babies. Clothing — shoes. Concepts — color. Rhyming text.

Firefighters in the dark ill. by Nicoletta Ceccoli. Houghton Mifflin, 2006. ISBN 0-618-55459-9 Subj: Bedtime. Careers — firefighters. Dreams.

Slingsby, Janet. *Hetty's 100 hats* ill. by Emma Dodd. Good Books, 2005. ISBN 1-56148-456-3 Subj: Behavior — collecting things. Birthdays. Clothing — hats. Counting, numbers.

Sloat, Teri. *I'm a duck!* ill. by author. Penguin, 2006. ISBN 0-399-24274-0 Subj: Behavior — growing up. Birds — ducks.

This is the house that was tidy and neat ill. by R. W. Alley. Henry Holt, 2005. ISBN 0-8050-6921-6 Subj: Character traits — cleanliness. Rhyming text.

Slonim, David. *He came with the couch* ill. by author. Chronicle, 2005. ISBN 0-8118-4430-7 Subj: Friendship. Furniture — couches, sofas.

Smalley, Elisa. *Zoe Sophia in New York: the mystery of the Pink Phoenix papers* (Mauner, Claudia)

Smallman, Steve. *The lamb who came for dinner* ill. by Joelle Dreidemy. Tiger Tales, 2007. ISBN 978-1-58925-067-3 Subj: Animals — sheep. Animals — wolves. Friendship.

The very greedy bee ill. by Jack Tickle. Tiger Tales, 2007. ISBN 978-1-58925-065-9 Subj: Behavior — greed. Behavior — sharing. Insects — bees.

Smalls, Irene. *My Nana and me* ill. by Cathy Ann Johnson. Little, Brown, 2005. ISBN 0-316-16821-1 Subj: Activities — playing. Ethnic groups in the U.S. — African Americans. Family life — grandmothers.

My Pop Pop and me ill. by Cathy Ann Johnson. Little, Brown, 2006. ISBN 0-316-73422-5 Subj: Activities — baking, cooking. Ethnic groups in the U.S. — African Americans. Family life — grandfathers. Rhyming text.

Smath, Jerry. *Sammy Salami* ill. by author. Abrams, 2007. ISBN 978-0-8109-9350-1 Subj: Activities — traveling. Activities — vacationing. Animals — cats. Pets.

Smee, Nicola. *No bed without Ted* ill. by author. Bloomsbury, 2005. ISBN 1-58234-963-0 Subj: Bedtime. Behavior — lost & found possessions. Format, unusual — toy & movable books. Toys — bears.

Smiley, Norene. *That stripy cat* ill. by Tara Anderson. Fitzhenry & Whiteside, 2007. ISBN 978-1-55005-164-3 Subj: Animals — cats.

Smith, Cynthia Leitich. *Santa knows* by Cynthia Leitich & Greg Leitich Smith; ill. by Steve Bjorkman. Penguin, 2006. ISBN 0-525-47757-8 Subj: Holidays — Christmas. Santa Claus.

Smith, Dana Kessimakis. *A brave spaceboy* ill. by Laura Freeman. Hyperion, 2005. ISBN 0-7868-0933-7 Subj: Imagination. Moving.

Smith, Greg Leitich. *Santa knows* (Smith, Cynthia Leitich)

Smith, Jada Pinkett. *Girls hold up this world* ill. by Donyell Kennedy-McCullough. Scholastic/Cartwheel, 2005. ISBN 0-439-08793-7 Subj: Gender roles. Rhyming text. Self-concept.

Smith, Lane. *John, Paul, George & Ben* ill. by author. Hyperion, 2006. ISBN 0-7868-4893-6 Subj: Humorous stories. U.S. history.

Smith, Lois T. *Carrie and Carl play* ill. by author. Candlewick, 2007. ISBN 978-0-7636-1690-8 Subj: Activities — playing. Format, unusual — toy & movable books.

Smith, Maggie (Margaret C.). *One naked baby: counting to ten and back again* ill. by author. Random House, 2007. ISBN 0-375-83329-3 Subj: Babies. Counting, numbers. Rhyming text.

Smith, Marie. *N is for our nation's capital: a Washington, DC alphabet* by Marie & Roland Smith; ill. by Barbara Leonard Gibson. Sleeping Bear, 2005. ISBN 1-58556-148-8 Subj: ABC books. Cities, towns. U.S. history.

Z is for zookeeper: a zoo alphabet by Marie & Roland Smith; ill. by Henry Cole. Sleeping Bear, 2005. ISBN 1-58536-158-5 Subj: ABC books. Zoos.

Smith, Roland. *N is for our nation's capital: a Washington, DC alphabet* (Smith, Marie)

Z is for zookeeper: a zoo alphabet (Smith, Marie)

Smith, Stu. *The bubble gum kid* ill. by Julia Woolf. Running Press, 2006. ISBN 0-7624-2046-4 Subj: Behavior — bullying. Rhyming text.

Sneed, Brad. *Deputy Harvey and the ant cow caper* ill. by author. Penguin, 2005. ISBN 0-8037-3023-3 Subj: Careers — sheriffs. Crime. Insects — ants. Mystery stories. U.S. history — frontier & pioneer life.

Sneed, Dani. *My even day* (Fisher, Doris)

One odd day (Fisher, Doris)

So, Sungwan. *Shanyi goes to China* ill. with photos. Frances Lincoln, 2006. ISBN 1-84507-470-X Subj: Foreign lands — China.

Sobel, June. *The goodnight train* ill. by Laura Huliska-Beith. Harcourt, 2006. ISBN 0-15-205436-7 Subj: Bedtime. Rhyming text. Trains.

Shiver me letters: a pirate ABC ill. by Henry Cole. Harcourt, 2006. ISBN 0-15-216732-3 Subj: ABC books. Pirates. Rhyming text.

Sockabasin, Allen. *Thanks to the animals* ill. by Rebekah Raye. Tilbury House, 2005. ISBN 0-88448-270-7 Subj: Animals. Babies. Behavior — lost. Family life — fathers. Indians of North America — Passamaquoddy.

Soto, Gary. *Chato goes cruisin'* ill. by Susan Guevara. Penguin, 2005. ISBN 0-399-23974-X Subj: Animals — cats. Animals — dogs. Boats, ships. Ethnic groups in the U.S. — Mexican Americans. Foreign languages. Illness.

My little car / Mi carrito ill. by Pam Paparone. Penguin, 2006. ISBN 0-399-23220-6 Subj: Automobiles. Ethnic groups in the U.S. —

Mexican Americans. Family life — grandfathers. Foreign languages. Toys.

Souhami, Jessica. *The little, little house* ill. by author. Frances Lincoln, 2006. ISBN 1-84507-108-5 Subj: Folk & fairy tales. Humorous stories. Problem solving.

Sausages ill. by author. Frances Lincoln, 2006. ISBN 1-84507-397-5 Subj: Behavior — wishing. Character traits — foolishness. Folk & fairy tales. Food.

Soule, Jean Conder. *Never tease a weasel* ill. by George Booth. Random House, 2007. ISBN 0-375-83420-2 Subj: Animals. Behavior — bullying. Character traits — kindness to animals. Humorous stories. Rhyming text.

Sperring, Mark. *The fairytale cake* ill. by Jonathan Langley. Scholastic/Chicken House, 2005. ISBN 0-439-68329-7 Subj: Birthdays. Books, reading. Food. Rhyming text.

Mermaid dreams ill. by The Pope Twins. Scholastic/Chicken House, 2006. ISBN 0-439-79610-5 Subj: Bedtime. Mythical creatures — mermaids, mermen. Sea & seashore.

Spinelli, Eileen. *The best time of day* ill. by Bryan Langdo. Harcourt, 2005. ISBN 0-15-205051-5 Subj: Animals. Careers — farmers. Farms. Rhyming text.

Callie Cat, ice skater ill. by Anne Kennedy. Albert Whitman, 2007. ISBN 978-0-8075-1042-1 Subj: Animals — cats. Contests. Sports — ice skating.

City angel ill. by Kyrsten Brooker. Penguin, 2005. ISBN 0-8037-2821-2 Subj: Angels. Cities, towns. Rhyming text.

Heat wave ill. by Betsy Lewin. Harcourt, 2007. ISBN 978-0-15-216779-0 Subj: Days of the week, months of the year. Weather.

Hero cat ill. by Jo Ellen McAllister Stammen. Marshall Cavendish, 2006. ISBN 0-7614-5223-0 Subj: Animals — cats. Character traits — bravery. Fire.

Polar bear, arctic hare: poems of the frozen north ill. by Eugenie Fernandes. Boyds Mills, 2007. ISBN 978-1-59078-344-3 Subj: Animals. Foreign lands — Arctic. Poetry.

Someday ill. by Rosie Winstead. Penguin, 2007. ISBN 978-0-8037-2941-4 Subj: Imagination.

When you are happy ill. by Geraldo Valerio. Simon & Schuster, 2006. ISBN 0-689-86251-2 Subj: Emotions. Family life.

Spirin, Gennady. *A apple pie* ill. by author. Penguin, 2005. ISBN 0-399-23981-2 Subj: ABC books. Nursery rhymes.

Martha ill. by author. Penguin, 2005. ISBN 0-399-23980-4 Subj: Birds — crows. Foreign lands — Russia.

We three kings ill. by author. Simon & Schuster/Atheneum, 2007. ISBN 978-0-689-82114-1 Subj: Holidays — Christmas. Religion — Nativity. Songs.

Spurr, Elizabeth. *Pumpkin hill* ill. by Whitney Martin. Holiday House, 2006. ISBN 0-8234-1869-3 Subj: Holidays — Halloween.

Stadler, Alexander. *Beverly Billingsly takes the cake* ill. by author. Harcourt, 2005. ISBN 0-15-205357-3 Subj: Activities — baking, cooking. Food. Imagination. Parties.

Stadler, John. *Take me out to the ball game: a pop-up book* ill. by author. Simon & Schuster/Little Simon, 2005. ISBN 0-689-85917-1 Subj: Format, unusual — toy & movable books. Songs. Sports — baseball.

Stainton, Sue. *The chocolate cat* ill. by Anne Mortimer. HarperCollins, 2007. ISBN 978-0-06-057245-7 Subj: Animals — cats. Food. Magic.

I love cats ill. by Anne Mortimer. HarperCollins, 2007. ISBN 978-0-06-085154-5 Subj: Animals — cats.

Stampler, Ann Redisch. *Shlemazel and the remarkable spoon of Pohost* ill. by Jacqueline M. Cohen. Houghton Mifflin, 2006. ISBN 0-618-36959-7 Subj: Character traits — laziness. Character traits — luck. Folk & fairy tales. Jewish culture.

Stanley, Diane. *The trouble with wishes* ill. by author. HarperCollins, 2007. ISBN 0-06-055451-7 Subj: Behavior — wishing. Careers — sculptors.

Stanley, Mandy. *Lettice the flower girl* ill. by author. Simon & Schuster, 2006. ISBN 1-4169-1157-X Subj: Animals — rabbits. Weddings.

Lettice the flying rabbit ill. by author. Simon & Schuster, 2004. ISBN 0-689-86234-2 Subj: Activities — flying. Airplanes, airports. Animals — rabbits.

Stanton, Karen. *Papi's gift* ill. by René King Moreno. Boyds Mills, 2007. ISBN 978-1-59078-422-8 Subj: Birthdays. Careers — migrant workers. Family life — fathers. Foreign lands — Latin America. Gifts.

Steffensmeier, Alexander. *Millie waits for the mail* ill. by author. Walker & Company, 2007. ISBN 978-0-8027-9662-2 Subj: Animals — bulls, cows. Careers — postal workers. Farms. Letters, cards.

Stein, David Ezra. *Cowboy Ned and Andy* ill. by author. Simon & Schuster, 2006. ISBN 978-1-4169-0041-2 Subj: Animals — horses, ponies. Cowboys, cowgirls. Friendship. U.S. history — frontier & pioneer life.

Leaves ill. by author. Penguin, 2007. ISBN 978-0-399-24636-4 Subj: Animals — bears. Hibernation. Seasons. Trees.

Monster hug! ill. by author. Penguin, 2007. ISBN 978-0-399-24637-1 Subj: Activities — playing. Hugging. Monsters.

Ned's new friend ill. by author. Simon & Schuster, 2007. ISBN 978-1-4169-2490-6 Subj: Animals — horses, ponies. Cowboys, cowgirls. Emotions — envy, jealousy. Friendship. U.S. history — frontier & pioneer life.

Stein, Mathilde. *Brave Ben* ill. by Mies van Hout. Boyds Mills, 2006. ISBN 1-932425-64-0 Subj: Character traits — bravery. Emotions — fear.

Mine! ill. by Mies van Hout. Boyds Mills, 2007. ISBN 978-1-59078-506-5 Subj: Behavior — sharing. Character traits — selfishness. Ghosts.

Monstersong ill. by Gerdien van der Linden. Boyds Mills, 2007. ISBN 978-1-932425-90-1 Subj: Animals — pigs. Bedtime. Monsters. Rhyming text.

Stemple, Heidi E. Y. *Sleep, black bear, sleep* (Yolen, Jane)

Stevens, April. *Waking up Wendell* ill. by Tad Hills. Random House, 2007. ISBN 978-0-375-83621-3 Subj: Communities, neighborhoods. Counting, numbers. Morning. Noise, sounds.

Stevens, Janet. *The great fuzz frenzy* by Janet Stevens & Susan Stevens Crummel; ill. by Janet Stevens. Harcourt, 2005. ISBN 0-15-204626-7 Subj: Animals — prairie dogs. Behavior — greed. Toys — balls.

Stevenson, Robert Louis. *Block city* ill. by Daniel Kirk. Simon & Schuster, 2005. ISBN 0-689-86964-9 Subj: Imagination. Poetry. Sea & seashore. Toys.

The moon ill. by Tracey Campbell Pearson. Farrar, Straus & Giroux, 2006. ISBN 0-374-35046-9 Subj: Moon. Poetry.

Stewart, Amber. *I'm big enough* ill. by Layn Marlow. Scholastic, 2007. ISBN 0-439-90666-0 Subj: Animals — rabbits. Behavior — growing up.

Rabbit ears ill. by Laura Rankin. Bloomsbury, 2006. ISBN 1-58234-959-2 Subj: Animals — rabbits. Character traits — cleanliness.

Stewart, Joel. *Dexter Bexley and the big blue beastie* ill. by author. Holiday House, 2007. ISBN 978-0-8234-2068-1 Subj: Character traits — cleverness. Friendship. Monsters.

Stewig, John Warren. *The animals watched: an alphabet book* ill. by Rosanne Litzinger. Holiday House, 2007. ISBN 978-0-8234-1906-7 Subj: ABC books. Animals. Boats, ships. Religion — Noah. Weather — floods. Weather — rain.

Stock, Catherine. *A porc in New York* ill. by author. Holiday House, 2007. ISBN 978-0-8234-1994-4 Subj: Activities — vacationing. Animals. Careers — farmers.

Stoeke, Janet Morgan. *The bus stop* ill. by author. Penguin, 2007. ISBN 978-0-525-47805-8 Subj: Buses. Rhyming text. School.

Minerva Louise and the colorful eggs ill. by author. Penguin, 2006. ISBN 0-525-47633-4 Subj: Birds — chickens. Eggs. Holidays — Easter.

Minerva Louise on Christmas Eve ill. by author. Penguin, 2007. ISBN 978-0-525-47857-7 Subj: Birds — chickens. Holidays — Christmas. Santa Claus.

Waiting for May ill. by author. Penguin, 2005. ISBN 0-525-47098-0 Subj: Adoption. Family life — brothers & sisters. Foreign lands — China.

Stohner, Anu. *Brave Charlotte* ill. by Henrike Wilson. Bloomsbury, 2005. ISBN 1-58234-690-9 Subj: Animals — dogs. Animals — sheep. Behavior — resourcefulness. Character traits — bravery.

Stowell, Penelope. *The greatest potatoes* ill. by Sharon Watts. Hyperion, 2005. ISBN 0-7868-5113-9 Subj: Activities — baking, cooking. Careers — chefs, cooks. Ethnic groups in the U.S. — Racially mixed. Food. Restaurants.

Straaten, Harmen van. *Duck's tale* trans. from Dutch by Marianne Martens; ill. by Harmen van Straaten. NorthSouth, 2007. ISBN 978-0-7358-2133-0 Subj: Animals. Birds — ducks. Books, reading. Friendship. Frogs & toads.

For me? ill. by author. NorthSouth, 2004. ISBN 978-0-7358-2163-7 Subj: Animals. Birds — ducks. Friendship. Frogs & toads. Letters, cards.

Strauss, Rochelle. *One well: the story of water on Earth* ill. by Rosemary Woods. Kids Can, 2007. ISBN 978-1-5533-7954-6 Subj: Water.

Stringer, Lauren. *Winter is the warmest season* ill. by author. Harcourt, 2006. ISBN 0-15-204967-3 Subj: Seasons — winter.

Stryer, Andrea Stenn. *Kami and the yaks* ill. by Bert Dodson. Bay Otter, 2007. ISBN 0-9778961-0-2 Subj: Animals — yaks. Character traits — bravery. Foreign lands — Nepal. Handicaps — deafness.

Sturges, Philemon. *How do you make a baby smile?* ill. by Bridget Strevens-Marzo. HarperCollins, 2007. ISBN 978-0-06-076072-4 Subj: Animals — babies. Rhyming text.

I love tools! ill. by Shari Halpern. HarperCollins, 2006. ISBN 0-06-009288-2 Subj: Activities — making things. Homes, houses. Rhyming text. Tools.

This little pirate ill. by Amy Walrod. Penguin, 2005. ISBN 0-525-46440-9 Subj: Animals — pigs. Parties. Pirates. Rhyming text.

Waggers ill. by Jim Ishikawa. Penguin, 2005. ISBN 0-525-47116-2 Subj: Animals — cats. Animals — dogs. Rhyming text.

Sugarman, Brynn Olenberg. *Rebecca's journey home* ill. by Michelle Shapiro. Lerner, 2006. ISBN 1-58013-157-3 Subj: Adoption. Family life. Foreign lands — Vietnam. Jewish culture.

Sullivan, Sarah. *Dear Baby: letters from your big brother* ill. by Paul Meisel. Candlewick, 2005. ISBN 0-7636-2126-9 Subj: Babies. Family life — brothers & sisters. Letters, cards.

Sutton, Jane. *The trouble with cauliflower* ill. by Jim Harris. Penguin, 2006. ISBN 0-8037-2707-0 Subj: Animals — koalas. Character traits — luck. Food. Friendship. Superstition.

Swaim, Jessica. *The hound from the pound* ill. by Jill McElmurry. Candlewick, 2007. ISBN 978-0-7636-2330-2 Subj: Animals — dogs. Emotions — loneliness. Pets. Rhyming text.

Swallow, Pamela Curtis. *Groundhog gets a say* ill. by Denise Brunkus. Penguin, 2005. ISBN 0-399-23876-X Subj: Animals — groundhogs. Holidays — Groundhog Day.

Sweet, Melissa. *Carmine: a little more red* ill. by author. Houghton Mifflin, 2005. ISBN 0-618-38794-3 Subj: ABC books. Activities — painting. Animals — dogs. Animals — wolves. Concepts — color. Family life — grandmothers. Folk & fairy tales.

Swinburne, Stephen R. *Turtle tide: the ways of sea turtles* ill. by Bruce Hiscock. Boyds Mills, 2005. ISBN 1-59078-081-7 Subj: Reptiles — turtles, tortoises.

Taback, Simms. *I miss you every day* ill. by author. Penguin, 2007. ISBN 978-0-670-06192-1 Subj: Emotions — loneliness. Emotions — love. Letters, cards. Rhyming text.

Kibitzers and fools: tales my zayda told me ill. by author. Penguin, 2005. ISBN 0-670-05955-2 Subj: Activities — storytelling. Folk & fairy tales. Jewish culture.

Taber, Norman. *Rufus at work* (Taber, Tory)

Taber, Tory. *Rufus at work* by Tory & Norman Taber; ill. by authors. Walker & Company, 2005. ISBN 0-80278984-6 Subj: Activities — working. Animals — cats.

Tafolla, Carmen. *What can you do with a rebozo?* ill. by Amy Cordova. Ten Speed, 2007. ISBN 978-1-58246-220-2 Subj: Clothing. Ethnic groups in the U.S. — Mexican Americans. Foreign lands — Mexico.

Tafuri, Nancy. *The busy little squirrel* ill. by author. Simon & Schuster, 2007. ISBN 978-0-689-87341-6 Subj: Animals — squirrels. Seasons — fall.

Five little chicks ill. by author. Simon & Schuster, 2006. ISBN 0-689-87342-5 Subj: Animals — babies. Birds — chickens.

Goodnight, my duckling ill. by author. Scholastic, 2005. ISBN 0-439-39881-9 Subj: Bedtime. Behavior — lost. Birds — ducks.

Whose chick are you? ill. by author. HarperCollins, 2007. ISBN 978-0-06-082515-7 Subj: Birds. Birds — swans. Eggs. Family life — mothers.

Tanaka, Shelley. *True friends: a tale from Tanzania* (Kilaka, John)

Tanaka, Shinsuke. *Wings* ill. by author. Purple Bear, 2006. ISBN 1-933327-19-7 Subj: Anatomy — wings. Animals — dogs. Imagination. Wordless.

Tang, Greg. *Math fables: lessons that count* ill. by Heather Cahoon. Scholastic, 2004. ISBN 0-439-45399-2 Subj: Counting, numbers. Rhyming text.

Math fables too: making science count ill. by Taia Morley. Scholastic, 2007. ISBN 978-0-439-78351-4 Subj: Animals. Counting, numbers. Rhyming text. Science.

Tankard, Jeremy. *Grumpy Bird* ill. by author. Scholastic, 2007. ISBN 978-0-439-85147-3 Subj: Animals. Behavior — bad day. Birds. Emotions.

Tarlow, Ellen. *Pinwheel days* ill. by Gretel Parker. Star Bright, 2007. ISBN 978-1-59572-059-7 Subj: Animals. Animals — donkeys. Friendship.

Tashiro, Chisato. *Five nice mice* trans. from Japanese by Sayako Uchida; adapt. by Kate Westerlund; ill. by Chisato Tashiro. Minedition, 2007. ISBN 978-0-698-40058-0 Subj: Animals — mice. Frogs & toads. Music.

Tatham, Betty. *Baby Sea Otter* ill. by Joan Paley. Henry Holt, 2005. ISBN 0-8050-7504-6 Subj: Animals — babies. Animals — otters.

Tauss, Marc. *Superhero* ill. by author. Scholastic, 2005. ISBN 0-439-62734-6 Subj: Cities, towns. Ethnic groups in the U.S. — African Americans. Problem solving. Robots.

Taylor, Eleanor. *Beep, beep, let's go!* ill. by author. Bloomsbury, 2005. ISBN 1-58234-973-8 Subj: Animals. Animals — dogs. Sea & seashore.

Taylor, Sean. *When a monster is born* ill. by Nick Sharratt. Macmillan, 2007. ISBN 978-1-59643-254-3 Subj: Babies. Behavior — growing up. Monsters.

Teckentrup, Britta. *Big smelly bear* ill. by author. Boxer, 2007. ISBN 978-1-905417-37-7 Subj: Activities — bathing. Animals — bears. Character traits — cleanliness.

Teevin, Toni. *What to do? What to do?* ill. by Janet Pedersen. Houghton Mifflin, 2006. ISBN 0-618-44632-X Subj: Activities — baking, cooking. Birds. Emotions — loneliness.

Tellis, Annabel. *If my dad were a dog* photos by Tracy Morgan; ill. by Annabel Tellis. Scholastic, 2007. ISBN 978-0-439-91387-4 Subj: Animals — dogs. Family life — fathers. Humorous stories. Rhyming text.

Thach, James Otis. *A child's guide to common household monsters* ill. by David Udovic. Boyds Mills, 2007. ISBN 978-1-932425-58-1 Subj: Emotions — fear. Monsters. Rhyming text.

Thaler, Mike. *Pig Little* ill. by Paige Miglio. Henry Holt, 2006. ISBN 0-8050-6977-1 Subj: Animals — pigs. Sea & seashore — beaches.

Thermes, Jennifer. *Sam Bennett's new shoes* ill. by author. Carolrhoda, 2006. ISBN 1-57505-822-7 Subj: Behavior — growing up. Clothing — shoes. Family life. Farms. U.S. history.

This little light of mine ill. by E. B. Lewis. Simon & Schuster, 2005. ISBN 0-689-83179-X Subj: Ethnic groups in the U.S. — African Americans. Songs.

Thomas, Eliza. *The red blanket* ill. by Joe Cepeda. Scholastic, 2004. ISBN 0-439-32253-7 Subj: Adoption. Emotions — love. Ethnic groups in the U.S. — Chinese Americans. Family life — single-parent families.

Thomas, Joyce Carol. *Shouting* ill. by Annie Lee. Hyperion, 2007. ISBN 0-7868-0664-8 Subj: Activities — dancing. Religion.

The six fools (Hurston, Zora Neale)

Thomas, Patricia. *Firefly mountain* ill. by Peter Sylvada. Peachtree, 2007. ISBN 978-1-56145-360-3 Subj: Insects — fireflies. Night. Seasons — summer.

Thomas, Shelley Moore. *Happy birthday, Good Knight* ill. by Jennifer Plecas. Penguin, 2006. ISBN 0-525-47184-7 Subj: Birthdays. Dragons. Friendship. Gifts. Knights.

Take care, Good Knight ill. by Paul Meisel. Penguin, 2006. ISBN 0-525-47695-4 Subj: Animals — cats. Books, reading. Character traits — helpfulness. Dragons. Knights.

Thomas, Valerie. *Winnie the witch* ill. by Korky Paul. Harper-Collins, 2007. ISBN 978-0-06-117312-7 Subj: Animals — cats. Concepts — color. Witches.

Thompson, Lauren. *The apple pie that Papa baked* ill. by Jonathan Bean. Simon & Schuster, 2007. ISBN 978-1-4169-1240-8 Subj: Cumulative tales. Food. Trees.

Ballerina dreams: a true story photos by James Estrin. Feiwel & Friends, 2007. ISBN 978-0-312-37029-9 Subj: Activities — dancing. Ballet. Handicaps — cerebral palsy.

Little Quack: dial-a-duck ill. by Derek Anderson. Simon & Schuster, 2006. ISBN 1-4169-0932-X Subj: Birds — ducks. Counting, numbers. Format, unusual — board books. Format, unusual — toy & movable books.

Little Quack's hide and seek ill. by Derek Anderson. Simon & Schuster, 2007. [board book]. ISBN 1-4169-0325-9 Subj: Birds — ducks. Counting, numbers. Family life — mothers. Format, unusual — board books. Games.

Little Quack's new friend ill. by Derek Anderson. Simon & Schuster, 2006. ISBN 0-689-86893-6 Subj: Activities — playing. Birds — ducks. Friendship. Frogs & toads. Lakes, ponds.

Mouse's first fall ill. by Buket Erdogan. Simon & Schuster, 2006. ISBN 0-689-85837-X Subj: Animals — mice. Seasons — fall.

Mouse's first snow ill. by Buket Erdogan. Simon & Schuster, 2005. ISBN 0-689-85836-1 Subj: Animals — mice. Family life — fathers. Seasons — winter. Weather — snow.

Mouse's first spring ill. by Buket Erdogan. Simon & Schuster, 2005. ISBN 0-689-85838-8 Subj: Animals — mice. Family life — mothers. Seasons — spring. Weather — wind.

Thong, Roseanne. *Gai see: what you can see in Chinatown* ill. by Yangsook Choi. Abrams, 2007. ISBN 978-0-8109-9337-2 Subj: Ethnic groups in the U.S. — Chinese Americans. Rhyming text. Seasons. Stores.

Tummy girl ill. by Sam Williams. Henry Holt, 2007. ISBN 0-8050-7609-3 Subj: Babies. Behavior — growing up. Rhyming text.

The three bears. *Goldilocks and the three bears* retold by Caralyn Buehner; ill. by Mark Buehner. Penguin, 2007. ISBN 978-0-8037-2939-1 Subj: Animals — bears. Folk & fairy tales.

The three little pigs. *The three little pigs / Los tres cerditos* adapt. by Merce Escardo i Bas; ill. by Pere Joan. Chronicle, 2006. ISBN 0-8118-5063-3 Subj: Animals — pigs. Animals — wolves. Character traits — cleverness. Folk & fairy tales. Foreign languages.

Tildes, Phyllis Limbacher. *Eye guess: a fold-out guessing game* ill. by author. Charlesbridge, 2005. ISBN 1-57091-650-0 Subj: Animals. Format, unusual — toy & movable books.

Tillman, Nancy. *On the night you were born* ill. by author. Feiwel & Friends, 2006. ISBN 978-0-312-34606-5 Subj: Birth. Night.

Timmers, Leo. *Who is driving?* ill. by author. Bloomsbury, 2007. ISBN 978-1-5999-0021-6 Subj: Activities — driving. Animals. Automobiles. Trucks.

Tingle, Tim. *When turtle grew feathers: a folktale from the Choctaw nation* ill. by Stacey Schuett. August House, 2007. ISBN 978-0-87483-777-3 Subj: Animals — rabbits. Behavior — trickery. Folk & fairy tales. Indians of North America — Choctaw. Reptiles — turtles, tortoises. Sports — racing.

Tinkham, Kelly A. *Hair for Mama* ill. by Amy June Bates. Penguin, 2007. ISBN 978-0-8037-2955-1 Subj: Emotions — love. Ethnic groups in the U.S. — African Americans. Hair. Illness — cancer.

Toft, Kim Michelle. *The world that we want* ill. by author. Charlesbridge, 2005. ISBN 1-58089-114-4 Subj: Animals. Ecology. Format, unusual.

Tokuda, Yukihisa. *I'm a pill bug* ill. by Kiyoshi Takahashi. Kane/Miller, 2006. ISBN 978-1-929132-95-9 Subj: Crustaceans .

Tomp, Sarah Wones. *Red, white, and blue goodbye* ill. by Ann Barrow. Walker & Company, 2005. ISBN 0-8027-8962-5 Subj: Careers — military. Family life — fathers.

Topek, Susan Remick. *Ten good rules* photos by Tod Cohen. Lerner, 2007. ISBN 978-1-58013-209-1 Subj: Religion — Moses.

Toten, Teresa. *Bright red kisses* ill. by Deirdre Betteridge. Annick, 2005. ISBN 1-55037-909-7 Subj: Character traits — helpfulness. Family life — mothers.

Tourville, Amanda Doering. *A crocodile grows up* ill. by Michael Denman & William J. Huiett. Picture Window, 2006. ISBN 978-1-4048-3157-5 Subj: Reptiles — alligators, crocodiles.

A giraffe grows up ill. by Michael Denman & William J. Huiett. Picture Window, 2006. ISBN 978-1-4048-3158-2 Subj: Animals — giraffes.

A jaguar grows up ill. by Michael Denman & William J. Huiett. Picture Window, 2006. ISBN 978-1-4048-6159-9 Subj: Animals — giraffes.

Train, Mary. *Time for the fair* ill. by Karel Hayes. Down East, 2005. ISBN 0-89272-694-6 Subj: Character traits — patience. Fairs, festivals. Seasons.

Trapani, Iza. *Here we go 'round the mulberry bush* ill. by author. Charlesbridge, 2006. ISBN 1-57091-663-2 Subj: Gardens, gardening. Songs.

Jingle bells ill. by author. Charlesbridge, 2005. ISBN 1-58089-095-4 Subj: Holidays — Christmas. Music. Songs.

Trice, Linda. *Kenya's word* ill. by Pamela Johnson. Charlesbridge, 2006. ISBN 1-57091-887-2 Subj: Ethnic groups in the U.S. — African Americans. Language.

Tripp, Paul. *Tubby the tuba* ill. by Henry Cole. Penguin, 2006. ISBN 0-525-47717-9 Subj: Frogs & toads. Musical instruments — orchestras. Musical instruments — tubas.

Trollinger, Patsi B. *Perfect timing: how Isaac Murphy became one of the world's greatest jockeys* ill. by Jerome Lagarrigue. Penguin, 2006. ISBN 0-670-06083-6 Subj: Animals — horses, ponies. Careers — jockeys. Ethnic groups in the U.S. — African Americans. Sports — racing.

Trotter, Deborah W. *How do you know?* ill. by Julie Downing. Houghton Mifflin, 2006. ISBN 0-618-46343-7 Subj: Emotions — love. Family life — mothers. Weather — fog.

Truss, Lynne. *Eats, shoots & leaves: why, commas really do make a difference!* ill. by Bonnie Timmons. Penguin, 2006. ISBN 0-399-24491-3 Subj: Language.

Turhan, Sedat. *Monkey business: fun with idioms* (Hambleton, Laura)

Turner, Glennette Tilley. *An apple for Harriet Tubman* ill. by Susan Keeter. Albert Whitman, 2006. ISBN 0-8075-0395-9 Subj: Ethnic groups in the U.S. — African Americans. Slavery. U.S. history.

Tyler, Anne. *Timothy Tugbottom says no!* ill. by Mitra Modarressi. Penguin, 2005. ISBN 0-399-24255-4 Subj: Character traits — stubbornness. Sleepovers.

Tyler, Michael. *The skin you live in* ill. by David Lee Csicsko. Chicago Children's Museum, 2005. ISBN 0-9759580-0-3 Subj: Anatomy — skin. Rhyming text. Self-concept.

Uchida, Sayako. *Five nice mice* (Tashiro, Chisato)

Uhlberg, Myron. *Dad, Jackie, and me* ill. by Colin Bootman. Peachtree, 2005. ISBN 1-56145-329-3 Subj: Ethnic groups in the U.S. — African Americans. Family life — fathers. Handicaps — deafness. Sports — baseball.

Umansky, Kaye. *I don't like Gloria!* ill. by Margaret Chamberlain. Candlewick, 2007. ISBN 978-0-7636-3202-1 Subj: Animals — cats. Animals — dogs. Emotions — envy, jealousy. Pets.

Urbanovic, Jackie. *Duck at the door* ill. by author. HarperCollins, 2007. ISBN 0-06-121438-8 Subj: Birds — ducks. Character traits — individuality. Pets.

Urbigkit, Cat. *A young shepherd* photos by author. Boyds Mills, 2006. ISBN 1-59078-364-6 Subj: Animals — sheep. Careers — ranchers. Careers — shepherds.

Vail, Rachel. *Righty and Lefty: a tale of two feet* ill. by Matthew Cordell. Scholastic, 2007. ISBN 978-0-439-63629-2 Subj: Anatomy — feet. Character traits — cooperation.

Valckx, Catharina. *Lizette's green sock* ill. by author. Houghton Mifflin, 2005. ISBN 0-618-45298-2 Subj: Birds. Clothing — socks.

Valentina, Marina. *Lost in the roses* ill. by author. Red Cygnet, 2007. ISBN 1-60108-014-X Subj: Birds — chickens. Flowers — roses.

Vallverdu, Josep. *Aladdin and the magic lamp / Aldino y la lampara maravillosa* ill. by Pep Montserrat. Chronicle, 2006. ISBN 0-8118-5061-7 Subj: Folk & fairy tales. Foreign lands — Arabia. Foreign languages. Magic.

Van Allsburg, Chris. *Probuditi!* ill. by author. Houghton Mifflin, 2006. ISBN 0-618-75502-0 Subj: Imagination. Magic.

Van Leeuwen, Jean. *Benny and beautiful baby Delilah* ill. by LeUyen Pham. Penguin, 2006. ISBN 0-8037-2891-3 Subj: Babies. Family life — new sibling.

Papa and the pioneer quilt ill. by Rebecca Bond. Penguin, 2007. ISBN 978-0-8037-3028-1 Subj: Family life. Quilts. U.S. history — frontier & pioneer life.

van Lieshout, Elle. *The wish* by Elle van Lieshout & Erik van Os; ill. by Paula Gerritsen. Boyds Mills, 2007. ISBN 978-1-932425-91-8 Subj: Behavior — solitude. Behavior — wishing. Emotions — love. Tractors.

van Os, Erik. *The wish* (van Lieshout, Elle)

Van Steenwyk, Elizabeth. *Prairie Christmas* ill. by Ronald Himler. Eerdmans, 2006. ISBN 0-8028-5280-7 Subj: Birth. Family life. Holidays — Christmas. U.S. history — frontier & pioneer life.

Varela, Barry. *Gizmo* ill. by Ed Briant. Macmillan, 2007. ISBN 978-1-59643-115-7 Subj: Inventions. Machines. Rhyming text.

Varon, Sara. *Chicken and Cat* ill. by author. Scholastic, 2006. ISBN 0-439-63406-7 Subj: Animals — cats. Birds — chickens. Friendship. Wordless.

Veit, Barbara. *Who stole my house?* trans. from German by Marianne Martens; ill. by AnnaLaura Cantone. NorthSouth, 2007. ISBN 978-0-7358-2122-4 Subj: Animals — snails. Homes, houses.

Verdick, Elizabeth. *Tails are not for pulling* ill. by Marieka Heinlen. Free Spirit, 2005. ISBN 1-57542-180-1 Subj: Format, unusual — board books. Pets.

Vere, Ed. *The getaway* ill. by author. Simon & Schuster, 2007. ISBN 978-1-4169-4789-9 Subj: Animals — elephants. Animals — mice. Behavior — stealing.

Vestergaard, Hope. *Hillside lullaby* ill. by Margie Moore. Penguin, 2006. ISBN 0-525-47215-0 Subj: Animals. Bedtime. Rhyming text.

What do you do when a monster says boo? ill. by Maggie Smith. Penguin, 2006. ISBN 0-525-47737-3 Subj: Monsters. Rhyming text.

Viorst, Judith. *Just in case* ill. by Diana Cain Bluthenthal. Simon & Schuster/Atheneum, 2006. ISBN 0-689-87164-3 Subj: Behavior — worrying.

Vischer, Phil. *Sidney and Norman: a tale of two pigs* ill. by Justin Gerard. Thomas Nelson, 2006. ISBN 1-4003-0834-8 Subj: Animals — pigs. Emotions — love. Religion.

Voake, Charlotte. *Hello twins* ill. by author. Candlewick, 2006. ISBN 0-7636-3003-9 Subj: Family life — brothers & sisters. Multiple births — twins.

Votaw, Carol. *Good morning, little polar bear* ill. by Susan Banta. NorthWord, 2005. ISBN 1-55971-932-X Subj: Animals. Foreign lands — Arctic. Morning.

Waking up down under ill. by Susan Banta. NorthWord, 2007. ISBN 978-1-55971-976-6 Subj: Animals. Foreign lands — Australia. Rhyming text.

Waddell, Martin. *Bee frog* ill. by Barbara Firth. Candlewick, 2007. ISBN 978-0-7636-3310-3 Subj: Behavior — running away. Frogs & toads. Imagination. Self-concept.

Sleep tight, Little Bear ill. by Barbara Firth. Candlewick, 2005. ISBN 0-7636-2439-X Subj: Animals — bears. Bedtime. Emotions — loneliness. Night. Sleep.

Waechter, Phillip. *Rosie and the nightmares* ill. by author. Handprint, 2005. ISBN 1-59354-130-9 Subj: Animals — rabbits. Emotions — fear. Monsters. Nightmares.

Wakeman, Daniel. *Ben's bunny trouble* ill. by Dirk van Stralen. Orca, 2007. ISBN 978-1-55143-611-1 Subj: Animals — rabbits. Space & space ships. Wordless.

Waldman, Debby. *A sack full of feathers* ill. by Cindy Revell. Orca, 2006. ISBN 1-55143-332-X Subj: Behavior — gossip. Folk & fairy tales. Jewish culture.

Wallace, Karen. *I am an ankylosaurus* ill. by Mike Bostock. Simon & Schuster/Atheneum, 2005. ISBN 0-689-87318-2 Subj: Dinosaurs.

Wallace, Nancy Elizabeth. *Alphabet house* ill. by author. Marshall Cavendish, 2005. ISBN 0-7614-5192-7 Subj: ABC books. Animals — rabbits.

The kindness quilt ill. by author. Marshall Cavendish, 2006. ISBN 0-7614-5313-X Subj: Character traits — kindness. Quilts.

Look! Look! Look! by Nancy Elizabeth Wallace & Linda K. Friedlaender; ill. by Nancy Elizabeth Wallace. Marshall Cavendish, 2006. ISBN 0-7614-5282-6 Subj: Animals — mice. Art. Letters, cards.

Shells! Shells! Shells! ill. by author. Marshall Cavendish, 2007. ISBN 978-0-7614-5332-1 Subj: Animals — bears. Sea & seashore — beaches.

Snow ill. by author. Marshall Cavendish, 2007. ISBN 978-0-7614-5362-8 Subj: Animals — rabbits. Format, unusual — board books. Seasons — winter. Weather — snow.

Wallner, Alexandra. *Lucy Maud Montgomery: the author of Anne of Green Gables* ill. by author. Holiday House, 2006. ISBN 0-8234-1549-X Subj: Activities — writing. Books, reading.

Walsh, Ellen Stoll. *Mouse shapes* ill. by author. Harcourt, 2007. ISBN 978-0-15-206091-6 Subj: Animals — mice. Concepts — shape.

Walsh, Melanie. *Do lions live on lily pads?* ill. by author. Houghton Mifflin, 2006. ISBN 0-618-47300-9 Subj: Animals. Character traits — questioning. Homes, houses. Nature.

Walton, Rick. *Bunny school: a learning fun-for-all* ill. by Paige Miglio. HarperCollins, 2005. ISBN 0-06-057509-3 Subj: Animals — rabbits. Rhyming text. School.

Just me and 6,000 rats: a tale of conjunctions ill. by Mike & Carl Gordon. Gibbs Smith, 2007. ISBN 978-1-4236-0219-4 Subj: Animals — rats. Humorous stories. Language.

The remarkable friendship of Mr. Cat and Mr. Rat ill. by Lisa McCue. Penguin, 2006. ISBN 0-399-23899-9 Subj: Animals — cats. Animals — rats. Friendship. Gifts.

Wang, Xiaohong. *One year in Beijing* ill. by Grace Lin. China Sprout, 2006. ISBN 0-9747302-5-4 Subj: Days of the week, months of the year. Foreign lands — China.

Ward, Helen. *Little Moon Dog* ill. by Wayne Anderson. Penguin, 2007. ISBN 978-0-525-47727-3 Subj: Animals — dogs. Fairies. Friendship. Moon.

Ward, Jennifer. *Forest bright, forest night* ill. by Jamichael Henterly. Dawn, 2005. ISBN 158469-066-6 Subj: Animals. Forest, woods.

Way up in the Arctic ill. by Kenneth J. Spengler. Rising Moon, 2007. ISBN 978-0-87358-928-4 Subj: Animals. Counting, numbers. Foreign lands — Arctic. Rhyming text.

Ward, Nick. *Don't eat the babysitter!* ill. by author. Random House, 2006. ISBN 0-385-75062-5 Subj: Activities — babysitting. Family life — brothers & sisters. Fish — sharks.

Wargin, Kathy-Jo. *The frog prince* (Grimm, Jacob)

Warhola, James. *If you're happy and you know it: jungle edition* ill. by author. Scholastic, 2007. ISBN 0-439-72766-9 Subj: Animals. Emotions — happiness. Jungles. Songs.

Waterton, Betty. *A bumblebee sweater* ill. by Kim LaFave. Fitzhenry & Whiteside, 2007. ISBN 1-55455-028-9 Subj: Activities — knitting. Clothing — sweaters. Theater.

Watt, Melanie. *Chester* ill. by author. Kids Can, 2007. ISBN 978-1-55453-140-0 Subj: Activities — drawing. Activities — writing. Animals — cats.

Scaredy Squirrel ill. by author. Kids Can, 2006. ISBN 1-55337-959-4 Subj: Animals — squirrels. Character traits — bravery. Emotions — fear.

Scaredy Squirrel makes a friend ill. by author. Kids Can, 2007. ISBN 978-1-55453-181-3 Subj: Animals — dogs. Animals — squirrels. Emotions — fear. Emotions — loneliness. Friendship.

Watters, Debbie. *Where's Mom's hair? A family journey through cancer* by Debbie, Haydn & Emmett Watters; photos by Sophie Hogan. Second Story, 2005. ISBN 1-896764-94-0 Subj: Family life — mothers. Hair. Illness — cancer.

Watters, Emmett. *Where's Mom's hair? A family journey through cancer* (Watters, Debbie)

Watters, Haydn. *Where's Mom's hair? A family journey through cancer* (Watters, Debbie)

Watts, Bernadette. *Jorinda and Jorindel* (Grimm, Jacob)

Watts, Leslie Elizabeth. *The Baabaasheep Quartet* ill. by author. Fitzhenry & Whiteside, 2005. ISBN 1-55041-890-4 Subj: Activities — singing. Animals — sheep. Cities, towns. Music.

Weatherford, Carole Boston. *Champions on the bench: the Cannon Street YMCA All Stars* ill. by Leonard Jenkins. Penguin, 2007. ISBN 0-8037-2987-1 Subj: Ethnic groups in the U.S. — African Americans. Prejudice. Sports — baseball. U.S. history.

Freedom on the menu: the Greensboro sit-ins ill. by Jerome Lagarrigue. Penguin, 2005. ISBN 0-8037-2860-3 Subj: Ethnic groups in the U.S. — African Americans. Prejudice. Restaurants. U.S. history.

Moses: when Harriet Tubman led her people to freedom ill. by Kadir Nelson. Hyperion, 2006. ISBN 0-7868-5175-9 Subj: Caldecott award honor books. Ethnic groups in the U.S. — African Americans. Slavery. U.S. history.

Weaver, Tess. *Cat jumped in!* ill. by Emily Arnold McCully. Houghton Mifflin, 2007. ISBN 978-0-618-61488-2 Subj: Animals — cats. Behavior — misbehavior.

Webster, Christine. *Otter everywhere* ill. by Tim Nihoff. Candlewick, 2007. ISBN 978-0-7636-2921-2 Subj: Activities — picnicking. Animals — otters. Sports — swimming.

Weeks, Sarah. *Be mine, be mine, sweet valentine* ill. by Fumi Kosaka. HarperCollins, 2005. ISBN 0-694-01514-8 Subj: Format, unusual — toy & movable books. Gifts. Holidays — Valentine's Day. Rhyming text.

Counting Ovejas ill. by David Diaz. Simon & Schuster/Atheneum, 2006. ISBN 0-689-86750-6 Subj: Animals — sheep. Bedtime. Concepts — color. Counting, numbers. Foreign languages.

Ella, of course! ill. by Doug Cushman. Harcourt, 2007. ISBN 978-0-15-204943-0 Subj: Animals — pigs. Ballet. Problem solving. Umbrellas.

I'm a pig ill. by Holly Berry. HarperCollins, 2005. ISBN 0-06-074344-1 Subj: Animals — pigs. Rhyming text. Self-concept.

Overboard! ill. by Sam Williams. Harcourt, 2006. ISBN 0-15-205046-9 Subj: Activities — playing. Animals — rabbits. Babies. Rhyming text.

Weigelt, Udo. *Super Guinea Pig to the rescue* ill. by Nina Spranger. Walker & Company, 2007. ISBN 978-0-8027-9705-6 Subj: Animals — guinea pigs. Disguises. Pets. Television.

Weis, Carol. *When the cows got loose* ill. by Ard Hoyt. Simon & Schuster, 2006. ISBN 0-689-85166-9 Subj: Animals — bulls, cows. Behavior — misbehavior. Circus.

Weiss, Mitch. *The hidden feast: a folktale from the American South* (Hamilton, Martha)

Priceless gifts: a folktale from Italy (Hamilton, Martha)

Wellington, Monica. *Mr. Cookie Baker* ill. by author. Penguin, 2006. ISBN 0-525-47763-2 Subj: Activities — baking, cooking. Careers — bakers. Food.

Pizza at Sally's ill. by author. Penguin, 2006. ISBN 0-525-47715-2 Subj: Activities — baking, cooking. Careers — chefs, cooks. Food. Restaurants.

Truck driver Tom ill. by author. Penguin, 2007. ISBN 978-0-525-47831-7 Subj: Careers — truck drivers. Transportation. Trucks.

Zinnia's flower garden ill. by author. Penguin, 2005. ISBN 0-525-47368-8 Subj: Flowers. Gardens, gardening.

Wells, Robert E. *Did a dinosaur drink this water?* ill. by author. Albert Whitman, 2006. ISBN 978-0-8075-8839-0 Subj: Science. Water.

Wells, Rosemary. *Carry me!* ill. by author. Hyperion, 2006. ISBN 0-7868-0396-7 Subj: Animals — rabbits. Emotions — love. Family life. Poetry.

The gulps ill. by Marc Brown. Little, Brown, 2007. ISBN 978-0-316-01460-1 Subj: Health & fitness. Health & fitness — exercise. Self-concept.

McDuff's wild romp ill. by Susan Jeffers. Hyperion, 2005. ISBN 0-7868-1930-8 Subj: Animals — cats. Animals — dogs.

Max counts his chickens ill. by author. Penguin, 2007. ISBN 0-670-06222-5 Subj: Animals — rabbits. Counting, numbers. Holidays — Easter. Sibling rivalry.

Max's ABC ill. by author. Penguin, 2006. ISBN 0-670-06074-7 Subj: ABC books. Animals — rabbits.

The miraculous tale of the two Maries ill. by Petra Mathers. Penguin, 2006. ISBN 0-670-05960-9 Subj: Foreign lands — France. Religion.

Weninger, Brigitte. *Bye-bye, Binky* trans. from German by Kathryn Bishop; ill. by Yusuke Yonezu. Minedition, 2007. ISBN 978-0-698-40048-1 Subj: Animals. Behavior — growing up.

Double birthday ill. by Stephanie Roehe. Minedition, 2005. ISBN 0-698-40015-1 Subj: Animals — mice. Birthdays. Gifts. Toys.

Good night, Nori trans. from German by Kathryn Bishop; ill. by Yusuke Yonezu. Minedition, 2007. ISBN 978-0-698-40065-8 Subj: Animals — cats. Bedtime.

Miko goes on vacation trans. by Charise Myngheer; ill. by Stephanie Roehe. Penguin, 2006. ISBN 0-698-40017-8 Subj: Animals — mice. Friendship. Sea & seashore — beaches. Sports — swimming. Toys.

Miko wants a dog ill. by Stephanie Roehe. Minedition, 2006. ISBN 0-698-40016-X Subj: Animals — mice. Pets.

"Mom, wake up and play!" ill. by Stephanie Roehe. Minedition, 2005. ISBN 0-689-40012-7 Subj: Animals — mice. Family life — mothers. Morning.

"No bath! No way!" ill. by Stephanie Roehe. Minedition, 2005. ISBN 0-689-40013-5 Subj: Activities — bathing. Animals — mice. Bedtime. Family life — mothers.

Westerlund, Kate. *Five nice mice* (Tashiro, Chisato)

Weston, Carrie. *If a chicken stayed for supper* ill. by Sophie Fatus. Holiday House, 2007. ISBN 978-0-8234-2067-4 Subj: Animals — foxes. Behavior — misbehavior. Birds — chickens. Counting, numbers. Night.

Wheeler, Lisa. *Castaway cats* ill. by Ponder Goembel. Simon & Schuster/Atheneum, 2006. ISBN 0-689-86232-6 Subj: Animals — cats. Behavior — lost. Rhyming text.

Dino-hockey ill. by Barry Gott. Carolrhoda, 2007. ISBN 978-0-8225-6191-0 Subj: Dinosaurs. Rhyming text. Sports — hockey.

Hokey pokey: another prickly love story ill. by Janie Bynum. Little, Brown, 2006. ISBN 0-316-00090-6 Subj: Activities — dancing. Animals — hedgehogs. Animals — porcupines. Friendship.

Jazz baby ill. by R. Gregory Christie. Harcourt, 2007. ISBN 0-15-202522-7 Subj: Babies. Music. Rhyming text.

Mammoths on the move ill. by Kurt Cyrus. Harcourt, 2006. ISBN 0-15-204700-X Subj: Animals — wooly mammoths. Rhyming text.

Wheeler, Valerie. *Yes, please! No, thank you!* ill. by Glin Dibley. Sterling, 2006. ISBN 1-4027-3929-X Subj: Character traits — questioning. Etiquette. Format, unusual — board books.

Whitehead, Kathy. *Looking for Uncle Louie on the Fourth of July* ill. by Pablo Torrecilla. Boyds Mills, 2005. ISBN 1-59078-061-2 Subj: Careers — police officers. Family life — aunts, uncles. Holidays — Fourth of July. Motorcycles. Parades.

Whitford, Rebecca. *Little yoga: a toddler's first book of yoga* ill. by Martina Selway. Henry Holt, 2005. ISBN 0-8050-7879-7 Subj: Health & fitness.

Sleepy little yoga: a toddler's sleepy book of yoga ill. by Martina Selway. Henry Holt, 2007. ISBN 978-0-8050-8193-0 Subj: Health & fitness.

Why did the chicken cross the road? ill. by Jon Agee & others. Penguin, 2006. ISBN 0-8037-3094-2 Subj: Birds — chickens. Humorous stories.

Whybrow, Ian. *Badness for beginners: a Little Wolf and Smellybreff adventure* ill. by Tony Ross. Carolrhoda, 2005. ISBN 1-57505-861-8 Subj: Animals — wolves. Behavior — misbehavior. Family life — brothers & sisters.

Bella gets her skates on ill. by Rosie Reeve. Abrams, 2007. ISBN 978-0-8109-9416-4 Subj: Animals — rabbits. Behavior — worrying. Seasons — winter. Sports — ice skating.

Faraway farm ill. by Alex Ayliffe. Carolrhoda, 2006. ISBN 1-57505-938-X Subj: Farms. Picture puzzles. Rhyming text.

Harry and the dinosaurs at the museum ill. by Adrian Reynolds. Penguin, 2005. ISBN 0-375-83338-2 Subj: Behavior — lost. Dinosaurs. Museums. Toys.

Harry and the dinosaurs go to school ill. by Adrian Reynolds. Random House, 2007. ISBN 978-0-375-84180-4 Subj: Dinosaurs. School — first day. Toys.

Wick, Walter. *Can you see what I see? Once upon a time* ill. by author. Scholastic, 2006. ISBN 0-439-61777-4 Subj: Folk & fairy tales. Picture puzzles. Rhyming text.

Can you see what I see? Seymour makes new friends: a search and find storybook ill. by author. Scholastic/Cartwheel, 2006. ISBN 0-439-61780-4 Subj: Picture puzzles. Toys.

I spy treasure hunt: a book of picture riddles by Walter Wick & Jean Marzollo; photos by Walter Wick. Scholastic, 2007. ISBN 978-0-439-02674-1 Subj: Mystery stories. Picture puzzles. Pirates. Rhyming text. Riddles & jokes.

Wiesner, David. *Flotsam* ill. by author. Houghton Mifflin, 2006. ISBN 0-618-19457-6 Subj: Caldecott award books. Imagination. Sea & seashore — beaches.

Wigersma, Tanneke. *Baby brother* ill. by Nynke Mare Talsma. Boyds Mills, 2005. ISBN 1-932425-55-1 Subj: Babies. Family life — grandmothers. Family life — new sibling. Letters, cards.

Wild, Margaret. *Bobbie Dazzler* ill. by Janine Dawson. Kane/Miller, 2007. ISBN 978-1-933605-46-3 Subj: Animals — wallabies. Character traits — perseverance. Foreign lands — Australia.

Piglet and Mama ill. by Stephen Michael King. Abrams, 2005. ISBN 978-0-8109-5869-2 Subj: Animals — pigs. Emotions — love. Family life — mothers. Farms.

Piglet and Papa ill. by Stephen Michael King. Abrams, 2007. ISBN 978-0-8109-1476-6 Subj: Animals — pigs. Emotions — love. Family life — fathers. Farms.

Willard, Nancy. *The flying bed* ill. by John Thompson. Scholastic, 2007. ISBN 0-590-25610-6 Subj: Activities — flying. Behavior — greed. Careers — bakers. Foreign lands — Italy. Furniture — beds. Magic.

Willems, Mo. *Don't let the pigeon stay up late!* ill. by author. Hyperion, 2006. ISBN 0-7868-3746-2 Subj: Bedtime. Birds — pigeons. Humorous stories.

Edwina, the dinosaur who didn't know she was extinct ill. by author. Hyperion, 2006. ISBN 0-7868-3748-9 Subj: Dinosaurs. Self-concept.

I am invited to a party! ill. by author. Hyperion, 2007. ISBN 978-1-4231-0687-6 Subj: Animals — elephants. Animals — pigs. Friendship. Parties.

Knuffle Bunny: a cautionary tale ill. by author. Hyperion, 2004. ISBN 0-7868-1870-0 Subj: Animals — rabbits. Behavior — lost & found possessions. Caldecott award honor books. Laundry. Toys.

Knuffle Bunny too: a case of mistaken identity ill. by author. Hyperion, 2007. ISBN 978-1-4231-0299-1 Subj: Animals — rabbits. Caldecott award honor books. School — nursery. Toys.

Leonardo the terrible monster ill. by author. Hyperion, 2005. ISBN 0-7868-5294-1 Subj: Friendship. Imagination. Monsters.

My friend is sad ill. by author. Hyperion, 2007. ISBN 1-4231-0297-5 Subj: Animals — elephants. Animals — pigs. Emotions — sadness. Friendship.

The Pigeon finds a hot dog! ill. by author. Hyperion, 2005. ISBN 0-7868-5248-8 Subj: Birds — ducks. Birds — pigeons. Food. Humorous stories.

The Pigeon has feelings, too! A smidgeon of pigeon ill. by author. Hyperion, 2005. ISBN 0-7868-3650-4 Subj: Birds — pigeons. Emotions. Format, unusual — board books. Humorous stories.

The Pigeon loves things that go! a smidgeon of pigeon ill. by author. Hyperion, 2005. ISBN 0-7868-3651-2 Subj: Birds — pigeons. Format, unusual — board books. Transportation.

There is a bird on your head! ill. by author. Hyperion, 2007. ISBN 978-1-4231-0686-9 Subj: Animals — elephants. Animals — pigs. Friendship.

Time to say "please"! ill. by author. Hyperion, 2005. ISBN 0-7868-5293-3 Subj: Animals — mice. Etiquette. Format, unusual — toy & movable books.

Today I will fly! ill. by author. Hyperion, 2007. ISBN 1-4231-0295-9 Subj: Activities — flying. Animals — elephants. Animals — pigs. Character traits — cooperation. Friendship.

Willey, Margaret. *A Clever Beatrice Christmas* ill. by Heather M. Solomon. Simon & Schuster/Atheneum, 2006. ISBN 0-689-87017-5 Subj: Behavior — trickery. Holidays — Christmas. Santa Claus.

Williams, Barbara. *Albert's gift for grandmother* ill. by Doug Cushman. Candlewick, 2006. ISBN 0-7636-2097-1 Subj: Birthdays. Family life — grandmothers. Gifts. Reptiles — turtles, tortoises.

Williams, Brenda. *Home for a tiger, home for a bear* ill. by Rosamund Fowler. Barefoot, 2007. ISBN 978-1-905236-81-7 Subj: Animals. Homes, houses. Rhyming text. Spiders.

Williams, Laura E. *The best winds* ill. by Eujin Kim Neilan. Boyds Mills, 2006. ISBN 1-59078-274-7 Subj: Ethnic groups in the U.S. — Korean Americans. Family life — grandfathers. Kites.

Williams, Sam. *That's love* ill. by Mique Moriuchi. Holiday House, 2007. ISBN 0-8234-2028-0 Subj: Emotions — love. Rhyming text.

Williams, Suzanne. *Ten naughty little monkeys* ill. by Suzanne Watts. HarperCollins, 2007. ISBN 978-0-06-059904-1 Subj: Animals — monkeys. Counting, numbers. Rhyming text.

Willis, Jeanne. *Delilah D. at the library* ill. by Rosie Reeve. Houghton Mifflin, 2007. ISBN 978-0-618-78195-9 Subj: Imagination. Libraries.

Gorilla! Gorilla! ill. by Tony Ross. Simon & Schuster/Atheneum, 2006. ISBN 1-4169-1490-0 Subj: Animals — gorillas. Animals — mice. Behavior — misunderstanding. World.

Misery Moo ill. by Tony Ross. Henry Holt, 2005. ISBN 0-8050-7672-7 Subj: Animals — bulls, cows. Animals — sheep. Emotions — happiness. Emotions — sadness. Friendship.

Tadpole's promise ill. by Tony Ross. Simon & Schuster, 2005. ISBN 0-689-86524-4 Subj: Frogs & toads. Insects — butterflies, caterpillars. Metamorphosis.

Willis, Nancy Carol. *Red knot: a shorebird's incredible journey.* Birdsong, 2006. ISBN 0-9662761-4-0 Subj: Birds — sandpipers. Migration.

Wilson, Karma. *Animal strike at the zoo, it's true!* ill. by Margaret Spengler. HarperCollins, 2006. ISBN 0-06-057503-4 Subj: Animals. Rhyming text. Zoos.

Bear feels sick ill. by Jane Chapman. Simon & Schuster, 2007. ISBN 978-0-689-85985-4 Subj: Animals. Animals — bears. Friendship. Illness.

Dinos in the snow! ill. by Laura Rader. Little, Brown, 2005. ISBN 0-316-00948-2 Subj: Dinosaurs. Rhyming text. Seasons — winter. Weather — snow.

Hello, Calico! ill. by Buket Erdogan. Simon & Schuster/Little Simon, 2007. ISBN 978-1-4169-1356-6 Subj: Animals — cats. Format, unusual — board books.

How to bake an American pie ill. by Raúl Colón. Simon & Schuster, 2007. ISBN 978-0-689-86506-0 Subj: Rhyming text. U.S. history.

Mama always comes home ill. by Brooke Dyer. HarperCollins, 2005. ISBN 0-06-057506-9 Subj: Animals. Family life — mothers. Rhyming text.

Moose tracks! ill. by Jack E. Davis. Simon & Schuster, 2006. ISBN 0-689-83437-3 Subj: Animals. Animals — moose. Rhyming text.

Mortimer's Christmas manger ill. by Jane Chapman. Simon & Schuster, 2005. ISBN 0-689-85511-7 Subj: Animals — mice. Holidays — Christmas. Religion — Nativity.

Princess me ill. by Christa Unzner. Simon & Schuster, 2007. ISBN 978-1-4169-4098-2 Subj: Imagination. Rhyming text. Royalty — princesses. Toys.

Sakes alive! A cattle drive ill. by Karla Firehammer. Little, Brown, 2005. ISBN 0-316-98841-3 Subj: Activities — driving. Animals — bulls, cows. Rhyming text.

Sleepyhead ill. by John Segal. Simon & Schuster, 2006. ISBN 1-4169-1241-X Subj: Animals — cats. Bedtime. Rhyming text. Toys — bears.

Sweet Briar goes to camp ill. by LeUyen Pham. Penguin, 2005. ISBN 0-8037-2971-5 Subj: Animals — porcupines. Animals — skunks. Camps, camping. Emotions — loneliness.

Whopper cake ill. by Will Hillenbrand. Simon & Schuster, 2007. ISBN 978-0-689-83844-6 Subj: Activities — baking, cooking. Birthdays. Food. Rhyming text. Tall tales.

Wing, Natasha. *Go to bed, monster!* ill. by Sylvie Kantorovitz. Harcourt, 2007. ISBN 978-0-15-205775-6 Subj: Activities — drawing. Bedtime. Imagination. Monsters.

Winget, Susan. *Tucker's four-carrot school day* ill. by author. HarperCollins, 2005. ISBN 0-06-054643-3 Subj: Animals — rabbits. Friendship. School — first day.

Winstead, Rosie. *Ruby and Bubbles* ill. by author. Penguin, 2006. ISBN 0-8037-3024-1 Subj: Behavior — bullying. Birds. Friendship. Pets.

Winter, Jeanette. *Angelina's island* ill. by author. Farrar, Straus & Giroux, 2007. ISBN 978-0-374-30349-5 Subj: Emotions — loneliness. Ethnic groups in the U.S. — Jamaican Americans. Immigrants.

Mama: a true story, in which a baby hippo loses his mama during a tsunami, but finds a new home ill. by author. Harcourt, 2006. ISBN 0-15-205495-2 Subj: Animals — hippopotamuses. Family life — mothers. Reptiles — turtles, tortoises. Tsunamis.

The tale of pale male: a true story ill. by author. Harcourt, 2007. ISBN 978-0-15-205972-9 Subj: Birds — hawks.

Winter, Jonah. *Dizzy* ill. by Sean Qualls. Scholastic, 2006. ISBN 0-439-50737-5 Subj: Careers — musicians. Ethnic groups in the U.S. — African Americans. Music.

Winthrop, Elizabeth. *Squashed in the middle* ill. by Pat Cummings. Henry Holt, 2005. ISBN 0-8050-6497-4 Subj: Ethnic groups in the U.S. — African Americans. Family life. Self-concept. Sleepovers.

Wise, William. *Zany zoo* ill. by Lynn Munsinger. Houghton Mifflin, 2006. ISBN 0-618-18891-6 Subj: Animals. Language. Zoos.

Wishinsky, Frieda. *Please, Louise!* ill. by Marie-Louise Gay. Groundwood, 2007. ISBN 0-88899-796-5 Subj: Animals — dogs. Behavior — wishing. Family life — brothers & sisters.

Wisnewski, Andrea. *Little Red Riding Hood* (Grimm, Jacob)

Withrow, Sarah. *Be a baby* ill. by Manuel Monroy. Groundwood, 2007. ISBN 978-0-88899-776-0 Subj: Babies. Bedtime. Lullabies.

Wolff, Ferida. *It is the wind* ill. by James Ransome. HarperCollins, 2005. ISBN 0-06-028192-8 Subj: Animals. Bedtime. Noise, sounds. Sleep.

Wolff, Nancy. *It's time for school with Tallulah* ill. by author. Henry Holt, 2007. ISBN 978-0-8050-7962-3 Subj: Activities — playing. Animals — cats. School.

Tallulah in the kitchen ill. by author. Henry Holt, 2005. ISBN 0-8050-7463-5 Subj: Activities — baking, cooking. Animals — cats. Food.

Wong, Janet S. *The dumpster diver* ill. by David Roberts. Candlewick, 2007. ISBN 978-0-7636-2380-7 Subj: Communities, neighborhoods. Ecology.

Hide and seek ill. by Margaret Chodos-Irvine. Harcourt, 2005. ISBN 0-15-204934-7 Subj: Behavior — hiding. Counting, numbers. Rhyming text.

Wood, Audrey. *Alphabet rescue* ill. by Bruce Wood. Scholastic/Blue Sky, 2006. ISBN 0-439-85316-8 Subj: ABC books. Careers — firefighters. Trucks.

The deep blue sea: a book of colors ill. by Bruce Wood. Scholastic/ Blue Sky, 2005. ISBN 0-439-75382-1 Subj: Concepts — color. Sea & seashore.

A dog needs a bone ill. by author. Scholastic, 2007. ISBN 978-0-545-00005-5 Subj: Animals — dogs. Rhyming text.

Silly Sally ill. by author. Harcourt, 2007. ISBN 978-0-15-205902-6 Subj: Activities — traveling. Animals. Cumulative tales. Format, unusual — board books. Poetry.

Wood, Douglas. *Nothing to do* ill. by Wendy Anderson Halperin. Penguin, 2006. ISBN 0-525-47656-3 Subj: Activities — playing.

The secret of saying thanks ill. by Greg Shed. Simon & Schuster, 2005. ISBN 0-689-85410-2 Subj: Emotions — happiness. Nature.

What Grandmas can't do ill. by Doug Cushman. Simon & Schuster, 2005. ISBN 0-689-84647-9 Subj: Family life — grandmothers.

Wood, Nancy C. *Mr. and Mrs. God in the creation kitchen* ill. by Timothy Basil Ering. Candlewick, 2006. ISBN 0-7636-1258-8 Subj: Creation. Religion.

Woodhull, Anne Love. *Every season* (Rotner, Shelley)

Woodruff, Elvira. *Small beauties: the journey of Darcy Heart O'Hara* ill. by Adam Rex. Random House, 2006. ISBN 0-375-92686-0

Subj: Family life. Foreign lands — Ireland. Immigrants. U.S. history.

Woodson, Jacqueline. *Show way* ill. by Hudson Talbott. Penguin, 2005. ISBN 0-399-23749-6 Subj: Ethnic groups in the U.S. — African Americans. Family life — mothers. Quilts. Slavery. U.S. history.

Wright, Chantal. *Princess Pigsty* (Funke, Cornelia)

Wright, Cliff. *Bear and ball* ill. by author. Chronicle, 2005. ISBN 0-8118-4819-1 Subj: Animals — bears. Format, unusual — board books. Rhyming text. Toys — balls.

Bear and kite ill. by author. Chronicle, 2005. ISBN 0-8118-4820-5 Subj: Animals — bears. Format, unusual — board books. Kites. Rhyming text.

Wright, Michael. *Jake stays awake* ill. by author. Feiwel & Friends, 2007. ISBN 978-0-312-36797-8 Subj: Bedtime. Rhyming text. Sleep.

Wynne-Jones, Tim. *The boat in the tree* ill. by John Shelley. Boyds Mills, 2007. ISBN 978-1-932425-49-9 Subj: Adoption. Boats, ships. Family life — brothers & sisters. Sibling rivalry.

Xinran, Xue. *Motherbridge of love* ill. by Josée Masse. Barefoot, 2007. ISBN 978-1-84686-047-8 Subj: Adoption. Emotions — love. Family life — mothers. Poetry.

Yaccarino, Dan. *The birthday fish* ill. by author. Henry Holt, 2005. ISBN 0-8050-7493-7 Subj: Birthdays. Fish. Pets.

Every Friday ill. by author. Henry Holt, 2007. ISBN 978-0-8050-7724-7 Subj: Family life — fathers.

Yamada, Utako. *The story of Cherry the pig* ill. by author. Kane/ Miller, 2007. ISBN 978-1-933605-25-8 Subj: Activities — baking, cooking. Animals — pigs. Contests. Foreign lands — Japan.

Yang, Belle. *Always come home to me* ill. by author. Candlewick, 2007. ISBN 978-0-7636-2899-4 Subj: Birds — doves. Family life — mothers. Foreign lands — China. Multiple births — twins.

Yarrow, Peter. *Puff, the magic dragon* by Peter Yarrow & Leonard Lipton; ill. by Eric Puybaret. Sterling, 2007. ISBN 978-1-4027-4782-3 Subj: Dragons. Music. Songs.

Yee, Paul. *Bamboo* ill. by Shaoli Wang. Simply Read, 2006. ISBN 1-89496-553-1 Subj: Folk & fairy tales. Foreign lands — China.

Yee, Wong Herbert. *Detective Small in the amazing banana caper* ill. by author. Houghton Mifflin, 2007. ISBN 978-0-618-47285-7 Subj: Animals. Careers — detectives. Crime. Rhyming text.

Who likes rain? ill. by Herbert Yee Wong. Henry Holt, 2007. ISBN 978-0-8050-7734-6 Subj: Ethnic groups in the U.S. — Asian Americans. Games. Rhyming text. Seasons — spring. Weather — rain.

Yi, Hu Yong. *Good morning China* ill. by author. Macmillan, 2007. ISBN 1-59643-240-6 Subj: Foreign lands — China. Morning.

Yin. *Brothers* ill. by Chris Soentpiet. Penguin, 2006. ISBN 0-399-23406-3 Subj: Ethnic groups in the U.S. — Chinese Americans. Family life — brothers & sisters. Friendship. Immigrants. Stores. U.S. history.

Yolen, Jane. *Baby Bear's big dreams* ill. by Melissa Sweet. Harcourt, 2007. ISBN 978-0-15-205291-1 Subj: Animals — bears. Behavior — growing up. Rhyming text.

Baby Bear's books ill. by Melissa Sweet. Harcourt, 2006. ISBN 0-15-205290-9 Subj: Animals — bears. Books, reading. Rhyming text.

Baby Bear's chairs ill. by Melissa Sweet. Harcourt, 2005. ISBN 0-15-205114-7 Subj: Animals — bears. Bedtime. Family life — fathers. Rhyming text.

Dimity Duck ill. by Sebastien Braun. Penguin, 2006. ISBN 0-399-24632-0 Subj: Activities — playing. Birds — ducks. Friendship. Frogs & toads. Rhyming text.

Grandma's hurrying child ill. by Kay Chorao. Harcourt, 2005. ISBN 0-15-201813-1 Subj: Babies. Birth. Family life — grandmothers.

How do dinosaurs eat their food? ill. by Mark Teague. Scholastic/ Blue Sky, 2005. ISBN 0-439-24102-2 Subj: Dinosaurs. Etiquette. Food. Rhyming text.

How do dinosaurs go to school? ill. by Mark Teague. Scholastic, 2007. ISBN 978-0-439-02081-7 Subj: Dinosaurs. Rhyming text. School.

How do dinosaurs learn their colors? ill. by Mark Teague. Scholastic/Blue Sky, 2006. ISBN 0-439-85653-1 Subj: Concepts — color. Dinosaurs. Rhyming text.

How do dinosaurs play with their friends? ill. by Mark Teague. Scholastic/Blue Sky, 2006. ISBN 0-439-85654-X Subj: Behavior. Dinosaurs. Friendship. Rhyming text.

Sleep, black bear, sleep by Jane Yolen & Heidi E. Y. Stemple; ill. by Brooke Dyer. HarperCollins, 2007. ISBN 0-06-081560-4 Subj: Animals. Bedtime. Hibernation. Lullabies. Seasons — winter.

Soft house ill. by Wendy Anderson Halperin. Candlewick, 2005. ISBN 0-7636-1697-4 Subj: Activities — playing. Animals — cats. Behavior — boredom. Family life — brothers & sisters.

Yoo, Paula. *Sixteen years in sixteen seconds: the Sammy Lee story* ill. by Dom Lee. Lee & Low, 2005. ISBN 1-58430-247-X Subj: Ethnic groups in the U.S. — Asian Americans. Sports — Olympics.

Yoo, Taeeun. *The little red fish* ill. by author. Penguin, 2007. ISBN 0-8037-3145-0 Subj: Fish. Libraries. Magic.

Young, Amy. *Belinda and the glass slipper* ill. by author. Penguin, 2006. ISBN 0-670-06082-8 Subj: Activities — dancing. Anatomy — feet. Ballet.

Belinda begins ballet ill. by author. Penguin, 2007. ISBN 978-0-670-06244-7 Subj: Activities — dancing. Anatomy — feet. Ballet.

Belinda in Paris ill. by author. Penguin, 2005. ISBN 0-670-03693-5 Subj: Activities — dancing. Anatomy — feet. Ballet. Clothing — shoes. Foreign lands — France.

Young, Ed. *My Mei Mei* ill. by author. Penguin, 2006. ISBN 0-399-24339-9 Subj: Adoption. Emotions — love. Ethnic groups in the U.S. — Chinese Americans. Family life — brothers & sisters. Sibling rivalry.

Zalben, Jane Breskin. *Hey, Mama Goose* ill. by Emilie Chollat. Penguin, 2005. ISBN 0-525-47097-2 Subj: Homes, houses. Nursery rhymes. Rhyming text.

Zane, Alexander. *The wheels on the race car* ill. by James Warhola. Scholastic/Orchard, 2005. ISBN 0-439-59080-9 Subj: Animals. Automobiles. Songs. Sports — racing.

Zecca, Katherine. *A puffin's year* ill. by author. Down East, 2007. ISBN 978-0-89272-742-1 Subj: Birds — puffins.

Zemach, Margot. *Eating up Gladys* ill. by Kaethe Zemach. Scholastic, 2005. ISBN 0-439-66490-X Subj: Behavior — bossy. Family life — brothers & sisters.

Ziefert, Harriet. *Be fair, share!* ill. by Pete Whitehead. Sterling, 2007. ISBN 978-1-4027-3422-9 Subj: Animals. Behavior — sharing.

Beach party! ill. by Simms Taback. Blue Apple, 2005. ISBN 1-59354-067-1 Subj: Animals. Concepts — motion. Format, unusual — board books. Rhyming text. Sea & seashore.

Bigger than Daddy ill. by Elliot Kreloff. Blue Apple, 2006. ISBN 1-59354-147-3 Subj: Concepts — size. Ethnic groups in the U.S. — African Americans. Family life — fathers.

The biggest job of all ill. by Lauren Browne. Blue Apple, 2005. ISBN 1-59354-100-7 Subj: Careers. Family life — mothers.

Buzzy had a little lamb ill. by Emily Bolam. Blue Apple, 2005. ISBN 1-59354-068-X Subj: Animals — donkeys. School. Toys.

Circus parade ill. by Tanya Roitman. Blue Apple, 2005. ISBN 1-59354-088-4 Subj: Circus. Parades.

Families have together ill. by Deborah Zemke. Blue Apple, 2005. ISBN 1-59354-071-X Subj: Family life. Rhyming text.

From Kalamazoo to Timbuktu! ill. by Tanya Roitman. Blue Apple, 2005. ISBN 1-59354-091-4 Subj: Activities — traveling. Rhyming text. Transportation.

Fun Land fun! ill. by Yukiko Kido. Sterling, 2007. ISBN 978-1-4027-3416-8 Subj: Friendship. Parks — amusement.

Grandma, it's for you! ill. by Lauren Browne. Blue Apple, 2006. ISBN 1-59354-109-0 Subj: Activities — making things. Clothing — hats. Family life — grandmothers. Gifts.

Knick-knack paddywhack ill. by Emily Bolam. Sterling, 2005. ISBN 1-40272292-3 Subj: Activities — making things. Animals — dogs. Counting, numbers. Cumulative tales. Format, unusual — board books. Songs.

Messy Bessie: where's my homework ill. by Roger De Muth. Blue Apple, 2007. ISBN 978-1-59354-181-1 Subj: Animals — mice. Behavior — messy. Format, unusual. Picture puzzles. Rhyming text. School.

Mommy, I want to sleep in your bed! ill. by Elliot Kreloff. Blue Apple, 2005. ISBN 1-59354-103-1 Subj: Animals — dogs. Bedtime. Family life — mothers. Sleep.

Murphy jumps a hurdle ill. by Emily Bolam. Blue Apple, 2006. ISBN 1-59354-174-0 Subj: Animals — dogs. Character traits — perseverance. Sports.

Surprise! ill. by Richard Brown. Sterling, 2007. ISBN 978-1-4027-3410-6 Subj: Character traits — generosity. Family life — mothers.

That's what grandmas are for ill. by Amanda Haley. Blue Apple, 2006. ISBN 1-59354-098-1 Subj: Family life — grandmothers.

That's what grandpas are for ill. by Deborah Zemke. Blue Apple, 2006. ISBN 1-59354-097-3 Subj: Family life — grandfathers.

There was a little girl who had a little curl ill. by Elliot Kreloff. Blue Apple, 2006. ISBN 1-59354-161-9 Subj: Behavior — misbehavior. Character traits — appearance. Hair.

William and the dragon ill. by Richard Brown. Blue Apple, 2005. ISBN 1-59354-089-2 Subj: Dragons. Rhyming text.

Zimmerman, Andrea Griffing. *Fire engine man* ill. by David Clemesha. Henry Holt, 2007. ISBN 978-0-8050-7905-0 Subj: Careers — firefighters. Family life — brothers & sisters.

Zoehfeld, Kathleen Weidner. *Dinosaur tracks* ill. by Lucia Washburn. HarperCollins, 2007. ISBN 978-0-06-029024-5 Subj: Dinosaurs. Fossils.

Zolotow, Charlotte (Shapiro). *A father like that* ill. by LeUyen Pham. HarperCollins, 2007. ISBN 978-0-06-027864-9 Subj: Ethnic groups in the U.S. — African Americans. Family life — fathers. Family life — single-parent families.

If it weren't for you ill. by G. Brian Karas. HarperCollins, 2006. ISBN 0-06-027875-7 Subj: Family life. Sibling rivalry.

Zuckerman, Linda. *I will hold you 'til you sleep* ill. by Jon J Muth. Scholastic, 2006. ISBN 0-439-43420-3 Subj: Emotions — love. Family life.

Zweibel, Alan. *Our tree named Steve* ill. by David Catrow. Penguin, 2005. ISBN 0-399-23722-4 Subj: Family life. Letters, cards. Trees.

Title Index

Titles appear in alphabetical sequence with the author's name in parentheses, followed by the page number of the full listing in the Bibliographic Guide. For identical title listings, the illustrator's name is given to further identify the version. In the case of variant titles, both the original and differing titles are listed.

I

N

O

T

Illustrator Index

Illustrators appear alphabetically in bold-face followed by their titles. Names in parentheses are authors of the titles when different from the illustrator. Page numbers refer to the full listing in the Bibliographic Guide.

H

I

N

X

Y

About the Authors

CAROLYN W. LIMA has created all previous editions of this best-selling subject guide to picture books. Previously, Carolyn was Children's Librarian at the San Diego Public Library, Branch Libraries Division, San Diego, California.

REBECCA L. THOMAS is an elementary school librarian, Shaker Heights City Schools, Ohio. She is the author of numerous reference books, including the *Popular Series Fiction* set for Libraries Unlimited (2004) and *Across Cultures* (Libraries Unlimited, 2007).